PRINCIPLES OF EUROPEAN FAMILY LAW REGARDING PROPERTY RELATIONS BETWEEN SPOUSES

European Family Law Series

Published by the Organising Committee of the Commission on European Family Law

Prof. Katharina Boele-Woelki (Utrecht)
Prof. Frédérique Ferrand (Lyon)
Prof. Cristina González Beilfuss (Barcelona)
Prof. Maarit Jänterä-Jareborg (Uppsala)
Prof. Nigel Lowe (Cardiff)
Prof. Dieter Martiny (Frankfurt/Oder)
Prof. Walter Pintens (Leuven)

PRINCIPLES OF EUROPEAN FAMILY LAW REGARDING PROPERTY RELATIONS BETWEEN SPOUSES

Katharina Boele-Woelki
Frédérique Ferrand
Cristina González Beilfuss
Maarit Jänterä-Jareborg
Nigel Lowe
Dieter Martiny
Walter Pintens

In collaboration with

Masha Antokolskaia, Anne Barlow, Bente Braat, Nina Dethloff, Ruth Farrugio, Miloš Haťapka, Milana Hrusaková, Achilles Koutsouradis, Kirsti Kurki-Suonio, Ingrid Lund-Andersen, Andrzej Mączyński, Jane Mair, Miguel Martín-Casals, Filip Melzer, Valentinas Mikelenas, Guilherme De Oliveira, Salvatore Patti, Marianne Roth, Ingeborg Schwenzer, Geoffrey Shannon, Tone Sverdrup, Orsolya Szeibert, Velina Todorova, Emilia Weiss

intersentia
Cambridge – Antwerp – Portland

Intersentia Publishing Ltd.
Trinity House | Cambridge Business Park | Cowley Road
Cambridge | CB4 0WZ | United Kingdom
Tel.: +44 1223 393 753 | Email: mail@intersentia.co.uk

Distribution for the UK:
NBN International
Airport Business Centre, 10 Thornbury Road
Plymouth, PL6 7 PP
United Kingdom
Tel.: +44 1752 202 301 | Fax: +44 1752 202 331
Email: orders@nbninternational.com

Distribution for the USA and Canada:
International Specialized Book Services
920 NE 58th Ave. Suite 300
Portland, OR 97213
USA
Tel.: +1 800 944 6190 (toll free)
Email: info@isbs.com

Distribution for Austria:
Stämpfli Verlag AG
Wölflistrasse 1
Postfach 5662
3001 Bern
Switserland
Tel.: +41 31 300 66 77
Email: verlag@staempfli.com

Distribution for other countries:
Intersentia Publishing nv
Groenstraat 31
2640 Mortsel
Belgium
Tel.: +32 3 680 15 50
Email: mail@intersentia.be

Principles of European Family Law Regarding Property Relations between Spouses
Katharina Boele-Woelki, Frédérique Ferrand, Cristina González Beilfuss, Maarit Jänterä-Jareborg, Nigel Lowe, Dieter Martiny and Walter Pintens

ISBN 978-1-78068-152-8
D/2013/7849/47
NUR 820

British Library Cataloguing in Publication Data. A catalogue record for this book is available from the British Library.

PREFACE

The Commission on European Family Law and its Principles of European Family Law

The Commission on European Family Law (CEFL), which was established in September 2001, drafts common principles that are thought to be the most suitable for the harmonisation of family law in Europe. The Principles of European Family Law regarding Divorce and Maintenance between Former Spouses were published in 2004[1] and the Principles regarding Parental Responsibilities in 2007.[2] This book contains the Principles regarding the Property Relations between Spouses.

Organisation

The CEFL comprises of the *Organising Committee* (Katharina Boele-Woelki (chair), Frédérique Ferrand, Cristina González Beilfuss, Maarit Jänterä-Jareborg, Nigel Lowe, Dieter Martiny and Walter Pintens) and the *Expert Group*, which at present has 26 members. The Organising Committee prepares and co-ordinates the work of the CEFL as a whole. The members of the Organising Committee are also members of the Expert Group. The Expert Group comprises specialists in the field of family and comparative law from most of the Member States of the European Union with the involvement of experts from other European countries, such as Norway, Russia and Switzerland.

The CEFL is a Foundation according to Dutch law. It has its seat at Utrecht University's Molengraaff Institute for Private Law, Janskerkhof 12, NL - 3512 BL Utrecht, www.ceflonline.nl. Dr. Bente Braat, legal counsel at the International Commission on Civil Status, heads CEFL's secretariat. Dr. Pia Lokin, university lecturer at the University of Nijmegen, acted as deputy secretary in 2009–2011 and Dr. Ian Curry-Sumner of Utrecht University held the position of webmaster until April 2012. He has been succeeded by Roderic ter Rele, student assistant of the Utrecht Centre for European Research into Family Law (UCERF) of the Molengraaff Institute for Private Law at Utrecht University's School of Law.

---

1 European Family Law Series No. 7.

2 European Family Law Series No. 16.

Aims and objectives

The CEFL's activities are intended to produce results that may be used for specific practical and academic purposes. First and foremost, the Principles are addressed to national legislators in their quest to modernise their national family law. They also function as a source of inspiration for both the European and international legislatures. The Principles are spelt out in provisions but these must be read in conjunction with comments, which elucidate the rules and offer comparative information. These comments are part and parcel of the Principles. The Principles could considerably facilitate the task of legislators because, on the one hand, CEFL's in-depth and comprehensive comparative research is easily accessible and, on the other hand, many of the rules have been drafted in a manner that legislators often consider to be appropriate. Some, but not all, of the Principles have been drafted so that they could be implemented in a national system. Second, research into the effectiveness of national solutions in the field of family law can largely profit from the CEFL's results. The drafting of the Principles is based on an evaluation of the legal institutions, legal solutions and norms of the various legal orders, which express the hierarchy of values inherent in every legal order, although to different degrees. It is to be expected that future scientific research in the field of the harmonisation of family law in Europe to be carried out by individual researchers or eventually research teams will necessarily refer to and compare national solutions with the CEFL Principles. Third, the CEFL's comparative material contains comprehensive information about twenty-six family law systems in Europe and it has been regularly consulted by practitioners. Specific information about, for instance, the divorce grounds in GREECE or the position of the new partner of the parent who holds parental responsibilities in respect of the child under FINNISH law or the administration of community property in THE NETHERLANDS is easily accessible and may help in those cases where lawyers seek information about the precise content of foreign family law. In addition, all national reports are written in English, which in most cases facilitates access to those national systems where the official language is not English, French or German. The often difficult legal translations have thus already been done by national experts.

Experts

The following persons contributed to the drafting of the Principles regarding Property Relations between Spouses through the writing of a national report and/or taking part in the discussions at the CEFL meetings. Several experts wrote their national reports together with co-authors. Their names are both mentioned on the CEFL's website and listed in the integrated version of all national reports.[3]

---

3 Boele-Woelki/Braat/Curry-Sumner, *European Family Law in Action, Volume IV: Property Relations Between Spouses*, European Family Law series No. 24, 2009, pp. vii-x.

AUSTRIA	*Prof. Marianne Roth* University of Salzburg
BELGIUM	*Prof. Walter Pintens* University of Leuven Secretary General of the International Commission on Civil Status
BULGARIA	*Dr. Velina Todorova* Plovdiv University, Sofia
CATALONIA	*Prof. Miquel Martin-Casals* University of Girona
CZECH REPUBLIC	*Prof. Milana Hrusaková* Palacký University, Olomouc *Dr. Filip Melzer* Palacký University, Olomouc
DENMARK	*Prof. Ingrid Lund-Andersen* University of Copenhagen
ENGLAND AND WALES	*Prof. Anne Barlow* University of Exeter *Prof. Nigel Lowe* Cardiff Law School, University of Cardiff
FINLAND	*Dr. Kirsti Kurki-Suonio* Office of the Parliamentary Ombudsman, Helsinki University of Helsinki
FRANCE	*Dr. Bente Braat* Legal Counsel at the International Commission on Civil Status *Prof. Frédérique Ferrand* University Jean Moulin Lyon 3
GERMANY	*Prof. Nina Dethloff* University of Bonn *Prof. em. Dieter Martiny* European University Viadrina Frankfurt (Oder) Guest researcher Max Planck Institute for comparative and international private law, Hamburg
GREECE	*Prof. Achilles G. Koutsouradis* University of Thessaloniki

HUNGARY	*Prof. Emila Weiss* University of Eötvös Loránd, Budapest *Dr. Orsolya Szeibert* University of Eötvös Loránd, Budapest
REPUBLIC OF IRELAND	*Prof. Geoffrey Shannon* Law Society of Ireland, Dublin
ITALY	*Prof. Salvatore Patti* University La Sapienza, Rome
LITHUANIA	*Prof. Valentinas Mikelenas* Baltic Legal Solutions, Lithuania University of Vilnius
MALTA	*Prof. Ruth Farrugia* University of Malta
THE NETHERLANDS	*Prof. Katharina Boele-Woelki* Utrecht University
NORWAY	*Prof. Tone Sverdrup* University of Oslo
POLAND	*Prof. Andrzej Mączyński* Jagiellonian University of Kraków
PORTUGAL	*Prof. Guilherme de Oliveira* University of Coimbra
RUSSIA	*Prof. Masha Antokolskaia* Free University of Amsterdam
SCOTLAND	*Dr. Jane Mair* University of Glasgow
SLOVAKIA	*Dr. Miloš Haťapka* Ministry of Justice of the Slovak Republic
SPAIN	*Prof. Cristina González Beilfuss* University of Barcelona
SWEDEN	*Prof. Maarit Jänterä-Jareborg* Uppsala University
SWITZERLAND	*Prof. Ingeborg Schwenzer* University of Basel

Meetings

The meetings of the Organising Committee during which the Principles regarding Property Relations between Spouses were prepared and drafted took place in:

BARCELONA	3–6 May 2007
OSLO	7 and 10 June 2007
CARDIFF	25–28 October 2007
BRUSSELS	3–5 October 2008
FRANKFURT/ODER	11–14 December 2008
SAARBRÜCKEN	28–31 May 2009
LYON	15–18 October 2009
BARCELONA	4–7 March 2010
UPPSALA	2–4 September 2010
UTRECHT	9–12 December 2010
HAMBURG	7–10 April 2011
LEUVEN	16–19 June 2011
SIGTUNA	4 September 2011
CARDIFF	1–4 December 2011
LYON	23–26 February 2012
UTRECHT	17–20 May 2012
LYON	11–14 October 2012

At the meetings in FRANKFURT/ODER (2008) and HAMBURG (2011) the members of the Organising Committee presented work-in progress reports at conferences, which were attended by legal scholars and practitioners. Initial results were also reported at the 4th CEFL conference in CAMBRIDGE in April 2010.

The meeting of the *Expert Group* during which the draft of the Principles regarding Property Relations between Spouses was discussed took place in:

SIGTUNA	1–3 September 2011

Conferences

The essence of the work carried out by the CEFL is such that it needs constant backing in a broader academic forum. For this purpose, the CEFL organises family law conferences on a regular basis. All conference proceedings were published in the European Family Law series. To date the following conferences took place:

UTRECHT	11–14 December 2002
UTRECHT	9–11 December 2004
OSLO	7–9 June 2007
CAMBRIDGE	8–10 April 2010
BONN	29–31 August 2013

European Family Law series

The CEFL's Organising Committee established the *European Family Law* series which includes comparative legal studies and materials as well as studies on the effects of international and European law-making within the national legal systems in Europe. The books in this series are published by the Belgian publisher Intersentia (Antwerp-Cambridge-New York) in cooperation with the Swiss publisher Stämpfli (Bern). Since March 2003, thirty-two volumes have been published in the series. Further information is available at CEFL's website.

Financial support

Financial support has been received from the Netherlands Organisation for Scientific Research (NWO), the Deutsche Forschungsgemeinschaft (DFG), the Ius Commune Research School, and the publishers Intersentia (Antwerp/ Cambridge) and Stämpfli (Bern). The Universities of Barcelona, Cardiff, Frankfurt/Oder, Leuven, Lyon, Uppsala and Utrecht finally met a significant part of the expenses incurred by the CEFL meetings. In addition the following institutions should be mentioned. The *Europa Institut* of Saarland University and the Max Planck Institute for comparative and international private law in Hamburg contributed to the expenses of the CEFL meetings which took place in 2009 and 2011 respectively. As a member of the *Institut Universitaire* de France Frédérique Ferrand received funding for attending and organizing CEFL meetings. Finally, the bulk of the costs of the expert meeting, which took place in Sigtuna, Sweden, in September 2011, was made possible due to the Huselius Donation to the Faculty of Law, Uppsala University.

The CEFL is very grateful to all these sponsors for their substantial contributions.

Katharina Boele-Woelki

Utrecht, April 2013

CONTENTS

THE WORK OF THE COMMISSION ON EUROPEAN FAMILY LAW

Unification and harmonisation of (international) family law within the European Union

For the 27 Member States of the European Union the general legal background in family law is not only subject to Human Rights Conventions but also to various European Treaties. The *Treaty of Lisbon of 2007*[4] restructured the European Union by amending the *Treaty on European Union* (TEU) and the *Treaty Establishing the European Community*[5] which became the *Treaty on the Functioning of the European Union* (TFEU). Both Treaties have founded the *Union* which replaced and succeeded the European Community. Article 18 TFEU contains the prohibition of discrimination on grounds of nationality whereas Article 20 TFEU establishes the citizenship of the Union for nationals of the Members States. According to Article 21(1) TFEU all citizens have the right to move and to reside freely within the Member States. This right of free movement together with the emerging European citizenship has gradually gained more significance in the discussion on the unification of private international law in family matters as well as the harmonisation of substantive family law.

Since 1998 the European legislator has been extremely active with regard to cross-border family relationships.[6] Article 81 TFEU (formerly Article 65 EC Treaty) provides the legal basis to legislate in civil matters having cross-border implications. Three Regulations containing rules on jurisdiction, applicable law and recognition and enforcement were adopted in the field of divorce, parental responsibilities[7] and maintenance.[8] In the near future additional Regulations

4 Official Journal 2007/C 306/01.

5 It entered into force on 1 December 2009 for all Member States.

6 See González Beilfuss, "The Unification of Private International Law in Europe: a Success Story?", in: Boele-Woelki/Miles/Scherpe (eds), *The Future of Family Property in Europe*, European Family Law Series No. 29, pp. 329–340.

7 Regulation (EC) No. 2201/2003 of 27 November 2003 concerning jurisdiction and the recognition and enforcement of judgments in matrimonial matters and the matters of parental responsibility, repealing Regulation (EC) No. 1347/2000 (*Brussels II bis*) and Regulation (EU) No 1259/2010 of 20 December 2010 implementing enhanced cooperation in the area of the law applicable to divorce and legal separation (*Rome III*).

8 Regulation (EC) No. 4/2009 of 18 December 2008 on jurisdiction, applicable law, recognition and enforcement of decisions and cooperation in matters relating to maintenance obligations.

will cover matters of succession,[9] matrimonial property regimes[10] and the property consequences of registered partnerships.[11] Moreover, the possibility of regulating the free movement of public documents and the recognition of the effects of civil status records is under discussion.[12]

The legal acts of the Union must meet the requirement of proportionality and compatibility with the principle of subsidiarity. Until now all adopted and envisaged European family law Regulations were considered as being necessary for the proper functioning of the internal market. They are in line with the principle of subsidiarity since the same results cannot be easily be achieved by the Member States.

In respect of substantive family law, it is generally accepted that the Union has *no* competence under the TFEU to unify or harmonise these areas.[13] Private international law and substantive law are, however, interrelated. The European family law instruments for cross-border relations will only be successful in the long run when there are greater similarities between the substantive family law systems. Thus, the harmonisation of substantive family law is the next natural step to be taken.[14] This step is prepared by the Commission on European Family Law (CEFL) which proposes common Principles of European Family Law in various areas. Based upon extensive comparative research the CEFL Principles demonstrate how family law in Europe could be harmonised. It goes without saying that all legislatures are free "to take it or leave it". If a national legislature takes the comparative material of the CEFL into account and – more importantly – finally decides to use the Principles as a source of inspiration when adopting new rules in family law, the ultimate goal of the CEFL has been achieved.

---

9 Regulation (EU) No. 650/2012 of 4 July 2012 on jurisdiction, applicable law, recognition and enforcement of decisions and authentic instruments in matters of succession and the creation of a European Certificate of Succession.

10 Proposal for a Regulation on jurisdiction, applicable law and the recognition and enforcement of decisions in matters of matrimonial property regimes, COM(2011) 126/2.

11 Proposal for a Regulation on jurisdiction, applicable law and the recognition and enforcement of decisions regarding the property consequences of registered partnerships, COM(2011) 127/2.

12 Green Paper on less bureaucracy for citizens: promoting free movement of public documents and recognition of the effects of civil status records, COM(2010) 747 final.

13 See the Communication of the European Commission on *Bringing legal clarity to property rights for international couples*, COM(2011) 125/3. See also Pintens, "Europeanisation of Family Law", in: Boele-Woelki, (ed.), *Perspectives for the Unification and Harmonisation of Family Law in Europe*, European Family Law Series No. 4, 2003, pp. 3–33 (22). See for a different view Boele-Woelki, *Unifying and Harmonizing Substantive Law and the Role of Conflict of Laws*, Hague Academy of International Law, 2010, no. 32.

14 See Martiny, "Is Unification of Family Law Feasible or even Desirable?", in: Hartkamp/Hesselink/Hondius/Mak/Du Perron (eds), *Towards a European Civil Code*, 2011, pp. 429–457.

National legislatures have already been inspired by the models proposed by the CEFL.[15] In 2008, the PORTUGUESE legislature, for example, in modernizing the law of divorce and parental authority took advantage of the work of the CEFL. As a result, some of the new PORTUGUESE rules are identical with the CEFL Principles.[16] Another example of CEFL's impact has been in the development in NORWEGIAN law. The NORWEGIAN Child Law Commission 2008 proposed alternating residence, and referred inter alia to the Principles regarding Parental Responsibilities and in particular to Principle 3:20 as part of their justification.[17] Not only do these examples illustrate that the final results are considered to be in accordance with the scientific standard for reliable and comprehensive comparative research but also that the Principles are not black letter rules, but guidelines to be "filtered" into national – or European – legislation.[18]

Divorce and Maintenance between Former Spouses

In 2004, the CEFL published its first two sets of Principles of European Family Law in the field of Divorce and Maintenance between Former Spouses.[19] On the basis of twenty-two national reports, the CEFL formulated ten Principles concerning Divorce (Part 1) and ten Principles concerning Maintenance between Former Spouses (Part 2).[20]

---

15 See BOELE-WOELKI, "Zwischen Konvergenz und Divergenz: Die CEFL Prinzipien zum Europäischen Familienrecht", *Rabels Zeitschrift für internationales und ausländisches Privatrecht* 2009, pp. 241–267.

16 See DE OLIVEIRA, "Changes Going on in Portuguese Family Law", *Zeitschrift für das gesamte Familienrecht* 2008, pp. 1712–1714.

17 *Norges offentlige utredninger* 2008:9, p. 82. On 9 April 2010 a provision on alternating residence was enacted, § 36 Children Act. See SVERDRUP, "Norway: Equal Parenthood: Recent Reforms in Child Custody Cases", *Yearbook of the International Society of Family Law* 2011, pp. 303–312.

18 See JÄNTERÄ-JAREBORG, "Europeanization of Law: Harmonization of Fragmentation – A Family Law Approach", *Tidskrift utgiven av Juridiska Föreningen i Finland*, 2010, pp. 504–515.

19 See BOELE-WOELKI/FERRAND/GONZÁLEZ BEILFUSS/JÄNTERÄ-JAREBORG/LOWE/MARTINY/PINTENS, *Principles of European Family Law Regarding Divorce and Maintenance Between Former Spouses*, European Family Law Series No. 7, 2004.

20 See FERRAND, "Les Principes de droit du divorce établis par la Commission de droit européen de la famille", *Revue Lamy Droit Civil* 2005, pp. 29–42; GÖTTING/HALLIK/UUSEN-NACKE, "Legal regulation of divorce in Estonia. Comparison with the Principles of European Family Law as regards divorce and maintenance of a divorced spouse", *Juridica* 2006, p. 244 -...; BOELE-WOELKI/MARTINY, Prinzipien zum Europäischen Familienrecht betreffend Ehescheidung und nachelicher Unterhalt, *Zeitschrift für Europäisches Privatrecht* 2006, pp. 6–20; ANTOKOLSKAIA, *Nederlands echtscheidingsrecht en the CEFL Principles on Divorce*, Free University Amsterdam 2006; ÖRÜCÜ/MAIR (eds), *Juxtaposing Legal Systems and the Principles of European Family Law on Divorce and Maintenance*, European Family Law Series No. 17, 2007; TOSCANO, *Ehescheidungen mit grenzüberschreitendem Bezug. Von divergierenden nationalen Scheidungsvoraussetzungen zu einem einheitlichen europäischen Scheidungsrecht?*, 2011.

Parental Responsibilities

In 2007, the CEFL published its third set of Principles of European Family Law in the field of Parental Responsibilities.[21] On the basis of twenty-two national reports, the CEFL formulated thirty-nine Principles.[22] These Principles constitute Part 3 of the CEFL Principles.

Property Relations between Spouses

In December 2006, the CEFL's Organising Committee decided that Part 4 of its Principles should address the property relations between spouses. When the CEFL commenced its activities in 2001 this field of law was considered to be too complicated an endeavour, given the great diversity of legal regimes within Europe and their different technical nature. Since then, however, important changes have taken place in the fields of private international law and substantive law within the Union.

First and foremost, the European Commission also considers the law of property relations between spouses and registered partners as an area where unified private international law rules will contribute to a better functioning of the internal market. To that end two Proposals for Regulations were published in March 2011.[23] In its accompanying Communication[24] on *Bringing legal clarity to property rights for international couples* the European Commission explains why legislative measures should be taken and why two different Regulations should be adopted, one for the property relations of spouses and the other for the property consequences of registered partnerships. In this Communication reference is also made to the *Stockholm Programme* published in 2010[25] in which

21 See Boele-Woelki/Ferrand/González Beilfuss/Jänterä-Jareborg/Lowe/Martiny/Pintens, *Principles of European Family Law Regarding Parental Responsibilities*, European Family Law Series No. 16, 2007.

22 See Boele-Woelki/Martiny, "The Commission on European Family Law (CEFL) and its Principles of European Family Law Regarding Parental Responsibilities", *ERA Forum* 1-2007; Örücü/Mair (eds), *Juxtaposing Legal Systems and the Principles of European Family Law on Parental Responsibilities*, European Family Law Series No. 27, 2010; Pintens, "Europäische Prinzipien zur elterlichen Verantwortung", in: Helms/Zeppernick (eds.), *Lebendiges Familienrecht. Festschrift für Rainer Frank zum 70. Geburtstag*, 2008, pp. 473–489; Jeppesen De Boer, *Joint Parental Authority, A comparative Legal Study on the Continuation of Joint Parental Authority after Divorce and the Breakup of a Relationship in Dutch and Danish Law and the CEFL Principles*, European Family Law Series No. 22, 2008; Boele-Woelki/Martiny, "Die CEFL und die Prinzipien zum europäischen Familienrecht betreffende elterliche Verantwortung: mehr Übereinstimmungen als Unterschiede", Zeitschrift für Europäisches Privatrecht, 2009, pp. 685–698; Fucik, "Das Kindschaftsrecht des ABGB und die Prinzipien zum europäischen Familienrecht betreffend elterliche Verantwortung", in: Fischer-Czermak/Hopf/Kathrein/Schauer (eds) *Festschrift 200 Jahre ABGB* 2011, pp. 1685–1701.

23 COM(2011) 126/2 and COM(2011) 127/2.

24 COM(2011) 125/3.

25 The Stockholm Programme – An open and secure Europe serving and protecting citizens, Official Journal 2010 C 115.

the European Council recommends extending the concept of mutual recognition to fields that are essential to everyday life, such as matrimonial property rights and the property consequences of the separation of couples, while taking into consideration Member States' legal systems, including public policy, and national traditions in this area. The two Proposals were preceded by a *Green Paper* published in 2006.[26] In order to prepare these legislative measures the legal situation in the Member States with regard to substantive and private international law was investigated.[27] Moreover, several other studies and overviews of European systems have been undertaken.[28] The *Green Paper* did not investigate the possibility as to whether one optional European matrimonial regime should be introduced even though the preparatory comparative study has strongly favoured this idea and which had been suggested earlier and supported by several distinguished experts in the field of matrimonial property law, private international law and comparative law.[29] It should also be mentioned that the European Group for Private International Law[30] shows in its answers to the questions posed in the *Green Paper* an interest in the establishment of a European matrimonial property regime which, for instance, could consist of two models amongst which the parties could choose: a community of property regime or a separation of property regime. Finally, by December 2006, all the Nordic states (DENMARK, FINLAND, ICELAND, NORWAY and SWEDEN) had acceded to the *Convention on the Amendment of the Rules on the Matrimonial Property Relations of Spouses*, included in the *Convention on Issues of Private International Law concerning Marriage, Adoption and Guardianship*, originally from 1931.[31]

---

26 COM (2006) 400 final.

27 This study was completed in 2002. It was carried out by researchers of the TMC Asser Institute in The Hague and researchers from the Belgian Catholic University at Louvain-la-Neuve. The research contains 16 national reports and a comparative analysis. See *Étude sur les regimes matrimoniaux des couples mariés et sur le patrimoine des couples non mariés dans le droit international privé et le droit interne des états members de l'union européen*, JAI/A3/2001/03 (2002).

28 See VERBEKE, "European Marital Property Law. Survey 1988–1994", European Review of Private Law 1995, pp. 445–482; HENRICH/SCHWAB, *Eheliche Gemeinschaft, Partnerschaft und Vermögen im europäischen Vergleich, Beiträge zum europäischen Familienrecht*, 1999; VERWILGHEN, "Régimes matrimoniaux, successions et libéralités dans les relations internationales et internes", Union Internationale du Notariat Latin, 2003; BRAAT, *Indépendance et interdépendance des époux dans le régime matrimonial légal des droits français, néerlandais et suisse*, European Family Law Series No. 6, 2004; BONOMI/STEINER, *Les régimes matrimoniaux en droit comparé et en droit international privé*, 2006.

29 See AGELL, "Towards Uniforming Spouses' Property Rights Especially in International Marriages?", Council of Europe, Proceedings of the 3rd European Conference on Family Law, 1995, pp. 63–80; VERBEKE, "Perspectives for an International Marital Contract", *Maastricht Journal of European and Comparative Law* 2001, pp. 189–200; HENRICH, "Zur Zukunft des Güterrechts in Europa", *Zeitschrift für das gesamte Familienrecht* 2002, pp. 1521–1526; MARTINY, "Ein zusätzlicher Güterstand für Europa?", in: HOFER/KLIPPEL/WALTER (eds.), *Perspektiven des Familienrechts – Festschrift für Dieter Schwab*, 2005, pp. 1189–1207; STEENHOFF, "A Matrimonial Property System for the European Union?", *International Family Law* 2005, pp. 74–77.

30 See: gedip-egpil.eu/documents/gedip-documents-26.html.

31 See MEURLING, "Less Surprise for Spouses Moving Between the Nordic Countries? Amendments to the 1931 Nordic Convention on Marriage", *Yearbook of Private International*

With regard to substantive law the bilateral *French-German Agreement* concluded in February 2010[32] deserves attention. This bilateral Agreement is primarily aimed at unifying substantive law. It introduces an additional community of accrued gains (*Wahl-Zugewinngemeinschaft/Le régime matrimonial optionnel de la participation aux acquêts*) as an optional matrimonial property regime.

Finally, particular attention should be paid to the current situation in the common law jurisdictions where there has been a consistent refusal to impose any formal regime of property rights upon entering into a marriage. Three ground-breaking decisions by the ENGLISH House of Lords in 2001[33] and 2006[34] have given rise to claims that ENGLAND AND WALES has in practice adopted a system akin to a deferred community of property.[35] In addition, pre-nuptial and post-nuptial agreements which currently are not enforceable in the event of a divorce under the law of ENGLAND AND WALES have attracted considerable attention after the judgment of the UK Supreme Court in *Granatino v Radmacher (formerly Granatino)*[36] which went further than ever before in recognising their significance. The Law Commission for ENGLAND AND WALES is considering reform of the law on marital property agreements.[37] In IRELAND the feasibility of adopting a community of property regime has also been discussed.[38] SCOTLAND, which is a mixed system, follows the common law jurisdictions to the extent that it has no formal matrimonial property regime but it does provide for a deferred community of acquests by means of statutory principles for the fair share of matrimonial property on divorce.[39]

Law 2009, pp. 385–394 and JÄNTERÄ-JAREBORG, "Inter-Nordic Exceptions in EU Regulations on Matters of Family and Inheritance Law. Legal 'Irritants' or Necessary Concessions in the Citizens' Interest?", *Confronting the Frontiers of Family and Succession Law, Liber Amicorum Walter Pintens*, 2012, pp. 745–749.

32 *Abkommen zwischen der Bundesrepublik Deutschland und der Französischen Republik über den Güterstand der Wahl-Zugewinngemeinschaft/Accord entre la République fédérale d'Allemagne et la République française instituant un régime matrimonial optionnel de la participation aux acquêts*. See the German Ratification Act of 15 March 2012, *Bundesgesetzblatt* 2012 Teil II p. 178 and the text of the Agreement of 4 February 2010, p. 180 and the French Ratification Act, LOI n° 2013-98 du 28 janvier 2013 autorisant la ratification de l'accord entre la République française et la République fédérale d'Allemagne instituant un régime matrimonial optionnel de la participation aux acquêts, JORF n°0024 du 29 janvier 2013 p. 1721. Entry into force on 1 May 2013.

33 *White v. White* [2001] I AC 596.

34 *Miller v. Miller: McFarlane v. McFarlane* [2006] UKHL 24, [2006] 2 AC 618. 24.

35 See COOKE/BARLOW/CALLUS, *Community of Property, A Regime for England and Wales?*, The Nuffield Foundation 2006.

36 [2010] UKSC 42, [2011] 1 AC 534.

37 See COOKE, "Marital property agreements and the work of the Law Commission for England and Wales", in: BOELE-WOELKI/MILES/SCHERPE (eds), *The Future of Family Property in Europe*, European Family Law Series No. 29, pp. 95–113. See also the Law Commission on "Matrimonial Property, Needs and Agreements A Supplementary Consultation Paper", September 2012.

38 See BUCKLEY, "Matrimonial Property and Irish Law: A Case for Community?", *Northern Ireland Legal Quarterly*, 2002, vol 53, no. 39.

39 See MAIR, Scottish Report, Q 1.

Finally, it should be noted that legal doctrine also has focused its attention on European and comparative matrimonial property law.[40]

All these developments signify a growing need to draft Principles of European Family Law regarding Property Relations between Spouses. The Principles contained in this volume are based on twenty-six national reports which were finalised in December 2008. The aim has also been to take into account later reforms and proposals. These concern the following jurisdictions: BULGARIA (2009),[41] CATALONIA (2010),[42] GERMANY (2009),[43] HUNGARY (proposal 2012),[44] THE NETHERLANDS (2012)[45] and SWEDEN (2011).[46]

---

40 See PINTENS, "Matrimonial Property Law in Europe", in: BOELE-WOELKI/MILES/SCHERPE (eds), *The Future of Family Property in Europe*, European Family Law Series No. 29, pp. 19–46 with extensive references in note 1 on p. 20.

41 The new Family Law Code entered into force on 1 October 2009. One of the major reforms concerns the matrimonial property regime. The compulsory regulation of matrimonial property regime was scrapped. The spouses now are free to choose a regime out of three options: separation, common ownership and matrimonial contract (Art. 18, para. 1 Family Code). The three regimes are also available to spouses, whose marriage has been contracted before the new law became effective. The new regulation applies only to married couples.

42 Catalonia enacted a new Book II of its Civil Code dealing with Family law in 2010 (Ley 25/2010, de 29 de Julio, del Libro Segundo del Código civil de Cataluña, relativo a la Persona y la Familia, DOGC nº 5686, de 5 de agosto de 2010) which substitutes the former Family law Code of 1998. The new Catalan law introduces fundamental changes with regard to the property relations between spouses. The default regime of separation of property comes closer to a system of (limited) participation in the acquisitions in so far as it provides for compensation in cases in which one of the spouses has contributed substantively more than the other to the care of the family. The legal regimes of Participation in the acquisitions and Community have as well been substantially reformed.

43 The Act on the Amendment of the Equalisation of Accrued Gains and the Law of Guardianship of 6 July 2009 (Bundesgesetzblatt 2009 part I p. 1696) amended the rules for the participation regime. Now debts that exist at the beginning of the community of accrued gains will be taken into consideration (§ 1374 German CC) and protection against fraudulent manoeuvres has been improved (§ 1385 German CC). The rights of the spouses to information concerning the other spouse's property have been strengthened (§ 1379 German CC). The rules on the allotment of household goods and the matrimonial home have been introduced into the Civil Code (§ 1586a *et seq.* German CC). The procedural rules have been incorporated into the Act on Family Law Matters and on Voluntary Jurisdiction of 2009 (§ 200 *et seq.*).

44 The Bill No T/7971 on the new Civil Code was submitted to the Parliament on July 11th, 2012. The matrimonial property rules are part of the Family Law Book (§§ 4:34 – 4:75 of the Sixth Title on Matrimonial Property Law, Second Part Marriage, Fourth Book Family Law). The proposed matrimonial property rules are detailed regulations primarily in the field of the default matrimonial property regime, which is the community of property regime. In addition new alternative matrimonial property regimes are proposed such as the separation of property and the community of accrued gains. Overall, however, the proposed matrimonial property rules are basically the same as in the Act No CXX 2009.

45 The amendment of a few provisions of Titles 6–8 of Book 1 of the Dutch Civil Code took effect on 1 January 2012. The universal community of property regime is still the default regime. The changes concern the administration of community property, introduce new rules on substitution of property and on compensation for different types of investment in the other spouse's assets. See BOELE-WOELKI/BRAAT, "Marital agreements and Partyautonomy in Dutch Law", in: SCHERPE (ed.), *Marital Agreements and Private Autonomy in a Comparative Perspective*, 2012, pp. 231–255.

46 Since 1 October 2011, the competent authority for the registration of marital property agreements in Sweden is Sweden's National Taxation Agency (*Skatteverket*), instead of a

Methodology

The CEFL adopted the same working method with regard to these Property Principles as it did for the previous sets of Principles.[47] On the basis of a detailed questionnaire containing 201 questions the expert members prepared twenty-six comprehensive national reports based on the law as it stood in 2008. These national reports, together with the relevant legal provisions, are available on CEFL's website www.ceflonline.net under working field 3. In addition, an integrated version of all the reports has been published.[48] On the basis of a systematic analysis of this comparative material, to which the comparative overviews comprehensively refer,[49] and the relevant international and European instruments in this field, the CEFL formulated fifty-eight Principles concerning Property Relations between Spouses. They were drafted by the Organising Committee and have been discussed with the drafters of the national reports at a meeting of the Expert Group in Sigtuna (Sweden) from 1st – 3rd September 2011.

Frame of reference

As with the previous sets of Principles, those regarding Property Relations between Spouses are primarily directed towards national, European and international legislators who are considering modernising the law in this field. They may serve as a frame of reference and inspiration. In using the CEFL Principles it should be kept in mind that the drafters lack a political mandate and that the members of the CEFL do not represent their national system. Instead they have distanced themselves from their own legal background because the European perspective ultimately prevails. In respect of the adopted results it is considered to be absolutely vital to reveal the criteria upon which the choices and the underlining policies were based. This aspect is one of the major objectives and concerns of the CEFL since its Principles may only aspire to be used not *ratione imperii*, but *imperio rationis*. Consequently the utmost care has been given to the explanation of both the commonly shared desires and the underlying considerations, which are either of a general or specific nature. The

district (first instance) court. This reform is a result of the Swedish government's policy to remove all primarily "administrative matters" from the courts' jurisdiction. If the Agency refuses the application of registration, its decision may, however, be appealed to court. See Swedish Marriage Code, Ch. 7 § 3 para. 3–4 and Ch. 16 § 5. See Jänterä-Jareborg, "Marital Agreements and Private Autonomy in Sweden", in: Scherpe (ed.), *Marital Agreements and Private Autonomy in a Comparative Perspective*, 2012, pp. 379–380.

47 See Boele-Woelki, "The Working Method of the Commission on European Family Law", in: Boele-Woelki (ed), *Common Core and Better Law in European Family Law*, European Family Law Series No. 10, 2005, pp. 15–38.

48 See Boele-Woelki/Braat/Curry-Sumner (eds), *European Family Law in Action, Volume IV: Property Relations between Spouses*, European Family Law Series No. 24, 2009.

49 Reference is made to the national reports by citing the author's name, the jurisdiction concerned and the number of the question where the specific answer is provided.

comments associated with each Principle contain this fundamental information. Finally, it should be emphasised that the CEFL Principles are not only aimed for Member States of the European Union but also for all jurisdictions in Europe. Hence, the comparative surveys in the preparatory work of the CEFL Principles included several European jurisdictions outside the EU.

Languages

The CEFL's working language is English. However, the Principles are formulated in three languages: English, French and German. No version is a translation of one of the two other languages. All three versions have not only been drafted at the same time, but have also influenced and improved each other. They are equally authentic. The present publication has been completed with a translation of the Principles into Dutch, Spanish and Swedish.

INTRODUCTION TO THE PRINCIPLES REGARDING PROPERTY RELATIONS BETWEEN SPOUSES

The current state of the law on property relations between spouses in Europe

The law regarding the property relations between spouses in the countries represented in the CEFL provides a varied picture. The most striking differences exist between the civil law and the common law approach.[50] Continental European systems generally regulate the property consequences of marriage through a specific set of rules commonly prescribed as matrimonial property law, whereas the common law does not have such a statutory body of law. In the common law jurisdictions represented in the CEFL marriage has no effect on the proprietary rights of the spouses. A default matrimonial property regime does not exist. Lack of similarity can also be discerned in respect of marital property agreements. In the civil law jurisdictions spouses enjoy a large degree of autonomy. They can choose their preferred matrimonial property regime or they can modify the default or any other regime either before or during the marriage. In contrast, in ENGLAND AND WALES and IRELAND pre-nuptial and post-nuptial agreements traditionally are not binding.[51] However, post-nuptial agreements have effect if they are fair[52] and the same applies since the ground-breaking judgment of the UK Supreme Court in *Granatino v Radmacher (formerly Granatino)*[53] in respect of pre-nuptial agreements. Moreover, the Law Commission for ENGLAND AND WALES is currently considering the legal effects of marital property agreements. Apart from the specific civil-common law dichotomy many differences exist among all the systems surveyed in respect of

---

50 See PINTENS, "Matrimonial Property Law in Europe", in: BOELE-WOELKI/MILES/SCHERPE (eds), *The Future of Family Property in Europe*, European Family Law Series No. 29, pp. 19–46; HERTEL, "Ehegüterrecht in Europa: Vergleich der gesetzlichen Güterstände und der Vermögensverteilung bei Scheidung", in: BENGEL/LIMMER/REIMANN (eds), *Festschrift Kanzleiter* 2010, pp. 207–226; SCHERPE (ed), *Marital Agreements and Private Autonomy in a Comparative Perspective, The legal status of pre-nuptial, post-nuptial and separation agreements*, 2012.

51 SCOTLAND does not fit clearly into either side of the dichotomy, being a mixed civil/common law system.

52 *MacLeod v. MacLeod* [2008] UKPC 64, [2010] 1 AC 298.

53 [2010] UKSC 42, [2011] 1 AC 534.

the categories of assets, the administration of assets and the distribution of assets upon dissolution of the marriage.

In order to make a comparison of the various systems possible the CEFL classified the different matrimonial property regimes currently applied in Europe. This classification was used by the experts in answering the questionnaire. The table below goes beyond the simple translation of the different systems into English. The commonly used term *community of acquisition*, for example, has been replaced by the more general term *community of property* which thus encloses several types of systems (universal community, community of acquisition, and other kinds of restricted communities). The same applies to the *community of accrued gains* which according to the CEFL classification can also be indicated as *participation in acquisitions*. For each country first the default statutory regime – if any – is indicated, followed by other statutory regimes.

TYPE OF REGIME	SOURCE	CLASSIFICATION AND TERMINOLOGY PROPOSED BY THE CEFL
	AUSTRIA	
Default statutory regime	Gütertrennung (§ 1237 Allgemeines Bürgerliches Gesetzbuch)	Deferred community
Other statutory regime	Gütergemeinschaft (§ 1233 Allgemeines Bürgerliches Gesetzbuch)	Community of property
	BELGIUM	
Default statutory regime	Wettelijk stelsel/Régime légal (Gemeenschap van aanwinsten/ Communauté des acquêts) (art. 1398 Code civil Belge)	Community of acquisitions
Other statutory regime	Scheiding van goederen/Séparation de biens (art. 1466 Code civil Belge)	Separation of property
Other statutory regime	Conventionele gemeenschap/ Communauté conventionnelle (art. 1451 Code civil Belge)	Community of property
	BULGARIA	
Default statutory regime	Съпружеска имуществена общност (art. 19 СЕМЕЕН КОДЕКС 1985)	Community of acquisition
	CATALONIA	
Default statutory regime	Separació de bens (arts. 232-1 to 232-12 Codi civil de Catalunya)	Separation of property
Other statutory regime	Participació en el guanys (arts. 232-13 to 232-27 (Codi civil de Catalunya)	Participation in acquisitions

TYPE OF REGIME	SOURCE	CLASSIFICATION AND TERMINOLOGY PROPOSED BY THE CEFL
Other statutory regime	Comunitat de bens (arts. 232-30 to 232-38 Codi Civil de Catalunya	Community of property
	CZECH REPUBLIC	
Default statutory regime	Společné jmění manželů; participation in acquisitions (§ 143-151 Občanský zákoník)	Community of property
Other statutory regime	Vyhrazení vzniku společného jmění manželů ke dni zániku manželství (§ 143a para. 2 Občanský zákoník)	Deferred community of property
	DENMARK	
Default statutory regime	Fælleseje Almindeligt formuefællesskab (§ 15 Ægteskabsloven)	Deferred community of property
Other statutory regime	Særeje (§ 28 Retsvirkningsloven)	Separation of property
	ENGLAND AND WALES	
	Financial relief Matrimonial Causes Act 1973 Part 2	Separation of property with distribution by the competent authority
	FINLAND	
Default statutory regime	Avio-oikeus (§ 35 Avioliittolaki)	Deferred community of property
Other statutory regime	Omaisuuden erillisyys (§ 41 Avioliittolaki)	Separation of property
	FRANCE	
Default statutory regime	Communauté légale (communauté réduite aux acquêts; art. 1401 Code civil français)	Community of property
Other statutory regime	Communauté conventionnelle (art. 1497 Code civil français)	Community of property
Other statutory regime	Séparation de biens (art. 1536 Code civil français)	Separation of property
Other statutory regime	Participation aux acquêts (art. 1569 Code civil français)	Participation in acquisitions
	GERMANY	
Default statutory regime	Zugewinngemeinschaft (§ 1363 Bürgerliches Gesetzbuch)	Participation in acquisition
Other statutory regime	Gütertrennung (§ 1414 Bürgerliches Gesetzbuch)	Separation of property
Other statutory regime	Gütergemeinschaft (§ 1415 Bürgerliches Gesetzbuch)	Community of property

TYPE OF REGIME	SOURCE	CLASSIFICATION AND TERMINOLOGY PROPOSED BY THE CEFL
	GREECE	
Default statutory regime	Περιουσιακή αυτοτέλεια των συζύγων (art. 1397 Οικογενειακο Δικαιο)	Separation of property with a claim of participation in acquisitions.
Other statutory regime	Κοινοκτημοσυνη (Art. 1403 Οικογενειακο Δικαιο)	Community of property
	HUNGARY	
Default statutory regime	Házastársi vagyonközösség (Art. 27 para. 1 Családjo törvény)	Community of property
	IRELAND	
	The Irish Family Law Act 1995, Part II and the Irish Family Law (Divorce) Act 1996, Part II	Separation of property with distribution by the competent authority
	ITALY	
Default statutory regime	Comunione dei beni (art. 177 Codice Civile Italiano)	Community of property
Other statutory regime	Comunione convenzionale (art. 210 Codice Civile Italiano)	Community of property
Other statutory regime	Separazione dei beni (art. 215 Codice Civile Italiano)	Separation of property
	LITHUANIA	
Default statutory regime	Bendroji jungtinė sutuoktinių nuosvybė (art. 3.87 Lietuvos civilinis kodeksas)	Community of property
Other statutory regime	Vedybų sutartimi nustatytas režimas (art. 3.104 Lietuvos civilinis kodeksas	Separation of property
	MALTA	
Default statutory regime	Community of acquests (art. 1316 Maltese Civil Code)	Community of property
Other statutory regime	Community of residue under separate administration (art. 1338 Maltese Civil Code)	Community of property
	THE NETHERLANDS	
Default statutory regime	Algemene gemeenschap van goederen (art. 1:93 Burgerlijk Wetboek)	Community of property
Other statutory regime	Gemeenschap van vruchten en inkomsten (art. 1:123 Burgerlijk Wetboek)	Community of property
Other statutory regime	Gemeenschap van winst en verlies (art. 1:128 Burgerlijk Wetboek)	Community of property
Other statutory regime	Verrekenbedingen van inkomsten of van vermogen (art. 1:132–143 Burgerlijk Wetboek)	Participation in acquisitions

TYPE OF REGIME	SOURCE	CLASSIFICATION AND TERMINOLOGY PROPOSED BY THE CEFL
	NORWAY	
Default statutory regime	Felleseie (Kapittel 6 og 12 Lov om ekteskap)	Deferred community of property
Other statutory regime*	Særeie (§ 42 Lov om ekteskap)	Separation of property
	POLAND	
Default statutory regime	Wspólność majątkowa (art. 3.104 Kodeks rodzinny i opiekuńczy)	Community of property
Other statutory regime	Rozdzielność majątkowa (art. 51 Kodeks rodzinny i opiekuńczy)	Separation of property
Other statutory regime	Rozdzielność majątkowa z wyrównaniem dorobków (art. 51 para. 2 Kodeks rodzinny i opiekuńczy)	Participation in acquisitions
	PORTUGAL	
Default statutory regime	Regime da comunhão de adquiridos (art. 1717 Código Civil Português)	Community of property
Other statutory regime	Regime da comunhão geral (art. 1732 Código Civil Português)	Community of property
Other statutory regime	Regime da separação (art. 1735 Código Civil Português)	Separation of property
	RUSSIA	
Default statutory regime	Законный режим имущества супругов (Статья 33 Семейный кодекс Российской Федерации) (Статья 42. Содержание брачного договора)	Community of property
	SCOTLAND	
	Scots Family law Act 1985, S 9	Separation of property with distribution by the competent authority
	SLOVAKIA	
Default statutory regime	Bezpodielové spoluvlastníctvo manželov (§ 143 a nasl. Občianskeho zákonníka)	Community of property
Other statutory regime	Vznik bezpodielového spoluvlastníctva ku dňu zániku manželstva (§ 143a ods. 2 Občianskeho zákonníka)	Deferred community of property
Other statutory regime	Zrušenie bezpodielového spoluvlastníctva manželov súdom (§ 148a ods. 2 Občianskeho zákonníka)	Separation of property (only upon a decision of the court in cases determined by the law)

TYPE OF REGIME	SOURCE	CLASSIFICATION AND TERMINOLOGY PROPOSED BY THE CEFL
	SPAIN	
Default statutory regime	Sociedad de ganaciales (art. 1344 Código Civil español)	Community of property
Other statutory regime	Régimen de participación (art. 1411 Código Civil español)	Participation in acquisitions
Other statutory regime	Régimen de separación de bienes (art. 1435 Código Civil español)	Separation of property
	SWEDEN	
Default statutory regime	Giftorättsgemenskap (Kap 7: § 1 Äktenskapsbalken)	Deferred community of property
Other statutory regime	Egendomsskillnad (Kap. 7 § 2 Äktenskapsbalken)	Separation of property
	SWITZERLAND	
Default statutory regime	Errungenschaftsbeteiligung/ Participation aux acquêts (art. 181 Code civil Suisse)	Participation in acquisitions
Other statutory regime	Gütergemeinschaft/ Communauté des biens (art. 221 Code civil Suisse)	Community of property
Other statutory regime	Gütertrennung/ Séparation des biens (art. 247 Code civil Suisse)	Separation of property

The concept of property relations between spouses

The term *property relations between spouses* which the CEFL has chosen for its Principles encompasses three different sets of rules: the general rights and duties of the spouses in relation to general property issues, such as the family home and household goods, marital property agreements and the matrimonial property regime. Under FRENCH law and GERMAN law, for instance, the spouses' general rights and duties are indicated as *régime primaire* or *allgemeine Ehewirkungen*, whereas the matrimonial property regime is called *régime secondaire* or *Ehegüterstand*. This part of the property relations between spouses constitutes the core of the whole set of Principles.

Based upon the jurisdictions represented in the CEFL five different regimes have been distinguished. They are listed below. The term "community of acquisitions" does not include the universal community of property which only functions in THE NETHERLANDS as the default regime. In other jurisdictions the term community of property is also used, however, such a community only comprises acquisitions. Differences also exit in respect of the community of accrued gains on the one hand and the participation in acquisitions on the other hand.

Although the CEFL recognizes these variations for the purpose of this work it is possible and useful to put the two regimes under the same category.

ENGLISH	FRENCH	GERMAN
Community of acquisitions	Communauté d'acquêts	Errungenschaftsgemeinschaft
Community of accrued gains/Participation in acquisitions	Participation aux acquêts	Zugewinngemeinschaft/ Errungenschaftsbeteiligung
Deferred community of property	Communauté de biens différée	Aufgeschobene Gütergemeinschaft
Separation of property	Séparation de biens	Gütertrennung
Separation of property with distribution by the competent authority	Séparation de biens avec répartition des biens par l'autorité compétente	Gütertrennung mit behördlicher Vermögensverteilung

- the *community of acquisitions* (AUSTRIA, BELGIUM, BULGARIA, CZECH REPUBLIC,[54] FRANCE, HUNGARY, ITALY, LITHUANIA, MALTA, POLAND, PORTUGAL, RUSSIA, SLOVAKIA and SPAIN)
- the *community of accrued gains/participation in acquisitions* (CATALONIA, GERMANY, GREECE, and SWITZERLAND)
- the *deferred community* (DENMARK, FINLAND, NORWAY, and SWEDEN)[55]
- the *separation of property*[56] (BELGIUM, CATALONIA, FRANCE, GERMANY, ITALY, MALTA, POLAND, PORTUGAL, SPAIN and SWITZERLAND)
- the *separation of property with distribution by the competent authority* (ENGLAND AND WALES, IRELAND and SCOTLAND).

Finally, it should be noted that CEFL's concept of property relations between spouses as used in these Principles does not include maintenance obligations between spouses, nor succession rights of a surviving spouse, nor the consequences of insolvency proceedings. Pension rights, too, fall outside the scope of the Principles. In some jurisdictions, pension rights can be covered by the applicable matrimonial property regime, whereas in others they fall outside. Pension rights may be intimately linked with post-divorce maintenance. They are also connected with social security law. In many jurisdictions specific rules

---

54 Erroneously, in the printed version of the national reports the CZECH system has been put under the community of accrued gains/participation in acquisitions, see BOELE-WOELKI/ BRAAT/CURRY-SUMNER (eds), *European Family Law in Action, Volume IV: Property Relations between Spouses*, European Family Law Series No. 24, 2009, pp. 603–753.

55 Separation of ownership prevails but at the moment of dissolution of the regime, the acquisitions are divided with a possibility of adjustment by the court.

56 In many other jurisdictions (also in the Nordic countries) the spouses can agree through marital property agreement on separation of property.

exist on damages due to domestic violence; they overlap with specific consequences of divorce which have an effect of marital property. Damages paid to a spouse qualify under the CEFL Principles as personal property, but are not otherwise dealt with.

International and European instruments

There are several international and European instruments in the field of the law of property relations between spouses which are to be taken into account. They address general rights and duties of the spouses, private international law issues and matters of substantive law. The most relevant organisations and their respective instruments are listed here. Under each Principle – if relevant – reference is made to any specific provision of these instruments.

a. The United Nations

The United Nations does not have an instrument directly regulating issues concerning matrimonial property law. However, the principle of equality between the spouses has been codified in various UN instruments.[57]

The *Universal Declaration of Human Rights 1948* includes in its Article 7 the principle of equality and the prohibition of discrimination. This provision also comprises the general right to own and administer property. Article 16 specifically entrenches the principle of equality between men and women, wherefrom the principle of equality between the spouses results.

Article 23 of the *International Covenant on Civil and Political Rights 1966* also codifies the principle of equality between the spouses.

The same counts for the *International Covenant on Economic, Social and Cultural Rights 1966*, in which in Articles 3 and 10 the equality of men and women is regulated.

Finally, Article 16 of the *Convention on the Elimination of All Forms of Discrimination against Women* 1979, provides for a clear, precise and extensive list of equal rights of men and women in family and husband and wife in marriage. Furthermore, is important to note that subsection *h* of the first paragraph of this Article states that 'both spouses have the same rights in respect of the ownership, acquisition, management, administration, enjoyment and disposition of property'. Without directly referring to standard subjects of

[57] All instruments listed in this paragraph are available at: untreaty.un.org.

matrimonial property law this Article clearly emphasises the equal basis upon which the marriage and property relations are determined.

b. The Hague Conference on Private International Law

The Hague Conference on Private International Law adopted two conventions in 1905 and 1978.[58] The *Convention Relating to Conflicts of Laws with regard to the Effects of Marriage on the Rights and Duties of the Spouses in their Personal Relationship and with regard to their Estates 1905* is still in force in ITALY, PORTUGAL and ROMANIA. This old Hague Convention determines which law governs the property relations between the spouses. Marital property agreements are specifically addressed. However, many former Contracting States (BELGIUM, GERMANY, FRANCE, THE NETHERLANDS, POLAND and SWEDEN) have denounced the Convention on account of Article 2, which determines that the national law of the husband is to be applied.

The *Convention on the Law Applicable to Matrimonial Property Regimes 1978* entered into force in 1992 for only FRANCE, LUXEMBOURG and THE NETHERLANDS. This Hague Convention focuses on the law applicable to the matrimonial property regimes. Despite the small number of Contracting States this Convention has influenced the lawmaking in other jurisdictions, for example in BELGIUM, FINLAND and SWEDEN. It has had an impact also on the drafting of international instruments, for example, the rules on matrimonial property relations in the *Convention between Denmark, Finland, Iceland, Norway and Sweden on Issues of Private International Law concerning Marriage, Adoption and Guardianship* as revised in 2006, and more recently on the current European Commission's Proposal for a Regulation on jurisdiction, applicable law and the recognition and enforcement of decisions in matters of matrimonial property regimes.[59]

c. The Council of Europe

The Council of Europe is an organisation under which many human rights instruments have been adopted.[60]

The most important instrument is the *European Convention on Human Rights and Fundamental Freedoms 1950.*[61] Article 8 contains the right to respect for private and family life and Article 14 contains the prohibition of discrimination on grounds of – amongst others – a person's sex. In the context of property

58 Both Conventions are available at: www.hcch.net.

59 Proposal for a Regulation on jurisdiction, applicable law and the recognition and enforcement of decisions in matters of matrimonial property regimes, COM(2011) 126/2.

60 All treaties listed in this paragraph are available at: conventions.coe.int.

61 All countries represented in the CEFL are bound by this Convention.

relations between spouses Article 6 of the Convention, which guarantees the right to a fair trial within reasonable time by an independent court, is of particular importance in cases where States and notaries have been held liable for delayed liquidations after the dissolution of the matrimonial property regime.[62]

The Convention also forbids all forms of discrimination as regards rights guaranteed by the additional Protocols supplementing the Convention. Article 5 of Protocol No. 7 prescribes that spouses shall enjoy equality of rights and responsibilities of a private law character between them, and in their relations with their children, during marriage and in the event of its dissolution. This Article, which includes property rights, shall, nevertheless, not prevent States from taking such measures as are necessary in the interests of the children. Furthermore, according to Article 1 of the first Protocol, every person is entitled to the peaceful enjoyment of his or her possessions. No one shall be deprived of his or her possessions except in the public interest and subject to the conditions provided for by law and by the general principles of international law.

In addition, the *European Social Charter of 1961 and 1996* is of relevance. Article 27 determines that all persons with family responsibilities and who are engaged or wish to engage in employment have a right to do so without being subject to discrimination and as far as possible without conflict between their employment and family responsibilities. In order to guarantee the equality of men and women in employment, States party to the Charter shall take appropriate measures to enable workers to fulfil their family responsibilities. The Charter does not directly deal with the spouses' duty to fulfil their family responsibilities. Not all of the jurisdictions surveyed, however, have ratified this Charter.[63]

In addition to these two Conventions several Declarations, Recommendations and Resolutions have been adopted by the Committee of Ministers and the Parliamentary Assembly concerning the property relations between spouses.[64] They are, nevertheless, not binding on Member States, and decades may have passed since they were concluded, which might limit their adequacy in modern society. Listed in chronological order the following instruments are of relevance:

- (CM) Resolution (78)37 of 27 September 1978 on equality of spouses in civil law;

62 See decisions of the European Court of Human Rights 3 October 2000 (*Kanoun/France*); 2 December 2003 (*Treial/ Estonia*); 27 April 2004 (*Janik/Poland*) and 25 May 2004 (*Szakaly/ Hungary*).

63 The 1961 Charter has not been ratified by BULGARIA, LITHUANIA, RUSSIA, and SWITZERLAND and the 1996 Charter has not been ratified by AUSTRIA, CZECH REPUBLIC, GERMANY, GREECE, POLAND, RUSSIA, SPAIN, SWITZERLAND and the UNITED KINGDOM.

64 These instruments are available at: www.coe.int.

- (CM) Recommendation (81)15 of 16 October 1981 on the rights of spouses relating to the occupation of the family home and the use of the household contents;
- (CM) Declaration of 16 November 1988 on equality of women and men;
- (CM) Recommendation (2007)17 of 21 November 2007 on gender equality standards and mechanisms;
- (CM) Declaration (2009)68 of 6 May 2009 on making gender equality a reality.

Section III of Resolution 78(37) on equality of spouses in civil law is of particular relevance since it contains provisions concerning the property and financial relations between spouses. In this Resolution the Committee of Ministers recommends the governments of the Member States to take all steps necessary to promote equality of the spouses in matrimonial property matters, for instance, by ensuring that "all household expenses are borne jointly by both spouses".[65] Under Paragraphs 12, 13 and 14 reference is made to three kinds of matrimonial property regimes: community of property, community of accrued gains and separation of property. With regard to spousal agency or representation it is stated under Paragraph 1 that the governments of the Member States should take necessary steps to ensure that civil law does not contain provisions by which a spouse is put in a more advantageous positions than the other spouse, for instance because this spouse has the sole right to represent the other spouse.

Recommendation (81)15 on the rights of spouses relating to the occupation of the family home and the use of the household contents is an additional document to the Resolution on equality of spouses in civil law 1978 and contains recommendations in the form of principles on the property relations of spouses with regard to the administration and occupation of community property.

d. The European Union

The competence of the European Union covers two relevant aspects regarding the property relations between spouses. First, the right to equality has been laid down in the *European Charter of Fundamental Rights 2000*, which the Lisbon Treaty "upgraded" to become a part of binding EU Treaty law. Article 23 explicitly determines that equality between men and women must be ensured in all areas.

Secondly, based upon Article 81 TFEU two new instruments regarding the property relations of international couples may be adopted by the European

65 See Section III, Paragraph 8 under I of the Resolution.

legislature in the form of a Regulation.[66] For the CEFL's purposes the Proposal for a *Regulation on jurisdiction, applicable law and the recognition and enforcement of decisions in matters of matrimonial property regimes*[67] is of significant importance. The second Proposal for a *Regulation on jurisdiction, applicable law and the recognition and enforcement of decisions regarding the property consequences of registered partnerships*[68] has not been taken into account since the CEFL Principles are restricted to proprietary aspects as a consequence of marriage concluded between different-sex or same-sex couples.

e. Other European cooperation

Some States have also concluded multilateral and bilateral conventions both in the field of private international law and substantive law concerning matrimonial property aspects.

In 2006, the choice of law rules concerning matrimonial property relations were revised in the *Convention between Denmark, Finland, Iceland, Norway and Sweden on Issues of Private International Law concerning Marriage, Adoption and Guardianship*,[69] which dates originally from 1931. The new rules, endorsing the spouses' and future spouses' right to choose the law applicable, entered into force in all the Nordic countries on 1 December 2008. Party autonomy was considered justified not least with regard to the increasing differences between the Nordic States in respect of substantive matrimonial property law. The Convention applies however only to spouses who at the date of their marriage are citizens in a Nordic State, upon marriage take their habitual residence in a Nordic State, and maintain their habitual residence and citizenship in one of the Nordic States. In this way, it aims at facilitating free movement between the Nordic countries which, since 1955, have a joint labour market for their citizens. If any of the above-mentioned requirements is missing, the situation falls outside the scope of the inter-Nordic Convention.

On 4 February 2010 FRANCE and GERMANY concluded an *Agreement on the establishment of an optional matrimonial property regime* prescribed as *Zugewinngemeinschaft* and *participation aux acquêts* respectively. It is the first

---

66 See MARTINY, "Die Kommissionsvorschläge für das Ehegüterrecht sowie für das Güterrecht eingetragener Partnerschaften", *Praxis des internationalen Privat- und Verfahrensrechts* 2011, pp. 437–458 with extensive references. FARRUGIA, "The future EU Regulation concerning matrimonial property regimes", in: CAMPUZANO DÍAZ/CZEPELAK/RODRÍGUEZ VÁQUEZ (eds), *Latest Developments in EU Private International Law*, Antwerp, 2011, pp. 63–82.

67 COM(2011) 126/2.

68 COM(2011) 127/2.

69 See MEURLING, "Less Surprise for Spouses Moving Between the Nordic Countries? Amendments to the 1931 Nordic Convention on Marriage", *Yearbook of Private International Law* 2009, pp. 385–394.

attempt to unify substantive matrimonial property law in Europe.[70] Under the Agreement couples whose matrimonial property relations – according to FRENCH or GERMAN conflict of law rules – are governed by either FRENCH or GERMAN law may also choose the special, optional matrimonial property regime. As a result, the Agreement is not limited to FRENCH or GERMAN spouses or to mixed FRENCH-GERMAN couples, but covers all spouses irrespective of their nationality who, according to the applicable choice of law in a concerned State, are free to choose FRENCH or GERMAN law as being applicable to their matrimonial property relations, given the spouses' or one of the spouse's connection to FRANCE or GERMANY. Interestingly enough, the Agreement does not exclude other Member States from becoming parties to it, following the ratification by FRANCE and GERMANY. Due to the growing mobility of persons within the European Union it is considered desirable that other Member States may accede to the Agreement once it has entered into force. The substantive rules of the Agreement have been extensively taken into account in the overview of international and European instruments listed under the relevant Principles.

Women's employment and the care for children

European societies develop at different pace and encounter different impediments. The economic situations of married couples within Europe vary to a great extent in respect of the level of women's labour participation, social welfare systems and tax regimes. However, the growth of women's employment and the dual-earner family model is a Europe-wide trend. Sociological studies show that dual-earnership is the rule rather than the exception in European families, and that it is increasingly common among families with young children.[71] Economic studies have shown that women's labour market participation is much more influenced by their family situation than men's.[72] The presence of (young) children and the time needed to care for those children

---

70 See FÖTSCHL, "The Common Matrimonial Property Regime of Germany and France: Epoch-Making in the Unification of Law", *European Review of Private Law* 2010, pp. 881–889 = *Yearbook of Private International Law* 2009, pp. 395–404; KLIPSTEIN, "Der deutsch-französische Wahlgüterstand der Wahl-Zugewinngemeinschaft", *Familie, Partnerschaft, Recht* 2010, pp. 510–515; MARTINY, "Der neue deutsch-französische Wahlgüterstand – Ein Beispiel optionaler bilateraler Familienrechtsvereinheitlichung", *Zeitschrift für Europäisches Privatrecht* 2011, pp. 577–600; MEYER, "Der neue deutsch-französische Wahlgüterstand", Zeitschrift für das gesamte Familienrecht 2010, pp. 612–617; SIMLER, "Le nouveau régime matrimonial optionnel franco-allemand de participation aux acquêts", *Droit de la famille* 2010 No. 5, pp. 9–19; DETHLOFF, "Der deutsch-französische Wahlgüterstand, Wegbereiter für eine Angleichung des Familienrechts?", *RabelsZ für ausländisches und internationales Privatrecht* 2012, pp. 509–539.

71 See MALINEN/KINNUNEN/TOLVANEN/RONKA/WIERDA-BOER/GERRIS, "Happy spouses, happy parents? Family relationships among Finnish and Dutch dual earners," *Journal of Marriage and Family* 2010, pp. 293–306.

72 See RUBERY/SMITH/FAGAN, *Women's Employment in Europe*, 1999.

in particular places a heavy restriction on mothers' participation in the labour market. Based on these results a wide range of measures have been taken to facilitate the combination of paid work and care tasks and to promote the so-called work-life balance. As various studies show, such measures do indeed stimulate women's labour market participation.[73] However, there are still major differences in participation between different family types and between European countries that cannot be explained by the availability or absence of work-life facilities such as child care and leave arrangements, as for instance the choice for part-time work as a strategy to combine work and family life. In this respect cultural, regional and educational factors may be involved. It is already known that the example set by mothers influences daughters' participation later in life,[74] but it is not yet known, whether this is true in all European countries.

While women have made progress in terms of career opportunities, both men and women are experiencing more time pressure and greater difficulties to balance work and family life.[75] Despite the increasing labour market participation of women, there is an enduring gender asymmetry in family care involvement, even in the more egalitarian Nordic countries. Workplaces, all over Europe, are still highly gendered and both vertical and horizontal segregation is still common. Reconciling work and family life (including the care for both children and the elderly) with competing demands coming from outside the family has become increasingly complicated.

Central questions and concerns

During the drafting process, the CEFL was confronted with several important questions regarding the content and the structure of the Principles: is it possible to establish only one single matrimonial property regime? If this is not the case, should another matrimonial property regime (which?) be drafted? If the answer to this question is in the affirmative, how should both regimes be presented? Should one regime be the default regime, and the other function as an optional regime? Which regime should be chosen as the default regime, and which as the optional regime? Should both regimes be presented as equal default regimes, meaning that they are applicable if the spouses have not otherwise agreed?

---

73 See Den Dulk/Van Doorne-Huiskes, "Social Policy in Europe: Its Impact on Families and Work" in: Crompton/Lewis/Lyonette, *Women, Men, Work and Family in Europe* 2007, pp. 35–57.

74 See Van Putten, *The role of intergenerational transfers in gendered labour patterns*, 2009.

75 Van der Lippe/De Jager/Kops, Work-family balance in European countries, *Acta Sociologica* 2006, pp. 303–319.

All these questions were extensively discussed amongst the members of the Organising Committee, who could not reach unanimity regarding all issues. Furthermore no clear solution concerning the various options emerged from the discussion with the expert group, though that meeting in Sigtuna in September 2011 highlighted additional important points, which were carefully considered.

Below, the answers to these crucial questions and final choices will be explained and justified.

Two regimes

The comparative research-based drafting of the Principles revealed that the elements of all national systems surveyed cannot be merged into one single matrimonial property regime. Within Europe, five different systems can be identified. Roughly speaking, it is possible to divide these into two main systems: a *community system* on the one side, and a *participation system* on the other side. The basic starting points are diametrically opposed. A community of property between the spouses automatically takes effect at the moment of concluding the marriage, whereas in a participation system, no community of property will ever arise by operation of law. The property of each spouse is treated as the owner's separate property. A clear common core in favour of either a community system or a participation system does not exist within the jurisdictions represented in the CEFL. Consequently, these fundamental differences must be acknowledged when constructing a model for Europe. As a result, the CEFL drafted two matrimonial property regimes: the participation in acquisitions and the community of acquisitions. The reduction of the number of systems to only two systems might show that, within these two systems, harmonisation of the law is possible. In view of the CEFL's aim of reducing the wide variation within Europe, such a result – and the resulting comparable simplicity – might be regarded as a major achievement.

Arguments in favour of a participation regime or a community regime

In the discussion regarding whether from a European point of view a choice between the two regimes should be made and, if so, which of the regimes should function as the default regime, all pros and cons have been weighed.

The main arguments in favour of a participation regime are that it:

- promotes the independence of spouses;
- is more suitable for spouses who both own property and/or are on the labour market;
- provides for a right to participate in the wealth acquired during the marriage.

The main arguments in favour of a community regime are that it:

- promotes solidarity between the spouses;
- is more suitable for a spouse who neither owns property nor is on the labour market;
- provides for a property title if assets are to be divided at the end of the marriage, which generally is considered to be stronger than a monetary claim.

From a harmonisation point of view the participation of acquistions regime is the best solution especially as it provides a bridge between the civil law systems and the common law systems but that argument is in itself not an argument in favour of that specific regime.

In assessing this decision it should be kept in mind that the CEFL has not undertaken any socio-economic research on care for children and elderly, women joining the labour market or, more generally, the distribution of labour between spouses in the various European societies.

Equality of both regimes

The CEFL has decided not to make a choice between either regime regarding their legal nature as a default regime. This decision is based on a careful evaluation of the various pros and cons of both regimes. It acknowledges that cases that are solved under one regime do not fundamentally change if they fall under the other regime. Similar results are achieved, although both regimes conceptually differ. Finally, from a strategic point of view, it is not desirable to promote one regime instead of the other. This would not reflect the various European approaches regarding property relations between spouses. Neither the one nor the other regime is the dominating regime in Europe. It is for national legislatures to decide whether they – if inspired by these Principles – opt for one of these regimes if a decision about a default or / and an optional regime is to be taken.

Both regimes have been put on an equal footing, although the participation regime precedes the community regime. No weight, however, should be put on the order in which the regimes are presented. Principles 4:16 and 4:33 make it clear that the respective system is applicable if the spouses have not agreed otherwise. Moreoever, it should be kept in mind that each matrimonial property regime, whether it functions as a default or as an optional regime, does not stand alone. The regime is strongly connected with the rights and duties of the spouses (Chapter 1) and the possibility for them to make a marital property agreement (Chapter 2). The rules of these two Chapters are aimed to be mandatory. They equally apply to both matrimonial property regimes. As a result it was possible to bring both regimes in line with each other, since they are bound by the same set of general principles. In this respect the attempt to provide a harmonising model for European matrimonial property law has been successful. Another characteristic feature of the Principles regarding property relations between spouses concerns the emphasis on the autonomy of the spouses. The spouses are free to agree otherwise and create their own solution according to their needs and expectations.

Underlying values of both regimes

As regards both regimes a restricted approach has been chosen. Property acquired *before* the marriage by the spouses will not be included into the division or distribution of property in the case of a dissolution of the marriage. The same applies to debts, which each spouse incurred *before* entering into marriage. They remain each spouse's personal debts. This restriction is expressed in the term of both regimes: *participation in acquisitions* and *community of acquistions*. The CEFL opts for this approach in order to enhance self-sufficiency and independence of both spouses. This reflects the modern tendency in the majority of jurisdictions surveyed. It is also in accordance with the standard set in Principle 2:2 of the Principles Regarding Divorce and Maintenance between Former Spouses. As a result only marital contribution justifies marital solidarity which is the main fundament upon which both CEFL matrimonial property regimes are built.[76] They are aimed to meet the needs of today's societies in Europe. The CEFL has tried to modernise both regimes by stipulating that generally the wealth which has been acquired during the marriage should be shared in a fair manner whereby hardship situations can also be taken into account. This leads to more flexibility.

The specific underlying values and concepts, which have guided the CEFL in its search of a well-balanced and consistent set of Principles, are explained in the comments on each individual Principle. In addition the Preamble and its comment provide explanations of the aims and objectives of this set of Principles.

The significance of the CEFL Principles for international couples

In the future, the Principles on European Family Law might contribute to the drafting of an optional European family law instrument. Such an instrument, once adopted by the European institutions, could be chosen by international

[76] See Boele-Woelki, "Ziel- und Wertvorstellungen der CEFL in ihren Prinzipien zum europäischen Familienrecht", in: Declerck/Helms/Scherpe/Senaeve/Verbeke (eds), *Confronting the Frontiers of Family and Succession Law, Liber Amicorum Walter Pintens*, 2012, pp. 167–185.

couples as the law governing their marriage or partnership, their general rights and duties, their property relations, their divorce etc.[77] The introduction of an optional European Matrimonial Property Regime was proposed already more than a decade ago.[78] The European Commission also considers that unified matrimonial property law, which has been established in the *French-German Agreement*, is one possible means of reducing legal uncertainty for international couples.[79] In following a truly European approach regarding the property relations of international couples, the CEFL Principles might also be used.[80]

Scope

These Principles regulate the property relations between spouses. They adopt the approach that there is a distinction between matrimonial property law on the one hand and maintenance between former spouses on the other and that both areas are considered as separate issues. Post-divorce maintenance has already been addressed in the Principles Regarding Divorce and Maintenance between Former Spouses where it has been specified that property settlement after divorce has an indirect influence on maintenance in nearly all jurisdictions surveyed insofar as a the division of property can influence the creditor's needs and the debtor's ability to pay.

Structure and content of the Principles regarding Property Relations between Spouses

This 4th set of CEFL's Principles of European Family Law contains a Preamble and 58 Principles contained in three Chapters.

- The *first Chapter* deals with the General Rights and Duties of the Spouses: General application (Principle 4:1), Equality of the spouses (Principle 4:2),

---

77 See Jänterä-Jareborg, "Europeanization of Law: Harmonization or Fragmentation – A Family Law Approach", *Tidskrift utgiven av Juridiska Föreningen i Finland* 2010, pp. 504–515 (512).

78 See Agell, "The Division of Property upon Divorce from a European Perspective", in: Liber amicorum Marie-Thérèse Meulders-Klein, *Droit comparé des personnes et de la famille*, 1998 pp. 1–20; Verbeke, "Perspectives for an International Marital Contract", *Maastricht Journal of European and Comparative Law*, 2001 pp. 189–200; Dethloff, "Die Europäische Ehe", *Zeitschrift für das Standesamtswesen* 2006, pp. 253–260. See also the European Economic Social Committee (EESC), in its Opinion of 21 September 2011, SOC/146 and SOC/147.

79 See Communication of the European Commission on Bringing Clarity to Property Rights of International Couples, Com 125/3.

80 See Dethloff, "Der deutsch-französische Wahlgüterstand, Wegbereiter für eine Angleichung des Familienrechts?", *RabelsZ für ausländisches und internationales Privatrecht* 2012, pp. 509–539; Boele-Woelki, "Cross-border Family Relationships in Europe: Towards a Common European Matrimonial Property Law based upon Cooperation between Private International Law and Substantive Law", in: Keirse/Loos (eds), *Alternative Ways to a New Ius Commune*, 2012, pp. 33–47.

Legal capacity of the spouses (Principle 4:3), Contributions to the needs of the family (Principle 4:4), Protection of the family home and household goods (Principle 4:5), Protection of the leased family home (Principle 4:6), Representation (Principle 4:7), Duty to inform (Principle 4:8) and Freedom to enter into marital property agreement (Principle 4:9).

- *Chapter two* addresses Marital Property Agreements: Concept (Principle 4:10), Form requirements (Principle 4:11), Disclosure (Principle 4:13), Obligations of the notary or other legal professionals with comparable functions (4:14), Effects as against third parties (Principle 4:14) and Exceptional hardship (Principle 4:15).
- *Chapter three* on Matrimonial Property Regimes consists of two Sections.
  - *Section A* on the Participation in Acquisitions consists of: Applicability of the participation in acquisitions regime (Principle 4:16), Concept of participation in acquisitions (Principle 4:17), Acquisitions (Principle 4:18), Reserved property (Principle 20), Presumption of joint ownership (Principle 4:20), Personal debts (Principle 4:21), Recovery of personal debts (Principle 4:22), Administration of property (Principle 4:23), Grounds for Dissolution (Principle) 4:24), Date of dissolution (Principle 4:25), Determination and valuation of acquisitions (Principle 4:26), Detrimental transactions (Principle 4:27), Compensation (Principle 4:28), Agreement on participation (Principle 4:29), Allocation of family home and household goods (Principle (4:30), Equal participation in the net aquisitions (Principle 4:31) and Adjustment by the competent authority (Principle (4:32).
  - *Section B* on the Community of Acquisitions consists of: Applicability of the community of acquisitions regime (Principle 4:33), Concept of the community of acquisitions (Principle 4:34), Community property (Principle 4:35), Personal property (Principle 4:36), Substitution (Principle (4:37), Investment or reinvestment (Principle 4:38), Presumption of community property (Principle 4:39), Community debts (Principle 4:40), Personal debts (Principle 4:41), Recovery of community debts (Principle 4:42), Recovery of personal debts (Principle 4:43), Administration of community property (Principle 4:44), Acts requiring joint administration (Principle 4:45), Annulment of acts of administration (Principle 4:46), Administration of personal property (Principle 4:47), Divestment of the right to administer community property (Principle 4:48), Grounds for dissolution (Principle 4:49), Date of dissolution (Principle 4:50), Administration after dissolution (Principle 4:51), Determination and valuation of the community property (Principle 4:52), Compensation (Principle 4:53), Ranking of debts (Principle 4:54), Agreement on distribution (Principle 4:55), Allocation of family home, household goods and professional assets

(Principle 4:56), Equal sharing and adjustment (Principle 4:57) and Recovery of community debts after distribution of the community (Principle 4:58).

Each Principle has four parts: (1) the black letter text of the Principle, (2) an overview of the INTERNATIONAL INSTRUMENTS, if any, on the issues dealt with under the concerned Principle, (3) a COMPARATIVE OVERVIEW of the issue addressed in the Principle and finally (4) an explanation as to *why* the Principle has been drafted as proposed – which information is provided in the COMMENT to each Principle. The comparative information compiled in this volume is drafted with the aim of covering all aspects of relevance for the regulation of property relations between spouses at least as far as the European systems represented in the CEFL are concerned.

PREAMBLE
PREAMBULE
PRÄAMBEL

PREAMBLE

Recognising that, notwithstanding the existing diversities between national family law systems, there is nevertheless a growing convergence of laws;
Recognising that the free movement of persons within Europe is hindered by the remaining differences;
Desiring to contribute to common European values regarding the equality of spouses;
Desiring to strike a balance between the spouses' private autonomy and their solidarity;
Desiring to contribute to the welfare of the family;
Desiring to secure the protection of the family home;
Desiring to guarantee each spouse a fair share in the property acquired during the marriage;
Desiring to contribute to the harmonisation of family law in Europe and to strengthen the rights of its citizens;
The Commission on European Family Law recommends the following Principles:

PREAMBULE

Reconnaissant que, malgré les diversités existant entre les systèmes nationaux de droit de la famille, la convergence entre les lois tend à s'accroître;
Reconnaissant que la libre circulation des personnes en Europe est entravée par les différences qui demeurent;
Souhaitant contribuer à des valeurs communes européennes concernant l'égalité des époux;
Souhaitant établir un équilibre entre l'autonomie de la volonté des époux et leur solidarité;
Souhaitant contribuer au bien être de la famille;
Souhaitant assurer la protection du logement de la famille;

Souhaitant garantir à chaque époux une part équitable dans le patrimoine acquis pendant le mariage;
Souhaitant contribuer à l'harmonisation du droit de la famille en Europe et renforcer les droits de ses citoyens;
La Commission pour le Droit Européen de la Famille recommande les Principes suivants:

PRÄAMBEL
In Anerkennung, dass es trotz der bestehenden Unterschiede der nationalen Familienrechte gleichwohl eine zunehmende Übereinstimmung gibt;
In Anerkennung, dass die bestehenden Unterschiede die Freizügigkeit der Personen in Europa behindern;
In dem Wunsch zu den gemeinsamen europäischen Werten in Bezug auf die Gleichheit der Ehegatten beizutragen;
In dem Wunsch einen Ausgleich zwischen der Privatautonomie der Ehegatten und ihrer Solidarität zu schaffen;
In dem Wunsch zum Wohl der Familie beizutragen;
In dem Wunsch den Schutz der Familienwohnung zu sichern;
In dem Wunsch jedem Ehegatten eine gerechte Teilhabe an dem während der Ehe erworbenen Vermögen zu garantieren;
In dem Wunsch zur Angleichung des Familienrechts in Europa beizutragen und die Rechte seiner Bürger zu stärken;
Empfiehlt die Kommission für Europäisches Familienrecht die folgenden Prinzipien:

COMMENT

1. Following the model set by the CEFL's Principles of European Family Law regarding Divorce, Maintenance between Former Spouses and Parental Responsibilities also the Principles regarding Property Relation between Spouses are preceded by a Preamble. This third Preamble also includes both generally acknowledged considerations and commonly felt desires with regard to the situation of family law in Europe as well as the European values regarding the equality of spouses which functioned as the main guideline in the drafting process.

2. The Preamble refers to the free movement of persons in Europe which is hindered by the existing divergencies of family law systems. It is generally acknowledged that, to date, in cross-border situations spouses cannot rely on the recognition of their matrimonial property regime when changing residence. The unification of the private international law rules (jurisdiction, applicable law,

recognition and enforcement) through a Regulation in matters of matrimonial property regimes is unable to completely eliminate the obstacles experienced by European citizens moving across jurisdictions.

3. The Preamble contains five specific considerations of which four address specific issues regarding the property relations between spouses and the family, whereas the fifth objective is of a general nature.

4. As regards the substance of the Principles regarding Property Relations between Spouses, *equality* between the spouses is the primary but by no means the only consideration that has been taken into account. Principles of *sharing* and *fairness*, *solidarity*, *flexibility*, *legal certainty*, *protection of the weaker spouse*, and the promotion of *party autonomy* are likewise of fundamental importance in this area of law. The drafting of the Principles, on the other hand, was specifically guided by concerns that the proposed system should be relatively easy to understand and that the proposed rules should be such as to enable spouses to settle their conflicts on their own without needing to engage lawyers and courts in the dispute. According to SWEDISH research,[81] for example, 75% of the couples who carry out a property division after their divorce divide their assets by themselves without the help or 'interference' by lawyers. Inquiries show that the couples who have managed to share their assets without legal assistance are clearly more satisfied with the outcome than those who have engaged a lawyer. It is assumed that couples who manage on their own avoid the often considerable costs that a legal dispute gives rise to. When rules are clear, there is less scope to quarrel. Hence, if a system is too complicated or contains too many details, couples will have difficulties to comprehend what the rules prescribe which, in turn, can be a seedbed for legal disputes.[82]

5. The crucial question is how to strike a balance between the different goals. Equal sharing might turn out to be unfair and in conflict with the aim of promoting party autonomy. Too much emphasis on the freedom of the spouses to determine their property relations might, on the other hand, lead to unfair results. The need to take the different concerns into account of necessity results in a certain complexity, even if the aim has been to draft simple rules.

---

81 BRATTSTRÖM, "Bodelning mellan makar – verklighetens betydelse för framtidens regelutformning? Delrapport 1 inom ramen för projektet Rättvis delning? Frågor om delningsrättens täckningsområde vid bodelning mellan makar och sambor", *Tidskrift for Familierett, Arverett og Barnevernsrettslige sporsmål (FAS)* 2011, pp. 56–100 (83).

82 BOELE-WOELKI/JÄNTERÄ-JAREBORG, "Initial Results of the Work of the CEFL in the Field of Property Relations between Spouses", in BOELE-WOELKI, MILES, SCHERPE (eds), *The Future of Family Property in Europe*, 2011, pp. 47–61 (51).

6. First and foremost, the CEFL wishes to contribute to the equality of spouses which is a commonly acknowledged principle throughout Europe by introducing rules which better live up to the goal of equal rights and equal opportunities. This Principle is of paramount importance and is indisputable. The Principles also strive to contribute to the spouses' private autonomy on the one hand and their duty of mutual solidarity on the other, even if tensions can arise between these two goals. This is one of the most difficult and therefore challenging problems to solve. In facing this tension the Principles strive to find a balance between the two goals.

7. The second objective expressed in the Preamble concerns the protection of the family home. Two Principles, contained in the general rights and duties of the spouses, specify how the family home is to be protected (Principles 4:6 and 4:7). In addition, two Principles contained in the respective matrimonial property regimes determine that the competent authority may allocate the family home to one of the spouses upon dissolution of the marriage by taking into account the interests of both spouses, paying particular consideration to the needs of the children of the family (Principles 4:30 and 4:56).

8. Upon dissolution of the matrimonial property regime, particularly because of divorce, disputes may arise about which spouse gets what and how much. This is the most complicated issue of the proprietary relationship of the spouses. In this context the CEFL Principles focus on the property that has been acquired during the marriage. The CEFL expresses its desire that according to its Principles, each spouse fairly participates in the wealth (earnings, capital and assets) acquired during the marriage, irrespective of the nature of his or her contribution to it (for example, paid employment, household work and/or child-rearing).

9. Consistency with the CEFL Principles regarding Divorce, Maintenance between former Spouses and Parental Responsibilities has been observed in respect of certain concepts (for example agreements, discretion of the competent authority) and the use of the same terminology (for example exceptional hardship).

10. As with the prevous sets of Principles the CEFL's main objective in drafting the Principles regarding Property Relations between Spouses is that they can be used in the harmonisation process of family law in Europe. If the CEFL Principles play a role in this development the ultimate goal has been achieved. Harmonisation will lead to more certainty in cross-border cases and will contribute to the development of a truly European area of law and justice. The beneficiaries of this will be the European citizens and the residents of Europe.

CHAPTER I: GENERAL RIGHTS AND DUTIES OF THE SPOUSES
CHAPITRE I: DROITS ET DEVOIRS GÉNÉRAUX DES ÉPOUX
KAPITEL I: RECHTE UND PFLICHTEN DER EHEGATTEN IM ALLGEMEINEN

Principle 4:1 General application
The Principles contained in this Chapter apply irrespective of the matrimonial property regime.

Principe 4:1 Application générale
Les Principes contenus dans ce Chapitre sont applicables quel que soit le régime matrimonial des époux.

Prinzip 4:1 Allgemeine Anwendbarkeit
Die Prinzipien dieses Kapitels sind unabhängig vom jeweiligen Güterstand anwendbar.

INTERNATIONAL INSTRUMENTS

There are currently no international instruments that regulate, on a global level, inter-spousal rights and duties by establishing a particular set of rules applicable to all marriages irrespective of the matrimonial property regime. Numerous international instruments confirm, nevertheless, certain basic principles of uttermost relevance to inter-spousal relationships, such as the principle of legal equality between the spouses and the prohibition of all discrimination on the basis of a person's sex. These instruments will be referred to whenever they are of particular relevance to any of the Principles introduced in this Chapter.

In Europe, the *European Convention on the Protection of Human Rights and Fundamental Freedoms of 1950*, along with its successive supplementing Protocols, are of particular importance. In addition, certain European soft law instruments strive to develop standards to promote the implementation, both in law and in practice, of the principle of legal equality between spouses, with a focus on their mutual and general rights and duties. These rights and duties often concern financial aspects of marriage which are independent of the applicable matrimonial property regime. In this sense, there is a clear link with their content and the Principles contained in Chapter I of the CEFL Principles. These instruments will be taken into account whenever they are relevant for the Principles contained in this Chapter.

Interestingly, Chapter III (Articles 4–6) of the *French-German Agreement of 2010*, which provides for an optional matrimonial property regime for marriages where the marital property relations are governed by either French or German law, contains general rules concerning the spouses' rights to administer, enjoy and dispose of their property. These provisions form a kind of a *régime primaire*, and the spouses cannot not set them aside through an agreement (Art. 3 para. 3). Article 4 establishes, as a starting point, the right for each spouse to administer his or her property independently. Article 5 introduces restrictions in respect of property constituting household goods or the family home. Article 6 confirms the right of each spouse independently to enter into transactions for the joint household or for the needs of the children, but which gives rise to joint responsibility with the other spouse. The placement of these provisions in a separate chapter not only demonstrates their significance but also the difficulty of drawing any clear line between what constitutes matrimonial property relations, and the general legal effects of the marriage or the legal effects of a separation or a divorce.[83] All these aspects are closely intertwined.

COMPARATIVE OVERVIEW

The law in the vast majority of the 26 jurisdictions[84] surveyed contains distinct rules concerning the general rights and duties of the spouses. This body of rules applies irrespective of whether a contractual or default matrimonial property regime governs the property relation of the spouses. These rules are, in other words, aimed to apply to all marriages. The rules concern various kinds of issues that are occasionally labelled as the *personal legal effects of marriage*, or as the *general legal effects of marriage* (such as instructions regarding marital cohabitation for the well-being of each spouse and the children, the duty to contribute to family expenses, protection of housing and powers of

[83] See Martiny, "Der neue deutsch-französische Wahlgüterstand – Ein Beispiel optimaler bilateraler Familienrechtsvereinheitlichung", *Zeitschrift für Europäisches Privatrecht*, 2011, pp. 585–587.

[84] See answers to Q 7 in the national reports.

representation). In some jurisdictions, in particular BELGIUM,[85] FRANCE[86] and SPAIN,[87] the importance of these rules is highlighted by their labelling as "a primary or basic mandatory regime" (*régime primaire*), which should be distinguished from the *secondary regime*, since the latter focuses on the property rights of the spouses and at permitting certain exercises of party autonomy.

COMMENT

1. The placement of this set of Principles in the first Chapter is motivated by their relevance and their intended general applicability to all marriages, irrespective of the applicable matrimonial property regime. The Principles strive to contribute to the creation of rules that meet the needs of the contemporary European societies, by identifying the different interests and values at stake in marriage, from both a spousal and a societal perspective, and to strike a reasonable balance between these concerns. In this way, the Principles strive also to contribute to common European values. In forming a separate chapter, this structure resembles the primary regime established in some of the jurisdictions, but has a more mixed content. The aim is to give the rights and duties contained in this Chapter a more prominent role than they have, at present, in many European jurisdictions.

2. The Principles contained in Chapter I, Principles 4:1–4:9, are intended to apply irrespective of whether the matrimonial property regime applicable between the spouses is a default regime, or is chosen in the form of an agreement. The rights and duties established by these Principles are intended to be mandatory and the spouses may not set them aside by an agreement. This approach is in line with the existing national regulations on the general rights and duties of the spouses and, in this sense, reflects the common core.

3. In addition to stating fundamental and established principles on the equality of the spouses and their autonomy, the basic Principles in Chapter I concern the spouses' contributions and liability for family expenses, protection of the family home, mutual authority of representation and mutual duty of information, as well as the freedom to enter into matrimonial property agreements. In part, they correspond to Chapter III (Art. 4–6) in the *French-German Agreement of 2010*; however, due to the variety of provisions encompassed, they also go beyond this *Agreement's* primary regime.

---

85 See PINTENS/ALLAERTS/SEYNS/PIGNOLET, Belgian Report, Q 7.

86 See FERRAND/BRAAT, French Report, Q 7.

87 See GONZÁLEZ BEILFUSS, Spanish Report, Q 2 and Q 7.

Principle 4:2 Equality of the spouses
Both spouses have equal rights and duties.

Principe 4:2 Egalité des époux
Chaque époux a les mêmes droits et devoirs.

Prinzip 4:2 Gleichheit der Ehegatten
Jeder Ehegatte hat die gleichen Rechte und Pflichten.

INTERNATIONAL INSTRUMENTS

Numerous international instruments, such as the *United Nations Declaration on Human Rights of 1948*, the *International Covenant on Civil and Political Rights of 1966* and the *International Covenant on Economic, Social and Cultural Rights of 1966*, confirm the principle of equality between men and women (and consequently, also between spouses), and forbid all forms of discrimination (for example, on the basis of a person's sex). The principle of legal equality between men and women in all fields of life, including marriage, is further developed and promoted by the *United Nations Convention on the Elimination of All Forms of Discrimination against Women of 1979*. In its Preamble, the Convention explicitly acknowledges that "extensive discrimination against women continues to exist", and emphasises that such discrimination "violates the principles of equality of rights and respect for human dignity". Article 15 para. 1 of the *Convention* obliges the contracting States to "accord to women equality with men before the law". Article 16 of the *Convention* confirms that "both spouses have the same rights in respect of the ownership, acquisition, management, administration, enjoyment and disposition of property". These international instruments also recognise the family as the fundamental unit within society, entitled to protection by both society and the state.

As regards European instruments, particular mention should be made of the *European Convention on the Protection of Human Rights and Fundamental Freedoms of 1950* and its successive supplementing Protocols. The Convention strives, for example, to safeguard equal rights for men and women, and forbids all forms of discrimination as regards the enjoyment of rights granted by the *Convention*. The Convention is effectively monitored by the European Court on Human Rights. In addition, the *European Social Charter of 1961*, along with its successive amendments, should be mentioned due to the special link that exists between social law and family life. The Charter aims, in particular, to promote equal rights for men and women in employment, and obliges the States Parties to enable all employees to combine work with family life and family responsibilities (Art. 27).

There are also European soft law instruments which strive to develop standards to promote the implementation, both in law and in practice, of the principle of legal equality between spouses, with a particular focus on the spouses' mutual rights and duties. Of special interest in this respect are several Resolutions and Recommendations adopted by the Council of Europe, particularly its *Resolution (78) 37 on Equality of Spouses in Civil Law, Recommendation (81) 15 on the Rights of Spouses Relating to the Occupation of the Family Home and the Use of the Household Contents*, and *Recommendation (89) 1 on Contributions Following Divorce*. In addition, one should mention the *Declaration on Equality of Women and Men of 1988, the Recommendation (2007) 17 on Gender Equality Standards and Mechanisms* and the *Declaration (2009) 68 on Making Gender Equality a Reality.*

COMPARATIVE OVERVIEW

In the prevailing law of all of the studied jurisdictions, the spouses are regarded as equal, with equal rights and duties, politically and legally. The notion of legal equality between spouses is by now regarded to be so self-evident in western societies that the law on marriage often contains no explicit provisions stating this. Marriage legislation puts both spouses on an equal footing, without referring to the spouse's gender. In several jurisdictions, the Constitution includes an explicit provision establishing and confirming legal equality between the spouses (for example CZECH REPUBLIC,[88] GERMANY,[89] GREECE,[90] HUNGARY,[91] PORTUGAL[92] and SPAIN[93]). In all jurisdictions, the rules on inter-spousal rights and duties, including marital property relations, strive to uphold the principle of legal equality between spouses. Full common core applies on this key issue.

The brief overviews within the national reports concerning historical developments illustrate how earlier provisions reflecting inequality in the marriage, for example, the husband's powers of administration of property in

88 Art. 1 para. 2 Constitution of 9 May, 1948. See MELZER, Czech Report, Q 2.
89 Art. 3 para. 2 German Constitution. See DETHLOFF/MARTINY, German Report, Q 2.
90 Art. 4 para. 2 Greek Constitution. See KOUTSOURADIS/KOTRONIS/HATZANTONIS, Greek Report, Q 2.
91 § 23(1) Hungarian Family Law Act.
92 Art. 36 para. 3 of Portuguese Constitution. See DE OLIVEIRA/MARTINS/VÍTOR, Portuguese Report, Q 2.
93 Art. 32 para. 1 and 14 of the Spanish Constitution. See GONZÁLEZ BEILFUSS, Spanish Report, Q 2.

the marriage (AUSTRIA,[94] FINLAND,[95] GERMANY,[96] NORWAY,[97] PORTUGAL,[98] SCOTLAND,[99] SPAIN[100] and SWEDEN[101]), or the restrictions on the wife's legal capacity (BELGIUM,[102] CATALONIA,[103] ENGLAND AND WALES,[104] FRANCE,[105] THE NETHERLANDS[106] and SCOTLAND[107]) were successively, during a period of more than 100 years starting in the mid-19th century, set aside by rules establishing equal rights and duties for the spouses. The previous patriarchal model was replaced by an equalitarian model. SPAIN[108] was last to join this "the equalitarian club" through amending the law in the early 1980s. Prevailing traditions and social factors, nevertheless, in reality, often prevent married women from exercising and enjoying the same autonomy as that of married men.

Importantly, on the basis of the national reports, it appears that the default regimes of the various jurisdictions have been justified with reference to legal equality between the spouses, irrespective of whether the applicable default regime is a community regime (for example, BULGARIA,[109] HUNGARY[110]), or a separation regime in the broad sense of the concept (for example, FINLAND,[111] GERMANY[112] and PORTUGAL[113]). With the purposes of safeguarding and implementing equality between the spouses, some of the jurisdictions contain special provisions aimed explicitly at protecting the wife, due to the fact that the wife is more likely than the husband to act as an unpaid home-maker, or to be the financially weaker party in the marriage (CATALONIA[114] and DENMARK[115]). Others set out gender-neutral provisions on protection of the weaker spouse which, in practice, are primarily applicable in safeguarding the wife's interests

94 See ROTH, Austrian Report, Q 2.
95 See KURKI-SUONIO, Finnish Report, Q 2.
96 See DETHLOFF/MARTINY, German Report, Q 2.
97 See SVERDRUP, Norwegian Report, Q 2.
98 See DE OLIVEIRA/MARTINS/VÍTOR, Portuguese Report, Q 2.
99 See MAIR, Scottish Report, Q 2.
100 Art. 66 of the Spanish Civil Code. See GONZÁLEZ BEILFUSS, Spanish Report, Q 2.
101 See JÄNTERÄ-JAREBORG/BRATTSTRÖM/WALLENG, Swedish Report, Q 2.
102 See PINTENS/ALLAERTS/SEYNS/PIGNOLET, Belgian Report, Q 2.
103 See MARTÍN-CASALS/RIBOT, Catalan Report, Q 2.
104 See BARLOW, English Report, Q 2.
105 See FERRAND/BRAAT, French Report, Q 2.
106 See BOELE-WOELKI/SCHONEWILLE/SCHRAMA, Dutch Report, Q 2.
107 See MAIR, Scottish Report, Q 2.
108 See GONZÁLEZ BEILFUSS, Spanish Report, Q 2.
109 See TODOROVA, Bulgarian Report, Q 2.
110 See WEISS/SZEIBERT, Hungarian Report, Q 2.
111 See KURKI-SUONIO, Finnish Report, Q 2.
112 See DETHLOFF/MARTINY, German Report, Q 2.
113 See DE OLIVEIRA/MARTINS/VÍTOR, Portuguese Report, Q 2.
114 See MARTÍN-CASALS/RIBOT, Catalan Report, Q 2. Until 1984, special restrictions applied, e.g. in CATALONIA, which restricted the wife's ability to enter into guarantees for the husband. See MARTÍN-CASALS/RIBOT, Catalan Report, Q 12.
115 § 11(1) Danish Act on the Legal Effects of Marriage (household debts etc.).

(ENGLAND AND WALES,[116] NORWAY,[117] PORTUGAL[118] and SWITZERLAND[119]). Nevertheless, the trend appears to be in favour of gender-neutral rules.

COMMENT

1. Principle 4:2 sets out the self-evident basis of all of the Principles, namely that of legal equality between the husband and the wife. In this respect, full common core exists among the jurisdictions. This Principle also finds support in all relevant global and European instruments. Safeguarding this equality in the form of a specific Principle is considered valuable having regard to the fact that all of the jurisdictions surveyed are pluralistic societies, where different groups might have divergent value systems. It also functions as a reminder that both spouses, not only on a legal level, but also in their actual lives, should enjoy equal rights and duties.

2. Equality between the spouses is a basic justification for any claims that a spouse can raise regarding, for example, participation in property acquired by the other spouse. Inequalities in the spouses' wealth can be evened out through rights relating to participation and sharing. Equality between the spouses forms the foundation for protecting the spouse against the other spouse's transactions, for example, relating to the family home and the household goods, or regarding the right to take over such property when the marriage ends. Irrespective of the form in which the spouses have contributed to the welfare of the family and to the acquisition of property during the marriage (for example, as breadwinners or as principal caretakers of the home), their contributions should, having regard to the equal rights and duties of the spouses, essentially carry the same weight. Today, married men and women have, increasingly, an equivalent education, but women's income tends to be lower than that of men. Furthermore, married women are not as gainfully active as married men. This is due, not least, to the existing socially constructed and stereotyped roles for women and men,[120] which lead to the situation in which women remain the principal caretakers of the family and the home, even if there are also marriages in which the spouses participate on equal terms both economically and in maintaining the welfare of the family. The CEFL Principles wish to promote the latter kind of marriages and to contribute to an increased equality between spouses in law and in practice.

---

116 English Matrimonial Causes Act 1973 Part II. See BARLOW, English Report, Q 2.
117 § 31 Norwegian Marriage Act. See SVERDRUP, Norwegian Report, Q 2.
118 Art. 1676 para. 2 Portuguese Civil Code.
119 See SCHWENZER/BOCK, Swiss Report, Q 2.
120 The Council of Europe Convention on preventing and combating violence against women and domestic violence, adopted in Istanbul in May 2011, draws special attention to the negative impact on women of socially constructed and stereotyped roles for men and women.

Principle 4:3 Legal capacity of the spouses
Subject to the following Principles, each spouse has full legal capacity and in particular is free to enter into legal transactions with the other spouse and with third persons.

Principe 4:3 Capacité juridique des époux
Sous réserve des principes suivants, chaque époux a la pleine capacité juridique, et peut en particulier conclure des actes juridiques avec l'autre époux ou avec des tiers.

Prinzip 4:3 Rechts-, Geschäfts- und Handlungsfähigkeit der Ehegatten
Vorbehaltlich der nachstehenden Prinzipien besitzt jeder Ehegatte vollständige Rechts-, Geschäfts- und Handlungsfähigkeit und kann insbesondere Rechtsgeschäfte mit dem anderen Ehegatten und mit Dritten vornehmen.

INTERNATIONAL INSTRUMENTS

In international instruments, full and equal legal capacity for spouses is directly linked with the spouses' right to enjoy equal rights and duties. Of particular relevance is the *United Nations Convention on the Elimination of All Forms of Discrimination against Women of 1979*. Article 15 para. 2 of the Convention obliges the Contracting States to "accord to women, in civil matters, a legal capacity identical to that of men and the same opportunities to exercise that capacity. In particular, they shall give women equal rights to conclude contracts and to administer property and shall treat them equally in all stages of procedure in courts and tribunals". According to Article 15 para. 3, the Contracting States agree "that all contracts and all other private instruments of any kind with a legal effect which is directed at restricting the legal capacity of women shall be deemed null and void". Article 16 of the *Convention* confirms that "both spouses have the same rights in respect of the ownership, acquisition, management, administration, enjoyment and disposition of property".

COMPARATIVE OVERVIEW

Basic points of departure

The now self-evident point of departure in all of the surveyed jurisdictions is that entering a marriage should not incapacitate either spouse, and that both spouses should have full and equal legal capacity. It follows that they are free to enter into transactions with each other (AUSTRIA,[121] CATALONIA,[122] CZECH REPUBLIC,[123] ENGLAND AND WALES,[124] FRANCE,[125] GERMANY,[126] ITALY,[127] LITHUANIA,[128] THE NETHERLANDS,[129] POLAND,[130] PORTUGAL,[131] RUSSIA,[132] SCOTLAND,[133] SPAIN,[134] SWEDEN[135] and SWITZERLAND[136]), and with a third person, in the same way as unmarried persons (for example DENMARK,[137] ENGLAND AND WALES,[138] FRANCE,[139] GREECE,[140] ITALY,[141] POLAND,[142] SCOTLAND,[143] SLOVAKIA,[144] SWEDEN[145] and SWITZERLAND[146]). Full common core exists concerning this basic approach. Unless special rules are contained in the law of marriage of a specific jurisdiction, the general law of obligations applies and special rules are not regarded as necessary.

Nevertheless, due to the special relationship which normally exists between spouses, namely a community of interests created by the marriage, a special concern arises as to how this community of interests and, usually, shared economy, affects, or should affect, the spouses' right to enter into transactions with each other and with third persons. Concerns include respect for the individual autonomy of each spouse, spousal solidarity, protection of the economically weaker spouse (or the children) through restrictions concerning the family home and household goods, protection of the third party (creditor,

121 See ROTH, Austrian Report, Q 14.
122 See MARTÍN-CASALS/RIBOT, Catalan Report, Q 14.
123 See MELZER, Czech Report, Q 14.
124 See BARLOW, English Report, Q 14.
125 See FERRAND/BRAAT, French Report, Q 14.
126 See DETHLOFF/MARTINY, German Report, Q 14.
127 Art. 781 Italian Civil Code. See PATTI/CARICATO/IRTI/IANNICELLI/SERA/DI STEFANO/PETÖ, Italian Report, Q 14.
128 See MIKELENAS, Lithuanian Report, Q 14.
129 See BOELE-WOELKI/SCHONEWILLE/SCHRAMA, Dutch Report, Q 14.
130 See MĄCZYŃSKI, Polish Report, Q 14.
131 See DE OLIVEIRA/MARTINS/VÍTOR, Portuguese Report, Q 2.
132 See ANTOKOLSKAIA, Russian Report, Q 14.
133 See MAIR, Scottish Report, Q 14.
134 Art. 1323 Spanish Civil Code. See GONZÁLEZ BEILFUSS, Spanish Report, Q 14.
135 See JÄNTERÄ-JAREBORG/BRATTSTRÖM/WALLENG, Swedish Report, Q 14.
136 See SCHWENZER/BOCK, Swiss Report, Q 14.
137 See LUND-ANDERSEN/MAGNUSSEN, Danish Report, Q 12.
138 See BARLOW, English Report, Q 12.
139 See FERRAND/BRAAT, French Report, Q 12.
140 See KOUTSOURADIS/KOTRONIS/HATZANTONIS, Greek Report, Q 12.
141 See PATTI/CARICATO/IRTI/IANNICELLI/SERA/DI STEFANO/PETÖ, Italian Report, Q 12.
142 See Mączyński, Polish Report, Q 12.
143 See MAIR, Scottish Report, Q 12, with special references to case law.
144 See HAŤAPKA, Slovakian Report, Q 12.
145 See JÄNTERÄ-JAREBORG/BRATTSTRÖM/WALLENG, Swedish Report, Q 12.
146 See SCHWENZER/BOCK, Swiss Report, Q 12.

purchaser) and, more generally, protection of "market interests". To address these kinds of concerns, special rules apply to some extent.

Full and equal legal capacity for spouses has not always existed. Historical overviews[147] demonstrate how the previous restrictions on married women's legal capacity, which were common in the past, have successively been removed (e.g. BELGIUM,[148] CATALONIA,[149] ENGLAND AND WALES,[150] FRANCE[151] and THE NETHERLANDS[152]). Many jurisdictions also used to impose restrictions on the wife's ability to undertake certain kinds of legal acts, such as guarantees on behalf of her husband, in order to protect the wife.[153]

Restrictions based on the nature of the assets

Most of the jurisdictions have special rules regarding transactions concerning the matrimonial home and the household goods. The essence of these rules is that these kinds of assets, which are so fundamental for the well-being of the family, should not be transferred to a third person without both spouses consenting to it. The applicable marital property regime is, in this respect, irrelevant.

It is much more uncommon that any other assets belonging to a married person are subject to similar rules, even if certain other restrictions do exist. These restrictions may concern real property in general, irrespective of the matrimonial property regime, or significant legal acts by a spouse which can affect the spouses' economy. The owner spouse's transactions require, in these cases, the other spouse's consent, or court permission, for the legal act to be valid. In marriages where a community regime applies, spouses can only dispose of the assets jointly.

Restrictions concerning specific transactions

Many of the jurisdictions apply restrictions regarding certain kinds of transactions between spouses in order to protect the spouses' creditors (for

147 See answers to Q 2.
148 See PINTENS/ALLAERTS/SEYNS/PIGNOLET, Belgian Report, Q 2.
149 See MARTÍN-CASALS/RIBOT, Catalan Report, Q 2.
150 See BARLOW, English Report, Q 2.
151 See FERRAND/BRAAT, French Report, Q 2.
152 See BOELE-WOELKI/SCHONEWILLE/SCHRAMA, Dutch Report, Q 2.
153 In, e.g. Catalonia, this applied until the amendment in 1984. See MARTÍN-CASALS/RIBOT, Catalan Report, Q 12.

example CATALONIA,[154] DENMARK,[155] FINLAND,[156] GERMANY,[157] HUNGARY,[158] IRELAND,[159] MALTA[160] and SWEDEN[161]). In BELGIUM[162] and PORTUGAL,[163] for example, a purchase agreement or a contract of sale between spouses is basically unenforceable. In many cases, however, the rules are there to protect the spouses themselves, or the interests of the family. If, for example, a spouse incurs debts or enters into guarantees in order to financially harm the other spouse, the legal act in question may be considered invalid, give the other spouse a right of compensation (GREECE[164] and ITALY[165]), or even result in the dissolution of the matrimonial property regime upon a decision by a competent authority (SWITZERLAND[166]). The special rules may also, more generally, strive to protect a spouse against debts and guarantees, and hire-purchases contracts, entered into by the other spouse (FRANCE,[167] THE NETHERLANDS[168] and SWITZERLAND[169]). Special form requirements may apply, which are aimed at protecting the spouse or spouses, as regards, for example, loan agreements or sureties (AUSTRIA[170] and HUNGARY[171]). It is common among the studied jurisdictions that gifts between spouses are subject to special rules regarding their validity and binding force, either in the interests of the spouses' creditors, the spouses themselves, or both (for example AUSTRIA,[172] CATALONIA,[173] CZECH REPUBLIC,[174] DENMARK,[175]

---

154 See MARTÍN-CASALS/RIBOT, Catalan Report, Q 14.
155 See LUND-ANDERSEN/MAGNUSSEN, Danish Report, Q 14.
156 See KURKI-SUONIO, Finnish Report, Q 14.
157 See, in particular, § 4 German Act on the Avoidance of Legal Acts by the Debtor Outside the Insolvency Proceedings. See DETHLOFF/MARTINY, German Report, Q 14.
158 See WEISS/SZEIBERT, Hungarian Report, Q 14.
159 See SHANNON, Irish Report, Q 14.
160 See FARRUGIA, Maltese Report, Q 14.
161 Ch. 8 § 1 para. 2 Swedish Marriage Code. See JÄNTERÄ-JAREBORG/BRATTSTRÖM/WALLENG, Swedish Report, Q 14.
162 See PINTENS/ALLAERTS/SEYNS/PIGNOLET, Belgian Report, Q 14.
163 In a broader sense, this position is a consequence of the principle of immutability of the applicable matrimonial property regime, to prevent spouse from being able to alter the composition of the property components. See DE OLIVEIRA/MARTINS/VÍTOR, Portuguese Report, Q 12.
164 See KOUTSOURADIS/KOTRONIS/HATZANTONIS, Greek Report, Q 12.
165 See PATTI/CARICATO/IRTI/IANNICELLI/SERA/DI STEFANO/PETÖ, Italian Report, Q 12.
166 Art. 185 Swiss Civil Code.
167 See FERRAND/BRAAT, French Report, Q 12.
168 Art. 1:88 para. 4 and 5 Dutch Civil Code. See BOELE-WOELKI/SCHONEWILLE/SCHRAMA, Dutch Report, Q 12.
169 Art. 494 Swiss Code of Obligations. See SCHWENZER/BOCK, Swiss Report, Q 12.
170 See ROTH, Austrian Report, Q 14.
171 See WEISS/SZEIBERT, Hungarian Report, Q 14.
172 See ROTH, Austrian Report, Q 14.
173 See MARTÍN-CASALS/RIBOT, Catalan Report, Q 14.
174 See MELZER, Czech Report, Q 14.
175 See LUND-ANDERSEN/MAGNUSSEN, Danish Report, Q 14.

FINLAND,[176] FRANCE,[177] HUNGARY,[178] LITHUANIA,[179] MALTA,[180] THE NETHERLANDS,[181] NORWAY,[182] SLOVAKIA[183] and SWEDEN[184]).

Marriage and majority

Traditionally, a marriage concluded by a minor resulted in the minor's emancipation. This position is less evident in Europe today, and we can instead see a trend to restrict, or even forbid, the right to marry before the age of majority. Because this issue is not specifically addressed in the national reports, it is not possible to give a comparative overview of how the various jurisdictions deal with the impact of a minor's marriage on his or her legal capacity.[185]

COMMENT

1. Principle 4:3 confirms the now self-evident principle that entering into a marriage does not affect either spouse's legal capacity, and that the spouses remain two independent individuals, with autonomy to enter into legal transactions with each other and with third persons. Stating this in the form of a specific Principle is considered valuable in as much as that all jurisdictions surveyed are pluralistic societies, where different traditions might coexist.

2. In the following Principles, certain exceptions have, nevertheless, been found to be necessary. These exceptions correspond to those in many of the studied jurisdictions. To cover all these situations, Principle 4:3 makes a general reference to the limitations that may be applied to the other Principles.

3. The impact of a marriage concluded by a minor on his or her legal capacity falls outside the scope of Principle 4:3. The law in the European jurisdictions surveyed appears to be in transition regarding this issue.

---

176 See Kurki-Suonio, Finnish Report, Q 14.
177 See Ferrand/Braat, French Report, Q 14.
178 See Weiss/Szeibert, Hungarian Report, Q 14.
179 See Mikelenas, Lithuanian Report, Q 14.
180 See Farrugia, Maltese Report, Q 14.
181 Art. 1:88 para. 1 sub b Dutch Civil Code. See Boele-Woelki/Schonewille/Schrama, Dutch Report, Q 12.
182 See Sverdrup, Norwegian Report, Q 14.
183 See Haťapka, Slovakian Report, Q 14.
184 See Jänterä-Jareborg/Brattström/Walleng, Swedish Report, Q 14.
185 Marriage and majority is, nevertheless, touched upon in the National Reports on parental responsibilities (answers to Q 3). See *European Family Law in Action, Volume III: Parental Responsibilities*, Boele-Woelki, Braat, Curry-Sumner, (eds.), 2005.

Principle 4:4 Contribution to the needs of the family

(1) Each spouse should contribute to the needs of the family according to his or her ability.

(2) The contribution to the needs of the family encompasses contributions to the running of the household, the personal needs of the spouses and the maintenance, upbringing and education of the children.

(3) If a spouse does not fulfill his or her obligation to contribute to the needs of the family the other spouse may request the competent authority to determine the contribution.

Principe 4:4 Contribution aux besoins de la famille

(1) Chaque époux contribue aux besoins de la famille à proportion de ses facultés.

(2) La contribution aux besoins de la famille comprend les contributions aux charges du ménage, aux besoins personnels des époux, à l'entretien et à l'éducation des enfants.

(3) Si un époux n'exécute pas son obligation de contribuer aux besoins de la famille, l'autre époux peut demander à l'autorité compétente de fixer le montant de la contribution.

Prinzip 4:4 Beitrag zum Lebensbedarf der Familie

(1) Jeder Ehegatte trägt nach seinen Fähigkeiten zum Lebensbedarf der Familie bei.

(2) Der Beitrag zum Lebensbedarf der Familie umfasst Beiträge zur Führung des Haushaltes, zu den persönlichen Bedürfnissen der Ehegatten, zum Unterhalt und zur Erziehung der Kinder.

(3) Erfüllt ein Ehegatte seine Verpflichtung zu den Familienausgaben beizutragen nicht, kann der andere Ehegatte von der zuständigen Behörde verlangen, den Beitrag zu bestimmen.

INTERNATIONAL INSTRUMENTS

Several international instruments adopted by the United Nations and the Council of Europe express concerns regarding gender equality, especially equality between spouses.[186] In particular, the *European Convention on Human Rights and Fundamental Freedoms of 1950* sets out, in Article 14, the prohibition of discrimination on grounds of – inter alia – sex. The *Convention* also forbids all forms of discrimination as regards the rights guaranteed by the additional

---

[186] See under the Introduction to these Principles and under Principle 4:1 the international instruments mentioned.

Protocols supplementing the Convention. Article 5 of Protocol No. 7 prescribes that before marriage, during marriage, and in the event of its dissolution, there shall be equality between spouses with regard to rights and responsibilities of a private law character, and in their relations with their children.

In addition, the *(CM) Resolution (78)37 on Equality of Spouses in Civil Law*, adopted by the Council of Europe on 27 September 1978, recommends that, in general matters, Member States should "take all necessary steps to ensure that the civil law does not contain provisions whereby a spouse is put in a more advantageous position than that of the other spouse".[187] Furthermore, with regard to matters concerning the property and financial relations of the spouses, the Resolution obliges the Member States to ensure "that household expenses are borne jointly by the spouses according to the means of each spouse, work in the house by one spouse being considered as a contribution to household expenses".[188] However, joint and several liability of each spouse for such debts is not expressly required by the Resolution.

The *French-German Agreement of 2010* on the choice of a matrimonial property regime contains a provision (Article 6) on legal transactions relating to family debts (*actes relatifs à l'entretien du ménage*), which states that each spouse is entitled to enter into legal transactions relating to the support of the household or to the children's education. These transactions bind both spouses jointly and severally (*ces contrats obligent solidairement l'autre époux*). An exception is set out in Article 6 para. 2, which states that if the debt is manifestly excessive in light of the standard of living of the spouses (*caractère manifestement excessif eu égard au train de vie des époux*), and the other contracting party knows, or should have known, about this, only the spouse who has entered into the transaction is liable.

Several other international instruments adopted by the Council of Europe in order to promote equality between the spouses could also be mentioned: the *(CM) Declaration of 16 November 1988 on equality of women and men*, the *(CM) Recommendation (2007)17 of 21 November 2007 on gender equality standards and mechanisms* and the (CM) *Declaration (2009)68 of 6 May 2009 on making gender equality a reality.*

On 18 December 1979, the United Nations General Assembly adopted the *Convention on the Elimination of All Forms of Discrimination against Women*, which is of relevance in this context.[189] In particular, Article 16 of the *Convention*

[187] Res. (78) 37, point 1.
[188] Res. (78) 37, point 8, i.
[189] For more details, see Principle 4:2 under International instruments.

aims to eliminate discrimination against women on all matters relating to marriage and family relations, and at ensuring equality between men and women.[190] For the purpose of considering the progress made in the implementation of this Convention, a Committee on the Elimination of Discrimination against Women has been established (see Art. 17 of the Convention).

COMPARATIVE OVERVIEW

The duty of the spouses to contribute to the needs of the family

A substantial majority of the twenty-six jurisdictions surveyed impose general rights and duties upon the spouses, independent of the specific property relationship between them (AUSTRIA,[191] BELGIUM,[192] CATALONIA,[193] CZECH REPUBLIC,[194] DENMARK,[195] ENGLAND AND WALES,[196] FINLAND,[197] FRANCE,[198] GERMANY,[199] GREECE,[200] HUNGARY,[201] IRELAND,[202] ITALY,[203] LITHUANIA,[204] THE NETHERLANDS,[205] NORWAY,[206] POLAND,[207] PORTUGAL,[208] RUSSIA[209] – but

190 See art. 16: (a) The same right to enter into marriage; (b) The same right freely to choose a spouse and to enter into marriage only with their free and full consent; (c) The same rights and responsibilities during marriage and at its dissolution; (d) The same rights and responsibilities as parents, irrespective of their marital status, in matters relating to their children; in all cases the interests of the children shall be paramount; (e) The same rights to decide freely and responsibly on the number and spacing of their children and to have access to the information, education and means to enable them to exercise these rights; (f) The same rights and responsibilities with regard to guardianship, wardship, trusteeship and adoption of children, or similar institutions where these concepts exist in national legislation; in all cases the interests of the children shall be paramount; (g) The same personal rights as husband and wife, including the right to choose a family name, a profession and an occupation; (h) The same rights for both spouses in respect of the ownership, acquisition, management, administration, enjoyment and disposition of property, whether free of charge or for a valuable consideration.

191 See Roth, Austrian Report, Q 7.

192 See Pintens/Allaerts/Seyns/Pignolet, Belgian Report, Q 7.

193 See Martín-Casals/, Catalan Report, Q 7.

194 See Melzer, Czech Report, Q 7.

195 See Lund-Andersen/Magnussen, Danish Report, Q 7.

196 See Barlow, English Report, Q 7.

197 See Kurki-Suonio, Finnish Report, Q 7.

198 See Ferrand/Braat, French Report, Q 7.

199 See Dethloff/Martiny, German Report, Q 7.

200 See Koutsouradis/Kotronis/Hatzantonis, Greek Report, Q 7.

201 See Weiss/Szeibert, Hungarian Report, Q 7.

202 See Shannon, Irish Report Q 7.

203 See Patti/Caricato/Irti/Iannicelli/Sera/Di Stefano/Petö, Italian Report, Q 7.

204 See Mikelenas, Lithuanian Report, Q 7.

205 See Boele-Woelki/Schonewille/Schrama, Dutch Report, Q 7.

206 See Sverdrup, Norwegian Report, Q 7.

207 See Mączyński, Polish Report, Q 7.

208 See De Oliveira/Martins/Vítor, Portuguese Report, Q 7.

209 See Antokolskaia, Russian Report, Q 7.

only non-patrimonial rights and duties -, SLOVAKIA,[210] SPAIN,[211] SWEDEN[212] and SWITZERLAND[213]). These jurisdictions also set out a legal obligation upon the spouses to contribute to household expenses, or at least to "contribute to the satisfaction of the needs in proportion to their economic situations".[214] The laws of ENGLAND AND WALES,[215] IRELAND,[216] RUSSIA[217] and SCOTLAND[218] do not state such a specific obligation; however, their statutory maintenance provisions impose a duty upon each spouse to maintain one another, and to support their children. In some legal systems, a distinction is made between the maintenance duty of each spouse and the contribution to the household expenses. In RUSSIA,[219] for example, there is no specific rule governing the obligation of the spouses to contribute to the household expenses, but the law allows child and spousal maintenance to be awarded during marriage where one spouse fails to provide for the needs of the family. In other jurisdictions, such as BELGIUM[220] and FRANCE,[221] there is a duty of assistance and support between spouses, as well as a second, separate duty to contribute to the marriage expenditure.[222]

The duty to contribute to household needs (also known as *family needs*,[223] *spouses' joint and personal needs*,[224] or *living costs of parents and children*)[225] expressly exists in twenty-two jurisdictions. In some instances, the formulation is general: in AUSTRIA, for example, a general provision requires that the spouses shall jointly contribute to meeting the needs that are deemed to be adequate given their economic situation, in accordance with each spouse's capability and the organization of their married community.[226] Sometimes, the terminology is more precise, as seen in BELGIUM,[227] BULGARIA,[228] CATALONIA,[229] CZECH

210 See HAŤAPKA, Slovakian Report, Q 7.
211 See GONZÁLEZ BEILFUSS, Spanish Report, Q 7.
212 See JÄNTERÄ-JAREBORG/BRATTSTRÖM/WALLENG, Swedish Report, Q 7.
213 See SCHWENZER/BOCK, Swiss Report, Q 7.
214 See e.g. § 94 para. 1 Austrian Civil Code.
215 See BARLOW, English Report, Q 8.
216 See SHANNON, Irish Report Q 8.
217 See ANTOKOLSKAIA, Russian Report, Q 8.
218 See MAIR, Scottish Report, Q 8.
219 See ANTOKOLSKAIA, Russian Report, Q 8.
220 See PINTENS/ALLAERTS/SEYNS/PIGNOLET, Belgian Report, Q 8.
221 See FERRAND/BRAAT, French Report, Q 8.
222 Contribution aux charges du mariage.
223 See MELZER, Czech Report, Q 8; HAŤAPKA, Slovakian Report, Q 8.
224 See JÄNTERÄ-JAREBORG/BRATTSTRÖM/WALLENG, Swedish Report, Q 8.
225 See GONZÁLEZ BEILFUSS, Spanish Report, Q 8.
226 § 94 para. 1 Austrian Civil Code.
227 Art. 221 Belgian Civil Code. See PINTENS/ALLAERTS/SEYNS/PIGNOLET, Belgian Report, Q 8.
228 Art. 18 Bulgarian Family Code. See TODOROVA, Bulgarian Report, Q 8.
229 Art. 5 para. 1 Catalan Family Code. See MARTÍN-CASALS/RIBOT, Catalan Report, Q 8.

REPUBLIC,[230] DENMARK,[231] FINLAND,[232] FRANCE,[233] GERMANY,[234] GREECE,[235] HUNGARY,[236] ITALY,[237] LITHUANIA,[238] MALTA,[239] THE NETHERLANDS,[240] NORWAY,[241] POLAND,[242] PORTUGAL,[243] SLOVAKIA,[244] SPAIN,[245] SWEDEN[246] and SWITZERLAND.[247] The statutory provisions of these jurisdictions expressly mention the contributions of the spouses to the "marriage expenses" (BELGIUM[248] and FRANCE[249]), the *family expenses* (for example, CATALONIA[250] and HUNGARY[251]), *family life expenses* (PORTUGAL[252]), *household expenses* (SLOVAKIA[253] and SPAIN[254]), the *needs of the family* (CZECH REPUBLIC,[255] LITHUANIA,[256] MALTA[257] and POLAND[258]), the *maintenance of the family* (DENMARK[259] and GERMANY[260]), the *common household of the family* (FINLAND[261]), the *support of the family*,[262] or even *spousal support, child support*

---

230 § 19 Czech Family Act. See MELZER, Czech Report, Q 8.

231 § 2 Danish Act on Legal Effects of Marriage. See LUND-ANDERSEN/MAGNUSSEN, Danish Report, Q 8.

232 § 46 Finnish Marriage Act and KURKI-SUONIO, Finnish Report, Q 8.

233 Art. 214 para. 1 French Code Civil. See FERRAND/BRAAT, French Report, Q 8.

234 § 1360 German Civil Code. See DETHLOFF/MARTINY, German Report, Q 8.

235 Art. 1390 Greek Civil Code. See KOUTSOURADIS/KOTRONIS, Greek Report, Q 8.

236 § 32 para. 1 first sentence Hungarian Family Code. See WEISS/SZEIBERT, Hungarian Report, Q 8.

237 Art. 143 para. 1 Italian Civil Code. See PATTI/CARICATO/IRTI/IANNICELLI/SERA/DI STEFANO/PETÖ, Italian Report, Q 8.

238 Art. 3:27 Lithuanian Civil Code. See MIKELENAS, Lithuanian Report, Q 8.

239 Art. 3 Maltese Civil Code. See FARRUGIA, Maltese Report, Q 8.

240 Art. 1:82 para. 1 first sentence and para. 2 and Art. 1:82 Dutch Civil Code. See BOELE-WOELKI/SCHONEWILLE/SCHRAMA, Dutch Report, Q 8.

241 § 38 Norwegian Marriage Act. See SVERDRUP, Norwegian Report, Q 8.

242 See MĄCZYŃSKI, Polish Report, Q 8.

243 Art. 1676 Portuguese Civil Code. See DE OLIVEIRA/MARTINS/VÍTOR, Portuguese Report, Q 8.

244 See HAŤAPKA, Slovakian Report, Q 8.

245 Art. 1318 Spanish Civil Code. See GONZÁLEZ BEILFUSS, Spanish Report, Q 8.

246 Ch. 6 § 1 Swedish Marriage Code. See JÄNTERÄ-JAREBORG/BRATTSTRÖM/WALLENG, Swedish Report, Q 8.

247 Art. 163 para. 1 Swiss Civil Code. See SCHWENZER/BOCK, Swiss Report, Q 8.

248 See PINTENS/ALLAERTS/SEYNS/PIGNOLET, Belgian Report, Q 8.

249 See FERRAND/BRAAT, French Report, Q 8.

250 See MARTÍIN-CASALS/RIBOT, Catalan Report, Q 8.

251 See WEISS/SZEIBERT, Hungarian Report, Q 8 (expenses of the family household).

252 See DE OLIVEIRA/MARTINS/VÍTOR, Portuguese Report, Q 8.

253 See HAŤAPKA, Slovakian Report, Q 8.

254 See GONZÁLEZ BEILFUSS, Spanish Report, Q 8.

255 See MELZER, Czech Report, Q 8.

256 See MIKELENAS, Lithuanian Report, Q 8.

257 See FARRUGIA, Maltese Report, Q 8.

258 See MĄCZYŃSKI, Polish Report, Q 8.

259 See LUND-ANDERSEN/MAGNUSSEN, Danish Report, Q 8.

260 See DETHLOFF/MARTINY, German Report, Q 8.

261 See KURKI-SUONIO, Finnish Report, Q 8. See SVERDRUP, Norwegian Report, Q 8 (joint household and other joint needs, the upbringing of the children and the particular needs of each spouse).

262 See SCHWENZER/BOCK, Swiss Report, Q 8.

and support for the family household (GREECE[263]). Some legislations mention the "maintenance needed to meet the spouses' joint and personal needs" (SWEDEN[264]), or the *common duty of the spouses to contribute for the welfare of the family and the rearing of the children* (BULGARIA[265]).

What is meant by "needs of the family"

Even if the terminology differs from jurisdiction to jurisdiction, the meaning is the same: the spouses are jointly responsible for the support of the family, which mostly encompasses the common needs of the spouses, the children's needs, and the personal needs of one spouse. Several national statutory provisions do not define the scope of "family needs" or "household expenses" (for example, AUSTRIA,[266] BELGIUM,[267] CZECH REPUBLIC,[268] FRANCE,[269] GREECE,[270] HUNGARY,[271] LITHUANIA,[272] MALTA,[273] POLAND[274] and PORTUGAL[275]), leaving case law and literature decide to elaborate. In contrast, others give a precise definition (e.g. CATALONIA,[276] GERMANY[277] and SPAIN[278]). In general, the concept of family or household expenses includes the living costs of the spouses, as well as the maintenance and education costs of the children (even the children of one spouse who live in the family home, like in BULGARIA,[279] CATALONIA,[280] THE NETHERLANDS[281] and SPAIN[282]).

263 See KOUTSOURADIS/KOTRONIS/HATZANTONIS, Greek Report, Q 8.
264 See JÄNTERÄ-JAREBORG/BRATTSTRÖM/WALLENG, Swedish Report, Q 8.
265 See TODOROVA, Bulgarian Report, Q 8.
266 See ROTH, Austrian Report, Q 8.
267 See PINTENS/ALLAERTS/SEYNS/PIGNOLET, Belgian Report, Q 8.
268 See MELZER, Czech Report, Q 8.
269 See FERRAND/BRAAT, French Report, Q 8.
270 See KOUTSOURADIS/KOTRONIS/HATZANTONIS, Greek Report, Q 8.
271 See WEISS/SZEIBERT, Hungarian Report, Q 8.
272 See MIKELENAS, Lithuanian Report, Q 8.
273 See FARRUGIA, Maltese Report, Q 8.
274 See MĄCZYŃSKI, Polish Report, Q 8.
275 See DE OLIVEIRA/MARTINS/VÍTOR, Portuguese Report, Q 8.
276 See Art. 4 para. 1 Catalan Civil Code (family expenses are those that are necessary to maintain the family according to usage and to the standard of living of the family. They include maintenance of the spouses, their children and relatives who live with them in the family home, insurance medical and healthcare expenses, expenses deriving from the maintenance of the dwellings and other assets of family use, the expenses deriving from the acquisition and the improvements to the dwellings and other assets of family use).,.
277 See § 1360a para. 1 German Civil Code (everything that is necessary according to the circumstances of the spouses to pay for the costs of the household and the personal needs of the spouses and their children.
278 See Art. 1362 Spanish Civil Code.
279 See TODOROVA, Bulgarian Report, Q 8.
280 See MARTÍN-CASALS/RIBOT, Catalan Report, Q 8, but only if those children cannot afford their expenses with their own financial resources.
281 See BOELE-WOELKI/SCHONEWILLE/SCHRAMA, Dutch Report, Q 8.
282 See GONZÁLEZ BEILFUSS, Spanish Report, Q 8.

Proportional contribution of each spouse according to ability

In all jurisdictions that set out a duty upon the spouses to contribute to the needs of the family, each spouse has to contribute according "to his or her possibilities" or "capabilities" or "ability". This means that the contribution of each of the spouses is not equal. To the contrary, the extent of each spouse's duty to contribute depends on his/her capabilities, property and income. As BULGARIAN law states,[283] an equal effort of the spouses is required, but not an equal contribution in terms of amount. The same is stated in BELGIUM[284] and CATALONIA (standard of proportional contribution, in accordance with the "economic resources" of each spouse[285]), and applies in the CZECH REPUBLIC,[286] DENMARK,[287] FINLAND,[288] FRANCE,[289] GREECE,[290] LITHUANIA,[291] MALTA,[292] THE NETHERLANDS,[293] POLAND,[294] SLOVAKIA[295] and SWEDEN.[296] In SWITZERLAND,[297] it is presumed that the spouses share the burden of support equally, but if the spouses cannot agree on their respective contributions, they can apply to the court, which will then determine the proper amount of the respective financial contributions.[298]

Determining what constitutes the appropriate support of the family largely depends on the circumstances of each case. In many jurisdictions, apart from the daily needs which are automatically included in the family needs (food, clothing, family home, health care, etc.), relevant factors include the economic situation of the family and the standard of living chosen by the spouses (for example in AUSTRIA,[299] BELGIUM,[300] BULGARIA,[301] THE CZECH

283 See TODOROVA, Bulgarian Report, Q 8.
284 See PINTENS/ALLAERTS/SEYNS/PIGNOLET, Belgian Report, Q 8.
285 See MARTÍN-CASALS/RIBOT, Catalan Report, Q 8.
286 According to the abilities, possibilities and property conditions of the spouses, see MELZER, Czech Report, Q 8.
287 See LUND-ANDERSEN/MAGNUSSEN, Danish Report, Q 8 (according to the spouses' individual means).
288 To the best of the spouses' abilities, see KURKI-SUONIO, Finnish Report, Q 8.
289 See FERRAND/BRAAT, French Report, Q 8 (in proportion to their respective means).
290 See KOUTSOURADIS/KOTRONIS/HATZANTONIS, Greek Report, Q 8.
291 See MIKELENAS, Lithuanian Report, Q 8.
292 See FARRUGIA, Maltese Report, Q 8 (each spouse in proportion to his or her means and his or her ability to work whether in the home or outside the home).
293 See BOELE-WOELKI/SCHONEWILLE/SCHRAMA, Dutch Report, Q 8 with a four-step system relating to the concrete contribution of each spouse.
294 See MĄCZYŃSKI, Polish Report, Q 8.
295 See HAŤAPKA, Slovakian Report, Q 8.
296 See JÄNTERÄ-JAREBORG/BRATTSTRÖM/WALLENG, Swedish Report, Q 8.
297 See SCHWENZER/BOCK, Swiss Report, Q 8.
298 Art. 173 Swiss Civil Code.
299 See ROTH, Austrian Report, Q 8.
300 See PINTENS/ALLAERTS/SEYNS/PIGNOLET, Belgian Report, Q 8.
301 See TODOROVA, Bulgarian Report, Q 8.

REPUBLIC,[302] DENMARK,[303] FRANCE,[304] GERMANY,[305] PORTUGAL,[306] SPAIN[307] and SWITZERLAND[308]).

May the spouses enter into agreement on the extent and content of the contribution?

Some jurisdictions allow the spouses to enter into an agreement on the extent and content of the contribution. For example, in SWITZERLAND,[309] CATALONIA[310] and in THE NETHERLANDS,[311] the spouses are free to decide on the extent and content of their respective contributions. In FRANCE,[312] an ante-nuptial agreement may regulate the contribution of the spouses to the marriage expenses. In GREECE,[313] such agreements between spouses are allowed, but are subject to the requirement that the principles of proportionality and the mutuality are not affected.

Possible judicial action if one spouse fails to fulfil his or her duty to contribute

Where a spouse does not fulfil his or her obligation to contribute to the family expenses, the other spouse is entitled to bring a claim before the court (BELGIUM,[314] CZECH REPUBLIC,[315] FRANCE,[316] NORWAY,[317] PORTUGAL[318] and SWITZERLAND[319]). The court must then determine the amount to be paid by the defendant spouse. Although some national reports do not expressly mention the possibility of such judicial action, or restrict it to a kind of "maintenance claim", the tendency in the jurisdictions surveyed appears to favour permitting one spouse to sue the other in order to allow the competent authority (usually a court) to determine the amount to be paid and to order the defendant to pay it.

---

302 See MELZER, Czech Report, Q 8.
303 See LUND-ANDERSEN/MAGNUSSEN, Danish Report, Q 8.
304 See FERRAND/BRAAT, French Report, Q 8.
305 See DETHLOFF/MARTINY, German Report, Q 8.
306 See DE OLIVEIRA/MARTINS/VÍTOR, Portuguese Report, Q 8.
307 See GONZÁLEZ BEILFUSS, Spanish Report, Q 8.
308 See SCHWENZER/BOCK, Swiss Report, Q 8.
309 See SCHWENZER/BOCK, Swiss Report, Q 8.
310 See MARTÍN-CASALS/RIBOT, Catalan Report, Q 8.
311 See BOELE-WOELKI/SCHONEWILLE/SCHRAMA, Dutch Report, Q 8 (such an agreement requires a written contract, see Art. 1:84 para. 3 Dutch Civil Code. It seldom happens).
312 Art. 214 French Civil Code.
313 See KOUTSOURADIS/KOTRONIS/HATZANTONIS, Greek Report, Q 8.
314 See PINTENS/ALLAERTS/SEYNS/PIGNOLET, Belgian Report, Q 8.
315 See MELZER, Czech Report, Q 8.
316 See FERRAND/BRAAT, French Report, Q 8.
317 See SVERDRUP, Norwegian Report, Q 8.
318 Art. 1676 para. 9 Portuguese Civil Code.
319 See SCHWENZER/BOCK, Swiss Report, Q 8.

Joint and several liability of both spouses for family debts, even if they were incurred only by one spouse

Everyday household debts are essential in the matrimonial context. Spouses often do not enter jointly into the transactions required to support the family's life. However, if each spouse contributes to the family debts in a fair way, meaning that each spouse contributes according to his or her ability and capabilities, can he or she be made liable for the debts incurred by the other spouse that relate to, and can be qualified, as family debts? Such joint and several liability of both spouses demonstrate their common responsibility for the support of the family. This issue is sometimes – but not always – combined with the powers of representation of each spouse (agency, for example in CATALONIA[320]).

Principle of joint and several liability

Of the twenty-two jurisdictions which set out the obligation on spouses to contribute to their family's needs, sixteen impose joint liability on both spouses for their family's debts, even when only one of spouses took the initiative to enter into the transaction. This is the case in BELGIUM,[321] BULGARIA,[322] CATALONIA,[323] CZECH REPUBLIC,[324] DENMARK,[325] FINLAND,[326] FRANCE,[327] GERMANY,[328] HUNGARY,[329] THE NETHERLANDS,[330] NORWAY,[331] POLAND,[332] PORTUGAL,[333] SLOVAKIA,[334] SPAIN[335] (with some restrictions) and SWITZERLAND.[336]

---

320 See Art. 3.2 Catalan Family Code (each spouse is empowered to incur in debts for the purpose of meeting ordinary family expenses). See also Principle 4:7 regarding agency.

321 See PINTENS/ALLAERTS/SEYNS/PIGNOLET, Belgian Report, Q 9.

322 See TODOROVA, Bulgarian Report, Q 9.

323 See MARTÍN-CASALS/RIBOT, Catalan Report, Q 9.

324 See MELZER, Czech Report, Q 9.

325 See LUND-ANDERSEN/MAGNUSSEN, Danish Report, Q 9.

326 § 52 para. 2–3 Finnish Marriage Act. See also KURKI-SUONIO, Finnish Report, Q 9. The joint responsibility is restricted to maintenance debts and does not cover monetary loans taken a spouse, credit card purchases included.

327 See FERRAND/BRAAT, French Report, Q 9.

328 See DETHLOFF/MARTINY, German Report, Q 9.

329 See WEISS/SZEIBERT, Hungarian Report, Q 9.

330 See BOELE-WOELKI/SCHONEWILLE/SCHRAMA, Dutch Report, Q 9.

331 See SVERDRUP, Norwegian Report, Q 9.

332 See MĄCZYŃSKI, Polish Report, Q 9.

333 See DE OLIVEIRA/MARTINS/VÍTOR, Portuguese Report, Q 9.

334 See HAŤAPKA, Slovakian Report, Q 9.

335 See GONZÁLEZ BEILFUSS, Spanish Report, Q 9. There is joint and several liability of the spouses only if the debts cannot be covered by common property or by the property of the spouse who incurred the debt. See also Art. 1319 Spanish Civil Code: any spouse may incur ordinary expenses for the household according to local usage and the circumstances of the family.

336 See SCHWENZER/BOCK, Swiss Report, Q 9.

In BELGIUM,[337] for example, everyday household debts automatically attach to both of the spouses, and hold them jointly liable, even if the debt was not necessary.[338] In BULGARIA, Article 25 para. 2 Bulgarian Family Code clearly states that "for debts incurred by one or both spouses for the satisfaction of family needs, both spouses are jointly responsible";[339] the same applies in HUNGARY,[340] LITHUANIA[341] and POLAND.[342] In CATALONIA, the same principle applies, subject to the condition that the expenses are "in accordance with the usage and the standard of living of the family" (if this is not the case, only the spouse who entered to obligation is liable).[343] In the CZECH REPUBLIC,[344] the activities of one spouse in managing the usual affairs of the family bind both spouses jointly and severally. The same rule also applies in DENMARK, under the condition that the spouses are still in marital cohabitation[345] and the contracts are to be concluded for the purpose of meeting day-to-day household needs, or the children's needs. Similar solutions are provided in DUTCH,[346] NORWEGIAN[347] and PORTUGUESE law.[348] The law of FRANCE also states a broad principle: (1) the power of each spouse to singularly make contracts which relate to the support of the household or the education of children, and (2) the joint and several liability of both spouses for debts deriving from such transactions[349] (however, some

337 See Art. 222 Belgian Civil Code. See PINTENS/ALLAERTS/SEYNS/PIGNOLET, Belgian Report, Q 9.

338 But there are some exceptions to this principle, see Art. 222 para. 2 Belgian Civil Code. See PINTENS/ALLAERTS/SEYNS/PIGNOLET, Belgian Report, Q 9.

339 See TODOROVA, Bulgarian Report, Q 9: the joint liability cannot be excluded by virtue of a spousal agreement.

340 See WEISS/SZEIBERT, Hungarian Report, Q 9.

341 See MIKELENAS, Lithuanian Report, Q 9.

342 Art. 30 para. 1 Polish Family and Guardianship Code. This liability cannot be excluded by the spouses. However, the court may, upon one spouse's request, order that only the spouse who has entered into a precise obligation is liable.

343 See Art. 8 Catalan Family Code. See MARTÍN-CASALS/RIBOT, Catalan Report, Q 9. Internally, the contribution of each spouse will be measured accordingly to their agreement or the standard of proportionality (Art. 5 Catalan Family Code).

344 See Art. 21 para. 2 Czech Family Act.

345 § 11 Danish Act on the Effects of Marriage. See LUND-ANDERSEN/MAGNUSSEN, Danish Report, Q 9. Solidarity does not apply if the third party knew, or should have known, that the contract was unreasonable. In addition, loans are not covered by the joint and several liability of the spouses.

346 See Art. 1:85 Dutch Civil Code. However, the non-acting spouse does not become party to the contract, and does not derive the power to exercise creditor's rights from Art. 1:85; see BOELE-WOELKI/SCHONEWILLE/SCHRAMA, Dutch Report, Q 9.

347 See § 41 Norwegian Marriage Act. See SVERDRUP, Norwegian Report, Q 9: a spouse may, during cohabitation, enter into agreements resulting in joint and several liability of both spouses. These are the agreements regarding the daily housekeeping and the upbringing of the children as well as ordinary agreements to cover the necessary requirement of the individual spouse. The leasing of the common residence belongs to such transactions that result in joint and several liability of both spouses.

348 Art. 1691 para. 1 sub b Portuguese Civil Code.

349 Art. 220 para. 1 French Civil Code. See FERRAND/BRAAT, French Report, Q 9.

contracts are excluded from such solidarity). In GERMANY, spouses have an implied agency which allows each of them to enter into a transaction in order to meet the necessities of the family;[350] the transactions entered into in this context lead to the joint and several liability of both spouses.[351] SWITZERLAND also provides a liability for "debts incurred for the day-to-day needs of the family".[352] For the debts incurred in meeting other needs of the family, the spouses are jointly and severally liable a) if the court or one spouse has authorized the other spouse to incur such a debt,[353] b) in urgent circumstances,[354] and c) if a third party relied on the fact that the debt was incurred for day-to-day needs even though it was in fact a debt incurred for other family needs.[355]

Exceptions to joint and several liability

The jurisdictions that do not provide joint liability of the spouses for the family debts independent of the matrimonial property relationship between them are AUSTRIA,[356] ENGLAND AND WALES,[357] IRELAND,[358] ITALY,[359] MALTA,[360] RUSSIA,[361] SCOTLAND[362] and SWEDEN.[363] In ITALY,[364] it is only under the legal community regime that a spouse is liable for the debts contracted by the other spouse in the interest of the family; the same applies in MALTA.[365] In RUSSIA,[366] there is no specific rule in the Russian Family Code governing liability for household debts incurred by the other spouse. Joint and several liability is only imposed for debts arising from the use of the family home.[367] In SWEDEN, each spouse is only liable for the debts incurred by him or her,[368] there is no special rule regarding liability for household debts. SWEDEN sets out a duty of both spouses to contribute to the

350 § 1357 German Civil Code.
351 §§ 421 to 425 German Civil Code. See DETHLOFF/MARTINY, German Report, Q 9.
352 Art. 166 para. 1 Swiss Civil Code.
353 Art. 166 para. 2 Swiss Civil Code.
354 Art. 166 para. 2 n°1 Swiss Civil Code.
355 Art. 166 para. 3 Swiss Civil Code.
356 See ROTH, Austrian Report, Q 9.
357 See BARLOW, English Report, Q 9.
358 See SHANNON, Irish Report, Q 9.
359 See PATTI/CARICATO/IRTI/IANNICELLI/SERA/DI STEFANO/PETÖ, Italian Report, Q 9.
360 See FARRUGIA, Maltese Report, Q 9.
361 See ANTOKOLSKAIA, Russian Report, Q 9.
362 See MAIR, Scottish Report, Q 9.
363 See JÄNTERÄ-JAREBORG/BRATTSTRÖM/WALLENG, Swedish Report, Q 9.
364 See PATTI/CARICATO/IRTI/IANNICELLI/SERA/DI STEFANO/PETÖ, Italian Report, Q 9.
365 See FARRUGIA, Maltese Report, Q 9.
366 See ANTOKOLSKAIA, Russian Report, Q 9.
367 Art. 31 para. 3 Russian Housing Code as well as Art. 292 para. 1 Russian Civil Code quoted in the national report. See ANTOKOLSKAIA, Russian Report, Q 9. Those rules are not mandatory and can be set aside by a marital property agreement.
368 Chap. 1 § 3 Swedish Marriage Code. See JÄNTERÄ-JAREBORG/BRATTSTRÖM/WALLENG, Swedish Report, Q 9.

family needs, however, those rules only refer to the inter-spousal relationship, and cannot be invoked by a creditor. AUSTRIA[369] has chosen a very specific model: for legal transactions in connection with the daily life of the household, § 96 Austrian Civil Code states that the spouse who manages the joint household and earns no income represents the other spouse in legal transactions relating to daily life (so-called *Schlüsselgewalt*). Therefore, it is only the other spouse (who did not personally enter into transaction) who becomes the contract partner and the debtor, and is personally liable.[370] Where both spouses are employed, only the spouse who enters into transaction becomes the contract partner and the debtor.

Conditions and exemptions to joint and several liability

In most of the jurisdictions that state a joint and several liability of both spouses, the debts which result in such a liability are those relating to the needs of the family. There is a great variety of terminology: *family debts* in CATALONIA,[371] *normal running of the household* in THE NETHERLANDS,[372] *ordinary expenses for the household* in SPAIN, *ordinary family life expenses* in PORTUGAL, *debts for the support of the household and the upbringing of the children* in BELGIUM[373] and FRANCE,[374] *day-to-day needs* in DENMARK[375] and SWITZERLAND,[376] *debts for the satisfaction of family needs* in BULGARIA[377] and POLAND[378] *standard needs of the family*, for the *maintenance of the family* in FINLAND, *the appropriate necessities of the family* in GERMANY.[379] In NORWAY,[380] more precisely, the debts resulting in joint and several liability of both spouses are those incurred in the *daily housekeeping and the upbringing of the children as well as the necessary requirements of the individual spouse.* The question of what constitutes the *normal running of the household* or *family needs* largely depends on the circumstances of each particular case, in which the nature of the expense, financial circumstances and family's lifestyle as it appears to the outside world are considered to be decisive factors (for example,

369 See ROTH, Austrian Report, Q 9.
370 However, if the third party cannot infer from the circumstances that the acting spouse is the representative, both parties are jointly liable for the household debts, see ROTH, Austrian Report, Q 9.
371 See MARTÍN-CASALS/RIBOT, Catalan Report, Q 9.
372 The costs which belong to the "normal running of the household" are less wide-ranging than the "costs of the household." See BOELE-WOELKI/SCHONEWILLE/SCHRAMA, Dutch Report, Q 9.
373 See PINTENS/ALLAERTS/SEYNS/PIGNOLET, Belgian Report, Q 9.
374 See FERRAND/BRAAT, French Report, Q 9.
375 See LUND-ANDERSEN/MAGNUSSEN, Danish Report, Q 9.
376 See SCHWENZER/BOCK, Swiss Report, Q 9.
377 See TODOROVA, Bulgarian Report, Q 9.
378 See MĄCZYŃSKI, Polish Report, Q 9.
379 See DETHLOFF/MARTINY, German Report, Q 9.
380 See SVERDRUP, Norwegian Report, Q 9.

BELGIUM,[381] CATALONIA,[382] FRANCE,[383] THE NETHERLANDS,[384] PORTUGAL,[385] SPAIN[386] and SWITZERLAND[387]). The concepts of *family needs* and the joint and several liability of both spouses are not limited to *in abstracto* necessary expenses (BELGIUM[388] and FRANCE[389]). Other jurisdictions appear to be more restrictive and to limit the joint liability of the spouses to the *standard needs of the family* (POLAND[390]). Several national reports do not mention the criteria used to evaluate whether the debt incurred by one spouse results in joint liability or not.

Many of the sixteen jurisdictions which set out the principle of a joint and several liability of both spouses for family debts make some exceptions to this basic rule. In BELGIUM[391] and FRANCE,[392] for example, there is no joint liability if the incurred debts are exorbitant (*manifestement excessives*) in view of the means of the family (the exorbitance is evaluated *in concreto* with regard to the standard of living of the couple). An exclusion of the joint and several liability of the spouses also applies in LITHUANIA,[393] where the price of transaction is clearly too high and unreasonable, in DENMARK the other spouse is not liable if the third party knew, or should have known, that the contract was unreasonable) and, implicitly, in CATALONIA[394] or PORTUGAL,[395] since the expenses are required to be in accordance with the usage (CATALONIA[396]) and the standard of living of the family (CATALONIA[397] and PORTUGAL[398]). The *French-German Agreement of 2010* on the choice of a matrimonial property regime (*régime matrimonial optionnel de la participation aux acquêts*) also states in Article 6 para. 2 that joint and several liability of the spouses is excluded if the debt is manifestly excessive with regard to the standard of

381 See PINTENS/ALLAERTS/SEYNS/PIGNOLET, Belgian Report, Q 9.
382 See MARTÍN-CASALS/RIBOT, Catalan Report, Q 9.
383 See FERRAND/BRAAT, French Report, Q 9.
384 See BOELE-WOELKI/SCHONEWILLE/SCHRAMA, Dutch Report, Q 9.
385 See DE OLIVEIRA/MARTINS/VÍTOR, Portuguese Report, Q 9.
386 See GONZÁLEZ BEILFUSS, Spanish Report, Q 9.
387 See SCHWENZER/BOCK, Swiss Report, Q 9.
388 See PINTENS/ALLAERTS/SEYNS/PIGNOLET, Belgian Report, Q 9.
389 See FERRAND/BRAAT, French Report, Q 9.
390 See MĄCZYŃSKI, Polish Report, Q 9.
391 Art. 222 para. 2 Belgian Civil Code and Art. 220 para. 2 French Civil Code.
392 Art. 220 para. 2 French Civil Code. See FERRAND/BRAAT, French Report, Q 9: the evaluation of whether a debt is manifestly excessive occurs is based upon three possible criteria: the standard of living of the household, the usefulness or uselessness of the transaction and the good or bad faith of the contracting third party.
393 See MIKELENAS, Lithuanian Report, Q 9.
394 See MARTÍN-CASALS/RIBOT, Catalan Report, Q 9.
395 See DE OLIVEIRA/MARTINS/VÍTOR, Portuguese Report, Q 9.
396 See MARTÍN-CASALS/RIBOT, Catalan Report, Q 9.
397 See MARTÍN-CASALS/RIBOT, Catalan Report, Q 9.
398 See DE OLIVEIRA/MARTINS/VÍTOR, Portuguese Report, Q 9.

living of the spouses, and the other contracting party knows, or should have known, about this, given the circumstances. According to CZECH law,[399] joint and several liability of the spouses can be expressely excluded by the spouse who did not enter into the transaction provided that the third party knew of this.

Joint and several liability of the spouses can also be excluded for *special kinds of transaction*. In several jurisdictions, monetary loans, for example, are not covered by such a liability (DENMARK,[400] FINLAND,[401] FRANCE[402] and LITHUANIA[403]); this may also be the case where goods are acquired on credit without the consent of the other spouse.

Another possible ground for the exclusion of the joint and several liability of the spouses is a *de facto* separation[404] between them. The issue is not always clearly solved in many jurisdictions (e.g. SPAIN[405]). In FINLAND,[406] there is no more spousal solidarity if the separation is due to a breakdown of the spouses' relationship and if the creditor was aware of the separation (which can be difficult to prove). In DENMARK,[407] GERMANY[408] and SWITZERLAND,[409] joint liability only applies if the spouses live in marital cohabitation.

The joint and several liability of both spouses with regard to family debts does not appear to be a possible matter of agreement between spouses (BELGIUM,[410] BULGARIA,[411] FRANCE,[412] LITHUANIA[413] and POLAND[414]). The other national reports do not deal with the issue of the validity of a spousal agreement which excludes the joint and several liability set out in the national statutory provisions.

---

399 Art. § 21 last para. Czech Family Act.
400 § 11 Danish Act on the Effects of Marriage. See LUND-ANDERSEN/MAGNUSSEN, Danish Report, Q 9.
401 See KURKI-SUONIO, Finnish Report, Q 9.
402 See FERRAND/BRAAT, French Report, Q 9, unless the amounts are reasonable and needed for the cants of everyday life, see Art. 220 para. 3 French Civil Code.
403 In LITHUANIA, there is no joint and several liability where one spouse, without the consent of the other, takes out a loan or acquires goods on credit which are not necessary for the needs of the family.
404 Joint and several liability self evidently ends upon divorce or nullity of marriage.
405 See GONZÁLEZ BEILFUSS, Spanish Report, Q 9: in case of a factual separation, the solution seems to depend on whether or not the separation is generally known by third parties.
406 See KURKI-SUONIO, Finnish Report, Q 9.
407 See LUND-ANDERSEN/MAGNUSSEN, Danish Report, Q 9.
408 § 1357 para. 3 German Civil Code.
409 See SCHWENZER/BOCK, Swiss Report, Q 9.
410 See PINTENS/ALLAERTS/SEYNS/PIGNOLET, Belgian Report, Q 9.
411 See TODOROVA, Bulgarian Report, Q 9.
412 See FERRAND/BRAAT, French Report, Q 9.
413 See MIKELENAS, Lithuanian Report, Q 9.
414 See MĄCZYŃSKI, Polish Report, Q 9.

COMMENT

1. Both spouses should contribute to the needs of the family on the grounds of solidarity between married people and the mutual duty to care for the family. Equity requires that the spouses do not contribute in equal shares, but in proportion to their respective ability and capabilities. This is a clear common core in the jurisdictions surveyed. Whether the extent and content of the contribution should be a possible matter of agreement between the spouses who should be free to organize their married life as they wish, is left to national law. The question of whether such an agreement can be entered into before marriage in a pre-nuptial contract, or can also be entered into during marriage, should also be left to national law.

2. Reflecting the position in all the jurisdictions surveyed, it is permissible under Principle 4:4 for a spouse to contribute in kind through the care of the home (housework) and the care of the children. The children whose care should be included in the category of family needs are the common children of the spouses, and/or the children of one spouse living in the family home.

3. The needs of the family encompass the expenditure relating to the "household", which includes the common needs of the spouses, as well as the personal needs of each spouse. Family needs also include the maintenance and education of the children of the spouses (or of one spouse if they live in the family home), as well as their health care.[415] The spousal duty to contribute to the needs of the family should cover all expenses which are necessary to maintain the family's standard of living.

4. Where one spouse fails to fulfil his or her duty to contribute, the other spouse should be entitled to bring a claim before court, or to summon his or her spouse to appear before the competent authority. The competent authority (court or administrative body) should determine the amount to be paid by the defendant spouse with regard to the capabilities of each spouse, their needs, and the standard of living of the family. With regard to the practical importance of the duty to contribute, it is desirable that the order delivered by the competent authority be immediately enforceable, notwithstanding a possible appeal. However, this issue is left to the national law of procedure and enforcement.

5. Although there exists a broad common core among the jurisdictions surveyed that spouse are jointly and severally liable for debts incurred in order to cover the needs of the family this has not been stated in Principle 4:4. Having

[415] See Principle 3:1 of the Principles of European Family Law Regarding Parental Responsibilities, which defines the concept of parental responsibilities.

regard to the better law approach, such a liability appears to be outdated, and was justified at a time when only the husband was employed, and the wife dedicated her life to home and children care. Furthermore, such joint and several liability gives the creditor a better position when he contracts with one spouse than when the contracting party is not married. There is no strong reason to maintain this rule in favour of the creditors.

Principle 4:5 Protection of the family home and household goods
(1) Any act of disposal of rights to the family home or household goods requires the consent of both spouses.
(2) Any act of disposal by one spouse without the consent of the other is valid if the latter ratifies it.
(3) If a spouse refuses or is unable to give consent, the other spouse may request authorisation by the competent authority.
(4) Any act of disposal in breach of the preceding paragraphs may be annulled by the competent authority upon the application of the non-consenting spouse.

Principe 4:5 Protection du logement de la famille et des meubles meublants
(1) Tout acte de disposition des droits sur le logement de la famille ou sur les meubles meublants requiert le consentement de chaque époux.
(2) Tout acte de disposition par un époux sans le consentement de l'autre est valide si ce dernier le confirme.
(3) Si un époux refuse son consentement ou n'est pas en mesure de le donner, l'autre époux peut solliciter l'autorisation de l'autorité compétente.
(4) Tout acte de disposition passé en violation des alinéas précédents peut être annulé par l'autorité compétente à la demande de l'époux qui n'a pas consenti.

Prinzip 4:5 Schutz der Familienwohnung und Haushaltsgegenstände
(1) Jedes Verpflichtungs- oder Verfügungsgeschäft bezüglich Rechten an der Familienwohnung oder bezüglich der Haushaltsgegenstände erfordert die Zustimmung beider Ehegatten.
(2) Jedes andere Verpflichtungs- oder Verfügungsgeschäft eines Ehegatten ohne Zustimmung des anderen Ehegatten ist wirksam, wenn der andere es genehmigt.
(3) Verweigert ein Ehegatte seine Zustimmung oder ist er nicht in der Lage, diese zu erteilen, kann der andere Ehegatte eine Ermächtigung bei der zuständigen Behörde beantragen.
(4) Jedes Verpflichtungs- oder Verfügungsgeschäft, das die vorangegangenen Absätze verletzt, kann auf Antrag des nicht zustimmenden Ehegatten von der zuständigen Behörde für nichtig erklärt werden.

INTERNATIONAL INSTRUMENTS

Recommendation No. R (81) 15 of the Committee of Ministers of the Council of Europe, which was adopted on 16th October 1981, deals with the *right of the spouses relating to the occupation of the family home and the use of the household contents*. Member States are encouraged to adapt their legislation to the principles set out in the appendix of the Recommendation.

Principle 1 of the Recommendation requires that any act by one spouse that directly prejudices the right of the other spouse to occupy the family home should be carried out with the consent of the latter. When such consent is unjustifiably withheld or impossible to obtain authorisation by a competent authority can be requested. Principle 2 provides that it should be possible to set aside acts in breach of the rule established in Principle 1. If the right of occupancy cannot be maintained other appropriate sanctions should be available. Principle 3 deals with the right of occupation of the family home in case of marriage breakdown. In the case of a divorce or a judicial separation this right may be assigned, in appropriate cases, exclusively to one of the spouses. Principle 4 states that the surviving spouse shall have the right to continue to occupy the family home. Principles 6 to 8 of the Recommendation deal with the rights of spouses to the use of furniture and other objects that are meant for the use of the family in the home. Any act carried out by one spouse without the consent of the other spouse that prejudices the right of the latter to use such items may be set aside or subject to any other appropriate sanction. In the case of divorce or legal separation the whole or part of the said household contents can be assigned exclusively to one spouse. The surviving spouse shall have the right to be granted the whole or part of the household contents.

The family home and the household goods are also protected in the *French-German Agreement of 2010* establishing the optional regime of participation in acquisitions. Article 5 (1) of this instrument provides that unilateral acts of disposal of rights to the family home and the household goods are void unless they are ratified by the non-consenting spouse. The competent authority can authorize one spouse to act alone if the other spouse lacks capacity to issue consent or wilfully refuses such consent not taking into account the interests of the family.

COMPARATIVE OVERVIEW

Protection of the family home

The family home is protected in many European systems regardless of the matrimonial property regime except in countries such as AUSTRIA,[416] CZECH

[416] See ROTH, Austrian Report, Q 10.

REPUBLIC,[417] DENMARK,[418] GREECE,[419] RUSSIA[420] and SLOVAKIA,[421] where the rules on the matrimonial home depend on the ownership of such property. In jurisdictions such as SCOTLAND[422] and IRELAND[423] there are special Family Home Protection Acts that apply to all married couples. Similarly, there are provisions in the English Family Law Act 1996 that protect non-owner spouses in ENGLAND AND WALES.[424] Under GERMAN law,[425] the protection of the family home is an issue of matrimonial property law.

The majority of European legal systems surveyed define the family home as the habitual dwelling place of the family (AUSTRIA,[426] BELGIUM,[427] BULGARIA,[428] CATALONIA,[429] DENMARK,[430] ENGLAND AND WALES,[431] FINLAND,[432] FRANCE,[433] GERMANY,[434] HUNGARY,[435] IRELAND,[436] ITALY,[437] LITHUANIA,[438] THE NETHERLANDS,[439] NORWAY,[440] PORTUGAL,[441] SCOTLAND,[442] SPAIN,[443] SWEDEN[444] and SWITZERLAND[445]). Some jurisdictions require that the family home be an immovable (e.g. BELGIUM[446]) while others also accept boats or caravans (e.g. ENGLAND AND WALES[447] and SCOTLAND[448]). There are discrepancies between jurisdictions that only recognise one immovable as the matrimonial home (e.g.

417 See MELZER, Czech Report, Q 10.
418 See LUND-ANDERSEN/MAGNUSSEN, Danish Report, Q 10.
419 See KOUTSOURADIS/KOTRONIS/HATZANTONIS, Greek Report, Q 10.
420 See ANTOKOLSKAIA, Russian Report, Q 10.
421 See HAŤAPKA, Slovakian Report, Q 10.
422 Matrimonial Homes (Family Protection) (Scotland) Act 1981.
423 Irish Family Home Protection Act 1976.
424 S. 30 and 31 of the English Familiy Law Act 1996. See BARLOW, English Report, Q 10.
425 See DETHLOFF/MARTINY, German Report, Q 10.
426 See ROTH, Austrian Report, Q 10.
427 See PINTENS/ALLAERTS/SEYNS/PIGNOLET, Belgian Report, Q 10.
428 See TODOROVA, Bulgarian Report, Q 10.
429 See MARTÍN-CASALS/RIBOT, Catalan Report, Q 10.
430 See LUND-ANDERSEN/MAGNUSSEN, Danish Report, Q 10.
431 See BARLOW, English Report, Q 10.
432 See KURKI-SUONIO, Finnish Report, Q 10.
433 See FERRAND/BRAAT, French Report, Q 10.
434 See DETHLOFF/MARTINY, German Report, Q 10.
435 See WEISS/SZEIBERT, Hungarian Report, Q 10.
436 S. 2 (1) Irish Family Home Protection Act 1976 See SHANNON, Irish Report, Q 10.
437 See PATTI/CARICATO/IRTI/IANNICELLI/SERA/DI STEFANO/PETÖ, Italian Report, Q 10.
438 See MIKELENAS, Lithuanian Report, Q 10.
439 See BOELE-WOELKI/SCHONEWILLE/SCHRAMA, Dutch Report, Q 10.
440 See SVERDRUP, Norwegian Report, Q 10.
441 See DE OLIVEIRA/MARTINS/VÍTOR, Portuguese Report, Q 10.
442 See MAIR, Scottish Report, Q 10.
443 See GONZÁLEZ BEILFUSS, Spanish Report, Q 10.
444 See JÄNTERÄ-JAREBORG/BRATTSTRÖM/WALLENG, Swedish Report, Q 10.
445 See SCHWENZER/BOCK, Swiss Report, Q 10.
446 See PINTENS/ALLAERTS/SEYNS/PIGNOLET, Belgian Report, Q 10.
447 S. 63 Family Law Act 1996.
448 See MAIR, Scottish Report, Q 10.

AUSTRIA[449] and BELGIUM[450]) while others accept that, for example, holiday homes may fall into the category (DENMARK[451] and ENGLAND AND WALES[452]). The acceptance in some jurisdictions that there can be more than one matrimonial home is subject to there being very special circumstances (SPAIN[453] and SWITZERLAND[454]) or requires that the second residence is regularly used (THE NETHERLANDS[455]).

Household goods

There is less convergence as regards the protection of household goods. They are however protected in BELGIUM,[456] CATALONIA,[457] FINLAND,[458] FRANCE,[459] IRELAND,[460] THE NETHERLANDS,[461] NORWAY,[462] PORTUGAL,[463] SCOTLAND,[464] SPAIN,[465] SWEDEN[466] and SWITZERLAND.[467]

Household goods are often not defined in legislation (BELGIUM,[468] BULGARIA,[469] CATALONIA,[470], ENGLAND AND WALES,[471] GREECE,[472] HUNGARY,[473] MALTA,[474] RUSSIA[475] and SLOVAKIA[476]), although there are some systems that give detailed

449 See ROTH, Austrian Report, Q 10.
450 See PINTENS/ALLAERTS/SEYNS/PIGNOLET, Belgian Report, Q 10.
451 See LUND-ANDERSEN/MAGNUSSEN, Danish Report, Q 10.
452 See BARLOW, English Report, Q 10.
453 See GONZÁLEZ BEILFUSS, Spanish Report, Q 10.
454 See SCHWENZER/BOCK, Swiss Report, Q 10.
455 See BOELE-WOELKI/SCHONEWILLE/SCHRAMA, Dutch Report, Q 10.
456 Art. 215 Belgian Civil Code. See PINTENS/ALLAERTS/SEYNS/PIGNOLET, Belgian Report, Q 11.
457 Art. 9 Catalan Family Code. See MARTÍN-CASALS/RIBOT, Catalan Report, Q 11.
458 § 39 Finnish Marriage Act. See KURKI-SUONIO, Finnish Report, Q 11.
459 Art. 215 para.3 and 1751 French Civil Code. See FERRAND/BRAAT, French Report, Q 11.
460 S. 9 Irish Family Home Protection Act. See SHANNON, Irish Report, Q 11.
461 See BOELE-WOELKI/SCHONEWILLE/SCHRAMA, Dutch Report, Q 11.
462 § 33 Norwegian Marriage Act. See SVERDRUP, Norwegian Report, Q 11.
463 Art. 1682 para.3 sub a Portuguese Civil Code. See DE OLIVEIRA/MARTINS/VÍTOR, Portuguese Report, Q11.
464 S. 25 of the Scots Family Law Act 1985. See MAIR, Scottish Report, Q 11.
465 Art. 1323 Spanish Civil Code. See GONZÁLEZ BEILFUSS, Spanish Report, Q 11.
466 Ch. 7 §§ 4–5 Swedish Marriage Code. See JÄNTERÄ-JAREBORG/BRATTSTRÖM/WALLENG, Swedish Report, Q 11.
467 See SCHWENZER/BOCK, Swiss Report, Q 11.
468 See PINTENS/ALLAERTS/SEYNS/PIGNOLET, Belgian Report, Q 11.
469 See TODOROVA, Bulgarian Report, Q 11.
470 See MARTÍN-CASALS/RIBOT, Catalan Report, Q 11.
471 See BARLOW, English Report, Q 11.
472 See KOUTSOURADIS/KOTRONIS/HATZANTONIS, Greek Report, Q 11.
473 See WEISS/SZEIBERT, Hungarian Report, Q 11.
474 See FARRUGIA, Maltese Report, Q 11.
475 See ANTOKOLSKAIA, Russian Report, Q 11.
476 See HAŤAPKA, Slovakian Report, Q 11.

definitions such as FRANCE[477] and IRELAND.[478] All systems include movables that are used inside the family home such as for example furniture and kitchen equipment (AUSTRIA,[479] BELGIUM,[480] DENMARK,[481] FINLAND,[482] IRELAND,[483] LITHUANIA,[484] NORWAY,[485] PORTUGAL,[486] SCOTLAND,[487] SPAIN,[488] SWEDEN[489] and SWITZERLAND[490]) while capital investments such as antiques, valuable paintings or jewellery are excluded (BELGIUM,[491] LITHUANIA,[492] NORWAY[493] and SPAIN[494]). Collections of pictures, which are displayed in galleries or special rooms are excluded in FRANCE.[495] However, pictures and statutes belong to household goods if they form part of the urniture of an apartment. There are differences as regards cars. These are considered household goods in BELGIUM[496] while there are provisions to the contrary in FRANCE,[497] SCOTLAND,[498] SPAIN[499] and SWEDEN.[500] Domestic animals are another difficult issue. They are considered household goods in IRELAND[501] but excluded from the concept of household goods in SCOTLAND[502] and SWITZERLAND.[503]

Protection of household goods is often effected by applying the same rules that protect the matrimonial home. Few jurisdictions have special rules. In IRELAND,[504] it is in the court's power to place a restriction on the disposal of household chattels. In SCOTLAND,[505] there is a presumption of equal shares in household goods.

---

477 Art. 534 French Civil Code.
478 S. 9 (7) Irish Home Protection Act 1976. See SHANNON, Irish Report, Q 11.
479 See ROTH, Austrian Report, Q 11.
480 See PINTENS/ALLAERTS/SEYNS/PIGNOLET, Belgian Report, Q 11.
481 See LUND-ANDERSEN/MAGNUSSEN, Danish Report, Q11.
482 See KURKI-SUONIO, Finnish Report, Q 11.
483 See SHANNON, Irish Report, Q 11.
484 See MIKELENAS, Lithuanian Report, Q 11.
485 See SVERDRUP, Norwegian Report, Q 11.
486 See DE OLIVEIRA/MARTINS/VÍTOR, Portuguese Report, Q 11.
487 See MAIR, Scottish Report, Q 11.
488 See GONZÁLEZ BEILFUSS, Spanish Report, Q 11.
489 See JÄNTERÄ-JAREBORG/BRATTSTRÖM/WALLENG, Swedish Report, Q 11.
490 See SCHWENZER/BOCK, Swiss Report, Q 11.
491 See PINTENS/ALLAERTS/SEYNS/PIGNOLET, Belgian Report, Q 11.
492 See MIKELENAS, Lithuanian Report, Q 11.
493 See SVERDRUP, Norwegian Report, Q 11.
494 Art. 1322 Spanish Civil Code.
495 Art. 534 para. 2 French Civil Code.
496 See PINTENS/ALLAERTS/SEYNS/PIGNOLET, Belgian Report, Q 11.
497 This can be derived from the definition provided in Art. 534 French Civil Code.
498 S. 25(3)(b) Family Law (Scotland) Act 1985.
499 Art. 346 Spanish Civil Code.
500 Ch. 7 § 4 para. 2 Swedish Marriage Code.
501 S. 9 (7) Irish Home Protection Act 1976.
502 Family Law (Scotland) Act 1985, s.25(3)(c).
503 Art. 651a para.1 Swiss Civil Code.
504 See SHANNON, Irish Report, Q 11.
505 See MAIR, Scottish Report, Q 11.

Acts of disposal

In most of the systems surveyed acts of disposal of the family home by one of the spouses require the consent of the other spouse, regardless of who is the actual owner of the home (BELGIUM,[506] BULGARIA,[507] CATALONIA,[508] DENMARK,[509] FINLAND,[510] FRANCE,[511] HUNGARY,[512] IRELAND,[513] LITHUANIA,[514] THE NETHERLANDS,[515] NORWAY,[516] PORTUGAL,[517] SCOTLAND,[518] SPAIN[519] and SWEDEN[520]). In civil law jurisdictions this is mostly achieved through a rule of the so-called *régime matrimonial primaire* from which spouses cannot derogate, while common law jurisdictions achieve the same effect by granting to non-owner spouses a right of occupancy in respect of the matrimonial home that protects them from sale to a third party without their knowledge (e.g. ENGLAND AND WALES[521]). The concept of acts of disposal is defined widely in most jurisdictions and covers any act that might deprive the family from the right to occupy the matrimonial home or which creates a risk that such a situation may arise in the future (e.g. BELGIUM[522], FRANCE[523], HUNGARY[524], THE NETHERLANDS[525], PORTUGAL,[526] SWITZERLAND[527] and SCOTLAND[528]).

If consent to a proposed act of disposal is unreasonably withheld or cannot be obtained, many systems provide that the competent authority has a power to dispense with such consent in the interest of the family at the request of the spouse who wishes to carry out the transaction (BELGIUM,[529] BULGARIA,[530]

506 Art. 21 Belgian Civil Code.
507 Art. 23 Bulgarian Family Code.
508 Art. 9 Catalan Family Code.
509 § 18 and § 19 Danish Act on Legal Effects of Marriage, provided that the home belongs to the deferred community property.
510 § 38(1) Finnish Marriage Act.
511 Art. 15 para. 3 French Civil Code.
512 See WEISS/SZEIBERT, Hungarian Report, Q 10.
513 S. 3 (1) of the 1976 Irish Family Home Protection Act.
514 Art. 3. 85 Lithuanian Civil Code.
515 Art. 1:88 para. 1 sub a Dutch Civil Code.
516 § 32 Norwegian Marriage Act.
517 Art. 1682A para. 2 Portuguese Civil Code.
518 S. 6 Scots Matrimonial Homes (Family Protection) Act 1981.
519 Art. 1320 Spanish Civil Code.
520 Ch. 7 § 5 Swedish Marriage Code.
521 See BARLOW, English Report, Q 10.
522 See PINTENS/ALLAERTS/SEYNS/PIGNOLET, Belgian Report, Q 10.
523 See FERRAND/BRAAT, French Report, Q 10.
524 See WEISS/SZEIBERT, Hungarian Report, Q 10.
525 See BOELE-WOELKI/SCHONEWILLE/SCHRAMA, Dutch Report, Q 10.
526 See DE OLIVEIRA/MARTINS/VÍTOR, Portuguese Report, Q 10.
527 See SCHWENZER/BOCK, Swiss Report, Q 10.
528 See MAIR, Scottish Report, Q 10.
529 See PINTENS/ALLAERTS/SEYNS/PIGNOLET, Belgian Report, Q 10.
530 Art. 23 Bulgarian Family Code.

CATALONIA,[531] DENMARK,[532] FINLAND,[533] NORWAY,[534] POLAND,[535] PORTUGAL,[536] SCOTLAND,[537] SPAIN[538] and SWEDEN[539]). In LITHUANIA authorization by the competent authority is always necessary if there are minor children.[540]

Acts of disposal carried out by one spouse unilaterally without the other spouse's consent can be nullified by the competent authority in systems that subject such acts to both spouses' consent (BELGIUM,[541] BULGARIA,[542] FRANCE,[543] NORWAY,[544] PORTUGAL,[545] SPAIN[546] and SWEDEN[547]). Where there has been a transfer for value to a third party that acted in good faith there is, however, a need to limit such possibility in order to protect the third party. This probably explains why some jurisdictions require that the spouses' consent to the transaction has to be given in writing prior to the transaction (FINLAND,[548] IRELAND,[549] THE NETHERLANDS[550] and NORWAY[551]). Jurisdictions such as SPAIN[552] in which consent can be express or tacit and take place before or after the transaction seem not to protect the non-owner spouse effectively in practice.

Actions for annulment of unilateral acts of disposal of the family home or the household goods are usually subject to time limitations. Under FRENCH law, for example, actions for annulment must be brought within the year after the day that the non-consenting spouse received knowledge of the transaction and cannot, in any event be instituted more than one year after the matrimonial

531 Art. 9 Catalan Family Code.
532 § 20 Danish Act on Legal Effects of Marriage.
533 § 40 Finnish Marriage Act.
534 § 32 para. 2 Norwegian Marriage Act.
535 See Mączyński, Polish Report, Q 10.
536 Art. 1684 para. 1 of Portuguese Civil Code, which refers to the possibility for the court to supply the consent of the aforementioned spouse. See DE OLIVEIRA/MARTINS/VÍTOR, Portuguese Report, Q 40 and Q145.
537 S. 7 Scots Matrimonial Homes (Family Protection) Act 1981.
538 Art. 1321 Spanish Civil Code.
539 Ch. 7 § 8 Swedish Marriage Code.
540 Art. 3.85.2 Lithuanian Civil Code.
541 See PINTENS/ALLAERTS/SEYNS/PIGNOLET, Belgian Report, Q 10.
542 See TODOROVA, Bulgarian Report, Q 10.
543 See FERRAND/BRAAT, French Report, Q 10.
544 See SVERDRUP, Norwegian Report, Q 10.
545 Art. 1687 para. 1 of Portuguese Civil Code. See DE OLIVEIRA/MARTINS/VÍTOR, Portuguese Report, Q 41 and Q146.
546 See GONZÁLEZ BEILFUSS, Spanish Report, Q 10.
547 See JÄNTERÄ-JAREBORG/BRATTSTRÖM/WALLENG, Swedish Report, Q 10.
548 See KURKI-SUONIO, Finnish Report, Q 10.
549 See SHANNON, Irish Report, Q 10.
550 See BOELE-WOELKI/SCHONEWILLE/SCHRAMA, Dutch Report, Q 10.
551 See SVERDRUP, Norwegian Report, Q 10.
552 See GONZÁLEZ BEILFUSS, Spanish Report, Q 10.

property regime was dissolved.[553] In SWEDEN[554] proceedings to have unilateral transactions declared void must be commenced in court within three months of the other spouse learning of the disposition of the property.

COMMENT

1. Principle 4:5 reflects the common core of the jurisdictions surveyed and is also in line with the Council of Europe Recommendation on the rights of spouses relating to the occupation of the family home and the use of the household goods and the *French-German Agreement of 2010* which provides for an optional matrimonial property regime.

2. The habitual dwelling place of the family is to be protected as the family home. Household goods cover movables that are used inside the family home such as, for example, furniture and kitchen equipment while capital investments such as antiques, valuable paintings or jewellery are excluded. In interpreting the concepts of family home and household goods the socio-economic conditions prevailing in the different jurisdictions should be taken into account. This may lead some national legislators to protect cars or holiday homes.

3. Principle 4:5(1) requires the consent of both spouses for any act that prejudices or risks prejudicing the use of the family home and the household goods. This rule is specifically tailored in order to protect the non-owner spouse. Acts envisaged under this rule are any acts of disposal of rights to the family home and the household goods. National legislators are free to further specify the acts covered.

4. In order to provide the necessary flexibility, Principle 4:5(2) provides that any acts of disposal of one spouse without the consent of the other can be ratified by the latter spouse at a later stage.

5. If a spouse unreasonably withholds consent or if the consent of one spouse cannot otherwise be obtained the other spouse can request the competent authority to grant authorisation for an envisaged act of disposal of the family home or the household goods. The Principle itself does not provide any further details on this procedure but authorisation should be granted if the proposed transaction is in the interest of the family.

---

553 See FERRAND/BRAAT, French Report, Q 10.

554 Ch.7 § 9 para. 2 Swedish Marriage Code.

6. Acts of disposal in breach of Principle 4:5 are voidable. The non-consenting spouse may request annulment by the competent authority.

7. The time limitations, to which actions for annulment are subject, are left to national law.

Principle 4:6 Protection of the leased family home

(1) Where the family home is leased to one spouse, the lease is deemed to belong to both spouses, even if it has been concluded before the marriage.

(2) One spouse may not terminate or modify the lease without the consent of the other.

(3) The landlord should notify both spouses to terminate the lease.

Principe 4:6 Protection du bail relatif au logement de la famille

(1) Si le contrat de bail du logement de la famille a été conclu par un seul des époux, ce bail est réputé appartenir à l'un et l'autre des époux même s'il a été conclu avant le mariage.

(2) Un époux ne peut, sans le consentement de l'autre, mettre fin au contrat de bail ou le modifier.

(3) Le bailleur notifie la résiliation du bail à chaque époux.

Prinzip 4:6 Schutz der gemieteten Familienwohnung

(1) Ist die Familienwohnung an einen der Ehegatten vermietet worden, erstreckt sich das Mietverhältnis auf beide Ehegatten, selbst wenn das Mietverhältnis vor der Ehe eingegangen worden ist.

(2) Ohne Zustimmung des anderen Ehegatten kann ein Ehegatte das Mietverhältnis nicht beenden oder ändern.

(3) Der Vermieter hat beiden Ehegatten zu kündigen, um das Mietverhältnis zu beenden.

INTERNATIONAL INSTRUMENTS

The *Council of Europe Recommendation of 18th October 1981 on the rights of spouses relating to the occupation of the family home and the use of the household contents* also deals with the leased family home. According to Principle 5, Principles 1 to 4 of the said Recommendation equally apply where the family home is held on leasehold by one of the spouses. This means that the consent of both spouses is required for any act that directly prejudices the right of the spouses to occupy the family home. If the consent of one spouse is unjustifiably withheld or impossible to obtain, the other spouse can request authorisation by the competent authority. Acts in breach of such rule can be set aside or be subject to other appropriate sanctions. In the case of marriage breakdown the right to occupy the leased family home can be assigned exclusively to one of the spouses. The surviving spouse has the right to continue occupying the leased family home even where the leasehold was held by the deceased spouse. Principle 5 para. 2 of the Recommendation guarantees that the spouse, who is not the leaseholder, can continue occupying the family home, in the event that the other spouse does not discharge the obligations of a leaseholder, provided he or she takes care of these obligations.

Article 5 of the *French-German Agreement of 2010* also covers the leased family home. Any act of disposal of rights to the family home requires the joint consent of the spouses. Consent can be given retrospectively. If one spouse is not able to issue consent or unreasonably withholds consent, the competent authority can authorize the other spouse to act alone.

COMPARATIVE OVERVIEW

Protection of the leased family home

The Questionnaire on which the national reports used for this Comparative Overview were based did not explicitly address the issue of the leased family home. Consequently the information referred to is taken mostly from other sources and is not as exhaustive and updated as in other Comparative Overviews.

In many European systems the leased matrimonial home is protected in the same spirit as the matrimonial home that is owned by the spouses. Sometimes the provisions on the leased matrimonial home are contained in tenancy law (e.g. SWITZERLAND[555])

A basic rule that is often established is that the lease is deemed to belong to both spouses even if only one of them actually entered into the contract. This rule also applies even where the tenancy was entered into before the marriage was celebrated (e.g. BELGIUM[556] and FRANCE[557]). This means that the landlord has both a contractual tenant and a legal tenant. Both spouses possess equal and undivided tenancy rights.

One consequence of this rule is that the landlord must notify both spouses to terminate the lease. In BELGIAN law it is clearly established by case law that notification to terminate the contract has to be addressed to both spouses independently[558] or that certain specific rules have to be followed that ensure that both spouses were clearly aware that the landlord has communicated his

[555] See SCHWENZER/BOCK, Swiss Report, Q 10.
[556] Art. 215 para. 2 Belgian Civil Code.
[557] Art. 1751 para. 1 French Civil Code.
[558] Decision by the Cour de Cassation of 6th October 1978.

or her intention to terminate the contract.[559] FRENCH law also provides that the notification of the contract that is addressed to only one spouse is not effective as against the other.[560] In SWITZERLAND[561] an agreement on the extension of the lease with the landlord is only valid if it was entered into by both spouses.

Termination of the lease

Since both spouses enjoy tenancy rights, neither spouse can terminate the contract without the consent of the other (e.g. DENMARK,[562] THE NETHERLANDS[563] and NORWAY[564]). Both spouses also have joint and several obligations to pay the rent. In PORTUGAL,[565] both the termination and modification of the lease, as well as the sub-lease of the family home, need the consent of both spouses.

In the case of divorce or judicial separation, the right to the lease of the matrimonial home may be allotted by the court to one of the spouses, subject to the rights of re-imbursement or indemnity for the benefit of the other spouse. In GERMAN law,[566] the court can decide that one of the spouses should continue as a tenant or that one of the spouses substitutes for the other spouse in the tenancy contract.

In case of death of one of the spouses, the surviving spouse has an exclusive right to the lease, except where he or she renounces it (e.g. FRANCE[567]).

In order to protect landlords some legal systems provide that rules protecting the family home only apply if the landlord knew that the tenant was married with the consequence that the tenant who marries must notify his new civil status to the landlord (BELGIUM[568]). In other systems, however, there is no such an obligation (e.g. FRANCE[569]).

---

559 See PINTENS, "Der Schutz der Familienwohnung nach belgischem Recht" in: HENRICH/SCHWAB (eds), *Der Schutz der Familienwohnung in Europäischen Rechtsordnungen*, 1995, pp. 12–13.

560 Cass. civ.III 6.5. 1971 and Cass. civ.III 20.1.1988.

561 Art. 273a Swiss Code of Obligations.

562 § 81 Danish Rent Act.

563 Art. 1:88 para. 1 sub a Dutch Civil Code.

564 § 32 Norwegian Marriage Act.

565 Art. 1682 (b) Portuguese Civil Code.

566 § 1568 a German BGB.

567 See Art. 1751 para. 3 French Civil Code and FERRAND, "Der Schutz der Familienwohnung im französischen Recht", in: HENRICH/SCHWAB (eds), *Der Schutz der Familienwohnung in Europäischen Rechtsordnungen*, 1995, p. 51.

568 Such a provision was introduced in 1991 in order to avoid that the landlord has to inform him or herself about the civil status of the lessor. See Art. 215 para. 2 Belgian Civil Code.

569 See FERRAND, "Der Schutz der Familienwohnung im französischen Recht", in: HENRICH/SCHWAB (eds), *Der Schutz der Familienwohnung in Europäischen Rechtsordnungen*, 1995, p. 51.

COMMENT

1. Principle 4:6 reflects a common core in Europe and goes beyond the *Recommendation of the Committee of Ministers of the Council of Europe* and the *French-German Agreement of 2010* because it specifically addresses the issue of the leased family home.

2. Principle 4:6(1) establishes that the spouse who did not enter the leasehold on the family home nevertheless holds the position of a legal tenant with the same rights and obligations as the contractual tenant. The rule applies regardless of whether the leasehold contract was celebrated before or after the marriage of the contractual tenant. The Principle does not establish any obligation to protect landlords by requiring that they be informed of a change in civil status of their tenant.

3. The consent of both spouses is required in order to terminate or modify the leasehold. This follows logically from the fact that both spouses are deemed to be parties to the leasehold contract.

4. Principle 4:6 does not preclude special rules applying in cases of domestic violence.

Principle 4:7 Representation
(1) One spouse may authorize the other spouse to represent him or her in legal transactions.
(2) When a spouse is unable to express his or her intentions, the competent authority may authorize the other spouse
(a) to act alone where the consent of his or her spouse would otherwise be required;
(b) to represent his or her spouse when the latter has the power to act alone.

Principe 4:7 Représentation
(1) Un époux peut donner mandat à l'autre époux de le représenter dans les actes juridiques.
(2) Si un époux est hors d'état de manifester sa volonté, l'autorité compétente peut autoriser l'autre époux
(a) à agir seul dans le cas où le consentement de son époux serait nécessaire;
(b) à représenter son époux dans le cas où ce dernier a le pouvoir d'agir seul.

Prinzip 4:7 Vertretung
(1) Ein Ehegatte kann den anderen Ehegatten ermächtigen, ihn bei rechtlichen Geschäften zu vertreten.
(2) Ist ein Ehegatte außerstande, seinen Willen zu äußern, kann die zuständige Behörde den anderen Ehegatten ermächtigen
(a) in den Fällen, in denen die Zustimmung seines Ehegatten erforderlich wäre, alleine zu handeln;
(b) seinen Ehegatten zu vertreten, wenn letzterer berechtigt ist, alleine zu handeln.

INTERNATIONAL INSTRUMENTS

The representation or agency[570] between spouses is not regulated by any convention. The *Hague Convention on the law applicable to matrimonial property regimes of 14 March 1978*[571] does not explicitly deal with matters relating to

[570] In the following the terms 'representation' and 'agency' are used interchangeably. The Draft Common Frame of Reference of 2009 prepared by the Study Group on a European Civil Code and the Research Group on EC Private Law (Acquis Group) defines a 'representative' as a person who has authority to affect directly the legal position of another person, the principal, in relation to a third party by acting on behalf of the principal. The Proposal for a Common European Sales Law (COM(2011) 635 final), however, does not regulate representation.

[571] The Convention entered into force on 1 September 1992 for three countries: FRANCE, LUXEMBURG and THE NETHERLANDS.

agency between spouses. Acting as agent for the other spouse requires legal capacity. Article 1 sub-paragraph 3 only determines that the Convention does not apply to this 'capacity of the spouses'. At the time the Convention was drafted, restrictions were imposed by certain laws on the capacity of the married woman such as the prohibition on intercession in favour of the husband (lack of capacity to guarantee obligations of the husband) and the requirement of the husband's authorisation from the exercise of a profession. Such questions are considered to be related to capacity in general or to the personal effects of marriage. The true purpose of the exclusion of the 'capacity of the spouses' is to show that the Convention does not require application of the law it designates to the capacity to enter into a marriage contract, or to choose the law applicable to the matrimonial property regime.[572]

The *Hague Convention on the law applicable to agency of 14 March 1978*[573] explicitly excludes spousal agency from its scope of application. Article 2 (c) determines that the Convention does not apply to 'agency by operation of law in family law, in matrimonial property regimes, or in the law of succession.'

COMPARATIVE OVERVIEW

The comparison of the twenty-six jurisdictions in respect of the question whether a spouse may act as an agent for the other spouses reveals that a distinction is to be made between jurisdictions that provide for general rules on agency only and jurisdictions that provide for specific rules on marital representation irrespective of the content of these rules. Twenty jurisdictions have specific rules on agency between spouses. However, not every national provision is as specific and, in some systems the general rules on agency apply as well.

General rules on representation

In ENGLAND AND WALES,[574] HUNGARY,[575] IRELAND,[576] RUSSIA,[577] SCOTLAND[578] and SWEDEN[579] there are no specific rules on marital agency at all. In ENGLAND AND WALES, IRELAND, SCOTLAND and SWEDEN the general rules on power of

---

572 Explanatory report by VON OVERBECK, Actes et Documents de la Treizième session, tome II Régimes matrimoniaux, no. 117 and 119.
573 The Convention entered into force on 1 May 1992 for four countries. From the jurisdictions surveyed FRANCE, THE NETHERLANDS and PORTUGAL belong to the contracting states.
574 See BARLOW, English Report, Q 13.
575 See WEISS/SZEIBERT, Hungarian Report, Q 13.
576 See SHANNON, Irish Report, Q 13.
577 See ANTOKOLSKAIA, Russian Report, Q 13.
578 See MAIR, Scottish Report, Q 13.
579 See JÄNTERÄ-JAREBORG/BRATTSTRÖM/WALLENG, Swedish Report, Q 13.

attorney apply, whereas it has been reported for HUNGARY and RUSSIA that there are no specific rules without further reference to the applicability of any general rules on agency.

Specific rules on marital representation

Most of the jurisdictions surveyed (AUSTRIA,[580] BELGIUM,[581] CATALONIA,[582] CZECH REPUBLIC,[583] DENMARK,[584] FINLAND,[585] FRANCE,[586] GERMANY,[587] ITALY,[588] LITHUANIA,[589] MALTA,[590] THE NETHERLANDS,[591] NORWAY,[592] POLAND,[593] PORTUGAL,[594] SLOVAKIA,[595] SPAIN[596] and SWITZERLAND[597]) have specific rules for marital agency. These rules specify in which situations and under which circumstances representation is possible, provide for the requirements for the conferment of the representation and regulate the aspects of liability and third party protection.

In some jurisdictions additional reference is made to the general rules on agency, for instance, in CATALONIA,[598] ITALY,[599] LITHUANIA[600] and THE NETHERLANDS.[601] The law of BULGARIA[602] and GREECE[603] simply have a rule that provides for the

580 § 96 Austrian Civil Code. See ROTH, Austrian Report, Q 13.
581 Art. 219 Belgian Civil Code.
582 Art. 3 para. 3 Catalan Family Code.
583 § 21 para. 1 Czech Family Act.
584 § 13 Danish Act on the Legal Effects of Marriage. See LUND-ANDERSEN/MAGNUSSEN, Danish Report, Q 13.
585 § 63 Finnish Marriage Act.
586 Art. 217 to 222 French Civil Code.
587 § 1353 together with § 1365 to 1370 German Civil Code.
588 Art. 185 and 217 Italian Civil Code. General rules on mandate: Art. 1710 to 1718 Italian Civil Code.
589 Art. 3.32, 3.94 and 3.97 para. 4 Lithuanian Civil Code.
590 Art. 1322 para. 6 Maltese Civil Code.
591 Art. 1:90 para. 3 and para. 4 Dutch Civil Code.
592 § 40 and 41 Norwegian Marriage Act 1991.
593 See MĄCZYŃSKI, Polish Report, Q 13.
594 Art. 1678 para. 2 (f) and (g) Portuguese Civil Code.
595 Art. 20 Slovakian Family Code. See HAŤAPKA, Slovakian Report, Q 13.
596 Art. 71 and 1439 Spanish Civil Code.
597 Art. 166 para. 1 and para. 2 Swiss Civil Code.
598 Art. 3 para. 4 Catalan Family Code explicitly refers to the general rules on mandate.
599 Art. 185 refers to art. 217 Italian Civil Code which refers to the general rules on mandate.
600 Art. 3.94 para. 3 of the Lithuanian Civil Code refers to the general rules on management of other's property and affairs. In short, the general rules on mandate.
601 Art. 1:90 para. 3 and art. 7:400 to 413 Dutch Civil Code.
602 See TODOROVA, Bulgarian Report, Q 13. Art. 22 para. 2 Bulgarian Family Code on the disposal of matrimonial community property refers to the requirement of exclusive authorization of the spouse acting as an agent for the other.
603 Art. 1399 Greek Civil Code. See KOUTSOURADIS/KOTRONIS/HATZANTONIS, Greek Report, Q 13.

possibility of spouses to act as an agent for each other. There are no further specific rules for marital agency and consequently only the general rules apply.[604]

Representation ex lege

Where a spouse can act for the other spouse as agent without his or her consent, the legal basis for the representation lies in statutory law and is not based upon the express consent of the spouses. In the jurisdictions surveyed the representation ex lege is either explicitly or implicitly regulated. The rules are explicit if they state that in a particular situation a spouse can 'represent' or 'act as an agent for' the other spouse. This is the case in AUSTRIA,[605] CATALONIA,[606] CZECH REPUBLIC,[607] NORWAY,[608] SLOVAKIA[609] and SWITZERLAND.[610] On the other hand, the representation ex lege can also be implicitly derived from the law if the represented spouse is bound by the legal transaction entered into by the other spouse. Most of the jurisdictions surveyed have chosen this approach: BELGIUM,[611] BULGARIA,[612] CATALONIA,[613] CZECH REPUBLIC,[614] DENMARK,[615] FRANCE,[616] FINLAND,[617] GERMANY,[618] HUNGARY,[619] ITALY,[620] LITHUANIA,[621] MALTA,[622] THE NETHERLANDS,[623] NORWAY,[624] POLAND,[625] PORTUGAL,[626] SLOVAKIA,[627] SPAIN,[628] SWEDEN[629] and

604 See KOUTSOURADIS/KOTRONIS/HATZANTONIS, Greek Report, Q 13 and TODOROVA, Bulgarian Report, Q 13.
605 § 96 Austrian Civil Code.
606 Art. 3 para. 2 and 3 para. 3 Catalan Family Code.
607 § 21 Czech Family Act.
608 § 41 Norwegian Marriage Act 1991.
609 Art. 20 Slovakian Family Code. See HAŤAPKA, Slovakian Report, Q 13.
610 Art. 166 para. 1 Swiss Civil Code.
611 Art. 222 and Art. 1408 Belgian Civil Code.
612 Art. 25 Bulgarian Family Code.
613 Art. 3 para. 2 Catalan Family Code.
614 § 21 para. 1 and para. 2 Czech Family Act.
615 See LUND-ANDERSEN/MAGNUSSEN, Danish Report, Q 9 and Q 13.
616 Art. 220 French Civil Code.
617 § 52 para. 2 Finnish Marriage Act.
618 § 1357 German Civil Code. See DETHLOFF/MARTINY, German Report, Q 13.
619 See WEISS/SZEIBERT, Hungarian Report, Q 9.
620 Arts. 186 to 190 Italian Civil Code. See PATTI/CARICATO/IRTI/IANNICELLI/SERA/DI STEFANO/PETÖ, Italian Report, Q 9.
621 Art. 3.109 para. 2 to para. 4 Lithuanian Civil Code. See MIKELENAS, Lithuanian Report, Q 9.
622 Art. 1327 (c) Maltese Civil Code. See FARRUGIA, Maltese Report, Q 9.
623 Art. 1:85 Dutch Civil Code.
624 § 41 Norwegian Marriage Act 1991. See SVERDRUP, Norwegian Report, Q 9.
625 Art. 30 para. 1 Polish Family and Guardianship Code. See MĄCZYŃSKI, Polish Report, Q 9.
626 Art. 1690 para. 1 and 1691 Portuguese Civil Code.
627 Art. 20 Slovakian Family Code. See HAŤAPKA, Slovakian Report, Q 13.
628 Art. 1319 Spanish Civil Code.
629 Art. 4 of Chapter 6 Swedish Marriage Act.

SWITZERLAND.[630] The ex lege representation is, however, restricted to certain actions and situations.

Joint household and family needs

In all jurisdictions where the ex lege representation is either based upon an explicit rule or on the liability of the other spouse who has been represented, a spouse can bind the other spouse in respect of actions relating to the joint household (AUSTRIA,[631] BELGIUM,[632] BULGARIA,[633] CATALONIA,[634] CZECH REPUBLIC,[635] DENMARK,[636] FINLAND,[637] FRANCE,[638] GERMANY,[639] LITHUANIA,[640] THE NETHERLANDS,[641] NORWAY,[642] POLAND,[643] PORTUGAL[644] and SLOVAKIA[645]). The Family Code of CATALONIA explicitly states that if the representing spouse is acting for the benefit of family needs, the consent of the other spouse is presumed.[646] There are no statutory provisions determining that a spouse is liable for the household debts incurred by the other spouse in, for example ENGLAND AND WALES,[647] IRELAND,[648] RUSSIA[649], SCOTLAND[650] and SWEDEN.[651]

Although the general provisions, which determine that the represented spouse is bound by the legal transaction relating to the maintenance of the common household entered into by the other spouse, are similar to a great extent, some differences exist in relation to additional requirements that must be met in order to establish liability. According to almost all jurisdictions spouses are liable for the debts incurred for the normal, usual or common needs or affairs of the

630 Art. 166 para. 1 Swiss Civil Code.
631 § 96 Austrian Civil Code.
632 Art. 222 Belgian Civil Code.
633 Art. 25 Bulgarian Family Code.
634 Art. 3 para. 2 Catalan Family Code.
635 § 21 para. 1 and para. 2 Czech Family Act.
636 See LUND-ANDERSEN/MAGNUSSEN, Danish Report, Q 9 and Q 13.
637 § 52 para. 2 Finnish Marriage Act.
638 Art. 220 French Civil Code.
639 § 1357 German Civil Code. See DETHLOFF/MARTINY, German Report, Q 13.
640 Art. 3.109 para. 2 to para. 4 Lithuanian Civil Code. See MIKELENAS, Lithuanian Report, Q 9.
641 Arts. 1:84 and 1:85 Dutch Civil Code.
642 § 41 Norwegian Marriage Act 1991. See SVERDRUP, Norwegian Report, Q 9.
643 Art. 30 para. 1 Polish Family and Guardianship Code. See MĄCZYŃSKI, Polish Report, Q 9.
644 Arts. 1690 para. 1 and 1691 para. 1 (b) Portuguese Civil Code.
645 Art. 20 Slovakian Family Code. See HAŤAPKA, Slovakian Report, Q 13.
646 Art. 4 Catalan Family Code describes what should be considered the ordinary family debts.
647 See BARLOW, English Report, Q 9.
648 See SHANNON, Irish Report, Q 9.
649 See HAŤAPKA, Slovakian Report, Q 9.
650 See MAIR, Scottish Report, Q 9.
651 See JÄNTERÄ-JAREBORG/BRATTSTRÖM/WALLENG, Swedish Report, Q 9.

family. However, the laws in AUSTRIA,[652] BELGIUM,[653] DENMARK,[654] FRANCE,[655] GERMANY,[656] LITHUANIA[657] and NORWAY[658] explicitly and additionally require that the debts incurred must be in accordance with the usual living standard of the family. In other words, expenses may not be excessive or unreasonably high. If this requirement is not fulfilled, the acting spouse does not bind the other spouse.

Absence, illness or incapacity of the represented spouse

Marital representation can take place without specific consent. If the represented spouse is ill, incapable or absent, his or her consent cannot be obtained. The jurisdictions of AUSTRIA,[659] BELGIUM,[660] CATALONIA,[661] CZECH REPUBLIC,[662] DENMARK,[663] FRANCE,[664] LITHUANIA,[665] MALTA,[666] THE NETHERLANDS,[667] POLAND,[668] PORTUGAL[669] and SWITZERLAND[670] provide specific rules for these situations. The SWEDISH Marriage Act[671] specifies that the ill or absent spouse may be represented by the other spouse, unless there already is an authorized agent, guardian, appointed representative or administrator.[672] In some systems, such as BELGIUM,[673] FRANCE,[674] LITHUANIA,[675] MALTA[676] and THE NETHERLANDS[677] the representation due to the absence, illness or incapacity of the other spouse needs judicial

---

652 § 96 Austrian Civil Code.
653 Art. 222 Belgian Civil Code.
654 See LUND-ANDERSEN/MAGNUSSEN, Danish Report, Q 9.
655 Art. 220 French Civil Code.
656 § 1357 para. 1 German Civil Code. This provision speaks of angemessenen Deckung des Lebensbedarf' (appropriate covering of the life needs).
657 Art. 3.109 Lithuanian Civil Code. See MIKELENAS, Lithuanian Report, Q 9.
658 § 41 Norwegian Marriage Act 1991.
659 § 96 Austrian Civil Code.
660 Art. 220 Belgian Civil Code.
661 Art. 3 para. 3 Catalan Family Code.
662 § 21 Czech Family Act.
663 § 13 Danish Marriage Act. See LUND-ANDERSEN/MAGNUSSEN, Danish Report, Q 13.
664 Art. 217 to 219 French Civil Code.
665 Art. 3.32 para. 1, 3.94 and 3.97 para. 4 and para. 5 Lithuanian Civil Code.
666 Art. 1322 and 1335 Maltese Civil Code.
667 Art. 1:88 para. 6 Dutch Civil Code.
668 See MĄCZYŃSKI, Polish Report, Q 13.
669 See DE OLIVEIRA/MARTINS/VÍTOR, Portuguese Report, Q 42 and Q 147.
670 Art. 166 para. 2 Swiss Civil Code.
671 Ch 6 § 4 Swedish Marriage Act.
672 See JÄNTERÄ-JAREBORG/BRATTSTRÖM/WALLENG, Swedish Report, Q 9 and 13.
673 Art. 220 Belgian Civil Code.
674 Art. 217 and 219 French Civil Code.
675 Art. 3.32 para. 2 and 3.94 para. 2 Lithuanian Civil Code.
676 Art. 1322 para. 6 Maltese Civil Code.
677 Art. 1:88 para. 6 Dutch Civil Code.

authorisation. In such a case the spouse requests the court to authorize him or her to act as an agent for the other.

Joint household

In some jurisdictions spouses can only bind each other by actions relating to the common household or in cases of urgency under the condition that they are still sharing a household. This requirement must be fulfilled in DENMARK,[678] FINLAND,[679] GERMANY,[680] NORWAY[681] and SWEDEN.[682]

Spousal authorisation

Consent of the spouse to be represented by the other spouse is generally presumed for actions related to the joint household and in cases of absence, illness or incapacity. For all other legal transactions explicit consent is needed. Either spouse may authorize the other to represent him or her and act on his or her behalf.

In BELGIUM,[683] CATALONIA,[684] FINLAND,[685] GREECE,[686] ITALY,[687] NORWAY,[688] PORTUGAL[689] and SPAIN[690] reference is made to the general rules on agency. In CATALONIA and SPAIN, for instance, the relevant provisions state that a spouse cannot represent the other without proper authorisation. In PORTUGAL and NORWAY, that spouse should be specically authorised or expressely mandated by the other spouse. In GREECE and FINLAND the spouse should be 'permitted' by the other spouse or the power should be 'transferred'. Finally, in ITALY explicit reference is made to the general rules on mandate and power of attorney. The spouses have to respect the contract they have established. All these provisions lack specific requirements and it is therefore assumed that the general rules on agency apply. In this respect they do not differ from those jurisdictions which have no specific rules concerning spousal representation at all which is the case

678 § 11 Danish Marriage Act. See LUND-ANDERSEN/MAGNUSSEN, Danish Report, Q 9.
679 Under the condition that the third person knew this was not the case. See § 52 para. 3 Finnish Marriage Act.
680 § 1357 para. 3 German Civil Code.
681 § 41 Norwegian Marriage Act 1991.
682 Ch 6 § 4 Swedish Marriage Act.
683 Art. 219 Belgian Civil Code.
684 Art. 3 para. 3 Catalan Family Code.
685 § 63 Finnish Marriage Act.
686 Art. 1399 Greek Civil Code.
687 Art. 217 Italian Civil Code.
688 § 40 Norwegian Marriage Act 1991.
689 Art. 1678 para. 2 (g) Portuguese Civil Code.
690 Art. 71 and 1320 Spanish Civil Code. See GONZÁLEZ BEILFUSS, Spanish Report, Q 13.

in ENGLAND AND WALES,[691] HUNGARY,[692] IRELAND,[693] RUSSIA,[694] SCOTLAND[695] and SWEDEN.[696]

Five jurisdictions prescribe the form of the spousal authorisation. In FRANCE,[697] LITHUANIA,[698] MALTA,[699] THE NETHERLANDS,[700] SLOVAKIA[701] and SWITZERLAND,[702] the representation has to be conferred in writing. This written authorization can for instance be taken up in a marital property agreement or laid down in a public or notarial deed (MALTA[703] and SLOVAKIA[704]).

Exclusion and withdrawal

In AUSTRIA,[705] BULGARIA,[706] CZECH REPUBLIC,[707] FRANCE,[708] ITALY,[709] and MALTA,[710] the specific marital agency provisions expressly determine that the represented spouse may exclude certain actions from the representation. If the third party knows of this exclusion, only the acting spouse is liable for these actions, and not the represented spouse (ITALY and MALTA). As a result the represented spouse can determine the scope of the other spouse's representational power. The consequence is that a proper exclusion avoids liability of the represented spouse for the particular act. Such provisions can be found in the laws of AUSTRIA,[711] CZECH REPUBLIC,[712] THE NETHERLANDS,[713]

---

691 See BARLOW, English Report, Q 13.
692 See WEISS/SZEIBERT, Hungarian Report, Q 13.
693 See SHANNON, Irish Report, Q 13.
694 See ANTOKOLSKAIA, Russian Report, Q 13.
695 See MAIR, Scottish Report, Q 13.
696 See JÄNTERÄ-JAREBORG/BRATTSTRÖM/WALLENG, Swedish Report, Q 13.
697 Art. 218 French Civil Code.
698 Art. 3.32 para. 1 and 3.92 para. 3 Lithuania Civil Code.
699 Art. 1322 para. 6 Maltese Civil Code.
700 Art. 1:88 para. 3 Dutch Civil Code.
701 See HAŤAPKA, Slovakian Report, Q 13.
702 Art. 166 para. 2 Swiss Civil Code. See SCHWENZER/BOCK, Swiss Report, Q 13.
703 Art. 1322 para. 6 Maltese Civil Code.
704 See HAŤAPKA, Slovakian Report, Q 13.
705 § 96 Austrian Civil Code.
706 Art. 22 (4) Bulgarian Family Code.
707 § 21 Czech Family Act.
708 Art. 217 to 219 French Civil Code. See FERRAND/BRAAT, French Report, Q 13. Under Art. 217 French Civil Code both spouses are liable, under Art. 219 only the acting spouse is liable.
709 Art. 217 para. 4 Italian Civil Code. See PATTI/CARICATO/IRTI/IANNICELLI/SERA/DI STEFANO/PETÖ, Italian Report, Q 13.
710 Art. 1335 to 1337 Maltese Civil Code.
711 § 96 Austrian Civil Code.
712 Art. 21 para. 3 Czech Family Act.
713 Art. 1:92 Dutch Civil Code.

POLAND,[714] SLOVAKIA[715] and SWITZERLAND.[716] Furthermore, in FINLAND,[717] FRANCE,[718] POLAND[719] and SLOVAKIA,[720] statutory provisions on the scope of the martial representation allow for the possibility to revoke the power of attorney, mandate or any other form of agency.

Judicial authorisation

Besides the general and specific rules on the conferment of agency, it may happen that a spouse is unable to obtain consent from the other spouse and therefore in principle lacks proper authority. For these situations the possibility of obtaining judicial authorisation has been created. Several jurisdictions adopted specific provisions regarding judicial authorisation (BELGIUM,[721] FRANCE,[722] LITHUANIA,[723] MALTA,[724] THE NETHERLANDS,[725] SPAIN[726] and SWITZERLAND[727]). In these jurisdictions a spouse can request a court to authorize him or her to represent the other spouse who is absent, ill or incapable.

However, it is not only in cases of impediment, illness or incapacity that the court can authorise the requesting spouse to act as an agent for the other spouse. In various jurisdictions 'other objective reasons' or the 'refusal of consent without proper reasoning' are – subject to certain conditions – valid situations to obtain judicial authorisation (BELGIUM,[728] FRANCE,[729] LITHUANIA[730] and MALTA[731]).

---

714 See MĄCZYŃSKI, Polish Report, Q 13.
715 Art. 20 Slovakian Family Code. See HAŤAPKA, Slovakian Report, Q 13.
716 Art. 166 para. 3 Swiss Civil Code.
717 § 63 para. 2 Finnish Marriage Act.
718 Art. 218 French Civil Code.
719 See MĄCZYŃSKI, Polish Report, Q 13.
720 See HAŤAPKA, Slovakian Report, Q 13.
721 Art. 220 Belgian Civil Code.
722 Arts. 217 and 219 French Civil Code.
723 Art. 3.92 para. 3 juncto 3.32 para. 2 Lithuanian Civil Code. See MIKELENAS, Lithuanian Report, Q 13.
724 Arts. 1322 para. 6 and 1323 para. 2 Maltese Civil Code.
725 Art. 1:88 para. 6 Dutch Civil Code.
726 Art. 1709 et seq. See GONZÁLEZ BEILFUSS, Spanish Report, Q 13.
727 Art. 166 para. 2 Swiss Civil Code.
728 Art. 215 para. 1 Belgian Civil Code.
729 Art. 217 French Civil Code.
730 Art. 3.93 Lithuanian Civil Code.
731 Art. 1323 Maltese Civil Code.

COMMENT

1. None of the twenty-six jurisdictions surveyed prohibit spousal representation. There is a clear common core that one spouse may represent the other. The minority of jurisdictions (six out of twenty-six) apply their general rules on agency or power of attorney whereas in all other systems specific rules for marital representation are to be applied. While there are some differences in the wording and content of these specific rules, a specific principle on marital representation constitutes the common core.

2. The law should clarify the situations, implications and requirements of the spouses' representational power. Generally, spouses trust each other and assume that they are authorises *ex lege* to act on behalf of each other due to their marital status. However, legal (trans-)actions differ in terms of financial risks, obligation and long-term commitment. Hence, in general, each spouse should have a say as to whether or not he or she is bound by legal actions carried out by the other spouse. It follows from the right to self-determination that the represented spouse's consent should be required since his or her legal position is affected.

3. Each spouse should have the freedom to decide whether or not the other spouse may represent him or her. Consequently, the mandate of the representing spouse can be revoked at any time. This starting point – no representation without consent – reflects the common core in the majority of the systems surveyed. Only a few jurisdictions, on the other hand, specify the formal requirements of the spousal consent to represent the other spouse. In this respect a common core cannot be discovered. Whether the spouses should explicitly give their consent either in writing or by notarial deed (for instance in a marital contract) or whether an implicit authorization suffices should be decided by national law.

4. According to Principle 4:7(2) a spouse should be able to obtain judicial authorisation to represent the other spouse who is unable to express his or her intentions in case of illness, impediment or incapacity. Only seven jurisdictions provide for specific rules in this respect. A common core does not exist. Nonetheless, it is desirable to specify the circumstances under which it should be possible to obtain judicial authorisation. The judicial replacement of the spousal consent should be subject to the condition that the action for which authorisation is requested is in accordance with the family interests. This is, for instance, the case when the legal action concerns the well-being of the spouse whose consent is to be replaced, such as decisions concerning his or her medical treatment or placement in a nursing home. Another example, which illustrates involvement of family interests, is where the family needs to find a new common residence

resulting from termination of the rent of their current home and which will rquire both spouses to enter into the transaction in respect of the new common residence. However, if one spouse is absent, ill or incapable, it would be detrimental to the family interests if there was no possibility to replace the spousal consent. Such family interests include, in particular, the interests of children living in the same household and those of the spouse who is under the obligation to act together with the other spouse.

Principle 4:8 Duty to inform
Each spouse has the duty to inform the other about his or her assets and debts and about significant acts of administration in so far as it is necessary to enable the other to exercise his or her rights.

Principe 4:8 Obligation d'information
Chaque époux est tenu d'informer l'autre époux de son patrimoine ainsi que des actes importants d'administration dans la mesure nécessaire pour permettre à l'autre époux d'exercer ses droits.

Prinzip 4:8 Informationspflicht
Jeder Ehegatte hat die Verpflichtung, den anderen über seine Vermögensgegenstände und Schulden sowie wesentliche Verwaltungshandlungen insoweit zu informieren, wie das notwendig ist, um dem anderen die Ausübung seiner Rechte zu ermöglichen.

INTERNATIONAL INSTRUMENTS

The *Council of Europe's Resolution (78) 37 on Equality of Spouses in Civil Law*, adopted in September 1978, recommends the Member States' governments to take the necessary steps to ensure, inter alia, that each spouse in under a duty to provide the other spouse with sufficient information concerning his or her own financial situation for the purpose of ascertaining the amount of his or her contribution to the household expenses. Furthermore, where a separation of property regime prevails, both spouses should have an equal right to be informed regarding the extent of property belonging to the other spouse, where the law requires such information to be given. Where the law, in contrast, provides for a community of property, each spouse should have the right to be informed by the other spouse regarding the actual extent of the common property. The importance of information between spouses is also emphasised in the *Recommendation No. R (89) by the Council of Europe on Contributions Following Divorce* (January 1989), with the aim of establishing whether a contribution by one spouse to the other should take place.

COMPARATIVE OVERVIEW

The extent to which spouses are under an obligation to inform each other about their assets and debts varies among the jurisdictions surveyed, and there is no common core to follow.

In SWITZERLAND,[732] each spouse may request that the other spouse provides information about his or her income, assets or debts, unless such information is protected by rules on professional secrecy. This applies as a general duty regardless of the applicable matrimonial property regime. In the case of a spouse's failure to comply,[733] the court may order him or her, or any third person, to provide the necessary information or documentation. In the Nordic jurisdictions, both spouses have a duty to provide each other with the information needed to assess the financial circumstances of the family, which is of relevance in ascertaining the necessary spousal contributions to the welfare of the family (DENMARK,[734] FINLAND,[735] NORWAY[736] and SWEDEN[737]). As in the case of SWITZERLAND, this duty is regarded as a general duty of the spouses, and it applies irrespective of the spouses' marital property regime. This does not, however, imply that the spouses have a duty to inform each other about their assets and debts in general. In SPAIN,[738] it follows from the spouses' duty to respect and assist each other, and to act in the interests of the family, that the spouses also have a duty to keep each other informed about their relevant economic circumstances. In GERMANY,[739] such a duty also appears to follow, at least to the extent of the conjugal community existing between the spouses, under general matrimonial law, whereas in CATALONIA,[740] this duty is more or less directly connected to the expectation of each spouse to be able to participate in the acquisitions of the other spouse. In common law jurisdictions, no clear distinction exists between general rights and duties of the spouses and their property relationship; however, once separation or divorce proceedings have been initiated, each spouse is under the obligation to provide information to the other spouse in respect of his or her assets (IRELAND[741] and ENGLAND AND WALES[742]). It remains uncertain whether any specific duty of information exists in these jurisdictions during the marriage, with the exception of the duty of disclosure upon the drafting of marital property agreements.

In pure separation regimes, whether applicable as a default regime or as an optional regime, spouses have no duty to inform each other about financial

[732] Art. 170 para. 1 and para. 3 Swiss Civil Code. See SCHWENZER/BOCK, Swiss Report, Q 74 and Q 144.
[733] Art. 172 Swiss Civil Code. See SCHWENZER/BOCK, Swiss Report, Q 74.
[734] § 10 Danish Act on the Legal Effects of Marriage.
[735] See KURKI-SUONIO, Finnish Report, Q 110.
[736] § 39 Norwegian Marriage Act. See SVERDRUP, Norwegian Report, Q 110.
[737] Ch. 1 § 4 Swedish Marriage Code.
[738] See GONZÁLEZ BEILFUSS, Spanish Report, Q 144 with reference to Art. 67 Spanish Civil Code.
[739] § 1353 para. 1 German Civil Code. See DETHLOFF/MARTINY, German Report, Q 74.
[740] See MARTÍN-CASALS/RIBOT, Catalan Report, Q 74.
[741] See SHANNON, Irish Report, Q 176.
[742] S. 37 English Matrimonial Causes Act 1973. See BARLOW, English Report, Q 176.

issues (e.g. AUSTRIA,[743] BELGIUM,[744] CATALONIA[745] and FRANCE[746]). However, in BELGIUM,[747] the competent authority can order a spouse to provide the other spouse with information about the administration of assets.

National reports describing community of property regimes focus, in particular, on the spouses' duty to inform each other about the administration of assets.[748] Even when the legislation lacks an explicit provision on this (AUSTRIA,[749] BELGIUM,[750] CZECH REPUBLIC,[751] FRANCE,[752] HUNGARY[753] and RUSSIA[754]), it is argued that both the management of the community property in the joint interests of the spouses and the family, and the aim of ensuring that acts of administration will not be disputed later on by the other spouse, require that each spouse informs the other about the administration of the community assets (BELGIUM,[755] FRANCE[756] and SLOVAKIA[757]). Furthermore, joint administration is, in several jurisdictions, regarded as presupposing that both of the spouses are informed (BULGARIA,[758] ITALY[759] and MALTA[760]). A duty to inform the other party may also be derived from the rules on extraordinary administration of common property. Regarding everyday routine matters of administration, in which each spouse can act alone, it is argued that a duty of mutual information is not necessary (BULGARIA,[761] ITALY[762] and MALTA[763]).

In THE NETHERLANDS,[764] there is a duty to provide information upon the request of the other spouse. Moreover, in other jurisdictions which also have community

743 See ROTH, Austrian Report, Q 144.
744 See PINTENS/ALLAERTS/SEYNS/PIGNOLET, Belgian Report, Q 144.
745 See MARTÍN-CASALS/RIBOT, Catalan Report, Q 144.
746 See FERRAND/BRAAT, French Report, Q 144.
747 Art. 221 Belgian Civil Code. See PINTENS/ALLAERTS/SEYNS/PIGNOLET, Belgian Report, Q 144.
748 This issue is explicitly addressed in the Questionnaire, see Q 39, 74, 110, 144 and 176.
749 See ROTH, Austrian Report, Q 39.
750 See PINTENS/ALLAERTS/SEYNS/PIGNOLET, Belgian Report, Q 39.
751 See MELZER, Czech Report, Q 74.
752 See FERRAND/BRAAT, French Report, Q 39.
753 See WEISS/SZEIBERT, Hungarian Report, Q 39.
754 See ANTOKOLSKAIA, Russian Report, Q 39.
755 See PINTENS/ALLAERTS/SEYNS/PIGNOLET, Belgian Report, Q 39.
756 See FERRAND/BRAAT, French Report, Q 39.
757 See HATÁPKA, Slovakian Report, Q 39.
758 See TODOROVA, Bulgarian Report, Q 39.
759 See PATTI/CARICATO/IRTI/IANNICELL/SERRA/DI STEFANO/PETÖ/BORTOLU, Italian Report, Q 39.
760 See FARRUGIA, Maltese Report, Q 39.
761 See TODOROVA, Bulgarian Report, Q 39.
762 See PATTI/CARICATO/IRTI/IANNICELL/SERRA/DI STEFANO/PETÖ/BORTOLU, Italian Report, Q 39.
763 See FARRUGIA, Maltese Report, Q 39.
764 See BOELE-WOELKI/SCHONEWILLE/SCHRAMA, Dutch Report, Q 39.

property regimes, an extensive, express duty of information applies (LITHUANIA,[765] POLAND,[766] PORTUGAL[767] and SPAIN[768]).

COMMENT

1. Principle 4:8 establishes the duty of each spouse to inform the other spouse regarding the owner spouse's assets and debts, as well as important acts of administration, to the *extent that this is necessary to enable the other spouse to exercise his or her rights.* The other spouse has a corresponding right to be informed. The duty to inform is not meant to be dependant on the other spouse's request. The issue how it is to be exercised is left to national law. The level and kind of information deemed to be necessary will depend on the circumstances of the spouses. To a varying degree, all of the jurisdictions require that the spouses provide each other with relevant information.

2. The placement of this Principle under Chapter I, which consists of the general rights and duties of the spouses, implies that this duty is meant to apply irrespective of the matrimonial property regime applicable between the spouses, whether this is a default regime, or a contractual regime. This duty cannot be excluded by an agreement to the contrary. As part of the *régime primaire*, the duty to inform and the right to be informed applies during the marriage, and it should be kept separate from, for example, the spouses' duty of disclosure upon the entry into a marital property contract under Principle 4:12.

3. The common core of all the studied jurisdictions is that a marriage carries with it the obligation on both spouses to contribute to the expenses of the family (each spouse according to his or her ability). The duty to contribute to family needs is expressly regulated by Principle 4:4. The "proportionality" of contribution cannot be achieved unless each spouse has sufficient knowledge about the other spouse's financial situation. A mutual duty of information is also anticipated to contribute to marital solidarity, community of interests and equality between the spouses.

4. With the exception of the common law jurisdictions, special rules apply in all jurisdictions concerning the effect of the marriage on the spouses' property relations. Irrespective of what kind of regime applies, a spouse can effectively exercise his or her rights, during the marriage, or upon the dissolution of the

---

765 See MIKELENAS, Lithuanian Report, Q 39.

766 Art. 36 para. 1 Polish Family and Guardianship Code, See MĄCZYŃSKI, Polish Report, Q 39.

767 See DE OLIVEIRA/MARTINS/VÍTOR, Portuguese Report, Q 39.

768 Art. 1383 Spanish Civil Code. See GONZÁLEZ BEILFUSS, Spanish Report, Q 39.

property regime, only if he or she has adequate knowledge of the other spouse's financial circumstances, including both assets and debts. The serious failure of a spouse to comply with this duty to provide information may result in an advanced dissolution of the regime, by decision of the competent authority, in accordance with Principles 4:24(d) and 4:49(d). In addition, in accordance with Principle 4:48(1)(c), it may result in a decision by the competent authority divesting the spouse of the right to administer the community property. The spouse suffering harm may also have the right to damages, due to the lack of relevant information.

5. Principle 4:8 explicitly mentions not only the duty of either spouse to inform the other spouse about his or her assets and debts, but also the duty to inform about significant acts of administration. This solution finds support in many of the jurisdictions surveyed. The degree of required information depends on what is necessary for the other spouse to exercise his or her rights. It is left to national law to decide what kinds of acts qualify as significant. Traditionally, however, the acquisition, alienation and encumbrance of immovable property are considered to be such acts, due to the special position enjoyed by this type of property in most jurisdictions. It may therefore be required that these acts are subject to particular restrictions of disposal, such as the consent of the other spouse, even when this property does not constitute a specially protected matrimonial home. Similar restrictions apply in respect of, for example, significant loan agreements entered into by a spouse, or significant gifts given by a spouse. The aim of this is to provide a safeguard against the risk that a spouse mismanages property belonging to him or her, or to the community, to the detriment of the other spouse, thus giving the other spouse the opportunity to take adequate legal measures.

Principle 4:9 Freedom to enter into marital property agreements
Spouses should be free to enter into agreements determining their marital property relationship.

Principe 4:9 Liberté de conclure des conventions patrimoniales
Les époux sont libres de conclure des conventions matrimoniales portant sur leurs relations patrimoniales.

Prinzip 4:9 Freiheit ehegüterrechtliche Vereinbarungen zu treffen
Die Ehegatten sind frei, Vereinbarungen zur Bestimmung ihrer ehelichen Vermögensbeziehungen zu treffen.

INTERNATIONAL INSTRUMENTS

The *Hague Convention on the law applicable to matrimonial property regimes of 14 March 1978* is not of direct relevance save that it provides for the applicable law for the formalities of "marriage contracts" without defining them (Art. 12, 13). The Proposal for a *Council Regulation on jurisdiction, applicable law and the recognition and enforcement of decisions in matters of matrimonial property regimes* of 16 March 2011 deals only with private international law. A *marriage contract* is defined as any agreement by which spouses organise their property relationships between themselves and in relation to third parties (Art. 2 (b)). The *French-German Agreement of 2010* provides for an additional optional matrimonial regime of participation in acquisitions in GERMAN and FRENCH family law (Art. 3 para. 1). The spouses may choose the matrimonial property regime through pre- and/or post-nuptial *marriage contracts* (Art. 3 para. 2). The *Convention between Denmark, Finland, Iceland, Norway and Sweden on Issues of Private International Law concerning Marriage, Adoption and Guardianship* as revised in 2006, also contains provisions on marital property agreements (Art. 3(c) and Art. 4).

COMPARATIVE OVERVIEW

Freedom to enter into agreements

Despite the differences in the jurisdictions surveyed spouses are basically free to enter into agreements to determine their property relationship. Nevertheless there are fundamental differences. In the civil law jurisdictions pre-nuptial agreements, made before marriage, and post-nuptial marital property agreements, made after marriage, are generally recognised (see Principle 4:10). The starting point of these jurisdictions is that spouses and prospective spouses are free to choose a matrimonial property regime and thus contract out the respective default regime and into an alternative form of sharing or into a "pure" separation of property. This matrimonial property regime may then be changed and modified. However, on closer examination there are many restrictions on entering and upon the content and validity of such agreements (see Principles 4:10 to 4:15) and, not to be forgotten, those imposed by the rules of the so-called primary regime (*régime primaire*) with mandatory provisions for all marriages, see Principles 4:1 to 4:8. In the Nordic systems of deferred community the function of marital agreements is to a great extent to modify the existing rules on participation at the end of a matrimonial property regime. In SCOTLAND,[769] pre-nuptial and post-nuptial agreements are recognised.

The starting point of the common law approach is a separation of property with the possibility of a distribution by the competent authority at the end of the marriage. This means that marriage does not affect the ownership of assets of spouses during the marriage (ENGLAND AND WALES[770] and IRELAND[771]), but that the court upon divorce has wide discretion regarding the distribution of assets. One effect of the assumption that there is basically no specific matrimonial property regime is that the spouses generally may make their own arrangements. However, such pre-nuptial agreements are not enforceable per se and not binding in court proceedings. The impact of marital property agreements is under discussion in ENGLAND AND WALES.[772]

In the jurisdictions surveyed there is no unanimity on the binding force of such agreements. There are jurisdictions where the binding force of pre- and post-nuptial agreements is not accepted (e.g. IRELAND[773]). Although this is also the case in ENGLAND AND WALES, recent case-law shows some willingness to take agreements of the spouses into account.[774] However, in the vast majority of legal systems matrimonial property law contains rules for several property regimes. The spouses may through pre- and/or post-nuptial agreements choose a statutory matrimonial property regime (e.g. AUSTRIA,[775] BELGIUM,[776] FRANCE,[777]

769 See MAIR, Scottish Report, Q 191 and Q 192.
770 See BARLOW, English Report, Q 161.
771 See SHANNON, Irish Report, Q 198.
772 See The Law Commission, Consultation Paper No 198, Marital Property Agreements, A Consultation Paper, 2011.
773 See SHANNON, Irish Report, Q 198.
774 *Granatino* v. *Radmacher (formerly Granatino)*, [2010] UKSC 42, [2011] 1 AC 534.
775 § 1233, 1237 Austrian Civil Code and ROTH, Austrian Report, Q 198.
776 See PINTENS/ALLAERTS/SEYNS/PIGNOLET, Belgian Report, Q 198.
777 Art. 1393 para. 1 French Civil Code. See FERRAND/BRAAT, French Report, Q 199.

GERMANY,[778] GREECE,[779] LITHUANIA,[780] MALTA,[781] THE NETHERLANDS,[782] PORTUGAL,[783] SLOVAKIA,[784] SPAIN,[785] and SWITZERLAND[786]). In the Nordic countries, the legislation on marital property permits both pre- and post-nuptial agreements, to deviate from these countries' deferred community property regimes (DENMARK,[787] FINLAND,[788] NORWAY[789] and SWEDEN[790]) and, even, to introduce full separation of property.

Marital property agreements

All the legal systems surveyed contain rules for marital property agreements with the exception of ENGLAND AND WALES and IRELAND. There are often special provisions on "marriage contracts" with which the spouses may choose between several existing statutory regimes (e.g. AUSTRIA,[791] BELGIUM,[792] CATALONIA,[793] FRANCE,[794] GERMANY,[795] GREECE,[796] ITALY,[797] LITHUANIA,[798] MALTA,[799] THE NETHERLANDS,[800] PORTUGAL,[801] SLOVAKIA,[802] SPAIN[803] and SWITZERLAND[804]). In the Nordic countries there is no choice between several property regimes.

778 § 1408 para. 1 German Civil Code. See DETHLOFF/MARTINY, German Report, Q 198.
779 KOUTSOURADIS/KOTRONIS/HATZANTONIS, Greek Report, Q 198.
780 Art. 3.104 Lithuanian Civil Code. See MIKELENAS, Lithuanian Report, Q 198.
781 Art. 1237 para. 2 Maltese Civil Code. See FARRUGIA, Maltese Report, Q 198.
782 Art. 93 Dutch Civil Code. See BOELE-WOELKI/SCHONEWILLE/SCHRAMA, Dutch Report, Q 198.
783 See DE OLIVEIRA/MARTINS/VÍTOR, Portuguese Report, Q 198.
784 Art. 143a para. 1 Slovak Civil Code. See HAŤAPKA, Slovakian Report, Q 198.
785 See GONZÁLEZ BEILFUSS, Spanish Report, Q 198.
786 Art. 181 Swiss Civil Code. See SCHWENZER/BOCK, Swiss Report, Q 198.
787 § 28 Danish Act on the Legal Effects of Marriage. See LUND-ANDERSEN/MAGNUSSEN, Danish Report, Q 198.
788 § 41 Finnish Marriage Act. See KURKI-SUONIO, Finnish Report, Q 198.
789 § 42, 43 Norwegian Marriage Act. See SVERDRUP Norwegian Report, Q 198.
790 Ch. 7 § 3 Swedish Marriage Code. See JÄNTERÄ-JAREBORG/BRATTSTRÖM/WALLENG, Swedish Report, Q 198.
791 § 1233, 1237 Austrian Civil Code. See ROTH, Austrian Report, Q 198.
792 See PINTENS/ALLAERTS/SEYNS/PIGNOLET, Belgian Report, Q 198.
793 Art. 15 para. 1 Catalan Family Code. See MARTÍN-CASALS/RIBOT, Catalan Report, Q 191.
794 Art. 1393 para. 1 French Civil Code. See FERRAND/BRAAT, French Report, Q 199.
795 § 1408 para. 1 German Civil Code. See DETHLOFF/MARTINY, German Report, Q 198.
796 See KOUTSOURADIS/KOTRONIS/HATZANTONIS, Greek Report, Q 198.
797 See PATTI/CARICATO/IRTI/IANNICELLI/SERRA/DI STEFANO/PETÖ/BORTOLU, Italian Report, Q 191.
798 Art. 3.104 Lithuanian Civil Code. See MIKELENAS, Lithuanian Report, Q 198.
799 Art. 1237 para. 2 Maltese Civil Code. See FARRUGIA, Maltese Report, Q 198.
800 Art. 93 Dutch Civil Code. See BOELE-WOELKI/SCHONEWILLE/SCHRAMA, Dutch Report, Q 198.
801 Art. 1698 Portuguese Civil Code. See DE OLIVEIRA/MARTINS/VÍTOR, Portuguese Report, Q.
802 Art. 143a para. 1 Slovak Civil Code. See HAŤAPKA, Slovakian Report, Q 198.
803 See GONZÁLEZ BEILFUSS, Spanish Report, Q 198.
804 Art. 181 Swiss Civil Code. See SCHWENZER/BOCK, Swiss Report, Q 198.

However, the spouses may by marital property agreements make considerable modifications of the legal rules and thus find individual solutions for their property relations (DENMARK,[805] FINLAND,[806] NORWAY[807] and SWEDEN[808]). In a few jurisdictions marriage contracts are also used for agreements on equalisation of pension rights (GERMANY[809]).

Freedom of the spouses to regulate participation

As a rule, under the existing regimes of *participation in acquisition/community of accrued gains* and the Nordic model of *deferred community property regime* the spouses are basically free to make agreements concerning the participation in the acquisitions. Certain restrictions may still apply, e.g. on the basis of what kind of assets are at stake, in order to protect the other spouse's interests as well as the interests of the family, minor children included. This applies in particular in relation to the matrimonial home and the household goods.

Under a *participation in acquisition/community of accrued gains* regime there are systems where basically all assets can give rise to an equalisation claim (for example GERMANY[810]) while others follow a more restricted approach and provide also for a category of separate property (for example SWITZERLAND[811]). In some of these jurisdictions where a category of separate property exists the spouses may designate business assets that would otherwise belong to the marital property as separate property (for example SWITZERLAND[812]). On the other hand, separate property may also be classified as marital property. The spouses may assign revenue generated from separate property to the separate property (for example SWITZERLAND[813]). It can also be agreed that certain assets, for example a company, may not be equalised at all (GERMANY[814]).

A general feature of *deferred community of property* regimes is that there exist marital property and separate property. In the jurisdictions with such a property regime the spouses may also modify categories of assets and restrict participation. They may provide that a portion of marital property is to be held

805 § 28 Danish Act on the Legal Effects of Marriage. See LUND-ANDERSEN/MAGNUSSEN, Danish Report, Q 198.
806 § 41 Finnish Marriage Act. See KURKI-SUONIO, Finnish Report, Q 198.
807 See SVERDRUP Norwegian Report, Q 198.
808 See JÄNTERÄ-JAREBORG/SINGER/SÖRGJERD, Swedish Report, Q 198.
809 § 1408 para. 2 German Civil Code. See DETHLOFF/MARTINY, German Report, Q 198.
810 § 1323 ff. German Civil Code. See DETHLOFF/MARTINY, German Report, Q 199.
811 See SCHWENZER/BOCK, Swiss Report, Q 199.
812 Art. 199 para. 1 Swiss Civil Code. See SCHWENZER/BOCK, Swiss Report, Q 199.
813 Art. 199 para. 2 Swiss Civil Code. See SCHWENZER/BOCK, Swiss Report, Q 199.
814 § 1408 para. 1 German Civil Code. See DETHLOFF/MARTINY, German Report, Q 89, 199.

as separate property (DENMARK[815] and NORWAY[816]). The parties may exclude from the category of marital property any property owned or later acquired by a spouse or agree that certain assets shall be transformed from marital property into separate property (DENMARK,[817] FINLAND,[818] NORWAY[819] and SWEDEN[820]).

COMMENT

1. Principle 4:9 reflects the common core of all jurisdictions surveyed that permit marital property agreements to be made. When spouses draft a marital property agreement they enjoy broad freedom to construct a system of their choice. The freedom of the spouses enables them to find their specific solution both for the daily management of their property and for its division if the couple separate or one of its members dies. The Principle recognises the autonomy of the spouses to enter into such agreements. Despite the unpredictability of the future the spouses have, by the ability to make their own arrangements, at least a chance to create some certainty. This concerns mainly the choice of an appropriate matrimonial property regime according to Principles 4:10 – 4:15. However, also within the framework of the single matrimonial property regime agreements are possible, mainly in respect to the dissolution of the regime of participation in acquisitions (Principle 4:16) and the regime of community of acquisitions (Principle 4:33).

2. The property relationship between spouses is primarily determined by the general rights and duties of the spouses applicable to all marriages (Principles 4:1 – 4:8) and secondly by the rules of the specific matrimonial regime (Principles 4:16 et seq.). These rules not only concern daily management of the property of the spouses and the situation at the termination of the regime but also have effect as against third parties, in particular creditors.

3. Freedom is exercised by making a marital property agreement in the sense of Principle 4:9. Such marital property agreements are subject to the Principles contained in Chapter II (Principles 4:10–4:15). A marital property agreement is an agreement by which spouses organise their property relationships between themselves and in relation to third parties. Although the broader term

---

815 See LUND-ANDERSEN/MAGNUSSEN, Danish Report, Q 199.

816 See SVERDRUP, Norwegian Report, Q 199.

817 Danish Act § 28 on the Legal Effects of Marriage. See LUND-ANDERSEN/MAGNUSSEN, Danish Report, Q 198.

818 § 41 para. 1 Finnish Marriage Act. See KURKI-SUONIO, Finnish Report, Q 199.

819 § 42–43 Norwegian Marriage Act. See SVERDRUP, Norwegian Report, Q 198.

820 Ch. 12 § 3 para. 1 Swedish Marriage Code. See JÄNTERÄ-JAREBORG/BRATTSTRÖM/WALLENG, Swedish Report, Q 199.

"agreement" is used rather than the term "contract", nevertheless the agreement has a contractual nature.

4. One of the purposes of matrimonial property law is to grant each spouse the right to obtain a fair share in the property of the other. Marital property agreements may endanger this purpose of matrimonial property law. The same is true for the protection of third parties against fraudulent manoeuvres. Despite the fact that no authorization of a competent authority is required and there is no specific Principle dealing with the validity of agreements and the control of its content there are several limits to party autonomy. The rules on general rights and duties (Principles 4:1–4:9) are by and large mandatory. There are also several Principles on marital property agreements concerning different protective aspects such as requirements as to form (Principle 4:11) and obligations of the notary or other persons with comparable functions to give independent advice (Principle 4:13). It is also important that both spouses fully disclose their assets to ensure fairness (Principle 4:12). A special provision on exceptional hardship shall prevent unfair results (Principle 4:15). One has also take into account that the overall unfairness of an agreement is sometimes derived from the context with other agreements concerning or denying maintenance after divorce and equalisation of pension rights.

5. Closely related to marital property agreements are maintenance agreements. Principle 2:10 of the Principles of European Family Law Regarding Divorce and Maintenance between Former Spouses deals with such agreements. According to these Principles spouses should be permitted to make an agreement about maintenance after divorce.

CHAPTER II: MARITAL PROPERTY AGREEMENTS
CHAPITRE II: CONVENTIONS MATRIMONIALES PORTANT SUR LES RELATIONS PATRIMONIALES DES ÉPOUX
KAPITEL II: EHEGÜTERRECHTLICHE VEREINBARUNGEN

Principle 4:10 Concept

(1) In a marital property agreement made before the marriage the future spouses may choose their matrimonial property regime.

(2) During the marriage the spouses may modify their matrimonial property regime or change it for another regime.

Principe 4:10 Notion

(1) Dans une convention conclue avant le mariage, les futurs époux peuvent choisir leur régime matrimonial.

(2) Au cours du mariage, les époux peuvent modifier leur régime ou en changer entièrement.

Prinzip 4:10 Begriff

(1) In einer vor der Eheschließung getroffenen Vereinbarung können die künftigen Ehegatten ihren Ehegüterstand wählen.

(2) Während der Ehe können die Ehegatten ihren Ehegüterstand abändern oder zu einem anderen Ehegüterstand überwechseln.

INTERNATIONAL INSTRUMENTS

The *Council of Europe's Resolution (78) 37 on Equality of Spouses in Civil Law*, adopted in September 1978, recommends inter alia that Member States' governments "take all necessary steps in relation to contract of marriage to ensure that the laws relating to such contracts do not contain provisions which discriminate against one spouse" and "to give both spouses equal rights and obligations concerning their common property where the operation of law provides for a matrimonial property regime of community of goods and in particular:

(i) the right to be informed by the other spouse of the actual extent of the common property;
(ii) an equal right to use, administer, receive profits or dispose of the common property and income as well as to share in the division of property;
(iii) equal obligations concerning debts."

In *Recommendation No. R (89) of the Council of Europe On Contributions Following Divorce* (January 1989), Member States are advised to enact appropriate rules relating to, inter alia, "matrimonial property regimes, in particular by granting to a former spouse the right to obtain a fair share of the property of the other."

The *French-German Agreement of 2010* provides for an additional optional matrimonial regime of participation in acquisitions in German and French family law (Art. 3 para. 1). The spouses may choose it through pre- and/or post-nuptial agreements (Art. 3 para. 2). The spouses have the freedom to modify the regime and may make modifications with respect to the equalisation claim (Art. 3 para. 3). However, the provisions belonging to the regime primaire are mandatory and spouses may not set them aside (Art. 3 para. 3).

COMPARATIVE OVERVIEW

Acceptance of pre- and post-nuptial agreements

There are jurisdictions where the binding force of pre- and post-nuptial agreements is not accepted (e.g. IRELAND[821]). This is also strictly the case in ENGLAND AND WALES,[822] although recent case law shows that there is agreater willingness to take agreements between the spouses into account. In many jurisdictions the spouses may, through pre- and post-nuptial agreements, choose a statutory matrimonial property regime.

In a few jurisdictions there is only one matrimonial property regime so that there is no choice between regimes (HUNGARY[823]). Despite the right of the

[821] See SHANNON, Irish Report, Q 198.
[822] *Granatino v. Radmacher (formerly Granatino)*, [2010] UKSC 42, [2011] 1 AC 534.
[823] SeeWEISS/SZEIBERT, Hungarian Report, Q 198 on Hungarian law before the reform of 20 November 2009.

spouses to deviate not only to a certain extent from the statutory rules regarding matrimonial property relations but also in full, introducing full separation of property also upon the dissolution of the regime, it may be argued that there is only one statutory regime in the Nordic countries (DENMARK,[824] FINLAND,[825] NORWAY[826] and SWEDEN[827]), namely that of deferred community of property. However, in the vast majority of legal systems matrimonial property law contains rules for several property regimes. The spouses may choose between several existing statutory regimes (e.g. AUSTRIA,[828] BELGIUM,[829] FRANCE,[830] GERMANY,[831] GREECE,[832] ITALY,[833] LITHUANIA,[834] MALTA,[835] THE NETHERLANDS,[836] PORTUGAL,[837] SLOVAKIA,[838] SPAIN[839] and SWITZERLAND[840]).

In some jurisdictions different combinations are possible. For example, different matrimonial property regimes may be combined in such a way that different regimes apply to different types of property or assets, for example, immovable property or specified chattels (e.g. LITHUANIA[841]). The same effect can be reached by excluding certain assets in DENMARK,[842] FINLAND,[843] NORWAY,[844] SWEDEN[845] and PORTUGAL.[846]

In their marriage contract the spouses sometimes define a matrimonial regime both in respect of their existing and future property. In some jurisdictions it is possible for one matrimonial property regime to apply for only for a certain

---

824 § 28 Danish Act on the Legal Effects of Marriage. See LUND-ANDERSEN/MAGNUSSEN, Danish Report, Q 198.
825 § 35 et seq. Finnish Marriage Act. See KURKI-SUONIO, Finnish Report, Q 198.
826 § 42 et seq. Marriage Act. See SVERDRUP, Norwegian Report, Q 198.
827 See JÄNTERÄ-JAREBORG/BRATTSTRÖM/WALLENG, Swedish Report, Q 198.
828 § 1233, 1237 Austrian Civil Code. See ROTH, Austrian Report, Q 198.
829 See PINTENS/ALLAERTS/SEYNS/PIGNOLET, Belgian Report, Q 198.
830 Art. 1393 para. 1 French Civil Code. See FERRAND/BRAAT, French Report, Q 199.
831 § 1408 para. 1 German Civil Code. See DETHLOFF/MARTINY, German Report, Q 198.
832 See KOUTSOURADIS/KOTRONIS/HATZANTONIS, Greek Report, Q 198.
833 See PATTI/CARICATO/IRTI/IANNICELLI/SERRA/DI STEFANO/PETÖ/BORTOLU, Italian Report, Q 191.
834 Art. 3.104 Lithuanian Civil Code. See MIKELENAS, Lithuanian Report, Q 198.
835 Art. 1237 para. 2 Maltese Civil Code. See FARRUGIA, Maltese Report, Q 198.
836 Art. 93 Dutch Civil Code. See BOELE-WOELKI/SCHONEWILLE/SCHRAMA, Dutch Report, Q 198.
837 Art. 1698 Portuguese Civil Code. See DE OLIVEIRA/MARTINS/VÍTOR, Portuguese Report, Q 198.
838 Art. 143a para. 1 Slovak Civil Code. See HAŤAPKA, Slovakian Report, Q 198.
839 See GONZÁLEZ BEILFUSS, Spanish Report, Q 198.
840 Art. 181 Swiss Civil Code. See SCHWENZER/BOCK, Swiss Report, Q 198.
841 Art. 3.104 Lithuanian Civil Code. See MIKELENAS, Lithuanian Report, Q 198.
842 See LUND-ANDERSEN/MAGNUSSEN, Danish Report, Q 198.
843 § 41 Finnish Marriage Act. See KURKI-SUONIO, Finnish Report, Q 198.
844 See SVERDRUP, Norwegian Report, Q 198.
845 See JÄNTERÄ-JAREBORG/BRATTSTRÖM/WALLENG, Swedish Report, Q 198.
846 See DE OLIVEIRA/MARTINS/VÍTOR, Portuguese Report, Q 198.

period of time and thereafter for the assets to be subject to another property regime (e.g. LITHUANIA[847] and RUSSIA[848]). The same result can be reached in DENMARK[849] and NORWAY.[850]

The emergence or termination of rights and duties may also be related to the fulfilment or omission of a certain condition stipulated in the marriage contract (LITHUANIA[851] and RUSSIA[852]).

How often are marital property agreements made?

In the majority of jurisdictions surveyed no official statistics are available. This is the case in AUSTRIA, BELGIUM, CZECH REPUBLIC, ENGLAND AND WALES,[853] GERMANY, GREECE, HUNGARY, IRELAND,[854] ITALY, LITHUANIA, MALTA, POLAND, RUSSIA, SCOTLAND, SLOVAKIA and SWITZERLAND. In a number of jurisdictions assumptions and estimates were made: this is the case for GERMANY (less than 10% of married couples conclude a marital property agreement),[855] SCOTLAND (agreements are used to resolve disputes in around one-third of the total number of divorces in any year)[856] and SWITZERLAND (only 5–10% of all spouses make a marital contract in which most of the couples choose separation of property).[857]

In those jurisdictions where statistical data about the number of marital contracts is available and has been provided, no distinction is made between pre- and post-nuptial agreements except in FRANCE where in 1996 16% of the spouses made a pre-nuptial agreement and 3% a post-nuptial agreement,[858] in LITHUANIA where after the entry into force in 2002 of the Register of Marriage Contract Act and until mid-2008, 1919 marriage contracts where registered (428 pre-nuptial and 1491 post-nuptial)[859] and in NORWAY where, according to the Register of

---

847 Art. 3.104 Lithuanian Civil Code. See MIKELENAS, Lithuanian Report, Q 198.

848 Art. 42 para. 2 Russian Family Code.

849 See LUND-ANDERSEN/MAGNUSSEN, Danish Report, Q 198.

850 See SVERDRUP, Norwegian Report, Q 198.

851 Art. 3.104 Lithuanian Civil Code. See MIKELENAS, Lithuanian Report, Q 198.

852 Art. 42 para. 2 Russian Family Code.

853 See BARLOW, English Report, Q 197: There is anecdotal evidence from solicitors that more people are making pre-nuptial agreements, particularly if they are remarrying, despite the lack of certainty surrounding enforceability.

854 See SHANNON, Irish Report, Q 197: Irish family lawyers experienced an increase in the level of client inquiries about pre-nuptial agreements since the coming into force of the Irish Divorce Act in 1997 particularly by those entering into a second marriage seeking protection for the properties they had before they married, between whom there is a significant asset inbalance and those where a foreign national was marrying an Irish person.

855 See DETHLOFF/MARTINY, German Report, Q 197 refers to research carried out in 1988 and 2001.

856 See MAIR, Scottish Report, Q 197 refers to a Scottish handbook published in 2006.

857 See SCHWENZER/BOCK, Swiss Report, Q 197 with no further references.

858 See FERRAND/BRAAT, French Report, Q 197.

859 See MIKELENAS, Lithuanian Report, Q 197.

Marriage Agreements, the annual number of nuptial agreements is approximately 3,500 of which 30% are pre-nuptial and 70% are post-nuptial. The number of unregistered nuptial agreements which, according to NORWEGIAN law are only binding on the spouses and their heirs,[860] is not known.[861]

The statistics for THE NETHERLANDS indicate that in 25% of the marriages concluded in 2003 a marital property agreement was drawn up,[862] whereas in PORTUGAL this percentage was 15% for the marriages celebrated in 2007.[863]

The general trend in jurisdictions with statistical data covering a longer period is that there has been a steady increase in the number of marital property agreements. The data, however, concern different periods.

More or less comparable in terms of the time span are the statistical data of CATALONIA, where since the end of the 1970s until 2003 the increase was about 700%,[864] of FINLAND, where the number of marital agreements increased from 10% in the 1970s to 25% after 2000[865] and of SPAIN, where according to research undertaken in 2001, the number of marital property agreements have particularly increased since 1975.[866]

The information provided for DENMARK covers thirteen years from 1992 (5,000 agreements) to 2005 (11,000 marriage agreements).[867] In LITHUANIA,[868] the number of registered agreements increased from 24 in 2002 to 600 in 2007. The statistics provided for SWEDEN cover the years 2003–2007, where the number of registered marital property agreements is fairly steady with about 10,800 per year (13,590 in 2003 and 10,464 in 2007). The authors rightly make the point that the number of marriages concluded in SWEDEN during these years does not necessarily correlate with the number of registered agreements. The statistics make no distinction between pre-nuptial and post-nuptial agreements and a registered agreement may also replace an earlier marital property agreement between the spouses. As a result it is not possible to draw conclusions as to how common it is in SWEDEN for spouses to completely set aside the deferred community of property regime.[869]

---

860 § 54 para. 3 Norwegian Marriage Act.
861 See SVERDRUP, Norwegian Report, Q 197.
862 See BOELE-WOELKI/SCHONEWILLE/SCHRAMA, Dutch Report, Q 197.
863 See DE OLIVEIRA/MARTINS/VÍTOR, Portuguese Report, Q 197.
864 See MARTÍN-CASALS/RIBOT, Catalan Report, Q 197.
865 See KURKI-SUONIO, Finnish Report, Q 197.
866 See GONZÁLEZ BEILFUSS, Spanish Report, Q 197.
867 See LUND-ANDERSEN/MAGNUSSEN, Danish Report, Q 197.
868 See MIKELENAS, Lithuanian Report, Q 197.
869 See JÄNTERÄ-JAREBORG/BRATTSTRÖM/WALLENG, Swedish Report, Q 197.

Some statistical information is provided in relation with the content of the marital property agreements.

In SWEDEN, in the vast majority of the registered agreements (about 90%) the couples prescribe which property they consider to be separate property. In 10% of the agreements they stipulate that separate property should be marital property.[870] In NORWAY,[871] agreements by which the spouses set aside the default regime, in full or in part, thereby transforming the concerned assets into separate property constitute approximately 85% of the total number of agreements. Similarly, in HUNGARY[872] spouses sometimes record in a document which assets belong to the separate property of a spouse before marriage. The infrequent use of matrimonial property agreements in this jurisdiction is due to the fact that the HUNGARIAN Family Act only contains one regime and does not provide for any other alternative property regime.

In SPAIN,[873] the agreements are made in order to establish separation of property, but, for example, in FINLAND,[874] they are made if the spouses want to deviate from the main principle of the Marriage Act which prescribes an equal distribution of property when the marriage is dissolved. In SWITZERLAND,[875] it is estimated that a substantial number of spouses enter into a combination of marital and testamentary contracts which modify the SWISS participation in acquisitions with the aim of ensuring the highest possible benefit for the surviving spouse. Against the background of the DUTCH default system of a total community of property,[876] it is notable that the percentage of marital property agreements containing a complete separation of property (*koude uitsluiting*) has considerably increased from 24,5% in 2004 to 34,3% in 2009.[877]

The statistical information on the frequency and the content of marital property agreements does not cover all jurisdictions surveyed since in many jurisdictions these data simply do not exist, whereas in others they are outdated, they are only available for a specific year or they cover different periods. Moreover, the reasons why spouses make use of the opportunity to deviate from the default regime differ. As a result, the data do not allow drawing any conclusions.

---

870 See JÄNTERÄ-JAREBORG/BRATTSTRÖM/WALLENG, Swedish Report, Q 197.

871 See SVERDRUP, Norwegian Report, Q 197.

872 See WEISS/SZEIBERT, Hungarian Report, Q 197.

873 See GONZÁLEZ BEILFUSS, Spanish Report, Q 197.

874 See KURKI-SUONIO, Finnish Report, Q 197.

875 See SCHWENZER/BOCK, Swiss Report, Q 197.

876 See BOELE-WOELKI/SCHONEWILLE/SCHRAMA, Dutch Report, Q 197.

877 See SCHOLS/HOENS, CNR-Huwelijksvoorwaardenonderzoek, deel I: algemeen en koude voorwaarden, WPNR 2012 nr. 6956.

Modification of matrimonial property regime

In nearly all jurisdictions the spouses are free to modify the statutory or chosen matrimonial property regime (e.g. AUSTRIA,[878] BELGIUM,[879] DENMARK,[880] FINLAND,[881] MALTA,[882] THE NETHERLANDS,[883] NORWAY,[884] PORTUGAL,[885] RUSSIA,[886] SLOVAKIA,[887] SPAIN,[888] SWEDEN[889] and SWITZERLAND[890]). There are, however, different kinds of restrictions.

Creation of new types of matrimonial property régimes

In some several of the reviewed jurisdictions the spouses can also create new types of matrimonial property regimes so as, for example, to follow the rules of a foreign regime or to create their own "tailor-made" regime (e.g. AUSTRIA,[891] BELGIUM,[892] FRANCE,[893] HUNGARY,[894] THE NETHERLANDS,[895] PORTUGAL[896] and RUSSIA[897]). In most jurisdictions, however, spouses cannot create their own regime (e.g. GERMANY,[898] ITALY,[899] MALTA,[900] SLOVAKIA,[901] SPAIN[902] and SWITZERLAND[903]).

---

878 See ROTH, Austrian Report, Q 198.
879 See PINTENS/ALLAERTS/SEYNS/PIGNOLET, Belgian Report, Q 198.
880 See LUND-ANDERSEN/MAGNUSSEN, Danish Report, Q 198.
881 § 41 Finnish Marriage Act. See KURKI-SUONIO, Finnish Report, Q 198.
882 Art. 1237 para. 2 Maltese Civil Code. See FARRUGIA, Maltese Report, Q 198.
883 See BOELE-WOELKI/SCHONEWILLE/SCHRAMA, Dutch Report, Q 198.
884 See SVERDRUP Norwegian Report, Q 198.
885 Art. 1698 Portuguese Civil Code. See DE OLIVEIRA/MARTINS/VÍTOR, Portuguese Report, Q 198.
886 Art. 42 Russian Family Code. See ANTOKOLSKAIA, Russian Report, Q 198, 199.
887 See HAŤAPKA, Slovakian Report, Q 198.
888 See GONZÁLEZ BEILFUSS, Spanish Report, Q 198.
889 Ch. 7 § 3 Swedish Marriage Code. See JÄNTERÄ-JAREBORG/BRATTSTRÖM/WALLENG, Swedish Report, Q 198.
890 See SCHWENZER/BOCK, Swiss Report, Q 198.
891 See ROTH, Austrian Report, Q 198.
892 See PINTENS/ALLAERTS/SEYNS/PIGNOLET, Belgian Report, Q 198.
893 See FERRAND/BRAAT, French Report, Q 198.
894 See WEISS/SZEIBERT, Hungarian Report, Q 198.
895 See BOELE-WOELKI/SCHONEWILLE/SCHRAMA, Dutch Report, Q 198.
896 Art. 1698, 1718 Portuguese Civil Code. See DE OLIVEIRA/MARTINS/VÍTOR, Portuguese Report, Q 198.
897 Art. 42 Russian Family Code. See ANTOKOLSKAIA, Russian Report, Q 198.
898 § 1409 German Civil Code. See DETHLOFF/MARTINY, German Report, Q 198.
899 See PATTI/CARICATO/IRTI/IANNICELLI/SERRA/DI STEFANO/PETÖ/BORTOLU, Italian Report, Q 191.
900 Art. 1237 para. 2 Maltese Civil Code. See FARRUGIA, Maltese Report, Q 198.
901 See HAŤAPKA, Slovakian Report, Q 198.
902 See GONZÁLEZ BEILFUSS, Spanish Report, Q 198.
903 Art. 181, 182 para. 2 Swiss Civil Code. See SCHWENZER/BOCK, Swiss Report, Q 198.

Pre-nuptial and post-nuptial property agreements

In many of the jurisdictions surveyed there is a more or less clear distinction between pre-nuptial and post-nuptial marital property agreements (e.g. AUSTRIA,[904] BELGIUM,[905] FRANCE,[906] ITALY,[907] LITHUANIA,[908] MALTA,[909] THE NETHERLANDS,[910] PORTUGAL,[911] SLOVAKIA,[912] SPAIN[913] and SWITZERLAND[914]). However, some jurisdictions do not differentiate between pre-nuptial and post-nuptial agreements, for example, DENMARK,[915] FINLAND,[916] GERMANY,[917] GREECE,[918] NORWAY,[919] RUSSIA[920] and SWEDEN.[921]

Pre-nuptial property agreements

Spouses may conclude pre-nuptial agreements prior to the marriage in order to regulate their property relationships (e.g. AUSTRIA,[922] BELGIUM,[923] DENMARK,[924] FINLAND,[925] FRANCE,[926] GERMANY,[927] GREECE,[928] HUNGARY,[929] ITALY,[930]

---

904 § 1217 Austrian Civil Code. See ROTH, Austrian Report, Q 191.
905 See PINTENS/ALLAERTS/SEYNS/PIGNOLET, Belgian Report, Q 191.
906 Art. 1393 para. 1 French Civil Code. See FERRAND/BRAAT, French Report, Q 199.
907 See PATTI/CARICATO/IRTI/IANNICELLI/SERRA/DI STEFANO/PETÖ/BORTOLU, Italian Report, Q 192.
908 Art. 3.104 Lithuanian Civil Code. See MIKELENAS, Lithuanian Report, Q 192.
909 Art. 1237 para. 2 Maltese Civil Code. See FARRUGIA, Maltese Report, Q 192.
910 Art. 93 Dutch Civil Code. See BOELE-WOELKI/SCHONEWILLE/SCHRAMA, Dutch Report, Q 192.
911 Art. 1698 Portuguese Civil Code. See DE OLIVEIRA/MARTINS/VÍTOR, Portuguese Report, Q.
912 Art. 143a para. 1 Slovak Civil Code. See HAŤAPKA, Slovakian Report, Q 192.
913 See GONZÁLEZ BEILFUSS, Spanish Report, Q 192.
914 Art. 181 Swiss Civil Code. See SCHWENZER/BOCK, Swiss Report, Q 192.
915 § 28 Danish Act on the Legal Effects of Marriage. See LUND-ANDERSEN/MAGNUSSEN, Danish Report, Q 191 and Q 192.
916 § 41 Finnish Marriage Act. See KURKI-SUONIO, Finnish Report, Q 198.
917 See DETHLOFF/MARTINY, German Report, Q 191.
918 See KOUTSOURADIS/KOTRONIS/HATZANTONIS, Greek Report, Q 192.
919 See SVERDRUP Norwegian Report, Q 191.
920 Art. 41 para. 1 Russian Family Code.
921 See JÄNTERÄ-JAREBORG/BRATTSTRÖM/WALLENG, Swedish Report, Q 191.
922 § 1217 Austrian Civil Code. See ROTH, Austrian Report, Q 191.
923 See PINTENS/ALLAERTS/SEYNS/PIGNOLET, Belgian Report, Q 191.
924 § 28 Danish Act on the Legal Effects of Marriage. See LUND-ANDERSEN/MAGNUSSEN, Danish Report, Q 191.
925 § 41 Finnish Marriage Act. See KURKI-SUONIO, Finnish Report, Q 198.
926 Art. 1393 para. 1 French Civil Code. See FERRAND/BRAAT, French Report, Q 199.
927 § 1408 para. 1 German Civil Code. See DETHLOFF/MARTINY, German Report, Q 191.
928 Art. 1403 para. 1 Greek Civil Code. See KOUTSOURADIS/KOTRONIS/HATZANTONIS, Greek Report, Q 191.
929 § 27 para. 2 Hungarian Family Law Act. See WEISS/SZEIBERT, Hungarian Report, Q 199.
930 See PATTI/CARICATO/IRTI/IANNICELLI/SERRA/DI STEFANO/PETÖ/BORTOLU, Italian Report, Q 191.

LITHUANIA,[931] MALTA,[932] THE NETHERLANDS,[933] NORWAY,[934] PORTUGAL,[935] RUSSIA,[936] SLOVAKIA,[937] SPAIN[938] and SWITZERLAND[939]). Pre-nuptial agreements are contracts and are therefore binding if they comply with the necessary requirements (e.g. AUSTRIA,[940] BELGIUM,[941] DENMARK,[942] FINLAND,[943] FRANCE,[944] GERMANY,[945] GREECE,[946] LITHUANIA,[947] MALTA,[948] THE NETHERLANDS,[949] NORWAY,[950] POLAND,[951] PORTUGAL,[952] RUSSIA,[953] SPAIN,[954] SWEDEN[955] and SWITZERLAND[956]). The stipulations may not violate mandatory rules, in particular *bonos mores* or public policy (e.g. BELGIUM,[957] FRANCE,[958] GERMANY,[959] THE NETHERLANDS[960] and RUSSIA[961]). In GERMANY the control of the content of such agreements has been considerably extended by the courts during recent years. In only a few civil law jurisdictions pre-marital property agreements are not permitted (e.g. ITALY[962] and SLOVAKIA[963]).

---

931 Art. 3.104 Lithuanian Civil Code. See MIKELENAS, Lithuanian Report, Q 191.
932 Art. 1237 para. 2 Maltese Civil Code. See FARRUGIA, Maltese Report, Q 191.
933 Art. 93 Dutch Civil Code. See BOELE-WOELKI/SCHONEWILLE/SCHRAMA, Dutch Report, Q 191.
934 See SVERDRUP Norwegian Report, Q 191.
935 Art. 1698 Portuguese Civil Code. See DE OLIVEIRA/MARTINS/VÍTOR, Portuguese Report, Q.
936 See ANTOKOLSKAIA, Russian Report, Q 191, 199.
937 Art. 143a para. 1 Slovak Civil Code. See HAŤAPKA, Slovakian Report, Q 191.
938 See GONZÁLEZ BEILFUSS, Spanish Report, Q 191.
939 Art. 181 Swiss Civil Code. See SCHWENZER/BOCK, Swiss Report, Q 191.
940 See ROTH, Austrian Report, Q 191.
941 See PINTENS/ALLAERTS/SEYNS/PIGNOLET, Belgian Report, Q 191.
942 § 28 Danish Act on the Legal Effects of Marriage. See LUND-ANDERSEN/MAGNUSSEN, Danish Report, Q 191.
943 § 41 Finnish Marriage Act. See KURKI-SUONIO, Finnish Report, Q 198.
944 Art. 1393 para. 1 French Civil Code. See FERRAND/BRAAT, French Report, Q 199.
945 § 1408 para. 1 German Civil Code. See DETHLOFF/MARTINY, German Report, Q 191.
946 See KOUTSOURADIS/KOTRONIS/HATZANTONIS, Greek Report, Q 191.
947 Art. 3.102 Lithuanian Civil Code. See MIKELENAS, Lithuanian Report, Q 191.
948 Art. 1237 para. 2 Maltese Civil Code. See FARRUGIA, Maltese Report, Q 191.
949 Art. 1:114 Dutch Civil Code. See BOELE-WOELKI/SCHONEWILLE/SCHRAMA, Dutch Report, Q 191.
950 Ch. 9 Norwegian Marriage Act. See SVERDRUP Norwegian Report, Q 191 and Q 193.
951 See MĄCZYŃSKI, Polish Report, Q 191.
952 Art. 1698 Portuguese Civil Code. See DE OLIVEIRA/MARTINS/VÍTOR, Portuguese Report, Q 191.
953 Art. 42 Russian Family Code. See ANTOKOLSKAIA, Russian Report, Q 191, 199.
954 Art. 1325, 1326 Spanish Civil Code. See GONZÁLEZ BEILFUSS, Spanish Report, Q 191.
955 See JÄNTERÄ-JAREBORG/BRATTSTRÖM/WALLENG, Swedish Report, Q 191.
956 Art. 182 Swiss Civil Code. See SCHWENZER/BOCK, Swiss Report, Q 191.
957 See PINTENS/ALLAERTS/SEYNS/PIGNOLET, Belgian Report, Q 191, 201.
958 See FERRAND/BRAAT, French Report, Q 191.
959 § 1408 para. 1 German Civil Code. See DETHLOFF/MARTINY, German Report, Q 191.
960 Art. 1:121 para. 1 Dutch Civil Code. See BOELE-WOELKI/SCHONEWILLE/SCHRAMA, Dutch Report, Q 191.
961 Art. 42 para. 2 Russian Family Code.
962 See PATTI/CARICATO/IRTI/IANNICELLI/SERRA/DI STEFANO/PETÖ/BORTOLU, Italian Report, Q 191.
963 See HAŤAPKA, Slovakian Report, Q 191.

In common law jurisdictions pre-nuptial agreements are permitted, but they are not strictly binding (ENGLAND AND WALES[964] and IRELAND[965]). However, they may have an effect as they will be taken into account as one of the circumstances of the case on divorce. In SCOTLAND such an agreement is binding.[966]

Post-nuptial property agreements

In the majority of jurisdictions surveyed the spouses may make a post-nuptial agreement (e.g. AUSTRIA,[967] BELGIUM,[968] DENMARK,[969] FRANCE,[970] GERMANY,[971] GREECE,[972] ITALY,[973] HUNGARY,[974] LITHUANIA,[975] MALTA,[976] THE NETHERLANDS,[977] NORWAY,[978] RUSSIA,[979] SLOVAKIA,[980] SPAIN,[981] SCOTLAND[982] and SWITZERLAND[983]). However, PORTUGAL does not allow such an agreement and follows instead the principle of immutability of property regimes.[984]

In GERMANY,[985] spouses are permitted to make a post-nuptial agreement revoking or changing their property regime. The requirements and effects of a post-nuptial agreement do not deviate from those of pre-nuptial agreements.

964 See BARLOW, English Report, Q 191. But see now *Granatino* v. *Radmacher (formerly Granatino)*, [2010] UKSC 42, [2011] 1 AC 534 and LOWE, "Prenuptial agreements. The Developing English Position", in: DECLERCK/HELMS/SCHERPE/SENAEVE/VERBEKE (eds.), *Confronting the Frontiers of Family and Succession Law, Liber Amicorum Walter Pintens*, 2012, pp. 867–885.

965 See SHANNON, Irish Report, Q 191.

966 See MAIR, SCOTTISH REPORT, Q 191.

967 § 1217 Austrian Civil Code. See ROTH, Austrian Report, Q 192.

968 See PINTENS/ALLAERTS/SEYNS/PIGNOLET, Belgian Report, Q 192.

969 § 28 Danish Act on the Legal Effects of Marriage. See LUND-ANDERSEN/MAGNUSSEN, Danish Report, Q 192.

970 Art. 1393 para. 1 French Civil Code. See FERRAND/BRAAT, French Report, Q 199.

971 § 1408 para. 1 German Civil Code. See DETHLOFF/MARTINY, German Report, Q 192.

972 See KOUTSOURADIS/KOTRONIS/HATZANTONIS, Greek Report, Q 192.

973 See PATTI/CARICATO/IRTI/IANNICELLI/SERRA/DI STEFANO/PETÖ/BORTOLU, Italian Report, Q 192.

974 § 27 para. 2 Hungarian Family Act. See WEISS/SZEIBERT, Hungarian Report, Q 192.

975 Art. 3.104 Lithuanian Civil Code. See MIKELENAS, Lithuanian Report, Q 192.

976 Art. 1237 para. 2 Maltese Civil Code. See FARRUGIA, Maltese Report, Q 192.

977 Art. 93 Dutch Civil Code. See BOELE-WOELKI/SCHONEWILLE/SCHRAMA, Dutch Report, Q 192.

978 See SVERDRUP, Norwegian Report, Q 192.

979 Art. 42 Russian Family Code. See ANTOKOLSKAIA, Russian Report, Q 192, 199.

980 Art. 143a para. 1 Slovak Civil Code. See HAŤAPKA, Slovakian Report, Q 192.

981 See GONZÁLEZ BEILFUSS, Spanish Report, Q 192.

982 See MAIR, SCOTTISH REPORT, Q 192.

983 Art. 181 Swiss Civil Code. See SCHWENZER/BOCK, Swiss Report, Q 192.

984 Art. 1714 Portuguese Civil Code. See DE OLIVEIRA/MARTINS/VÍTOR, Portuguese Report, Q 192.

985 § 1408 para. 1 German Civil Code.

In FRANCE,[986] spouses do not have complete freedom to modify their matrimonial property regime during the marriage by simple agreement. Several requirements must be fulfilled. FRENCH law knows a form of slightly controlled mutability.[987] A modification is only possible after two years of application of a matrimonial property regime. Additionally, the amendment (or entire change) must be made in the interest of the family.[988] The amendment or entire change should also not be fraudulent against the rights of third parties, especially creditors.

In common law jurisdictions spouses are permitted to make a post-nuptial agreement regulating or changing their property relationship, providing it does not restrict the right to apply to the court. It is not necessarily strictly binding as it cannot oust the jurisdiction of the court (ENGLAND AND WALES[989] and IRELAND[990]). In SCOTLAND,[991] such an agreement is binding.

Separation agreement

In some of the jurisdictions surveyed a distinction is drawn between post-nuptial agreements and separation agreements. A separation agreement is permissible under IRISH law and is governed by contract law.[992] In fact, an Irish divorce court is directed to have regard to a separation agreement on the granting of ancillary orders. Separation agreements, more commonly labelled as agreements preceding a divorce, are also recognized under Nordic law (e.g. SWEDEN[993]). However, spouses can only make such an agreement if a divorce is envisaged in the near future. In such an agreement the spouses may, for example, agree on the future allocation of property, deductions of debts, evaluation of property, etc.

Restrictions

Despite their general autonomy, spouses' freedom is often restricted. For instance, the choice of certain matrimonial property regimes is not possible where the spouses have children (PORTUGAL[994]) or where one of the spouses is

[986] Art. 1396 para. 3 French Civil Code. See FERRAND/BRAAT, French Report, Q 192.
[987] Art. 1397 French Civil Code. See FERRAND/BRAAT, French Report, Q 192.
[988] Art. 1397 para. 1 French Civil Code. See FERRAND/BRAAT, French Report, Q 192.
[989] S. 34 English Matrimonial Causes Act 1973. See BARLOW, English Report, Q 192.
[990] See SHANNON, Irish Report, Q 191.
[991] See MAIR, SCOTTISH REPORT, Q 192.
[992] See SHANNON, Irish Report, Q 191.
[993] Ch. 9 § 13 Swedish Marriage Code. See JÄNTERÄ-JAREBORG/BRATTSTRÖM/WALLENG, Swedish Report, Q 192.
[994] Art. 1699 para. 2 Portuguese Civil Code. See DE OLIVEIRA/MARTINS/VÍTOR, Portuguese Report, Q 198.

over sixty years of age (PORTUGAL[995]). The freedom of the parties is also curtailed by so-called mandatory rules, that is a rule from which the parties cannot deviate. Such restrictions exist particularly with respect to the rules on the regime primaire but, depending on the single matrimonial property regime, also to the patrimonial regime as such. If spouses are permitted to modify through pre- and/or post-nuptial agreements a statutory regime or create their own regime, those modifications can be made to several aspects. However, there are some jurisdictions which do not allow modifications (for example, POLAND[996]). If modifications are allowed the type and the extent of modifications often depend on the single matrimonial property regime.

Categories of assets

In a *community of property regime* there are generally several *categories of assets*: common property and one or even two categories of personal property. In some legal systems it is not possible to make modifications regarding the categories of assets (LITHUANIA[997]). However, in many other jurisdictions the spouses may modify the assets or the categories of assets that belong to the common property (e.g. AUSTRIA,[998] BELGIUM,[999] CZECH REPUBLIC,[1000] FRANCE,[1001] GERMANY,[1002] GREECE,[1003] HUNGARY,[1004] RUSSIA,[1005] SLOVAKIA[1006] and SWITZERLAND[1007]). Particularly under a community of property regime the parties may extend the assets which fall into the community property (SWITZERLAND[1008]) or stipulate that property personal by nature falls into the community (FRANCE[1009] and SPAIN[1010]). Providing for the opposite is also possible. The spouses may, by a marital property agreement, restrict community of property to the gains accrued during marriage (SWITZERLAND[1011]). By agreement, the spouses may also exclude from the community of property specific assets or types of assets, such

995 Art. 1720 para. 1 lit. b Portuguese Civil Code. See DE OLIVEIRA/MARTINS/VÍTOR, Portuguese Report, Q 198.
996 See MĄCZYŃSKI, Polish Report, Q 199.
997 See MIKELENAS, Lithuanian Report, Q 199.
998 § 1235 Austrian Civil Code. See ROTH, Austrian Report, Q 199.
999 See PINTENS/ALLAERTS/SEYNS/PIGNOLET, Belgian Report, Q 199.
1000 Art. 143a para. 1 Czech Civil Code.
1001 See FERRAND/BRAAT, French Report, Q 199.
1002 § 1418 para. 2 Nr. 1 German Civil Code. See DETHLOFF/MARTINY, German Report, Q 199.
1003 See KOUTSOURADIS/KOTRONIS/HATZANTONIS, Greek Report, Q 199.
1004 See WEISS/SZEIBERT, Hungarian Report, Q 191, 199.
1005 See ANTOKOLSKAIA, Russian Report, Q 199.
1006 Art. 143a para. 1 Slovak Civil Code. See HAŤAPKA, Slovakian Report, Q 199.
1007 Art. 223–224 Swiss Civil Code. See SCHWENZER/BOCK, Swiss Report, Q 199.
1008 See SCHWENZER/BOCK, Swiss Report, Q 199.
1009 See FERRAND/BRAAT, French Report, Q 199.
1010 Art. 1355 Spanish Civil Code. See GONZÁLEZ BEILFUSS, Spanish Report, Q 199.
1011 Art. 223 para. 1 Swiss Civil Code. See SCHWENZER/BOCK, Swiss Report, Q 199.

as land, or assets used to practise a profession or run a business (SPAIN[1012] and SWITZERLAND[1013]).

There are also, however, some restrictions against reducing community property. Whereas in some legal systems it is possible to exclude a spouse's income from work from the community (SWITZERLAND[1014]), in others this is not permitted (BELGIUM[1015]). In THE NETHERLANDS a spouse cannot be made responsible for a larger share of the liabilities than that spouse shares in the community of property.[1016]

The issue of relevant assets also arises in the *participation in acquisition (community of accrued gains)* regimes. There are systems where basically all assets can give rise to an equalisation claim (e.g. GERMANY[1017]) while others follow a more restricted approach. In SWITZERLAND,[1018] where a category of separate property exists, the spouses may designate business assets that would otherwise belong to the marital property as separate property. Conversely, separate property may also be classified as marital property. The spouses may assign revenue generated from separate property to the separate property.[1019] It can also be agreed that certain assets, for example a company, may not be equalised at all (GERMANY[1020]).

Under the *deferred community of property regimes* the spouses' property is generally marital property, but there may be separate property as well because, for example, the spouses have agreed in the form of a marital property agreement that all or certain assets shall be the owner spouse's separate property. In the jurisdictions with such a property regime the spouses may also modify categories of assets and restrict participation.

Modifications to the administration of assets

It has become a basic principle of matrimonial property law for both spouses to have within the frame of the respective property regime, the power of

---

1012 See GONZÁLEZ BEILFUSS, Spanish Report, Q 199.

1013 Art. 224 para. 1 Swiss Civil Code. See SCHWENZER/BOCK, Swiss Report, Q 199.

1014 Art. 224 para. 1 Swiss Civil Code. See SCHWENZER/BOCK, Swiss Report, Q 199.

1015 See PINTENS/ALLAERTS/SEYNS/PIGNOLET, Belgian Report, Q 199.

1016 Art. 1:121 para. 2 Dutch Civil Code. See BOELE-WOELKI/SCHONEWILLE/SCHRAMA, Dutch Report, Q 199.

1017 § 1323 ff. German Civil Code. See DETHLOFF/MARTINY, German Report, Q 199.

1018 Art. 199 para. 1 Swiss Civil Code. See SCHWENZER/BOCK, Swiss Report, Q 199.

1019 Art. 199 para. 2 Swiss Civil Code. See SCHWENZER/BOCK, Swiss Report, Q 199.

1020 § 1408 para. 1 German Civil Code. See DETHLOFF/MARTINY, German Report, Q 89, 199.

disposal. In MALTA[1021] and PORTUGAL,[1022] it is expressely stated that it is not lawful for the future spouses to make an agreement that one of them is the head of the family. However, the spouses can make *modifications* to the *administration* of assets (for example, AUSTRIA,[1023] GERMANY,[1024] GREECE,[1025] LITHUANIA,[1026] THE NETHERLANDS,[1027] SCOTLAND,[1028] SLOVAKIA[1029] and SPAIN[1030]).

Spouses are free to mandate each other with the administration of the assets by an ordinary contract irrespective of the applicable property regime (for example GERMANY,[1031] PORTUGAL[1032] and SWITZERLAND[1033]). Such a contract is not considered to be a marital property agreement but one which is governed by the general provisions on mandate (e.g. GERMANY[1034] and SWITZERLAND[1035]).

In FRANCE,[1036] the spouses can modify the default administration of assets rules of community. They may agree to jointly administer the community. In such a case, the instruments of disposition and administration of common assets must be signed by both spouses, and they carry as a matter of law solidarity of obligations. Instruments preserving rights from extinction may be made separately by each spouse. However, it is also argued that an agreement that the community property be administered by only one of the spouses contravenes the principle of equality of the spouses and is not accepted (RUSSIA[1037]). In other jurisdictions this question is disputed (SPAIN[1038]). In some jurisdictions modifications of the rules about administration of the couple's assets cannot be subject of a pre-nuptial agreement (HUNGARY[1039] and PORTUGAL[1040]) or are restricted (BELGIUM[1041]).

1021 Art. 1238 Maltese Civil Code and FARRUGIA, Maltese Report, Q 199.
1022 Art. 1671 Portuguese Civil Code and Art. 36 para. 3 Portuguese Constitution.
1023 See ROTH, Austrian Report, Q 199.
1024 § 1421 German Civil Code. See DETHLOFF/MARTINY, German Report, Q 199.
1025 Art. 1399, 1404 Greek Civil Code. See KOUTSOURADIS/KOTRONIS/HATZANTONIS, Greek Report, Q 199.
1026 See MIKELENAS, Lithuanian Report, Q 199.
1027 See BOELE-WOELKI/SCHONEWILLE/SCHRAMA, Dutch Report, Q 199.
1028 See MAIR, SCOTTISH REPORT, Q 199.
1029 Art. 143a para. 1 Slovak Civil Code. See HAŤAPKA, Slovakian Report, Q 199.
1030 See GONZÁLEZ BEILFUSS, Spanish Report, Q 199.
1031 See DETHLOFF/MARTINY, German Report, Q 199.
1032 See DE OLIVEIRA/MARTINS/VÍTOR, Portuguese Report, Q 13, Q 36 and Q 141.
1033 See SCHWENZER/BOCK, Swiss Report, Q 199.
1034 See DETHLOFF/MARTINY, German Report, Q 199.
1035 Art. 195 para. 1 Swiss Civil Code. See SCHWENZER/BOCK, Swiss Report, Q 199.
1036 Art. 1503 French Civil Code. See FERRAND/BRAAT, French Report, Q 199.
1037 See ANTOKOLSKAIA, Russian Report, Q 199.
1038 See GONZÁLEZ BEILFUSS, Spanish Report, Q 199.
1039 See WEISS/SZEIBERT, Hungarian Report, Q 199.
1040 Art. 1699 para. 1 sub c Portuguese Civil Code. See DE OLIVEIRA/MARTINS/VÍTOR, Portuguese Report, Q 199.
1041 See PINTENS/ALLAERTS/SEYNS/PIGNOLET, Belgian Report, Q 199.

Under a *deferred community of property regime* contractual modifications in the administration fall outside what the parties may stipulate in the form of a pre- or post-nuptial matrimonial property agreement, since matrimonial property agreements under this regime normally only serve the function of labelling the assets of the spouses as belonging either to the marital property or separate property (DENMARK,[1042] FINLAND,[1043] NORWAY[1044] and SWEDEN[1045]). In NORWAY,[1046] however, modifications can be made to the administration of particular assets: The spouses may stipulate in a marital property agreement, that the restrictions on the spouses' right to dispose of the common residence shall not apply to assets which are separate property.

Modifications to the distribution of assets

At the end of the matrimonial property regime the issue of distribution arises. In general the spouses also can make *modifications to the distribution of assets* (for example AUSTRIA,[1047] NETHERLANDS,[1048] RUSSIA[1049] and SLOVAKIA[1050]). They may change the method of valuation and the respective quotas or fix some amounts of money to be paid. This applies also to the community of property (GREECE,[1051] SPAIN[1052] and SWITZERLAND[1053]).

Under the *participation in acquisition/community of accrued gains* regime, the general rule of a 50:50 division may be modified (e.g. GERMANY[1054] and SWITZERLAND[1055]). However, there are also restrictions. For example, such agreements may not adversely affect the inheritance rights of children who are not the spouses' common children or their descendents (SWITZERLAND[1056]). In the system of separation of property with distribution by the competent authority, such as in SCOTLAND,[1057] the parties may agree on the division of property on divorce by means of a Minute of Agreement. This can only be set

1042 See LUND-ANDERSEN/MAGNUSSEN, Danish Report, Q 199.
1043 See KURKI-SUONIO, Finnish Report, Q 199.
1044 See SVERDRUP, Norwegian Report, Q 199.
1045 See JÄNTERÄ-JAREBORG/BRATTSTRÖM/WALLENG, Swedish Report, Q 199.
1046 § 32, 33 and 37 Marriage Act. See SVERDRUP Norwegian Report, Q 199.
1047 See ROTH, Austrian Report, Q 199.
1048 Art. 1:121 Dutch Civil Code. See BOELE-WOELKI/SCHONEWILLE/SCHRAMA, Dutch Report, Q 199.
1049 See ANTOKOLSKAIA, Russian Report, Q 199.
1050 See HAŤAPKA, Slovakian Report, Q 199.
1051 See KOUTSOURADIS/KOTRONIS/HATZANTONIS, Greek Report, Q 199.
1052 Art. 1315, 1325 Spanish Civil Code. See GONZÁLEZ BEILFUSS, Spanish Report, Q 199.
1053 Art. 241, 242 Swiss Civil Code. See SCHWENZER/BOCK, Swiss Report, Q 199.
1054 See DETHLOFF/MARTINY, German Report, Q 199.
1055 Art. 216 para. 1 Swiss Civil Code. See SCHWENZER/BOCK, Swiss Report, Q 199.
1056 Art. 216 para. 2 Swiss Civil Code. See SCHWENZER/BOCK, Swiss Report, Q 199.
1057 See MAIR, SCOTTISH REPORT, Q 198.

aside by the court if it can be shown to have been unfair at the time of entering into the agreement.

Issues of distribution also arise in a *deferred community of property regime*. In DENMARK,[1058] FINLAND,[1059] NORWAY[1060] and SWEDEN,[1061] the spouses may totally exclude the participation (the *marital right*) in the property of the other spouse in the form of a marital property agreement. The spouses may, alternatively agree that certain assets may be exempted from the equal division. In DENMARK,[1062] a marital property agreement may also stipulate that a certain fixed portion of the spouses' or a spouse's property shall be exempted. In SWEDEN,[1063] at the moment of property division the spouses may agree on unequal shares, for example, 60% of the value of the marital property is allocated to one spouse and 40% to the other spouse. Such an agreement cannot, however, be made in the form of a marital property agreement in advance of the property division. In DENMARK,[1064] FINLAND[1065] and NORWAY,[1066] it is possible to limit the effects of a marital property agreement, excluding participation, to situations where the marriage ends in divorce. In contrast, in SWEDEN,[1067] the competent authority has refused to allow registration of such agreements.

Ground of dissolution of the marriage

A matrimonial property regime generally ends with the death of one of the spouses or with a divorce. The spouses may take this in to account in their agreement and their stipulations [modifications] may depend upon the *ground of dissolution of the marriage* (for example, AUSTRIA,[1068] FINLAND,[1069] THE NETHERLANDS,[1070] NORWAY,[1071] PORTUGAL,[1072] SCOTLAND[1073] and

1058 § 28 Danish Act on the Legal Effects of Marriage and LUND-ANDERSEN/MAGNUSSEN, Danish Report, Q 198.
1059 § 41 Finnish Marriage Act. See KURKI-SUONIO, Finnish Report, Q 198.
1060 § 42–43 Norwegian Marriage Act. See SVERDRUP, Norwegian Report, Q 198.
1061 Ch. 7 § 3 para. 1 Swedish Marriage Code. See JÄNTERÄ-JAREBORG/BRATTSTRÖM/WALLENG, Swedish Report, Q 192 and Q 198.
1062 See LUND-ANDERSEN/MAGNUSSEN, Danish Report, Q 199.
1063 See JÄNTERÄ-JAREBORG/BRATTSTRÖM/WALLENG, Swedish Report, Q 199.
1064 See LUND-ANDERSEN/MAGNUSSEN, Danish Report, Q 199.
1065 See judgment of the Finnish Supreme Court KKO 2000:100 and KURKI-SUONIO, Finnish Report, Q 199.
1066 § 42 para. 2 Norwegian Marriage Act. See SVERDRUP, Norwegian Report, Q 199.
1067 See JÄNTERÄ-JAREBORG/BRATTSTRÖM/WALLENG, Swedish Report, Q 199.
1068 See ROTH, Austrian Report, Q 199.
1069 See KURKI-SUONIO, Finnish Report, Q 198, 199.
1070 Art. 121 Dutch Civil Code. See BOELE-WOELKI/SCHONEWILLE/SCHRAMA, Dutch Report, Q 199.
1071 See SVERDRUP, Norwegian Report, Q 198.
1072 See DE OLIVEIRA/MARTINS/VÍTOR, Portuguese Report, Q 56, Q 160 and Q 199 d.
1073 See MAIR, Scottish Report, Q 199.

SWITZERLAND[1074]). Different forms of dissolution may lead to different legal consequences. In other jurisdictions this possibility is denied (GREECE,[1075] HUNGARY,[1076] RUSSIA[1077] and SLOVAKIA[1078]). Sometimes, there is a restriction that agreements varying the statutory participation in acquisitions are valid only if the marital property agreement expressly so provides (SWITZERLAND[1079]).

Under a *deferred community of property regime* the question of modifications also arises. SWEDISH law[1080] does not permit marital property contracts in which spouses stipulate that the classification of the assets in a future property division as marital property or separate property will depend upon the ground of dissolution of the marriage (for example, that property shall be marital property when property division is occasioned by the death of a spouse, but separate property in case of divorce). In DENMARK,[1081] NORWAY[1082] and FINLAND,[1083] however, the marital property agreement for separate property may be limited so as only to be effective upon the division of matrimonial property in both spouses' lifetime (divorce separate property).[1084]

Where the marriage is dissolved by death special modifications are also allowed. In DENMARK,[1085] the marital property agreement may provide that total separation property can only be granted if one of the spouses dies, to the surviving spouse or to his heirs. Similar provisions exist in NORWAY.[1086] Under SWEDISH law,[1087] the surviving spouse has the right, ex lege, to request that no division or only partial division of the spouses' marital property shall take place; this option is of relevance in particular in those situations where the surviving spouse owns most of the spouses' marital property. This result is also possible to achieve by agreement in NORWAY.[1088]

1074 See SCHWENZER/BOCK, Swiss Report, Q 199.
1075 See KOUTSOURADIS/KOTRONIS/HATZANTONIS, Greek Report, Q 199.
1076 See WEISS/SZEIBERT, Hungarian Report, Q 199.
1077 See ANTOKOLSKAIA, Russian Report, Q 199.
1078 See HAŤAPKA, Slovakian Report, Q 199.
1079 Art. 217 Swiss Civil Code. See SCHWENZER/BOCK, Swiss Report, Q 199.
1080 Ch. 12 § 2 Swedish Marriage Code. See JÄNTERÄ-JAREBORG/BRATTSTRÖM/WALLENG, Swedish Report, Q 199.
1081 See LUND-ANDERSEN/MAGNUSSEN, Danish Report, Q 198 and 199.
1082 §§ 42–43 Norwegian Marriage Act. See SVERDRUP, Norwegian Report, Q 198.
1083 See Finnish Supreme Court Decision KKO/HD 2000:100. See KURKI-SUONIO, Finnish Report, Q 198 and Q 199.
1084 See LUND-ANDERSEN/MAGNUSSEN, Danish Report, Q 198 and 199.
1085 § 28 para. 1 no. 2 Danish Act on the Legal Effects of Marriage. See LUND-ANDERSEN/MAGNUSSEN, Danish Report, Q 198 and 199.
1086 See SVERDRUP Norwegian Report, Q 198 and Q 199.
1087 Ch. 12 § 2 Swedish Marriage Code. See JÄNTERÄ-JAREBORG/BRATTSTRÖM/WALLENG, Swedish Report, Q 199 and Q 128.
1088 See SVERDRUP, Norwegian Report, Q 198.

Change of matrimonial property regime

Where it is possible to change the statutory regime there are different legal approaches. In some jurisdictions the property regime itself may only be modified where the law explicitly so provides (e.g. SWITZERLAND[1089]). In other jurisdictions there is more contractual freedom (e.g. BELGIUM[1090]). The change has often to occur in the form of marital property agreement (e.g. AUSTRIA,[1091] BELGIUM,[1092] DENMARK,[1093] GERMANY,[1094] GREECE,[1095] ITALY,[1096] LITHUANIA,[1097] MALTA,[1098] THE NETHERLANDS,[1099] NORWAY,[1100] RUSSIA,[1101] SLOVAKIA,[1102] SPAIN[1103] and SWITZERLAND[1104]). In only a few jurisdictions does the change have to be authorized by the competent authority in certain circumstances (FRANCE[1105]). The purpose of such a restriction is to protect the interests of the children of one or both of the spouses and of creditors.

COMMENT

1. Principle 4:10 allows spouses to choose a matrimonial property regime and recognises pre-marital and post-marital property agreements. It reflects the common core of the jurisdictions surveyed that permit marital property agreements to be made.

2. According to Principle 4:10 spouses are entitled to choose a property regime for all their property. They may restrict their choice of a property regime to a certain part of their assets, for example immovable property or chattels. By a marital property agreement, the spouses may also exclude from the community of acquisitions/participation in acquisitions, specific assets or types of assets,

1089 Art. 182 para. 2 Swiss Civil Code. See SCHWENZER/BOCK, Swiss Report, Q 198.
1090 See PINTENS/ALLAERTS/SEYNS/PIGNOLET, Belgian Report, Q 198.
1091 § 1217 Austrian Civil Code. See ROTH, Austrian Report, Q 192.
1092 See PINTENS/ALLAERTS/SEYNS/PIGNOLET, Belgian Report, Q 192.
1093 § 28 Danish Act on the Legal Effects of Marriage. See LUND-ANDERSEN/MAGNUSSEN, Danish Report, Q 192.
1094 § 1408 para. 1 German Civil Code. See DETHLOFF/MARTINY, German Report, Q 192.
1095 See KOUTSOURADIS/KOTRONIS/HATZANTONIS, Greek Report, Q 192.
1096 See PATTI/CARICATO/IRTI/IANNICELLI/SERRA/DI STEFANO/PETÖ/BORTOLU, Italian Report, Q 192.
1097 Art. 3.104 Lithuanian Civil Code. See MIKELENAS, Lithuanian Report, Q 192.
1098 Art. 1237 para. 2 Maltese Civil Code. See FARRUGIA, Maltese Report, Q 192.
1099 Ar. 93 Dutch Civil Code. See BOELE-WOELKI/SCHONEWILLE/SCHRAMA, Dutch Report, Q 192.
1100 See SVERDRUP, Norwegian Report, Q 192.
1101 Art. 42 Russian Family Code. See ANTOKOLSKAIA, Russian Report, Q 192, 199.
1102 Art. 143a para. 1 Slovak Civil Code. See HAŤAPKA, Slovakian Report, Q 192.
1103 See GONZÁLEZ BEILFUSS, Spanish Report, Q 192.
1104 Art. 181 Swiss Civil Code. See SCHWENZER/BOCK, Swiss Report, Q 192.
1105 Art. 1397 French Civil Code. See FERRAND/BRAAT, French Report, Q 199.

such as land, a spouse's income from work or assets used to practise a profession or run a business. Such special property may then be agreed to be "non-marital" (separate) property. There may be legitimate family or business interests for making such an agreement.

3. The spouses may by a marital property agreement restrict their matrimonial regime to a limited period of time.

4. In all cases, the choice outlined in the Principles must be made by a marital property agreement. Principle 4:10 establishes the concept of a marital property agreement. Some important details are dealt with in other Principles: Form requirements (Principle 4:11), disclosure (Principle 4:12), obligations of the notary or other persons with comparable functions (Principle 4:13), effects as against third parties (Principle 4:14) and exceptional hardship (Principle 4:15). Principles 4:29 and 4:55 deal specifically with agreements on distribution.

5. An agreement between the spouses or prospective spouses may be concluded at any time. In other words, no fundamental distinction is drawn between pre-nuptial and post-nuptial agreements.

6. In a marital property agreement made before the marriage in the form of a pre-nuptial agreement the prospective spouses may choose their matrimonial property regime. This is mainly appropriate if there is considerable property, there are assets used for an economic or professional purpose and/or if there have been several marital relationships and there are children from former relationships. Sometimes coordination with company law and/or testamentary dispositions is also advisable.

7. The matrimonial property regimes that may be chosen under this Principle are participation in acquisitions or community of acquisitions. It is left to national law to determine whether other property regimes may exist and be chosen.

8. A change from one regime to another is possible. According to Principle 4:10(2) the spouses may change their matrimonial property regime for another regime during the marriage. This change must made by a marital property agreement in accordance with Principles 4:11 and 4:12.

9. The second basic rule of Principle 4:10(2) is that the spouses are entitled to modify a property regime which has been chosen or is the default regime. The spouses should be given sufficient freedom to shape the property regime according to their situation and needs. The modifications must also be made by a marital property agreement.

10. Where no choice of a matrimonial property regime has been made, the rules of the default regime apply. However, if a choice is subsequently exercised in accordance with Principles 4:11 and 4:12 there will be a consequential change of the matrimonial property regime.

Principle 4:11 Form requirements
Marital property agreements should be drawn up by a notary or other legal professional with comparable functions, be dated and should be signed by both spouses.

Principe 4:11 Conditions de forme
Les conventions matrimoniales portant sur les relations patrimoniales entre époux doivent être dressées par un notaire ou un autre professionnel du droit exerçant des fonctions comparables, être datées et doivent signées par chaque époux.

Prinzip 4:11 Formerfordernisse
Ehegüterrechtliche Vereinbarungen sind von einem Notar oder einer anderen rechtskundigen Person mit vergleichbaren Funktionen auszufertigen, zu datieren und von beiden Ehegatten zu unterzeichnen.

INTERNATIONAL INSTRUMENTS

The *Hague Convention on the law applicable to matrimonial property regimes of 14 March 1978* is of broad relevance in as much as Articles 12 and 13 provide respectively that as a minimum requirement, marriage contracts and designations of applicable law contained in such contracts must be "in writing, dated and signed by the spouses." A similar position is adopted in the *Proposal for a Council Regulation on jurisdiction, applicable law and the recognition and enforcement of decisions in matters of matrimonial property regimes* (COM (2011) 126/2), Article 20 of which states that while the form of a marriage contract shall be that prescribed by the law applicable to the matrimonial property regime or by the law of the State where the contract is drawn up, it "must at least be set out in a document dated and signed by both spouses."

The *Convention between Denmark, Finland, Iceland, Norway and Sweden on Issues of Private International Law concerning Marriage, Adoption and Guardianship*, as revised in 2006, is relevant to the extent that Article 4 requires marital property agreements to comply with the formalities set out either by the Contracting State whose law is applicable to the spouses' property relations or of the state where both or either of the spouses was a citizen.

COMPARATIVE OVERVIEW

Need for writing

In all the jurisdictions surveyed that permit marital property agreements to be made, such agreements have at least to be made in writing. In many, the requirement is that at any rate pre-marital property agreements have to be drawn up in a notarial deed (sometimes expressed as a public deed authorized by a notary) or at least drawn up in the presence of a notary: AUSTRIA,[1106] BELGIUM,[1107] CATALONIA,[1108] FRANCE,[1109] GERMANY,[1110] GREECE,[1111] ITALY,[1112] LITHUANIA,[1113] THE NETHERLANDS,[1114] POLAND,[1115] RUSSIA,[1116] SPAIN[1117] and SWITZERLAND.[1118] In HUNGARY,[1119] the agreement either has to be a public document or a private one signed by a lawyer. In PORTUGAL,[1120] the agreement must be made through an official of the Civil Registry Office or by a public deed. In MALTA,[1121] the agreement must be made by a public deed. A different position is taken in Nordic countries where notaries do not exist. In DENMARK,[1122] the marriage agreement must be written, signed by the parties and registered and a similar position applies in FINLAND[1123] and SWEDEN.[1124] In NORWAY,[1125] the agreement must be in writing, signed by the spouses in the presence of witnesses but it need not be registered to

1106 § 1a Austrian Notarial Deed Act, though notarial confirmation by appending the private document to the so-called covering instrument (*Mantelakt*) may be sufficient. See ROTH, Austrian Report, Q 193.

1107 Art. 1392 Belgian Civil Code. See PINTENS/ALLAERTS/SEYNS/PIGNOLET, Belgian Report, Q 193.

1108 Art. 17 para. 1 Catalan Family Code. See MARTÍN-CASALS/RIBOT, Catalan Report, Q 193.

1109 See FERRAND/BRAAT, French Report, Q 193.

1110 See § 1410 German Civil Code. See DETHLOFF/MARTINY, German Report, Q 193.

1111 See KOUTSOURADIS/KOTRONIS/HATZANTONIS, Greek Report, Q 193.

1112 In so far as marital property agreements are permissible, see PATTI/CARICATO/IRTI/IANNICELL/SERRA/DI STEFANO/PETÖ/BORTOLU, Italian Report, Q 191.

1113 See MIKELENAS, Lithuanian Report, Q 193.

1114 Art. 1:115 para. 1 Dutch Civil Code. See BOELE-WOELKI/SCHONEWILLE/SCHRAMA, Dutch Report, Q 193.

1115 See MĄCZYŃSKI, Polish Report, Q 193.

1116 See ANTOKOLSKAIA, Russian Report, Q 193.

1117 Art. 1327 and 1280 Spanish Civil Code. See GONZÁLEZ BEILFUSS, Spanish Report, Q 193.

1118 Art. 184 Swiss Civil Code. See SCHWENZER/BOCK, Swiss Report, Q 193.

1119 See WEISS/SZEIBERT, Hungarian Report, Q 193.

1120 Art. 1710 Portuguese Civil Code and Art. 189 para. 1 Portuguese Code of Civil Registry. See DE OLIVEIRA/MARTINS/VÍTOR, Portuguese Report, Q 193.

1121 See FARRUGIA, Maltese Report, Q 193.

1122 § 35 Danish Act on the Legal Effects of Marriage. See LUND-ANDERSEN/MAGNUSSEN, Danish Report, Q 193.

1123 § 42–46 and 66 of the Finnish Marriage Act. See KURKI -SUONIO, FINNISH REPORT, Q 193.

1124 Though there is no longer the requirement that the spouses' signatures have to be witnessed, see Ch. 7 § 3 para. 2 – 3 Swedish Marriage Code. See JÄNTERÄ-JAREBORG/BRATTSTRÖM/WALLENG, Swedish Report, Q 193.

1125 § 54 Norwegian Marriage Act. See SVERDRUP, Norwegian Report, Q 193.

be binding between the spouses. Similarly, in SCOTLAND[1126] the agreement (referred to as a Minute of Agreement) must be in writing but it need not be registered to be enforceable, though, if it is not, it is necessary to go to court to enforce it. In ENGLAND AND WALES, where pre-nuptial agreements are of relevance but are not binding,[1127] given the need for independent legal advice before agreements may be taken into account, such agreements will in practice have been drawn up by a lawyer. A similar position is likely to be taken by IRELAND.[1128]

Distinctions between pre-martial and post-marital property agreements

From the point of view of formalities, most of the jurisdictions referred to above make no distinction between pre-marital property agreements and post-marital property agreements (though in SLOVAKIA,[1129] where only post-marital property agreements are permitted, they must take the form of a notarial deed). In BELGIUM,[1130] however, the spouses can agree by notarial deed on modification to their matrimonial property regime. In SPAIN,[1131] modification of a previous agreement requires a note to be attached to the previous notarial deed indicating that the agreement has been modified. In FRANCE,[1132] notarial instruments embodying post-marital property agreements have in some circumstances to be submitted to the court of the spouses' domicile for approval. Similarly, in LITHUANIA,[1133] a marriage contract can only be amended with court leave. In MALTA[1134] too, post-marital property agreements have to be authorized by the competent court. A similar position formerly obtained in THE NETHERLANDS,[1135] but the court requirement has now been abandoned.[1136] Nevertheless divorce covenants must be in writing if the spouses agree therein to derogate from equal share distribution of the community property. In ENGLAND AND WALES,[1137] post-marital property agreements only become enforceable following confirmation by a court order.

1126 See MAIR, Scottish Report, Q 193. Although there is no requirement to register the agreement, if it is, the agreement can be enforced without reference to the court.

1127 See *Granatino* v. *Radmacher (formerly Granatino)*, [2010] UKSC 42, [2011] 1 AC 534.

1128 See SHANNON, Irish Report, Q 193.

1129 See HATÁPKA, Slovakian Report, Q 193 and Q 191.

1130 Art. 1394 Belgian Civil Code (as re-written in 2008). See PINTENS/ALLAERTS/SEYNS/PIGNOLET, Belgian Report, Q 193. The 2008 amendments have greatly simplified the rules on modification of marital property agreements by eliminating the need to distinguish large, medium and small modifications.

1131 Art. 1332 Spanish Civil Code. See GONZÁLEZ BEILFUSS, Spanish Report, Q 193.

1132 Art. 1397 French Civil Code, FERRAND/BRAAT, French Report, Q 193.

1133 Art. 3.103 Lithuanian Civil Code and MIKELENAS, Lithuanian Report, Q 193.

1134 See FARRUGIA, Maltese Report, Q 193.

1135 Art. 1:100 para. 1 Dutch Civil Code. See BOELE-WOELKI/SCHONEWILLE/SCHRAMA, Dutch Report, Q 193.

1136 Act of 18 April 2011, Staatsblad 2011, 205.

1137 See BARLOW, English Report, Q 193.

COMMENT

1. It is the clear common core that marital property agreements, whether made before or after marriage (Principle 4:11 makes no distinction between pre-marital property and post-marital property agreements), have to embodied in a formal agreement to be binding between the spouses. The formal requirement that such agreements have to be drawn up by a notary or other legal professional with comparable functions also reflects the clear common core, at any rate outside the Nordic jurisdictions. The rationale underlying this requirement is to ensure that the parties have independent advice before making such agreements, which is a stance further emphasised by Principle 4:13.

2. The general requirement, reflected by Principle 4:11, is that such agreements, which as a consequence of having to be drawn up by a notary or other legal professional with comparable functions will have to be in writing and must be dated and signed by the spouses.

3. To accommodate those jurisdictions where notaries, as such, are unknown, Principle 4:11 refers to 'other legal professional with comparable functions' by which is primarily meant, the legal practitioners involved in drafting or advising in the drafting of the marital property agreement.

4. It will be noted that Principle 4:11 does not require that the spouses' signatures be witnessed (jurisdictions take different stances on this requirement) nor does it require registration or court approval even for post-marital property agreements, as is the case in some jurisdictions. However, Principle 4:11 does not prevent national law from adding further requirements as is felt appropriate and in this way accommodates those jurisdictions that distinguish pre-marital and post-marital property agreements.

Principle 4:12 Disclosure
When entering into a marital property agreement the spouses should be under a mutual duty to disclose their assets and debts.

Principe 4:12 Révélation du patrimoine
Lorsque les époux concluent une convention matrimoniale, chacun d'eux est tenu de révéler à l'autre la composition de son patrimoine.

Prinzip 4:12 Offenlegung des Vermögens
Bei Abschluss einer ehegüterrechtlichen Vereinbarung unterliegen die Ehegatten einer gegenseitigen Verpflichtung ihre Vermögensgegenstände und Schulden offenzulegen.

INTERNATIONAL INSTRUMENTS

None of particular relevance.

COMPARATIVE OVERVIEW

Duty to disclose

In the overwhelming majority of jurisdictions that permit marital property agreements there is no duty upon the spouses to disclose of their assets and debts prior to the making of the agreement. This is the case in AUSTRIA,[1138] CATALONIA,[1139] DENMARK,[1140] FINLAND,[1141] FRANCE,[1142] GREECE,[1143] HUNGARY,[1144] ITALY,[1145] LITHUANIA,[1146] MALTA,[1147] NORWAY,[1148] POLAND,[1149]

1138 See ROTH, Austrian Report, Q 195.
1139 See MARTÍN-CASALS/RIBOT, Catalan Report, Q 195.
1140 See LUND-ANDERSEN/MAGNUSSEN, Danish Report, Q 195.
1141 See KURKI–SUONIO, FINNISH REPORT, Q 195.
1142 See FERRAND/BRAAT, French Report, Q 193.
1143 See KOUTSOURADIS/KOTRONIS/HATZANTONIS, Greek Report, Q 195.
1144 See WEISS/SZEIBERT, Hungarian Report, Q 195.
1145 In so far as marital property agreements are permissible, ie when spouses opt in to an alternative statutory matrimonial property regime, see PATTI/CARICATO/IRTI/IANNICELL/SERRA/DI STEFANO/PETÖ/BORTOLU, Italian Report, Q 195.
1146 See MIKELENAS, Lithuanian Report, Q 195.
1147 See FARRUGIA, Maltese Report, Q 195.
1148 See SVERDRUP, Norwegian Report, Q 195.
1149 See MĄCZYŃSKI, Polish Report, Q 195.

PORTUGAL,[1150] RUSSIA,[1151] SLOVAKIA,[1152] SPAIN[1153] and SWEDEN.[1154] In THE NETHERLANDS,[1155] however, although post-marital property agreements no longer require court approval,[1156] it is still assumed that the spouses remain under a duty to disclose all their assets and debts. In BELGIUM,[1157] a distinction is also drawn between pre-marital property agreements, where there is no duty of disclosure, and post-marital property agreements where, if one spouse so requests, the agreement will be preceded by an inventory of all movable and immovable properties and all debts of the spouses. The inventory is obligatory, when the new regime implies the liquidation of the former one. Similarly, in SWITZERLAND[1158] each spouse may request the other's participation in the making of an inventory (in the form of a public deed). In GERMANY,[1159] while, strictly, there may be no general duty of disclosure, upon marriage there is, as between the spouses, a general duty of respect, out of which, there can be spelt out an entitlement to be informed about each other's property assets and debts and, hence a duty of disclosure when making post-marital property agreements.

In contrast to the above, there is a general duty of disclosure in IRELAND,[1160] while in SCOTLAND,[1161] lack of full disclosure can, in the context of divorce, be a ground for challenging the validity of marital property agreements, upon the basis that the agreement was not fair and reasonable at the time it was entered into. In ENGLAND AND WALES, full disclosure is normally required for pre-marital property agreements to be taken into account by the court,[1162] while in the case of post-marital property agreements, which require court approval to be binding, it is well established[1163] that the spouses owe a duty of full disclosure to the court.

1150 See DE OLIVEIRA/MARTINS/VITOR, Portuguese Report, Q 195.
1151 See ANTOKOLSKAIA, Russian Report, Q 195.
1152 In so far as marital property agreements are permissible, see HATÁPKA, Slovakian Report, Q 195.
1153 See GONZÁLEZ BEILFUSS, Spanish Report, Q 195.
1154 Where the duty to supply information under Ch 1 § 4 of the Swedish marriage is a moral one only, see JÄNTERÄ-JAREBORG/ BRATTSTRÖM/WALLENG, Swedish Report, Q 195.
1155 Art. 1:119 para. 1 Dutch Civil Code. See BOELE-WOELKI/SCHONEWILLE/SCHRAMA, Dutch Report, Q 195.
1156 Act of 18 April 2011, Staatsblad 2011, 205.
1157 Art. 1394 para. 2 Belgian Civil Code. See PINTENS/ALLAERTS/SEYNS/PIGNOLET, Belgian Report, Q 195.
1158 Art. 184 Swiss Civil Code. See SCHWENZER/BOCK, Swiss Report, Q 193.
1159 See DETHLOFF/MARTINY, German Report, Q 195.
1160 See SHANNON, Irish Report, Q 195.
1161 See MAIR, Scottish Report, Q 195. Although there is no requirement to register the agreement, if it is, the agreement can be enforced without reference to the court.
1162 Though there was not full disclosure in *Granatino v. Radmacher (formerly Granatino)*, [2010] UKSC 42, [2011] 1 AC 534.
1163 *Livesey (formerly Jenkins) v Jenkins* [1985] AC 424.

COMMENT

1. In providing that spouses should be under a general duty to disclose their assets and debts when making marital property agreements, Principle 4:12 does not adopt the common core. However, it follows from the general principle, Principle 4:8, by which spouses are under a mutual duty to inform each other about his or her assets and debts in so far as it is necessary to enable one spouse to exercise his or her rights, that there should be a mutual duty of disclosure when making marital property agreements during the marriage. Furthermore, given the increased incidence of cohabitation before marriage, it no longer makes sense to distinguish pre-marital property agreements from agreements made after marriage.

2. In line with the general policy of these Principles no distinction is drawn between pre-marital property agreements and post-marital property agreements.

3. Reflecting the fact that disclosure is not the common core, Principle 4:12 is silent on the effect of the consequences of non-disclosure, leaving that issue to be determined by national law. Suffice to say that in those jurisdictions where disclosure is required, agreements can be set aside for non-disclosure.

Principle 4:13 Obligations of a notary or other legal professional with comparable functions
The notary or other legal professional with comparable functions should
(a) give impartial advice to each spouse separately,
(b) ensure that each spouse understands the legal consequences of the marital property agreement, and
(c) ensure that both spouses freely consent to the agreement.

Principe 4:13 Obligations du notaire ou du professionnel du droit exerçant des fonctions comparables
Le notaire ou le professionnel du droit exerçant des fonctions comparables
(a) conseille chaque époux séparément, en toute impartialité,
(b) s'assure que chaque époux comprend les conséquences juridiques de la convention matrimoniale, et
(c) s'assure que le consentement des deux époux est libre.

Prinzip 4:13 Pflichten des Notars oder einer anderen rechtskundigen Person mit vergleichbaren Funktionen
Der Notar oder eine andere rechtskundige Person mit vergleichbaren Funktionen soll
(a) jeden Ehegatten unparteiisch und getrennt beraten,
(b) sicherstellen, dass jeder Ehegatte die rechtlichen Folgen der ehegüterrechtlichen Vereinbarung versteht, und
(c) sicherstellen, dass beide Ehegatten die Vereinbarung freiwillig treffen.

INTERNATIONAL INSTRUMENTS

None of particular relevance.

COMPARATIVE OVERVIEW

Notaries' duties

The common broad position among jurisdictions where marital property agreements are made by notarial deed is that the notary must be satisfied that the spouses understand the nature and consequences of their agreement and freely consent to it. However, while breach of that duty might render the notary liable in damages and/or to professional disciplinary action, the agreement itself is not normally thereby invalidated. There are, however, detailed differences between the jurisdictions.

In AUSTRIA,[1164] the notary is obliged to examine each spouse's personal ability and entitlement at the time of concluding the contract; to instruct them of the purposes and consequences of it, and be convinced that the deed represents the parties' intentions. However, the parties can waive this duty because, for example, they have previously received legal advice or that they themselves are familiar with the law. Lack of instruction does not affect the validity of the marriage contract but the notary can be liable in damages.[1165] In BELGIUM,[1166] the notary has to inform the parties entirely and objectively. If the terms of the agreement are unbalanced or there is a threat of a conflict of interests, the notary must indicate that each party is able to seek the assistance of a lawyer or a second notary. Failure to discharge this duty can render the notary liable in damages. In CATALONIA,[1167] the public notary is under a duty to inform the parties of the meaning and scope of their agreement and to be satisfied that they freely agree to it. The notary is also under a duty to give specific legal assistance to the party that needs it more. Failure to meet this duty will render the notary liable to disciplinary action but there is nevertheless a rebuttable presumption that the agreement is valid and effective.[1168] In FRANCE,[1169] the notary has a duty to inform and advise the parties and failure to do so can result in professional liability. A similar position exists in PORTUGAL.[1170] In GERMANY,[1171] the notary must advise the parties about the legal scope of their agreement but must also ensure that the inexperienced spouse or one not conversant in such matters is not disadvantaged. Failure to discharge this duty renders the notary liable in damages but does not normally render the agreement invalid. In GREECE,[1172] the notary is under a general duty to advise the parties and ensure that that they freely consent to it. Failure to do so renders the notary liable to disciplinary action but does not invalidate the agreement.[1173] In THE NETHERLANDS,[1174] too, the civil notary has a duty to inform the parties about the contract and its consequences. Breach of this duty can render the notary both professionally liable to disciplinary action and to pay compensatory damages. There are similar

1164 See ROTH, Austrian Report, Q 196.
1165 § 52 Austrian Notarial Act.
1166 Art. 9 Belgian Law on the Notarial Profession. See PINTENS/ALLAERTS/SEYNS/PIGNOLET, Belgian Report, Q 196.
1167 Art. 147 Catalan Notary Regulations. See MARTÍN-CASALS/RIBOT, Catalan Report, Q 196.
1168 Art. 446 et seq Catalan Notary Regulations.
1169 See FERRAND/BRAAT, French Report, Q 196.
1170 Art. 4 para. 1 and Art. 61 Portuguese Code of the Notary and Art. 61 Portuguese Statute of the Notary. See DE OLIVEIRA/MARTINS/VÍTOR, Portuguese Report, Q 196.
1171 § 17 para. 1 German Notarial Recording Act. See DETHLOFF/MARTINY, German Report, Q 196.
1172 Art. 5 No 2 Law No.2830/2000. See KOUTSOURADIS/KOTRONIS/HATZANTONIS, Greek Report, Q 196.
1173 Art. 42 pp Law No.2830/2000.
1174 See BOELE-WOELKI/SCHONEWILLE/SCHRAMA, Dutch Report, Q 196.

duties of advice and of ensuring that the parties consent to the agreement in RUSSIA,[1175] SPAIN[1176] and SWITZERLAND.[1177]

In contrast to the above mentioned jurisdictions, in ITALY[1178] and SLOVAKIA,[1179] in so far as marital property agreements are permitted, the notary is not required to provide information to the parties. In LITHUANIA,[1180] breach of the duty to inform the parties of the context and consequences of their agreement can lead to the agreement's subsequent annulment. In MALTA[1181] too, failure to inform the parties about the content and consequences of the agreement can nullify the agreement.

Position where notaries are unknown or not involved

In other jurisdictions where notaries are either unknown or not used in relation to the making of marital property agreements, the general position is that where the parties seek legal advice, the legal advisor is obliged to inform the client of his or her legal position and of the effect and wisdom of making the agreement. This is essentially the position in ENGLAND AND WALES,[1182] SCOTLAND[1183] and IRELAND,[1184] where each spouse is advised to seek independent legal advice before making an agreement.

In DENMARK,[1185] FINLAND,[1186] NORWAY[1187] and SWEDEN,[1188] where there is no necessity to consult lawyers or notaries before making an agreement, some control over the form and content of the agreement lies with the registering competent authority, although that authority has no general obligation to inform the parties about the content of their agreement nor to advise them about its legal consequences.

1175 See ANTOKOLSKAIA, Russian Report, Q 196. Failure to discharge the duty can lead to the notary being liable in damages.

1176 Art. 147 Reglamento Notarial. See GONZÁLEZ BEILFUSS, Spanish Report, Q 196. Failure to discharge the duties can render the notary liable in damages but the agreement remains valid.

1177 See SCHWENZER/BOCK, Swiss Report, Q 196. Failure to discharge the duties can render the notary liable in damages but the agreement remains valid.

1178 See PATTI/CARICATO/IRTI/IANNICELL/SERRA/DI STEFANO/PETÖ/BORTOLU, Italian Report, Q 196.

1179 See HATÁPKA, Slovakian Report, Q 196.

1180 See MIKELENAS, Lithuanian Report, Q 196.

1181 See FARRUGIA, Maltese Report, Q 196.

1182 See BARLOW, English Report, Q 196.

1183 See MAIR, Scottish Report, Q 196.

1184 See SHANNON, Irish Report, Q 196.

1185 See LUND-ANDERSEN/MAGNUSSEN, Danish Report, Q 196.

1186 See KURKI -SUONIO, Finnish Report, Q 196.

1187 See SVERDRUP, Norwegian Report, Q 196.

1188 See JÄNTERÄ-JAREBORG/ BRATTSTRÖM/WALLENG, Swedish Report, Q 196.

COMMENT

1. Principle 4:13 reflects the clear common core that a notary or other legal professional with comparable functions (the meaning of which is discussed in Comment 3 to Principle 4:11) should explain to each spouse the applicable law and choices available so as to ensure that the spouses understand the legal consequences of their marital property agreement and that they freely consent to it. On grounds of practicality and costs the Principle stops short of requiring that each spouse be given independent advice by different notaries or legal professionals with comparable functions. However, it does not prevent national law from so providing.

2. In line with the general policy of these Principles no distinction is drawn between pre-marital property agreements and post-marital property agreements.

3. Principle 4:13 is silent on the effects of any breach of duty by a notary or comparable legal professional leaving that issue to be determined by national law. However, the common position is that such a breach renders the notary or comparable legal professional liable to disciplinary action and/or liable to pay compensatory damages, but that the agreement itself is not thereby invalidated.

Principle 4:14 Effects as against third parties
As against third parties marital property agreements are binding if at the time of making the transactions with a spouse

(a) such information is publically documented; or
(b) they knew of the relevant parts of the agreement.

Principe 4:14 Effets à l'égard des tiers
Les conventions matrimoniales portant sur les relations patrimoniales entre époux sont opposables aux tiers si, au moment de la conclusion d'une convention avec un époux,

(a) ces informations sont contenues dans un document public; ou
(b) les tiers avaient connaissance des clauses pertinentes de la convention matrimoniale.

Prinzip 4:14 Wirkungen gegenüber Dritten
Gegenüber Dritten wirken ehegüterrechtliche Vereinbarungen, wenn im Zeitpunkt des Abschlusses des Rechtsgeschäfts mit einem Ehegatten

(a) derartige Informationen öffentlich dokumentiert waren; oder
(b) sie die relevanten Teile der Vereinbarung kannten.

INTERNATIONAL INSTRUMENTS

The *Hague Convention on the law applicable to matrimonial property regimes of 14 March 1978* is of relevance in as much as it provides rules for the protection of third parties. Article 9 in particular provides that while the effects of the matrimonial property regime on legal relations between a spouse and a third party are governed by the law applicable to the regime in accordance with the Convention, States may nevertheless provide that the regime may not be relied upon by a spouse against a third party unless "(1) any requirements of publicity or registration specified by that law have been complied with, or (2) the legal relations between the spouse and the third party arose at a time when the third party either knew or should have known of the law applicable to the matrimonial property regime." Article 35 (2) of the *Proposal for a Council Regulation on jurisdiction, applicable law and the recognition and enforcement of decisions in matters of matrimonial property regimes* (COM (2011) 126/2) similarly states that "the law of a Member State may provide that the law applicable to the matrimonial property regime may not be relied upon by a spouse in dealings with a third party if one or other has their habitual residence in the territory of that Member State and the conditions of disclosure or registration provided for in the law of that State are not satisfied, unless the third party was aware of or ought to have been aware of the law applicable to the matrimonial property regime."

COMPARATIVE OVERVIEW

Although there are considerable differences between jurisdictions,[1189] in broad terms marital property agreements are generally only enforceable against third parties if they are contained in a publicly registered or recorded document, although in some jurisdictions it can be sufficient that the third party knows of the relevant part of the agreement when making the transaction.

Requiring registration

In DENMARK,[1190] marital property agreements must be registered with the competent authority to be binding between the spouses and on third parties. In NORWAY,[1191] an agreement whereby one spouse transfers property to the other spouse must be made not only in the form of a marital property agreement but also registered with the competent authority to become binding upon creditors; other marital property agreements do not require registration. In FINLAND,[1192] the marital agreement needs to be submitted to the local magistracy for registration before it becomes binding even between the spouses. Similarly in SWEDEN,[1193] marital property agreements must be registered at the civil registry to be binding both between the spouses and third parties. In all the Nordic jurisdictions, an agreement that must be registered takes effect as of the date when the application for registration was received by the competent authority. In GERMANY,[1194] to be binding upon third parties, the marital property agreement, or its subsequent modification, must be entered into the matrimonial property register which is kept by the local court. It is for the spouses to apply for registration. In the absence of registration, third parties will only be bound by an agreement if they were actually aware of it at the time making a contract with the spouses. In GREECE[1195] marital property agreements are only binding against third parties after they have been registered in a public register. Similarly, in LITHUANIA,[1196] marriage contracts and any subsequent amendments must normally be registered (in the register of marriage contracts) to be binding upon third parties, but such parties will also be bound if they knew of the contract and

1189 See generally MARTINY, "The Effects of Marital Property Agreements in Respect of Third Parties", in: DECLERCK/HELMS/SCHERPE/SENAEVE/VERBEKE (eds), *Confronting the Frontiers of Family and Succession Law, Liber Amicorum Walter Pintens*, 2012, pp. 903–927.

1190 See LUND-ANDERSEN/MAGNUSSEN, Danish Report, Q 194.

1191 § 55 para. 1 Norwegian Marriage Act and SVERDRUP, Norwegian Report, Q 194.

1192 § 42, 43, 44 and 66 of the Finnish Marriage Act. See KURKI –SUONIO, Finnish REPORT, Q 194.

1193 Ch 7 § 3 para. 2 – 3 and Ch 16 Swedish Marriage Code as amended from 1 October 2011. Until then, all marital property agreements needed to be registered at a district court.

1194 § 1412 para. 1 and para. 2 German Civil Code. See DETHLOFF/MARTINY, German Report, Q 194.

1195 See KOUTSOURADIS/KOTRONIS/HATZANTONIS, Greek Report, Q 192.

1196 Art. 3.103 Lithuanian Civil Code. See MIKELENAS, Lithuanian Report, Q 194.

its amendments at the time of the contract with the spouses. In MALTA,[1197] the notary has to register the agreement (whereupon it becomes public and accessible through the Public Registry) for it to be binding upon third parties. In THE NETHERLANDS,[1198] marital property agreements concerning the property relationship between the spouses are only effective against third parties if they have been registered in the Matrimonial Property Register.[1199] In PORTUGAL,[1200] to be binding upon third parties, pre-nuptial agreements need to be registered (registration is effected by their mention on the text of the marriage entry) as do subsequent amendments (achieved through an annotation of the marriage entry). In each case the agreement only becomes effective upon registration.

Distinguishing types of property

Some jurisdictions draw a distinction according to the type of property that the agreements concern or to the status of the spouses. In NORWAY,[1201]for example, while in general marriage agreements that transfer property from one spouse to another are only legally protected from the spouses' creditors if they are registered in the Register of Marriage Agreements, those that only transform deferred community to separate property and vice versa do not require registration. Moreover, agreements in which immovable property is transferred from one spouse to the other must be judicially registered by the registrar for judicial registration of title to real property.[1202] In SPAIN,[1203] agreements are only enforceable against third parties if they are recorded[1204] in the Civil Register (agreements take effect at the date of registration), unless the third party has actual knowledge of the agreement. However, if the agreement concerns immovable property, it must be recorded in the Property Register and where the spouses are business partners, the agreement also needs to recorded in the Commercial Register. Not dissimilarly, in CATALONIA,[1205] modifications to the matrimonial property regime, before or after the marriage, must generally be recorded in the Register of Births, Marriages and Deaths before they can become binding upon third parties. But in the case of immovable property, for example,

1197 Art. 1246 and 1247 Maltese Civil Code. See FARRUGIA, Maltese Report, Q 194.

1198 See BOELE-WOELKI/SCHONEWILLE/SCHRAMA, Dutch Report, Q 194.

1199 The Matrimonial Property Register is kept at the clerk's off in the district within whose jurisdiction the marriage is entered into, Art. 1:116 para. 1 Dutch Civil Code.

1200 Art. 1711 para. 1 Portuguese Civil Code and Art. 191 para. 1 Portuguese Code of Civil Registration (pre-nuptial agreements) and Art. 190 para. 1 and para. 2 Portuguese Code of Civil Registration (subsequent amendments). See DE OLIVEIRA/MARTINS/VÍTOR, Portuguese Report, Q 194.

1201 § 55 para. 1 Norwegian Marriage Act. See SVERDRUP, Norwegian Report, Q 194.

1202 § 55 para. 2 Norwegian Marriage Act.

1203 See GONZÁLEZ BEILFUSS, Spanish Report, Q 194.

1204 The Civil Register does not reproduce the whole agreement leaving third parties with a legitimate interest to seek further details from the notary.

1205 Art. 17 para. 2 Catalan Family Code. See MARTÍN-CASALS/RIBOT, Catalan Report, Q 194.

the agreement must also be registered in the Register of Property. In AUSTRIA,[1206] registration is only provided for by spouses of a business owner, whose company is registered in the company register. In such cases, each spouse can enter the marriage contract in the company register.

Distinguishing pre- and post-marital property agreements

Some jurisdictions also make some distinction between pre-marital and post-marital property agreements as well as the nature of the agreement. In BELGIUM,[1207] for example, pre-nuptial agreements have to be duly recorded in the marriage certificate to be binding upon third parties, unless such parties actually know of the agreement. Those agreements containing an immediate transfer of immovable property or of immovable property rights need also to be registered in the registers of the land and mortgage registry.[1208] If one of the spouses is a business partner, an extract of the agreement needs also to be registered in the register of commerce and therefore the notary is obliged to send the extract to the court registry at the Court of Commerce. So far as post-nuptial agreements are concerned, they need to be mentioned in the margin of the marriage certificate to be binding. Furthermore the notary is responsible for its publication in the Belgian Bulletin of Acts and Decrees. Publication is not, however, required in relation to the appointment of a surviving spouse as an heir. In FRANCE,[1209] in the case of pre-nuptial agreements, the system is for spouses to give a certificate of the agreement, drawn up by a notary, to the registrar at the time of the wedding. Having done so, that agreement binds third parties. Even if the registrar is not given the certificate, third parties are bound provided the spouses brought their agreement to the third party's attention at the time of the transaction between them. In the case of post-marital property agreements, third parties are bound three months after the modification has been added to the marriage certificate,[1210] or if the spouses mentioned the modification to the third party at the time of the transaction between them. In the case of agreements concerning immovable property, the land register may also need to be changed.

No registration requirement

A number of jurisdictions do not have a system of registration. SWITZERLAND,[1211] for example, abolished the need to register marital property agreements in 1998,

---

1206 § 36 Austrian Business Enterprise Code. See ROTH, Austrian Report, Q 194.

1207 Art. 76 and Art. 101 Belgian Civil Code (pre-nuptial agreements) and art. 106 (post-nuptial agreements). See PINTENS/ALLAERTS/SEYNS/PIGNOLET, Belgian Report, Q 194.

1208 Art. 1, 1e Belgian Law of Mortgages.

1209 See FERRAND/BRAAT, French Report, Q 194.

1210 Art. 1397 para. 6 French Civil Code.

1211 See SCHWENZER/BOCK, Swiss Report, Q 194.

it being sufficient that they are entered into by notarial deed and signed by both spouses. In both POLAND[1212] and SLOVAKIA,[1213] agreements are only binding upon third parties if they knew of them at the time of making a contact with spouses. In RUSSIA,[1214] on the other hand, the spouses are obliged to inform third parties of any agreement. Failure to do so, means that such agreements will not bind third parties. In HUNGARY,[1215] there are no special rules about the enforceability of marital property agreements against third parties save that they must be countersigned by a lawyer.

In SCOTLAND,[1216] while there is no necessity to register the Minute of Agreement, if the agreement is not so registered, it can only be enforced by a court order.

COMMENT

1. Principle 4:14 reflects the clear common core by providing that third parties can only be bound by marital property agreements because either they are deemed to know them by reason of their inclusion in a publicly available document or because they actually knew of them before entering into the transaction with the spouses. In this regard, in line with the general policy of these Principles, no distinction is drawn between pre-marital property agreements and post-marital property agreements. Furthermore no distinction is drawn between the types of property included in the agreement.

2. Principle 4:14 does not attempt to prescribe how information about the agreements should be "publicly documented," leaving that issue for national law to determine. Although it is common for jurisdictions to provide for some form of registration that is by no means a universal solution and Principle 4:14 reflects that choice by not insisting upon such a scheme. Furthermore, it preserves the position taken in some jurisdictions only to fix third party liability upon actual knowledge.

3. Principle 4:14 does not say at what point third parties will be bound by a marital property agreement, again leaving that to be determined by national law. Where liability is dependent upon the agreement's inclusion in a publicly available document, it usually dates from the time of its formal registration or recording, but that is not the generally accepted position.

1212 See MĄCZYŃSKI, Polish Report, Q 194.
1213 See HATÁPKA, Slovakian Report, Q 194.
1214 See ANTOKOLSKAIA, Russian Report, Q 194.
1215 § 27 para. 5 Hungarian Family Act. See WEISS/SZEIBERT, Hungarian Report, Q 194.
1216 See MAIR, Scottish Report, Q 194.

Principle 4:15 Exceptional hardship
Having regard to the circumstances when the agreement was concluded or those subsequently arising, the competent authority may, in cases of exceptional hardship, set aside or adjust a marital property agreement.

Principe 4:15 Dureté exceptionnelle
En cas de dureté exceptionnelle, l'autorité compétente peut, en tenant compte des circonstances dans lesquelles la convention matrimoniale a été conclue ou de circonstances postérieures, écarter ou adapter la convention matrimoniale.

Prinzip 4:15 Außergewöhnliche Härte
Unter Berücksichtigung der Umstände bei Zustandekommen der Vereinbarung oder später entstandener Umstände kann die zuständige Behörde in Fällen außergewöhnlicher Härte die ehegüterrechtliche Vereinbarung für unwirksam erklären oder anpassen.

INTERNATIONAL INSTRUMENTS

None of particular relevance.

COMPARATIVE OVERVIEW

General contract law

In most the legal systems surveyed marital property agreements have the status of binding contractual provisions that cannot be modified or set aside by a competent authority except on grounds of general contract law.[1217] The general rules on misrepresentation, fraud, duress etc. apply and it is therefore possible to set aside an agreement or a provision thereof on the basis of such general grounds of invalidity (e.g. AUSTRIA,[1218] BELGIUM,[1219] DENMARK,[1220] FRANCE,[1221]

1217 See in general MOMBERG URIBE, *The effect of a change of circumstances on the binding force of contracts: comparative persepectives*, Ius Commune Series, No. 94, 2011.
1218 See ROTH, Austrian Report, Q 201.
1219 See PINTENS/ALLAERTS/SEYNS/PIGNOLET, Belgian Report, Q 201.
1220 See LUND-ANDERSEN/MAGNUSSEN, Danish Report, Q 201.
1221 See FERRAND/BRAAT, French Report, Q 201.

GREECE,[1222] POLAND,[1223] PORTUGAL,[1224] RUSSIA,[1225] SCOTLAND,[1226] SPAIN[1227] and SWITZERLAND[1228]). Contractual provisions, which are contrary to public order or morality or against imperative provisions, are null and void (e.g. BELGIUM[1229]). In some cases general rules on impossibility or hardship allow a court to amend or set aside a marital property agreement due to an unexpected change of circumstances (e.g. RUSSIA[1230] and THE NETHERLANDS[1231]). This, however, requires that the change of circumstances be substantial and unforeseeable.

Family law

In some systems it is not only possible to set aside marital property agreements or provisions thereof on the basis of general contract law, but also because special family law provisions allow the competent authority to intervene.

In CATALONIA[1232] and LITHUANIA,[1233] detailed provisions have been enacted specifying the circumstances (such as mistake, fraud, threats, bad faith and abuse of rights, violation of mandatory legislative rules, good morals or public order), in which the court must declare null and void agreements that infringe the principle of legal equality between the spouses. Other situations which are explicitly enumerated by the CATALAN and LITHUANIAN legislator are: (1) one of the spouses is left in a situation where after the marriage breakdown he or she cannot appropriately take care of his or her needs; (2) circumstances existing at the moment when the agreement was made changed in an unforeseeable manner and (3) the principle of equal shares in the community property is jeopardized. In PORTUGAL[1234] and SWITZERLAND,[1235] where principally the court cannot override a marital property agreement an exception is made if a contract concerning the distribution of the common assets or the settlement of matrimonial property in a divorce contract violates the imperative "rule of the half" or where "clarity, completeness and obvious inadequacy" require judicial

1222 See KOUTSOURADIS/KOTRONIS/HATZANTONIS, Greek Report, Q 201.
1223 See MĄCZYŃSKI, Polish Report, Q 201.
1224 See DE OLIVEIRA/MARTINS/VÍTOR, Portuguese Report, Q 201.
1225 Art. 44 para. 1 Russian Family Code.
1226 See MAIR, Scottish Report, Q 201.
1227 See GONZÁLEZ BEILFUSS, Spanish Report, Q 201.
1228 See SCHWENZER/BOCK, Swiss Report, Q 201.
1229 See PINTENS/ALLAERTS/SEYNS/PIGNOLET, Belgian Report, Q 201.
1230 Art. 451 Russian Civil Code. See ANTOKOLSKAIA, Russian Report, Q 201.
1231 See BOELE-WOELKI/SCHONEWILLE/SCHRAMA, Dutch Report, Q 201.
1232 Art. 15 para. 1 Catalan Family Code.
1233 Art. 3.105 Lithuanian Civil Code.
1234 Art. 1730 Portuguese Civil Code.
1235 Art. 140 para. 2 Swiss Civil Code.

scrutiny. In RUSSIA,[1236] the court can also declare a marital property agreement or certain provisions thereof void if the agreement or a certain provision thereof places one of the spouses in an extremely unfavourable position.

In some other legal systems there is a possibility to make adjustments on grounds of fairness. Under FINNISH law,[1237] a spouse can request an adjustment to the distribution if it would otherwise lead to an unreasonable result or to the other spouse receiving an unjust financial benefit. The procedure is a strict one since both the preconditions for such an adjustment and the measures that can be taken are specified by the law. Likewise under SWEDISH law,[1238] the adjustment of the terms in a marital property agreement is considered to be the last alternative, when it is not possible to achieve an equitable result through any other solution.

According to GERMAN case-law,[1239] it is well established that although the equalisation of accrued gains is, in principle, open to contractual regulation, the protective purpose of the statutory provisions cannot be undermined at will. A so-called "core area" of the law on the consequences of divorce has to be respected. In practice this however means that the threshold for invalidating the agreement is very high and that the spouses are able to conclude very far-reaching agreements. Traditionally in ENGLAND AND WALES, the court had discretion as to whether to give effect to the agreement. When the agreement was fair there was a tendency to take it into account. After *Granatino v Radmacher (formerly Granatino)*[1240] this discretion has become more limited in that a marital property agreement entered into by each party with a full appreciation of its implications has effect, unless in the circumstances prevailing it would not be fair to hold the parties to their agreement.

COMMENT

1. The concept of exceptional hardship has also been used in Principle 1:9 of the Divorce Principles (Exceptional hardship to the petitioner) and Principle 2:6 of the Maintenance between Former Spouses Principles (Exceptional hardship to the debtor spouse) as well as in Principle 4:32 (Adjustment by the competent authority) and Principle 4:57 (Equal sharing and adjustment). As in these latter Principles regarding property relations of spouses a hardship under Principle

---

1236 Art. 42 para. 3 Russian Family Code.

1237 § 103 b Finnish Marriage Act. See KURKI-SUONIO, Finnish Report, Q 127 and Q 201.

1238 Ch. 12 § 3 Marriage Code.

1239 See DETHLOFF/MARTINY, German Report, Q 201.

1240 [2010] UKSC 42, [2011] 1 AC 534.

4:15 is not be limited to *extreme* exceptional cases, but can take account of the particular circumstances of the other spouse.

2. In most of legal systems surveyed setting aside a marriage contract on grounds of unfairness is not possible since marital property agreements are contractually binding. Principle 4:15, however, opts for allowing the competent authority to set aside or adjust a marital property agreement in cases of exceptional hardship because such agreements should for several reasons be distinguished from other contracts. First, it should be taken into account that the parties are emotionally dependent on each other and trust in their relationship and its future which may lead them to disregard any negative side aspects of the agreement. Second, the influence of other family members whom the parties want to please should not to be underestimated. Thirdly, these agreements are meant to be long lasting and very often do not take into account the changes that circumstances can force on the relationship, especially when it comes to issues such as childrearing and unforeseen illness of a family member, which may force one of the spouses, generally the wife, to leave the job market or to reduce gainful activity for the benefit of the family.

3. For these reasons Principle 4:15 allows the setting aside or adjustment of the marital property agreement in cases of exceptional hardship. This Principle is to be interpreted strictly in order not to undermine the contractual status of the agreement. The main objective of the competent authority should be to respect so far as possible the parties' common intention. Only if circumstances have arisen, that would cause exceptional hardship to one or both spouses should the agreement be respected in its entirety, is it possible to depart from it. If such is the case, intervention by the competent authority should be as minimal as possible. The first choice should be to set aside parts of the agreement. Completely setting aside of an agreement should only be the option of last resort. The competent authority, however, enjoys discretion with regard to the consequences of its intervention. Depending on the circumstances it may set aside any aspect covered by the agreement. It might even allocate the family home to the non-owner spouse without compensation.

4. Given that the circumstances of the specific situation are decisive, Principle 4:15 does not attempt to define what might be considered exceptional hardship. What it does provide, however, is that in determining that question, regard should be had to *all* the circumstances be they those when the agreement was made, those subsequently arising, or the overall circumstances.

CHAPTER III: MATRIMONIAL PROPERTY REGIMES
CHAPITRE III: RÉGIMES MATRIMONIAUX
KAPITEL III: EHEGÜTERSTÄNDE

SECTION A: PARTICIPATION IN ACQUISITIONS
SECTION A: PARTICIPATION AUX ACQUÊTS
ABSCHNITT A: ERRUNGENSCHAFTSBETEILIGUNG

Principle 4:16 Applicability of the participation in acquisitions regime
The participation in acquisitions regime applies if the spouses have not agreed otherwise in accordance with Chapter II.

Principe 4:16 Applicabilité du régime de participation aux acquêts
Le régime de la participation aux acquêts s'applique si les époux n'ont pas conclu de convention contraire conformément au Chapitre II.

Prinzip 4:16 Anwendbarkeit des Güterstands der Errungenschaftsbeteiligung
Der Güterstand der Errungenschaftsbeteiligung gilt, sofern die Ehegatten nicht etwas anderes gemäß Kapitel II vereinbart haben.

INTERNATIONAL INSTRUMENTS

The *Council of Europe's Resolution (78) 37 on Equality of Spouses in Civil Law*, adopted in September 1978, recommends that the Member States' governments "ensure that, where a matrimonial property regime of separation of goods arises by the operation of law, a spouse, on the termination of the marriage by a judicial decree of divorce or nullity, has a legal right to obtain a fair share in the property of his former spouse, or a fixed sum, for any financial inequalities which have arisen during the course of the marriage". In the *Recommendation No. R (89) by the Council of Europe on Contributions Following Divorce* (January 1989), the Member States are advised to enact appropriate rules relating to, inter alia, "matrimonial property regimes, in particular by granting to a former spouse the right to obtain a fair share of the property of the other".

The *French-German Agreement of 2010* provides for an optional matrimonial property regime, based on participation in accrued gains, for marriages in which the marital property relations are governed by either FRENCH or GERMAN law.

COMPARATIVE OVERVIEW

Of the twenty-six jurisdictions surveyed, fifteen were categorised, in accordance with the CEFL's classification of matrimonial property regimes, as *community of property* regimes.[1241] The remaining eleven jurisdictions fall under four different systems which, interpreted broadly, can be categorised as *regimes based on separation of property.* The common feature of these systems is that they do not create any community of property *during* the regime; the spouses' ownership of property remaining separate, whereas upon dissolution of the regime, some form of property distribution or sharing of property takes place. In this latter respect, the systems differ widely. Their solutions will be compared and, where appropriate, used as models for the drafting of the Principles in Chapter III, Section A, which sets out a system based on *participation in acquisitions.*

The first system viewed as belonging to the separation of property regimes consists of the *participation in acquisitions regime* and *the regime on a community of accrued gains.* A participation in acquisitions regime applies as a default regime in SWITZERLAND[1242] and GERMANY,[1243] while in GREECE[1244] a community of accrued gains operates as their default regime. This latter regime is also introduced by the *French-German Agreement of 2010* as the joint optional marital property regime of FRANCE and GERMANY, for spouses whose property relations are subject to either FRENCH or GERMAN law. For this choice of regime to be applicable, it must be selected by the spouses or the future spouses through a marital property agreement.[1245] In CATALONIA,[1246] FRANCE[1247] and THE NETHERLANDS,[1248] optional regimes are also available to be chosen through a marital property agreement between the spouses.

1241 See the Table in the INTRODUCTION, pp. 10-14.
1242 Art. 181 Swiss Civil Code. See SCHWENZER/BOCK, Swiss Report, Q 16.
1243 § 1363 para. 1 German Civil Code. See DETHLOFF/MARTINY, German Report, Q 16.
1244 Arts. 1397, 1400 para.1 and Art. 1403 para. 1 Greek Civil Code. See KOUTSOURADIS/KOTRONIS/HATZANTONIS, Greek Report, Q 16.
1245 See Art. 3 of the Agreement.
1246 See MARTÍN-CASALS/RIBOT, Catalan Report, Q 57. Nevertheless, answer to Q 62 gives at hand that this regime is hardly ever used in practice in Catalonia.
1247 See Ferrand, French Report, Q 198.
1248 See BOELE-WOELKI/SCHONEWILLE/SCHRAMA, Dutch Report, Q 18.

The second system is the *deferred community of property regime*,[1249] which applies as a default regime in DENMARK,[1250] FINLAND,[1251] NORWAY[1252] and SWEDEN[1253] and in part as an optional regime in ITALY.[1254]

The third system is a *pure separation of property regime*,[1255] which applies as the default regime in AUSTRIA[1256] and CATALONIA[1257] and as an optional regime in BELGIUM,[1258] FRANCE,[1259] GERMANY,[1260] POLAND,[1261] PORTUGAL,[1262] SPAIN[1263] and SWITZERLAND.[1264] Certain rights of compensation may, nevertheless, arise under this system. In addition, this regime can also be selected, in full or in part, in DENMARK,[1265] FINLAND,[1266] NORWAY[1267] and SWEDEN,[1268] through the use of marital property agreements which exclude or limit the spouses' right to participate in each other's property.

The fourth system is classified as *separation of property with distribution by the competent authority*.[1269] This approach is followed in ENGLAND AND WALES,[1270] IRELAND[1271] and, with modifications, in SCOTLAND.[1272] This model is, strictly speaking, not a *regime* of matrimonial property relations. It is a system based on separation of property in which the courts enjoy a wide discretion to distribute the spouses' assets on the basis of ancillary relief upon dissolution of the marriage (this functions in a more restricted sense in SCOTLAND[1273]).

1249 In the Questionnaire, Q 91–128 concern this system.
1250 See LUND-ANDERSEN/MAGNUSSEN, Danish Report, Q 16.
1251 See KURKI-SUONIO, Finnish Report, Q 16.
1252 § 56 Norwegian Marriage Act. See SVERDRUP, Norwegian Report, Q 16.
1253 See JÄNTERÄ-JAREBORG/BRATTSTRÖM/WALLENG, Swedish Report, Q 16.
1254 See PATTI/CARICATO/IRTI/IANNICELLI/SERA/DI STEFANO/PETÖ, Italian Report, Q 91.
1255 In the Questionnaire Q 129–160 concern this system.
1256 See ROTH, Austrian Report, Q 16.
1257 Art. 37–47 Catalan Family Code. See MARTÍN-CASALS/RIBOT, Catalan Report, Q 16.
1258 Art. 1466–1469 Belgian Civil Code.
1259 Art. 1536–1543 French Civil Code.
1260 See DETHLOFF/MARTINY, German Report, Q 17.
1261 See MĄCZYŃSKI, Polish Report, Q 17.
1262 Art. 1735 Portuguese Civil Code.
1263 Art. 1437 Spanish Civil Code.
1264 Art. 247 et seq. Swiss Civil Code.
1265 See LUND-ANDERSEN/MAGNUSSEN, Danish Report, Q 198.
1266 See KURKI-SUONIO, Finnish Report, Q 199 and Q 198.
1267 § 42 and § 43 Norwegian Marriage Act. See SVERDRUP, Norwegian Report, Q 17 and Q 18.
1268 See JÄNTERÄ-JAREBORG/BRATTSTRÖM/WALLENG, Swedish Report, Q 198.
1269 In the Questionnaire, Q 161–190 refer to this system.
1270 See BARLOW, English Report, Q 16.
1271 See SHANNON, Irish Report, Q 16.
1272 See MAIR, Scottish Report, Q 16.
1273 See MAIR, Scottish Report, Q 181.

COMMENT

1. Principle 4:16 states that the participation in acquisitions regime applies when the spouses have not agreed otherwise in accordance with Chapter II. This means that it is a default regime. A corresponding Principle for the community of acquisitions regime is provided by Principle 4:33.

2. The participation in acquisitions regime is designated as a system based on a separation of property during the marriage, but which still includes a sharing of certain property upon dissolution of the regime. Labelling the chosen system as a "participation in acquisitions regime" reflects the core of the system, namely that upon dissolution of the regime, both spouses participate in the acquisitions made during the regime by sharing them as specified by Principle 4:17(3) and its reference to Principle 4:31.

CONCEPT
NOTION
BEGRIFF

Principle 4:17 Concept of participation in acquisitions
(1) Participation in acquisitions is a matrimonial property regime during which property is owned separately by the spouses.
(2) Each spouse's property comprises acquisitions and reserved property.
(3) Upon dissolution of the regime each spouse participates in the acquisitions made by the other during the regime in accordance with Principle 4:31.

Principe 4:17 Notion de participation aux acquêts
(1) La participation aux acquêts est un régime matrimonial pendant la durée duquel les époux sont chacun propriétaires de leur patrimoine.
(2) Le patrimoine de chaque époux se compose d'acquêts et de biens réservés.
(3) Lors de la dissolution du régime matrimonial, et conformément au Principe 4:31 chaque époux participe aux acquêts réalisés pendant la durée du régime.

Prinzip 4:17 Begriff der Errungenschaftsbeteiligung
(1) Die Errungenschaftsbeteiligung ist ein Güterstand, während dessen jeder Ehegatte Eigentümer seines Vermögens ist.
(2) Das Vermögen jedes Ehegatten umfasst die Errungenschaft und das Vorbehaltsvermögen.
(3) Bei Beendigung des Güterstands ist jeder Ehegatte an der während des Güterstands erworbenen Errungenschaft des anderen gemäß Prinzip 4:31 beteiligt.

INTERNATIONAL INSTRUMENTS

The *Council of Europe's Resolution (78) 37 on Equality of Spouses in Civil Law*, (September 1978), and the *Recommendation No. R (89) by the Council of Europe on Contributions Following Divorce* (January 1989), focus, inter alia, on situations in which a separation regime arises through operation of law. Where this is the case, there should be rules granting each spouse, upon termination of the regime, a right to obtain a fair share in the property of the other spouse. This mitigates any financial inequalities which may have arisen during the course of the marriage (or the regime). The purpose of these rules is to enable, where possible, each spouse to be economically independent and self-supporting after divorce. The *French-German Agreement of 2010*, which provides for an optional regime of participation in accrued gains, defines such a regime in Article 2. Under this regime, all property owned by either spouse remains the owner's separate property during the regime. However, upon the regime's dissolution, the spouses have a claim to equal participation in the net value of the accrued gains made during the regime.[1274] The participation focuses on the difference (surplus) between the final assets (*Endvermögen*) of each spouse, compared with the spouse's initial assets (*Anfangsvermögen*). Upon dissolution of the regime, the claim for participation is determined by comparing both spouses' accrued gains. The regime grants the spouse with less accrued gains the right to claim, from the spouse with more such gains, half of the value of the difference.

COMPARATIVE OVERVIEW

Separate and individual ownership

A common characteristic of all systems of *separation of property* is that this regime does not, in itself, give rise to any *community of property* (common property). Instead, a separation of ownership prevails during the regime, with each spouse solely owning the property belonging to him or her. Equally, all debts incurred by a spouse are his or her own debts, and each spouse independently administers property owned by him or her. The terminology used to describe the separation of property systems, particularly when translated into English, often interchangeably employs terms such as a spouse's *separate property* or *personal property* or *individually owned property.*

Separately and individually owned property may still belong to different categories

Notwithstanding the separation of ownership, the property owned by each spouse may still, depending on the regime, belong to different categories of property. The issue of to which category an asset belongs is of special relevance upon dissolution of the regime. Once the regime is dissolved, a right may arise for each spouse to take part in property belonging to the other spouse. The scope and content of this right varies among the various regimes.

1274 See in particular Chapter 4, Articles 7–14 of the Agreement.

Under the system of *deferred community of property*, which applies as the default regime in the Nordic jurisdictions (DENMARK,[1275] FINLAND,[1276] NORWAY[1277] and SWEDEN[1278]), each spouse individually and separately owns all property which he or she brought into the regime, or which he or she has acquired during the regime, irrespective of the manner of acquisition (for example, as income or as a bequest). This individual and separate ownership of property applies despite the fact that, unless the spouses have stipulated otherwise through a marital property agreement, *all* their assets belong to a so-called *deferred community*, meaning that the net value of the assets shall, according to the main rule, be divided equally upon dissolution of the regime.[1279] It is only in NORWAY,[1280] following a law reform carried out in 1991, that assets that can clearly be traced back to the spouses' pre-marital assets, inheritance or gifts received during marriage, are excluded from the main rule of equal division.

In SWITZERLAND,[1281] under the *participation in acquisitions regime*, each spouse's property is classified as either *separate property* (*Eigengut*),[1282] or as *acquisitions* (*Errungenschaft*),[1283] with the result that in a marriage where this regime applies, four different categories of property exist.[1284] Upon dissolution of the regime, each asset is assigned to one of the four categories. A spouse may claim half the positive balance of the *acquisitions* of the other spouse, and the respective financial claims between the spouses are set off against each other.[1285] In GERMANY,[1286] the default system of *accrued gains* focuses on a distinction between each spouse's *initial assets* and his or her *final assets*. The *accrued gains* is the amount by which the *final assets* of a spouse exceeds his or her *initial assets*, after subtraction of debts. If, upon dissolution of the regime, the *accrued gains* of one spouse exceed the *accrued gains* of the other spouse, the latter is entitled to the value of half the surplus as an equalisation claim.[1287] In GREECE,[1288] certain assets are excluded from the compensatory settlement, such

1275 See LUND-ANDERSEN/MAGNUSSEN, Danish Report, Q 91.
1276 See KURKI-SUONIO, Finnish Report, Q 91.
1277 See SVERDRUP, Norwegian Report, Q 91.
1278 See JÄNTERÄ-JAREBORG/BRATTSTRÖM/WALLENG, Swedish Report, Q 91.
1279 In addition, a third party can, in a bequest to another person, stipulate that the property shall fall outside any future property division in the recipient's marriage.
1280 See SVERDRUP, Norwegian Report, Q 91 and Q 116.
1281 See SCHWENZER/BOCK, Swiss Report, Q 57.
1282 Art. 198 Swiss Civil Code.
1283 Art. 197 Swiss Civil Code.
1284 Alternatively, in contrast with *gains accrued during the marriage* and *marital property* (*Errungenschaft*), terms such as *individual property* (*Eigengut*) are used to describe the system.
1285 Art. 215 Swiss Civil Code.
1286 See DETHLOFF/MARTINY, German Report, Q 57.
1287 § 1378 German Civil Code.
1288 Article 1400 para. 3 Greek Civil Code. See KOUTSOURADIS/KOTRONIS/HATZANTONIS, Greek Report, Q 57.

as those owned by either spouse before the regime, and assets acquired as gifts or inheritance during the regime. The available optional regimes qualifying as *participation in acquisition regimes* or *regimes on a community of accrued gains* in the various jurisdictions (for example, those of FRANCE[1289] or CATALONIA[1290]) are inspired by either the GERMAN or the SWISS model.

Under a *pure separation of property regime*, applicable either as a default regime or as an optional regime (AUSTRIA,[1291] BELGIUM,[1292] CATALONIA,[1293] FRANCE,[1294] GERMANY,[1295] MALTA,[1296] POLAND,[1297] PORTUGAL,[1298] SPAIN[1299] and SWITZERLAND[1300]), although the spouses' entire property is regarded as the owner spouse's separate property during the regime, a right to compensation claims may arise upon the dissolution of the regime. In AUSTRIA,[1301] the separation of property is altered by the principle of marital participation rights to the assets. In CATALONIA,[1302] the spouse who has worked for the household or for the other spouse without payment is entitled to economic compensation from the other spouse. In THE NETHERLANDS,[1303] special clauses have been developed in notarial practice to exclude situations where a spouse would have to leave the marriage empty-handed due to a marital property agreement excluding the otherwise applicable community regime.

Under the common law system of *separation of property with distribution by the competent authority*, there are no legally distinct categories of property as such (ENGLAND AND WALES[1304] and IRELAND[1305]). However, upon divorce, the court has a wide discretion regarding the distribution of the assets and may, for example, pay special regard to when (before or during the marriage) and how (bequest or income) property of a spouse has been acquired.[1306] A similar position applies in SCOTLAND,[1307] but with a more restricted judicial discretion.

1289 Art. 1569 et seq. French Civil Code.
1290 See Martín-Casals/Ribot, Catalan Report, Q 57.
1291 1233 and 1237 Austrian civil code. See Roth, Austrian Report, Q 12.
1292 See Pintens/Allaerts/Seyns/Pignolet, Belgian Report, Q 129.
1293 Art. 37 Catalan Family Code.
1294 See Ferrand/Braat, French Report, Q 129.
1295 See Dethloff/Martiny, German Report, Q 129.
1296 See Farrugia, Maltese Report, Q 129.
1297 See Mączyński, Polish Report, Q 129.
1298 See De Oliveira/Martins/Vítor, Portuguese Report, Q 129.
1299 Art.1437 Spanish Civil Code.
1300 See Schwenzer/Bock, Swiss Report, Q 129.
1301 See Roth, Austrian Report, Q 148.
1302 Art. 41 para. 1 Catalan Civil Code and Martín-Casals/Ribot, Catalan Report, Q 148.
1303 See Boele-Woelki/Schonewille/Schrama, Dutch Report, Q 57.
1304 See Barlow, English Report, Q 162.
1305 See Shannon, Irish Report, Q 162.
1306 See answers to Q 182.
1307 See Mair, Scottish Report, Q 182.

The relevance of the time and origin of assets

In determining the category to which an asset belongs, and whether it should be taken into account in a claim of participation upon the dissolution of the regime, both the time when the asset was acquired and the origin of the asset are key considerations. Under the GERMAN default system,[1308] these elements determine whether the asset belongs to either the *initial assets*, or the *final assets*. Equally, under the SWISS system[1309] of participation in acquisitions, these factors decide whether the asset is to be regarded as a spouse's *separate individual property*, or as a spouse's *acquisition* during the regime. Assets which a spouse has acquired before the regime, or as a gift, or through inheritance or a bequest, during the regime, are added to the initial assets of that spouse (GERMANY), or belong to the category of *separate individual property* (SWITZERLAND). In the default community regimes, with the exception of NORWAY,[1310] these elements are less important, but may still affect the outcome of, for example, a court's decision in respect of claims for adjustment of the property division. In ENGLAND AND WALES,[1311] while the court has the power to take all the spouses' property into account, increasingly a distinction is made between "matrimonial property" and "non-matrimonial property", such that an uneven distribution is permissible where the origin of the property lies outside the marriage (for example, in cases of gifts or inheritance). In SCOTLAND,[1312] matrimonial property includes all assets acquired during marriage, with the exception of those acquired by gift or inheritance from a third party.

COMMENT

1. Although the participation in acquisitions regime strives to promote self-sufficiency, gender equality and the autonomy of the spouses, it also pays regard to the need of inter-spousal solidarity and fairness between the spouses, both during the regime, and upon its dissolution. This is achieved through the separation of ownership which prevails during the regime, giving each spouse a considerable autonomy in respect of assets owned by him or her. The separation of ownership during the regime creates a need for both spouses to have assets of their own which, in turn, may require that both of them are gainfully active. This promotes gender equality, as the spouses are expected to assume equal responsibilities in ensuring the welfare of the family. It also protects each spouse

1308 See DETHLOFF/MARTINY, German Report, Q 57.
1309 See SCHWENZER/BOCK, Swiss Report, Q 57.
1310 See SVERDRUP, Norwegian Report, Q 91 and Q 116.
1311 See *Miller v. Miller: McFarlane v. McFarlane* [2006] UKHL 24, [2006] 2 AC 618 and BARLOW, English Report, Q 182.
1312 See MAIR, Scottish Report, Q 182.

against the consequences of economic losses by the other spouse, as their own assets and liabilities remain unaffected. These are fundamental differences in relation to the community in acquisitions regime, defined under Section B.

2. The necessary inter-spousal solidarity is achieved by giving each spouse a protected right to take part in the acquisitions of the other spouse which were made during the regime. Compared to a pure separation regime, and the common law system of separation of property with distribution by the competent authority, the difference here is that the participation in acquisitions regime not only establishes an explicit right for both spouses to share in the acquisitions upon dissolution of the regime, but also creates the model for facilitating this. In this manner, it recognises each spouse's direct or indirect contributions to these acquisitions, in addition to providing an increased predictability in respect of the outcome. The main difference in relation to deferred community property regimes, which upon the regime's dissolution normally take all the spouses' property into account, is that the assets to be shared are limited to assets qualifying as acquisitions of either spouse (and thus linked to the regime's existence). In this way, it reflects a more limited and, with regard to the needs of the contemporary European societies, a seemingly more adequate notion, of marital solidarity.

3. Principle 4:17 provides a general definition of the content of the *participation in acquisitions regime*. During the regime a separation of ownership of property prevails, meaning that each spouse alone owns all his or her property. Under this regime, a spouse's property can consist of two categories of property: either acquisitions as defined by Principles 4:18, or reserved property, in accordance with Principle 4:19. Importantly, a certain sharing of the property of the spouses takes place upon dissolution of the regime, with each spouse participating in the acquisitions made by the other spouse in accordance with Principle 4:31.

4. The classification of each spouse's assets as belonging either to the category of *acquisitions* or to the category of *reserved property*, is of crucial importance, primarily upon the dissolution of the regime. Principle 4:17(2) therefore explicitly states that the assets of each spouse can only fall under these two different categories of property. No additional categories exist.

5. Upon dissolution of the regime, the spouses participate equally in the acquisitions made during the regime, as laid down in Principle 4:31. Neither spouse has any claim for participation regarding assets which do not qualify as acquisitions: this is the reserved property. In certain cases, a right to compensation from one category of property to the other may exist, as provided by Principle 4:28.

ASSETS
L'ACTIF
AKTIVA

Principle 4:18 Acquisitions

(1) The acquisitions comprise the assets acquired during the regime, other than the reserved property. In particular, the acquisitions include

(a) each spouse's income and gains whether derived from earnings or property;

(b) assets acquired by means of either spouse's income or gains.

(2) Assets are presumed to be acquisitions unless they are proved to be reserved property.

Principe 4:18 Acquêts

(1) Les acquêts comprennent les biens acquis pendant le régime et qui ne sont pas des biens réservés. Les acquêts comprennent notamment

(a) les revenus et gains de chaque époux, qu'ils proviennent de salaires ou de son patrimoine;

(b) les biens acquis au moyen de revenus ou gains d'un époux.

(2) Les biens sont présumés acquêts sauf preuve contraire.

Prinzip 4:18 Errungenschaft

(1) Die Errungenschaft umfasst während des Güterstands erworbene Vermögensgegenstände mit Ausnahme des Vorbehaltsvermögens. Die Errungenschaft umfasst insbesondere

(a) das Einkommen und die Gewinne eines jeden Ehegatten erzielt aus dem Einkommen oder dem Vermögen;

(b) Vermögensgegenstände, die mit Mitteln aus dem Einkommen oder dem Gewinn eines Ehegatten erworben worden sind.

(2) Es wird vermutet, dass Vermögensgegenstände Errungenschaften sind, es sei denn, es wird bewiesen, dass sie Vorbehaltsvermögen sind.

INTERNATIONAL INSTRUMENTS

The optional regime of participation in accrued gains, provided for the *French-German Agreement of 2010*, draws a distinction between the initial assets and the final assets of each spouse. Initial assets are the assets which either spouse had at the beginning of the regime. The final assets are those which a spouse has at the time of the dissolution of the regime. In this regime, the *fruits ("Früchte")* of the initial assets are included among the final assets.[1313] One example is the rental income of an apartment which a spouse acquired before the regime.[1314] The increase in value of initial assets during the regime is included, with the exception of an increase in value of immovable property belonging to a spouse's initial assets, which is generally not the result of economic activities of the spouses.[1315] Assets acquired through inheritance, gift or bequest, or as compensation for pain or suffering, are included among the initial assets. On the other hand, gifts and bequests which a spouse has given to a direct heir from his or her initial assets are not added to the initial assets. If no inventory has been drawn of the initial assets of each spouse, all the property of each spouse is presumed to have been acquired during the regime, and is subject to claims of participation by the other spouse.[1316]

COMPARATIVE OVERVIEW

Categories of assets

The GERMAN default regime[1317] distinguishes between each spouse's *initial assets* and his or her *final assets*, but not between acquisitions and reserved property. Initial assets consist of the net assets which the spouse had at the beginning of the regime, and those that have been accumulated during the regime by way of gift, will or bequest during the regime.[1318] The final assets of each spouse are his or her assets at the time of the dissolution of the regime, after subtraction of liabilities and debts.[1319] The assessment of the initial and the final assets of each spouse is based on the market value of the assets. In order to prevent an increase in value purely as a result of inflation, the value of the initial assets is indexed.[1320] The accrued gains of each spouse, to which the other spouse has a claim of participation, are calculated for the entirety of the spouse's property, including the initial assets. It follows that spouses also participate in any increase in value

1313 Art. 8 para. 3.
1314 Explanatory Report, Article 8 para. 3.
1315 See Art. 9 para. 2 and FÖTSCHL, "The Common Optional Regime of Germany and France, Epoch-Making in the Unification of Law", *Yearbook of Private International Law*, 2009, p. 400.
1316 Art. 8 para. 5.
1317 See DETHLOFF/MARTINY, German Report, Q 57.
1318 § 1374 para. 1 German Civil Code.
1319 § 1375 para. 1 German Civil Code.
1320 See DETHLOFF/MARTINY, German Report, Q 82.

of the initial assets during the regime, which is an expression of a far-reaching matrimonial solidarity.[1321] The GREEK approach is similar.[1322]

In SWITZERLAND,[1323] under the *participation in acquisitions* regime, each spouse's property is classified as either *separate property* (*Eigengut*),[1324] or as *acquisitions* (*Errungenschaft*),[1325] with the result that there exist four different categories of property. Upon dissolution of the regime, each asset is assigned to one of the four categories. Assets which a spouse has acquired prior to the regime, acquired as a gift or through inheritance or bequest during the regime, or accumulated by investments, as well as compensation for personal damages and injury suffered by the spouse, constitute the owner spouse's *separate property*. All other assets are regarded as *acquisitions*. In contrast to GERMAN law, acquisitions made under the regime do not include the increase in value of assets which are separate property because they were acquired before the regime, or for other reasons belong to the category of separate property of either spouse.[1326] Instead a possible increase in value is allocated proportionally in relation to the contributions. The concept of "increase in value" only encompasses a surplus that is derived from market variations (an "economic" or "market" accretion), but not a surplus that was generated by the contributions of an individual spouse (an "industrial" accretion).[1327] The "industrial" accretion is equivalent to income from work, and is therefore treated as a part of the acquisitions. In the other jurisdictions surveyed, the corresponding optional regime is inspired by either the GERMAN or the SWISS model.

The *deferred community property regime* of DENMARK,[1328] FINLAND[1329] and SWEDEN[1330] includes, as a rule, *all* the spouses' assets, irrespective of when and how they were acquired. It follows that, according to the main rule, assets which a spouse owned at the time of the marriage, as well those which a spouse has acquired during the marriage through gift, inheritance or bequest, are also included in the regime *and* in a property division upon its dissolution, in addition to property that a spouse or the spouses otherwise acquired during the marriage

1321 See DETHLOFF/MARTINY, German Report, Q 82.

1322 See KOUTSOURADIS/KOTRONIS/HATZANTONIS, Greek Report, Q 82; PINTENS, "Matrimonial Property Law in Europe", in BOELE-WOELKI, MILES, SCHERPE (eds), *The Future of Family Property in Europe*, 2011, p. 31.

1323 See SCHWENZER/BOCK, Swiss Report, Q 57.

1324 Art. 198 Swiss Civil Code.

1325 Art. 197 Swiss Civil Code.

1326 See PINTENS, "Matrimonial Property Law in Europe", in BOELE-WOELKI, MILES, SCHERPE (eds), *The Future of Family Property in Europe*, 2011, p. 31.

1327 See SCHWENZER/BOCK, Swiss Report, Q 83.

1328 See LUND-ANDERSEN/MAGNUSSEN, Danish Report, Q 91.

1329 See KURKI-SUONIO, Finnish Report, Q 91.

1330 See JÄNTERÄ-JAREBORG/BRATTSTRÖM/WALLENG, Swedish Report, Q 91.

(for example, through income from gainful employment or from property). Nevertheless, there is *reserved property* which falls outside the property division on two different grounds. Firstly, the spouses may agree through a marital property agreement that all, or certain parts, of their property shall fall outside the regime. Secondly, this can also be achieved by stipulation of a third person who donates or bequeaths property, to the effect that the transferred property shall be the recipient's *reserved property*. In NORWAY,[1331] since a law reform carried out in 1991, assets that can clearly be traced back to the spouses' pre-marital assets, inheritances or gifts received during marriage, constitute reserved property.

A *pure separation of property regime*, applicable either as a default regime or, more commonly, as an optional regime, (AUSTRIA,[1332] BELGIUM,[1333] CATALONIA,[1334] FRANCE,[1335] GERMANY,[1336] MALTA,[1337] POLAND,[1338] PORTUGAL,[1339] SPAIN[1340] and SWITZERLAND[1341]) could appear to lack different categories of property. Yet, depending on the jurisdiction, various kinds of rules on compensation may enable the spouses to participate in each other's property upon dissolution of the regime.

Under the common law systems (ENGLAND AND WALES[1342] and IRELAND[1343]), all assets held individually or jointly by the spouses qualify as the personal property (separate property) of each spouse. Upon divorce, on the other hand, the court has wide discretion regarding the distribution of the assets. Similarly, in SCOTLAND,[1344] distribution of property upon divorce must be justified by statutory principles. The first principle is the fair sharing of matrimonial property.

Presumptions regarding the category of assets

In systems where the time of the acquisition, or the origin of the property is relevant, the question arises how such relevant elements are proved. Under the

---

1331 See SVERDRUP, Norwegian Report, Q 91 and Q 116.
1332 Art. 1233 and 1237 Austrian Civil Code. See ROTH, Austrian Report, Q 12.
1333 See PINTENS/ALLAERTS/SEYNS/PIGNOLET, Belgian Report, Q 129.
1334 Art. 37 Catalan Family Code.
1335 See FERRAND/BRAAT, French Report, Q 129.
1336 See DETHLOFF/MARTINY, German Report, Q 129.
1337 See FARRUGIA, Maltese Report, Q 129.
1338 See MĄCZYŃSKI, Polish Report, Q 129.
1339 See DE OLIVEIRA/MARTINS/VÍTOR, Portuguese Report, Q 129.
1340 Art. 1437 Spanish Civil Code.
1341 See SCHWENZER/BOCK, Swiss Report, Q 129.
1342 See BARLOW, English Report, Q 162.
1343 See SHANNON, Irish Report, Q 162.
1344 See MAIR, Scottish Report, Q 182.

GERMAN default regime,[1345] the drawing up of an inventory of the initial assets is required for the property to qualify as such. In the absence of such an inventory, the assets become subject to participation claims. Under the SWISS system, all assets are regarded as acquisitions of a spouse, unless proved otherwise. In GREECE,[1346] there is also a rebuttable presumption, according to which property belongs to a spouse's accrued gains.

Income and gains

A spouse's *income* can be derived from earnings from, for example, gainful employment or from his or her property (for example, rental income of an apartment belonging to the spouse), or from any other capital. In the SWISS system of participation in acquisitions, categorising the income of a spouse follows the general rules of the regime, whereby the source of the income and its timing are of relevance. In contrast, under the GERMAN[1347] default regime, the accrued gains that are shared upon dissolution of the regime also include the increased value of the initial assets (and any income from these) during the regime.

In the SWISS system of participation in acquisitions, the notion of gains appears to be very limited, (for example, money won in lottery games). According to the SWISS Federal Supreme Court, lottery prizes should be included in the division if the lottery ticket was bought with money forming part of the acquisitions.[1348] In contrast, under the GERMAN[1349] default regime of accrued gains, a different and much broader notion is employed, which includes the value increase of all property of the spouses. Therefore, the rules on substitution can be applied.[1350]

Professional activities

Since under GERMAN law[1351] the difference between initial and final assets is decisive, the value of, for example, a medical practice will thus be included. This takes into account not only capital assets, such as buildings and equipment, but

1345 § 1377 German Civil Code.

1346 Art. 1400, para. 1 Greek Civil Code, according to which the contribution of the one spouse, in order to increase the property of the other, is presumed to amount to one-third of this increase. See KOUTSOURADIS/KOTRONIS/HATZANTONIS, Greek Report, Q 82. See also PINTENS "Matrimonial Property Law in Europe", BOELE-WOELKI/MILES/SCHERPE (eds.), *The Future of Family Property in Europe,* 2011, p. 32.

1347 § 1377 German Civil Code.

1348 See SCHWENZER/BOCK, Swiss Report, Q 61.

1349 § 1377 German Civil Code.

1350 See SCHWENZER/BOCK, Swiss Report, Q 61.

1351 See §§ 1375 para. 1, 1376 para. 2, 1378 para. 1 German Civil Code.

also the goodwill of a practice or a business.[1352] Under SWISS law,[1353] the goodwill is included as an "industrial accretion" insofar as it is the result of the activities of the spouse and is a part of the acquisitions.

COMMENT

1. The core of the participation in acquisitions regime is that property which qualifies as acquisitions, because any claim to take part in the property of the other spouse upon dissolution of the regime focuses on such assets. The approach taken in Principle 4:18(1) is that all assets acquired during the regime, with the exception of property qualifying as so-called reserved property under Principle 4:19, qualify as acquisitions of a spouse. The type of assets at stake, for example moveable and immovable property, is irrelevant.

2. In order to further clarify this regime, Principe 4:18(1) specifies in a non-exhaustive manner forms of acquisitions. Principles 4:18(1)(a) mentions each spouse's income and gains, whether derived from earnings or from property. It follows that all income and gains of either spouse, *if made during the regime*, are included irrespective of when – or how – the *source* of the income or gain was acquired, and whether, as a result, that property qualifies as an acquisition under the regime, or as reserved property. For example, royalties received by a spouse during the regime for works created by him or her *before* the regime are included in acquisitions of the regime as earnings, comparable to any other income made during the regime. The income received during the regime through, for example, the wife's booming consultation business, which was founded before the marriage, would also be taken into account. Where the source of the income belongs to the category of reserved property, there is no common core on this issue, and the position taken in the Principles reflects a better law approach, based on concerns of promoting a marital community of interests and marital solidarity by treating all income alike. Were this position to result in exceptional hardship, the competent authority may, in accordance with Principle 4:32, adjust the participation.

3. "Gains" might best be described as "windfall assets", acquired with the use of an acquisition or reserved property, such as winnings acquired from betting, lotteries or draws. "Gains", however, do not include *inherent* increases in value of assets that fall within reserved property, for example, the increase in value of pre-marital property resulting from market valuations (as opposed to the

1352 See Federal Supreme Court 9 February 2011, FamRZ 2011, 622 annotation KOCH, annotation BORTH, FamRZ 2011, 705.

1353 See SCHWENZER/BOCK, Swiss Report, Q 83.

spouse's contributions), and thus falls outside any notions of family solidarity. Therefore, acquisitions under Principle 4:18 only include the increase in value of the assets qualifying as acquisitions under this Principle. Increases in value of reserved property generally remain reserved property (see Principle 4:19(f)). However, in exceptional circumstances (see Principle 4:32), the value existing in reserved property may be treated as income.

4. Included among acquisitions is increase in value of property qualifying as acquisitions, but not the increase in value of assets qualifying as reserved property. This restriction is expressly confirmed by Principle 4:19(e). The justification for not including the value increase of reserved property during the regime is that such property falls outside all claims of participation, and that its increase in value is normally a result of market valuations and has nothing to do with spousal contributions (in other cases, a right to compensation in accordance with Principle 4:28 may arise). In this manner, the Principles strive to achieve a fair balance between various interests. The chosen approach reflects a more narrow understanding of marital solidarity than the one promoted in the system of community of accrued gains (for example, the default regime of GERMANY, and the optional regime adopted by the *French-German Agreement of 2010*), and is more in line with the SWISS approach.

5. In order to simplify the system and follow an established model of identifying which assets should be subject to participation claims (when not all the spouses' assets are to be included, as is the case in the deferred community property systems), Principle 4:18(2) states that the assets of the spouses are presumed to be acquisitions unless proved to be reserved property. This position is of particular relevance upon the dissolution of the regime (see Principle 4:26), but can also be expected to contribute to marital solidarity during the course of the regime. The spouse who claims that an asset is not an acquisition, but his or her reserved property, has the burden of proof to demonstrate this. It is left to national law to decide what qualifies as sufficient proof regarding a property's classification as reserved property under Principle 4:19.

Principle 4:19 Reserved property

Reserved property comprises

(a) assets acquired before the commencement of the regime;
(b) gifts, inheritances and bequests acquired during the regime;
(c) assets substituting reserved property;
(d) assets that are personal in nature;
(e) assets exclusively acquired for a spouse's profession;
(f) increases in value of the property included in (a) to (e).

Principe 4:19 Propriété réservée

La propriété réservée comprend

(a) les biens acquis avant le début du régime matrimonial;
(b) les donations, successions et legs intervenus durant le régime;
(c) les biens acquis en substitution de biens réservés;
(d) les biens personnels par nature;
(e) les biens acquis exclusivement pour la profession d'un époux;
(f) les plus values des biens visés aux points (a) à (e).

Prinzip 4:19 Vorbehaltsvermögen

Vorbehaltsvermögen umfasst

(a) vor Beginn des Güterstands erworbene Vermögensgegenstände;
(b) während des Güterstands erworbene Schenkungen, Erbschaften und Vermächtnisse;
(c) Vorbehaltsvermögen ersetzende Vermögensgegenstände;
(d) Vermögensgegenstände persönlicher Natur;
(e) ausschließlich für die Berufstätigkeit eines der Ehegatten erworbene Vermögensgegenstände;
(f) Wertsteigerungen der in (a) bis (e) genannten Vermögensgegenstände.

INTERNATIONAL INSTRUMENTS

According to the *French-German Agreement of 2010* providing for an optional regime of participation in accrued gains, property owned by each spouse at the date of the regime's entry into force is excluded from the claims of participation upon dissolution of the regime, in addition to property that a spouse has received during the regime through inheritance, will, bequest or as compensation for pain and suffering.[1354]

[1354] Art. 8 para. 1 and para. 2. The inclusion for *compensation for pain and suffering* has been inspired by French law.

COMPARATIVE OVERVIEW

The existence of "reserved property"

The regimes based on a *participation in acquisitions* or a community of accrued gains include a category of property, characterised by the fact that, upon dissolution of the regime, the concerned assets are protected from the other spouse's participation claims. In GERMANY[1355] and, essentially, also in GREECE,[1356] the "initial assets", consisting of the assets acquired before the regime and of gifts, inheritances and bequests acquired during the regime, serve this function. The category encompassing each spouse's *separate property* (*Eigengut*)[1357] serves a similar function in the default regime of SWITZERLAND. Established separately for each spouse, this category of property consists of the concerned spouse's personal assets, assets acquired before the regime, those acquired gratuitously during the marriage, and those accumulated by investments, as well as compensation for personal damages and injury suffered by the spouse.[1358] Assets replacing previously owned assets (substitution) are, as a rule, allocated to the same category as the asset it replaces; in this respect, the decisive factor is the means by which the assets were acquired.[1359] The position taken in respect of assets acquired for either spouse's profession or trade is more complex. The general rule of the SWISS[1360] system is that they qualify as acquisitions if acquired during the regime, unless otherwise agreed between the spouses in the form of a matrimonial property agreement.

The *deferred community property regime* of DENMARK,[1361] FINLAND[1362] and SWEDEN[1363] includes, as a rule, *all* the spouses' assets, irrespective of when and how they were acquired. Nevertheless, there can be *reserved property*, normally referred to as *separate property* (in contrast to *marital property*), falling outside the property division on two different grounds. Firstly, the spouses may agree through a marital property agreement that all, or certain parts of, their property shall fall outside the regime, and thus, outside of property division. Secondly, this can also be achieved in the form of a stipulation by a third person donating

1355 See DETHLOFF/MARTINY, German Report, Q 57 and Q 59.
1356 See KOUTSOURADIS/KOTRONIS/HATZANTONIS, Greek Report, Q 57.
1357 Art. 198 Swiss Civil Code.
1358 See SCHWENZER/BOCK, Swiss Report, Q 57. See also PINTENS, "Matrimonial Property Law in Europe", in BOELE-WOELKI/ MILES/SCHERPRE, (eds), *The Future of Family Property in Europe*, 2011, p. 31.
1359 See SCHWENZER/BOCK, Swiss Report, Q 61.
1360 Art. 199 Swiss Civil Code.
1361 See LUND-ANDERSEN/MAGNUSSEN, Danish Report, Q 91.
1362 See KURKI-SUONIO, Finnish Report, Q 91.
1363 See JÄNTERÄ-JAREBORG/BRATTSTRÖM/WALLENG, Swedish Report, Q 91.

or bequesting property, to the effect that the transmitted property shall not be included in any property division upon the recipient's (eventual) marriage.[1364] In NORWAY,[1365] assets that can be clearly traced back to the spouses' pre-marital assets, inheritance or gifts received during marriage, are excluded from the main rule of equal division. In all of these jurisdictions,[1366] a spouse's assets which are personal in nature, for example, intended only for a spouse's highly-personal use or, more importantly, are not assignable, are not included in the deferred community of property.

In a *pure separation of property regime*, applicable either as a default regime or, more commonly, as an optional regime (AUSTRIA,[1367] BELGIUM,[1368] CATALONIA,[1369] FRANCE,[1370] GERMANY,[1371] MALTA,[1372] POLAND,[1373] PORTUGAL,[1374] SPAIN[1375] and SWITZERLAND[1376]), all property is regarded as the owner spouse's separate property. This does not, however, mean that the owner spouse is protected from all claims of sharing by the other spouse upon dissolution of the regime.

Under the common law systems (ENGLAND AND WALES[1377] and IRELAND[1378]), all assets held individually or jointly by the spouses qualify as the personal property (*separate property*) of each spouse. Upon divorce, on the other hand, the court has a wide discretion regarding the distribution of the assets. In principle, all assets of the spouses are taken into account by the court. However, where assets exceed needs, it is less likely that the court will redistribute pre-marital assets, inheritances or gifts to a spouse (ENGLAND AND WALES[1379] and IRELAND[1380]). The first principle of financial provision in SCOTLAND[1381] is, that there should be fair sharing of matrimonial property, which is broadly defined as assets acquired by either party during the marriage.

1364 It is not uncommon that, in particular, parents and grandparents making bequests for the children of the family make such conditions, irrespective of the children's age and civil status.
1365 See SVERDRUP, Norwegian Report, Q 91 and Q 116.
1366 See answers to Q 91.
1367 Art. 1233 and 1237 Austrian civil code. See ROTH, Austrian Report, Q 12.
1368 See PINTENS/ALLAERTS/SEYNS/PIGNOLET, Belgian Report, Q 129.
1369 Art. 37 Catalan Family Code.
1370 See FERRAND/BRAAT, French Report, Q 129.
1371 See DETHLOFF/MARTINY, German Report, Q 129.
1372 See FARRUGIA, Maltese Report, Q 129.
1373 See MĄCZYŃSKI, Polish Report, Q 129.
1374 See DE OLIVEIRA/MARTINS/VÍTOR, Portuguese Report, Q 129.
1375 Art.1437 Spanish Civil Code.
1376 See SCHWENZER/BOCK, Swiss Report, Q 129.
1377 See BARLOW, English Report, Q 162.
1378 See SHANNON, Irish Report, Q 162.
1379 See BARLOW, English Report, Q 182.
1380 See SHANNON, Irish Report, Q 182.
1381 See MAIR, Scottish Report, Q 182.

The existence of "reserved property" must be proved

Reserved property in the continental European sense of the term is "the exception". As a result, it is required that the owner spouse must be able to prove that the concerned assets qualify as property that should *not* to be included in the property division. For this purpose, the owner spouse may be required to present a special inventory of such property (GERMANY[1382] and GREECE[1383]), or at least, it must be possible to clearly trace the original source or means of the assets (SWITZERLAND[1384] and NORWAY[1385]). In all circumstances, a spouse claiming certain assets to be of this nature, or that these replace earlier assets, must be able to prove this.

COMMENT

1. Principle 4:19 defines the reserved property of either spouse as the property that is not included among the acquisitions set out in Principle 4:18. Reserved property qualifies, by its nature, as property that is protected against claims of participation by the other spouse upon dissolution of the regime. It can consist of any type of asset, namely: movable or immovable property, tangible and intangible property, or intellectual property rights. All the civil law jurisdictions surveyed recognise that spouses may have property that will not be included in a property division. This reflects a strong common core.

2. The grounds for classifying property as belonging to the category of reserved property include the *period of time* when the property was acquired (that is, before the commencement of the regime), Principle 4:19(a) (*the temporal element*). The justification is that the other spouse has not contributed to the acquisition of this property.

3. When a spouse has received assets from a third person as a gift, bequest or inheritance in accordance with Principle 4:19(b) (*the source element*), it can generally be assumed that the third person wished the property to remain the recipient's reserved property to which an eventual spouse has no claim. Often the property comes from the earlier generations within the family, in particular from parents to children. The other spouse has not contributed to the acquisition of this property. Principle 4:19(b) does not apply if the property has been given to a spouse or the spouses on condition that it shall belong to their acquisitions.

1382 § 1377 para. 1 German Civil Code. See DETHLOFF/MARTINY, German Report, Q 64.

1383 See PINTENS, "Matrimonial Property Law in Europe", in BOELE-WOELKI, MILES, SCHERPE (Eds), *The Future of Family Property in Europe*, 2011, p. 32.

1384 See SCHWENZER/BOCK, Swiss Report, Q 64.

1385 See SVERDRUP, Norwegian Report, Q 100 and Q 101.

4. Rules on *substitution* apply. As a result property acquired during the regime which substitutes the owner spouse's reserved property continues to be his or her reserved property, Principle 4:19(c). This is a standard position among jurisdictions. A substitution may take place both directly, for example, when an insurance company pays compensation for a destroyed object which was reserved property, or indirectly, when one object belonging to this category of property has been substituted by another object. If an asset has been funded partly by acquisitions, and partly by reserved property, the category from which the largest amount of the funding originated should be decisive. In case of doubt, it is presumed that the asset belongs to the acquisitions (see Principle 4:18(2)). Rights of compensation may arise in accordance with Principle 4:28, which permits taking into account any contribution from one category of assets to another category of assets.

5. In addition, according to Principle 4:19(d), assets that are personal in nature belong to each spouse's reserved property, even when acquired during the regime (*the personal nature element*). Assets are personal in nature when they are intended for a spouse's personal use only, such as clothing and jewellery (except for those deemed to be of an extraordinary nature given the spouses' standard of living). An investment on jewellery may, nevertheless, give rise to a right to compensation under Principle 4:28 if a spouse's acquisitions have been used for this investment. Damages paid to a spouse for that spouse's pain and suffering, or for personal or moral injury caused to that spouse, qualify as personal assets of that spouse, because of the damages' special link with the compensated spouse, and the purpose of offering individual relief and remedy to him or her. In addition, rights of a spouse that cannot be assigned to another person qualify as assets that are personal in nature.

6. According to Principle 4:19(e), assets exclusively acquired for a spouse's profession, such as a dentist's special equipment or a plumber's plumbing machines, also belong to the category of reserved property, even when acquired during the regime (*the professional asset element*). In cases such as these, it appears evident that such assets have been acquired exclusively for professional purposes. The justification for qualifying them as reserved property is that such assets are used exclusively by one of the spouses to enable that spouse to pursue his or her profession; if this qualification is not met, the assets qualify as acquisitions. On the other hand, all income and gains from the profession and the professional assets are included among the acquisitions according to Principle 4:18(1). If assets qualifying as acquisitions under Principle 4:18 have been used to acquire the professional tools, a right of compensation will arise in accordance with Principle 4:28.

7. Increases in the value of the assets qualifying as reserved property remain outside the reach of any participation claims by the other spouse, Principle 4:19(f). The reason behind this is that such increases are, normally, the result of general market developments, without requiring any particular investments or other measures by the owner of the property. These occur, for example, because of the attractive location of the concerned property (for example, a piece of land). Since such increases in value have nothing to do with the contributions by the other spouse, the position taken in the Principles is that the notions of family solidarity and sharing should not be extended to cover them, but instead benefit the owner. By treating the increases in value of the assets enlisted under Principle 4:19(a)-(e) as reserved property, Principle 4:19 reflects a better law approach.

Principle 4:20 Presumption of joint ownership
Assets are presumed to be owned jointly by both spouses unless otherwise proved.

Principe 4:20 Présomption d'indivision
Sauf preuve contraire, les biens sont présumés appartenir en indivision aux deux époux.

Prinzip 4:20 Vermutung von Miteigentum
Es wird vermutet, dass Vermögensgegenstände Miteigentum beider Ehegatten sind, es sei denn, das Gegenteil wird bewiesen.

INTERNATIONAL INSTRUMENTS

None of particular relevance.

COMPARATIVE OVERVIEW

In all systems based on separation of property during the marriage, each spouse is considered to be the owner of the property acquired by him or her. It is however quite common the case, that spouses are not able to prove between themselves and against third parties, who is actually the owner of a certain asset when this issue becomes relevant.

Presumption of joint ownership

In the systems classified as *participation in acquisitions*, formal ownership determines who owns the property: in case of doubt the law rebuttably presumes that the asset belongs to both spouses in equal shares in CATALONIA[1386] and THE NETHERLANDS,[1387] while in GERMANY[1388] and SWITZERLAND,[1389] the general presumption of ownership for the possessor applies. There can be exceptions to the general rule, for example, movable property for the personal use of a spouse is presumed to belong to that spouse (e.g. CATALONIA[1390] and GERMANY[1391]). In

1386 See MARTÍN-CASALS/RIBOT, Catalan Report, Q 64.
1387 Art. 1:131 para. 1 Dutch Civil Code.
1388 § 1006 BGB. See DETHLOFF/MARTINY, German Report, Q 64.
1389 Art.930 Swiss Civil Code.
1390 Art. 40 Catalan Family Code. See MARTÍN-CASALS/RIBOT, Catalan Report, Q 64.
1391 § 1362 BGB. See DETHLOFF/MARTINY, German Report, Q 64.

some jurisdictions like in GERMANY,[1392] there are special presumptions protecting creditors: movables in the possession of either or both spouses are presumed to belong to the debtor spouse. In other legal systems the same presumptions apply both between spouses and against third parties (e.g. SWITZERLAND[1393]).

In pure *separation systems* presumptions are also common. The law of BELGIUM,[1394] CATALONIA,[1395] FRANCE,[1396] PORTUGAL[1397] and SPAIN[1398] provides that when the ownership of an asset cannot be proved, the asset is presumed to be joint property. This presumption also often applies between the spouses as well as against third parties. It is quite common in those systems to allow spouses to include clauses of presumption of ownership in their marital property agreements (e.g. FRANCE[1399] and PORTUGAL[1400]).

In systems that can be categorized as *deferred community systems*, rules also exist in connection to this issue. The FINNISH Marriage Act[1401] contains a presumption according to which spouses own movable objects jointly with equal rights. This presumption applies to household goods. A court can also declare that a particular item of property belongs to both spouses even though it is registered in the name of one spouse only, if this was the intention of the spouses at the moment of acquisition. Under NORWEGIAN law[1402] if both spouses have made a direct contribution to the purchase price of an item, there is a presumption that the spouses have made a tacit agreement of co-ownership even although only one spouse is the actual buyer. Similarly, under the law of SWEDEN[1403] a hidden or *caveat* joint ownership can arise. Even if a property item is acquired in the name of one spouse only, a hidden joint property arises if it is proved that the spouses intended that the property be jointly owned, the non formal owner made some financial contribution to the acquisition and the spouse who acquires title was aware of the intention of sharing ownership. The principle of *caveat* joint ownership applies to immovable and movable property. Normally, however, there is a presumption that property other than joint household goods belongs to the spouse who both paid for the property and uses it.[1404]

1392 § 1362 para. 1 sent. 1 BGB. See DETHLOFF/MARTINY, German Report, Q 65.
1393 See SCHWENZER/BOCK, Swiss Report, Q 65.
1394 Art. 1468 para. 2 Belgian Civil Code.
1395 Art. 40 Catalan Family Code.
1396 Art. 1538 para. 3 French Civil Code.
1397 Art.1736 para.2 Portuguese Civil Code.
1398 Art. 1441 Spanish Civil Code.
1399 Art. 1548 para. 2 French Civil Code. See FERRAND/BRAAT, French Report, Q 135.
1400 See DE OLIVEIRA/MARTINS/VÍTOR, Portuguese Report, Q 135.
1401 § 89 Finnish Marriage Act. See KURKI-SUONIO, Finnish Report, Q 100.
1402 See SVERDRUP, Norwegian Report, Q 100.
1403 See JÄNTERÄ-JAREBORG/BRATTSTRÖM/WALLENG, Swedish Report, Q 96.
1404 See JÄNTERÄ-JAREBORG/BRATTSTRÖM/WALLENG, Swedish Report, Q 100.

In the common law systems of *separation with distribution by the competent authority* the general approach is that ownership will be established according to the general rules of property law. There are however some exceptions under, for example, SCOTS law,[1405] as regards household goods, which are presumed to be owned in equal shares unless there is proof to the contrary, and as regards money or property acquired with money, which is derived from an allowance provided for joint household expenses, that is also considered to be jointly owned.

COMMENT

1. In all systems based on separation of property during the marriage, each spouse is considered to be the owner of the property acquired by him or her. It is, however, quite commonly the case, that spouses are not able to prove between themselves and against third parties, who is actually the owner of a particular asset when this issue becomes relevant. Principle 4:20 follows the common core and establishes a rebuttable presumption that all assets are owned jointly by both spouses. The presumption is justified on grounds of practicality, since in many cases it will not be possible to prove, who the actual owner of an item or an asset is.

2. The presumption contained in Principle 4:20 should be distinguished from that established in Principle 4:18(2). The latter Principle applies when there is dispute as to which category of assets an item belongs to. If there is no proof to the contrary, assets will be included in the category of acquisitions. The presumption contained in Principle 4:20 deals with the question of ownership to an asset. If ownership of an item of property cannot be proved it will be considered to be the spouses' joint property.

3. In most cases the presumption will apply to movables since ownership of immovable property will normally be recorded in a special manner, such as in a public registry where the record proves ownership. However, where exceptionally ownership of immovable property is hard to establish, the presumption of joint ownership also applies.

4. The burden lies with the spouse who claims to be the owner of the asset. Principle 4:20 does not attempt to prescribe the means of proof, leaving that to be determined by national law.

5. Although no distinction is made between proof as between spouses and proof with regard to third parties, by not prescribing evidential rules Principle 4:20 nevertheless preserves the freedom of jurisdictions to make such a distinction.

1405 See MAIR, Scottish Report, Q 166.

DEBTS
DETTES
VERBINDLICHKEITEN

Principle 4:21 Personal debts
Debts incurred by one spouse are his or her personal debts.

Principe 4:21 Dettes personnelles
Les dettes souscrites par un époux lui sont personnelles.

Prinzip 4:21 Persönliche Verbindlichkeiten
Verbindlichkeiten eines Ehegatten sind seine persönlichen Schulden.

INTERNATIONAL INSTRUMENTS

Although there is no express provision on debts in the *French-German Agreement of 2010* it follows from several of its provisions that all debts are personal debts. Article 2 clearly establishes that the common FRENCH-GERMAN regime of participation in the acquisitions is defined by the fact that the property of the spouses remains separate until the matrimonial property regime is terminated. According to Article 4, each spouse independently administers and disposes over his or her personal property alone, which logically means that debts contracted by this spouse are his or her personal debts. Article 6 establishes by way of exception that debts incurred in order to meet family needs are joint debts which further confirms that generally each spouse's debts are his or her personal debts.

COMPARATIVE OVERVIEW

All matrimonial property regimes outside the *community system* have in common that the spouses own and administer their property separately while the regime is in force. Logically, the debts incurred by one spouse are his or her personal debts.

In *participation systems* all debts incurred by one spouse personally, are his or her personal debts. Spouses are joint debtors only for the debts incurred jointly or by one spouse with the express consent of the other. The only exceptions are debts related to family debts (e.g. CATALONIA,[1406] GERMANY[1407] and SWITZERLAND[1408]) which are always joint debts, independently of the spouse who incurred them.

In the Nordic systems of *deferred community* each spouse is solely liable for a debt incurred by him or her before or during the marriage (e.g. SWEDEN[1409]). Only debts incurred jointly or to cover ordinary family expenses are joint debts (DENMARK,[1410] FINLAND[1411] and NORWAY[1412]). In *separation systems* all debts are in principle personal debts (e.g. FRANCE[1413]). Joint debts are created from legal transactions which the spouses conclude jointly, or from transactions in order to meet family expenses (e.g. SPAIN[1414]). In common law jurisdictions marriage has no effect on personal liability. All debts are therefore personal unless incurred jointly (ENGLAND AND WALES,[1415] IRELAND[1416] and SCOTLAND[1417]).

COMMENT

1. Principle 4:21 follows the common core. In all matrimonial property regimes based on separation of property debts incurred by one spouse are his or her personal debts.

2. Because of the nature of the relationship between spouses it is quite common that spouses incur debts jointly. Such joint debts follow the general law of obligations.

1406 Art. 8 Catalan Family Code.
1407 § 1357 para. 3 German Civil Code.
1408 Art. 166 para. 1 Swiss Civil Code.
1409 Ch. 1 § 3 Swedish Marriage Code.
1410 See LUND-ANDERSEN/MAGNUSSEN, Danish Report, Q 103.
1411 § 52 Finnish Marriage Act. See KURKI-SUONIO, Finnish Report, Q 102 and 103.
1412 §§ 40 and 41 Norwegian Marriage Act. See SVERDRUP, Norwegian Report, Q 102 and Q 103.
1413 Art. 1536 para. 2 French Civil Code. See FERRAND/BRAAT, French Report, Q 136.
1414 Art. 1319 Spanish Civil Code. See GONZÁLEZ BEILFUSS, Spanish Report, Q 137.
1415 See BARLOW, English Report, Q 168 – 171.
1416 See SHANNON, Irish Report, Q 168–171.
1417 See MAIR, Scottish Report, Q 168–171.

Principle 4:22 Recovery of personal debts
Personal debts are recoverable from the debtor spouse's acquisitions and his or her reserved property.

Principe 4:22 Recouvrement des dettes personnelles
Les dettes personelles peuvent être recouvrées sur les acquêts et la propriéte réservée de l'époux débiteur.

Prinzip 4:22 Haftung für persönliche Verbindlichkeiten
Für persönliche Verbindlichkeiten haften die Errungenschaft und das Vorbehaltsvermögen des verpflichteten Ehegatten.

INTERNATIONAL INSTRUMENTS

As was mentioned in connection with Principle 4:21 it follows from the *French-German Agreement of 2010* that all debts are personal debts. Although the issue is not specifically dealt with it follows logically that they are only recoverable from the debtor's personal property.

COMPARATIVE OVERVIEW

In all matrimonial property regimes outside the *community system*, personal debts can only be recovered from the debtor spouse's personal property. Rules about the recovery of joint debts differ.

In *participation systems* personal debts are recoverable from the personal property of the debtor spouse (e.g. CATALONIA[1418]). Under SWISS law,[1419] each spouse is liable for his or her personal debts with all of his or her assets, regardless of whether they are classified as separate or marital property. Similarly, in the Nordic systems of *deferred community*, personal debts can be recovered from all the assets that belong to the debtor spouse, irrespective of whether the property is marital property or separate property (e.g. SWEDEN[1420] and NORWAY[1421]).

1418 See MARTÍN-CASALS/RIBOT, Catalan Report, Q 68.
1419 Art. 202 Swiss Civil Code.
1420 See JÄNTERÄ-JAREBORG/BRATTSTRÖM/WALLENG, Swedish Report, Q 104.
1421 See SVERDRUP, Norwegian Report, Q 105.

In *separation systems* personal debts can only be recovered from personal assets of the debtor spouse (e.g. AUSTRIA[1422]). In jurisdictions such as BELGIUM[1423] and PORTUGAL,[1424] joint debts can only be recovered from the assets of each spouse to the extent of his or her part in the joint debt, while under SWISS law,[1425] a creditor may choose to recover his or her debt from one spouse only. In common law jurisdiction marriages, personal debts can be recovered from all assets belonging to the debtor spouse (ENGLAND AND WALES[1426] and IRELAND[1427]). The same applies to SCOTLAND.[1428]

COMMENT

1. Principle 4:22 follows the common core. In all matrimonial property regimes based on separation of property personal debts can only be recovered from the debtor spouse's property. The debtor spouse's property consists of his or her acquisitions and reserved property.

2. If a debt was incurred jointly by both spouses the general law of obligations determines how such debts are to be recovered.

1422 See ROTH, Austrian Report, Q 138.

1423 Art. 1220 Belgian Cvill Code. See PINTENS/ALLAERTS/SEYNS/PIGNOLET, Belgian Report, Q 139.

1424 Art. 1695 para.2 Portuguese Civil Code. See DE OLIVEIRA/MARTINS/VÍTOR, Portuguese Report, Q 139.

1425 See SCHWENZER/BOCK, Swiss Report, Q 139.

1426 See BARLOW, English Report, Q 168 – 171.

1427 See SHANNON, Irish Report, Q 168–171.

1428 See MAIR, Scottish Report, Q 168–171.

ADMINISTRATION
ADMINISTRATION
VERWALTUNG

Principle 4:23 Administration of property
Subject to Principles 4:6 and 4:7, each spouse is entitled to administer his or her property independently.

Principe 4:23 Administration des biens
Sous réserve des principes 4:6 et 4:7, chaque époux est habilité à administrer seul ses biens.

Prinzip 4:23 Verwaltung des Vermögens
Vorbehaltlich der Prinzipien 4:6 und 4:7 ist jeder Ehegatte berechtigt, sein Vermögen allein zu verwalten.

INTERNATIONAL INSTRUMENTS

The *Council of Europe's Recommendation No. R(81) 15 on the Rights of Spouses Relating to the Occupation of the Family Home and the Use of Household Contents*, adopted in October 1981, recommends Member States to take legislative measures to ensure, inter alia, that legal acts by one spouse concerning the family home or the household contents can only be carried out with the consent of the other spouse. Alternatively, where this consent is unjustifiably withheld or impossible to obtain, the legal act can be authorized by a competent authority.

Article 4 of the *French-German Agreement of 2010* providing for an optional regime of participation in acquisitions establishes that each spouse administers his or her personal property independently and freely disposes of it. There are, however, limitations on the right of free disposal in connection to the family home and the household goods because the consent of both spouses is required (Art. 5).

COMPARATIVE OVERVIEW

Independent administration

As a rule, under the existing participation regimes such as participation in acquisition and community of accrued gains, the system of pure separation, the Nordic model of *deferred community property regime* and the common law system of *separation of property with distribution by the competent authority*, the owner spouse is, basically, free to administer his or her assets independently of the other spouse. Certain restrictions may, however, still apply, for example on the basis of what type of assets are at stake, in order to protect the other spouse's interests as well as the interests of the family including those of minor children. This applies in particular in relation to the matrimonial home and the household goods of the spouses.

In participation systems such as CATALONIA[1429] and GERMANY,[1430] each spouse has an independent right to administer his or her assets but he or she has the duty to inform the other sufficiently and adequately.[1431] The consent of the non-owner spouse is required for transactions concerning the matrimonial home and the household assets.[1432] In a pure separation system each spouse has the exclusive right to administer his or her property (AUSTRIA,[1433] BELGIUM,[1434] CATALONIA,[1435] FRANCE,[1436] GERMANY,[1437] ITALY,[1438] MALTA,[1439] PORTUGAL,[1440] SPAIN[1441] and SWITZERLAND[1442]). There are however important limitations in the interest of the family. As regards the family home and the household goods most legal systems require the consent of both spouses for acts of disposal (e.g. BELGIUM,[1443] CATALONIA[1444] and FRANCE[1445]).

1429 Art. 49 Catalan Family Code.
1430 § 1364 German Civil Code.
1431 See MARTÍN-CASALS/RIBOT, Catalan Report, Q 74. See DETHLOFF/MARTINY, German Report, Q 70.
1432 See MARTÍN-CASALS/RIBOT, Catalan Report, Q 72. See DETHLOFF/MARTINY, German Report, Q 72.
1433 See ROTH, Austrian Report, Q 140.
1434 Art. 1466 Belgian Civil Code.
1435 Art. 37 Catalan Family Code.
1436 Art. 1536 para. 2 French Civil Code.
1437 See DETHLOFF/MARTINY, German Report, Q 140.
1438 See Art. 217 para. 1 Italian Civil Code.
1439 Art. 1334 Maltese Civil Code.
1440 Art. 1678 para. 1 and Art. 1735 Portuguese Civil Code.
1441 Art. 1437 Spanish Civil Code.
1442 Art. 247 Swiss Civil Code.
1443 See PINTENS/ALLAERTS/SEYNS/PIGNOLET, Belgian Report, Q 142.
1444 See MARTÍN-CASALS/RIBOT, Catalan Report, Q 142.
1445 See FERRAND/BRAAT, French Report, Q 142.

In the Nordic model of *deferred community property*, the starting point of the owner spouse's free administration of the whole of his or her property is subject to the owner spouse's obligation to pay due regard to the other spouse's interests. Hence, in DENMARK,[1446] FINLAND[1447] and NORWAY,[1448] special rules apply obliging each spouse to administer his or her property (belonging to the deferred community property regime) in such a manner as not to expose it to the risk of deterioration to the detriment of the other spouse. The owner spouse's maladministration of his or her property gives the other spouse the right to claim compensation in a future dissolution of the regime.

In addition, in the Nordic model of the *deferred community property*, the spouse owning the matrimonial home may not convey it without the consent of the other spouse (DENMARK,[1449] FINLAND,[1450] NORWAY[1451] and SWEDEN[1452]). Special restrictions may also apply in respect of immovable property owned by a spouse (DENMARK[1453] and SWEDEN[1454]) even when this property does not constitute the matrimonial home but only on condition that that property is part of the deferred community property regime. Restrictions concerning the owner spouse's administration of his or her immovable property were formerly more common in the Nordic systems, but have successively been removed. Administration of household goods is subject to restrictions in all of these jurisdictions (DENMARK,[1455] FINLAND,[1456] NORWAY[1457] and SWEDEN[1458]).

In the common law system of "separation of property with distribution by the competent authority" each spouse administers his or her property freely (ENGLAND AND WALES,[1459] IRELAND[1460] and SCOTLAND[1461]). There are however restrictions as regards the matrimonial home. The IRISH Family Home Protection

1446 § 17 and § 23 Danish Act on the Legal Effects of Marriage. See LUND-ANDERSEN/MAGNUSSEN, Danish Report, Q 106 and Q 108.
1447 § 37 and § 94 Finnish Marriage Act. See KURKI-SUONIO, Finnish Report, Q 106.
1448 § 63 para. 2 Norwegian Marriage Act. See SVERDRUP, Norwegian Report, Q 112.
1449 See LUND-ANDERSEN/MAGNUSSEN, Danish Report, Q 91 and Q 106.
1450 See KURKI-SUONIO, Finnish Report, Q 91 and Q 106.
1451 § 32 Norwegian Marriage Act. See SVERDRUP, Norwegian Report, Q 108.
1452 See JÄNTERÄ-JAREBORG/BRATTSTRÖM/WALLENG, Swedish Report, Q 91.
1453 § 18 Danish Act on the Legal Effects of Marriage. See LUND-ANDERSEN/MAGNUSSEN, Danish Report, Q 108.
1454 See JÄNTERÄ-JAREBORG/BRATTSTRÖM/WALLENG, Swedish Report, Q 108.
1455 § 19 Danish Act on the Legal Effects of Marriage. See LUND-ANDERSEN/MAGNUSSEN, Danish Report, Q 108.
1456 § 39 Finnish Marriage Act. See KURKI-SUONIO, Finnish Report, Q 11.
1457 § 33 Norwegian Marriage Act. See SVERDRUP, Norwegian Report, Q 108.
1458 Ch. 7 § 4.2 Swedish Marriage Code. See JÄNTERÄ-JAREBORG/BRATTSTRÖM/WALLENG, Swedish Report, Q 11 and Q 108.
1459 See BARLOW, English Report, Q 172.
1460 See SHANNON, Irish Report, Q 172.
1461 See MAIR, Scottish Report, Q 172.

Act,[1462] for example, prevents the spouse in whose name the title to the family home is vested from dealing with his or her interest in the family home without the prior written consent of the other spouse. Similarly in SCOTLAND,[1463] there are restrictions on dealings with a third party in respect of the matrimonial home.

COMMENT

1. Principle 4:23 establishes that each spouse should be able to independently administer his or her property. This means that a spouse does not, as a rule, need the consent of the other spouse for the administrative measures he or she takes in respect of his or her property.

2. It would however be wrong to ignore the protection of the family home. There are limitations on this freedom of independent administration. It should be kept in mind that Principle 4:5 is fully applicable. Consequently any act of disposal of rights to the family home or the household goods intended for the spouses' joint use requires the consent of both spouses, irrespective of whether the family home or the household goods are acquisitions or reserved property of one spouse. The owner spouse should not therefore be able to administer these assets freely but must have the consent of the other spouse for purposes of disposal.

3. Each spouse is under a general duty to administer his or her property responsibly, in order to safeguard the other spouses' right to participate in the acquisitions. This duty can be enforced upon dissolution of the regime (see Principle 4:24(d)). Detrimental transactions can also be taken into account in calculating the acquisitions (Principle 4:27).

1462 See SHANNON, Irish Report, Q 174.

1463 See MAIR, Scottish Report, Q 174.

DISSOLUTION
DISSOLUTION
BEENDIGUNG

Principle 4:24 Grounds for dissolution

The regime on the participation in acquisitions is dissolved by

(a) the death of a spouse;
(b) the annulment of the marriage, divorce or legal separation;
(c) the change of the matrimonial property regime by agreement between the spouses; or
(d) the decision of the competent authority based upon serious grounds.

Principe 4:24 Motifs de dissolution

Le régime de participation aux acquêts est dissous par

(a) le décès d'un époux;
(b) l'annulation du mariage, le divorce ou la séparation de corps;
(c) le changement de régime matrimonial par accord entre les époux; ou
(d) la décision de l'autorité compétente, fondée sur des motifs graves.

Prinzip 4:24 Gründe für die Beendigung

Der Güterstand der Errungenschaftsbeteiligung wird beendet durch

(a) den Tod eines Ehegatten;
(b) die Nichtigerklärung der Ehe, die Ehescheidung oder die gesetzliche Trennung;
(c) die Änderung des Güterstands durch die Ehegatten; oder
(d) die Entscheidung der zuständigen Behörde aus wichtigen Gründen.

INTERNATIONAL INSTRUMENTS

Article 7 of the *French-German Agreement of 2010*, which provides for an optional regime of participation in accrued gains, establishes that this regime is dissolved by the death or the declaration of the death of one of the spouses, by a change of that matrimonial property regime to another regime, or by a judgment on divorce or by any other judicial decision resulting in the dissolution of the regime.

COMPARATIVE OVERVIEW

The separation of property regimes (see Comparative Overview under Principle 4:16) may be dissolved on several grounds. Strictly speaking, it is misleading to refer to the dissolution of a matrimonial property regime in common law jurisdictions.

Dissolution of the regime by the death of a spouse

The most common ground leading to the dissolution of any separation of property regime is the death of a spouse. In this respect, a common core exists. The regime is dissolved *ex lege*, directly by force of law, upon the death of the first spouse. A declaration of death in situations where there is reason to expect a spouse to have died likewise dissolves the regime (e.g. CATALONIA[1464] and SWITZERLAND[1465]), but the cut-off date may vary in such circumstances (see the Comparative Overview under Principle 4:25).

Dissolution of the regime through marriage annulment or divorce

A clear common core exists in relation to divorce. In all of the jurisdictions surveyed, divorce dissolves, *ex lege*, the applicable matrimonial property regime, even if the date when this takes effect varies (see the Comparative Overview under Principle 4:25). An additional common ground, *ex lege*, for the dissolution of the marital property regime is the annulment of the marriage, except in FINLAND[1466] and SWEDEN,[1467] which no longer provide for marriage annulment in their domestic legislation, but continue to recognise it through provisions of private international law.

Dissolution of the regime through legal or factual separation between the spouses

Another common ground leading to the dissolution of the regime is the legal separation between the spouses, whereby a judicial decree formalises the weakening of the marital ties between the spouses, without dissolving the marriage itself. However, this legal remedy is no longer provided by the domestic laws of FINLAND[1468] and SWEDEN,[1469] although both jurisdictions continue to recognise, through provisions of private international law, legal separations that have taken place abroad. In other jurisdictions, legal separation brings the applicable

1464 See MARTÍN-CASALS/RIBOT, Catalan Report, Q 79.
1465 Art. 38 para. 2 Swiss Civil Code. See SCHWENZER/BOCK, Swiss Report, Q 79.
1466 See KURKI-SUONIO, Finnish Report, Q 1(f).
1467 See See JÄNTERÄ-JAREBORG/BRATTSTRÖM/WALLENG, Swedish Report, Q 1(f).
1468 See KURKI-SUONIO, Finnish Report, Q 1(c).
1469 See JÄNTERÄ-JAREBORG/BRATTSTRÖM/WALLENG, Swedish Report, Q 1(c).

matrimonial property regime to an end, *ex lege*, at a specific date (CATALONIA,[1470] DENMARK,[1471] THE NETHERLANDS,[1472] NORWAY,[1473] SWITZERLAND[1474] and SPAIN[1475]). Factual separation of a certain duration can also, upon application, lead to the termination of the regime. Both GERMAN[1476] and GREEK[1477] law require, in such instances, the completion of a separation period of three years before the dissolution of the regime on accrued gains may take place. In contrast, according to the law of CATALONIA,[1478] de facto separation of at least one year is sufficient.

Spousal agreement

It is widely acknowledged among the jurisdictions surveyed that the applicable regime may be dissolved through an agreement to this effect between the spouses. In these cases, a spousal agreement changes the applicable regime to another regime. Normally, this is done in the form of a marital property agreement, in which the spouses agree to change the applicable regime to another regime (AUSTRIA,[1479] BELGIUM,[1480] CATALONIA,[1481] FRANCE,[1482] GERMANY,[1483] THE NETHERLANDS,[1484] SPAIN[1485] and SWITZERLAND[1486]). In the Nordic jurisdictions,[1487] the legislation does not provide for any alternative matrimonial property regimes to these jurisdictions' default regime of deferred community of property. However, an existing deferred community of property regime can effectively be terminated during the course of the marriage by the spouses introducing, in the form of a marital property agreement, a *pure* separation of property into the marriage. Similarly, the spouses may, during the

1470 Art. 51 Catalan Family Code. See also Art. 10 para. 2 as regards the Catalan system of separation of property. See MARTÍN-CASALS/RIBOT, Catalan Report, Q 148.
1471 § 16 para. 2 Danish Act on the Legal Effects of Marriage. See LUND-ANDERSEN/MAGNUSSEN, Danish Report, Q 114.
1472 See BOELE-WOELKI/SCHONEWILLE/SCHRAMA, Dutch Report, Q 78 as regards the so-called netting covenants regime.
1473 § 57 Norwegian Marriage Act. See SVERDRUP, Norwegian Report, Q 114.
1474 Art. 204 Swiss Civil Code. See SCHWENZER/BOCK, Swiss Report, Q 78.
1475 Art. 95 Spanish Civil Code. See GONZÁLEZ BEILFUSS, Spanish Report, Q 148.
1476 § 1385 para. 1 German Civil Code. See DETHLOFF/MARTINY, German Report, Q 78.
1477 Art. 1400 para. 2 and 1413 para. 1 Greek Civil Code. See KOUTSOURADIS/KOTRONIS/HATZANTONIS, Greek Report, Q 78.
1478 Art. 52 Catalan Family Code and MARTÍN-CASALS/RIBOT, Catalan Report, Q 78.
1479 § 1217 Austrian Civil Code. See ROTH, Austrian Report, Q 148.
1480 See PINTENS/ALLAERTS/SEYNS/PIGNOLET, Belgian Report, Q 148.
1481 Art. 51 Catalan Family Code. See MARTÍN-CASALS/RIBOT, Catalan Report, Q 78.
1482 See FERRAND/BRAAT, French Report, Q 148, with reference to the optional regime of separation of property in France.
1483 §§ 1408–1412 German Civil Code. See DETHLOFF/MARTINY, German Report, Q 78.
1484 See BOELE-WOELKI/SCHONEWILLE/SCHRAMA, Dutch Report, Q 78.
1485 Art. 1325 Spanish Civil Code. See GONZÁLEZ BEILFUSS, Spanish Report, Q 148.
1486 Art. 204 para. 1 Swiss Civil Code. See SCHWENZER/BOCK, Swiss Report, Q 78.
1487 This situation is explicitly mentioned by SVERDRUP, Norwegian Report, Q 114, but also applies in the other Nordic countries.

course of the marriage, set aside a previous marital property agreement stipulating pure separation of property, by concluding a new marital property agreement introducing the regime of deferred community of property into their marriage. In SWEDEN,[1488] the spouses may also agree without any requirement of a marital property agreement, following notification of the competent authority, to dissolve the default regime of deferred community of property, and distribute the property accordingly during the marriage.

Decision by a competent authority

In many of the jurisdictions surveyed, a decision by a competent authority is required to dissolve the regime *during the marriage*. Such decisions are often a result of serious mismanagement by one of the spouses of his or her property, which jeopardizes the interests of the other spouse, or a spouse's failure to provide information about his or her financial situation (e.g. CATALONIA,[1489] NORWAY[1490] and SWITZERLAND[1491]). In addition, in SWITZERLAND,[1492] a spouse's permanent incapability to give required consent qualifies as a ground for dissolution of the participation in the acquisitions regime. In all these cases, the decision is taken upon application, normally by the spouse whose interests are endangered. In several of the jurisdictions, a spouse's *bankruptcy* may provide a ground to terminate the regime. In FINLAND,[1493] the other spouse may within a year of the bankruptcy, make an announcement to a competent authority to the effect that neither spouse shall have any right to the other spouse's property; no property distribution will then take place.[1494] In DENMARK,[1495] a spouse's bankruptcy also constitutes a ground for the dissolution of the regime by the decision of the competent authority. In SWITZERLAND,[1496] the fact that a spouse is over-indebted, or that his or her acquisitions are distrained, qualify as grounds for the competent authority to dissolve the default regime of participation in acquisitions.

In ENGLAND AND WALES,[1497] IRELAND[1498] and SCOTLAND[1499] there is no regime to dissolve. However, a spouse's maladministration of assets may be a factor to be

1488 Ch. 9 § 1 para. 2 Swedish Marriage Code. See JÄNTERÄ-JAREBORG/BRATTSTRÖM/WALLENG, Swedish Report, Q 114.
1489 Art. 52 Catalan Family Code. See MARTÍN-CASALS/RIBOT, Catalan Report, Q 78.
1490 § 57 (c) Norwegian Marriage Act. See SVERDRUP, Norwegian Report, Q 114.
1491 Art. 185 para. 2. See SCHWENZER/BOCK, Swiss Report, Q 78.
1492 Art. 185 para. 2. See SCHWENZER/BOCK, Swiss Report, Q 78.
1493 See KURKI-SUONIO, Finnish Report, Q 114.
1494 This right of a spouse, as a result of the other spouse's bankruptcy, is sometimes called a *one-sided marital settlement*.
1495 § 38(2) Danish Act on Legal Effects of Marriage.
1496 Art. 185 para. 2 Swiss Civil Code.
1497 See BARLOW, English Report, Q 178.
1498 See SHANNON, Irish Report, Q 178.
1499 See MAIR, Scottish Report, Q 178.

taken into account when the court redistributes the spouses' property upon divorce.

COMMENT

1. Principle 4:24(a) establishes the most common ground for dissolution of any matrimonial property regime, namely the death of a spouse. In this case, the dissolution of the regime takes place *ex lege*, the marriage ending upon the death of the first spouse (see Principle 4:25(a)).

2. According to Principle 4:24(b) the annulment of the marriage, divorce or legal separation between the spouses also lead to dissolution of the participation in acquisitions regime. In these cases, the dissolution of the regime takes place *ex lege*, at the date specified by Principle 4.25(b). Divorce, marriage annulment and legal separation are all events demonstrating that, in economic terms, the marital community of interests and the solidarity between the spouses have come to an end, requiring the dissolution of the applicable matrimonial property regime. This is a widely accepted solution in the jurisdictions surveyed. This effect is also usually accepted in respect of foreign decrees on legal separation and marriage annulment in those few jurisdictions whose domestic laws have abolished such remedies. In these relevant respects, a common core thus exists.

3. Factual separation does not qualify as a ground for dissolution according to Principle 4:24 because, inter alia, it is difficult to prove when the separation started, with spouses often moving "out and in" of the matrimonial home, as a result of marital disharmony followed by reconciliation, even if short-lived. A common core does not exist because not all of the jurisdictions consider factual separation as a ground which leads to the dissolving of the applicable matrimonial property regime. In addition, it is relevant that the participation in acquisitions regime is based upon separation of ownership during the regime, making it less crucial, compared with a community in acquisitions regime, to take a factual separation into account.

4. Principle 4:24(c) acknowledges the spouses' right to change the participation in acquisitions regime to another matrimonial property regime in the form of an agreement during the marriage, normally a marital property agreement. This is an important expression of the recognition of the spouses' autonomy in respect of their matrimonial property relations (see Principle 4:10(b)). The agreement brings forth the dissolution of the participation in acquisitions regime, whereby the newly agreed regime takes over. It follows that the agreement must involve the replacement of the existing regime by another regime, and not just the modification of certain provisions in the current regime. In this respect, Principle 4:24(c) can be

seen as an important clarification and, in some cases, as an extension of the scope of the permitted spousal party autonomy. With the exception of the position of the common law jurisdictions, Principle 4:24(c) builds upon an existing common core.

5. Principle 4:24(d) provides for the dissolution of the regime by a decision of a competent authority where there are serious grounds for doing so. As demonstrated by the prevailing national law of the jurisdictions surveyed, serious grounds includes serious mismanagement of a spouse's property, or a spouse's unwillingness to sufficiently inform the other spouse of economic issues of relevance, thereby jeopardising the financial interests of the other spouse. Other grounds can include a spouse's bankruptcy or over-indebtedness. These examples are not exhaustive, but leave scope for national law. For example, a combination of various grounds could be held decisive in deciding to order the dissolution of the regime. The competent authority's decision can usually be expected to take place upon the application of the spouse whose interests are threatened, with the decision taken primarily to protect that spouse's interests. Since the decision terminates the regime, neither spouse can make any claims on the sharing of property acquired by the other spouse after the decision.

6. Where the participation in acquisitions regime is dissolved by the decision of a competent authority, in accordance with Principle 4:24(d), the reasons behind this decision can also constitute a ground for a competent authority to adjust the participation rights of the spouses in accordance with Principle 4:32.

Principle 4:25 Date of dissolution

The dissolution of the regime on the participation in acquisitions takes effect

(a) at the date of the death of a spouse;
(b) in the case of annulment of the marriage, divorce or legal separation, at the date of the application;
(c) in the case of an agreement to change to another matrimonial property regime, at the date of the change; and
(d) in the case of a decision by the competent authority, at the date of the application.

Principe 4:25 Date de dissolution

La dissolution du régime de participation aux acquêts prend effet

(a) à la date du décès d'un époux;
(b) en cas d'annulation du mariage, de divorce ou de séparation de corps, à la date de la demande;
(c) en cas de convention de changement de régime matrimonial, à la date du changement; et
(d) en cas de décision de l'autorité compétente, à la date de la demande.

Prinzip 4:25 Zeitpunkt der Beendigung

Die Beendigung des Güterstands der Errungenschaftsbeteiligung wird wirksam im Zeitpunkt

(a) des Todes eines Ehegatten;
(b) im Fall der Nichtigerklärung der Ehe, der Ehescheidung oder der gesetzlichen Trennung der Ehegatten im Zeitpunkt der Antragstellung;
(c) im Fall einer vereinbarten Änderung des Güterstands im Zeitpunkt der Änderung; und
(d) im Fall einer Entscheidung der zuständigen Behörde im Zeitpunkt der Antragstellung.

INTERNATIONAL INSTRUMENTS

According to the *French-German Agreement of 2010*, the regime is terminated when a decisive event takes place, or when any other ground for the termination of the regime occurs.[1500] These events and grounds are specified in the Agreement.

[1500] See Art. 7 in combination with Art. 10.

COMPARATIVE OVERVIEW

The date of dissolution determines which assets (and debts) are to be taken into account in the dissolution of the regime. Only assets (and debts) that existed at this precise date – the *cut off-date* or the critical *date* – are taken into account. As regards the grounds of dissolution, see Comparative Overview under Principle 4:24.

Dissolution by death of a spouse

In all of the surveyed jurisdictions, if the marriage is dissolved by the *death of a spouse*, then the date of the deceased spouse's death constitutes the decisive date. A common core thus exists among the jurisdictions. In the case of a declaration of death, judging from the little information provided by the national reports, the relevant date appears to vary. If divorce proceedings were pending at the time of the death, the decisive date may, in contrast, be the date when the divorce proceedings were initiated (e.g. SWEDEN[1501]).

Dissolution by divorce, marriage annulment or legal separation

When *divorce* constitutes the ground for dissolution, there are differences in respect of how the decisive date is established. In many of the jurisdictions, the decisive date is that when the divorce proceedings were initiated (CATALONIA,[1502] FINLAND,[1503] THE NETHERLANDS,[1504] SWITZERLAND[1505] and SWEDEN[1506]), meaning the date of the application for divorce to the competent authority. In NORWAY[1507] the date when the spouses ceased to live together is decisive if this took place before the application date for the divorce. In others, it is the date when the divorce decree becomes final (GERMANY,[1508] GREECE,[1509] BELGIUM,[1510]

1501 Ch. 9 § 2 para. 2 Swedish Marriage Code. See JÄNTERÄ-JAREBORG/BRATTSTRÖM/WALLENG, Swedish Report, Q 115.

1502 See MARTÍN-CASALS/RIBOT, Catalan Report, Q 79 and Q 149.

1503 KURKI-SUONIO, Finnish Report, Q 115.

1504 Art. 1:142 para. 1 sub (a)-(g) Dutch Civil Code. See BOELE-WOELKI/SCHONEWILLE/SCHRAMA, Dutch Report, Q 79.

1505 Art. 204 para. 2 Swiss Civil Code. See SCHWENZER/BOCK, Swiss Report, Q 79 and Q 149.

1506 See JÄNTERÄ-JAREBORG/BRATTSTRÖM/WALLENG, Swedish Report, Q 115.

1507 See SVERDRUP, Norwegian Report, Q 115.

1508 § 1564 German Civil Code. See DETHLOFF/MARTINY, German Report, Q 79 and Q 149.

1509 See KOUTSOURADIS/KOTRONIS/HATZANTONIS, Greek Report, Q 79.

1510 Art. 1278 para. 1 Belgian Judicial Code. To become effective against a third party, the dissolution of the regime must be registered and applies from the date of registration. See PINTENS/ALLAERTS/SEYNS/PIGNOLET, Belgian Report, Q 149.

DENMARK,[1511] ITALY[1512] and SPAIN[1513]). The approach chosen by each jurisdiction is also used to establish the relevant date when the dissolution of the regime takes place due to legal separation or the annulment of the marriage.

Dissolution by spousal agreement

In many of the jurisdictions surveyed, if the dissolution results from an *agreement between the spouses to change the regime* into another regime, the date of the agreement or of a notarial deed is decisive as regards the effect of the change between the spouses (BELGIUM,[1514] CATALONIA,[1515] GERMANY,[1516] NORWAY,[1517] SWITZERLAND[1518] and SPAIN[1519]). In relation to third parties, another date may be decisive for the change to take effect, as, for example, the date of the required registration of the change (CATALONIA[1520] and MALTA[1521]). It may also be the day of the official publication of an excerpt of the stipulated changes, unless the spouses have informed the third parties of the modification, in which case the change applies from the date the information was provided (BELGIUM[1522]). In addition, there are also jurisdictions in which the agreement takes effect on the same date, both in relation to the spouses and in relation to third parties. Thus, in SWEDEN,[1523] the date in which a new matrimonial property agreement is registered with the civil registry or, if the spouses simply agree to dissolve the regime during marriage, the date of notification to the registry of this agreement, is decisive in both instances.[1524] In DENMARK[1525] and FINLAND,[1526] it is not the date of the marital property agreement, but its

1511 See LUND-ANDERSEN/MAGNUSSEN, Danish Report, Q 115.

1512 See PATTI/CARICATO/IRTI/IANNICELLI/SERA/DI STEFANO/PETÖ, Italian Report Q 149.

1513 Art. 95 para. 1 Spanish Civil Code. See GONZÁLEZ BEILFUSS, Spanish Report, Q 149.

1514 See PINTENS/ALLAERTS/SEYNS/PIGNOLET, Belgian Report, Q 44.

1515 See MARTÍN-CASALS/RIBOT, Catalan Report, Q 79.

1516 See DETHLOFF/MARTINY, German Report, Q 79 and Q 149.

1517 See SVERDRUP, Norwegian Report, Q 115 and Q 149.

1518 Art. 204 para. 1 Swiss Civil Code. See SCHWENZER/BOCK, Swiss Report, Q 79 and Q 149. Basically, Swiss law permits the spouses also to agree upon the date.

1519 See GONZÁLEZ BEILFUSS, Spanish Report, Q 149.

1520 Art. 17 para. 2 Catalan Family Code. See MARTÍN-CASALS/RIBOT, Catalan Report, Q 79 and Q 149.

1521 See FARRUGIA, Maltese Report, Q 149.

1522 See PINTENS/ALLAERTS/SEYNS/PIGNOLET, Belgian Report, Q 44.

1523 Ch. 7 § 3 para. 3 and Ch. 9 § 2 para. 2 Swedish Marriage Code. See JÄNTERÄ-JAREBORG/BRATTSTRÖM/WALLENG, Swedish Report, Q 115.

1524 In fact, since under Swedish law, a marital property agreement does not affect ownership rights to property or debts, it is, strictly speaking, irrelevant from the point of view of third persons, as its legal effects are limited to the spouses. See JÄNTERÄ-JAREBORG/BRATTSTRÖM/WALLENG, Swedish Report, Q 194 and AGELL, *Nordisk äktenskapsrätt, En jämförande studie av dansk, finsk, isländsk, norsk och svensk rätt med diskussion av reformbehov och harmoniseringsmöjligheter*, Nord 2003:2, pp. 190 f.

1525 See LUND-ANDERSEN/MAGNUSSEN, Danish Report, Q 194.

1526 § 44 Finnish Marriage Act. See KURKI-SUONIO, Finnish Report, Q 191.

registration with, or publication by, the competent authority, which makes the agreement valid between the spouses and third parties. The relevant date of registration is determined on the basis of the application for registration to the competent authority.

Dissolution by the decision of the competent authority

In many cases, a competent authority intervenes and orders dissolution of the regime, following an application by the spouse whose interests are threatened (see Comparative Overview under Principle 4:24). Differences exist regarding the date which is decisive for the regime's dissolution. It may be the date when the application was made (e.g. DENMARK,[1527] NORWAY[1528] and SWITZERLAND[1529]), or it may be the date when the decision establishing the dissolution becomes final (GERMANY[1530]).

COMMENT

1. Whereas Principle 4:24 lists the grounds for dissolution of the participation in acquisitions regime, Principle 4:25 provides the date from which each such ground becomes effective.

2. Principle 4:25(a) reflects the common core. When the regime is dissolved upon the death of a spouse, the date of the spouse's death constitutes the critical *cut-off date*, for ascertaining what property is to be included in the regime to be dissolved. The justification for this solution is that the spouse's death immediately terminates the marriage itself, bringing its legal effects to an end. The Principle does not touch upon the situation in which proceedings for divorce, marriage annulment or legal separation were pending at the time of the death of the spouse, with the result that there may be a number of concurrent critical dates. The solution to be adopted is left to the national law to determine.

3. Marriage annulment, divorce, and even legal separation mark the end of the marital community of interests and spousal solidarity. When an application is granted by the competent authority, the question arises as to whether it should be the date of the application, or the date of the final decree, which should be decisive as the critical date for the dissolution of the regime. According to Principle 4:25(b), the date of the application is decisive. This means that once the

1527 See LUND-ANDERSEN/MAGNUSSEN, Danish Report, Q 115.

1528 § 57 (c) and § 60 para. 1 Norwegian Marriage Act. See SVERDRUP, Norwegian Report, Q 115.

1529 Art. 204 para. 2 Swiss Civil Code. See SCHWENZER/BOCK, Swiss Report, Q 79.

1530 § 1388 German Civil Code. See DETHLOFF/MARTINY, German Report, Q 79.

annulment of the marriage, divorce or legal separation is granted, the decree takes effect retroactively from the date of the application. This solution, although it is supported for its simplicity and fairness, does not form part of any existing common core, since approximately half of the jurisdictions regard the date of the final decision to be as decisive. However, one advantage of the solution adopted by Principle 4:25(b) is that a spouse objecting to the divorce, annulment or legal separation cannot, through time-consuming appeals, influence the scope of the acquisitions to be taken into account. This promotes foreseeability in a situation where inter-spousal solidarity has come to an end. Furthermore, there is no reason to burden the Principles with criteria that many (almost half) of the jurisdictions have found to be unnecessary. In this sense, the solution is based on a better law-approach.

4. In contrast to Principle 4:50(b) concerning the community in acquisitions regime, Principle 4:25 does not take into account, in the case of factual separation between the spouses, the date when the spouses separated. A crucial difference is that the participation in acquisitions regime is based upon separation of ownership, making the mutual economic dependency and solidarity between the spouses less evident than under the community in acquisitions regime. The Principle also strives to be as simple as possible. A factual separation between the spouses can, nevertheless, depending on the circumstances, qualify as exceptional hardship which, according to Principle 4:32, gives the competent authority the power to adjust the participation.

5. The majority of the jurisdictions acknowledge that the spouses may, during the marriage, change the applicable regime to another regime through an agreement. As acknowledged by Principle 4:24(c), such change of necessity dissolves the previously existing regime. According to Principle 4:25(c), the date of the change is decisive. As the comparative overview shows, a different date may be relevant, such as the date when the change takes place between the spouses, or when the change takes place in relation to third parties. This date can, nevertheless, also be the same for both relationships. In order to keep the drafting as simple as possible, and having regard to the existing differences of approach, Principle 4:25(c) leaves it to national law to decide the date on which the change takes place, in relation between the spouses, and in relation to third parties.

6. When a jurisdiction provides for the dissolution of the regime by the decision of a competent authority on serious grounds, the date of the application constitutes the common core regarding the decisive cut-off event. This approach is also followed in Principle 4:25(d). As under Principle 4:25(b), this solution is not only simple, but also has the advantage that the other spouse cannot postpone the date of the regime's dissolution through appeals, and consequently, influence what assets (and debts) are to be taken into account. By taking this position, Principle 4:25(d) protects the applicant spouse whose financial interests may be threatened.

7. It follows from the separation of ownership and the separation of debts under the participation in acquisitions regime that, in contrast to the community of acquisitions regime and the solutions promoted by Principle 4:50(b)-(d), there is no need for special dates for the dissolution of the regime in relation to third persons. Instead, the same dates apply as in the interspousal relationship. The drafting of Principle 4:25(b)-(d) is therefore, in these respects, simpler and less detailed than that of Principle 4:50(b)-(d).

LIQUIDATION
LIQUIDATION
AUSEINANDERSETZUNG

Principle 4:26 Determination and valuation of acquisitions
(1) The acquisitions of each spouse should be determined at the date of the dissolution of the regime, as specified by Principle 4:25.
(2) The acquisitions should be valued at the date of the liquidation of the regime.

Principe 4:26 Détermination et évaluation des acquêts
(1) Les acquêts de chaque époux sont déterminés à la date de dissolution du régime, telle que précisée au Principe 4:25.
(2) Les acquêts sont évalués à la date de liquidation du régime.

Prinzip 4:26 Feststellung und Bewertung der Errungenschaft
(1) Die Errungenschaft jedes Ehegatten wird im Zeitpunkt der Beendigung des Güterstands festgestellt, wie in Prinzip 4:25 bestimmt.
(2) Die Errungenschaft wird im Zeitpunkt der Auseinandersetzung des Güterstands bewertet.

INTERNATIONAL INSTRUMENTS

The rules of the *French-German Agreement of 2010* relating to the determination and valuation of assets reflect those of a regime based on a system of participation in accrued gains. It follows that a distinction is made between the initial assets and the final assets of each spouse. The *initial assets* of each spouse consist of his or her assets (including debts) at the time of the regime's entry into force, as well as of assets which the spouse has acquired subsequently as a gift, inheritance or bequest, or as damages for suffered pain (Art. 8). The valuation of the initial assets is based on their value at the date of the regime's entry into force or, if they have been acquired after that date, the date of their acquisition (Art. 9). When the dissolution of the regime takes place at a later date, the valuation is adjusted to the changes in the concerned Contracting State's general consumer price index. Immovable property, with some exceptions, is valued at the date of the dissolution of the regime. If such property has been disposed of, or replaced, during the course of the regime, its valuation is based on the date of the disposition or replacement. The *final assets* of each spouse consist of his or her assets (debts included) at the date of the dissolution of the regime (Art. 10), and should be given the value they have at that date (Art. 11). Gifts given by a spouse are subject to special rules regarding both the extent to which they are to be included among the final assets, and their valuation (Art. 10–11). Under this regime, the spouses have a claim for equal participation in the net value of the accrued gains made during the regime.[1531]

COMPARATIVE OVERVIEW

General characteristics

The surveyed systems which, broadly speaking, qualify as separation systems due to the separation of ownership prevailing during the existence of the matrimonial property regime, differ greatly as regards the extent and the manner in which the spouses participate in each other's assets once the regime is dissolved. These differences have consequences for the determination and valuation of the assets to be shared. The date of the dissolution of the regime is normally decisive regarding which assets are subject to any participation claims. This date can also be used in deciding the value to be given to the included assets. Alternatively, this valuation can be based on another date, usually the date of the liquidation of the regime. This difference in approach is of particular relevance when the value of the assets changes, positively or negatively, during the lapse of time between the regime's dissolution and its liquidation. To what extent, and on which ground, should the spouses share in the increase or decrease in the value of the assets (debts included) after the critical date?

Regimes on the participation in acquisitions or community of accrued gains

Under the SWISS system,[1532] when the regime on participation in acquisitions is dissolved, each asset and liability has to be allocated to one of four different categories of property, the separate property (*Eigengut*)[1533] and the acquisitions (*Errungenschaft*)[1534] of each spouse. The decisive date for the valuation of each asset is the date of the settlement of the regime.[1535] If, however, such a settlement is subject to court proceedings, the date of the judgment is decisive. The market value of the assets is decisive,[1536] but ascertained in various ways,

1531 See in particular Chapter 4, Articles 7–14 of the Agreement.
1532 Art. 207 para. 1 Swiss Civil Code. See SCHWENZER/BOCK, Swiss Report, Q 82.
1533 Art. 198 Swiss Civil Code.
1534 Art. 197 Swiss Civil Code.
1535 Art. 214 Swiss Civil Code. See SCHWENZER/BOCK, Swiss Report, Q 82.
1536 Art. 211 Swiss Civil Code. See SCHWENZER/BOCK, Swiss Report, Q 81.

depending on the asset in question. For example, in order to ensure that a farming enterprise can be continued by the farming spouse, the farm is valued on the basis of a capitalised earnings value, which is more favourable to that spouse.[1537] In this system, after the date of the dissolution of the regime and the allocation of the assets to the four different categories, the value of the assets may have changed.[1538] An increase in the value of an asset belongs to the category of assets to which the asset is allocated, but is limited to a surplus derived from market variations, and is not generated by the contributions of a spouse.[1539]

According to the GERMAN default regime,[1540] the accrued gains to be shared by the spouses are established by determining the amount by which the final assets of each spouse exceed his or her initial assets after subtraction of debts. This means that both the initial and the final assets have to be determined and valued. The relevant date for the determination and valuation of the initial assets is the date at which the regime came into force. For subsequent acquisitions belonging to the category of initial assets, the value at the time of the acquisition is decisive.[1541] In both cases, the market value of the assets is decisive. The relevant date for the determination and valuation of the final assets is the date of the dissolution of the regime, with the exception of divorce, in which case the date of the application is decisive for the calculation of the accrued gains.[1542] The increase in value of the initial assets is also to be shared, with the exception of a value increase solely due to inflation. On the other hand, any agricultural or forestry asset which is to be taken into account for the computation of the initial or final assets, is calculated according to the value of its produce.

In GREECE,[1543] a distinction is made between the initial value of the assets at the commencement of the regime and their value at the time of the dissolution of the regime (i.e. the death of a spouse or a final decision on divorce or marriage annulment). An alternative view, however, is, that the date of the application for marriage dissolution should be decisive.[1544] In the case of separation between the spouses preceding the dissolution of the marriage, there is a rebuttable presumption that one third of the property acquired after the separation should be taken into account.

1537 Art. 212 Swiss Civil Code. See SCHWENZER/BOCK, Swiss Report, Q 80.
1538 See SCHWENZER/BOCK, Swiss Report, Q 82.
1539 Art. 206 and 209 Swiss Civil Code. See SCHWENZER/BOCK, Swiss Report, Q 81.
1540 § 1373 German Civil Code. See DETHLOFF/MARTINY, German Report, Q 81.
1541 § 1376 para. 1.2 German Civil Code. See DETHLOFF/MARTINY, German Report, Q 82.
1542 § 1384 German Civil Code. See DETHLOFF/MARTINY, German Report, Q 82.
1543 See KOUTSOURADIS/KOTRONIS/HATZANTONIS, Greek Report, Q 82.
1544 See KOUTSOURADIS/KOTRONIS/HATZANTONIS, Greek Report, Q 82.

The optional *participation in acquisition regimes* or *regimes on the community of accrued gains* which are available in various jurisdictions (e.g. FRANCE[1545] and CATALONIA[1546]) are inspired by either the SWISS model or the GERMAN model.

Deferred community property regimes

Under the *deferred community property regimes*, the assets which will be subject to participation claims are determined on the basis of the date of the dissolution of the regime (DENMARK,[1547] FINLAND,[1548] NORWAY[1549] and SWEDEN[1550]). However, it should be noted that in the case of divorce, the determination of this date can vary between the jurisdictions, from the date on which the spouse ceased to live together, to the date on which the divorce proceedings were initiated, or to the date of the final decree on divorce (see the Comparative Overview under Principle 4:25).

As regards the decisive date for the valuation of the assets to be included in the property division, in all of the jurisdictions surveyed, the spouses are free to agree on the relevant date.[1551] Where there is no agreement, there is wide support for regarding the date of the property distribution as decisive (DENMARK,[1552] FINLAND,[1553] NORWAY[1554] and SWEDEN[1555]). More precisely, NORWEGIAN law[1556] makes a distinction between the date of the valuation of assets which belong to one spouse, and are retained by him or her in the property distribution, and the other assets. In the former case, the date of the dissolution of the regime is decisive for the valuation of the assets, since the owner spouse does not need to share any subsequent increase in the value of the assets with the other spouse, and other spouse is not concerned with the risk that the value of these assets decreases. In other cases, under NORWEGIAN law, the date of the allocation of the property into portions for each spouse is decisive. In SWEDEN,[1557] the prevailing practice is that assets are valued at the date when the content of the spouses'

1545 Art. 1569 et seq. French Civil Code.
1546 See MARTÍN-CASALS/RIBOT, Catalan Report, Q 57.
1547 See LUND-ANDERSEN/MAGNUSSEN, Danish Report, Q 117.
1548 See KURKI-SUONIO, Finnish Report, Q 117.
1549 § 69 para. 2 Norwegian Marriage Act. See SVERDRUP, Norwegian Report, Q 117 and AGELL, *Nordisk äktenskapsrätt*, TemaNord 2003:2, p. 269.
1550 See JÄNTERÄ-JAREBORG/BRATTSTRÖM/WALLENG, Swedish Report, Q 117.
1551 See AGELL, *Nordisk äktenskapsrätt*, TemaNord 2003:2, p. 268. LUND-ANDERSEN/MAGNUSSEN, Danish Report, Q 117.
1552 See LUND-ANDERSEN/MAGNUSSEN, Danish Report, Q 117.
1553 See KURKI-SUONIO, Finnish Report, Q 117.
1554 § 60 Norwegian Marriage Act. See SVERDRUP, Norwegian Report, Q 117.
1555 See JÄNTERÄ-JAREBORG/BRATTSTRÖM/WALLENG, Swedish Report, Q 117.
1556 § 60 Norwegian Marriage Act. See SVERDRUP, Norwegian Report, Q 117.
1557 See JÄNTERÄ-JAREBORG/BRATTSTRÖM/WALLENG, Swedish Report, Q 117.

assets is decided upon. Essentially, this is also the FINNISH[1558] position. Valuation is based on the market value of the assets (DENMARK,[1559] FINLAND,[1560] NORWAY[1561] and SWEDEN[1562]). In all of the jurisdictions, a considerable period of time may have passed between the dissolution of the regime, the determination of which assets should be included, and their valuation. In legal literature, it is recommended that the valuation of assets and liabilities should take place as close as possible in time to the actual distribution of the assets.[1563]

Regimes on pure separation of property

In *pure separation systems*, a distinction must be drawn between those systems where the property of the spouses is not shared after dissolution of the regime, and those where some sort of participation or reallocation takes place. In the former, there is no need to determine and value any assets after the dissolution of the regime, since each spouse retains his or her separate property, and joint property is divided according to ordinary civil law rules (BELGIUM,[1564] FRANCE,[1565] GERMANY,[1566] PORTUGAL[1567] and SPAIN[1568]). In jurisdictions such as AUSTRIA or CATALONIA, where separation of property is the default rule, an adjustment takes place after dissolution. In AUSTRIA,[1569] a division of the matrimonial property and marital savings takes place after dissolution of the matrimonial property regime for which the ownership relationships are not relevant. This division is governed by the principle of marital participation in the assets owned by the other spouse; it would appear that the date of the dissolution of the regime is also decisive for the valuation of these assets.

Separation of property with discretion for the competent authority

Upon divorce, the common law systems (ENGLAND AND WALES[1570] and IRELAND[1571]) provide the competent authority with a discretionary power of redistribution of the entire property owned by the spouses, in accordance with statutory guidelines. This implies that all assets and liabilities are subsequently

1558 See KURKI-SUONIO, Finnish Report, Q 117.
1559 See LUND-ANDERSEN/MAGNUSSEN, Danish Report, Q 116.
1560 See KURKI-SUONIO, Finnish Report, Q 116.
1561 § 69 para. 1 Norwegian Marriage Act. See SVERDRUP, Norwegian Report, Q 116.
1562 See JÄNTERÄ-JAREBORG/BRATTSTRÖM/WALLENG, Swedish Report, Q 116.
1563 See JÄNTERÄ-JAREBORG/BRATTSTRÖM/WALLENG, Swedish Report, Q 117.
1564 See PINTENS/ALLAERTS/SEYNS/PIGNOLET, Belgian Report, Q 150.
1565 See FERRAND/BRAAT, French Report, Q 150.
1566 See DETHLOFF/MARTINY, German Report, Q 150.
1567 See DE OLIVEIRA/MARTINS/VÍTOR, Portuguese Report, Q 150.
1568 See GONZÁLEZ BEILFUSS, Spanish Report, Q 150.
1569 See ROTH, Austrian Report, Q 150.
1570 Matrimonial Causes Act (1973) S. 25. See BARLOW, English Report, Q 181.
1571 See SHANNON, Irish Report, Q 182.

determined and valued.[1572] In SCOTLAND,[1573] primarily only the assets which are acquired during the marriage are subject to a sharing upon dissolution of the regime, even if the court may also take other assets into account. This implies that the relevant date for the valuation of the assets is the date of the marriage dissolution.

COMMENT

1. Principle 4:26(1) refers to the date of the dissolution of the regime, as specified by Principle 4:25, as being decisive in determining which acquisitions should be taken into account in the liquidation of the regime. A cut-off date applies in this respect, fixing the assets to be included, in line with the prevailing common core. Once the regime has come to an end, irrespective of the ground of dissolution, no subsequent acquisitions should be taken into account.

2. The choice of the relevant date for the valuation of the acquisitions is less self-evident, since there is often a lapse of time between the regime's dissolution and its liquidation. During this period, the value of the spouses' acquisitions may increase or decrease. If the valuation of the acquisitions is linked with the date of the dissolution of the regime, the advantage is that a spouse cannot influence the outcome by delaying the actual liquidation. Furthermore, by taking into account a decisive event which marks the end of an inter-spousal community of economic interests and solidarity, or the entry into force of a new agreed regime, predictability is promoted. The disadvantage is that this solution can turn out to be unfair to either one of the spouses in cases in which, between the regime's dissolution and its liquidation, the market value of the acquisitions changes considerably.

3. The approaches taken by the surveyed jurisdictions regarding the decisive date of valuation are divided between the regime's date of dissolution and the date of its liquidation. It is therefore not possible to perceive any clear new trend in favour of either. By choosing the date of the liquidation for the valuation of the acquisitions, and thus giving regard to the current value of the acquisitions, Principle 4:26(2) strives to promote fairness between both spouses. As a result, both spouses equally share the risks relating to the changes in the value of the acquisitions of either spouse after the date of the regime's dissolution. The sooner the liquidation takes place, the smaller the difference between the approaches. If the result would lead to exceptional hardship for a spouse, the

[1572] See BARLOW English Report, Q 182 and SHANNON, Irish Report, Q 182.
[1573] See MAIR, Scottish Report, Q 182.

outcome may be adjusted by decision of a competent authority in accordance with Principle 4:32.

4. Principle 4:26 leaves to national law to determine how the acquisitions should be valued, whether in accordance with their apparent market value, or by following some other method (for example, with regard to farms or other enterprises).

Principle 4:27 Detrimental transactions

In calculating the acquisitions of each spouse account should be taken of

(a) excessive gifts;
(b) dissipation of assets;
(c) other acts that have intentionally diminished the value of the acquisitions to the detriment of the other spouse.

Principe 4:27 Opérations préjudiciables

Lors du calcul des acquêts de chaque époux, il est tenu compte

(a) des donations excessives;
(b) des biens dissipés;
(c) d'autres actes ayant intentionnellement diminué la valeur des acquêts au détriment de l'autre époux.

Prinzip 4:27 Benachteiligende Handlungen

Bei der Berechnung der Errungenschaft jedes Ehegatten werden berücksichtigt

(a) übermäßige Schenkungen;
(b) Verschwendung von Vermögensgegenständen;
(c) andere Handlungen, die den Wert der Errungenschaft zum Nachteil des anderen Ehegatten absichtlich vermindert haben.

INTERNATIONAL INSTRUMENTS

Article 10 para. 2 of the *French-German Agreement of 2010* contains a rule against detrimental actions of one spouse. It provides that the value of assets that were the object of transactions undertaken by one spouse to the detriment of the other, or that were squandered, has to be added to the final assets of that spouse. This produces the result of increasing the amount of the property that has to be shared thereby rendering detrimental actions ineffective.

COMPARATIVE OVERVIEW

Protection against detrimental actions

In *participation systems* each spouse has a claim to sharing the gains of the other spouse. In these systems there are therefore rules that protect one spouse against detrimental actions taken by the other. GERMAN law[1574] provides that the final assets of a spouse include notional amounts by which such assets were

[1574] § 1375 para. 2 and 3 German Civil Code. See DETHLOFF/MARTINY, German Report, Q 81.

diminished with the consequence that these amounts qualify as gains that spouses have to share. Detrimental acts are further specified as unjustified gifts or transactions undertaken with the intention of causing a detriment to the other spouse. There are, however, limitations to such rules. The amount of the property diminution is not included in the final assets if it occurred at least ten years before the termination of the matrimonial property regime or if the other spouse gave his or her consent to the detriment. Under the optional CATALAN regime of participation,[1575] the value of unilateral extraordinary gifts or of assets that have been destroyed or transferred with the aim of diminishing the gains fraudulently will be included in the patrimony of the concerned spouse. If after assessing the participation credit the debtor spouse has not the means to pay it, there is a possibility for the creditor spouse to request the rescission of those alienations. SWISS law[1576] provides that if a spouse has made significant gratuitous donations (exceeding customary gifts) without the consent of the other spouse during the five years preceding the dissolution of the regime, or if a spouse has deliberately squandered his or her marital property to diminish the financial claims of the other spouse, such divestments are added to the marital property.

In the *deferred community systems* spouses also have a claim after dissolution to sharing the property owned by the other spouse, which needs to be protected. Under FINNISH law,[1577] for example, it is possible to compensate an essential decrease in the net value of the marital property caused by a spouse who has mismanaged his or her financial affairs or misused his or her right to administer the marital property or other inappropriate action.

There are rules with a similar function in common law systems since spouses also receive financial provision after divorce. In ENGLAND AND WALES,[1578] maladministration of assets can be equated to inequitable conduct and this factor will be taken into account by the competent authority on redistribution of the property after divorce. Under SCOTS law,[1579] the principle of equal sharing after divorce can be departed from when determining the amount of financial provision, if it can be argued that the maladministration of one spouse has affected the value of the property which is available for sharing. After financial provision there is also the possibility of applying to the court for setting aside or varying any property transaction brought about by the other spouse within the

1575 Arts. 55 (b) and (c) and 60 para. 1 Catalan Family Code. See MARTÍN-CASALS/RIBOT, Catalan Report, Q 72.
1576 Art. 208 Swiss Civil Code. See SCHWENZER/BOCK, Swiss Report, Q 72.
1577 § 94 Finnish Marriage Act. See KURKI-SUONIO, Finnish Report, Q 118.
1578 See BARLOW, English Report, Q 178.
1579 See MAIR, Scottish Report, Q 178.

previous five years, if such transaction had the effect of defeating in whole or in part the claim for financial provision (so called avoidance transactions).

COMMENT

1. Principle 4:27 seeks to protect a spouse whose claim to participation in the acquisitions of the other spouse has been unduly reduced by the actions or omissions of the other spouse. It provides that when calculating the latter spouse's acquisitions, account should be taken of any excessive gifts, dissipation of assets and any other acts that have intentionally diminished the value of the acquisitions to the detriment of the other spouse.

2. A gift is by definition a gratuitous transaction that diminishes the acquisitions. There are however gifts that are permissible because they are normal in the social environment of the spouses. When gifts go beyond what is normal they cause undue detriment to the other spouse's participation claim. Whether a gift is or is not excessive may be disputed between the spouses. If they cannot reach agreement the matter will have to be decided by the competent authority.

3. Dissipation can be equated with extravagant and excessive spending and will also vary depending on the social environment. Disputes are again to be solved by the competent authority.

4. Other transactions need to fulfill two requirements in order to fall under Principle 4:27. They need firstly to have been undertaken with the intention of diminishing the value of the acquisitions and, secondly, such transactions must have resulted in a diminution of the value of the acquisitions that runs contrary to the other spouse's participation claim.

Principle 4:28 Compensation

(1) The acquisitions of a spouse should be compensated for any contribution profiting his or her reserved property.

(2) The reserved property of a spouse should be compensated for any contribution profiting his or her acquisitions.

(3) Debts encumber the property in relation to which they were incurred. In cases of doubt they are presumed to encumber the acquisitions.

(4) In the case of investment for the acquisition, improvement or preservation of an asset the calculation of the compensation should take into account any resulting increase or decrease in the value of the asset.

(5) The compensation should be paid in money, unless the spouses agree otherwise.

Principe 4:28 Compensation

(1) Une récompense est due pour toute contribution des acquêts d'un époux réalisée au profit de ses biens réservés.

(2) Une récompense est due pour toute contribution des biens réservés d'un époux réalisée au profit de ses acquêts.

(3) Les dettes grèvent le patrimoine en rapport avec lequel elles sont nées. En cas de doute, elles sont présumées grever les acquêts.

(4) En cas d'investissement en vue de l'acquisition, de l'amélioration ou de la conservation d'un bien, il est tenu compte, lors du calcul du montant de la récompense, de la plus-value ou de la moins-value du bien au profit duquel l'investissement a été réalisé.

(5) La récompense est due sous forme monétaire, sauf accord contraire des époux.

Prinzip 4:28 Ausgleich

(1) Die Errungenschaft eines Ehegatten erhält einen Ausgleich für jeden Beitrag zugunsten seines Vorbehaltsvermögens.

(2) Das Vorbehaltsvermögen eines Ehegatten erhält einen Ausgleich für jeden Beitrag zugunsten seiner Errungenschaft.

(3) Verbindlichkeiten belasten das Vermögen in Bezug auf welches sie eingegangen wurden. Im Zweifel wird vermutet, dass sie die Errungenschaft belasten.

(4) Im Fall der Anlage für den Erwerb, die Verbesserung oder den Erhalt eines Vermögensgegenstands ist bei der Berechnung des Ausgleichs der gestiegene oder gesunkene Wert des Vermögensgegenstands in Betracht zu ziehen.

(5) Der Ausgleich ist in Geld zu zahlen, sofern die Ehegatten nichts anderes vereinbaren.

INTERNATIONAL INSTRUMENTS

None of particular relevance.

COMPARATIVE OVERVIEW

The need for compensation

In participation regimes making a distinction between the reserved property and the acquisitions of a spouse these categories of property are not always kept separate by the spouses. It may occur that assets belonging to the reserved property of the spouses have been invested into the acquisitions and vice versa or that assets belonging to one category have been used for the payment of debts of the other. Before the acquisitions can be calculated a balance between the payments by the reserved property and by the acquisitions has to be drawn up in order to avoid unjust enrichment. Therefore, the SWISS participation regime[1580] prescribes compensation if assets belonging to one category of property have been invested in the other category. Compensation also applies where debts related to one category of property have been paid by the other.[1581] A debt encumbers the property in relation to which it was incurred. When it is not possible to prove this relationship, the debt is presumed to encumber the acquisitions.[1582]

The need for compensation does not arise in the GERMAN and GREEK participation systems because those systems do not make a distinction between reserved property and acquisitions but equalize the difference between the final and initial property of each spouse (see the Comparative Overview under Principle 4:31).

In deferred community systems compensation is applied. In DENMARK,[1583] a spouse may claim compensation if he or she has used assets from his or her reserved property to acquire or improve community property (marital property). He or she may have priority in claiming compensation from the community property. If a spouse used community assets (marital property) to acquire or improve his or her reserved property, the other spouse may claim compensation from the residuary community property or may claim that the deficit is paid out

---

1580 Art. 209 para. 3 Swiss Civil Code.

1581 Art. 209 para. 1 Swiss Civil Code.

1582 Art. 209 para. 2 Swiss Civil Code. See Hausheer/Aebi-Müller, in Basler Kommentar, Zivilgesetzbuch I, 3rd ed. Basel, 2006, Art. 209.

1583 § 23 para. 2 Danish Act on the Legal Effects of Marriage. See LUND-ANDERSEN/MAGNUSSEN, Danish Report, Q 118.

of the reserved property. Comparable rules exist in FINLAND[1584] and NORWAY.[1585] In SWEDEN,[1586] some differentiation is necessary. If a spouse without the consent of the other spouse reduces his or her community property (marital property) to a significant extent to increase the reserved property, the other spouse's share of the community property is calculated as if the transfer did not take place. This rule only applies in case of divorce and is restricted to actions within three years before the divorce application.[1587] There is no special rule of compensation if a spouse has used his or her reserved property for the benefit of the community property. But this transfer can be taken into account through the general rule on adjustments of property division.[1588] In DENMARK,[1589] FINLAND[1590] and NORWAY[1591] compensation applies also if assets belonging to one category of property have been used for payment of debts related to the other category of property.

In CATALONIA,[1592] where the separation of property regime is the default rule, a spouse who has worked for the household or for the other spouse without payment is entitled to receive economic compensation if this has produced a situation of inequality between the patrimonies of both spouses which implies an unjust enrichment.

In common law systems there is no specific right to compensation, but the fact that one spouse has invested money in the other spouse's assets is taken into account by the competent authority in the exercise of its discretionary powers of redistribution upon divorce. This is established by case law in ENGLAND AND WALES.[1593] In IRELAND,[1594] statutory law permits the court when making ancillary orders to take into account the contributions which a spouse made to the property and financial resources of the other spouse. SCOTS law[1595] also requires that fair account be taken of any economic advantage derived by either spouse from the contributions of the other.

1584 § 92 and 95 Finish Marriage Act.

1585 See SVERDRUP, Norwegian Report, Q 118.

1586 Ch. 11 § 4 para. 1 Swedish Marriage Code.

1587 See JÄNTERÄ-JAREBORG/BRATTSTRÖM/WALLENG, Swedish Report, Q 118.

1588 Ch. 12 § 1 Swedish Marriage Code. See JÄNTERÄ-JAREBORG/BRATTSTRÖM/WALLENG, Swedish Report, Q 118.

1589 § 23 para. 2 Danish Act on the Legal Effects of Marriage. See LUND-ANDERSEN/MAGNUSSEN, Danish Report, Q 118.

1590 § 95 Finnish Marriage Act. See KURKI-SUONIO, Finnish Report, Q 119.

1591 § 61 Norwegian Marriage Act. See SVERDRUP Norwegian Report, Q 119.

1592 Art. 41 para. 1 Catalan Family Code. See MARTÍN-CASALS/RIBOT, Catalan Report, Q 151.

1593 B v B (Ancillary Relief) (No 2) [2008] EWCA Civ 483, [2008] 2 FLR 1645. See BARLOW, English Report, Q 185.

1594 S.16 (2) f of the Irish Family Law Act 1995 and S. 20(2) (f) of the Irish Family Law (Divorce) Act 1996.

1595 S.9(1)(b) Scots Family Law Act 1985.

Calculation of the compensation

The compensation is usually calculated at the nominal value, but SWISS law[1596] makes an exception for assets belonging to one category of property if they have contributed to the acquisition, improvement or preservation of assets belonging to the other category of property. If the value of the latter assets has increased or decreased, the compensation is calculated according to the value of the assets at the time of the liquidation or their disposal. In DENMARK[1597] there is also nominal compensation, but there is a possibility for a more discretionary settlement. In NORWAY inflation can be taken into account.[1598]

COMMENT

1. In order to avoid unjust enrichment Principle 4:28 establishes a compensation rule between the reserved property and the acquisitions of each spouse. Any contributions to the reserved property originating from the acquisitions and vice versa need to be taken into account when determining the acquisitions (Principle 4:28(1) and (2)). This exercise should be undertaken for each spouse separately.

2. The contributions cover both direct profits deriving from investments as well as indirect profits deriving from the paying off of debts. What is essential is that resources belonging to one category of property are used to the benefit of the other category.

3. Principle 4:28(3) clarifies that debts encumber the property in relation to which they were incurred. This means, for example, that a debt relating to inherited property encumbers the reserved property since this category of property comprises the inheritances (see Principle 4:19(b)). If it cannot be proved to which category a debt is related, it is presumed to be related to the acquisitions, since all assets are presumed to be acquisitions, if they cannot be proved to belong to the reserved property (see Principle 4:18(2)).

4. The compensation is calculated at its nominal value. This applies, for example, when the acquisitions have paid a debt incurred by the reserved property.

5. In the case of investment, improvement or preservation of an asset the increase or decrease of the market value of this asset is taken into account

1596 Art. 209 para. 3 Swiss Civil Code.

1597 See LUND-ANDERSEN/MAGNUSSEN, Danish Report, Q 118.

1598 See SVERDRUP Norwegian Report, Q 118.

(Principle 4:28(4)). This rule guarantees that a profit made by a category of property also benefits the other category and that both categories of property have to share the consequences of a decrease of the value of the asset. An example: spouse A inherits a house having a value of 400.000 units. This house belongs to his reserved property (Principle 4:19(b)). Spouse A immediately invests 100.000 units from his acquisitions to improve the house. As a result of this investment the house has a market value of 500.000 units and this means that spouse A has invested one fifth of the value of the house. At the date of dissolution of the regime the house has a market value of 600.000 units. The reserved property has to pay compensation to the acquisitions taking into account the market value of the house at the date of the dissolution of the regime (Principle 4:28(1) and (4)). Since the acquisitions contributed one fifth to the market value of the house, the compensation has to be fixed at one fifth of the market value at the date of dissolution of the regime being 120.000 units. If due to a decrease of the market the house only has a market value of 300.000 units at the date of the dissolution of the regime, the compensation has also to be fixed at one fifth of this market value being 60.000 units.

6. Principle 4:28(5) states that the compensation claim has a monetary character but allows the spouses to agree otherwise.

PARTICIPATION
PARTICIPTATION
BETEILIGUNG

Principle 4:29 Agreement on participation
Spouses are free to agree on the participation in the acquisitions.

Principe 4:29 Convention sur la participation
Les époux peuvent conclure une convention sur la participation aux acquêts.

Prinzip 4:29 Vereinbarung über die Beteiligung
Die Ehegatten können eine Vereinbarung über die Errungenschaftsbeteiligung treffen.

INTERNATIONAL INSTRUMENTS

The *French-German Agreement of 2010* establishes a participation régime. The spouses are free to choose this matrimonial property regime (Art. 3 para. 1) and they may deviate from the rules of the Agreement (Art. 3 para. 3).

COMPARATIVE OVERVIEW

Modification of rules on division

Equal sharing is the basic principle for the *participation in acquisitions/ community of accrued gains* regime. However, the general rule of a 50:50 division may be modified (e.g. GERMANY[1599] and SWITZERLAND[1600]). In FINLAND,[1601] as well as in the other Nordic jurisdictions, the spouses may totally exclude the participation (the *marital right*) in the property of the other spouse. However, modifications are also subject to restrictions. For example, such agreements must not adversely affect the statutory inheritance entitlements of children who

---

1599 See DETHLOFF/MARTINY, German Report, Q 199.
1600 Art. 216 para. 1 Swiss Civil Code. See SCHWENZER/BOCK, Swiss Report, Q 199.
1601 § 41 para. 1 Finnish Marriage Act. See KURKI-SUONIO, Finnish Report, Q 199.

are not the common issue of the spouses or those of the issue of such children (SWITZERLAND[1602]).

Under a *deferred community of property* regime spouses may agree that certain assets may be exempted from the equal division (NORWAY[1603]). The spouses cannot, however, agree that assets shall be divided other than equally (NORWAY[1604]). In SWEDEN,[1605] however, in a property division the spouses may also agree that each shall take property with different shares, for example, 60% of the value of the marital property to one spouse and 40% of the value of the marital property to the other spouse.

Modifications in relation to the end of the matrimonial property regime

A matrimonial property regime generally ends with the death of one of the spouses or with a divorce. The spouses may take this in to account in their agreement and their modifications may depend upon the *ground of dissolution of the marriage* (SWITZERLAND[1606]). Different forms of dissolution may lead to different legal consequences. In some other jurisdictions this possibility is denied (GREECE[1607]).

Often special modifications can be made for the end of the marriage by divorce (FINLAND[1608]). Sometimes, there is a restriction that agreements varying the statutory participation in acquisitions are valid only if the matrimonial property agreement expressly so provides (SWITZERLAND[1609]).

Under a *deferred community of property* regime the question of modifications also arises. SWEDISH law[1610] does not permit marital property contracts where spouses stipulate that the classification of the property in a future property division shall depend upon the ground of dissolution of the marriage (for example, that property shall be marital property when property division is occasioned by the death of a spouse, but separate property in case of divorce). In DENMARK[1611] the marital property agreement for separate property may be

---

1602 Art. 216 para. 2 Swiss Civil Code. See SCHWENZER/BOCK, Swiss Report, Q 199.

1603 § 42 Norwegian Marriage Act. See SVERDRUP, Norwegian Report, Q 199.

1604 See SVERDRUP, Norwegian Report, Q 199.

1605 Ch. 12 § Swedish Marriage Code. See JÄNTERÄ-JAREBORG/BRATTSTRÖM/WALLENG, Swedish Report, Q 199.

1606 See SCHWENZER/BOCK, Swiss Report, Q 199.

1607 See KOUTSOURADIS/KOTRONIS/HATZANTONIS, Greek Report, Q 199.

1608 See KURKI-SUONIO, Finnish Report, Q 198, 199.

1609 Art. 217 Swiss Civil Code. See SCHWENZER/BOCK, Swiss Report, Q 199.

1610 Ch. 12 § Swedish Marriage Code. See JÄNTERÄ-JAREBORG/BRATTSTRÖM/WALLENG, Swedish Report, Q 199.

1611 See LUND-ANDERSEN/MAGNUSSEN, Danish Report, Q 198, 199.

limited so as only to be effective upon the division of matrimonial property in both spouses' lifetime (divorce separate property). In NORWAY,[1612] special modifications are allowed where the marriage is dissolved by death. In DENMARK,[1613] the marital property agreement may provide that absolute separate property can only be granted if one of the spouses dies, to a specifically designated spouse or to the surviving spouse. Under SWEDISH law,[1614] the surviving spouse has the right to request that no division or only partial division of the spouses' marital property shall take place. This is also possible under FINNISH law[1615] and by agreement in NORWAY.[1616]

In SCOTLAND,[1617] where the court may distribute property on divorce on the application of the either party, the principle is that the matrimonial property should be shared fairly. Fair sharing is taken to be equal sharing except where special circumstances apply. Special circumstances may include, for example, the source, nature or use of the assets and the existence of an agreement between the parties.

COMMENT

1. The spouses are free to agree on the extent of the participation in the acquisitions after the regime has been dissolved. This principle follows the common core of the legal systems surveyed and allows the spouses to agree on the participation in the acquisitions and to set aside or adjust the general rules of participation. An agreement may concern the assets which are subject to the participation of acquisitions or which belong to the reserved property. It is also permitted to make an agreement concerning the evaluation of assets, compensation claims and the participation in kind or in money. Agreements may be made particularly in the context of a divorce. The date of dissolution is determined in accordance with Principle 4:25. After the dissolution of the regime the spouses may also exclude participation totally. However, before dissolution, such an agreement would amount to a change of the matrimonial property regime to a pure separation of assets.

2. The Principle is another manifestation of the general autonomy of the spouses to enter into agreements with each other (see Principle 4:9). However, in

1612 See SVERDRUP Norwegian Report, Q 198.
1613 See LUND-ANDERSEN/MAGNUSSEN, Danish Report, Q 198, 199.
1614 Ch. 12 § 2 Swedish Marriage Code. See JÄNTERÄ-JAREBORG/BRATTSTRÖM/WALLENG, Swedish Report, Q 199.
1615 § 103 para. 2 Finnish Marriage Act.
1616 See SVERDRUP, Norwegian Report, Q 198.
1617 See MAIR, Scottish Report, Q 181.

cases of exceptional hardship the competent authority can set aside or modify the agreement in accordance with Principle 4:32.

3. The requirements as to the form of agreements on participation are left to national law.

Principle 4:30 Allocation of the family home and household goods
The competent authority may, in the interest of the family and subject to payment of compensation, allocate the family home and household goods to one of the spouses.

Principe 4:30 Attribution du logement de la famille et de meubles meublants
L'autorité compétente peut, dans l'intérêt de la famille et moyennant compensation financière, attribuer à l'un des époux le logement de la famille et des meubles meublants.

Prinzip 4:30 Zuteilung der Familienwohnung und Haushaltsgegenstände
Die zuständige Behörde kann, im Interesse der Familie und vorbehaltlich einer Ausgleichszahlung, die Familienwohnung und Haushaltsgegenstände einem der Ehegatten zuteilen.

INTERNATIONAL INSTRUMENTS

None of particular relevance.

COMPARATIVE OVERVIEW

Protecting the family home and household assets

In *particiption systems* there are different rules as regards the allocation of the family home when it comes to paying out the participation claim, which in most cases is a monetary claim. Spouses do not generally have preferential rights over the family home and the household assets under GERMAN law.[1618] However in, for example, cases of separation, either spouse may plead severe hardship and apply for exclusive possession of the family home on this ground.[1619] Under SWISS law,[1620] if both spouses collectively own an asset the court may assign the asset to the spouse whose interest prevails against appropriate compensation. Common children, professional or health considerations may constitute such an overriding interest. The law of CATALONIA[1621] provides that payment of certain assets may be requested unilaterally by the debtor or by the creditor spouse. The judge will grant it if there is an interest worthy of consideration.

1618 See DETHLOFF/MARTINY, German Report, Q 85.
1619 § 1361 and § 1568 (a) and (b)German Civil Code.
1620 See SCHWENZER/BOCK, Swiss Report, Q 85.
1621 Art. 59 para. 1 Catalan Family code.

In *deferred community systems*, where the debtor can choose between a payment in kind and a payment in money, there are usually specific rules on the issue. In the law of DENMARK,[1622] immovable property, which is used as the matrimonial home, may be taken by one spouse if the children do primarily live with that spouse. In NORWAY,[1623] a spouse may also demand to take over the family home and the household goods when there are special reasons for doing so. The needs of the spouses and their children are important factors when considering whether these special reasons exist. The same applies in SWEDEN.[1624] The spouse who has the greater need of the joint dwelling or household goods has the right to be allocated this property following a divorce. However, if this property is owned by the other spouse such allocation can only take place if it is reasonable for the owner spouse, having regard to the overall circumstances.[1625]

COMMENT

1. Principle 4:30 constitutes an exception to the general rule contained in Principle 4:31(4) according to which the participation claim is a monetary claim. It specifically allows the competent authority to order the allocation of the family home and the household assets subject to payment of compensation. Such a result can also be reached through an agreement between the spouses according to Principle 4:29. There can also be a compensation claim between reserved property and acquisitions according to Principle 4:28. The Principle is silent with regard to the situation where the family has more than one home. It is left to the competent authority to determine how best to resolve the allocation.

2. Although the issue is not specifically mentioned in Principle 4:30 the competent authority will mostly intervene at the request of one of the spouses, who can be either the debtor or the creditor spouse.

3. The decision in favour of allocating the family home and household goods to one of the spouses requires a careful consideration of the interests of the family, particularly the interests of each spouse and the children. Amongst the factors to consider will be the financial and personal situation of each spouse. A separate issue arises when the family home is also the place of business if, for example, one of the spouses has his or her practice in the family home. The competent authority should also give special consideration to the needs of the children of

---

1622 See LUND-ANDERSEN/MAGNUSSEN, Danish Report, Q 123.
1623 See SVERDRUP, Norwegian Report, Q 123.
1624 Ch. 11 § 8 Swedish Marriage Code.
1625 See JÄNTERÄ-JAREBORG/BRATTSTRÖM/WALLENG, Swedish Report, Q 123.

the family, particularly accommodation for them during their minority and stability as regards the home environment.

4. The allocation of the family home and the household goods should be distinguished from other provisions that exist under national law and which provide that one of the spouses has, for certain reasons, commonly because he or she is the residential parent, the use of the matrimonial home. This is not the issue that is dealt with here. Principle 4:30 is a rule about property redistribution and therefore requires that the value of the property that is transferred corresponds to the amount granted to the spouse who receives it on grounds of his or her claim to participation in the acquisitions of the debtor spouse. Otherwise the spouse who receives the assets will have to pay compensation for the surplus he or she has received.

Principle 4:31 Equal participation in the net acquisitions

(1) If one spouse's net acquisitions exceed the value of that of the other, the latter participates in the surplus to the amount of one half.

(2) Net acquisitions are the value of the acquisitions after deducting the debts.

(3) Losses made by one spouse exceeding his or her acquisitions at the date of the dissolution of the regime, should not be shared by the other spouse.

(4) The claim of participation is a monetary one, unless the spouses agree otherwise.

(5) Upon request of the debtor spouse the competent authority may, where there are serious grounds for doing so, authorize payments to be deferred or payable in instalments.

Principe 4:31 Participation égale aux acquêts nets

(1) Si les acquêts nets d'un époux dépassent en valeur ceux de l'autre époux, ce dernier participe à l'accroissement pour moitié.

(2) Les acquêts nets correspondent à la valeur des acquêts après déduction des dettes.

(3) Les pertes réalisées par un époux qui, à la date de la dissolution du régime, sont supérieures à ses acquêts, ne sont pas partagées avec l'autre époux.

(4) La créance de participation est de nature monétaire, sauf accord contraire des époux

(5) A la requête de l'époux débiteur, l'autorité compétente peut, en présence de motifs graves, autoriser des délais de paiement ou des paiements échelonnés.

Prinzip 4:31 Gleiche Beteiligung an der Netto-Errungenschaft

(1) Übersteigt der Wert der Netto-Errungenschaft eines Ehegatten den Wert der des anderen, ist letzterer zur Hälfte des übersteigenden Betrages beteiligt.

(2) Netto-Errungenschaft ist der Wert der Errungenschaft nach Abzug der Schulden.

(3) Verluste eines Ehegatten, die seine Errungenschaft im Zeitpunkt der Beendigung des Güterstands übersteigen, werden nicht mit dem anderen Ehegatten geteilt.

(4) Der Anspruch auf Beteiligung ist ein Anspruch in Geld, sofern die Ehegatten nichts anderes vereinbaren.

(5) Auf Antrag des verpflichteten Ehegatten kann die zuständige Behörde aus schwerwiegenden Gründen einen Zahlungsaufschub oder eine Zahlung in Raten gewähren.

INTERNATIONAL INSTRUMENTS

According to the *French-German Agreement of 2010* the accrued gains of both spouses are compared. If the accrued gains of a spouse exceed the one of the other spouse, the latter can claim half of the difference (Art. 12 (1)). The participation claim is a monetary one, but on application of a spouse the court can order the transfer of assets, if fairness requires it (Art. 12 (2)). Those rules apply independently of the grounds of dissolution of the regime. But in cases of dissolution by divorce or by another judicial decision, the participation claim is calculated taking into account the composition and the value of the spouses' property at the moment of the application to the court (Art. 13). The participation claim is in principle restricted to half the value of the debtor's property after deduction of his or her debts. But fictitious additions due to donations or detrimental acts can correct this rule (Art. 14).

COMPARATIVE OVERVIEW

Calculation of the participation claim

The matrimonial property regime of *participation in the acquisitions* entitles each spouse, when the regime dissolves, to participate in the acquisitions of the other spouse during the time the regime has been in effect. According to CATALAN law,[1626] if only one spouse has net acquisitions, the other spouse is entitled to half the value of those; if both spouses made acquisitions the spouse who has obtained less, is entitled to half of the difference between the value of his or her acquisitions and the acquisitions of the other spouse. GERMAN law[1627] provides for the equalization of the accrued gains. In case of dissolution of the participation regime by the death of a spouse the accrued gains are not calculated but the statutory hereditary portion of the surviving spouse is raised by one quarter.[1628] This rule applies even if the deceased has no accrued gains. In case of dissolution on other grounds the accrued gains have to be calculated.[1629] First, the final assets of each spouse are determined and valuated. These assets include notional amounts by which such assets were diminished due to certain acts detrimental to the other spouse.[1630] Then the value of the initial assets of each spouse is subtracted from his or her final assets. The result is the accrued gains of each spouse. The accrued gains of both spouses are compared and if the accrued gains of one spouse exceed those of the other, the latter is entitled to half of the

---

1626 Art. 232–21 Catalan Civil Code.
1627 § 1378 para. 1. German Civil Ccode.
1628 § 1371 para. 1 German Civil Code.
1629 § 1372–1390 German Civil Code. See DETHLOFF/MARTINY, German Report, Q 80.
1630 § 1375 para. 2 German Civil Code.

surplus as an equalization claim. The amount of the equalization claim is limited to the value of the assets which exist upon termination of the matrimonial regime, after the deduction of any obligations.[1631] According to SWISS law,[1632] the acquisitions of each spouse have to be shared. Therefore, each spouse's property acquired during the marriage, the value of dispositions made without consideration during the five years preceding the dissolution of the regime and the value of the assets disposed with the intention of diminishing the share of the other spouse have to be added.[1633] The remaining total value after deduction of the debts constitutes the surplus.[1634] A deficit is not taken into account.[1635] Each spouse or his or her heirs is or are entitled to the half of the surplus of the other spouse.[1636] Both claims are set-off.[1637]

In *deferred community systems* a deferred community comes into existence at the moment of dissolution of the regime. This community is then divided between the spouses. Only the net balance of assets of each spouse is included in the community. A spouse is not liable for the debts of the other spouse (DENMARK,[1638] FINLAND,[1639] NORWAY[1640] and SWEDEN[1641]). In SWEDEN,[1642] in a liquidation of the deferred community property regime when one of the spouses is bankrupt, both spouses may keep their own property, and the debtor spouse cannot, against the wishes of the other spouse, make any claims for participation in the other spouse's property.[1643] As a result, the regime's main rule of equal property division is set aside. Unless the spouses are in agreement, the decision is taken, upon application of a spouse, by a specially appointed property distributor, or the competent authority.

In common law jurisdictions, the court has a discretionary power to make property adjustments upon divorce. This power is provided for in ENGLAND AND WALES by the Matrimonial Causes Act 1973, about which there have been significant case-law developments. While before 2001, the court restricted the

1631 § 1378 para.2 German Civil Code.
1632 Art. 215 para. 1 Swiss Civil Code. See SCHWENZER/BOCK, Swiss Report, Q 80 and 81.
1633 Art. 207 and 208 Swiss Civil Code.
1634 Art. 210 para. 1 Swiss Civil Code.
1635 Art. 210 para. 2 Swiss Civil Code.
1636 Art. 215 para. 1 Swiss Civil Code.
1637 Art. 215 para. 2 Swiss Civil Code.
1638 See LUND-ANDERSEN/MAGNUSSEN, Danish Report, Q 91.
1639 See KURKI-SUONIO, Finnish Report, Q 91.
1640 See SVERDRUP, Norwegian Report, Q 91.
1641 See JÄNTERÄ-JAREBORG/BRATTSTRÖM/WALLENG, Swedish Report, Q 91.
1642 Ch. 12 § 1.1 Swedish Marriage Code.
1643 It is disputed in SWEDISH legal literature whether this is automatically the case when the other spouse makes a request to keep his or her property, or whether there must be additional grounds for this exception to apply. See AGELL/BRATTSTRÖM, *Äktenskap, Samboende, Partnerskap*, 4th ed., 2008, pp. 195–196 and 212–213.

weaker spouse's application to that which would satisfy his or her "reasonable requirements", in *White v. White*[1644] the House of Lords underlined that in seeking to achieve a fair outcome, there should be no discrimination between husband and wife and their respective roles. If both spouses have contributed equally to the welfare of the family, then it matters not which of them earned the money and built up the assets. Under such circumstances there should be in principle an equal division of both parties' property at the point of divorce.[1645] In *Miller v Miller and McFarlane* v. *McFarlane*,[1646] the House of Lords further developed this line of reasoning and distinguished according to the origin of property between matrimonial and non-matrimonial property or between family assets and other assets. Matrimonial property should in principle be shared, although the court retains a discretionary power to achieve a fair outcome according to the circumstances of the case.

Monetary claim

In *participation systems* the participation claim is generally a monetary claim (e.g. GERMANY[1647] and SWITZERLAND[1648]). In *deferred community systems*, the claim can be a *right in rem* unless otherwise agreed. Under DANISH law,[1649] each spouse may claim possession of items of property from the estate. If both spouses claim possession of the same item the spouse to whose property that asset belonged when it was contributed to the marriage is entitled to it. If this cannot be determined the spouse who is to take possession may be chosen by lot. In FINLAND,[1650] the spouse who is obliged to hand over property decides what property he or she will give. It is open to him or her to pay this in money.

In common law systems the court may make a range of orders, depending on the circumstances of the case. It can order a capital sum payment which can be made at the time of the divorce or within a specified period or it can order one party to transfer property to the other. Periodical payment orders or pension orders are also possible (e.g. ENGLAND AND WALES[1651] and SCOTLAND[1652]).

1644 [2001] 1 AC 596 (HL).
1645 See BARLOW, English Report, Q 161.
1646 [2006] UKHL 24, [2006] 2 AC 618.
1647 See DETHLOFF/MARTINY, German Report, Q 57.
1648 See SCHWENZER/BOCK, Swiss Report, Q 80.
1649 See LUND-ANDERSEN/MAGNUSSEN, Danish Report, Q 122.
1650 See KURKI-SUONIO, Finnish Report, Q 122.
1651 S. 23 and S. 24B – S. 24G Matrimonial Causes Act of 1973.
1652 See MAIR, Scottish Report, Q 181.

Methods of payment

In GERMANY,[1653] the court can grant payment by instalments or postpone it, if immediate payment would occur at an unreasonable time, if, for example, the housing and living conditions of common children would deteriorate with lasting effect. If such postponement is granted the debtor must be ordered to pay interest. The Family court may upon application order that the debtor furnish security for a postponed claim. In SWITZERLAND,[1654] the debtor may request a deferral, if immediate payment would cause him or her serious difficulties.

COMMENT

1. Principle 4:31(1) guarantees each spouse participation in the acquisitions of the other spouse. To the extent that one spouse's net acquisitions exceed the value of that of the other, the latter participates in the surplus to the amount of one half. This Principle reflects the common core of different systems that provide for sharing after the dissolution of the regime. The rule also reflects the principle of equality between the spouses. Regardless of who actually is the title holder of the assets that have been accumulated during the regime and independently of the different roles the spouses might have played, both spouses are deemed to have made equally valuable contributions. Detrimental transactions are taken into account under Principle 4:27.

2. The value of the acquisitions is determined according to Principle 4:26.

3. Principle 4:31(2) defines the net acquisitions as the value of the acquisitions minus the debts. Joint debts have to be taken into account on a proportional basis.

4. Principle 4:31(3) states that deficits are to be disregarded. The participation claim does not include the losses made by one spouse exceeding his or her acquisitions. This means that the participation claim is always a positive value and corresponds to the rules that can be found in participation and deferred community systems.

5. The Participation claim is a monetary one (Principle 4:31(4)). Spouses can however reach agreements that provide for payment in kind according to Principle 4:29. A monetary claim has the advantage that the ownership of the assets does not change.

1653 § 1382 German Civil Code. See DETHLOFF/MARTINY, German Report, Q 80.
1654 Art. 218 para. 1 Swiss Civil Code.

6. If there are serious grounds for doing so and upon request of the debtor spouse the competent authority may according to Principle 4:31(5) authorise the deferral of payment or the payment in installments. The Principle is silent on whether such deference generates an obligation to pay interest or as to whether the creditor spouse is entitled to request surety in such cases. These issues should be dealt with in national law.

7. Two examples may clarify the preceding rules.

Example A: The acquisitions of spouse A are 60.000 units, and his or her debts are 10.000 units. The acquisitions of spouse B are 40.000 units and his or her debts are 20.000 units. It follows that the net acquisitions of spouse A amount to 50.000 units whereas the corresponding figure for spouse B is 20.000 units. In comparison, the net acquisitions of spouse A exceed those of the spouse B by 30.000 units. This means that spouse B will have the claim to participate in half of this amount. Of the net acquisitions of spouse A altogether 15.000 units shall, as a result, be transferred to spouse B, and both spouses have in the end 35.000 units.

Example B: The acquisitions of spouse A are 60.000 units, and his or her debts are 10.000 units. The acquisitions of spouse B are 40.000 units and his or her debts are 50.000 units. The net acquisitions of spouse A amount to 50.000 units whereas the balance for spouse B, whose debts exceed his or her acquisitions, is set up at zero. In comparison, the net acquisitions of spouse A exceed those of spouse B by 50.000 units. This means that spouse B will have the claim to participate in half of this amount. Of spouse A's net acquisitions, 25.000 units shall be transferred to spouse B. In the end, both spouses have 25.000 units.

Principle 4:32 Adjustment by the competent authority
In cases of exceptional hardship the competent authority can
(a) adjust the participation;
(b) set aside or modify any spousal agreement made in accordance with Principle 4:29.

Principe 4:32 Adaptations par l'autorité compétente
En cas de dureté exceptionnelle, l'autorité compétente peut
(a) procéder à des adaptations de la participation;
(b) écarter ou modifier toute convention conclue entre les époux en vertu du Principe 4:29.

Prinzip 4:32 Anpassung durch die zuständige Behörde
In Fällen außergewöhnlicher Härte kann die zuständige Behörde
(a) die Beteiligung anpassen;
(b) jede nach Prinzip 4:29 getroffene Vereinbarung der Ehegatten aufheben oder abändern.

INTERNATIONAL INSTRUMENTS

None of particular relevance.

COMPARATIVE OVERVIEW

As a rule, under the existing regimes of *participation in acquisition/community of accrued gains*, the Nordic model of *deferred community property regime* and the common law system of *separation of property with distribution by the competent authority*, there can be a certain adjustment but this is not the case for all legal systems.

Adjustment by the competent authority

In some *systems of participation in acquisition* a refusal on grounds of gross inequity is possible under exceptional circumstances. The debtor may refuse to fulfil an equalisation claim to the extent that the equalisation of accrued gains would be grossly inequitable in the circumstances of the case (GERMANY[1655]). Gross inequity can exist particularly if the spouse who made trivial gains over a considerable period negligently failed to carry out the economic obligations

1655 § 1381 para. 1 German Civil Code. See DETHLOFF/MARTINY, German Report, Q 89.

which are inherent in marital relations (GERMANY[1656]). Under GREEK law,[1657] the court can use the general rule of Article 297 GREEK Civil Code to order a return in kind, for example the return of specific assets or the percentage of co-ownership. Other legal systems do not provide for such an adjustment (CATALONIA[1658]). In SWITZERLAND,[1659] only a restricted control can be based on the general provision prohibiting an abuse of a right.

The approach in *deferred community property regimes* is that an adjustment is possible in some cases. However, the general rules of distribution tend to take the facts of the single cases into account. In DENMARK,[1660] in the case of a divorce a deviation from the generally applicable rules is possible if an equal division of the property would be obviously unfair. In FINLAND[1661] and in SWEDEN,[1662] the distribution may be adjusted if it would otherwise lead to an unreasonable result or to the other spouse receiving an unjust financial benefit. Special attention is paid to the duration of the marriage, the activities of the spouses in their common household and the accumulation and preservation of the property as well as other comparable facts regarding the finances of the spouses. In NORWAY,[1663] if the right to withhold assets that can clearly be traced back to pre-marital assets, inheritance or gifts will lead to an "obviously unfair result" under the "unequal division rule", this right may be set aside entirely or partly. A spouse may also be awarded the right to exempt assets from equal division that should otherwise be divided equally, if "strong reasons" so indicate.

In systems of *pure separation* there is no participation claim and the spouses are free to make an agreement with respect to their assets. The competent authority is, however, bound by the general rules on the validity of agreements (BELGIUM[1664]). A preliminary issue is whether the agreement, which provides for separate property, is valid. In FINLAND,[1665] in the case of a separation of property, the participation can also be adjusted.[1666] For this purpose the conditions for the deferred community are to be applied.

1656 § 1381 para. 2 German Civil Code. See DETHLOFF/MARTINY, German Report, Q 89.
1657 Art. 297 Greek Civil Code. See KOUTSOURADIS/KOTRONIS/HATZANTONIS, Greek Report, Q 89.
1658 Art. 50 Catalan Family Code. See MARTÍN-CASALS/RIBOT, Catalan Report, Q 89.
1659 Art. 2 para. 2 Swiss Civil Code. See SCHWENZER/BOCK, Swiss Report, Q 89.
1660 § 69a Danish Division of Family Assets Act. See LUND-ANDERSEN/MAGNUSSEN, Danish Report, Q 127.
1661 § 103 b (1) Finnish Marriage Act. See KURKI-SUONIO, Finnish Report, Q 127.
1662 Ch. 12 § 1 Swedish Marriage Code. See JÄNTERÄ-JAREBORG/BRATTSTRÖM/WALLENG, Swedish Report, Q 127.
1663 § 59 para. 2 and 3 Norwegian Marriage Act. See SVERDRUP, Norwegian Report, Q 127 and Q 91.
1664 See PINTENS/ALLAERTS/SEYNS/PIGNOLET, Belgian Report, Q 159.
1665 § 107 and § 103 b Finnish Marriage Act. See KURKI-SUONIO, Finnish Report, Q 127.
1666 § 107 Finnish Marriage Act. See KURKI-SUONIO, Finnish Report, Q 127.

In the *common law system of separation of property with distribution* by the competent authority the particular facts of the case have to be taken into account (ENGLAND AND WALES[1667] and IRELAND[1668]).

Adjustment in the case of an agreement

An adjustment by a court is also possible in the case of an agreement of the spouses. In DENMARK[1669] and in SWEDEN,[1670] a marriage settlement may be adjusted by a judicial decree or held not be binding if it is deemed to have been unreasonable for either spouse at the time of its making or with regard to the overall circumstances. The same can occur generally for marriage contracts in NORWAY,[1671] particularly for contracts made in divorce cases.[1672] Similarly, in SWITZERLAND,[1673] the court may intervene in extreme cases where a divorce convention does deny any claims without reason. In THE NETHERLANDS,[1674] if the spouses have agreed on a participation regime the court may only in rare cases, namely where the results are contrary to reasonableness and fairness, modify or set aside the marital contract.

COMMENT

1. The basic principle regarding distribution of acquisitions is equal participation in the net acquisitions (Principle 4:31). However, there may be exceptional circumstances where the competent court may adjust the distribution. The adjustment can mean that despite the fact that the requirements for equal sharing are met an equalisation claim is denied or reduced.

2. The precondition for such a claim is exceptional hardship for one spouse. This could be the extremely short duration of the marriage or a patrimonial damage based on extremely unfair behaviour of the other party. However, the importance of this Principle is limited. According to Principle 4:24(d) the regime on the participation in acquisitions may be dissolved by a decision of the competent authority based on serious grounds. The existence of such a serious ground is not sufficient in itself for the application of Principle 4:32.

1667 See BARLOW, English Report, Q 161.
1668 See SHANNON, Irish Report, Q 161.
1669 See LUND-ANDERSEN/MAGNUSSEN, Danish Report, Q 127.
1670 Ch. 12 § 3 Swedish Marriage Code.
1671 § 46 para. 2 Marriage Act. See SVERDRUP Norwegian Report, Q 127.
1672 § 65 Marriage Act. See SVERDRUP Norwegian Report, Q 127.
1673 See SCHWENZER/ BOCK, Swiss Report, Q 89.
1674 See BOELE-WOELKI/SCHONEWILLE/SCHRAMA, Dutch Report, Q 89.

3. There are other Principles which give the competent authority the power to take special circumstances into account. According to Principle 4:27 detrimental transactions shall be taken into account. Based on Principle 4:30 on the allocation of family home and household goods the competent authority may, subject to payment of compensation, allocate the family home and household goods to one of the spouses. Upon request by the debtor spouse the competent authority may, where there are serious grounds for doing so, authorize payments to be deferred or payable in instalments.

4. Principle 4:32(2) takes into account that such exceptional hardship may exist and that in those cases a deviation from an equal split of the acquisitions may be justified. The competent authority may deviate from an equal distribution and even deviate from Principle 4:30 and allocate the family home and the household goods without compensation.

SECTION B: COMMUNITY OF ACQUISITIONS
SECTION B: COMMUNAUTÉ D'ACQUÊTS
ABSCHNITT B: ERRUNGENSCHAFTSGEMEINSCHAFT

Principle 4:33 Applicability of the community of acquisitions regime
The community of acquisitions regime applies if the spouses have not agreed otherwise in accordance with Chapter II.

Principle 4:33 Applicabilité du régime de communauté d'acquêts
Le régime de communauté d'acquêts s'applique si les époux n'ont pas conclu de convention contraire conformément au Chapitre II.

Prinzip 4:33 Anwendbarkeit des Güterstands der Errungenschaftsgemeinschaft
Der Güterstand der Errungenschaftsgemeinschaft gilt, sofern die Ehegatten nicht etwas anderes gemäß Kapitel II vereinbart haben.

INTERNATIONAL INSTRUMENTS

The *Council of Europe's Resolution (78) 37 on Equality of Spouses in Civil Law*, adopted in September 1978, recommends that the Member States' governments "give both spouses equal rights and obligations concerning their common property where the operation of law provides for a matrimonial property regime of community of goods and in particular:

- the right to be informed by the other spouse of the actual extent of the common property;
- an equal right to use, administer, receive profits or dispose of the common property and income as well as to share in the division of the property;
- equal obligations concerning debts."

It also recommends that Member States "ensure that where the operation of law provides for the sharing of the property acquired during the marriage and, where applicable, the property belonging to one spouse, the legal provisions protecting the rights of the spouses in such property, for example, the prohibition of gifts of great value, should be the same for both spouses." In *Recommendation No. R (89) by the Council of Europe on Contributions Following Divorce* (January 1989), the Member States are advised to enact appropriate rules relating to, inter alia, "matrimonial property regimes, in particular by granting to a former spouse the right to obtain a fair share of the property of the other."

COMPARATIVE OVERVIEW

Of the twenty six jurisdictions surveyed, thirteen have what may be considered a community of property regime operating as the default regime where spouses have not made a marital agreement: BELGIUM,[1675] BULGARIA,[1676] CZECH REPUBLIC,[1677] FRANCE,[1678] HUNGARY,[1679] ITALY,[1680] LITHUANIA,[1681] MALTA,[1682] POLAND,[1683] PORTUGAL,[1684] RUSSIA,[1685] SLOVAKIA[1686] and SPAIN.[1687] In addition, in many jurisdictions a community of property regime exists as a statutory optional regime: AUSTRIA,[1688] BELGIUM,[1689] CATALONIA,[1690] FRANCE,[1691] GERMANY,[1692] GREECE,[1693] POLAND,[1694] PORTUGAL,[1695] RUSSIA[1696] and SWITZERLAND.[1697] Finally, there is the special case of THE NETHERLANDS,[1698] in which, upon marriage, a universal community of property regime exists by operation of law.

1675 See PINTENS/ALLAERTS/SEYNS/PIGNOLET, Belgian Report, Q 20.

1676 Note that BULGARIAN law was changed in this respect by Art. 18 Bulgarian Family Code, which came into force on 1 October 2009 and thus supersedes the references in TODOROVA, Bulgarian Report, Q 20.

1677 See HRUŠÁKOVÁ/WESTPHALOVA, "Czech Republic", in: PINTENS (ed), *Family and Succession Law, in International Encyclopaedia of Laws*, 2011, p. 163 and 171 ff. See also MELZER, Czech Report, Q 20.

1678 See FERRAND/BRAAT, French Report, Q 20.

1679 See WEISS/SZEIBERT, Hungarian Report, Q 20.

1680 See PATTI/CARICATO/IRTI/IANNICELLI/SERRA/DI STEFANO/PETÖ/BORTULU, Italian Report, Q 20.

1681 See MIKELENAS, Lithuanian Report, Q 20.

1682 See FARRUGIA, Maltese Report, Q 20.

1683 See MĄCZYŃSKI, Polish Report, Q 20.

1684 See DE OLIVEIRA/MARTINS/VÍTOR, Portuguese Report, Q 20.

1685 See ANTOKOLSKAIA, Russian Report, Q 20.

1686 See HATÁPKA, Slovakian Report, Q 20.

1687 See GONZÁLEZ BEILFUSS, Spanish Report, Q 20.

1688 See ROTH, Austrian Report, Q 17.

1689 Arts. 1454 – 1465 Belgian Civil Code. See PINTENS/ALLAERTS/SEYNS/PIGNOLET, Belgian Report, Q 17.

1690 Arts. 66–75 Catalan Family Code See MARTÍN-CASALS/RIBOT, Catalan Report, Q 17.

1691 Arts. 1497 – 1528 French Civil Code. See FERRAND/BRAAT, French Report, Q 17.

1692 See DETHLOFF/MARTINY, German Report, Q 17.

1693 Art. 1403 para. 1 Greek Civil Code. See KOUTSOURADIS/KOTRONIS/HATZANTONIS, Greek Report, Q 17.

1694 See MĄCZYŃSKI, Polish Report, Q 17.

1695 See DE OLIVEIRA/MARTINS/VÍTOR, Portuguese Report, Q 17.

1696 Art. 42 para. 2 Russian Family Code. See ANTOKOLSKAIA, Russian Report, Q 17.

1697 Art. 182 para. 2 Swiss Civil Code. See SCHWENZER/BOCK, Swiss Report, Q 17.

1698 See BOELE-WOELKI/SCHONEWILLE/SCHRAMA, Dutch Report, Q 20.

COMMENT

1. Principle 4:33 states that the community of acquisitions regime applies when the spouses have not agreed otherwise in accordance with Chapter II. A corresponding Principle for the participation in acquisitions regime is provided by Principle 4:16.

2. The community of acquisitions regime is based on systems in which property acquired during the marriage, other than that acquired by gift, inheritance or bequest, is considered community property and which is shared upon dissolution of the regime. The label of the chosen system as a "community of acquisitions regime" was thought preferable to the more commonly used label "community of property" since the community in these Principles is a restricted one, see Principle 4:34.

3. The community of acquisitions regime promotes solidarity and fairness between the spouses both during the regime and upon its dissolution. It achieves this by regarding *all* post marital earnings and gains and *all* assets acquired either jointly or individually from those earnings, and all property acquired during the marriage (with the exception of property substituting to personal property or purchased with one spouse's personal property) as community property. Community property is shared equally upon the dissolution of the regime.

4. The community of acquisitions regime is the very antithesis of pure separation regimes and fundamentally differs from the participation in acquisitions regime defined in Section A in that *immediately* upon marriage, post marital earnings and gains are community owned assets. One important advantage of this regime is that it better protects the spouse who neither owns property nor is or remains on the labour market during the marriage. Moreover, providing for a property title if assets are to be divided at the end of the marriage is generally is considered to give stronger protection than a monetary claim.

5. Another advantage of the community of acquisitions regime is that it provides greater certainty both for the spouses and third parties during the marriage and, arguably, the distribution of assets upon the dissolution of the regime is much simpler as compared with the participation and the common law regimes.

6. Like the participation in acquisition regime, the community regime promotes gender equality, as the spouses are expected to take equal responsibility for the welfare of the family. It also protects each spouse against the consequences of economic losses by the other spouse in that the spouse's personal property and liabilities remain unaffected.

CONCEPT
NOTION
BEGRIFF

Principle 4:34 Concept of the community of acquisitions
(1) The community of acquisitions is a matrimonial property regime comprising community property and personal property.
(2) Community property is property acquired during the community of acquisitions and which is not personal property.
(3) Personal property is each spouse's own property.

Principe 4:34 Notion de communauté d'acquêts
(1) La communauté d'acquêts est un régime matrimonial qui comprend le patrimoine commun et le patrimoine personnel.
(2) Le patrimoine commun est le patrimoine acquis durant la communauté d'acquêts et qui n'est pas patrimoine personnel.
(3) Le patrimoine personnel est le patrimoine propre de chaque époux.

Prinzip 4:34 Begriff der Errungenschaftsgemeinschaft
(1) Die Errungenschaftsgemeinschaft ist ein Güterstand bestehend aus gemeinschaftlichem Vermögen und persönlichem Vermögen.
(2) Gemeinschaftliches Vermögen ist Vermögen, das während der Errungenschaftsgemeinschaft erworben wurde und nicht persönliches Vermögen ist.
(3) Persönliches Vermögen ist das eigene Vermögen jedes der Ehegatten.

INTERNATIONAL INSTRUMENTS

None of particular relevance.

COMPARATIVE OVERVIEW

In functional terms all of the jurisdictions surveyed distinguish community assets from the spouses' individually held personal assets. There are of course linguistic differences among the majority of jurisdictions referring to either 'the community' or 'the community of property or assets' (BELGIUM,[1699] BULGARIA,[1700] FRANCE,[1701] ITALY,[1702] LITHUANIA,[1703] POLAND,[1704] RUSSIA,[1705] SLOVAKIA[1706] and SPAIN[1707]) but with others referring to 'common' assets, property or fund or joint property regime (see respectively PORTUGAL,[1708] AUSTRIA[1709], HUNGARY[1710], MALTA[1711] and CZECH REPUBLIC[1712]). In THE NETHERLANDS[1713] it is referred to as the *universal community.*

COMMENT

Principle 4:34 provides a basic definition of 'the community of acquisitions' and, apart from its name (see the comment to Principle 4:33 above), reflects the position in all of surveyed States, namely, that the regime comprises two categories of property: the community property and the personal property of each spouse. No additional categories exist.

1699 See PINTENS/ALLAERTS/SEYNS/PIGNOLET, Belgian Report, Q 20.
1700 See TODOROVA, Bulgarian Report, Q 20 and 21.
1701 Art. 1400 French Civil Code. See FERRAND/BRAAT, French Report, Q 20.
1702 The position in ITALY is slightly more complicated since it distinguishes between the immediate community (assets, other than personal assets that the spouses purchase during the marriage) and the deferred community (assets existing at the moment of the dissolution of the Community deriving from profits from private assets, income from each spouse's separate activities: assets used by one spouse's enterprise established before the marriage and the growth of an enterprise, even if established before the marriage). See PATTI/CARICATO/IRTI/IANNICELLI/SERRA/DI STEFANO/PETÖ/BORTULU, Italian Report, Q 21.
1703 Arts. 3.88 and 3.89 Lithuanian Civil Code. See MIKELENAS, Lithuanian Report, Q 20 and 22.
1704 Art. 31 para. 1 and Art 33 Polish Family and Guardianship Code. See MĄCZYŃSKI, Polish Report, Q 20.
1705 Art. 256 para. 2 Russian Civil Code and Art. 34 para. 2 Russian Family Code. See ANTOKOLSKAIA, Russian Report, Q 20.
1706 See HATÁPKA, Slovakian Report, Q 20.
1707 See GONZÁLEZ BEILFUSS, Spanish Report, Q 20.
1708 Art. 1722 para. 1 and 2 Portuguese Civil Code. See DE OLIVEIRA/MART.INS/VÍTOR, Portuguese Report, Q 20.
1709 See ROTH, Austrian Report, Q 20.
1710 § 27 para. 1 and § 28 para. 1–2 Hungarian Family Act. See WEISS/SZEIBERT, Hungarian Report, Q 20.
1711 See FARRUGIA, Maltese Report, Q 20.
1712 See MELZER, Czech Report, Q 57.
1713 Art. 1:93 and Art. 1:94 Dutch Civil Code. See BOELE-WOELKI/SCHONEWILLE/SCHRAMA, Dutch Report, Q 20.

ASSETS
L'ACTIF
AKTIVA

Principle 4:35 Community property

(1) Community property comprises any property movable and immovable acquired during the regime that is not the personal property of one of the spouses.

(2) In particular, community property includes

(a) the spouses' income and gains whether derived from earnings, community property or personal property;

(b) assets acquired either jointly or individually by the spouses during the community of acquisitions by means of the spouses' income and gains;

(c) gifts and bequests to both spouses or to one spouse on condition that they belong to community property.

Principe 4:35 La communauté

(1) La communauté comprend tout bien meuble et immeuble acquis durant le régime et qui n'est pas propre à un des époux.

(2) En particulier, la communauté comprend

(a) les revenus et gains provenant soit de l'activité professionnelle des époux, soit de leur patrimoine commun ou personnel;

(b) les biens acquis en commun ou séparément par les époux durant la communauté d'acquêts au moyen des revenus et gains des époux;

(c) les donations et legs faits aux deux époux, ou à un seul époux sous condition qu'ils tombent dans la communauté.

Prinzip 4:35 Gemeinschaftliches Vermögen

(1) Gemeinschaftliches Vermögen besteht aus beweglichem und unbeweglichem Vermögen, das während des Güterstands erworben wird und das nicht persönliches Vermögen eines der Ehegatten ist.

(2) Insbesondere umfasst das gemeinschaftliche Vermögen

(a) Einkommen und Gewinne erzielt aus Verdienst, gemeinschaftlichem oder persönlichem Vermögen;

(b) Vermögensgegenstände, die entweder gemeinsam oder getrennt von den Ehegatten während der Errungenschaftsgemeinschaft mit Mitteln aus Einkommen und Gewinnen erworben werden.

(c) Schenkungen und Zuwendungen von Todes wegen an beide Ehegatten oder an einen Ehegatten unter der Bedingung, dass sie zum gemeinschaftlichen Vermögen gehören.

INTERNATIONAL INSTRUMENTS

None of particular relevance.

COMPARATIVE OVERVIEW

The two key elements in determining whether assets fall into the community are first, the timing of their acquisition (*the temporal element*) and secondly, the nature and/or source of the assets themselves (*the specific asset element*).

The temporal element

With regard to the temporal element there is, with the exception of HUNGARY and THE NETHERLANDS, common agreement that only assets (whether movables or immovables) acquired during the community (which in most cases means during the marriage) can qualify as community assets. In HUNGARY,[1714] however, property acquired during pre-marital cohabitation becomes community property upon the parties' marriage, while in THE NETHERLANDS,[1715] pre-maritally acquired assets generally belong to the community upon the parties' marriage.

The specific asset element: assets acquired during the marriage not falling into community property

It is accepted by all fifteen of the jurisdictions surveyed that not all assets acquired during the marriage fall into the community. The principal exclusions[1716] are:

i. Gifts or bequests made to one spouse[1717] (which is the position in all fifteen of the surveyed States, though in AUSTRIA,[1718] the donor or testator has to add a

[1714] See WEISS/SZEIBERT, Hungarian Report, Q 22.
[1715] See BOELE-WOELKI/SCHONEWILLE/SCHRAMA, Dutch Report, Q 25.
[1716] In the CZECH REPUBLIC special provision is made for the restitution of property confiscated during the Communist regime. See MELZER, Czech Report, Q 57.
[1717] Unless made on condition that it should belong to the community.
[1718] See ROTH, Austrian Report, Q 27.

specific condition obliging the benefited spouse to make an agreement with the other spouse that the asset will be separate property), and

ii. Assets acquired for personal or professional use of one of the spouses (subject to the proviso in some States that assets for personal use should not include luxury items or be out of proportion to the spouse's standard of living (see respectively BULGARIA[1719] and RUSSIA[1720]).
iii. Other assets that are personal by nature, principally one spouse's intellectual rights, damages for personal injury and maintenance claims.
iv. Property substituting or substantially financed by personal property.

The specific asset element: assets falling into the community

The following analysis focuses upon what community assets actually comprise as opposed to what they exclude. The narrowest regime of those surveyed is BULGARIA[1721] where the community is confined to property, rights in properties (for example, occupation rights, building lease) and bank deposits (that is savings accounts) acquired by the spouses during their marriage as a result of their 'common contribution' (which is widely defined as comprising investment of means and labour and care for the children and work in the household). This means, for example, that the spouses' earnings are their personal property unless and until they are invested in a community asset when they become community assets.

At the other end of the spectrum is THE NETHERLANDS[1722] where the community comprises all present and future assets (both movables and immovables) of both spouses, save for gifts and bequests to one of them provided that the deceased or donor has explicitly determined that the asset should not fall into the community property, assets that have a close affinity with one of the spouses, the right of usufruct and pension rights. Although spouses' earnings are not specifically regulated, because they are 'assets', they fall within the community.

In the case of the remaining thirteen jurisdictions there is broad agreement that community assets comprise:

i. Assets (other than 'personal assets' see above) acquired against payment either jointly or individually by the two spouses during the marriage. This is

1719 See TODOROVA, Bulgarian Report, Q 22.
1720 Art. 36 Russian Family Code. See ANTOKOLSKAIA, Russian Report, Q 22.
1721 See TODOROVA, Bulgarian Report, Q 25.
1722 Arts. 1:93 and 1:94 para. 1 and para. 2 Dutch Civil Code. See BOELE-WOELKI/SCHONEWILLE/SCHRAMA, Dutch Report, Q 25.

the position for instance in BELGIUM,[1723] CZECH REPUBLIC,[1724] FRANCE,[1725] HUNGARY,[1726] ITALY,[1727] LITHUANIA,[1728] POLAND,[1729] PORTUGAL,[1730] RUSSIA[1731] and SPAIN.[1732]

ii. The spouses' earnings during the marriage.
This is specifically provided for in the relevant Codes, as in BELGIUM,[1733] CZECH REPUBLIC,[1734] FRANCE,[1735] LITHUANIA,[1736] MALTA,[1737] POLAND,[1738] PORTUGAL,[1739] RUSSIA[1740] and SPAIN.[1741] In the case of AUSTRIA[1742] and SLOVAKIA,[1743] however, it is by case law that such earnings constitute community property. In HUNGARY,[1744] there are no specific rules governing spouses' earnings. In ITALY,[1745] earnings are not treated as community property per se but instead only become so in respect of 'gains' not used up at the moment of the community's dissolution (*comunione de residuo*). Not dissimilarly, POLAND[1746] only considers salaries and earnings that have been accrued during the marriage to be community property. In contrast, in FRANCE,[1747] it is now clear that profits and earnings are common assets even before they are collected or, in the case of intellectual rights, even before they have been exploited. In some jurisdictions, earnings etc are widely defined to include, in the case of BELGIUM,[1748] income or compensation replacing or supplementing earned income and income from public or private mandates.

1723 In the sense that all assets not proved to belong to one spouse, belong to the community: Art. 1405 No. 4 Belgian Civil Code.

1724 § 143 Czech Civil Code. See MELZER, Czech Report, Q 61.

1725 Art. 1401 French Civil Code.

1726 In the sense that all assets not proved to belong to one spouse, belong to the community: § 27 para. 1 Hungarian Family Act.

1727 Art. 177 Italian Civil Code.

1728 Art. 3.88 Lithuanian Civil Code. See MIKELENAS, Lithuanian Report, Q 25.

1729 Art. 31 para. 1 sentence 1 Polish Family and Guardianship Code.

1730 Art. 1724 sub a Portuguese Civil Code.

1731 Art. 34 and 36 Russion Family Code.

1732 Art. 1347 Spanish Civil Code.

1733 Art. 1405 Belgian Civil Code.

1734 See MELZER, Czech Report, Q 57.

1735 Art. 1401 French Civil Code.

1736 Art. 3.86 Lithuanian Civil Code.

1737 Art. 1334 para. 4 Maltese Civil Code.

1738 Art. 31 para. 2 point 2 Polish Civil Code – but see further below.

1739 Art. 1724 sub a Portuguese Civil Code.

1740 Art. 34 Russion Family Code.

1741 Art. 1347 para. 1 Spanish Civil Code.

1742 See ROTH, Austrian Report, Q 25.

1743 See HATÁPKA, Slovakian Report, Q 25.

1744 See WEISS/SZEIBERT, Hungarian Report, Q 25.

1745 See PATTI/CARICATO/IRTI/IANNICELLI/SERRA/DI STEFANO/PETÖ/BORTULU, Italian Report, Q 25.

1746 See MĄCZYŃSKI, Polish Report, Q 25.

1747 Art. L 212–9 para. 2 French Intellectual Property Code.

1748 Art. 1405 No 1 Belgian Civil Code.

A similar position exists in FRANCE.[1749] In PORTUGAL,[1750] reference is made to the revenues derived from the labour of the spouses including awards for productivity and intellectual property rights. A similar position exists in SPAIN,[1751] except that prizes won in lotteries or other games of chance are also included.[1752] MALTA[1753] similarly considers lottery winnings as belonging to the community (the assumption being that the money to buy the ticket came from community funds). In SLOVAKIA,[1754] case law establishes that winnings and assets acquired during the marriage from betting, lotteries or draws (whether monetary or not) are considered to be community property regardless of when the purchase was made.

iii. Income and interest from personal property.
As in the case of spouses' earnings, the inclusion of income and interest from personal property as community property is expressly provided for in the relevant codes as in BELGIUM,[1755] FRANCE,[1756] HUNGARY,[1757] MALTA,[1758] PORTUGAL[1759] and SPAIN.[1760] In LITHUANIA,[1761] the prevailing view is that earnings only become community property when they are actually received, but this question is a matter of some debate in the CZECH REPUBLIC.[1762] In ITALY,[1763] the position is that only the proceeds from personal assets that have been received and not used up at the moment of the dissolution of the community, fall into the community.

iv. Gifts or bequests to both spouses or one spouse on condition that they belong to the community.
Gifts and bequests to both spouses are commonly treated as community property. This rule is occasionally expressly provided for by statute as in BELGIUM[1764] and SPAIN.[1765] Many jurisdictions also permit the donor or testator to specify that the gift or bequest be assigned to the community:

1749 See FERRAND/BRAAT, French Report, Q 25.
1750 See Art. 1724 sub a Portuguese Civil Code.
1751 Art. 1342 para. 1 Spanish Civil Code.
1752 Art. 1351 Spanish Civil Code. See GONZÁLEZ BEILFUSS, Spanish Report, Q 25.
1753 See FARRUGIA, Maltese Report, Q 20.
1754 See HATÁPKA, Slovakian Report, Q 20.
1755 Art. 1405 Belgian Civil Code.
1756 Art. 1401 French Civil Code.
1757 § 27 para. 1 second sentence, Hungarian Family Act, which specifically mentions having first to deduct costs and other burdens of administration and maintenance of the separate property.
1758 Art. 1334 para. 3 Maltese Civil Code.
1759 Art. 1728 para. 1 and Art. 1733 para. 2 Portuguese Civil Code.
1760 Art. 1347 para. 2 and Art. 1349 Spanish Civil Code.
1761 See MIKELENAS, Lithuanian Report, Q 25.
1762 See MELZER, Czech Report, Q 57.
1763 Art. 177 Italian Civil Code.
1764 Art. 1405 Belgian Civil Code.
1765 Art. 1353 Spanish Civil Code.

BELGIUM,[1766] FRANCE,[1767] HUNGARY,[1768] ITALY,[1769] LITHUANIA,[1770] POLAND,[1771] PORTUGAL[1772] and SPAIN.[1773]

v. Miscellaneous assets

In ITALY,[1774] community property also includes gains and growth of companies (or 'enterprises' as they sometimes referred to) run by both spouses (regardless of whether it is owned jointly or by just one spouse). Enterprises established after the marriage but which are controlled by both spouses fall into the community. In SPAIN,[1775] too, enterprises and establishments funded by one spouse but with community property is considered community property. SPAIN and PORTUGAL also make express provision for assets acquired both out of personal and community funding. In PORTUGAL,[1776] if the community funding constitutes the greater part, the new asset belongs to the community, whereas in SPAIN,[1777] the community is entitled to the amount that is proportionate to the contribution. SPAIN[1778] also provides that improvements made to common assets accrue to the community regardless of which property financed them.

COMMENT

1. Principle 4:35 is intended to provide a broad general definition of community property encompassing both the nature and source of the assets (*the specific asset element*) and the timing of their acquisition (*the temporal element*). The definition of community property needs to be considered together with Principle 4:36 which defines personal property.

2. Reflecting the common core, Principle 4:35(1) defines community property as comprising both movable and immovable property in general and, as provided for by Principle 4:35(2)(a), the spouses' income (including earnings derived from

1766 Art. 1405 No 3 Belgian Civil Code. See PINTENS/ALLAERTS/SEYNS/PIGNOLET, Belgian Report, Q 27.

1767 Art. 1405 para. 2 French Civil Code. See FERRAND/BRAAT, French Report, Q 27.

1768 See WEISS/SZEIBERT, Hungarian Report, Q 27.

1769 See PATTI/CARICATO/IRTI/IANNICELLI/SERRA/DI STEFANO/PETÖ/BORTULU, Italian Report, Q 27.

1770 Art. 3.89 Lithuanian Civil Code. See MIKELENAS, Lithuanian Report, Q 27.

1771 Art. 33 para. 2 Polish Family and Guardianship Code. See MĄCZYŃSKI, Polish Report, Q 27.

1772 See DE OLIVEIRA/MARTINS/VÍTOR, Portuguese Report, Q 27.

1773 See GONZÁLEZ BEILFUSS, Spanish Report, Q 27.

1774 See PATTI/CARICATO/IRTI/IANNICELLI/SERRA/DI STEFANO/PETÖ/BORTULU, Italian Report, Q 25.

1775 Art. 1347 para. 5 Spanish Civil Code.

1776 See DE OLIVEIRA/MARTINS/VÍTOR, Portuguese Report, Q 25.

1777 See GONZÁLEZ BEILFUSS, Spanish Report, Q 25.

1778 Art. 1360 Spanish Civil Code.

intellectual property rights) and gains derived from earnings or community property or personal property, in particular. It also comprises, as provided for by Principle 4:35(2)(b), assets acquired by the spouse either jointly or individually, during the community of acquisitions by means of the spouses' income or gains.

3. By 'gains' is meant what might best be described as 'windfall assets' acquired with the use of community or personal property such as winnings acquired from betting, lotteries or draws. 'Gains', however, do not include *inherent* increases in value of assets that fall within personal property, for example, the increase in value of pre-marital property resulting from market valuations since that has nothing to do with the spouse's contributions and thus falls outside any notions of family solidarity.

4. So far as the temporal element is concerned, again adopting the common core, to constitute community property, the assets must be acquired during the community. Principle 4:35(1) does not therefore accommodate the exceptional position taken in some jurisdictions with regard to pre-marital assets.

5. Reflecting the clear common core of the jurisdictions surveyed, Principle 4:35(2)(c) includes in the definition of community property, gifts and bequests made to both spouses or to one of them on condition that they belong to community property.

Principle 4:36 Personal property
Personal property comprises:

(a) Assets acquired before entering into the community of acquisitions;
(b) Gifts, inheritances and bequests acquired during the regime;
(c) Assets acquired through substitution, investment or reinvestment in accordance with Principles 4:37 and 4:38;
(d) Assets personal in nature, acquired during the regime;
(e) Assets exclusively acquired for a spouse's profession.

Principe 4:36 Patrimoine propre
Le patrimoine propre comprend:

(a) les biens acquis avant l'existence de la communauté d'acquêts;
(b) les successions et les libéralités échues pendant le régime;
(c) les biens acquis par échange, emploi ou remploi conformément aux Principes 4:37 et 4:38;
(d) les biens personnels par nature, acquis durant le régime;
(e) les biens acquis exclusivement pour l'activité professionnelle d'un époux.

Prinzip 4:36 Persönliches Vermögen
Persönliches Vermögen umfasst

(a) vor Beginn der Errungenschaftsgemeinschaft erworbene Vermögensgegenstände;
(b) während des Güterstands durch Schenkung und von Todes wegen erworbenes Vermögen;
(c) in Folge der Prinzipien 4:37 und 4:38 durch Ersetzung, Anlage oder Wiederanlage erworbene Vermögensgegenstände;
(d) während des Güterstands erworbene persönliche Vermögensgegenstände;
(e) ausschließlich für die Berufstätigkeit eines Ehegatten erworbene Vermögensgegenstände.

INTERNATIONAL INSTRUMENTS

None of particular relevance.

COMPARATIVE OVERVIEW

Pre-marital assets

Although expressed differently, in all the jurisdictions surveyed,[1779] except for THE NETHERLANDS (see further below), personal assets comprise, inter alia, all assets acquired, from whatever source, before the marriage or, more technically, before the creation of the community. THE NETHERLANDS apart, the only variations are HUNGARY,[1780] in which assets acquired during pre-marital cohabitation are regarded as part of the community assets following the parties' marriage; and MALTA,[1781] where the "fruits" of a pre-marital gift or bequest received during the marriage is part of the community. THE NETHERLANDS,[1782] alone of the jurisdictions surveyed, treats pre-marital assets and assets acquired by gift or bequest, unless otherwise specified by the testator or donor, as belonging to the community upon the parties' marriage.

Gifts, inheritances and bequests

In general, all the jurisdictions surveyed regard gifts, inheritances and bequests to an individual as being the beneficiary spouse's personal assets.[1783] In AUSTRIA,[1784] however, this is the position only where the donor or testator has specifically added a condition obliging the benefited spouse to make an agreement with the other spouse that the asset will be separate property. In contrast, as already discussed in the context of defining community property for the purposes of Principle 4:35, many jurisdictions permit the donor or testator to specify that the gift or bequest be assigned to the community (BELGIUM,[1785]

1779 See ROTH, Austrian Report, Q 22; PINTENS/ALLAERTS/SEYNS/PIGNOLET, Belgian Report, Q 22: TODOROVA, Bulgarian Report, Q 22; MELZER, Czech Report, Q 57; FERRAND/BRAAT, French Report, Q 22; PATTI/CARICATO/IRTI/IANNICELLI/SERRA/DI STEFANO/PETÖ/BORTULU, Italian ReportQ 22; MIKELENAS, Lithuanian Report, Q 22; MĄCZYŃSKI, Polish Report, Q 22; DE OLIVEIRA/MARTÍNS/VÍTOR, Portuguese Report, Q 22; ANTOKOLSKAIA, Russian Report, Q 22; HATÁPKA, Slovakian Report, Q 22 and GONZÁLEZ BEILFUSS, Spanish Report, Q 22.

1780 See WEISS/SZEIBERT, Hungarian Report, Q 22.

1781 See FARRUGIA, Maltese Report, Q 22.

1782 See BOELE-WOELKI/SCHONEWILLE/SCHRAMA, Dutch Report, Q 25.

1783 See PINTENS/ALLAERTS/SEYNS/PIGNOLET, Belgian Report, Q 27; TODOROVA, Bulgarian Report, Q 27; MELZER, Czech Report, Q 57; FERRAND/BRAAT, French Report, Q 27; PATTI/CARICATO/IRTI/IANNICELLI/SERRA/DI STEFANO/PETÖ/BORTULU, Italian Report, Q 27; MIKELENAS, Lithuanian Report, Q 27; FARRUGIA, Maltese Report, Q 27; MĄCZYŃSKI, Polish Report, Q 27; ANTOKOLSKAIA, Russian Report, Q 27; DE OLIVEIRA/MART.INS/VÍTOR, Portuguese Report, Q 27; HATÁPKA, Slovakian Report, Q 27 and GONZÁLEZ BEILFUSS, Spanish Report, Q 27.

1784 See ROTH, Austrian Report, Q 27.

1785 See PINTENS/ALLAERTS/SEYNS/PIGNOLET, Belgian Report, Q 27.

FRANCE,[1786] HUNGARY,[1787] ITALY,[1788] LITHUANIA,[1789] POLAND,[1790] PORTUGAL[1791] and SPAIN[1792]). In the CZECH REPUBLIC,[1793] however, third parties have no power to stipulate into what category of assets their gift or bequest should fall. In RUSSIA,[1794] the donor or testator cannot stipulate that a gift or bequest to an individual spouse is anything other than that spouse's personal property; while in SLOVAKIA[1795] the donor or testator cannot stipulate that the gift or bequest be assigned to the community though he or she can stipulate that the spouses are the co-owners of a particular asset. In POLAND,[1796] gifts or bequests of ordinary household assets are treated as community property unless the donor or testator specifies otherwise.

Gifts and bequests to both spouses are commonly treated as community property. But in BULGARIA,[1797] such bequeathed assets belong to the spouses jointly rather than to the community. In SPAIN,[1798] gifts obtained on marriage are presumed to be personal assets and, unless the donor specifies otherwise, if made to both spouses, are divided into equal shares.

Assets for personal use

It is commonly accepted that clothing and objects for a spouse's personal use are that spouse's personal property. This is frequently expressly stated in the relevant Code as, for example, in BELGIUM,[1799] BULGARIA,[1800] FRANCE,[1801] LITHUANIA,[1802] PORTUGAL,[1803] RUSSIA[1804] and SPAIN[1805] (in some other jurisdictions, for

1786 See FERRAND/BRAAT, French Report, Q 27.
1787 See WEISS/SZEIBERT, Hungarian Report, Q 27.
1788 See PATTI/CARICATO/IRTI/IANNICELLI/SERRA/DI STEFANO/PETÖ/BORTULU, Italian Report, Q 27.
1789 See MIKELENAS, Lithuanian Report, Q 27.
1790 See MĄCZYŃSKI, Polish Report, Q 27.
1791 See DE OLIVEIRA/MARTINS/VÍTOR, Portuguese Report, Q 27.
1792 See GONZÁLEZ BEILFUSS, Spanish Report, Q 27.
1793 See MELZER, Czech Report, Q 63.
1794 Art. 26 Russian Family Code. See ANTOKOLSKAIA, Russian Report, Q 27.
1795 See HATÁPKA, Slovakian Report, Q 27.
1796 See WEISS/SZEIBERT, Hungarian Report, Q 27.
1797 See TODOROVA, Bulgarian Report, Q 27. But the position with regard to gifts has been a matter of debate.
1798 Art. 1353 Spanish Civil Code. See GONZÁLEZ BEILFUSS, Spanish Report, Q 27.
1799 Art. 1401 Belgian Civil Code. See PINTENS/ALLAERTS/SEYNS/PIGNOLET, Belgian Report, Q 22.
1800 See TODOROVA, Bulgarian Report, Q 22.
1801 Art. 1404 French Civil Code. See FERRAND/BRAAT, French Report, Q 22.
1802 Art. 3.39 Lithuanian Civil Code. See MIKELENAS, Lithuanian Report, Q 22.
1803 Art. 1733 para.1 Portuguese Civil Code. See DE OLIVEIRA/MARTINS/VÍTOR, Portuguese Report, Q 22. See.
1804 Art. 36 Russian Family Code. See ANTOKOLSKAIA, Russian Report, Q 22.
1805 Art. 1346.7 Spanish Civil Code. See GONZÁLEZ BEILFUSS, Spanish Report, Q 22.

example, ITALY[1806] and SLOVAKIA,[1807] reference is simply made to the spouses' 'personal needs'). The only qualifications on this position is in RUSSIA,[1808] where the Family Code expressly excludes jewellery and other luxury items; SPAIN,[1809] which similarly expressly excludes items of extraordinary value having regard to the spouses' standard of living and BULGARIA[1810] whose Code refers to assets for a spouse's 'ordinary' use, thereby excluding extraordinary items. HUNGARY,[1811] too, has regard to the spouses' standard of living and also to proportionality between the spouses in assessing whether to characterise personal items as personal property.

Other assets that are personal by nature

A number of jurisdictions include other assets beyond those for personal or professional use within the broad concept of assets being considered as personal by nature (as expressed in FRANCE[1812]), but also referred to as *special assets* in AUSTRIA,[1813] *strict personal rights* (as in BELGIUM[1814]) or as *assets having a close affinity with one spouse* (as in THE NETHERLANDS[1815]) or simply as being personal to one spouse (as in PORTUGAL[1816] and SPAIN[1817]). An alternative strategy is for the relevant Code to include as personal property, specific assets, for example, damages for personal injury (as in ITALY[1818] and LITHUANIA[1819]). However, this is an area where there is less overall common ground both in the sense of whether there is a specifically established position (either under a Code or by case-law) and, if so, on how the asset should be classified. Nevertheless, it is not unusual for the following assets (in order of commonality) to be expressly dealt with: intellectual rights; damages for personal or moral injury; inalienable claims or rights and personal effects.

1806 Art. 179 Italian Civil Code. See PATTI/CARICATO/IRTI/IANNICELLI/SERRA/DI STEFANO/PETÖ/BORTULU, Italian Report, Q 22.
1807 See HATÁPKA, Slovakian Report, Q 22.
1808 See ANTOKOLSKAIA, Russian Report, Q 22.
1809 Art. 1346.7 Spansh Civil Code.
1810 See TODOROVA, Bulgarian Report, Q 22.
1811 See WEISS/SZEIBERT, Hungarian Report, Q 22.
1812 Art. 1401 para. 1 French Civil Code. See FERRAND/BRAAT, French Report, Q 22.
1813 See ROTH, Austrian Report, Q 22.
1814 Art. 1401 Belgian Civil Code. See PINTENS/ALLAERTS/SEYNS/PIGNOLET, Belgian Report, Q 22.
1815 Art. 1:94 para. 3 Dutch Civil Code. See BOELE-WOELKI/SCHONEWILLE/SCHRAMA, Dutch Report, Q 22.
1816 See DE OLIVEIRA/MARTINS/VÍTOR, Portuguese Report, Q 22.
1817 See GONZÁLEZ BEILFUSS, Spanish Report, Q 22.
1818 Art. 179 Italian Civil Code. See PATTI/CARICATO/IRTI/IANNICELLI/SERRA/DI STEFANO/PETÖ/BORTULU, Italian Report, Q 22.
1819 Art. 3.89 Lithuanian Civil Code. See MIKELENAS, Lithuanian Report, Q 22.

So far as intellectual rights are concerned, where these are provided for, they are classified as personal assets in AUSTRIA,[1820] BULGARIA[1821] (where all economic rights apart from property rights are treated as personal), POLAND,[1822] PORTUGAL[1823] (which refers to moral authorship rights, but see below) and SLOVAKIA[1824] (as established by case-law). In contrast, intellectual property rights fall within the community in THE NETHERLANDS,[1825] while in LITHUANIA[1826] and RUSSIA,[1827] although the objects of intellectual property themselves are the personal property of their author, income received as a result of the exploitation of such objects is regarded as community property. In BELGIUM[1828] (where the Code refers to industrial property rights as well as literary and artistic rights), FRANCE,[1829] PORTUGAL[1830] and SPAIN[1831] too, income from intellectual property rights are considered as community assets.

Of the jurisdictions that deal with damages for personal or moral injury, the following regard the ensuing assets as personal assets, namely BELGIUM,[1832] FRANCE,[1833] ITALY,[1834] LITHUANIA[1835] and PORTUGAL.[1836] BULGARIA[1837] also recognises personal injury damages as being personal assets but on the basis that all economic rights apart from property rights are treated as personal. Only THE NETHERLANDS,[1838] among the jurisdictions surveyed, regard damages for personal injuries as falling within the community.

1820 See ROTH, Austrian Report, Q 22.
1821 See TODOROVA, Bulgarian Report, Q 22.
1822 Art. 33 Polish Family and Guardianship Code. See MĄCZYŃSKI, Polish Report, Q 21.
1823 See DE OLIVEIRA/MARTINS/VÍTOR, Portuguese Report, Q 22.
1824 See HATÁPKA, Slovakian Report, Q 22.
1825 See BOELE-WOELKI/SCHONEWILLE/SCHRAMA, Dutch Report, Q 22.
1826 Art. 3.89 Lithuanian Civil Code. See MIKELENAS, Lithuanian Report, Q 22.
1827 Arts. 36 and 256 para. 2 Russian Family Code, as amended. See ANTOKOLSKAIA, Russian Report, Q 22.
1828 Art. 1405 Belgian Civil Code. See PINTENS/ALLAERTS/SEYNS/PIGNOLET, Belgian Report, Q 25.
1829 Art. L 121–9 para. 2 French Code of Intellectual Property. See FERRAND/BRAAT, French Report, Q 25.
1830 Art. 1724 sub a Portuguese Civil Code. See DE OLIVEIRA/MART.INS/VÍTOR, Portuguese Report, Q 25.
1831 Art 1347 para. 5 Spanish Civil Code. See GONZÁLEZ BEILFUSS, Spanish Report, Q 22.
1832 Art. 1401 Belgian Civil Code and Art. 1401 Belgian Civil Code. See PINTENS/ALLAERTS/SEYNS/PIGNOLET, Belgian Report, Q 22.
1833 Art. 1404 para. 1 French Civil Code. See FERRAND/BRAAT, French Report, Q 22.
1834 Art. 179 Italian Civil Code. See PATTI/CARICATO/IRTI/IANNICELLI/SERRA/DI STEFANO/PETÖ/BORTULU, Italian Report, Q 22.
1835 Art. 3.89 Lithuanian Civil Code. See MIKELENAS, Lithuanian Report, Q 22.
1836 Art. 1733 para. 1 (d) of Portuguese Civil Code. See DE OLIVEIRA/MARTINS/VÍTOR, Portuguese Report, Q 22.
1837 See TODOROVA, Bulgarian Report, Q 22.
1838 See BOELE-WOELKI/SCHONEWILLE/SCHRAMA, Dutch Report, Q 22.

So far as alienable rights (other than intellectual rights) of one spouse are concerned, AUSTRIA[1839] regards maintenance claims and retirement interest and interests in succession as personal property; BELGIUM[1840] treats only the entitlement of pensions and annuities held by one spouse to be that spouse's personal assets. A spouse's membership rights are also regarded as personal property. In FRANCE,[1841] some annuities and life insurance policies (for example, those undertaken by one spouse for the benefit of the surviving spouse) are treated as personal assets and in SPAIN,[1842] where maintenance and pension rights are regarded as personal assets.

So far as personal effects are concerned, both FRANCE[1843] and PORTUGAL[1844] regard items such as honorary distinctions, diplomas, letters and family heirlooms as personal property.

Assets for professional use

Movable assets that are necessary for the spouse's professional use are also normally treated as that spouse's personal property (BELGIUM,[1845] FRANCE[1846] and BULGARIA[1847]). In RUSSIA,[1848] this problem is not regulated by statutory law but legal doctrine favours their qualification as personal property.

COMMENT

1. Principle 4:36 provides a broad definition of personal property and in doing so adopts the clear common core of the jurisdictions surveyed.

2. As mentioned in Comment 1 to Principle 4:35, the definition of personal property is integral to the definition of community property in so far as it determines what assets fall outside the community. The definition of personal property mirrors that of community property in that it encompasses both the timing of the acquisition of the assets and the nature and source of the assets

---

1839 See ROTH, Austrian Report, Q 22.
1840 Art. 1401 Belgian Civil Code. See PINTENS/ALLAERTS/SEYNS/PIGNOLET, Belgian Report, Q 22.
1841 Art. L. 132-16 French Insurances Code. See FERRAND/BRAAT, French Report, Q 22.
1842 Art. 1346.5 Spanish Civil Code. See GONZÁLEZ BEILFUSS, Spanish Report, Q 22.
1843 See FERRAND/BRAAT, French Report, Q 22.
1844 See DE OLIVEIRA/MARTINS/VÍTOR, Portuguese Report, Q 22.
1845 Art. 1400 No. 6 Belgium Civil Code. See PINTENS/ALLAERTS/SEYNS/PIGNOLET, Belgian Report, Q 22.
1846 Art. 1404 para. 2 French Civil Code. See FERRAND/BRAAT, French Report, Q 22.
1847 See TODOROVA, Bulgarian Report, Q 22.
1848 See ANTOKOLSKAIA, Russian Report, Q 22.

acquired, which becomes important if the assets are acquired during the community of acquisitions.

3. Principle 4:36(a) straightforwardly provides that assets (whether comprising movable or immovable property) acquired before entry into the community are to be regarded as personal property. This position reflects the clear common core. Indeed, only THE NETHERLANDS takes a completely different position.

4. Principle 4:36(b) also adopts the standard position that gifts, inheritances or bequests made to one of the spouses are to be regarded as that spouse's personal property whenever they are made unless they are made on condition that they belong to the community so as to bring them within the scope of Principle 4:35(2)(c). Principle 4:36(b) refrains from making any provision prescribing any limitations or conditions on the donor's or testator's ability to make such gifts or bequests, leaving that issue to be determined by national law.

5. Principle 4:36(c) makes it clear, again in line with the common core, that assets acquired through the substitution, investment or re-investment of personal property continue to be treated as personal property provided they fall within Principles 4:37 or 4:38.

6. Principle 4:36(d) adopts the generally accepted position that assets, such as clothing and objects for a spouse's personal use, or which are otherwise personal in nature, are to be regarded as that spouse's personal property even if they are acquired during the community of acquisitions. The Principle does not define what constitutes assets of a personal nature and in particular whether it includes intellectual rights (though in this respect a distinction has to be made between the rights themselves and income derived from those rights; the latter, when received during the community, being part of community assets, see Comment 2 on Principle 4:35) or personal damages, nor does it expressly deal with luxury items or assets of extraordinary value. In each case that is left to national law to determine.

7. Principle 4:36(e) adopts the common core position that assets that are necessary for a spouse's professional use are to be regarded as that spouse's personal property, again regardless of when those assets were acquired.

Principle 4:37 Substitution
(1) Any asset substituting personal assets without extra payment should be regarded as personal property.
(2) Any asset substituting personal assets with additional payment should be regarded as personal property unless the payment provided by community property equals or exceeds the value of the substituted asset.
(3) Where additional payment is made by one category of property, compensation is payable by the other.

Principe 4:37 Substitution
(1) Tout bien qui se substitue à un bien propre sans paiement additionnel est lui-même propre.
(2) Tout bien qui se substitue à un bien propre avec paiement additionnel est lui-même propre, sauf si le payement additionnel fait par la communauté est égal à la valeur du bien remplacé ou l'excède.
(3) En cas de paiement additionnel fait par un des patrimoines, une récompense est due par l'autre.

Prinzip 4:37 Ersetzung
(1) Jeder Vermögensgegenstand, der ohne zusätzliche Zahlung persönliche Vermögensgegenstände ersetzt, wird als persönliches Vermögen angesehen.
(2) Alle Vermögensgegenstände, die mit zusätzlicher Zahlung persönliche Vermögensgegenstände ersetzen, werden als persönliches Vermögen angesehen, es sei denn, die aus dem gemeinschaftlichen Vermögen erfolgende Zahlung hat den gleichen oder einen höheren Wert der ersetzten Vermögensgegenstände.
(3) Erfolgt eine zusätzliche Zahlung aus einem Vermögen, ist dem anderen Vermögen ein Ausgleich zu zahlen.

INTERNATIONAL INSTRUMENTS

None of particular relevance.

COMPARATIVE OVERVIEW

Jurisdictions vary in the degree of specific regulation of the issues concerning substitution of personal assets. In some there are no specific regulations as in

AUSTRIA,[1849] HUNGARY,[1850] THE NETHERLANDS,[1851] RUSSIA[1852] and SLOVAKIA,[1853] though in most of the aforementioned jurisdictions there is some case law and/or developed practice. In other jurisdictions, FRANCE[1854] being a particularly outstanding example, there are detailed provisions.

In so far as there is clear law on substitution, it is commonly the case that property (whether movable or immovable) replacing personal property (sometimes referred to as real subrogation) as, for example, insurance payments taking the place of the destroyed asset or compensating some damage and assets acquired by way of exchange for a personal asset, or a new property funded by the proceeds of the existing asset, remain the personal property of the spouse concerned. This is clearly the case in BELGIUM,[1855] FRANCE,[1856] POLAND,[1857] PORTUGAL[1858] and SPAIN.[1859] Case law in SLOVAKIA[1860] establishes much the same position. A similar position obtains in BULGARIA,[1861] save that assets that serve either the spouse's personal use or which are necessary for professional use cannot be substituted. It is similarly doubted in THE NETHERLANDS,[1862] whether assets having a close affinity with a spouse can be substituted.

In ITALY,[1863] a distinction is made between movable and immovable assets. In the former case the only formality that is required is a declaration by the owning spouse. In the case of immovables and registered movables the consent of the non-owning spouse is required.

The outstanding exception to the above position is that obtaining in MALTA[1864] where alienation of personal assets are subsumed into community property but the value of the personal asset ranks as a credit in favour of the property owning spouse.

1849 See ROTH, Austrian Report, Q 23.
1850 See WEISS/SZEIBERT, Hungarian Report, Q 23.
1851 See BOELE-WOELKI/SCHONEWILLE/SCHRAMA, Dutch Report, Q 23.
1852 See ANTOKOLSKAIA, Russian Report, Q 23.
1853 See HATÁPKA, Slovakian Report, Q 23.
1854 See FERRAND/BRAAT, French Report, Q 23.
1855 Art. 1400, No. 5 Belgian Civil Code.
1856 Art. 1406 al. 2 and 1407 French Civil Code.
1857 Art. 33 para. 10 Polish Family and Guardianship Code.
1858 Art. 1723 sub a Portuguese Civil Code.
1859 Art. 1346.3 Spanish Civil Code.
1860 See HATÁPKA, Slovakian Report, Q 23.
1861 Art. 21 para. 1 Bulgarian Family Code.
1862 See BOELE-WOELKI/SCHONEWILLE/SCHRAMA, Dutch Report, Q 23.
1863 Art. 179 para. 2 Italian Civil Code.
1864 Art. 1320 sub e Maltese Civil Code.

COMMENT

1. Apart from opting to make express provision, Principle 4:37(1) adopts the clear common core position with respect to the rule regarding substitution of personal assets where no additional payments are involved. It should be noted, however, that the Principle makes no substantive law distinction between movable and immovable property nor are there are special rules concerning the substitution of assets for personal or professional use.

2. Principle 4:37(2) deals with the position where substitution takes place with the aid of additional payments, that is, where more money is used to make the new purchase than is raised by the sale of the substituted asset. Paragraph 2 adopts the position that any asset substituting a personal asset will be considered personal property unless the additional payment provided by the community property *equals* or exceeds the value of the substituted asset. By way of example under this rule where the new asset is acquired for 100 units, it will remain personal property provided 51 or more units were provided by the sale of the substituted asset or otherwise raised from personal assets but it will be considered community property if 50 or more units were provided out of community assets. The underlying rationale is that the substituting asset should belong to the category of property that provided the majority funding but where the funding is equal the community should be favoured. Principle 4:37(2) is subject to Principle 4:37(3) which deals with compensation.

3. Principle 4:37(3) deals in general terms with the question of compensation (more specific rules on compensation are provided by Principle 4:53) and provides that any additional payment made by the category of assets to which the substituted property does not belong has to be compensated by the category to which it does belong. So, for example, where the substituted property was purchased for 100 units using 75 units from personal assets and 25 units from community assets, the latter category would be entitled to compensation from the beneficiary spouse's personal assets for one quarter of the value of the substituted property at the date of the dissolution of the regime.

Principle 4:38 Investment or reinvestment
(1) Any asset acquired solely through the investment or reinvestment of personal assets should be regarded as personal property.
(2) Any asset acquired partly through the investment or reinvestment of personal assets and partly through community assets should belong to the personal property unless the payment provided by community property equals or exceeds the value of the investment or reinvestment.
(3) Where additional investment of reinvestment is made by one category of property, compensation is payable by the other.

Principe 4:38 Emploi ou remploi
(1) Tout bien acquis exclusivement par emploi ou remploi de biens propres est lui-même propre.
(2) Tout bien acquis en partie par emploi ou remploi de biens propres et en partie par des biens communs, appartient au patrimoine propre sauf si le paiement fait par la communauté est égal à la valeur de l'emploi ou du remploi ou bien l'excède.
(3) En cas d'emploi ou de remploi additionnel fait par un des patrimoines, une récompense est due par l'autre.

Prinzipe 4:38 Anlage oder Wiederanlage
(1) Jeder ausschließlich durch Anlage oder Wiederanlage persönlicher Vermögensgegenstände erworbene Vermögensgegenstand ist als persönliches Vermögen anzusehen.
(2) Jeder teilweise durch Anlage oder Wiederanlage persönlicher Vermögensgegenstände und teilweise durch gemeinschaftliche Vermögensgegenstände erworbene Vermögensgegenstand gehört zum persönlichen Vermögen, es sei denn, die aus dem gemeinschaftlichen Vermögen erfolgende Zahlung hat den gleichen oder einen höheren Wert der erfolgten Anlage oder Wiederanlage.
(3) Erfolgt eine zusätzliche Anlage oder Wiederanlage aus einem Vermögen, ist dem anderen Vermögen ein Ausgleich zu zahlen.

INTERNATIONAL INSTRUMENTS

None of particular relevance

COMPARATIVE OVERVIEW

As with substitution, jurisdictions vary in their degree of specific regulation of issues concerning investment of personal property. In some States there are no specific regulations as in AUSTRIA,[1865] POLAND[1866] and SLOVAKIA.[1867] At the other end of the spectrum, both BELGIUM[1868] and FRANCE[1869] have detailed statutory rules on investments.

So far as investments are concerned the general rule is that property acquired solely through the investment or re-investment of personal property remains the personal property of the owning spouse though that will sometimes also require an appropriate declaration by the owning spouse. This is the basic position in BELGIUM,[1870] BULGARIA,[1871] FRANCE,[1872] HUNGARY,[1873] ITALY,[1874] MALTA,[1875] THE NETHERLANDS,[1876] PORTUGAL[1877] and SPAIN.[1878] Where new assets are acquired partly funded by personal assets and partly by the community then their categorisation will commonly depend on the proportion of investment, that is, if one fund provides the greater source of funding, it will belong to that fund but with compensation being payable. A similar approach applies to improving etc community property with private assets in as much as the community will be liable to pay compensation.

COMMENT

1. Apart from opting to make express provision, Principle 4:38 adopts the clear common core position with respect to the rules regarding the investment or re-investment of personal assets. It should be noted, however, that the Principle makes no substantive law distinction between movable and immovable property nor are there any special rules concerning the investment or reinvestment of assets for personal or professional use.

1865 See ROTH, Austrian Report, Q 24.

1866 See MĄCZYŃSKI, Polish Report, Q 24.

1867 See HATÁPKA, Slovakian Report, Q 24.

1868 See PINTENS/ALLAERTS/SEYNS/PIGNOLET, Belgian Report, Q 24.

1869 See FERRAND/BRAAT, French Report, Q 24.

1870 Art. 1400, No. 5 Belgian Civil Code. See PINTENS/ALLAERTS/SEYNS/PIGNOLET, Belgian Report, Q 24.

1871 See TODOROVA, Bulgarian Report, Q 24.

1872 Art. 1434 French Civil Code. See FERRAND/BRAAT, French Report, Q 24.

1873 § 31 para. 2 Hungarian Family Act. See WEISS/SZEIBERT, Hungarian Report, Q 21, 23 and 24.

1874 Art. 179 sub f Italian Civil Code. See PATTI/CARICATO/IRTI/IANNICELLI/SERRA/DI STEFANO/PETÖ/BORTULU, Italian Report, Q 24.

1875 Art. 1334 para. 2 Maltese Civil Code. See FARRUGIA, Maltese Report, Q 24.

1876 Art. 1:95 Dutch Civil Code. See BOELE-WOELKI/SCHONEWILLE/SCHRAMA, Dutch Report, Q 24.

1877 Art. 1723 sub c Portuguese Civil Code. See DE OLIVEIRA/MARTINS/VÍTOR, Portuguese Report, Q 24. In PORTUGAL, the intervention of both spouses is required.

1878 Art. 1383 Spanish Civil Code. See GONZÁLEZ BEILFUSS, Spanish Report, Q 24.

2. Principle 4:38(1) provides for the straightforward position that assets acquired solely through investment or reinvestment of personal assets are to be regarded as personal property.

3. Principle 4:38(2) deals with the position of mixed investments or reinvestments and, as provided for substitution by Principle 4:37(2), adopts the position that assets acquired partly through investment or reinvestment of personal assets and partly with community assets will belong to personal property unless the payment provided by community property equals or exceeds the value of the investment or reinvestment.

4. With regard to compensation, Principle 4:38(3) mirrors the general position provided for by Principle 4:37(3), namely, that, subject to Principle 4:53, any additional payments made by the category of assets to which the investment or reinvestment does not belong has to be compensated by the category to which it does belong.

Principle 4:39 Presumption of community property
Assets are presumed to be community property unless they are proved to be personal property in accordance with Principles 4:35 to 4:38.

Principe 4:39 Présomption de communauté
Les biens sont présumés communs sauf si leur caractère propre est prouvé conformément aux Principes 4:35 à 4:38.

Prinzip 4:39 Vermutung gemeinschaftlichen Vermögens
Es wird vermutet, dass Vermögensgegenstände gemeinschaftliches Vermögen sind, es sei denn, es wird bewiesen, dass sie nach den Prinzipien 4:35 bis 4:38 persönliches Vermögen sind.

INTERNATIONAL INSTRUMENTS

None of particular relevance.

COMPARATIVE OVERVIEW

Rebuttable presumption

In the majority of jurisdictions there is, as between the spouses, a rebuttable presumption that their assets are community property with the result that assertions that particular assets are personal have to be proved. This is the position in AUSTRIA,[1879] BELGIUM,[1880] BULGARIA,[1881] FRANCE,[1882] HUNGARY,[1883] ITALY,[1884] LITHUANIA,[1885] THE NETHERLANDS[1886] and SPAIN.[1887] In PORTUGAL[1888] and RUSSIA,[1889] there is only a rebuttable presumption in respect of movables. In contrast in both POLAND[1890] and SLOVAKIA,[1891] there are no specific rules and no

1879 At least with respect to current property § 1233 and 1177 Austrian Civil Code.
1880 Art. 1405, No. 4 Belgian Civil Code.
1881 Art. 19 para. 1 Bulgarian Family Code 1985.
1882 Art. 1402 French Civil Code.
1883 As a matter of practice, see WEISS/SZEIBERT, Hungarian Report, Q 28.
1884 Art. 219 para. 2 Italian Civil Code.
1885 See MIKELENAS, Lithuanian Report, Q 28.
1886 Art. 1:94 para. 1 and para. 3 Dutch Civil Code.
1887 Art. 1361 Spanish Civil Code.
1888 Art. 1725 Portuguese Civil Code.
1889 Art. 34 Russian Family Code.
1890 See MĄCZYŃSKI, Polish Report, Q 28.
1891 See HATÁPKA, Slovakian Report, Q 28.

presumptions. In MALTA,[1892] there are special rules governing the withdrawal of money from the spouses' joint bank account in as much as no enquiry is made as to which category of assets such sums fall.

In most of the above jurisdictions, presumptions apart (where applicable), there are no special rules of evidence but in both FRANCE[1893] and ITALY,[1894] there is some relaxation with regard to the need for written evidence, while in SPAIN,[1895] there is a high threshold to rebut the presumption of community of property.

Matters of proof

In some jurisdictions, and in particular in the CZECH REPUBLIC,[1896] FRANCE,[1897] LITHUANIA,[1898] THE NETHERLANDS[1899] and RUSSIA,[1900] no distinction is made between proof between the spouses and proof between spouses and third parties. In HUNGARY,[1901] a similar standpoint is taken, save that when making contracts with third parties, the spouses are obliged to reveal that assets which are affected by the contract, are the personal property of one of the spouses. In ITALY,[1902] the relaxation of the evidential rules (referred to above) cannot be applied to the prejudice of third parties, whilst in SPAIN,[1903] while the presumption applies equally as between the spouses and between spouses and third parties, a unilateral declaration by one spouse that a particular asset is a personal asset is insufficient as against third parties to rebut the presumption in favour of community. In SLOVAKIA,[1904] in contrast to the position as between the spouses, there is a presumption of community property at least in the sense that spousal agreements on limiting or extending the community are only binding upon third parties if they know about the agreement. In PORTUGAL,[1905] the presumption that movables are community property applies equally as between spouses and third parties.

1892 Art. 132 para. 1(4) Maltese Civil Code. See FARRUGIA, Maltese Report, Q 29.
1893 Art. 1402 para. 2 French Civil Code. See FERRAND/BRAAT, French Report, Q 28.
1894 Art. 2725 para. 2 Italian Civil Code. See PATTI/CARICATO/IRTI/IANNICELLI/SERRA/DI STEFANO/PETÖ/BORTOLU, Italian Report, Q 28.
1895 See GONZÁLEZ BEILFUSS, Spanish Report, Q 28.
1896 See MELZER, Czech Report, Q 64.
1897 Art. 1402 French Civil Code. See FERRAND/BRAAT, French Report, Q 29.
1898 See MIKELENAS, Lithuanian Report, Q 29.
1899 See BOELE-WOELKI/SCHONEWILLE/SCHRAMA, Dutch Report, Q 29 and the general application of Art. 150 Dutch Code of Civil Procedure.
1900 See ANTOKOLSKAIA, Russian Report, Q 29.
1901 See WEISS/SZEIBERT, Hungarian Report, Q 29.
1902 See PATTI/CARICATO/IRTI/IANNICELLI/SERRA/DI STEFANO/PETÖ/BORTOLU, Italian Report, Q 29.
1903 Art. 1361 Spanish Civil Code. See GONZÁLEZ BEILFUSS, Spanish Report, Q 29.
1904 See HATÁPKA, Slovakian Report, Q 29.
1905 Art. 1725 Portuguese Civil Code. See DE OLIVEIRA/MARTINS/VITOR, Portuguese Report, Q 29.

In both AUSTRIA[1906] and BELGIUM,[1907] the evidential rules themselves are stricter, for example, that witness evidence is not allowed in cases involving third parties. In BULGARIA,[1908] third parties are not permitted to rebut the presumption in favour of community property by proof that the property was not acquired by the spouses' mutual contribution.

COMMENT

1. It is quite commonly the case that when the issue of ownership becomes relevant, the spouses are not able to prove between themselves nor against third parties, whether specific assets belong to personal or community property. Principle 4:39 adopts the broad common core that there is a rebuttable presumption that assets are community property. The presumption is justified on the grounds of practicality since in many cases, especially over a period of time and particularly with regard to movable property, it will not be possible to prove who the actual owner of an item or an asset is.

2. Although difficulties of proving ownership are most likely only to concern movable property, the presumption expressed in Principle 4:39 applies to both movable and immovable property to cover the case where, exceptionally, ownership of immovable property is hard to establish.

3. Principle 4:39 does not attempt to prescribe the means of proof, leaving that to be determined by national law. Although no distinction is made between proof as between spouses and proof with regard to third parties by not prescribing evidential rules, Principle 4:39 nevertheless preserves the freedom of jurisdictions to make such a distinction.

[1906] At least with respect to current property § 1233 and 1177 Austrian Civil Code. See ROTH, Austrian Report, Q 29.

[1907] Art. 1399 para. 2 Belgian Civil Code. See PINTENS/ALLAERTS/SEYNS/PIGNOLET, Belgian Report, Q 29.

[1908] See TODOROVA, Bulgarian Report, Q 29.

DEBTS
DETTES
VERBINDLICHKEITEN

Principle 4:40 Community debts
The community debts are
- (a) debts incurred jointly by both spouses;
- (b) debts incurred by one spouse in order to meet the appropriate family needs;
- (c) debts related to the maintenance of children;
- (d) debts incurred by one spouse for the use or administration of community assets or in the interest of the community property;
- (e) debts related to a spouse's professional activities;
- (f) debts related to gifts and bequests belonging to community property;
- (g) debts that have not been proved to be personal debts.

Principe 4:40 Passif de la communauté
Le passif de la communauté se compose
- (a) des dettes contractées conjointement par les deux époux;
- (b) des dettes contractées par un époux pour les besoins appropriés de la famille;
- (c) des dettes d'aliments envers les enfants;
- (d) des dettes contractées par un époux pour l'usage ou l'administration des biens communs ou dans l'intérêt de la communauté;
- (e) des dettes relatives à l'activité professionnelle d'un époux;
- (f) des dettes relatives aux donations ou legs faisant partie de la communauté;
- (g) des dettes dont il n'est pas prouvé qu'elles sont des dettes personnelles.

Prinzip 4:40 Gemeinschaftliche Verbindlichkeiten
Gemeinschaftliche Verbindlichkeiten sind
- (a) von beiden Ehegatten gemeinsam eingegangene Verbindlichkeiten;
- (b) von einem der Ehegatten für den angemessenen Lebensbedarf der Familie eingegangene Verbindlichkeiten;
- (c) Unterhaltsverpflichtungen gegenüber Kindern;
- (d) von einem der Ehegatten für den Gebrauch oder die Verwaltung von gemeinschaftlichen Vermögengegenständen oder im Interesse des gemeinschaftlichen Vermögens eingegangene Verbindlichkeiten;

(e) Verbindlichkeiten in Bezug auf die berufliche Tätigkeit eines Ehegatten;
(f) im Zusammenhang mit einer Schenkung oder Zuwendung von Todes wegen an das gemeinschaftliche Vermögen entstandene Verbindlichkeiten;
(g) Verbindlichkeiten, von denen nicht bewiesen ist, dass sie persönliche Verbindlichkeiten sind.

INTERNATIONAL INSTRUMENTS

None of particular relevance.

COMPARATIVE OVERVIEW

What do community debts encompass?

Community debts are generally those either entered into jointly by the spouses, or incurred in meeting the needs of the family (in BULGARIA,[1909] BELGIUM,[1910] FRANCE,[1911] HUNGARY,[1912] ITALY,[1913] LITHUANIA,[1914] PORTUGAL[1915] and SPAIN,[1916] these are the costs and expenses connected with the subsistence of the family, the maintenance and education of common children and of the children of one spouse who live in the family home, and health care expenses adjusted in accordance with social usage and the circumstances of the family) or in the administration and the use of common property (e.g. in AUSTRIA,[1917] the debts

1909 Art. 25 para. 2 Bulgarian Family Code. See TODOROVA, Bulgarian Report, Q 31.

1910 See PINTENS/ALLAERTS/SEYNS/PIGNOLET, Belgian Report, Q 31 (debts arising from the housekeeping and the education of the children).

1911 See FERRAND/BRAAT, French Report, Q 31 (debts arising from the housekeeping and the education of the children),.

1912 See WEISS/SZEIBERT, Hungarian Report, Q 31.

1913 Art. 186 Italian Civil Code.

1914 Art. 3:109 Lithuanian Civil Code. See MIKELENAS, Lithuanian Report, Q 31.

1915 See DE OLIVEIRA/MARTINS/VÍTOR, Portuguese Report, Q 31.

1916 Art. 1362 para. 1 Spanish Civil Code. See GONZÁLEZ BEILFUSS, Spanish Report, Q 31. See ANTOKOLSKAIA, Russian Report, Q 31: maintenance of the matrimonial home but also debts incurred by one spouse for the benefit of the family. See HAŤAPKA, Slovakian Report, Q 31: distinction between ordinary and extraordinary matters; only transactions entered into by one spouse in ordinary matters do not require the other spouse's consent for their validity.

1917 See ROTH, Austrian Report, Q 31. The same ideas underlie BELGIAN law that contains in Art. 1409 Belgian Civil Code a long list enumerating the community debts. See PINTENS/ALLAERTS/SEYNS/PIGNOLET, Belgian Report, Q 31. See also PATTI/CARICATO/IRTI/IANNICELLI/SERRA/DI STEFANO/PETÖ/BORTULU; Italian Report, Q 31 and Art. 186 Italian Civil Code: all charges for the administration and the costs for the maintenance of the family

entered into jointly by both spouses and debts relating to administration and use of the common property; BELGIUM[1918] and ITALY[1919]). There is a clear common core in the fifteen jurisdictions surveyed (especially in AUSTRIA,[1920] BELGIUM,[1921] BULGARIA,[1922] CZECH REPUBLIC,[1923] HUNGARY[1924] and SPAIN[1925]).

As for the personal debts of one spouse, the degree of detail provided by national law varies between jurisdictions. Some use only vague terminology (BULGARIA[1926] and RUSSIA[1927]) whereas other legal systems enumerate a long list of what community debts comprise (BELGIUM,[1928] LITHUANIA,[1929] PORTUGAL[1930] and SPAIN[1931]). However, the basic ideas that underlie the definition of community debts appear to be similar.

Some jurisdictions provide a precise list of community debts. For example, this is the case in BELGIUM,[1932] where Article 1408 Belgian Civil Code enumerates (non-exhaustively): 1) debts incurred by both spouses jointly and severally; 2) debts incurred by one of the spouses for the benefit of the housekeeping and the education of the children; 3) debts incurred by one spouse for the purpose of the community property; 4) debts arising out of donations or bequests belonging to the community property; 5) interests on personal debts; 6) maintenance debts towards relatives of the spouse's direct line; and 7) debts that have not been proved to belong to one spouse's property.

In FRANCE,[1933] the statutory provisions are not very clear. Article 1409 French Civil Code states that community debts encompass "definitively, maintenance owed by the spouses, and debts incurred by them in supporting the household and the education of children, under Article 220; definitively or subject to reimbursement, according to the circumstances, other debts arising during the

as well as for the instruction and education of the children; also all cases where an obligation has been contracted jointly by both spouses.

1918 See PINTENS/ALLAERTS/SEYNS/PIGNOLET, Belgian Report, Q 31.
1919 Art. 186 Italian Civil Code and PATTI/CARICATO/IRTI/IANNICELLI/SERRA/DI STEFANO/PETÖ/BORTULU, Italian Report, Q 31.
1920 See ROTH, Austrian Report, Q 31.
1921 See PINTENS/ALLAERTS/SEYNS/PIGNOLET, Belgian Report, Q 31.
1922 See TODOROVA, Bulgarian Report, Q 31.
1923 See MELZER, Czech Report, Q 31.
1924 See WEISS/SZEIBERT, Hungarian Report, Q 31.
1925 See GONZÁLEZ BEILFUSS, Spanish Report, Q 31.
1926 See TODOROVA, Bulgarian Report, Q 31.
1927 See ANTOKOLSKAIA, Russian Report, Q 30 (no definition is provided by legal statutes in Russia).
1928 See PINTENS/ALLAERTS/SEYNS/PIGNOLET, Belgian Report, Q 31.
1929 See MIKELENAS; Lithuanian Report, Q 31.
1930 See DE OLIVEIRA/MARTINS/VÍTOR, Portuguese Report, Q 31.
1931 See GONZÁLEZ BEILFUSS, Spanish Report, Q 31.
1932 See PINTENS/ALLAERTS/SEYNS/PIGNOLET, Belgian Report, Q 31.
1933 See FERRAND/BRAAT, French Report, Q 31.

community". This means that maintenance debts of both spouses, and debts related to the household and the education of the children, are automatically community debts, whereas other debts arising during marriage can either be community debts (subject to their nature or purpose), or personal debts of one spouse that can be paid by the community, but are subject to compensation upon the liquidation of the community.

PORTUGAL[1934] appears to have opted for the broadest definition of community debts, encompassing: 1) debts incurred before or after marriage, by both spouses or by one of them with the consent of the other; 2) debts incurred by either spouse, before or after marriage, in order to cover the normal expenses of family life; 3) debts incurred during marriage by the administrating spouse for the common benefit of the couple and within the limits of the administrative powers of the spouses; 4) debts incurred by either spouse in the course of trade;[1935] 5) debts related to inheritances, bequests or donations belonging to the community property; 6) debts related to community assets; and 7) debts related to personal assets of one spouse, if originating from the reception of the respective revenues.

SPAIN[1936] also has a broad conception of community debts, including debts incurred by both spouses jointly (or by one with the consent of the other spouse),[1937] debts connected with the subsistence of the family,[1938] the acquisition, administration or use of community assets,[1939] or the tortuous debts incurred by one spouse acting for the benefit of the community,[1940] but also debts incurred in the ordinary administration of personal assets[1941] and ordinary debts incurred in the context of the professional activity of one spouse.[1942]

Only two jurisdictions appear to depart from the common core set out above: THE NETHERLANDS,[1943] where the legal matrimonial regime is part of an extensive community of property, where all debts incurred before or during marriage by one or both spouses are considered to be community debts

---

1934 Art. 1691, 1693 and 1694 Portuguese Civil Code. See DE OLIVEIRA/MARTINS/VÍTOR, Portuguese Report, Q 31.

1935 Except if proven that the debt was not incurred for the common benefit of the couple, see Art. 1691 para. 1 sub d Portuguese Civil Code.

1936 See GONZÁLEZ BEILFUSS, Spanish Report, Q 31.

1937 Art. 1367 Spanish Civil Code.

1938 Art. 1362 para. 1 Spanish Civil Code.

1939 Art. 1362 para. 2 Spanish Civil Code.

1940 Art. 1366 Spanish Civil Code.

1941 Art. 1362 para. 3 Spanish Civil Code. This rule is explained by the fact that the fruits, rental payments and interests obtained from personal assets during marriage belong to the community.

1942 Art. 1362 para. 4 Spanish Civil Code, since the earnings of the spouses belong to the community.

1943 See BOELE-WOELKI/SCHONEVILLE/SCHRAMA, Dutch Report, Q 31.

(however, there is an express exception for debts closely related to one spouse).[1944] POLAND[1945] also takes a different position, since community debts are those incurred by the spouses acting together (corresponding to the common core), or debts incurred by one spouse acting with the other spouse's consent[1946] (which is not the criterion in the other jurisdictions).

A community debt can be incurred by one spouse

In all jurisdictions surveyed, community debts can also be entered into by only one spouse. If all debts incurred jointly by the spouses are community debts, a debt contracted by a sole spouse can also, due to its nature or to its purpose, belong to the community. All debts connected with the family's needs, maintenance, upbringing and education of the common children (and in some jurisdictions, the children of one spouse living with the family, for example, SPAIN[1947]) are community debts, regardless of whether just the one spouse, or both, incurred them (for example, in PORTUGAL[1948]).

This issue is closely connected with the issue of the administration of the community (common administration by both spouses, or competing administration – *gestion concurrente* in FRENCH law[1949] – by each spouse) and/or the power of representation of one spouse (for example, BULGARIA[1950]).

Professional debts

Not all national reports expressly address the issue of professional debts. However, from the criteria stated by the national provisions concerning community debts, it can be inferred that, for example, in AUSTRIA[1951] and BULGARIA[1952] (debts incurred in connection with the commercial activities of one spouse), ITALY[1953] (in case of a separate activity), LITHUANIA,[1954] POLAND[1955] (where the debt was incurred without the consent of the other spouse) and

---

1944 Art. 1:94 para. 2 Dutch Civil Code.
1945 See MĄCZYŃSKI, Polish Report, Q 31.
1946 Art. 41 para. 1 Polish Family and Guardianship Code.
1947 See GONZÁLEZ BEILFUSS, Spanish Report, Q 31.
1948 Such debts should be largely considered, due to their nature or purpose, as a sub-section of community debts, see DE OLIVEIRA/MARTINS/VÍTOR, Portuguese Report, Q 31.
1949 Art. 1421 para. 1 French Civil Code.
1950 See TODOROVA, Bulgarian Report, Q 31.
1951 See ROTH, Austrian Report, Q 30 and Q 31.
1952 See TODOROVA, Bulgarian Report, Q 30 (any debt that is not incurred to meet the family needs is personal to the spouse who incurred it).
1953 Art. 189 para. 1 Italian Civil Code. See PATTI/CARICATO/IRTI/IANNICELLI/SERRA/DI STEFANO/PETÖ/BORTULU; Italian Report, Q 30.
1954 See MIKELENAS, Lithuanian Report, Q 31.
1955 See MĄCZYŃSKI, Polish Report, Q 31.

RUSSIA,[1956] professional debts are personal to the spouse who incurred them. In contrast, in a number of jurisdictions, professional debts are community debts, for example, in BELGIUM[1957] (but with some exceptions), FRANCE,[1958] THE NETHERLANDS,[1959] PORTUGAL[1960] (debts incurred by any of the spouses in the course of trade is a community debt, except if proved not to have been incurred for the common benefit of the couple) and SPAIN[1961] (the earnings of the spouses belong to the community property, but in the case of a *commercial* activity, the Spanish Commercial Code applies and the creditor will not be able to recover against all the community assets, only the community assets acquired with the benefits of his or her commercial activity).[1962]

Possible presumption that a debt is a community debt

A presumption that a debt, of which a personal character has not been proved, is deemed to be a community debt, is stated by a number of national laws, such as of BELGIUM,[1963] FRANCE[1964] and HUNGARY.[1965]

COMMENT

1. There is clearly a common core concerning the qualification of debts incurred jointly by both spouses as community debts. The participation of both spouses in the transaction is deemed to prove their willingness to be bound by it.

2. In order to meet the family's needs without systematically requiring the participation of both spouses in the transaction, debts incurred by one spouse which aim at satisfying the family's needs should also qualify as community debts with regard to their purpose.

1956 See ANTOKOLSKAIA, Russian Report, Q 30.

1957 Art. 1407 Belgian Civil Code *a contrario* that states that "the debts incurred by the exercise of a professional activity that had been prohibited to the spouse on the ground of Art. 216 remain personal to that spouse".

1958 See FERRAND/BRAAT, French Report, Q 31 and PETERKA, Régimes matrimoniaux, Dalloz 2008, p. 171.

1959 See BOELE-WOELKI/SCHONEWILLE/SCHRAMA, Dutch Report, Q 30.

1960 Art. 1691 para. 1 sub d Portuguese Civil Code; see also DE OLIVEIRA/MARTINS/VÍTOR, Portuguese Report, Q 31.

1961 Art. 1362 para. 4 Spanish Civil Code; see also GONZÁLEZ BEILFUSS, Spanish Report, Q 31.

1962 Art. 6–11 Spanish Commercial Code; see also GONZÁLEZ BEILFUSS, Spanish Report, Q 31.

1963 Art. 1408 *in fine* Belgian Civil Code.

1964 Art. 1416 French Civil Code. See FERRAND/BRAAT, French Report, Q 31.

1965 See WEISS/SZEIBERT, Hungarian Report, Q 31.

3. A maintenance debt towards a child qualifies as a community debt. This applies even if the child (who is creditor of such maintenance) is the child of only one spouse, and regardless of whether the child lives at the family home. Such a solution favours equal treatment of children. Principle 4:40 (c) applies to children of a former marriage as well as to children of the current one. However, if the child, who is creditor of the maintenance, is the child of only one spouse, the maintenance should not be recovered from the personal property of the other spouse. See also Principle 4:41. By contrast, maintenance due to an ex-spouse is regarded as a debt incurred before the new marriage, and will therefore qualify as a personal debt. The same applies to a maintenance debt towards a parent or grand-parent, since this qualifies as a "personal debt by nature" within the meaning of Principle 4:41 (d).

4. In many legal systems, each spouse may use and administer the community property. Therefore, the debts incurred through such use or administration should belong to the community debts. The same should apply to the debts related to the acquisition of community property, since the acquisition will enrich the community of property. Principle 4:40 (d) could, for example, apply in cases of a liability related to a common asset.

5. Professional debts qualify as community debts, since the earnings of the spouses belong to the community property.

6. In cases where assets obtained through bequest or donation fall into the community of property, it is logical that the debts related to these assets qualify as community debts.

7. In order to solve unclear cases there should be a presumption that the debts incurred by one spouse are community debts, unless it can be proved that these are personal debts. This solution underlines the principle of solidarity which is one of the main features of the community of acquisitions regime, and should be regarded as a "counterweight" or an instrument of balance to Principle 4:39.

Principle 4:41 Personal debts

Personal debts of a spouse are

(a) debts incurred before entering into the community of acquisitions;
(b) debts related to gifts, inheritances and bequests acquired by one spouse during the regime;
(c) debts related to personal property;
(d) debts which are personal by nature;
(e) debts incurred without the required consent of the other spouse.

Principe 4:41 Dettes propres

Les dettes propres d'un époux sont

(a) les dettes contractées avant l'existence de la communauté d'acquêts;
(b) les dettes grevant les successions et libéralités échues à l'époux pendant le régime;
(c) les dettes relatives aux biens propres;
(d) les dettes personnelles par leur nature;
(e) les dettes contractées sans le consentement nécessaire de l'autre époux.

Prinzip 4:41 Persönliche Verbindlichkeiten

Persönliche Verbindlichkeiten eines Ehegatten sind

(a) vor Eintritt in die Errungenschaftsgemeinschaft eingegangene Verbindlichkeiten;
(b) Verbindlichkeiten, die im Zusammenhang mit einer während des Güterstands erworbenen Schenkung oder einem Erbfall entstanden sind;
(c) Verbindlichkeiten, die sich auf das persönliche Vermögen beziehen;
(d) Verbindlichkeiten persönlicher Art;
(e) ohne die erforderliche Zustimmung des anderen Ehegatten eingegangene Verbindlichkeiten.

INTERNATIONAL INSTRUMENTS

None of particular relevance.

COMPARATIVE OVERVIEW

Link between personal assets and personal debts

Fifteen of the twenty-six jurisdictions surveyed indicated that community of property is one of the main matrimonial property regimes under their national law (AUSTRIA,[1966] BELGIUM,[1967] BULGARIA,[1968] CZECH REPUBLIC,[1969] FRANCE,[1970] HUNGARY,[1971] ITALY,[1972] LITHUANIA,[1973] MALTA,[1974] THE NETHERLANDS,[1975] POLAND,[1976] PORTUGAL,[1977] RUSSIA,[1978] SLOVAKIA[1979] and SPAIN[1980]). In these jurisdictions, community of property is either the legal regime, or is a conventional regime which the spouses may opt for. With regard to the classification of the debts within the community of property, the debts can either be designated as community debts, or personal to one spouse.

There is an important link between the personal assets of one spouse and his or her personal debts. Most of the fifteen jurisdictions surveyed regarding community of property (especially AUSTRIA,[1981] BELGIUM,[1982] FRANCE,[1983] HUNGARY,[1984] LITHUANIA[1985] and PORTUGAL[1986]) state that the personal debts of one spouse are:

- pre-marital debts,
- debts related to inheritances, bequests and donations to one spouse,

---

1966 See ROTH, Austrian Report, Q 30.
1967 See PINTENS/ALLAERTS/SEYNS/PIGNOLET, Belgian Report, Q 30.
1968 See TODOROVA, Bulgarian Report, Q 30.
1969 See MELZER, Czech Report, Q 30.
1970 See FERRAND/BRAAT, French Report, Q 30.
1971 See WEISS/SZEIBERT, Hungarian Report, Q 30.
1972 See PATTI/CARICATO/IRTI/IANNICELLI/SERRA/DI STEFANO/PETÖ/BORTULU, Italian Report, Q 30.
1973 See MIKELENAS, Lithuanian Report, Q 30.
1974 See FARRUGIA, Maltese Report, Q 30.
1975 See BOELE-WOELKI/SCHONEVILLE/SCHRAMA, Dutch Report, Q 30.
1976 See MĄCZYŃSKI, Polish Report, Q 30.
1977 See DE OLIVEIRA/MARTINS/VÍTOR, Portuguese Report, Q 30.
1978 See ANTOKOLSKAIA, Russian Report, Q 30.
1979 See HAŤAPKA, Slovakian Report, Q 30.
1980 See MARTÍN-CASALS/, Spanish Report, Q 30.
1981 See ROTH, Austrian Report, Q 30.
1982 See PINTENS/ALLAERTS/SEYNS/PIGNOLET, Belgian Report, Q 30.
1983 See FERRAND/BRAAT, French Report, Q 30.
1984 See WEISS/SZEIBERT, Hungarian Report, Q 30.
1985 See MIKELENAS, Lithuanian Report, Q 30.
1986 Art. 1692 to 1694 Portuguese Civil Code. See DE OLIVEIRA/MARTINS/VÍTOR, Portuguese Report, Q 30.

- debts related to the personal assets of the spouse (see also CZECH REPUBLIC,[1987] ITALY,[1988] MALTA,[1989] SLOVAKIA[1990] and RUSSIA[1991]).
- debts incurred by one spouse as a result of tort liability or criminal sentence.

It is the clear common core that pre-marital debts are the personal debts of one spouse. Personal debts can also be the debts which one spouse enters into alone, or which relate only to him or her personally (AUSTRIA[1992]), such as tort debts (AUSTRIA,[1993] BELGIUM,[1994] FRANCE,[1995] HUNGARY,[1996] LITHUANIA,[1997] PORTUGAL[1998] and SLOVAKIA[1999]), maintenance debts, or debts resulting from a divorce dispute (AUSTRIA[2000]). Some jurisdictions provide an exhaustive enumeration of the spouses' own debts (BELGIUM[2001] and FRANCE[2002]), while other jurisdictions refrain from doing so (BULGARIA,[2003] HUNGARY[2004] and RUSSIA,[2005] where no definitions of personal debts are provided).

1987 See MELZER, Czech Report, Q 66.

1988 See PATTI/CARICATO/IRTI/IANNICELLI/SERRA/DI STEFANO/PETÖ/BORTULU, Italian Report, Q 30: personal debts are the ones that each spouse contracts in the interest of his or her own or another person's estate, and those deriving from a separate activity (Art. 189 para. 2 Italian Civil Code). The same applies to debts incurred through extraordinary administration carried out without the other spouse's consent.

1989 Debts incurred by one spouse related to his/her property are personal debts; the same applies where the debt is incurred by extraordinary administration carried out without the other spouse's consent. Art. 1329 Maltese Civil Code. See FARRUGIA, Maltese Report, Q 30.

1990 Debts incurred by one spouse before marriage; debts not related to the community property, e.g. guarantee, tort damages, maintenance for children from a previous relationship, see HAŤAPKA, Slovakian Report, Q 30.

1991 See ANTOKOLSKAIA, Russian Report, Q 30 and Q 31.

1992 See ROTH, Austrian Report, Q 30.

1993 See ROTH, Austrian Report, Q 30.

1994 See PINTENS/ALLAERTS/SEYNS/PIGNOLET, Belgian Report, Q 30.

1995 See FERRAND/BRAAT, French Report, Q 30.

1996 See WEISS/SZEIBERT, Hungarian Report, Q 30.

1997 See MIKELENAS, Lithuanian Report, Q 30.

1998 See DE OLIVEIRA/MARTINS/VÍTOR, Portuguese Report, Q 30.

1999 See HAŤAPKA, Slovakian Report, Q 30.

2000 See ROTH, Austrian Report, Q 30.

2001 Art. 1406 and 1407 Belgian Civil Code. See PINTENS/ALLAERTS/SEYNS/PIGNOLET, Belgian Report, Q 30.

2002 Art. 1410 et seq French Civil Code. See FERRAND/BRAAT, French Report, Q 30.

2003 See TODOROVA, Bulgarian Report, Q 30: only through an a *contrario* interpretation of Art. 25 para. 2 Bulgarian Family Code, can it be asserted that personal debts of one spouse are all the debts that are not incurred in meeting the needs of the family.

2004 See WEISS/SZEIBERT, Hungarian Report, Q 30.

2005 See ANTOKOLSKAIA, Russian Report, Q 31. However, the same categories are to be found as in most jurisdictions: debts incurred by one spouse before marriage; debts incurred by one spouse during marriage with regard to his/her personal property; strictly personal debts of each spouse (tort, maintenance).

Some more specific distinctions

The jurisdictions that stipulate which debts are personal to one spouse often make a distinction between personal debts which designated as such because of their origin, and those that are designated due to their nature or purpose. This is, for example, the case in BELGIUM[2006] and FRANCE.[2007] In BELGIUM,[2008] personal debts defined as such because of their origin are the debts dating from the period before the marriage, and debts arising out of inheritances, bequests and gifts obtained during marriage by one spouse. Personal debts which arise due to their nature are contractual and (quasi-)delictual debts incurred by one spouse during marriage. In FRANCE, the definition of personal debts because of their nature is the same as under BELGIAN law,[2009] except that it also includes fines incurred by penal infractions, tort liability and debts contracted by one spouse by disregarding duties imposed by marriage. Under FRENCH law,[2010] personal debts classified as such due to their purpose are the debts contracted in the personal interest of one spouse, such as the acquisition, preservation and improvement of separate property.

In SPAIN,[2011] personal debts are defined in a negative way: a debt that does not qualify as a community debt is personal to one spouse. Personal debts are also (controversially) considered to be debts arising from guarantees given by one spouse on behalf of a third party, unless these were incurred in the interest of the family. Personal debts are also those incurred to satisfy the maintenance and education costs of the children of one spouse who do not live with the family; this is the personal debt of the spouse who is the parent of the child. However, the spouses may agree that such debts are to be considered as community debts.

Only in THE NETHERLANDS,[2012] – where a broad system of universal community applies – do all debts fall within the community, regardless of whether they were incurred before, or during, marriage. However, there are exceptions namely: 1) a

---

2006 See PINTENS/ALLAERTS/SEYNS/PIGNOLET, Belgian Report, Q 30.

2007 See FERRAND/BRAAT, French Report, Q 30.

2008 Art. 1407 Belgian Civil Code: Personal debts defined as such due to their nature are debts incurred by one spouse for the exclusive purpose of his/her personal property; debts arising from a personal or commercial security provided by one spouse in an interest other that the one of the community property; debts due to forbidden professions or forbidden acts; debts arising from a criminal sentence or from a wrongful act committed by one spouse.

2009 Art. 1410 French Code Civil. See FERRAND/BRAAT, French Report, Q 30. However, in contrast to BELGIAN law, the capital and the interest of those debts remain personal to the spouse, whereas in Belgium only the capital is a personal debt. Art. 1408 Belgian Civil Code. See PINTENS/ALLAERTS/SEYNS/PIGNOLET, Belgian Report, Q 30.

2010 Art. 1416 French Civil Code.

2011 See GONZÁLEZ BEILFUSS, Spanish Report, Q 30.

2012 See BOELE-WOELKI/SCHONEVILLE/SCHRAMA, Dutch Report, Q 30.

debt contracted in relation to a personal asset is a personal debt;[2013] and 2) a debt relating to an inheritance acquired under an exclusion clause is also a personal debt.[2014]

Some peculiarities can be found in various jurisdictions. In BELGIUM,[2015] for example, only the capital of personal debts is personal to one spouse; the interest accrued during the marriage is paid at the expense of the community property.[2016] In some jurisdictions, debts whose own character has not been proved are deemed to be community debts.[2017] There is rebuttable presumption in the law that the debt is a community debt.

This comparative overview shows that there is a common core with regard to what should be considered to be the personal debts of one spouse, namely: 1) debts incurred by one spouse before marriage; 2) debts related to inheritances, bequests of donation made to one spouse during marriage; 3) debts which are personal by nature, such as tort liability and fines pronounced against one spouse by a criminal sentence; 4) incurred by one spouse for the exclusive purpose of his or her personal property. Some jurisdictions (ITALY,[2018] MALTA,[2019] POLAND[2020] and CZECH REPUBLIC[2021]) also include debts which have been incurred by one spouse without the consent of the other spouse, where that consent was necessary. According to FRENCH law,[2022] this is, for example, the case for risky transactions, such as guarantees or monetary loans solely entered into by one spouse.

COMMENT

1. Logically, all debts incurred by one spouse before marriage should remain personal to him or her. This corresponds to the clear common core in the jurisdictions surveyed. The same applies to debts relating to inheritances, bequests and donations to one spouse during marriage, since the assets acquired

2013 Art. 1:94 para. 3 Dutch Civil Code.
2014 See BOELE-WOELKI/SCHONEVILLE/SCHRAMA, Dutch Report, Q 30.
2015 See PINTENS/ALLAERTS/SEYNS/PIGNOLET, Belgian Report, Q 30.
2016 See PINTENS/ALLAERTS/SEYNS/PIGNOLET, Belgian Report, Q 30 and Art. 1408 Belgian Civil Code.
2017 Art. 1408 para. 7 Belgian Civil Code.
2018 Art. 189 para. 1 Italian Civil Code: in cases of extraordinary administration carried out by one spouse without the consent of the other spouse.
2019 Art. 1329 Maltese Civil Code.
2020 See MĄCZYŃSKI, Polish Report, Q 30.
2021 See MELZER, Czech Report, Q 66: the debts whose extent exceeds the level of reasonable property condition of the spouses which were incurred by only one spouse without the consent of the other, are personal debts.
2022 Art. 1415 French Civil Code.

in such a way are the personal assets of the spouse. The same reasoning leads to the same solution for debts arising from the personal property of one spouse. In these three cases, a close correlation exists between assets and debts. Consequently, debts relating to personal assets remain personal to the spouse who is the owner of the asset. This also applies to the maintenance of a former spouse after divorce.

2. Other debts are personal due to their nature or purpose: damages to be paid by one spouse on the ground of a tort liability, a fine to be paid on the basis of a criminal sentence, or maintenance owed by one spouse to a parent or grandparent. These solutions should also apply to acts which can have important consequences for the family: guarantees given by one spouse to a third person, or monetary loans where they have been entered into without the formal consent of the other spouse. This aims at protecting the community property from unreflected transactions entered into by one spouse. Therefore, gambling debts are also the personal debts of the spouse who incurred them, since the community property has no interest in taking such risks and is endangered by them.

3. More generally, where national law requires the consent of both spouses with regard to especially significant transactions, the debt incurred is personal to the spouse who enters alone into such a transaction. This is, for example, the case for loan agreements, guarantees or sureties, which are acts requiring joint administration by both spouses under Principle 4:45. This does not preclude the question of whether the creditors can seize assets belonging to the community (in this case, the debtor spouse is liable to reimburse the community upon its liquidation to compensate the payment of the debt). Providing that debts are personal to one spouse does not mean that only the personal assets of that spouse can be seized by the creditor. This is of special significance in the many jurisdictions where the earnings of the spouses, which often are the most important source of income, belong to the community assets.

Principle 4:42 Recovery of community debts
(1) Community debts can be recovered from the community property and from the personal property of the spouse who incurred the debt.
(2) If the spouses are jointly and severally liable, the debt may also be recovered from the personal property of either spouse.

Principe 4:42 Recouvrement des dettes de la communauté
(1) Les dettes de la communauté peuvent être recouvrées sur les biens communs et sur les biens propres de l'époux qui a contracté la dette.
(2) Si les époux sont solidairement tenus, la dette peut être recouvrée également sur les biens propres de l'un ou l'autre époux.

Prinzip 4:42 Haftung für gemeinschaftliche Verbindlichkeiten
(1) Für gemeinschaftliche Verbindlichkeiten haftet das gemeinschaftliche Vermögen und das persönliche Vermögen des Ehegatten, der die Verbindlichkeit eingegangen ist.
(2) Sind die Ehegatten gesamtschuldnerisch verpflichtet, haftet für die Verbindlichkeit ebenfalls das persönliche Vermögen jedes Ehegatten.

INTERNATIONAL INSTRUMENTS

None of particular relevance.

COMPARATIVE OVERVIEW

Assets from which community debts may be recovered

There is a clear common core in most of the jurisdictions surveyed that community debts may be recovered from the common assets as well as from the personal assets of each spouse or at least of the spouse who incurred the debt. Community debts may be recovered from the common assets and from the personal assets of each spouse in AUSTRIA,[2023] BELGIUM with some

[2023] See ROTH, Austrian Report, Q 33: for debts entered jointly by the spouses and common property debts (e.g. debts from a purchase for the use of the common property).

exceptions,[2024] BULGARIA,[2025] CZECH REPUBLIC,[2026] HUNGARY,[2027] ITALY,[2028] LITHUANIA,[2029] MALTA,[2030] PORTUGAL[2031] and RUSSIA.[2032]

In other jurisdictions, a distinction is made with regard to whether both spouses are liable (FRANCE,[2033] THE NETHERLANDS[2034] and SPAIN[2035]), or whether both spouses have acted together (or one has acted alone with the consent of the other), or whether one spouse has acted alone without the other spouse's consent (POLAND[2036]). In THE NETHERLANDS,[2037] if only one spouse is liable, the creditor can recover the debt from the common assets and from the personal assets of the debtor spouse. If both spouses are liable (regardless of who contracted with the creditor), the debt can also be recovered from the personal assets of the non-contracting spouse. The same applies in FRANCE.[2038] The creditor may recover the community debts from the common assets and from the personal assets of the spouse who incurred the debt. The personal assets of the other spouse may only be seized if there is joint and several liability.[2039] However, FRENCH law provides for some exceptions: 1) In the case of a fraud by the debtor spouse and of bad faith of the creditor, the debt may not be enforced on community assets;[2040] 2) profits and earnings of the spouse who did not incur the debt may not be seized by the creditor unless the obligation was contracted to ensure the upkeep of the family household or the children's education;[2041] 3) the entry into a loan or surety by only one spouse binds only that spouse's personal assets and

2024 See PINTENS/ALLAERTS/SEYNS/PIGNOLET, Belgian Report, Q 33.
2025 Art. 121–127 Bulgarian Obligations and Contracts Act. See TODOROVA, Bulgarian Report, Q 33.
2026 Art. 145 para. 3 Czech Civil Code. See MELZER, Czech Report, Q 69. A debt which falls under joint property, even if incurred by only one spouse, leads to joint and several liability of the spouses.
2027 See WEISS/SZEIBERT, Hungarian Report, Q 33.
2028 See PATTI/CARICATO/IRTI/IANNICELLI/SERRA/DI STEFANO/PETÖ/BORTULU, Italian Report, Q 33. But the creditor must first claim against the community assets.
2029 Art. 3.113 Lithuanian Civil Code. See MIKELENAS, Lithuanian Report, Q 33.
2030 Art. 1327, 1330 and 1331 Maltese Civil Code. See FARRUGIA, Maltese Report, Q 31.
2031 See DE OLIVEIRA/MARTINS/VÍTOR, Portuguese Report, Q 33.
2032 Art. 45 para. 2 Russian Family Code. See ANTOKOLKAIA, Russian Report, Q 33.
2033 See FERRAND/BRAAT, French Report, Q 33.
2034 See BOELE-WOELKI/SCHONEWILLE/SCHRAMA, Dutch Report, Q 33.
2035 See GONZÁLEZ BEILFUSS, Spanish Report, Q 33.
2036 See MĄCZYŃSKI, Polish Report, Q 33.
2037 Art. 1:95 para. 1 and Art. 1:85 Dutch Civil Code. See BOELE-WOELKI/SCHONEWILLE/SCHRAMA, Dutch Report, Q 33.
2038 See FERRAND/BRAAT, French Report, Q 33.
2039 Like under Art. 220 French Civil Code: joint and several liability of both spouses for debts related to the household, the upbringing and education of children, even if only one spouse incurred the debt.
2040 The question of whether the debt may be enforced on the personal assets of the debtor spouse is debated in FRANCE.
2041 However, if the profits and earnings are in a bank account, see Art. 48 of the Decree n°92–755 of 31 July 1992: the creditor cannot seize the equivalent of one month's salary.

income unless the other spouse gave his or her consent to the act, in which case the community assets and the personal assets of the contracting spouse are also bound, but not the personal assets of the non-contracting spouse who gave his or her consent.[2042]

A similar solution is set out in SPANISH law.[2043] Community debts may be recovered from the common assets and from the personal property of the spouse who incurred the debt. The personal assets of the non-contracting spouse can only be seized where the debt relates to household expenses.[2044] In BELGIUM,[2045] where the basic rule is that community debts may be recovered from the common assets and from the personal assets of each spouse, the creditor may only recover some community debts from the common assets and from the contracting spouse's personal property if they are: 1) debts incurred by one spouse for housekeeping and the education of the children which lead to excessive obligations with regard to the family's means of support; 2) interest on a spouse's personal debt; 3) debts incurred by one spouse in his or her professional practice; 4) maintenance debts towards a spouse's relative in the descendant line.

POLISH law[2046] restricts the field of the assets that can be seized by the creditor. If the debt was incurred by the spouses acting together (or by one spouse acting with the consent of the other), the debt can be recovered from the common property and from the personal property of the spouse(s) who incurred the debt. If the debt was incurred by one spouse without the consent of the other, only the personal property of the acting spouse and some special common assets (that is, the earnings of the acting spouse) can be seized by the creditor.

Order of ranking to be followed by the creditor

Some jurisdictions do not state any special order of ranking that the creditor should follow (BELGIUM,[2047] BULGARIA,[2048] FRANCE[2049] and RUSSIA[2050]), while

2042 Art. 1415 French Civil Code.

2043 If the creditor recovers the community debt from a personal asset of the debtor spouse, that spouse has a legal compensation right against the community property. See GONZÁLEZ BEILFUSS, Spanish Report, Q 33.

2044 Art. 1319 Spanish Civil Code. See GONZÁLEZ BEILFUSS, Spanish Report, Q 33. The personal assets of the non-contracting spouse may only be seized if the creditor cannot recover from the community assets or the personal assets of the contracting spouse.

2045 Art. 1414 para. 2 Belgian Civil Code. The listed cases are exhaustive.

2046 Art. 41 para. 3 Polish Family and Guardianship Code. See MĄCZYŃSKI, Polish Report, Q 33.

2047 See PINTENS/ALLAERTS/SEYNS/PIGNOLET, Belgian Report, Q 33.

2048 See TODOROVA, Bulgarian Report, Q 33.

2049 See FERRAND/BRAAT, French Report, Q 33.

2050 See ANTOKOLSKAIA, Russian Report, Q 33.

other legal systems express some form of preference. In ITALY,[2051] for example, the creditor must first claim against the community assets. If these are insufficient, the creditor can claim against the personal assets of each spouse (each for half of the debt). The same applies in LITHUANIA.[2052] If the community property is not sufficient to satisfy the creditor, his or her claim may be discharged from the personal property of the spouses. Similarly, in PORTUGAL, community assets shall first be used to satisfy the creditor; if these are insufficient, personal assets of both spouses can be seized because the spouses are jointly liable.[2053] The same solution applies in RUSSIA.[2054] In SPAIN,[2055] if the expense is related to the household, the personal assets of the non-contracting spouse may only be seized if the creditor cannot recover from the community assets or the personal assets of the contracting spouse.[2056]

COMMENT

1. It is the clear common core in the jurisdictions surveyed that community debts may at least be recovered from the *whole* community property of the spouses and from the personal assets of the spouse who incurred the debt. There is an important difference between joint ownership in the framework of a participation regime, and in the community of property regime: in the participation regime, the creditor can only seize the debtor spouse's share in the joint property, whereas in the community regime the creditor can seize *all* the community property without distinguishing between the shares of the individual spouses.

2. Even though the majority of the jurisdictions surveyed also extend the recovery to the personal assets to the non-contracting spouse, is seems more reasonable to distinguish – as some legal systems do – between debts for which both spouses are joint and severally liable, and those without such joint liability. The property from which community debts may be recovered therefore reflects the concept of "community debt" as stated in Principle 4:40.

2051 See PATTI/CARICATO/IRTI/IANNICELLI/SERRA/DI STEFANO/PETÖ/BORTULU, Italian Report, Q 33.

2052 See MIKELENAS, Lithuanian Report, Q 33.

2053 Art. 1695 para. 1 Portuguese Civil Code. See DE OLIVEIRA/MARTINS/VÍTOR, Portuguese Report, Q 33. If the common assets are not sufficient, the creditor may subsequently request the payment in totality from any one of the spouses.

2054 See ANTOKOLSKAIA, Russian Report, Q 33.

2055 Art. 1369 Spanish Civil Code. See GONZÁLEZ BEILFUSS, Spanish Report, Q 33.

2056 If the debt is not related to a household expense, the creditor may only recover the debt from the common assets and from the personal assets of the contracting spouse, see Art. 1369 Spanish Civil Code.

3. Maintenance debts towards a child can be recovered from community property and from the personal assets of each spouse if the child is common to the spouses. Maintenance debts towards the child of only one spouse (either living or not living in the family home) can be recovered from community property and on the personal property of the spouse who is the parent of the child. A similar solution applies in the case of professional debts of one spouse: such professional debts may only be recovered from the personal property of the spouse exercising the profession and on the community property, but not from the personal property of the other spouse.

4. The personal assets of the non-contracting spouse can only be used to recover community debts for which both spouses are jointly and severally liable. This is, for example, the case where one spouse incurs a debt in order to meet appropriate family needs (see Principle 4:5), or where both spouses incur a community debt.

5. Whether a specific order of ranking should be followed by the creditor is left to national law.

Principle 4:43 Recovery of personal debts

(1) Debts which are personal to one spouse can be recovered from

- (a) the debtor spouse's personal property;
- (b) the debtor spouse's income and gains;
- (c) the community assets to the extent of their merger with the debtor spouse's personal property.

(2) Personal debts related to tort or crime can also be recovered from half of the net value of the community property where the debtor spouse's personal property, income and gains are insufficient for recovery.

Principe 4:43 Recouvrement des dettes propres

(1) Les dettes propres d'un époux peuvent être recouvrées sur

- (a) les biens propres de cet époux;
- (b) ses gains et salaires;
- (c) les biens communs dans la mesure de leur confusion avec les biens propres de l'époux débiteur.

(2) Les dettes personnelles résultant d'un délit civil ou d'une infraction pénale peuvent également être recouvrées sur la moitié de la valeur nette de la communauté, si les biens personnels ainsi que les gains et salaires de l'époux débiteur ne suffisent pas pour le recouvrement.

Prinzip 4:43 Haftung für persönliche Verbindlichkeiten

(1) Für persönliche Verbindlichkeiten eines Ehegatten haften

- (a) das persönliche Vermögen dieses Ehegatten;
- (b) seine Einkünfte und sein Gewinn;
- (c) die gemeinschaftlichen Vermögensgegenstände bis zum Ausmaß ihrer Vermischung mit dem persönlichen Vermögen des verpflichteten Ehegatten.

(2) Für persönliche Verbindlichkeiten aus deliktischem oder strafbarem Handeln haftet auch die Hälfte des Nettowerts des gemeinschaftlichen Vermögens, wenn das persönliche Vermögen, das Einkommen und die Gewinne des verpflichteten Ehegatten für die Haftung nicht ausreichen.

INTERNATIONAL INSTRUMENTS

None of particular relevance.

COMPARATIVE OVERVIEW

Recovery of personal debts from the personal property of the debtor spouse and from the community assets

In most of the fifteen jurisdictions surveyed, debts which are personal to one spouse can be recovered by the creditor from the personal property of that spouse, and from community assets: AUSTRIA,[2057] BULGARIA,[2058] CZECH REPUBLIC,[2059] but with some nuances (namely, the creditor must first claim recovery from the personal property of the debtor spouse – if the debt cannot be satisfied from those personal assets, and if certain conditions are met, the joint property can be seized; FRANCE,[2060] with some exceptions; HUNGARY,[2061] by recovering a personal debt on the spouse's personal assets and on his or her share from the community assets; ITALY,[2062] LITHUANIA,[2063] by recovering a debt which is personal to one spouse on the personal assets of that spouse, and on that spouse's share in the community property; THE NETHERLANDS,[2064] POLAND,[2065] (where only some specific community assets may be seized by the creditor) and PORTUGAL,[2066] where recovery must first be taken from the personal assets of the debtor spouse, secondly from specific community assets, and finally from half of the community assets if the former assets are not sufficient. A similar position is taken in RUSSIA,[2067] SLOVAKIA[2068] and SPAIN.[2069] In SPAIN,[2070] the debt must first be recovered from the personal assets of the

2057 See ROTH, Austrian Report, Q 32 (which only deals with the general community of property).

2058 Art. 502–506 Bulgarian Civil Procedure Code and Art. 26 para. 3 Bulgarian Family Code. See TODOROVA, Bulgarian Report, Q 32.

2059 Art. 266a and 267 para. 1 Czech Civil Procedure Code. See MELZER, Czech Report, Q 68.

2060 Art. 1413 French Civil Code and FERRAND/BRAAT, French Report, Q 32.

2061 See WEISS/SZEIBERT, Hungarian Report, Q 32.

2062 See PATTI/CARICATO/IRTI/IANNICELLI/SERRA/DI STEFANO/PETÖ/BORTULU, Italian Report, Q 32.

2063 Art. 3.110 Lithuanian Civil Code. See MIKELENAS, Lithuanian Report, Q 32.

2064 Art. 1:96 para. 1 Dutch Civil Code: Recovering from the personal assets of the debtor spouse and from the community of property, but in that latter case with a legal duty for the debtor spouse to compensate the community (Art. 1:96 para. 2 Dutch Civil Code). See BOELE-WOELKI/SCHONEWILLE/SCHRAMA, Dutch Report, Q 32.

2065 Art. 41 para. 3 Polish Family and Guardianship Code. See MĄCZYŃSKI, Polish Report, Q 32.

2066 Art. 1696 para. 1 and 2 Portuguese Civil Code. See DE OLIVEIRA/MARTINS/VÍTOR, Portuguese Report, Q 32.

2067 Art. 45 para. 1 Russian Family Code and Art. 255 Russian Civil Code. See ANTOKOLSKAIA, Russian Report, Q 32: In the first place, the personal debt shall be recovered from the personal assets of the debtor spouse; but if they are insufficient, the creditor may request the division of the community property and will be paid from the share of the debtor spouse in the community of property. These rules are mandatory.

2068 See HAŤAPKA, Slovakian Report, Q 32: Recovering of a personal debts from the personal assets of the debtor spouse and from the common assets except for the the other spouse's wages.

2069 See GONZÁLEZ BEILFUSS, Spanish Report, Q 32.

2070 Art. 1373 Spanish Civil Code.

debtor spouse. If these are insufficient, community assets can be seized; the other spouse may request that the seizure be limited to the share of the debtor spouse in the community property (in such a case, the community is dissolved). In BELGIUM,[2071] the creditor can only seize the personal assets of the debtor spouse and his earnings which belong to the common assets. Only in some exceptional cases[2072] may the other common assets of the spouse also be used by the creditor to recover the debt: this applies, for example, in the case of debts related to tort or crime[2073] and the personal property of the debtor spouse is insufficient for recovering (the aim of this exceptional rule is to protect the victim and to guarantee that she will be compensated). In FRANCE,[2074] the rule is the opposite to that in BELGIUM: the payments of debts for which a spouse is obligated, for whatever reason, may always be enforced against the common assets;[2075] however, this main rule does not apply in several special cases: 1) an important exception is that the rule does not apply to debts which are personal according to Article 1410 French Civil Code[2076] – in principle, the creditor may only enforce payment on the separate property of the debtor spouse and on his or her income; 2) in case of fraudulent entente between the debtor spouse and the creditor,[2077] the common assets may not be seized; 3) in instances where the community assets are seized by the creditor, FRENCH law excludes the seizure of the profits and earnings (*gains et salaires*) of the non-debtor spouse,[2078] unless the obligation was contracted for family expenses (household, maintenance and upbringing of the children);[2079] 4) a spouse may bind only his or her personal assets and his or her income by surety or loan, unless these have been contracted with the express consent of the other spouse who, in such an instance, does not bind his or her personal assets.[2080] In MALTA,[2081] the creditors of a spouse for debts which are not chargeable to the community of acquests can, where their

2071 Art. 1409 Belgian Civil Code. See PINTENS/ALLAERTS/SEYNS/PIGNOLET, Belgian Report, Q 32. The other common assets may only be seized in exceptional cases.

2072 See PINTENS/ALLAERTS/SEYNS/PIGNOLET, Belgian Report, Q 32: Debts which are recoverable against the community property are: prenuptial debts and obligations of gifts and inheritances; debts by virtue of forbidden professions or forbidden acts; debts arising from a criminal sentence or from a wrongful act; debts incurred by both spouses in a different capacity.

2073 Art. 1411 and 1412 Belgian Civil Code.

2074 See FERRAND/BRAAT, French Report, Q 32.

2075 Art. 1413 French Civil Code.

2076 These are debts owed by one spouse at the date of the marriage and the debts with which inheritances and gifts made to one spouse during the marriage; see FERRAND/BRAAT, French Report, Q 32.

2077 Art. 1413 French Civil Code.

2078 Art. 1414 French Civil Code.

2079 For a specific rule where the earnings of the non-debtor spouse are contained in a deposit account at the bank, see Art. 1414 para. 2 French Civil Code and Art. 48 of the Decree n°92–755 of 31 July 1992. See FERRAND/BRAAT, French Report, Q 32.

2080 Art. 1415 French Civil Code.

2081 Art. 1329 Maltese Civil Code. See FARRUGIA, Maltese Report, Q 30.

claim cannot be satisfied against the property that belongs separately to the spouses (paraphernal property), enforce their claim *in subsidium* against the assets forming part of the community of acquests, but only to the extent of the value of the share in it.[2082]

In all these legal systems, the personal assets of the spouse who did not incur the debt are protected from a possible claim of the creditor.

Limits to recovery from community assets

Even though a large majority of the legal systems surveyed allow the recovery of a debt which is personal to one spouse on the community assets of the spouses, there are differences with regard to the question of whether all the community assets, or only part of them, may be seized by the creditor.

Some jurisdictions have opted for a general community of property which allows the creditor to recover a personal debt of one spouse from the personal property of that spouse and from all community assets (AUSTRIA[2083] and THE NETHERLANDS[2084]). In the CZECH REPUBLIC,[2085] although the creditor must first recover the debt from the personal property of the debtor spouse, under certain conditions, community property may be seized if the debt was incurred during the marriage. In this case, execution on the community property can be carried out without any express limitation in the recovering of a personal debt of one spouse. The same applies when the spouse entered into a debt which surpasses the property conditions of the spouses, and therefore did not become a part of the community property regime.[2086] However, CZECH law[2087] gives the non-debtor spouse a special action which in some cases excludes enforcement against the common assets; two conditions must be fulfilled: (1) the debt is exclusively the responsibility of one spouse; (2) the debt was incurred while using or administering property that was not part of the common property.

In BULGARIA,[2088] community assets may be seized by the creditor; however, if a community asset is seized by the creditor and auctioned, the non-debtor spouse receives half of the price, while the other half goes to the creditor.[2089] As in BULGARIA, other jurisdictions allow the creditor to recover a debt which is

2082 The debtor's spouse has the right to seek the judicial separation of property, see Art. 1329 para. 2 Maltese Civil Code.

2083 See ROTH, Austrian Report, Q 32.

2084 See BOELE-WOELKI/SCHONEWILLE/SCHRAMA, Dutch Report, Q 32.

2085 See MELZER, Czech Report, Q 32.

2086 See MELZER, Czech Report, Q 32.

2087 See MELZER, Czech Report, Q 32.

2088 See TODOROVA, Bulgarian Report, Q 32.

2089 Art. 504 Bulgarian Civil Procedure Code. See TODOROVA, Bulgarian Report, Q 32.

personal to one spouse both on the personal assets of that spouse, and on his/her share in the community property: this is the case in HUNGARY,[2090] ITALY,[2091] LITHUANIA,[2092] MALTA,[2093] PORTUGAL,[2094] RUSSIA[2095] and SPAIN.[2096]

In FRANCE,[2097] POLAND[2098] and SLOVAKIA,[2099] some community assets are excluded. In POLAND,[2100] the creditor can only recover the debt from the personal property of the debtor spouse and from some specified assets which are the earnings of the debtor spouse from employment, copyright or any other activity.[2101] In SLOVAKIA,[2102] all community assets can be used to satisfy a personal debt with exception of the garnishment of the wages of the other spouse.[2103] FRENCH law[2104] is complex: debts which are personal according to Article 1410 French Civil Code can only be enforced against the personal assets of the debtor spouse and on his or her income[2105] (which qualifies as community property). Other debts may be enforced against the community assets, other than the profits and earnings of the non-debtor spouse.[2106] If these earnings, however, are paid into a joint bank account, which the creditor seizes, the non debtor spouse may request that an amount corresponding to his/her last month's salary will be left out of the seizure.[2107] There are also other limitations with regard to loans or sureties entered into by one spouse: if these have been entered into by only one spouse without the express consent of the other, the debtor spouse binds only his or her personal assets and income. If the other spouse gave his or her consent, the personal assets and the income of the debtor spouse, as well as the community assets are bound; the personal assets of the other spouse are protected.[2108]

2090 See WEISS/SZEIBERT, Hungarian Report, Q 32.
2091 See PATTI/CARICATO/IRTI/IANNICELLI/SERRA/DI STEFANO/PETÖ/BORTULU, Italian Report, Q 32.
2092 See MIKELENAS, Lithuanian Report, Q 32.
2093 See FARRUGIA, Maltese Report Q 32.
2094 See DE OLIVEIRA/MARTINS/VÍTOR, Portuguese Report, Q 32.
2095 See ANTOKOLSKAIA, Russian Report Q 32.
2096 See GONZÁLEZ/RIBOT, Spanish Report, Q 32.
2097 See FERRAND/BRAAT, French Report, Q 32.
2098 See MĄCZYŃSKI, Polish Report, Q 32.
2099 See HAŤAPKA, Slovakian Report, Q 32.
2100 See MĄCZYŃSKI, Polish Report, Q 32.
2101 See Art. 41 para. 3 Polish Family and Guardianship Code.
2102 See HAŤAPKA, Slovakian Report, Q 32.
2103 See HAŤAPKA, Slovekian Report, Q 32.
2104 See FERRAND/BRAAT, French Report, Q 32.
2105 Art. 1411 para. 1 French Civil Code.
2106 Art. 1414 para. 1 French Civil Code. This means that the other spouse's salary may not be seized directly from the employer.
2107 Art. 1414 para. 2 French Civil Code and Art. 48 of the Decree n°92–755 of 31 July 1992.
2108 Art. 1415 French Civil Code.

Order to be followed by the creditor

Many of the jurisdictions surveyed do not impose any order of ranking between the personal property of one spouse and common property (AUSTRIA,[2109] BELGIUM[2110] with regard to personal property and earnings of the debtor spouse; BULGARIA,[2111] FRANCE,[2112] HUNGARY,[2113] THE NETHERLANDS[2114] with the legal duty of the debtor spouse to compensate the community if the debt has been recovered from common assets,[2115] POLAND[2116] and SLOVAKIA[2117]) for the earnings of the debtor spouse.

Other legal systems state an order of ranking: the personal debt of one spouse must first be recovered from his or her personal assets, and only subsequently, if the personal assets are insufficient, can it then be recovered from community assets. This is the case in, for example, the CZECH REPUBLIC,[2118] MALTA,[2119] PORTUGAL,[2120] RUSSIA[2121] and SPAIN.[2122] In RUSSIA,[2123] if the personal assets of the debtor spouse appear to be insufficient, the creditor may request the division of the community property. In SPAIN,[2124] in such a situation, the creditor may request the seizure of community assets; the other spouse can either accept that community property will be used to cover a personal debt of the other spouse, or request that the seizure be limited to the debtor spouse's share in the community property. In that latter case, the community is dissolved.[2125]

Consequences of the recovery from community assets

In some jurisdictions, such as BULGARIA,[2126] if the creditor starts a procedure for the recovery of a personal debt on community assets, the community of property on the particular asset is terminated and converted into joint ownership with

2109 See ROTH, Austrian Report, Q 32.
2110 See PINTENS/ALLAERTS/SEYNS/PIGNOLET, Belgian Report, Q 32.
2111 See TODOROVA, Bulgarian Report, Q 32.
2112 See FERRAND/BRAAT, French Report, Q 32.
2113 See WEISS/SZEIBERT, Hungarian Report, Q 32.
2114 See BOELE-WOELKI/SCHONEWILLE/SCHRAMA, Dutch Report, Q 32.
2115 Art. 1:96 para. 2 Dutch Civil Code.
2116 See MĄCZYŃSKI, Polish Report, Q 32.
2117 See HAŤAPKA, Slovakian Report, Q 32.
2118 See MELZER, Czech Report, Q 32.
2119 Art. 1329 para. 1 Maltese Civil Code.
2120 See DE OLIVEIRA/MARTINS/VÍTOR, Portuguese Report, Q 32.
2121 Art. 45 para. 1 Russian Family Code.
2122 See GONZÁLEZ BEILFUSS/RIBOT, Spanish Report, Q 32.
2123 See ANTOKOLSKAIA, Russian Report, Q 32.
2124 See GONZÁLEZ BEILFUSS/RIBOT, Spanish Report, Q 32.
2125 Art. 1373 Spanish Civil Code.
2126 See TODOROVA, Bulgarian Report, Q 32.

equal shares.[2127] The non-debtor spouse may pay the debtor spouse's share of the asset to the creditor in order to prevent an auction and to become an owner in person of the asset.[2128] If the asset is auctioned, the non-debtor spouse receives half of the proceeds and the other half goes to the creditor.[2129] In LITHUANIA,[2130] the creditor who wants to recover the debt from community assets shall establish the share of the debtor spouse in the community property, so that a division of community property will occur. In RUSSIA,[2131] the creditor has to request the division of the community property if he wishes to recover the debt from the debtor spouse's share.[2132] In SPAIN,[2133] if the non-debtor spouse requests that the seizure should be limited to the debtor spouse's share in the community property, the community is dissolved and the creditor will recover the debt from the property attributed to the debtor spouse.

Most of the jurisdictions surveyed do not provide for any special consequence in instances where common assets of the spouses are seized to recover a debt which is personal to one spouse. However, national law can opt for a legal duty of compensation for the debtor spouse whose personal debt was paid from community property (for example, FRANCE,[2134] PORTUGAL[2135] and THE NETHERLANDS[2136]).

COMMENT

1. A debt which is personal to one spouse should be primarily recovered from the personal assets of that spouse. However, in many cases, the major property of one spouse will consist of his or her income. Therefore, in order to prevent the personal creditor of one spouse from being disadvantaged, the income and profits of the debtor spouse should also satisfy the payment of the debt, even if these qualify as the spouses' community assets. In contrast to several jurisdictions surveyed, the creditor should not be allowed to seize the other community assets, since the debt has a personal character. This choice – which reflects a better law approach – aims both to respect the balance between the spouses and to discharge the community property from debts with which it has no connection.

2127 Art. 26 para. 3 Bulgarian Family Code.
2128 Art. 505 Bulgarian Code of Civil Procedure and Art. 20 para. 1 Bulgarian Family Code.
2129 Art. 504 Bulgarian Code of Civil Procedure.
2130 See MIKELENAS, Lithuanian Report, Q 32.
2131 See ANTOKOLSKAIA, Russian Report, Q 32.
2132 Art. 45 para. 1 Russian Family Code and Art. 255 Russian Civil Code.
2133 See GONZÁLEZ, Spanish Report, Q 32.
2134 Art. 1413 in fine French Civil Code.
2135 Art. 1697 para. 2, Portuguese Civil Code.
2136 Art. 1:96 para. 2 Dutch Civil Code.

2. Income and gains should be understood in a broad sense, that is, not only salaries from employment, but also earnings from other activities such as intellectual property rights, lottery wins etc.

3. Debts which are personal to one spouse should also be recoverable from community property to the extent of the merger of the debtors spouse's personal property with community property. It can happen that a personal asset of one spouse is merged with community assets (for example, where household goods are mixed within the family home and the debtor spouse cannot prove that some household goods are his or her personal property, or the personal money of one spouse is placed on a private bank account, and then subsequently moved to the spouses' community bank account).

4. It does not seem useful to create a special order of ranking between the personal assets of the debtor spouse and his or her profits and earnings for the purposes of recovering the debt by the creditor. Therefore, Principle 4:43(1) provides no hierarchy. This issue should be left to national law.

5. A special rule aimed at protecting the victim should apply in cases where there is a debt related to tort or crime in which the debtor spouse's personal property, income and gains are insufficient for recovery. The debt should then be recovered from half of the net value of the community property. In this case, there is a ranking, since the debt should primarily be recovered from the debtor's personal property, income and gains. Only subsequently, where there is not sufficient property, may a part of the value of the community property be seized.

6. Where both spouses agree that a personal debt of one spouse should be satisfied from common assets, the debtor spouse has a duty to compensate at the dissolution of the community. This rule aims at safeguarding financial equality between both spouses, and at preventing the community from becoming impoverished because of the personal debts of one spouse.

ADMINISTRATION
ADMINISTRATION
VERWALTUNG

Principle 4:44 Administration of community property

(1) Each spouse is entitled to administer community property, but important acts require joint administration.

(2) If one spouse refuses to consent to an act requiring joint administration, the other spouse may apply to the competent authority for authorisation to act alone.

Principe 4:44 Administration de la communauté

(1) Chaque époux a le droit d'administrer les biens communs. Toutefois, les actes importants requièrent une administration conjointe.

(2) Si un époux refuse de donner son consentement à un acte nécessitant une administration conjointe, l'autre époux peut solliciter de l'autorité compétente l'autorisation de passer l'acte seul.

Prinzip 4:44 Verwaltung des gemeinschaftlichen Vermögens

(1) Jeder Ehegatte ist zur Verwaltung gemeinschaftlichen Vermögens berechtigt. Wichtige Geschäfte erfordern jedoch eine gemeinsame Verwaltung.

(2) Lehnt ein Ehegatte ab, einem Geschäft zuzustimmen, das gemeinschaftliche Verwaltung erfordert, so kann der andere Ehegatte eine Ermächtigung bei der zuständigen Behörde beantragen, das Geschäft alleine vorzunehmen.

INTERNATIONAL INSTRUMENTS

According to Article 16 (1) (h) of the *UN Convention on the Elimination of All Forms of Discrimination against Women of 18 December 1979* States Parties shall ensure the same rights for both spouses in respect of the ownership, acquisition, management, administration, enjoyment and disposition of property.

COMPARATIVE OVERVIEW

Administration of property affects the disposal of property during the matrimonial property regime. The main issues at stake are which spouse is entitled for acts of administration, what kind of acts are covered, what are the prerequisites for such acts and where are the limits?

Consent of the other spouse

In conformity with the basic principle of joint ownership the administration of the common property is in some legal systems undertaken by both spouses jointly (AUSTRIA,[2137] HUNGARY,[2138] LITHUANIA,[2139] RUSSIA[2140] and SPAIN[2141]). If the consent of the other spouse is needed, a practical important question is whether there was really consent of the other spouse or not. However, it would be cumbersome if for every act of administration it had to be proved that both spouses consented. Therefore in some jurisdictions it suffices that one spouse acts with the express or tacit consent of the other spouse (SPAIN[2142]). With regard to ordinary transactions there is sometimes a rebuttable presumption that there is spousal consent for transactions entered into between either of the spouses and a third party (HUNGARY,[2143] LITHUANIA[2144] and RUSSIA[2145]). Another solution adopted by many jurisdictions is that each of the spouses is entitled to act alone. This, however, has to be restricted mainly in the interest of the other spouse. Consequently, there is often a distinction between different types of administration and different acts of administration. A distinction between concurring and joint administration is made in BELGIUM,[2146] FRANCE[2147] and PORTUGAL.[2148]

In the first category of administration, comprising specified ordinary or concurring administration, one spouse can act alone. These acts of administration generally concern *everyday* transactions and do not always have far reaching consequences. The ordinary administration of the community assets and the right to sue or to be sued in respect of such ordinary administration is vested in either

2137 See ROTH, Austrian Report, Q 35.
2138 See WEISS/SZEIBERT, Hungarian Report, Q 35.
2139 See MIKELENAS, Lithuanian Report, Q 35.
2140 See ANTOKOLSKAIA, Russian Report, Q 35, 41.
2141 See GONZÁLEZ BEILFUSS, Spanish Report, Q 35, 37.
2142 See GONZÁLEZ BEILFUSS, Spanish Report, Q 35.
2143 § 30 para. 1 Hungarian Family Act. See WEISS/SZEIBERT, Hungarian Report, Q 35, 37.
2144 See MIKELENAS, Lithuanian Report, Q 35, 37.
2145 See ANTOKOLSKAIA, Russian Report, Q 35.
2146 See PINTENS/ALLAERTS/SEYNS/PIGNOLET, Belgian Report, Q 35.
2147 See FERRAND/BRAAT, French Report, Q 35.
2148 See DE OLIVEIRA/MARTINS/VÍTOR, Portuguese Report, Q 35.

spouse (BULGARIA,[2149] CZECH REPUBLIC,[2150] FRANCE,[2151] ITALY,[2152] MALTA,[2153] POLAND,[2154] PORTUGAL[2155] and SLOVAKIA[2156]). For the second category see Principle 4:45. Under DUTCH law,[2157] property within the community is subject to the administration of the spouse from whom it originated, insofar as the spouses have not agreed otherwise in a marriage contract.

The costs of the maintenance and the administration of chattels belonging to the community property are covered primarily from the community property. However, if that is not sufficient then both spouses are obliged to contribute to the costs (HUNGARY[2158]).

There are restrictions on acts of joint administration where the consent of both spouses is necessary to perform these acts. The rules on joint administration apply to important transactions (see Principle 4:45). Where there are special rules for the administration in the case of professional activities there are rules on sole or exclusive administration (see Principle 4:47).

Not all legal administration issues depend on a single matrimonial property regime. In some jurisdictions there are specific rules governing acquisition and transactions in respect of the matrimonial or family home irrespective of the matrimonial property regime (see Principles 4:6 and 4:7).

Internal and external relationship

The internal relationship between the spouses themselves and the external relationship with third parties must be distinguished. In their internal relationship spouses are generally free to conclude an agreement specifying or modifying the conditions of the administration of community property. For the external relationship with third parties and particularly concerning the issue of disposal of assets of the community is important. Contracts concluded with third parties by one of the spouses for the administration of the community property are also binding the other spouse by law (BULGARIA[2159]).

2149 See TODOROVA, Bulgarian Report, Q 35.
2150 See MELZER, Czech Report, Q 70.
2151 Art. 1421 French Civil Code. See FERRAND/BRAAT, French Report, Q 35.
2152 Art. 180 para. 1 Italian Civil Code. See PATTI/CARICATO/IRTI/IANNICELLI/SERRA/DI STEFANO/PETÖ/BORTOLU, Italian Report, Q 35.
2153 Art. 1322 para. 1 Maltese Civil Code. See FARRUGIA, Maltese Report, Q 35.
2154 Art. 36 para. 2 Polish Family and Guardianship Act. See MĄCZYŃSKI, Polish Report, Q 35.
2155 See DE OLIVEIRA/MARTINS/VÍTOR, Portuguese Report, Q 35.
2156 See HAŤAPKA, Slovakian Report, Q 35.
2157 See BOELE-WOELKI/SCHONEWILLE/SCHRAMA, Dutch Report, Q 35.
2158 See WEISS/SZEIBERT, Hungarian Report, Q 35.
2159 See TODOROVA, Bulgarian Report, Q 35.

It is possible that one spouse may refuse to an act envisaged by the other spouse. The refusal is valid with regard to third parties if they knew about the refusal before the act was performed (POLAND[2160]). In this context it should be mentioned that many jurisdictions have special provisions dealing with the good faith of a third party, see Principle 4:46.

Dispute Resolution

One has to distinguish between different kinds of property and different situations. So far as personal property is concerned, it is generally only the owner of the property who can decide matters of administration. The other spouse in general cannot object (e.g. RUSSIA[2161]). However, in special cases, if, for example, the family home is concerned, the other spouse may object (BELGIUM[2162]).

As far as community property is concerned it often depends whether general rules on administration of property apply. If this is the case then, in principle, one spouse may act alone but the other spouse may intervene. There is an exception where no refusal is possible for minor transactions concluded in everyday life and acts aimed at fulfilling the regular needs of the family (POLAND[2163] and SPAIN[2164]).

Joint administration requires the consent of both spouses. If one of the spouses refuses his or her consent to an act of extraordinary administration or to another act where consent is necessary, this has to be respected in principle. However, the other spouse may apply to the competent court for authorisation when the act is necessary in the interests of the family (BELGIUM,[2165] FRANCE,[2166] ITALY,[2167] LITHUANIA,[2168] MALTA,[2169] POLAND,[2170] PORTUGAL[2171] and SPAIN[2172]). Then the consent is substituted by a court decision.

2160 See MĄCZYŃSKI, Polish Report, Q 35.
2161 See ANTOKOLSKAIA, Russian Report, Q 40.
2162 See PINTENS/ALLAERTS/SEYNS/PIGNOLET, Belgian Report, Q 40.
2163 See MĄCZYŃSKI, Polish Report, Q 35.
2164 Art. 1319 Spanish Civil Code. See GONZÁLEZ BEILFUSS, Spanish Report, Q 35.
2165 Art. 1420 Belgian Civil Code. See PINTENS/ALLAERTS/SEYNS/PIGNOLET, Belgian Report, Q 40.
2166 Art. 217 French Civil Code. See FERRAND/BRAAT, French Report, Q 40.
2167 Art. 181 Italian Civil Code. See PATTI/CARICATO/IRTI/IANNICELLI/SERRA/DI STEFANO/PETÖ/BORTOLU, Italian Report, Q 35, 40.
2168 See MIKELENAS, Lithuanian Report, Q 35, 40 (without a distinction of different kinds of administration).
2169 Art. 1323 para. 1 Maltese Civil Code. See FARRUGIA, Maltese Report, Q 40.
2170 See MĄCZYŃSKI, Polish Report, Q 40.
2171 Art. 1684 para. 3 Portuguese Civil Code. See DE OLIVEIRA/MARTINS/VÍTOR, Portuguese Report, Q 40.
2172 See GONZÁLEZ BEILFUSS, Spanish Report, Q 40.

In rare cases lack of consent can result in the dissolution of the community (e.g. BULGARIA,[2173] HUNGARY,[2174] RUSSIA[2175] and SPAIN[2176]). If one spouse is incapable for the management of the property a removal from managing the assets also may be a consequence (LITHUANIA[2177]). See also the comparative overview under Principle 4:49.

Disputes between spouses concerning the administration of personal or community property may generally be resolved in court proceedings (e.g. BULGARIA,[2178] SLOVAKIA[2179] and SPAIN[2180]). In some jurisdictions there are special rules for the solution of such disputes in matrimonial property law (e.g. THE NETHERLANDS[2181]). In other jurisdictions such disputes have to be solved according to general rules of matrimonial law (CZECH REPUBLIC[2182]). In some jurisdictions such disputes have to be solved in non-contentious proceedings in the competent courts (AUSTRIA[2183]). Sometimes measures of alternative dispute treatment are explicitly offered (MALTA[2184]).

In many jurisdictions there are special procedural provisions to protect one spouse against acts of the other. In BELGIUM,[2185] a restraining order of the justice of the peace is possible.

COMMENT

1. The equality and independence of the spouses prevail in the regulation of the management and administration of community property (see Principles 4:2 and 4:3). The consequence is that both spouses have to decide on management and administration. It would be, however, difficult, if for every transaction both spouses should act together. Therefore the practicality of the rules on administration of property is essential and leads to a restriction of the requirement of acting jointly.

2. The rules on the administration of community property have to reflect the fact that the assets are generally the joint property of the spouses. Administration

2173 See TODOROVA, Bulgarian Report, Q 40.
2174 See WEISS/SZEIBERT, Hungarian Report, Q 40.
2175 See ANTOKOLSKAIA, Russian Report, Q 40.
2176 See GONZÁLEZ BEILFUSS, Spanish Report, Q 40.
2177 See MIKELENAS, Lithuanian Report, Q 40.
2178 See TODOROVA, Bulgarian Report, Q 40.
2179 See HAŤAPKA, Slovakian Report, Q 35, 40.
2180 See GONZÁLEZ BEILFUSS, Spanish Report, Q 40.
2181 See BOELE-WOELKI/SCHONEWILLE/SCHRAMA, Dutch Report, Q 40.
2182 See MELZER, Czech Report, Q 75.
2183 See ROTH, Austrian Report, Q 40.
2184 Art. 1323 para. 1 Maltese Civil Code. See FARRUGIA, Maltese Report, Q 40.
2185 See PINTENS/ALLAERTS/SEYNS/PIGNOLET, Belgian Report, Q 40.

of assets concerns a wide range of different acts and situations. It includes all acts of disposal (alienation, transfer or title, encumbrance) and pure management of property, for example repair of a movable.

3. A distinction is made between different types of administration. There are three kinds of administration: concurring, joint and exclusive administration.

4. As regards assets which form part of the community property, each spouse is, according to the first part of Principle 4:44(1) independently authorised to conduct acts of administration. Concurring administration generally applies to day-to-day transactions. The acts of ordinary management may be performed by each of the spouses independently. It is the task of the spouses to come to an understanding in their internal relationship on an allocation of responsibilities and to make substantial decisions on property issues.

5. There are, however, also cases of joint administration, which are dealt with in the second part of Principle 4:44(1). This applies to certain important acts and acts of extraordinary management, both of which require the consent from the other spouse (see Principle 4:45).

6. Exclusive administration means that one spouse, to the exclusion of the other, is assigned decision-making authority in whole or in part of the community property (see Principle 4:47).

7. Principle 4:44(2) is based on the assumption that there is an implicit mutual obligation of the spouses to cooperate in the carrying out of measures required for a proper administration of community property. The rules on the administration of property shall not be an obstacle when either spouse needs to do or to perform an act. Matrimonial law must provide for different solutions when either spouse refuses consent or is unable to manage and administer his or her property.

8. The necessary consent of the other spouse may not be unreasonably withheld. If one of the spouses refuses his or her consent to an act of extraordinary administration, the other spouse may apply to the competent authority for authorisation. The competent authority will decide in the interest of the community. If the spouse obtains an authorisation to act alone, the authorisation is restricted, to this act.

9. There are also specific rules governing acquisition and transactions in respect of household goods and the lease of the family home irrespective of the matrimonial property regime (see Principles 4:5 and 4:6). Other rules govern transactions entered into by one spouse irrespective of the matrimonial property regime (e.g. entering into guarantees, incurring debts), see Principles 4:3. According to Principle 4:7 one spouse may authorise the other to represent him or her.

Principle 4:45 Acts requiring joint administration
Subject to Principles 4:4 to 4:8 and taking into account the economic circumstances of the spouses, acts requiring joint administration include in particular the following:
(a) acquisition, alienation and encumbrance of immovable property;
(b) entering into significant loan agreements, guarantees and sureties;
(c) making significant gifts.

Principe 4:45 Actes nécessitant une administration conjointe
Sous réserve des Principes 4:4 à 4:8 et en tenant compte de la situation économique des époux, les actes nécessitant une administration conjointe englobent notamment:
(a) l'acquisition, l'aliénation et la charge de biens immeubles;
(b) la conclusion de contrats de prêts, de garanties et de sûretés de valeur significative;
(c) les donations de valeur significative.

Prinzip 4:45 Gemeinschaftliche Verwaltung erfordernde Geschäfte
Vorbehaltlich der Prinzipien 4:4 bis 4:8 und unter Berücksichtigung der wirtschaftlichen Verhältnisse der Ehegatten, gehören zu den gemeinschaftliche Verwaltung erfordernden Geschäften insbesondere die folgenden:
(a) Erwerb, Veräußerung und Belastung unbeweglichen Vermögens;
(b) Eingehung bedeutender Darlehensverträge, Bürgschaften und Garantien;
(c) Gewährung bedeutender Geschenke.

INTERNATIONAL INSTRUMENTS

None of particular relevance.

COMPARATIVE OVERVIEW

General rules on joint administration

Not all legal issues in the field of joint administration depend on the matrimonial property regime. Some jurisdictions have specific rules governing acquisition and transactions in respect of the matrimonial or family home irrespective of the matrimonial property regime (see Principles 4:6 and 4:7). There is a protection of the family home which limits the decision-making power of the spouse (BELGIUM,[2186] BULGARIA[2187] and FRANCE[2188]). Similarly, the consent of the other spouse is required for contracts for the disposal end encumbrance of the home (THE NETHERLANDS[2189] and PORTUGAL[2190]). In some jurisdictions there are also specific rules governing acquisition and transactions in respect of household goods irrespective of the matrimonial property regime (see Principle 4:5). In THE NETHERLANDS,[2191] the consent of the other spouse is always required for contracts for the disposal and encumbrance of household effects.

Some jurisdictions have other rules governing certain transactions entered into by one spouse irrespective of the matrimonial property regime (e.g. entering into guarantees, incurring debts), see Principle 4:3. The consent of the other spouse is required for significant gifts (THE NETHERLANDS[2192]). Sometimes the consent of the other spouse is also required for the provision of security for third parties other than in the normal conduct of the spouse's profession or business (THE NETHERLANDS[2193]), hire-purchase contracts, except for things which serve for the normal conduct of the spouse's profession of business (THE NETHERLANDS[2194]).

In many jurisdictions important acts concerning personal property require the consent of the other spouse according to community property law. In some jurisdictions all kinds of disposals of matrimonial property concerning property and property rights are distinguished from simple acts of administration. For them it is required that both spouses agree (BULGARIA[2195]). In certain jurisdictions the restrictions for personal and community property are nearly the same (PORTUGAL[2196]).

In other jurisdictions the only restrictions are in respect of the disposal of the matrimonial/family home (BELGIUM,[2197] FRANCE,[2198] HUNGARY,[2199]

2186 Art. 215 Belgian Civil Code. See PINTENS/ALLAERTS/SEYNS/PIGNOLET, Belgian Report, Q 37.
2187 See TODOROVA, Bulgarian Report, Q 41.
2188 Art. 215 French Civil Code. See FERRAND/BRAAT, French Report, Q 37.
2189 Art. 1:88 para. 1 Dutch Civil Code. See BOELE-WOELKI/SCHONEWILLE/SCHRAMA, Dutch Report, Q 37.
2190 See DE OLIVEIRA/MARTINS/VÍTOR, Portuguese Report, Q 37.
2191 Art. 1:88 para. 1 Dutch Civil Code. See BOELE-WOELKI/SCHONEWILLE/SCHRAMA, Dutch Report, Q 37.
2192 Art. 1:88 para. 1 Dutch Civil Code. See BOELE-WOELKI/SCHONEWILLE/SCHRAMA, Dutch Report, Q 37.
2193 Art. 1:88 para. 1 Dutch Civil Code. See BOELE-WOELKI/SCHONEWILLE/SCHRAMA, Dutch Report, Q 37.
2194 Art. 1:88 para. 1 Dutch Civil Code. See BOELE-WOELKI/SCHONEWILLE/SCHRAMA, Dutch Report, Q 37.
2195 See TODOROVA, Bulgarian Report, Q 35, 37.
2196 See DE OLIVEIRA/MARTINS/VÍTOR, Portuguese Report, Q 37.
2197 See PINTENS/ALLAERTS/SEYNS/PIGNOLET, Belgian Report, Q 37.
2198 Art. 215 para. 3 French Civil Code. See FERRAND/BRAAT, French Report, Q 37.
2199 See WEISS/SZEIBERT, Hungarian Report, Q 37.

LITHUANIA,[2200] MALTA[2201] and SPAIN[2202]). The disposal of personal movables jointly used by the spouses in the household is sometimes also restricted (FRANCE,[2203] PORTUGAL[2204] and SPAIN[2205]), but in other jurisdictions, there is no such restriction (AUSTRIA,[2206] POLAND[2207] and SLOVAKIA[2208]).

For community property the issue of the necessary consent of the other spouse for certain transactions depends on the question if there is a strict rule of common administration. If there is a basic rule that consent of the other spouse is generally necessary then there is a general restriction at least within the internal relationship of the spouses (AUSTRIA[2209]).

In jurisdictions where there is no general rule that one spouse may act alone the absence of the requirement of consent of the other spouse for a specific act is of crucial importance. All acts which go beyond the level of ordinary administration need consent of both spouses (CZECH REPUBLIC[2210]) and in many jurisdictions there is a rule that important acts concerning community property require the consent of the other spouse (BELGIUM,[2211] FRANCE,[2212] ITALY,[2213] MALTA[2214] and PORTUGAL[2215]).

Extraordinary transactions

It is necessary to define the type of transactions for which the consent of the other spouse is regularly required. These acts are generally economically important transactions where it is necessary to protect valuable assets and where the transaction would have serious consequences. Sometimes all transactions requiring the form of a notarial deed are named (RUSSIA[2216]). Other jurisdictions use the category of transactions which surpass the limits of ordinary

2200 See MIKELENAS, Lithuanian Report, Q 37.
2201 See FARRUGIA, Maltese Report, Q 37.
2202 See GONZÁLEZ BEILFUSS, Spanish Report, Q 37.
2203 Art. 215 para. 3 French Civil Code. See FERRAND/BRAAT, French Report, Q 37.
2204 See DE OLIVEIRA/MARTINS/VÍTOR, Portuguese Report, Q 37.
2205 Art. 1320 Spanish Civil Code. See GONZÁLEZ BEILFUSS, Spanish Report, Q 37.
2206 See ROTH, Austrian Report, Q 37.
2207 See MĄCZYŃSKI, Polish Report, Q 37.
2208 See HAŤAPKA, Slovakian Report, Q 37.
2209 See ROTH, Austrian Report, Q 37.
2210 See MELZER, Czech Report, Q 72.
2211 See PINTENS/ALLAERTS/SEYNS/PIGNOLET, Belgian Report, Q 37.
2212 Art. 1422 ff. French Civil Code. See FERRAND/BRAAT, French Report, Q 35, 37.
2213 Art. 180 para. 2 Italian Civil Code. See PATTI/CARICATO/IRTI/IANNICELLI/SERRA/DI STEFANO/PETÖ/BORTOLU, Italian Report, Q 37.
2214 Art. 1322 para. 2 Maltese Civil Code. See FARRUGIA, Maltese Report, Q 37.
2215 See DE OLIVEIRA/MARTINS/VÍTOR, Portuguese Report, Q 35, 37.
2216 See ANTOKOLSKAIA, Russian Report, Q 35, 37.

administration in a similar way as for underage persons (ITALY[2217]). However, matrimonial property law often contains a statutory list of cases of extraordinary administration where a joint action of the spouses is necessary (e.g. BELGIUM,[2218] MALTA[2219] and POLAND[2220]).

Only few jurisdictions leave the distinction between "ordinary" and "extraordinary" matters simply to case law (e.g. SLOVAKIA[2221]). Where there are definitions, they vary greatly from jurisdiction to jurisdiction. However, some typical transactions can be named. One kind of these transactions are acts granting the personal use of assets (ITALY[2222]).

An act of extraordinary administration is also an act whereby rights in immovable property are acquired or alienated (CZECH REPUBLIC,[2223] FRANCE,[2224] LITHUANIA,[2225] MALTA,[2226] POLAND[2227] and SLOVAKIA[2228]). Acts constituting or affecting the mortgaging of property are frequently included in the respective list (BELGIUM,[2229] FRANCE,[2230] LITHUANIA,[2231] MALTA,[2232] POLAND[2233] and RUSSIA[2234]). In some jurisdictions acts granting rights of use and, or, enjoyment over immovable property are on the list (FRANCE,[2235] MALTA,[2236] POLAND,[2237] PORTUGAL[2238] and RUSSIA[2239]). Transactions concerning the acquisition or the lease of a farm can also be an extraordinary transaction (POLAND[2240]).

2217 Art. 180 para. 2 Italian Civil Code. See PATTI/CARICATO/IRTI/IANNICELLI/SERRA/DI STEFANO/PETÖ/BORTOLU, Italian Report, Q 35.
2218 Art. 1417 para. 2, 1418, 1419 Belgian Civil Code. See PINTENS/ALLAERTS/SEYNS/PIGNOLET, Belgian Report, Q 37.
2219 Art. 1322 Maltese Civil Code. See FARRUGIA, Maltese Report, Q 37.
2220 Art. 37 para. 1 Polish Family and Guardianship Act. See MĄCZYŃSKI, Polish Report, Q 37.
2221 See HAŤAPKA, Slovakian Report, Q 37.
2222 Art. 180 para. 2 Italian Civil Code. See PATTI/CARICATO/IRTI/IANNICELLI/SERRA/DI STEFANO/PETÖ/BORTOLU, Italian Report, Q 35.
2223 See MELZER, Czech Report, Q 70.
2224 Art. 1424 French Civil Code. See FERRAND/BRAAT, French Report, Q 37.
2225 See MIKELENAS, Lithuanian Report, Q 35.
2226 Art. 1322 para. 3 lit. a Maltese Civil Code.
2227 See MĄCZYŃSKI, Polish Report, Q 37.
2228 See HAŤAPKA, Slovakian Report, Q 37.
2229 Art. 1418 no. 1 lit. a Belgian Civil Code. See PINTENS/ALLAERTS/SEYNS/PIGNOLET, Belgian Report, Q 37.
2230 See FERRAND/BRAAT, French Report, Q 37.
2231 See MIKELENAS, Lithuanian Report, Q 35.
2232 Art. 1322 para. 3(b) Maltese Civil Code.
2233 Art. 37 para. 1 no. 1 Polish Family and Guardianship Act.
2234 Art. 35 para. 3 Russian Family Code.
2235 Art. 1425 French Civil Code and FERRAND/BRAAT, French Report, Q 37.
2236 Art. 1322 para. 3 lit. d Maltese Civil Code.
2237 See MĄCZYŃSKI, Polish Report, Q 37.
2238 Art. 1682-A para. 1 lit. a Portuguese Civil Code.
2239 Art. 35 para. 3 Russian Family Code.
2240 See MĄCZYŃSKI, Polish Report, Q 37.

Very often the making of gifts other than those of minor importance needs the consent of the other spouse (BELGIUM,[2241] CZECH REPUBLIC,[2242] FRANCE,[2243] MALTA,[2244] POLAND,[2245] SLOVAKIA[2246] and SPAIN[2247]). Such a transaction may even be void ab initio if no consent was given before the donation was made (SPAIN[2248]).

Guaranteeing with community property for the debt of a third party is another example of an act of extraordinary administration (FRANCE[2249]). Other examples are borrowing or lending money (BELGIUM[2250]), the contracting of any suretyship (MALTA[2251]), or the giving of a pledge (MALTA[2252]). Participation in companies may also be restricted, e.g. entering with unlimited liability in a commercial partnership, or subscribing to or acquisition of any shares in a limited liability company which are not fully paid up (MALTA[2253]), the transfer of a business concern as well as the transfer of shares in a commercial partnership (LITHUANIA[2254] and MALTA[2255]). In some jurisdictions a special form for the spousal consent is required, e.g. the form demanded for a power of attorney (PORTUGAL[2256]).

Bank accounts

Some jurisdictions have special provisions on bank accounts (BULGARIA,[2257] FRANCE,[2258] MALTA[2259] and PORTUGAL[2260]). For third parties it is often impossible to find out whether money or investment instruments belong to the community property. Despite the aim of protection of the other spouse in this respect free disposal is given preference. Accordingly each spouse may, without the consent of the other, open a deposit account and a securities account in his or

2241 See PINTENS/ALLAERTS/SEYNS/PIGNOLET, Belgian Report, Q 37.
2242 See MELZER, Czech Report, Q 70.
2243 Art. 1422 para. 1 French Civil Code. See FERRAND/BRAAT, French Report, Q 37.
2244 Art. 1322 para. 3 lit. e Maltese Civil Code.
2245 Art. 37 para. 1 no. 4 Polish Family and Guardianship Act. See MĄCZYŃSKI, Polish Report, Q 37.
2246 See HAŤAPKA, Slovakian Report, Q 37.
2247 See GONZÁLEZ BEILFUSS, Spanish Report, Q 35, 37.
2248 See GONZÁLEZ BEILFUSS, Spanish Report, Q 37.
2249 Art. 1422 para. 2 French Civil Code. See FERRAND/BRAAT, French Report, Q 37.
2250 See PINTENS/ALLAERTS/SEYNS/PIGNOLET, Belgian Report, Q 37.
2251 Art. 1322 para. 3 lit. h Maltese Civil Code.
2252 Art. 1322 para. 3 lit. i Maltese Civil Code.
2253 Art. 1322 para. 3 lit. j Maltese Civil Code.
2254 See MIKELENAS, Lithuanian Report, Q 35.
2255 Art. 1322 para. 3 lit. k Maltese Civil Code.
2256 Art. 1684 para. 2 Portuguese Civil Code.
2257 Art. 22 para. 5 Bulgarian Family Code. See TODOROVA, Bulgarian Report, Q 35.
2258 Art. 221 French Civil Code. See FERRAND/BRAAT, French Report, Q 14.
2259 Art. 1322 para. 4, 5 Maltese Civil Code.
2260 Art. 1680 Portuguese Civil Code.

her personal name (FRANCE,[2261] LITHUANIA,[2262] MALTA[2263] and PORTUGAL[2264]). With regard to the depositary, the depositor is always considered to have free disposal of the funds and of the securities on deposit (FRANCE[2265]). These rules apply even after dissolution of the community or the marriage.

Protection of the family home

There are sometimes specific provisions in matrimonial property law dealing with the necessary consent for the disposal, the encumbrance or the lease of the family home (BULGARIA[2266] and PORTUGAL[2267]). The disposal of community movables jointly used by the spouses in the household can also be restricted (PORTUGAL[2268]). In other jurisdictions there are no such restrictions either in general matrimonial law or in matrimonial property law. The family home and household goods are treated as ordinary assets (e.g. SLOVAKIA[2269]); see the comparative overviews under Principles 4:6 and 4:7.

Urgent measures

There are exceptions to the requirement of consent if, inter alia, there is a need for urgent measures to protect community property or to cope with extraordinary situations (LITHUANIA,[2270] PORTUGAL[2271] and SPAIN[2272]), see the comparative overview under Principle 4:44.

COMMENT

1. The spouses should be able to participate in economic and social life without unnecessary restrictions. However, for the protection of the other spouse and having regard to the distinction between ordinary administration and extraordinary administration there need to be restrictions on the power of administration of the spouses. Acts of extraordinary administration require the

2261 Art. 221 para. 1 French Civil Code. See FERRAND/BRAAT, French Report, Q 14.
2262 See MIKELENAS, Lithuanian Report, Q 35.
2263 Art. 1322 para. 4 Maltese Civil Code.
2264 Art. 1680 Portuguese Civil Code.
2265 Art. 221 para. 2 French Civil Code. See FERRAND/BRAAT, French Report, Q 14.
2266 Art. 23 Bulgarian Family Code. See TODOROVA, Bulgarian Report, Q 41.
2267 See DE OLIVEIRA/MARTINS/VÍTOR, Portuguese Report, Q 37.
2268 See DE OLIVEIRA/MARTINS/VÍTOR, Portuguese Report, Q 37.
2269 See HAŤAPKA, Slovakian Report, Q 37.
2270 See MIKELENAS, Lithuanian Report, Q 35.
2271 Art. 1679 Portuguese Civil Code. See DE OLIVEIRA/MARTINS/VÍTOR, Portuguese Report, Q 42.
2272 Art. 1386 Spanish Civil Code. See GONZÁLEZ BEILFUSS, Spanish Report, Q 35.

consent of both spouses. The consent of the other spouse may be express or implied. It can also be given retrospectively.

2. Acts of extraordinary administration may have far reaching legal and economic consequences and may affect the interests of both spouses. Principle 4:45 provides a non-exhaustive list of such acts. Such significant acts include in particular the acquisition, alienation and encumbrance of immovable property (Principle 4:45(a)). Transactions concerning movables are, as such, not covered by this exception. Other examples include entering into significant loan agreements, guarantees and sureties (Principle 4:45(b)). Making significant gifts is another example of extraordinary administration (Principle 4:45(c)). Although it might be helpful to have a precise definition of what may be considered to be *significant*, the great diversity of the single transactions and their intimate relationship with national contract and property law precludes giving an exhaustive list. Nevertheless an indication may be given by the critieria for contributions to the family expenditures according to Principle 4:4.

3. Each spouse may open, without the consent of the other spouse, a deposit account and a securities account in his or her personal name. This is, however, not stated expressly in Principle 4:45, but it follows from Principle 4:3 according to which the spouses may act independently.

Principle 4:46 Annulment of acts of administration
Acts requiring joint administration may be annulled by the competent authority upon the application of the non-consenting spouse.

Principe 4:46 Annulation des actes d'administration
Les actes nécessitant une administration conjointe peuvent être annulés par l'autorité compétente à la requête de l'époux qui n'a pas consenti à l'acte.

Prinzip 4:46 Nichtigerklärung von Geschäften
Geschäfte, die gemeinschaftliche Verwaltung erfordern, können auf Antrag des nicht zustimmenden Ehegatten von der zuständigen Behörde für nichtig erklärt werden.

INTERNATIONAL INSTRUMENTS

None of particular relevance.

COMPARATIVE OVERVIEW

Consequences of violation of the rules on administration of property

The consequences of acts performed in violation of the rules regarding the administration of property concern different issues, namely, the existence of a contract of the spouse with a third party, the relationship between the spouses themselves and protection of the other spouse in the future. The consequences may also differ with respect to categories of property involved (registered property, movables and other non-registered property) and the kind of transaction (gifts etc.).

Not all jurisdictions provide special rules for the consequences if a spouse violates the rules governing the administration of personal property (e.g. SLOVAKIA[2273]). In other jurisdictions a court decision may deprive the spouse of his or her decision-making authority concerning his or her personal property (BELGIUM[2274]). This is possible if the spouse harms the family interests in respect of his or her personal property (BELGIUM[2275]).

2273 See HAŤAPKA, Slovakian Report, Q 41.
2274 Art. 1426 Belgian Civil Code. See PINTENS/ALLAERTS/SEYNS/PIGNOLET, Belgian Report, Q 40.
2275 Art. 1426 Belgian Civil Code. See PINTENS/ALLAERTS/SEYNS/PIGNOLET, Belgian Report, Q 34.

If a spouse manages his or her personal property in such a negligent or unreasonable way that it endangers the interests of the family, an administrator for the property may be appointed (LITHUANIA[2276]). If one spouse disposes or encumbers the personal property of the other spouse, the transaction is null and void (PORTUGAL[2277]). There may also be a compensation claim (FRANCE[2278]). The rules on the alienation of property of another may also be applicable (PORTUGAL[2279]).

The possible consequences of a spouse violating the rules governing the administration of community property depend on the type of violation. In cases of normal administration the problem does not in principle arise for those jurisdictions which accept that there is an autonomous decision by each of the spouses. Such transactions are valid against third parties (ITALY[2280]).

Protection is required particularly in cases where the consent of both spouses is necessary. If one of the spouses exceeds his or her powers over community property, it must be determined how far such a transaction is legally effective. Where such a transaction is entered into only by one spouse it has to be determined whether it is nevertheless legally effective. There can be relative invalidity which means that the other spouse who is affected by the act may question the act but can also rely on it (BELGIUM,[2281] BULGARIA,[2282] CZECH REPUBLIC,[2283] FRANCE,[2284] LITHUANIA,[2285] THE NETHERLANDS,[2286] POLAND,[2287] SLOVAKIA,[2288] RUSSIA[2289] and SPAIN[2290]). Consent may be given generally retroactively.

Generally, the other spouse, unless he or she has ratified the act, may apply for an annulment or invalidation of the act (BULGARIA,[2291] CZECH REPUBLIC,[2292]

2276 See MIKELENAS, Lithuanian Report, Q 34, 40, 41.
2277 See DE OLIVEIRA/MARTINS/VÍTOR, Portuguese Report, Q 41.
2278 See FERRAND/BRAAT, French Report, Q 41.
2279 Art. 1687 para. 3 Portuguese Civil Code. See DE OLIVEIRA/MARTINS/VÍTOR, Portuguese Report, Q 41.
2280 See PATTI/CARICATO/IRTI/IANNICELLI/SERRA/DI STEFANO/PETÖ/BORTOLU, Italian Report, Q 35, 41.
2281 See PINTENS/ALLAERTS/SEYNS/PIGNOLET, Belgian Report, Q 37, 41.
2282 See TODOROVA, Bulgarian Report, Q 37, 41.
2283 See MELZER, Czech Report, Q 76.
2284 Art. 1427 French Civil Code. See FERRAND/BRAAT, French Report, Q 37.
2285 See MIKELENAS, Lithuanian Report, Q 35, 37.
2286 See BOELE-WOELKI/SCHONEWILLE/SCHRAMA, Dutch Report, Q 37.
2287 Art. 37 para. 3, 4 Polish Family and Guardianship Act. See MĄCZYŃSKI, Polish Report, Q 37.
2288 See HAŤAPKA, Slovakian Report, Q 35, 37.
2289 See ANTOKOLSKAIA, Russian Report, Q 37.
2290 See GONZÁLEZ BEILFUSS, Spanish Report, Q 35, 37.
2291 See TODOROVA, Bulgarian Report, Q 41.
2292 § 145 para. 2 sent. 2. Czech Civil Code. See MELZER, Czech Report, Q 76.

FRANCE,[2293] ITALY,[2294] LITHUANIA,[2295] MALTA,[2296] RUSSIA,[2297] SLOVAKIA[2298] and SPAIN[2299]). The period of limitation for such an action differs from a period of six months (BULGARIA[2300] and PORTUGAL[2301]), to one year (ITALY[2302] and LITHUANIA[2303]), two years (FRANCE[2304]) or four years (SPAIN[2305]) beginning with the date when the spouse became aware of the transaction. There is also a limitation in time that the action for annulment may not be brought, for example, more than two years after the dissolution of the community as in FRANCE[2306] or more than three years after the performance of the act as in PORTUGAL.[2307] In POLAND,[2308] the consent of the other spouse may be requested. If it is refused, then the transaction is invalid. In some jurisdictions the proceedings for family disputes are applicable (SLOVAKIA[2309]).

In some jurisdictions damaging gratuitous transactions (donations and gifts) are always void without the consent of the other spouse (e.g. SPAIN[2310]).

Relationship with third parties

One of the problems that must also be solved in a community property regime is the relationship with third parties if only one of the spouses has entered into the transaction. The outside relationship is not an easy question since there are links with other rules dealing with restrictions of disposal and general provisions dealing with acquisitions based on good faith.

The first issue is whether the transaction can be valid. If this is the case then there is a claim against the acting spouse and a liability of his or her personal

2293 See FERRAND/BRAAT, French Report, Q 41.
2294 See PATTI/CARICATO/IRTI/IANNICELLI/SERRA/DI STEFANO/PETÖ/BORTOLU, Italian Report, Q 35, 41.
2295 See MIKELENAS, Lithuanian Report, Q 41.
2296 See FARRUGIA, Maltese Report, Q 41.
2297 See ANTOKOLSKAIA, Russian Report, Q 41.
2298 See HAŤAPKA, Slovakian Report, Q 41.
2299 Art. 1322 Spanish Civil Code. See GONZÁLEZ BEILFUSS, Spanish Report, Q 41.
2300 See TODOROVA, Bulgarian Report, Q 41.
2301 Art. 1687 para. 2 Portuguese Civil Code. See DE OLIVEIRA/MARTINS/VÍTOR, Portuguese Report, Q 41.
2302 See PATTI/CARICATO/IRTI/IANNICELLI/SERRA/DI STEFANO/PETÖ/BORTOLU, Italian Report, Q 41.
2303 See MIKELENAS, Lithuanian Report, Q 41.
2304 Art. 1427 French Civil Code. See FERRAND/BRAAT, French Report, Q 42.
2305 See GONZÁLEZ BEILFUSS, Spanish Report, Q 37.
2306 Art. 1427 French Civil Code. See FERRAND/BRAAT, French Report, Q 42.
2307 Art. 1687 para. 2 Portuguese Civil Code. See DE OLIVEIRA/MARTINS/VÍTOR, Portuguese Report, Q 41.
2308 Art. 38 para. 3 Polish Family and Guardianship Act. See MĄCZYŃSKI, Polish Report, Q 41.
2309 See HAŤAPKA, Slovakian Report, Q 41.
2310 Art. 1322 Spanish Civil Code. See GONZÁLEZ BEILFUSS, Spanish Report, Q 41.

property (POLAND[2311]). In some jurisdictions there are special provisions dealing with the good faith of a third party where there is only consent of one of the spouses. Some jurisdictions make a distinction in cases where the third party acted in bad faith (LITHUANIA,[2312] THE NETHERLANDS,[2313] POLAND[2314] and RUSSIA[2315]). If the other party to the transaction knew that the person with whom he or she was entering into the transaction was married, he or she can only withdraw from the transaction if the spouse had misrepresented the existence of the other spouse's consent (LITHUANIA[2316]). The protection accorded to third parties dealing in good faith with the spouse may be based on a special rule in matrimonial property law. However, some jurisdictions declare the general rules on acquisition in good faith for a person having no title applicable (POLAND[2317]). Another technique is to restrict the annulment of the transaction to the context of voidability. In the case of an alienation or encumbrance of a non-registered movable by only one of the spouses, the valdity of the transaction may not be opposed against a third party acting in good faith (PORTUGAL[2318]). The community may also be liable for the amount of the portion of the acting spouse if there was an extraordinary transaction without consent of the other spouse (ITALY[2319]). Such a rule broadens the accessibility of spousal property to creditors.

COMMENT

1. Spouses need protection against acts which require the consent of both spouses but which have been performed by one spouse without the consent of the other. However, absolute invalidity may be an inappropriate sanction. It is sufficient that these acts may be annulled by the competent authority at the request of the other spouse. According to the protective purpose the invalidity should occur ab initio. This is in line with Principle 4:5 on the protection of the family home and household goods, where any acts of disposal in breach of the protecting rules are voidable but may be subsequently approved.

2. Third parties must also be protected in respect of transactions regarding community assets, but entered into only by one of the spouses. In line with the

2311 Art. 41 para. 2 Polish Family and Guardianship Act.

2312 See MIKELENAS, Lithuanian Report, Q 41.

2313 See BOELE-WOELKI/SCHONEWILLE/SCHRAMA, Dutch Report, Q 41.

2314 Art. 38 Polish Family and Guardianship Act.

2315 See ANTOKOLSKAIA, Russian Report, Q 41.

2316 See MIKELENAS, Lithuanian Report, Q 35, 37.

2317 Art. 38 Polish Family and Guardianship Act.

2318 Art. 1687 para. 3 Portuguese Civil Code. See DE OLIVEIRA/MARTINS/VÍTOR, Portuguese Report, Q 41.

2319 Art. 189 Italian Civil Code.

general approach, Principle 4:46 does not address the consequences for the relationship with third parties. The questions whether the third party is bound and can acquire ownership if he acted in good faith are left to national law. It is also left to national law to decide whether third parties should have the right to avoid a contract prior to the consent of the other spouse and to what extent his or her good faith for a purchase of rights can play a role. The problems of third party rights are so interrelated with general issues of contract and property law that the Principles do not contain provisions on these issues.

3. Principle 4:46 does not attempt to prescribe time limits, leaving that to be determined by national law.

Principle 4:47 Administration of personal property
Subject to Principles 4:6 and 4:7 each spouse is entitled to administer his or her personal property independently.

Principe 4:47 Administration du patrimoine propre
Sous réserve des principes 4:6 et 4:7, chaque époux a le pouvoir d'administrer seul ses biens propres.

Prinzip 4:47 Verwaltung des persönlichen Vermögens
Vorbehaltlich der Prinzipien 4:6 und 4:7 ist jeder Ehegatte berechtigt, sein persönliches Vermögen allein zu verwalten.

INTERNATIONAL INSTRUMENTS

None of particular relevance.

COMPARATIVE OVERVIEW

General rules on personal administration

Not all legal issues concerning the property relations of the spouses during marriage and the administration of personal property depend on a specific matrimonial property regime. Rules under the primary regime can be particularly influential. In some jurisdictions there are specific rules governing the acquisition and transactions in respect of the matrimonial/family home irrespective of the matrimonial property regime (see the comparative overview under Principles 4:6 and 4:7). Some legal systems also provide specific rules governing the acquisition and transactions in respect of household goods irrespective of the matrimonial property regime (see the comparative overview under Principle 4:5). Sometimes there are also other rules governing transactions entered into by one spouse irrespective of the matrimonial property regime (e.g. entering into guarantees, incurring debts), see the comparative overview under Principles 4:3 and 4:44.

The provisions on the administration of property are generally based on a division of different types of property. In particular, the rules differentiate between the administration of personal property and community property. What is considered to be personal property differs in the reviewed jurisdictions; these are particularly assets of a strictly personal nature and property owned already before the marriage (e.g. ITALY[2320]), see the comparative overview under Principle 4:36. A spouse's separate assets essentially consist of the property owned or claimed by the spouse before marriage and the property acquired by the spouse during the marriage by gift, inheritance or bequest.

The starting point in all of the jurisdictions examined is that, in principle, each spouse may independently manage and administer the property which forms part of that spouse's own private property. Personal assets are administered autonomously by the spouse to whom such assets belong without any interference by the other spouse in AUSTRIA,[2321] BELGIUM,[2322] BULGARIA,[2323] CZECH REPUBLIC,[2324] FRANCE,[2325] HUNGARY,[2326] ITALY,[2327] LITHUANIA,[2328] MALTA,[2329] THE NETHERLANDS,[2330] POLAND,[2331] PORTUGAL,[2332] RUSSIA,[2333] SLOVAKIA[2334] and SPAIN.[2335]

Administration of personal property includes in general all powers of management, enjoyment and disposition. This comprises the possibility to sell the assets or to encumber the assets with debts (e.g. BELGIUM,[2336] THE NETHERLANDS[2337] and RUSSIA[2338]).

2320 Art. 185 Italian Civil Code. See PATTI/CARICATO/IRTI/IANNICELLI/SERRA/DI STEFANO/PETÖ/BORTOLU, Italian Report, Q 34.
2321 See ROTH, Austrian Report, Q 34.
2322 Art. 1425 Belgian Civil Code. See PINTENS/ALLAERTS/SEYNS/PIGNOLET, Belgian Report, Q 34.
2323 See TODOROVA, Bulgarian Report, Q 34.
2324 See MELZER, Czech Report, Q 70.
2325 See FERRAND/BRAAT, French Report, Q 34.
2326 See WEISS/SZEIBERT, Hungarian Report, Q 34.
2327 Art. 185 Italian Civil Code. See PATTI/CARICATO/IRTI/IANNICELLI/SERRA/DI STEFANO/PETÖ/BORTOLU, Italian Report, Q 34.
2328 See MIKELENAS, Lithuanian Report, Q 34.
2329 Art. 1334 para. 2 Maltese Civil Code: The management of paraphernal property shall appertain exclusively to the spouse to whom such property belongs.
2330 Art. 1:90 Dutch Civil Code. See BOELE-WOELKI/SCHONEWILLE/SCHRAMA, Dutch Report, Q 34.
2331 See MĄCZYŃSKI, Polish Report, Q 34.
2332 Art. 1678 para. 1 Portuguese Civil Code and DE OLIVEIRA/MARTINS/VÍTOR, Portuguese Report, Q 34.
2333 See ANTOKOLSKAIA, Russian Report, Q 34.
2334 See HAŤAPKA, Slovakian Report, Q 34.
2335 See GONZÁLEZ BEILFUSS, Spanish Report, Q 34.
2336 Art. 1425 Belgian Civil Code and PINTENS/ALLAERTS/SEYNS/PIGNOLET, Belgian Report, Q 34.
2337 See BOELE-WOELKI/SCHONEWILLE/SCHRAMA, Dutch Report, Q 34.
2338 See ANTOKOLSKAIA, Russian Report, Q 34.

Administration of professional assets

In some jurisdictions there are no special rules for the administration of professional assets (AUSTRIA,[2339] LITHUANIA,[2340] MALTA,[2341] HUNGARY,[2342] POLAND,[2343] RUSSIA[2344] and SPAIN[2345]). Other jurisdictions classify professional assets as personal property of the spouse exercising the profession. Consequently, the general rules on administration apply and the respective spouse administers them freely without interference from the other spouse (BULGARIA[2346] and SPAIN[2347]).

Still other jurisdictions provide special rules for professional assets (CZECH REPUBLIC,[2348] FRANCE,[2349] ITALY,[2350] THE NETHERLANDS[2351] and PORTUGAL[2352]). This kind of administration is sometimes called exclusive or sole administration since the other spouse is excluded from decision-making authority (BELGIUM[2353] and FRANCE[2354]). This question is sometimes covered by the rules of the primary regime and supplemented by provisions of the single matrimonial regime (BELGIUM[2355]).

Generally, in the group of jurisdictions with special rules on professional assets, a distinction is made between the different categories of property to which the assets belong. For example, in ITALY[2356] and PORTUGAL,[2357] a spouse may administer her or his personal property which is used for professional purposes. One spouse may also administer community property

2339 See ROTH, Austrian Report, Q 38.
2340 See MIKELENAS, Lithuanian Report, Q 38.
2341 Art. 1324 Maltese Civil Code. See FARRUGIA, Maltese Report, Q 38.
2342 See WEISS/SZEIBERT, Hungarian Report, Q 38.
2343 See MĄCZYŃSKI, Polish Report, Q 38.
2344 See ANTOKOLSKAIA, Russian Report, Q 38.
2345 See GONZÁLEZ BEILFUSS, Spanish Report, Q 38.
2346 See TODOROVA, Bulgarian Report, Q 38.
2347 See GONZÁLEZ BEILFUSS, Spanish Report, Q 38.
2348 § 145, 146 Czech Civil Code. See MELZER, Czech Report, Q 70.
2349 Art. 1421 para. 2 French Civil Code. See FERRAND/BRAAT, French Report, Q 35, 38.
2350 Art. 178 Italian Civil Code. See PATTI/CARICATO/IRTI/IANNICELLI/SERRA/DI STEFANO/PETÖ/BORTOLU, Italian Report, Q 38.
2351 See BOELE-WOELKI/SCHONEWILLE/SCHRAMA, Dutch Report, Q 35, 38.
2352 Art. 1678 Portuguese Civil Code. See DE OLIVEIRA/MARTINS/VÍTOR, Portuguese Report, Q 38.
2353 See PINTENS/ALLAERTS/SEYNS/PIGNOLET, Belgian Report, Q 35, 38.
2354 Art. 1421 para. 2 French Civil Code. See FERRAND/BRAAT, French Report, Q 35, 38.
2355 Art. 217 para. 2 and 1417 para. 1 Belgian Civil Code. See PINTENS/ALLAERTS/SEYNS/PIGNOLET, Belgian Report, Q 35, 38.
2356 Art. 178 Italian Civil Code. See PATTI/CARICATO/IRTI/IANNICELLI/SERRA/DI STEFANO/PETÖ/BORTOLU, Italian Report, Q 38.
2357 Art. 1678 para. 2 lit. e Portuguese Civil Code. See DE OLIVEIRA/MARTINS/VÍTOR, Portuguese Report, Q 38.

insofar as it concerns transactions which are considered to constitute normal business or professional conduct (PORTUGAL[2358]). Sometimes it is merely provided that community property may be used for professional purposes (HUNGARY[2359]).

The use of professional assets has a close relationship with professional and economic activities as such. Therefore a similar solution is, that if a spouse commences an entrepreneurial activity, he or she needs the consent of the other spouse. Community property remains part of the community assets. However, subsequent transactions relating to such an activity no longer require the consent of the other spouse (SLOVAKIA[2360]).

Professional assets may also be used for credit transactions. Accordingly, in some legal systems any spouse is free to borrow community money for activities related to the exercise of his or her profession (SPAIN[2361]).

Protection of the family home and household goods

There are, however, some limits to the administration of personal property. Such restrictions mainly concern the family home owned by one of the spouses (BELGIUM,[2362] BULGARIA,[2363] FRANCE,[2364] PORTUGAL[2365] and SPAIN[2366]). There is also a special protection for a leased family home (BELGIUM[2367] and PORTUGAL[2368]) and sometimes also for household assets (SPAIN[2369] and PORTUGAL[2370]). In some legal systems these restrictions are based on the primary regime of matrimonial property law (BELGIUM[2371] and FRANCE[2372]).

2358 Art. 1678 para. 2 lit. e Portuguese Civil Code. See De Oliveira/Martins/Vítor, Portuguese Report, Q 38.
2359 See Weiss/Szeibert, Hungarian Report, Q 38.
2360 See Haťapka, Slovakian Report, Q 38.
2361 See González Beilfuss, Spanish Report, Q 35.
2362 Art. 215 para. 1 Belgian Civil Code. See Pintens/Allaerts/Seyns/Pignolet, Belgian Report, Q 34.
2363 See Todorova, Bulgarian Report, Q 34, 41.
2364 See Ferrand/Braat, French Report, Q 34.
2365 See De Oliveira/Martins/Vítor, Portuguese Report, Q 37.
2366 See González Beilfuss, Spanish Report, Q 34.
2367 Art. 215 para. 2 Belgian Civil Code. See Pintens/Allaerts/Seyns/Pignolet, Belgian Report, Q 34.
2368 Art. 1683 para. 13 Portuguese Civil Code.
2369 See González Beilfuss, Spanish Report, Q 34.
2370 See De Oliveira/Martins/Vítor, Portuguese Report, Q 11 and Q 37.
2371 See Pintens/Allaerts/Seyns/Pignolet, Belgian Report, Q 34.
2372 See Ferrand/Braat, French Report, Q 34.

COMMENT

1. There are different categories of property. Personal property belongs individually to the spouses. Therefore either spouse may administer his or her personal property without interference of the other spouse. This is in accordance with the common core of the legal systems.

2. However, there may be restrictions in the interest of the marriage and the family. Principle 4:47 recognises that the independence of the spouses must give way to the protection of the family home and the household goods (see also Principles 4:6 and 4:7).

3. There is no special principle for the administration of professional assets, i.e. property which is used for professional purposes. Assets exclusively acquired for either spouse's profession are part of his or her personal property according to Principle 4:36(e). If there is community property, then the performance of professional und business activities of the spouses can be reached by application of the general rules on administration of community property (Principle 4:44(1)). A spouse, who follows a separate profession, has the sole power to perform acts of administration and disposition necessary for it.

Principle 4:48 Divestment of the right to administer community property

(1) Upon application by one spouse the competent authority may divest the other spouse of the right to administer in whole or in part the community property on the grounds of

(a) inability to express his or her intentions;

(b) serious maladministration; or

(c) serious failure to comply with the duty to inform in accordance with Principle 4:8.

(2) To the extent that one spouse has been divested of the right to administer the community property the power vests exclusively in the other spouse.

(3) Upon application of either spouse the competent authority may reinstate the divested spouse.

Principe 4:48 Retrait du droit d'administrer la communauté

(1) A la requête d'un époux, l'autorité compétente peut priver l'autre époux du droit d'administrer tout ou partie de la communauté en raison

(a) d'une impossibilité de manifester sa volonté;

(b) de graves fautes d'administration; ou

(c) d'une grave violation de l'obligation d'information énoncée au Principe 4:8.

(2) L'autre époux est seul habilité à administrer la communauté dans la mesure de la privation du droit d'administration de son conjoint.

(3) A la demande de l'un ou l'autre époux, l'autorité compétente peut restituer à l'époux destitué son droit d'administration.

Prinzip 4:48 Entziehung des Rechts zur Verwaltung des gemeinschaftlichen Vermögens

(1) Auf Antrag eines Ehegatten kann die zuständige Behörde dem anderen das Recht, das gemeinschaftliche Vermögen zu verwalten, ganz oder teilweise entziehen wegen

(a) Unfähigkeit, den eigenen Willen zu äußern;

(b) schwerwiegender mangelhafter Verwaltung; oder

(c) schwerwiegender Verletzung der Verpflichtung zur Information nach Prinzip 4:8.

(2) In dem Ausmaß, in dem einem der Ehegatten das Recht zur Verwaltung des gemeinschaftlichen Vermögens entzogen wird, steht die Befugnis dem anderen allein zu.

(3) Auf Antrag jedes der Ehegatten kann die zuständige Behörde dem Ehegatten das ihm entzogene Recht zur Verwaltung wieder einräumen.

INTERNATIONAL INSTRUMENTS

Protective measures may be ordered under the *Hague Convention on the Protection of Adults of 2000*. The competent authority may deal in particular with the designation and functions of any person or body having charge of the adult's property, representing or assisting the adult, the administration, conservation or disposal of the adult's property and the authorisation of a specific intervention for the protection of the property of the adult (Article 3(d), (f) and (g)). However, the Convention does not apply to property regimes in respect of marriage (Article 4 1)(c)).

COMPARATIVE OVERVIEW

Consequences of a violation of the rules for administration

In addition to the invalidity of acts there may be several other consequences as a result of a violation of the rules for administration. In some jurisdictions protective measures of the court against damaging administrative transactions may be prescribed (FRANCE[2373]). Also a formal declaration by the court that a spouse is excluded from administration is possible (BELGIUM[2374] and ITALY[2375]).

In cases where it can be proved that the rights of the other spouse in the community are endangered, the ultimate remedy is to dissolve the community (BELGIUM,[2376] THE NETHERLANDS,[2377] PORTUGAL[2378] and SPAIN[2379]). An alternative is for the share of the maladministrating spouse in the community property to be reduced (LITHUANIA[2380]).

Several claims based on general civil law and on special provisions of matrimonial property law may also exist between the spouses. Under general civil law in some jurisdictions possessory actions are admissible (AUSTRIA[2381]). The *actio negatoria* is also possible for the other spouse (AUSTRIA[2382]). The *actio*

2373 See FERRAND/BRAAT, French Report, Q 41.
2374 Art. 1426 Belgian Civil Code. See PINTENS/ALLAERTS/SEYNS/PIGNOLET, Belgian Report, Q 40.
2375 Art. 183 para. 1 Italian Civil Code. See PATTI/CARICATO/IRTI/IANNICELLI/SERRA/DI STEFANO/PETÖ/BORTOLU, Italian Report, Q 41.
2376 Art. 1472 Belgian Civil Code. See PINTENS/ALLAERTS/SEYNS/PIGNOLET, Belgian Report, Q 40.
2377 Art. 1:109 Dutch Civil Code. See BOELE-WOELKI/SCHONEWILLE/SCHRAMA, Dutch Report, Q 41.
2378 See DE OLIVEIRA/MARTINS/VÍTOR, Portuguese Report, Q 41.
2379 See GONZÁLEZ BEILFUSS, Spanish Report, Q 40.
2380 See MIKELENAS, Lithuanian Report, Q 41.
2381 See ROTH, Austrian Report, Q 41.
2382 See ROTH, Austrian Report, Q 41.

publicana is another remedy under civil law (AUSTRIA[2383]). Compensation claims based on the general rules of civil law or on special provisions may exist (AUSTRIA,[2384] BELGIUM,[2385] THE NETHERLANDS,[2386] POLAND,[2387] RUSSIA[2388] and SPAIN[2389]). The compensation claim generally is in favour of the community. According to the law of non-contractual obligations an action for unjust enrichment is also conceivable (AUSTRIA[2390] and MALTA[2391]).

Inability to administer property

Problems in the administration of property may be caused in a variety of ways. For example, one spouse may, in an enduring way, be unable to express his or her wish, or may imperil the interests of the family, either by allowing his or her separate property to waste away or by dissipating or embezzling the income withdrawn from them. This is relevant if it removes or limits the competence to perform legal acts. One reason for incapability of administration is mental disorder but in other (less common) cases a spouse may be absent or a minor.

The inability of the spouse may only be a factual one where he or she cannot act autonomously or there may be a court decision declaring legal incapability or incompetence. In the latter case, at least, there is a strong relationship with the law of protection of handicapped persons. In some jurisdictions matrimonial law does not contain a specific regulation on this matter (POLAND[2392] and RUSSIA[2393]). However, most legal systems provide for solutions in matrimonial property law when a spouse is unable to manage and administer his or her property.

Inability to administer personal property

One possible consequence if a spouse is unable to administer his or her personal property is that upon the other spouse's application, the incapable spouse may be divested of the rights of administration and enjoyment (FRANCE[2394]). Similarly, in other jurisdictions a formal declaration by the court that the incapable spouse

---

[2383] See ROTH, Austrian Report, Q 41.
[2384] Art. 372 et seq. Austrian Civil Code. See ROTH, Austrian Report, Q 41.
[2385] See PINTENS/ALLAERTS/SEYNS/PIGNOLET, Belgian Report, Q 40.
[2386] See BOELE-WOELKI/SCHONEWILLE/SCHRAMA, Dutch Report, Q 41.
[2387] See MĄCZYŃSKI, Polish Report, Q 41.
[2388] See ANTOKOLSKAIA, Russian Report, Q 41.
[2389] Art. 1322 Spanish Civil Code. See GONZÁLEZ BEILFUSS, Spanish Report, Q 41.
[2390] See ROTH, Austrian Report, Q 41.
[2391] See FARRUGIA, Maltese Report, Q 41.
[2392] See MĄCZYŃSKI, Polish Report, Q 42.
[2393] See ANTOKOLSKAIA, Russian Report, Q 42.
[2394] Art. 1429 French Civil Code. See FERRAND/BRAAT, French Report, Q 42.

is excluded from administration is possible (ITALY[2395]). Generally, the appointment of a judicial administrator, curator, trustee or a guardian will follow (AUSTRIA,[2396] BELGIUM,[2397] BULGARIA,[2398] CZECH REPUBLIC,[2399] FRANCE,[2400] HUNGARY,[2401] LITHUANIA,[2402] MALTA,[2403] RUSSIA[2404] and SLOVAKIA[2405]). It is also possible for the other spouse to become the administrator or guardian and legal representative of the incapacitated spouse (RUSSIA[2406] and SPAIN[2407]).

It is also possible for a judgment to grant the applicant spouse the power to administer the separate property of the divested spouse (BELGIUM,[2408] FRANCE,[2409] and THE NETHERLANDS[2410]). From the time of the application, the deprived spouse may only dispose alone of the bare ownership of his or her property (FRANCE[2411]). However, he or she may, subsequently, request the court to order restitution of his or her rights, if he or she establishes that the causes which had justified the divesting no longer exist (FRANCE[2412]).

There are also situations where one spouse may act for the personal property of the other in the case of factual incapability of the other spouse without being authorized by a court decision (PORTUGAL[2413]).

Inability to administer community property

The consequences of the inability of a spouse to administer community property are mainly the same as for personal property. One possible consequence is the

2395 Art. 183 para. 1 Italian Civil Code. See PATTI/CARICATO/IRTI/IANNICELLI/SERRA/DI STEFANO/PETÖ/BORTOLU, Italian Report, Q 42.
2396 See ROTH, Austrian Report, Q 42.
2397 Art. 1426 Belgian Civil Code. See PINTENS/ALLAERTS/SEYNS/PIGNOLET, Belgian Report, Q 42.
2398 See TODOROVA, Bulgarian Report, Q 42.
2399 See MELZER, Czech Report, Q 77.
2400 See FERRAND/BRAAT, French Report, Q 42.
2401 See WEISS/SZEIBERT, Hungarian Report, Q 42.
2402 See MIKELENAS, Lithuanian Report, Q 42.
2403 See FARRUGIA, Maltese Report, Q 42.
2404 Arts. 32 and 33 Russian Civil Code.
2405 See HAŤAPKA, Slovakian Report, Q 42.
2406 See ANTOKOLSKAIA, Russian Report, Q 42.
2407 See GONZÁLEZ BEILFUSS, Spanish Report, Q 42.
2408 Art. 1420 Belgian Civil Code. See PINTENS/ALLAERTS/SEYNS/PIGNOLET, Belgian Report, Q 42.
2409 Art. 1429 French Civil Code. See FERRAND/BRAAT, French Report, Q 42.
2410 See BOELE-WOELKI/SCHONEWILLE/SCHRAMA, Dutch Report, Q 42.
2411 Art. 1429 French Civil Code. See FERRAND/BRAAT, French Report, Q 42.
2412 Art. 1429 French Civil Code. See FERRAND/BRAAT, French Report, Q 42.
2413 Art. 1678 para. 2 lit. F and Art. 1679 Portuguese Civil Code. See DE OLIVEIRA/MARTINS/VÍTOR, Portuguese Report, Q 42.

appointment of a curator, guardian or trustee (AUSTRIA,[2414] BELGIUM,[2415] BULGARIA,[2416] CZECH REPUBLIC,[2417] HUNGARY,[2418] ITALY,[2419] LITHUANIA,[2420] MALTA,[2421] RUSSIA[2422] and SLOVAKIA[2423]). Another possibility is that the other spouse may act alone if there is a court decision declaring that he or she may administer the community property individually (BELGIUM,[2424] THE NETHERLANDS[2425] and SPAIN[2426]). The same result may be reached having regard to the needs of the household (LITHUANIA[2427]).

An alternative solution without the formalities of a guardianship exists under matrimonial law. Where one of the spouses is, in an enduring way, unable to express his or her wish, or if his or her management of the community reveals unfitness or fraud, the other spouse may request in court to be substituted for him or her in the exercise of those powers (FRANCE[2428] and POLAND[2429]). In many jurisdictions the other spouse may be authorized to administer the community property individually (SPAIN[2430]). The legal basis for such judicial measures is sometimes found in the provisions of the so-called regime primaire (BELGIUM[2431] and FRANCE[2432]).

A spouse thus entitled by court has the same powers which the spouse whom he or she replaces would have had; he or she may, with the authorisation of the court, enter into transactions for which his or her consent would have been required if a substitution had not taken place (FRANCE[2433]). A spouse who is divested of his or her powers may subsequently apply to a court for the restitution of their rights, by establishing that their transfer to the other spouse is no longer

2414 See ROTH, Austrian Report, Q 42.
2415 Art. 1426 Belgian Civil Code. See PINTENS/ALLAERTS/SEYNS/PIGNOLET, Belgian Report, Q 42.
2416 See TODOROVA, Bulgarian Report, Q 42.
2417 See MELZER, Czech Report, Q 77.
2418 See WEISS/SZEIBERT, Hungarian Report, Q 42.
2419 Art. 182 para. 1 Italian Civil Code. See PATTI/CARICATO/IRTI/IANNICELLI/SERRA/DI STEFANO/PETÖ/BORTOLU, Italian Report, Q 42.
2420 See MIKELENAS, Lithuanian Report, Q 42.
2421 See FARRUGIA, Maltese Report, Q 42.
2422 Art. 32 and 33 Russian Civil Code.
2423 See HAŤAPKA, Slovakian Report, Q 42.
2424 Art. 1420 Belgian Civil Code. See PINTENS/ALLAERTS/SEYNS/PIGNOLET, Belgian Report, Q 42.
2425 See BOELE-WOELKI/SCHONEWILLE/SCHRAMA, Dutch Report, Q 42.
2426 See GONZÁLEZ BEILFUSS, Spanish Report, Q 35, 42.
2427 Art. 3.32 para. 2 Lithuanian Civil Code. See MIKELENAS, Lithuanian Report, Q 34, 35, 42.
2428 See FERRAND/BRAAT, French Report, Q 42.
2429 See MĄCZYŃSKI, Polish Report, Q 42.
2430 See GONZÁLEZ BEILFUSS, Spanish Report, Q 42.
2431 See PINTENS/ALLAERTS/SEYNS/PIGNOLET, Belgian Report, Q 42.
2432 Art. 217 French Civil Code. See FERRAND/BRAAT, French Report, Q 42.
2433 See FERRAND/BRAAT, French Report, Q 42.

justified (FRANCE[2434]). Some jurisdictions also allow one spouse to act for community property in the case of factual inability of the other spouse without being authorised by a court decision (PORTUGAL[2435]).

The legal incompetence of a spouse may also be a ground for the dissolution of the community of property during the marriage (e.g. BULGARIA[2436] and SLOVAKIA[2437]), see the comparative overview under Principle 4:26.

Maladministration of personal property

In cases of simple maladministration of personal property by waste, dissipation or embezzling the income drawn from such assets, several remedies are possible. Upon application of the other spouse, the spouse may be dispossessed of his or her rights of administration and enjoyment (FRANCE[2438] and POLAND[2439]). A court decision confers on the plaintiff spouse the power to administer the separate property of the dispossessed spouse. The appointment of a judicial administrator is also possible (FRANCE[2440]).

As far as community property is concerned several reactions are possible. A court may prescribe urgent measures to protect the family interests (FRANCE[2441]). The spouse who managed the property may be obliged to answer to his or her faults (FRANCE[2442]); his or her transactions could not be enforced against the other spouse (FRANCE[2443]).

Another sanction is that his or her powers of administration could be transferred to the other spouse (FRANCE[2444]). The other spouse may sue in court for dissolution of the community or separation of property (FRANCE,[2445] ITALY,[2446] PORTUGAL[2447] and SPAIN[2448]).

2434 See FERRAND/BRAAT, French Report, Q 42.
2435 Art. 1678 para. 2 lit. f and Art. 1679 Portuguese Civil Code. See DE OLIVEIRA/MARTINS/VÍTOR, Portuguese Report, Q 42.
2436 See TODOROVA, Bulgarian Report, Q 42.
2437 See HAŤAPKA, Slovakian Report, Q 42.
2438 See FERRAND/BRAAT, French Report, Q 41.
2439 Art. 40 Polish Family and Guardianship Act.
2440 See FERRAND/BRAAT, French Report, Q 41.
2441 See FERRAND/BRAAT, French Report, Q 41.
2442 Art. 1421 French Civil Code. See FERRAND/BRAAT, French Report, Q 41.
2443 Art. 1421 French Civil Code. See FERRAND/BRAAT, French Report, Q 41.
2444 Art. 1426 French Civil Code. See FERRAND/BRAAT, French Report, Q 41.
2445 Art. 1443 French Civil Code. See FERRAND/BRAAT, French Report, Q 41.
2446 Art. 193 Italian Civil Code.
2447 See DE OLIVEIRA/MARTINS/VÍTOR, Portuguese Report, Q 41.
2448 See GONZÁLEZ BEILFUSS, Spanish Report, Q 41.

A narrowing of the assets forming the community property of the spouses to the common furnishings of the common household is sometimes possible (CZECH REPUBLIC[2449]). There can also be protective measures if there is an execution against the personal property of the spouse (HUNGARY[2450]).

COMMENT

1. There must be a protection for the future against acts which require the consent of both spouses but which have been performed by one spouse without the consent of the other spouse. In respect of past acts, protection is offered in the form of an annulment of acts of administration (Principle 4:46). Protection is also necessary where one of the spouses is not able to participate in the management of the community property.

2. The competent authority may, at the request of a spouse, order the exclusion of the other spouse either generally or limitedly for particular purposes or acts, from the administration of the community of property. This should be restricted to three cases. One is where the spouse is not competent to administer (Principle 4:48(1)(a)). Inability mainly encompasses cases of mental disorder or absence. Other situations include the inability to administer the property properly for other reasons. There are close links with the general rules on incapacity and also with the protection of incapacitated persons. It is, however, useful to have a separate rule also in matrimonial property law. The details for final and interim protective measures are left to national law. Incapacity can also lead to a dissolution of the community of acquisitions, see Principle 4:49(d).

3. The second case is where the spouse has mismanaged the community property (Principle 4:48(1)(b)). Mismanagement in a broad sense covers different cases of financial mismanagement, for example gross or minor mismanagement, wilful or reckless dissipation of community property, endangering the matrimonial property or seriously diminishing its value. Mismanagement can also lead to a dissolution of the community of acquisitions, see Principle 4:49(d). The third case is where the duty to inform has not been performed and there is a serious violation of this duty (Principle 4:48 (1) (c)).

4. Even if one spouse is incapacitated or otherwise unable to participate in the administration of community property, the administration of the community of property must be secured. According to Principle 4:48(2) the power to

2449 § 148 Czech Civil Code. See MELZER, Czech Report, Q 76.
2450 See WEISS/SZEIBERT, Hungarian Report, Q 41.

administer vests, to the extent to which a spouse has been excluded, exclusively in the other spouse who may assume sole powers of administration.

5. According to Principle 4:48(3) changed circumstances have to be taken into account. The spouse who has been excluded from administering common property may, if the grounds upon which he or she has been excluded no longer subsist, request the competent authority to reinstate him or her in the administration

6. The possible consequences if a spouse is incapable of administering his or her personal property and community property should be broadly the same. Special measures and an appointment of a guardian may be necessary. However, no separate principle on the administration of personal property in case of incapacity has been developed since this issue is better considered as belonging to the protection of incapacitated adults which does not fall into the scope of these Principles.

DISSOLUTION
DISSOLUTION
BEENDIGUNG

Principle 4:49 Grounds for dissolution
The community of acquisitions regime is dissolved by
- (a) the death of a spouse;
- (b) the annulment of the marriage, divorce or legal separation;
- (c) the change of the matrimonial property regime by agreement between the spouses; or
- (d) the decision of the competent authority based upon serious grounds ordering separation of property.

Principe 4:49 Causes de dissolution
Le régime de communauté d'acquêts est dissous par
- (a) le décès d'un époux;
- (b) l'annulation du mariage, le divorce ou la séparation de corps;
- (c) le changement de régime matrimonial par convention entre les époux; ou
- (d) la séparation de biens ordonnée par l'autorité compétente pour motifs graves.

Prinzip 4:49 Gründe für die Beendigung
Die Errungenschaftsgemeinschaft wird beendet durch
- (a) den Tod eines Ehegatten;
- (b) die Nichtigerklärung der Ehe, Ehescheidung oder gesetzliche Trennung;
- (c) die Änderung des Güterstands durch Vertrag zwischen den Ehegatten; oder
- (d) die aus wichtigen Gründen Gütertrennung anordnende Entscheidung der zuständigen Behörde.

INTERNATIONAL INSTRUMENTS

None of particular relevance.

COMPARATIVE OVERVIEW

There are several grounds upon which the community of acquisitions is dissolved. In the case of most of these grounds, especially when the community is dissolved as a consequence of the dissolution of the marriage, the dissolution of the community operates *ex lege*. For other grounds a decision by a competent authority is necessary.

Death

In all the jurisdictions surveyed the community property regime is dissolved by death of a spouse.[2451] The dissolution operates *ex lege*. In cases where a body has not been found but from the circumstances it can be concluded that death is certain, a competent authority may issue a declaration of death as in BELGIUM,[2452] CZECH REPUBLIC,[2453] FRANCE,[2454] PORTUGAL,[2455] RUSSIA[2456] and SPAIN.[2457]

Absence

Most jurisdictions equate a declaration of absence of a spouse with dissolution by death. This is, for example, the case in BELGIUM,[2458] FRANCE,[2459] ITALY,[2460] LITHUANIA,[2461] PORTUGAL,[2462] SLOVAKIA[2463] and SPAIN.[2464] In THE NETHERLANDS the community property regime is dissolved where a spouse's existence is uncertain in conformity with Article 1:412–425 Dutch Civil Code and the other spouse remarries or enters into a registered partnership.[2465]

Annulment of the marriage

Some jurisdictions expressly state in their matrimonial property law that the community property regime is dissolved by annulment of the marriage as in

2451 See all national reports, Q 43.
2452 Art. 126 Belgian Civil Code.
2453 § 22 para. 1 Czech Family Act. See MELZER, Czech Report, Q 78.
2454 Art. 88 French Civil Code.
2455 Art. 114 Portuguese Civil Code.
2456 Art. 45 Russian Civil Code.
2457 Art. 1392 para. 1 Spanish Civil Code.
2458 Art. 121 § 1 para. 2 Belgian Civil Code.
2459 Art. 1441 French Civil Code.
2460 See PATTI/CARICATO/IRTI/IANNICELLI/SERRA/DI STEFANO/PETÖ/BORTULU, Italian Report, Q 43.
2461 Art. 3.100 Lithuanian Civil Code.
2462 See DE OLIVEIRA/MARTINS/VÍTOR, Portuguese Report, Q 43.
2463 Art. 3.100 Lithuanian Civil Code.
2464 Art. 1392 para. 1 Spanish Civil Code.
2465 See BOELE-WOELKI/SCHONEWILLE/SCHRAMA, Dutch Report, Q 43.

AUSTRIA,[2466] BULGARIA,[2467] ITALY,[2468] LITHUANIA,[2469] PORTUGAL,[2470] RUSSIA[2471] and SPAIN.[2472] In other legal systems, such as BELGIUM[2473] and FRANCE,[2474] matrimonial property law does not expressly state that the annulment of the marriage is a ground for dissolution of the community property regime. But also it is clear nevertheless that in these legal systems the annulment dissolves the regime since this annulment erases all effects of the marriage. In POLAND,[2475] the law states that in case of annulment the proprietary consequences of the marriage are regulated as in case of divorce, which means that the community is dissolved.

Divorce

In all the jurisdictions surveyed divorce dissolves the community regime.[2476]

In ITALY,[2477] a distinction is made between a civil marriage and a canon marriage with civil effects. In the former case divorce dissolves the marriage and the community regime. In the latter case a divorce does not dissolve the marriage but only terminates her civil effects including the community regime.

Legal separation

Legal separation or separation *a mensa e thoro* does not dissolve the marriage but formalizes a separation. Since the *affectio maritalis* has ceased, the legal separation is a ground for dissolution of the community property regime *ex lege* in BELGIUM,[2478] FRANCE,[2479] ITALY,[2480] THE NETHERLANDS,[2481] PORTUGAL[2482] and SPAIN.[2483] Similarly, in MALTA,[2484] legal separation may dissolve the

2466 § 1265 Austrian Civil Code. See ROTH, Austrian Report, Q 43.
2467 Art. 26 para. 1 Bulgarian Family Law.
2468 Art. 191 Italian Civil Code.
2469 Art. 3.100 Lithuanian Civil Code.
2470 See DE OLIVEIRA/MARTINS/VÍTOR, Portuguese Report, Q 43.
2471 Art. 30 para. 2 Russian Family Code; with retroactive effect.
2472 Art. 1392 para. 2 Spanish Civil Code.
2473 Argument from Art. 201 Belgian Civil Code.
2474 Argument from Art. 201 French Civil Code.
2475 Art. 21 Polish Family and Guardianship Code.
2476 See Q 43.
2477 See PATTI/CARICATO/IRTI/IANNICELLI/SERRA/DI STEFANO/PETÖ/BORTULU, Italian Report, Q 43.
2478 Art. 1427 Belgian Civil Code.
2479 Art. 1441 French Civil Code.
2480 Art. 191 Italian Civil Code. The separation can be judicial or consensual (Art. 150 Italian Civil Code). But a consensual separation can only have legal effects after homologation by the court (Art. 158 Italian Civil Code).
2481 Art. 1:99 para. 1 Dutch Civil Code.
2482 See DE OLIVEIRA/MARTINS/VÍTOR, Portuguese Report, Q 43.
2483 Art. 1392.3 Spanish Civil Code.
2484 Art. 55 para. 1 Maltese Civil Code.

community. The court may, however, where in its opinion circumstances so warrant, direct that an asset or assets comprised in the community be not partitioned before the lapse of such period after the cessation of the community as it may in its direction determine.[2485] In POLAND,[2486] the community is also dissolved and separation of property is established.[2487] But the spouses can agree to continue the community regime.

Factual separation

In most legal systems factual separation is not a ground for dissolution of the community property regime. The exceptions are LITHUANIA[2488] and HUNGARY,[2489] where the community of property regime is dissolved when the matrimonial community of life terminates.[2490] In BULGARIA,[2491] a factual separation that creates inconvenience for the spouses to use and administer the community assets can be a serious reason for a judicial separation of property. But the court can also decide to restrict the dissolution to certain assets. In SPAIN,[2492] a factual separation of one year is a ground for a judicial separation of property, although there is case law favouring dissolution without spousal request in case of a prolonged separation.

Change of the matrimonial property regime by the spouses

In all the jurisdictions surveyed the community property regime can be dissolved by a change of the matrimonial regime that necessitates the liquidation of the former one.[2493] For this to occur a specific procedure has to be followed. This applies in AUSTRIA,[2494] BELGIUM,[2495] FRANCE,[2496] HUNGARY,[2497] ITALY,[2498]

2485 Art. 55 para. 7 Maltese Civil Code.
2486 Art. 54 para. 2 Polish Family and Guardianship Code.
2487 Art. 54 para. 1 Polish Family and Guardianship Code.
2488 See MIKELENAS, Lithuanian Report, Q 43.
2489 The last or final termination has the above-mentioned consequence.
2490 § 43 para. 2 Family Act. See WEISS/SZEIBERT, Hungarian Report, Q 43.
2491 See TODOROVA, Bulgarian Report, Q 43.
2492 Art. 1393.3 Spanish Civil Code. See GONZÁLEZ BEILFUSS, Spanish Report, Q 43.
2493 Portugal is an exception. According to the principle of immutability, the matrimonial regime cannot be changed after the celebration of marriage, except in cases relating to Art. 1715 of the Portuguese Civil Code.
2494 See ROTH, Austrian Report, Q 43.
2495 Art. 1427 Belgian Civil Code.
2496 Art. 1441 French Civil Code.
2497 § 27 para. 2 Hungarian Family Act.
2498 See PATTI/CARICATO/IRTI/IANNICELLI/SERRA/DI STEFANO/PETÖ/BORTULU, Italian Report, Q 43.

LITHUANIA,[2499] THE NETHERLANDS,[2500] POLAND,[2501] RUSSIA[2502] and SPAIN.[2503] In BULGARIA this possibility exists since 2009.[2504]

Decision by a competent authority ordering separation of property

In most of the jurisdictions surveyed a spouse can apply to the competent authority for a separation of property as in BELGIUM,[2505] BULGARIA,[2506] FRANCE,[2507] HUNGARY,[2508] ITALY,[2509] LITHUANIA,[2510] MALTA,[2511] THE NETHERLANDS,[2512] POLAND,[2513] PORTUGAL,[2514] RUSSIA,[2515] SLOVAKIA[2516] and SPAIN.[2517] In AUSTRIA,[2518] a unilateral request for such separation is not allowed.

Serious reasons for making such applications are necessary. In most jurisdictions the law does not detail what kind of reasons can be invoked but uses a general clause, mostly focusing on maladministration in a broad sense by one spouse endangering the interests of the other spouse as in BELGIUM,[2519] BULGARIA[2520] and FRANCE.[2521] In other jurisdictions the law is more detailed and comprises other additional grounds as in SPAIN.[2522] Exceptionally, the law does not offer the possibility to request a separation of property on the basis of a general clause or of a large list of specific grounds left to the appreciation of the court but only allows a separation of property on a few specific grounds operating *ex lege* as in the CZECH REPUBLIC.[2523]

2499 Art. 3.100 Lithuanian Civil Code.
2500 Art. 1:99 para. 1 Dutch Civil Code.
2501 Art. 47 Polish Family and Guardianship Code.
2502 See ANTOKOLSKAIA, Russian Report, Q 43.
2503 Art. 1392 para. 4 Spanish Civil Code. See GONZÁLEZ BEILFUSS, Spanish Report, Q 43.
2504 Art. 27 para. 3 Bulgarian Family Code of 2009.
2505 Art. 1427 Belgian Civil Code.
2506 Art. 26 para. 2 Bulgarian Family Code.
2507 Art. 1441 and 1443 French Civil Code.
2508 § 31 para. 1 Hungarian Family Act.
2509 Art. 193 Italian Civil Code.
2510 Art. 3.100 Lithuanian Civil Code.
2511 Art. 1332 Maltese Civil Code.
2512 Art. 1:99 para. 1 Dutch Civil Code.
2513 Art. 52 Polish Family and Guardianship Code.
2514 See DE OLIVEIRA/MARTINS/VÍTOR, Portuguese Report, Q 43.
2515 Art. 38 para. 2 Russian Family Code.
2516 See HAŤAPKA, Slovakian Report, Q 43.
2517 Art. 1393 Spanish Civil Code.
2518 See ROTH, Austrian Report, Q 43.
2519 Art. 1470 Belgian Civil Code.
2520 Art. 27 para. 3 Bulgarian Family Code.
2521 Art. 1443 French Civil Code.
2522 Art. 1393 Spanish Civil Code. See GONZÁLEZ BEILFUSS, Spanish Report, Q 43.
2523 See MELZER, Czech Report, Q 78.

The main ground for a separation of property is the maladministration of personal and community assets which defrauds the community property or damages or endangers the rights of the other spouse in the community. Examples are BELGIUM,[2524] FRANCE,[2525] ITALY,[2526] PORTUGAL,[2527] SLOVAKIA[2528] and SPAIN.[2529] Prodigality can also be considered to be maladministration (SPAIN[2530]).

Some legal systems use a broader concept and accept as a serious reason the irresponsible behaviour of a spouse that jeopardises the interests of the other family members as in BULGARIA.[2531] In ITALY,[2532] a separation of property is admitted when certain actions damage the interests of a spouse. Examples under SLOVAKIAN law[2533] are situations where a spouse does not contribute to the formation of the community, avoids to work, does not live permanently with his family and does not attend to the needs of the family. In SPAIN,[2534] a criminal conviction of abandoning the family is a serious reason.

In SPAIN,[2535] a spouse can also request a separation of property if a final court decision has incapacitated the other spouse. The same rule exists in SLOVAKIA.[2536] In BULGARIA,[2537] a separation of property is possible when a spouse becomes incapable to administer his or her personal and community assets. Furthermore, in SPAIN,[2538] a request for separation of property is possible when a spouse has been declared absent and a declaration of insolvency is a specific legal ground.

In a few legal systems, a specific rule provides for the possibility of requesting a separation of property in cases of factual separation. SPANISH law[2539] offers this possibility after a one year separation. In BULGARIA,[2540] the factual separation that creates inconvenience for the spouses to use and administer the community

2524 Art. 1470 Belgian Civil Code.
2525 Art. 1443 Spanish Civil Code.
2526 See PATTI/CARICATO/IRTI/IANNICELLI/SERRA/DI STEFANO/PETÖ/BORTULU, Italian Report, Q 43.
2527 See DE OLIVEIRA/MARTINS/VÍTOR, Portuguese Report, Q 41.
2528 See PATTI/CARICATO/IRTI/IANNICELLI/SERRA/DI STEFANO/PETÖ/BORTULU, Italian Report, Q 43.
2529 Art. 1393 para. 3 Spanish Civil Code. See GONZÁLEZ BEILFUSS, Spanish Report, Q 43.
2530 See GONZÁLEZ BEILFUSS, Spanish Report, Q 43.
2531 See TODOROVA, Bulgarian Report, Q 43.
2532 See PATTI/CARICATO/IRTI/IANNICELLI/SERRA/DI STEFANO/PETÖ/BORTULU, Italian Report, Q 43.
2533 See HAŤAPKA, Slovakian Report, Q 43.
2534 Art. 1393 para. 1 Spanish Civil Code. See GONZÁLEZ BEILFUSS, Spanish Report, Q 43.
2535 Art. 1393 Spanish Civil Code. See GONZÁLEZ BEILFUSS, Spanish Report, Q 43.
2536 See HAŤAPKA, Slovakian Report, Q 43.
2537 Supreme Court Judgment N° 5/1972. See TODOROVA, Bulgarian Report, Q 43.
2538 Art. 1393 Spanish Civil Code.
2539 Art. 1393.3 Spanish Civil Code. See GONZÁLEZ BEILFUSS, Spanish Report, Q 43.
2540 See TODOROVA, Bulgarian Report, Q 43.

assets is a serious reason for a separation of property. In SLOVAKIA,[2541] the factual separation as such is not a ground for a separation of property – it is only when the court establishes that the separation is permanent and irreversible and has an influence on the further continuation of the marriage, that it can be qualified as a serious ground. In addition, SLOVAKIAN law[2542] provides that a spouse may apply for separation of property if the other spouse starts a business or has received a permit to do so.

Bankruptcy and insolvency

In some legal systems, bankruptcy is a ground for *ex lege* dissolution as in AUSTRIA,[2543] CZECH REPUBLIC,[2544] ITALY[2545] POLAND,[2546] PORTUGAL[2547] and SLOVAKIA.[2548] In AUSTRIA[2549] and BULGARIA,[2550] the commencement of an insolvency procedure against a spouse dissolves the community property regime.

In other legal systems insolvency can only be a ground for a separation of property (see above).

Action by a creditor

In BULGARIAN law,[2551] the execution of a personal debt against community assets terminates *ex lege* the community property regime but only regarding those assets. In LITHUANIA,[2552] a creditor can request the dissolution and liquidation of the community.

Forfeiture of property

A few legal systems dissolve the community *ex lege* when in criminal proceedings a spouse is punished with the sanction of forfeiture of property as in the CZECH REPUBLIC[2553] and SLOVAKIA.[2554]

2541 See HAŤAPKA, Slovakian Report, Q 43.
2542 See HAŤAPKA, Slovakian Report, Q 43.
2543 § 1262 Austrian Civil Code.
2544 § 268 para. 1 Czech Insolvency Law.
2545 See PATTI/CARICATO/IRTI/IANNICELLI/SERRA/DI STEFANO/PETÖ/BORTULU, Italian Report, Q 43.
2546 Art. 53 para. 1 Polish Family and Guardianship Code.
2547 See DE OLIVEIRA/MARTINS/VÍTOR, Portuguese Report, Q 43.
2548 See HAŤAPKA, Slovakian Report, Q 43.
2549 § 1262 Austrian Civil Code. See ROTH, Austrian Report, Q 43.
2550 Art. 27 para. 5 Bulgarian Family Code. See TODOROVA, Bulgarian Report, Q 43.
2551 Art. 26 para. 3 Bulgarian Family Code. See TODOROVA, Bulgarian Report, Q 43.
2552 See MIKELENAS, Lithuanian Report, Q 43.
2553 § 52 para. 2 Czech Criminal Code. See MELZER, Czech Report, Q 78.
2554 See HAŤAPKA, Slovakian Report, Q 43.

Incapacity

Only a few legal systems, for example POLAND,[2555] have a rule dissolving the community property regime *ex lege* in cases of incapacity of a spouse whereas in other jurisdictions, incapacity can be a serious ground upon which a decision ordering separation of property may be based (see above).

COMMENT

1. Principle 4:49 reflects the common core of the legal systems by listing the grounds by which dissolution of the community of acquisitions takes place.

2. Principle 4:49(a) determines that the death of a spouse is a ground for dissolution. However, this ground does not apply to missing and absent persons. Instead this issue is left to national law to decide since many legal systems do not regulate their consequences in matrimonial property law but in the law on persons.

3. In accordance with the common core, the annulment of the marriage, divorce and legal separation are listed under Principle 4:49(b) as grounds for the dissolution of the community of acquisitions.

4. Dissolution by the change of the matrimonial regime as listed under Principle 4:49(c) reflects also the common core of the systems surveyed. Only the complete change of a regime into another regime leads to the dissolution of the previous regime. The change of the matrimonial regime needs a marital property agreement (see Principle 4:10(2)). Principle 4:11 sets out the requirements as to the form of such an agreement.

5. Principle 4:49(d) regarding the dissolution by decision of the competent authority ordering separation of property upon serious grounds reflects the common core of almost all the legal systems surveyed. Principle 4:49(d) does not detail those grounds although several legal systems do so. Given the large variety of reasons established by national legislation and case law, it is advisable to leave the enumeration of the reasons to the competent authority.

6. The comparative overview offers the necessary examples of serious reasons. The main category relates to the maladministration of the community (see Principle 4:48). Another category is linked to the marriage and covers neglect of

---

2555 Art. 53 para. 1 Polish Family and Guardianship Code.

marital duties and factual separation. A third category of reasons concerning the status of a spouse can be identified as, for example, absence and incapacity.

7. As stated in the comparative overview some legal systems allow dissolution on other specific grounds such as factual separation, bankruptcy, insolvency, action by a creditor, forfeiture of property or incapacity. Since those jurisdictions do not represent the common core of the legal systems surveyed and do not reflect a better law approach those grounds are not specified as independant dissolution grounds. Neverthless they can be taken into account as serious grounds for a decision ordering separation of property under Principle 4:49(d).

8. In the case of dissolution by death, divorce and legal separation the dissolution operates *ex lege* as a consequence of the dissolution. In the case of judicial separation of property a decision by a competent authority is necessary. In the case of change of the matrimonial property regime a specific procedure has to be followed (see Principles 4:11 to 4:14).

Principle 4:50 Date of dissolution
The dissolution of the community of acquisitions regime takes effect
(a) at the date of the death of a spouse;
(b) in the case of annulment of the marriage, divorce or legal separation as between the spouses, either at the date of the application or, if the spouses separated earlier, at the date of their separation and as against third persons, at the date of the registration of the decision of the competent authority;
(c) in the case of an agreement to change to another matrimonial property regime as between the spouses, at the date of the change and as against third persons, at the date of the publication of the agreement;
(d) in the case of separation of property ordered by the competent authority as between the spouses, at the date of the application and against third persons, at the date of the publication of the application.

Principe 4:50 Date de la dissolution
La dissolution du régime de communauté d'acquêts prend effet
(a) au moment du décès d'un époux;
(b) en cas d'annulation du mariage, de divorce ou de séparation de corps, entre époux à la date de la demande ou, si les époux se sont séparés antérieurement à cette date, à la date de leur séparation, à l'égard des tiers à la date de l'enregistrement de la décision rendue par autorité compétente;
(c) en cas de convention de changement de régime matrimonial, entre époux à la date de la convention et à l'égard des tiers à la date de la publication de la convention;
(d) en cas de séparation de biens prononcée par l'autorité compétente, entre époux à la date de la demande et à l'égard des tiers, à la date de la publication de la demande.

Prinzip 4:50 Zeitpunkt der Beendigung
Die Beendigung der Errungenschaftsgemeinschaft wird wirksam im Zeitpunkt
(a) des Todes eines Ehegatten;
(b) im Fall der Nichtigerklärung der Ehe, Ehescheidung oder gesetzlichen Trennung der Ehegatten, zwischen den Ehegatten im Zeitpunkt der Antragstellung, oder, wenn sich die Ehegatten vorher getrennt haben, im Zeitpunkt ihrer Trennung und gegenüber Dritten im Zeitpunkt der Eintragung der Entscheidung der zuständigen Behörde;
(c) im Fall einer vereinbarten Änderung des Güterstands, zwischen den Ehegatten im Zeitpunkt der Vereinbarung und gegenüber Dritten im Zeitpunkt der Bekanntmachung der Vereinbarung;

(d) im Fall der Gütertrennung durch die zuständige Behörde, zwischen den Ehegatten im Zeitpunkt der Antragstellung und gegenüber Dritten im Zeitpunkt der Bekanntmachung des Antrags.

INTERNATIONAL INSTRUMENTS

None of particular relevance.

COMPARATIVE OVERVIEW

Dissolution by death

In all the jurisdictions surveyed the date of dissolution in the case of death is the date of death.[2556]

Most of the legal systems have special rules for missing and absent persons. In BELGIUM,[2557] when a missing person is declared dead, the judgment indicates the date of death taking into account all the circumstances of the case. If this is not possible the judgment will indicate the date of disappearance as the date of death. If a person is declared absent, the judgment has effect from the date of the entry into the registers of civil status as, for example, in BELGIUM[2558] and FRANCE.[2559] In the CZECH REPUBLIC[2560] and SLOVAKIA,[2561] the date of dissolution is the date of the judgment having legal force. In ITALY,[2562] there are different legal theories. The most widespread theory argues that both in the cases of missing and absent persons, the date of dissolution of the community is the date of the declaration of death or absence. In SPAIN,[2563] also there are two theories. The first argues that the community is dissolved on the date at which the judgment becomes final, the other favours the date of the presumed death indicated in the judgment of declaration of death. In PORTUGAL,[2564] the community is dissolved when the spouse of the absent spouse demands an inventory and distribution of the community after the legal absence has been declared.

2556 See all national reports, Q 44.
2557 Art. 131 Belgian Civil Code.
2558 Art. 122 § 2 para. 2 Belgian Civil Code.
2559 Art. 128 para. 1 French Civil Code.
2560 See MELZER, Czech Report, Q 78 and 79.
2561 See HAŤAPKA, Slovakian Report, Q 44.
2562 See PATTI/CARICATO/IRTI/IANNICELLI/SERRA/DI STEFANO/PETÖ/BORTULU, Italian Report, Q 44.
2563 See GONZÁLEZ BEILFUSS, Spanish Report, Q 44.
2564 Art. 108 Portuguese Civil Code and Art. 1103 et seq. Portuguese Code of Civil Procedure. See DE OLIVEIRA/ MARTINS/VÍTOR, Portuguese Report, Q 44.

Divorce

In the case of dissolution of the community property regime by divorce most legal systems do not, for the purposes of determining property relations between the spouses, consider the date of dissolution upon which the divorce was granted to be relevant. Instead they commonly accept that the dissolution date is the date when successful divorce proceedings were commenced. But, as against third parties, the date of registration of the divorce in the registers of civil status is decisive. In FRANCE,[2565] when the divorce is granted by mutual consent, the date of the agreement regulating the consequences of the divorce is decisive, unless the agreement provides otherwise. In the case of a divorce for irretrievable breakdown of the marriage or for fault, the date of the decree of non-reconciliation is decisive.[2566] In BELGIUM,[2567] the rules are similar. In the case of a divorce by mutual consent the judgment has retroactive effect from the date of the initiation of the divorce proceedings, i.e. the date of the first appearance of the spouses before the president of the court. In the case of divorce on the ground of irretrievable breakdown of the marriage, the date of the initiation of the proceedings is decisive for the proprietary consequences of the divorce.[2568] In both legal systems the judge can order further retroactivity. In FRANCE,[2569] the judge may on request of one or both spouses postpone the effect of the judgment from the date of their factual separation and collaboration. In BELGIUM,[2570] specific assets acquired during the factual separation or debts incurred during this period can be kept separate. In LITHUANIA,[2571] the community is dissolved on the date of the divorce application or on the date of the factual separation. In PORTUGAL[2572] the same rule applies.

Other legal systems take the date of the final divorce judgment into account as in AUSTRIA,[2573] BULGARIA,[2574] CZECH REPUBLIC,[2575] RUSSIA[2576] and SLOVAKIA.[2577] In HUNGARY,[2578] this date is decisive, but if the matrimonial community of life terminated before the date of the divorce then the date of the

2565 Art. 262-1 French Civil Code.
2566 Art. 262-1 French Civil Code.
2567 Art. 1304 Belgian Judicial Code. See PINTENS/ALLAERTS/SEYNS/PIGNOLET, Belgian Report, Q 44.
2568 Art. 1278 para. 2 Belgian Judicial Code. See PINTENS/ALLAERTS/SEYNS/PIGNOLET, Belgian Report, Q 44.
2569 Art. 1442 French Civil Code.
2570 Art. 1278 para. 4 Belgian Judicial Code.
2571 Art. 3.67 Lithuanian Civil Code.
2572 Art. 1789 paras. 1 and 2 Portuguese Civil Code. See DE OLIVEIRA/MARTINS/VÍTOR, Portuguese Report, Q 44.
2573 See ROTH, Austrian Report, Q 44.
2574 Art. 325 and Art. 330 para. 5 Bulgarian Civil Procedure Code.
2575 See MELZER, Czech Report, Q 79.
2576 See ANTOKOLSKAIA, Russian Report, Q 44.
2577 See HAŤAPKA, Slovakian Report, Q 44.
2578 § 31 para. 2 Hungarian Family Act.

termination is taken into account. In SPAIN,[2579] the date on which the divorce judgment becomes final is decisive, but legal doctrine advocates the date of the initiation of the divorce proceedings or the date of the factual separation.

In some systems as in ITALY[2580] and THE NETHERLANDS,[2581] there is no retroactivity of the divorce judgment and the only decisive date is the one of the registration of the judgment in the registers of civil status.

Legal separation

In all the legal systems surveyed, the same rules apply to the dissolution by legal separation as in case of dissolution by divorce, as for example, in BELGIUM,[2582] THE NETHERLANDS[2583] and SPAIN.[2584]

Decision ordering separation of property

In BELGIUM[2585] and FRANCE,[2586] the decision ordering separation of property has retroactive effect between the spouses as well as against third parties from the date of the initiation of the procedure. In HUNGARY, the date mentioned in the judgment is decisive.[2587]

In DUTCH law,[2588] as between the spouses the community is dissolved with retroactive effect from the date of the request, whereas, as against third parties, the judgment takes effect from the publication in the Official Gazette and the registration in the matrimonial property register.[2589] In SPAIN,[2590] the date of the judgment is decisive whereas in PORTUGAL,[2591] the date of distribution of the community is decisive.

2579 See GONZÁLEZ BEILFUSS, Spanish Report, Q 44.

2580 See PATTI/CARICATO/IRTI/IANNICELLI/SERRA/DI STEFANO/PETÖ/BORTULU, Italian Report, Q 44.

2581 Art. 1:99 para. 1 a (old) Dutch Civil Code. See BOELE-WOELKI/SCHONEWILLE/SCHRAMA, Dutch Report, Q 44. This has been changed since 1 January 2012. The decisive date is the date when divorce proceedings were initiated, Art. 1:99 para. 1 under b and c Dutch Civil Code.

2582 Art. 311*bis* Belgian Civil Code and Art. 1306 Belgian Judicial Code. See PINTENS/ALLAERTS/SEYNS/PIGNOLET, Belgian Report, Q 44.

2583 Art. 1:173 Dutch Civil Code.

2584 Art. 95 para. 1 Spanish Civil Code.

2585 Art. 1472 Belgian Civil Code.

2586 Art. 1445 para. 2 French Civil Code.

2587 See WEISS/SZEIBERT, Hungarian Report, Q 44.

2588 Art. 1:111 Dutch Civil Code.

2589 Art. 1:116 Dutch Civil Code.

2590 Art. 1394 Spanish Civil Code. See GONZÁLEZ BEILFUSS, Spanish Report, Q 44.

2591 Art. 1770 Portuguese Civil Code.

Change of the matrimonial regime

In most of the legal systems surveyed, a change of the matrimonial property regime which results in its dissolution is effective between spouses from the date of the deed of change and against third parties from the date of the prescribed publication. This is, for example, the case in BELGIUM[2592] and ITALY.[2593] The rules are similar in FRANCE,[2594] but the dissolution is only effective against third persons three months after publication. In DUTCH law,[2595] the community is dissolved between the spouses the day after the deed but they may fix another date. Against third persons the modification is effective two weeks after the registration in the matrimonial property register.

COMMENT

1. In the case of dissolution by death, the date of dissolution is the date of death. Principle 4:50(a) does not provide a rule concerning missing and absent persons because in most legal systems such a rule is contained in the law of persons. Therefore it does not seem necessary to include a specific Principle in a set of matrimonial property law Principles.

2. In the case of dissolution by divorce, Principle 4:50 follows the common core of the legal systems and makes a distinction between the date of dissolution as between spouses and as against third parties. Principle 4:50(a) applies the rules on divorce to the legal separation and reflects the common core of the legal systems. This Principle also applies the same rules to annulments of marriage.

3. Between spouses the dissolution of the marriage has a retroactive effect from the date of the initiation of the divorce proceedings. If there is a factual separation before the initiation of those proceedings, the dissolution has retroactive effect from the beginning of the separation. Principle 4:50(b) is in accordance with the philosophy of a community regime. The community for life and the corresponding solidarity between spouses are at the basis of every community regime. The initiation of divorce proceedings or the factual separation indicates that the community of life and the solidarity between the spouses have come to an end. The spouses have separate households and live of separate incomes. An extension of the community would mean that property acquired with this income after the initiation of the divorce proceedings or after

2592 See PINTENS/ALLAERTS/SEYNS/PIGNOLET, Belgian Report, Q 44.
2593 See PATTI/CARICATO/IRTI/IANNICELLI/SERRA/DI STEFANO/PETÖ/BORTULU, Italian Report, Q 44.
2594 Art. 1397 para. 5 French Civil Code.
2595 Art. 120 Dutch Civil Code.

the separation would fall in the community. Spouses would even have the possibility to indebt the community. There is no justification for this further solidarity. The proof of the factual separation is a matter for national law.

4. Against third parties, under Principle 4:50(b), the decisive date is the date of registration of the divorce judgment in the registers of civil status. This principle reflects the common core of the legal systems surveyed and guarantees the protection of third parties.

5. In the case of a change of the matrimonial property regime, Principle 4:50(c) follows the common core of the legal systems and makes a distinction between the date of dissolution between the spouses and against third parties. With regard to the date of dissolution between the spouses, Principle 4:50(c) opts for the date of the new marital property agreement. Against third parties, the date of publication is decisive. Publication measures are left to national law. They can consist of, for example, a publication in the margin of the marriage certificate, registration in a matrimonial property register or publication in an official gazette.

6. In the case of a decision by the competent authority ordering separation of property there is a common core concerning the date of dissolution between the spouses: the decision has retroactive effect from the date of initiation of the proceedings. Principle 4:50(d) follows this common core since this is the only effective protection for the applicant.

7. There is no common core concerning the effect of the dissolution against third parties in the case of separation of property ordered by the competent authority. A better law approach has to be applied. The protection of the interests of the applicant spouse can only be effective when there is also retroactivity against third parties. The reason for the application is the disorder in the financial affairs and the outstanding debts of the other spouse. Without retroactivity against third parties there is a real danger that during the proceedings the situation will become increasingly detrimental for the applicant. But the interests of third parties also require protection. Retroactivity from the date of the application does not guarantee this protection. Principle 4:50(d) accordingly opts for retroactivity from the date of publication of the application. The specific requirements for publication are left to national law.

Principle 4:51 Administration after dissolution
After the dissolution of the community of acquisitions the general rules of joint ownership apply to administration.

Principe 4:51 Administration après dissolution
Postérieurement à la dissolution de la communauté d'acquêts, l'administration est soumise aux règles générales relatives à l'indivision.

Prinzip 4:51 Verwaltung nach Beendigung
Nach Beendigung der Errungenschaftsgemeinschaft finden die allgemeinen Regeln über das Miteigentum auf die Verwaltung Anwendung.

INTERNATIONAL INSTRUMENTS

None of particular relevance.

COMPARATIVE OVERVIEW

The effects of dissolution of the community

In a clear majority of the jurisdictions surveyed the dissolution of the community converts this community into a post-communal joint ownership. The rules on the administration of the community are no longer applicable and the general law on joint property applies. This is the rule in BELGIUM,[2596] where the administration of joint property implies that a joint owner can only perform acts of maintenance and provisional administration. All other acts require the consent of all joint owners. The FRENCH legislation was modernised in 2006.[2597] Any joint owner may perform acts of preservation, even if they are not urgent. Acts of administration and disposition no longer require the consent of all joint owners, but a two third majority suffices for certain acts of administration. Similarly, in BULGARIA,[2598] ITALY,[2599] MALTA,[2600] THE NETHERLANDS,[2601]

[2596] Art. 577-2 Belgian Civil Code. See PINTENS/ALLAERTS/SEYNS/PIGNOLET, Belgian Report, Q 48.
[2597] Art. 815-3 French Civil Code. See FERRAND/BRAAT, French Report, Q 48.
[2598] Art. 27 Bulgarian Family Code. See TODOROVA, Bulgarian Report, Q 48.
[2599] See PATTI/CARICATO/IRTI/IANNICELLI/SERRA/DI STEFANO/PETÖ/BORTULU, Italian Report, Q 48. Some authors defend the applicability of the rules on administration of the community.
[2600] See FARRUGIA, Maltese Report, Q 48.
[2601] Art. 3:170 Dutch Civil Code. See BOELE-WOELKI/SCHONEWILLE/SCHRAMA, Dutch Report, Q 48.

POLAND[2602] and SPAIN,[2603] the legal rules on joint property apply. SPAIN[2604] differentiates between dissolution by death and dissolution by divorce, legal separation and judicial separation. In the former case the rules on joint property and on succession law apply by analogy. In the latter case the court will decide on the rules of administration in the judgment.

Other jurisdictions apply matrimonial property law until the community is liquidated and the assets are distributed as in RUSSIA[2605] and SLOVAKIA.[2606] In HUNGARY,[2607] certain matrimonial property rules concerning the disposal of the community assets apply. This is the case for the rule prescribing that the chattels belonging to the community assets can only be alienated with the consent of both spouses. Since this rule is felt as unpractical, the proposal for a new HUNGARIAN Civil Code maintains the regulation but lists the acts that can be performed without both spouses' consent.[2608]

In PORTUGAL,[2609] case law is divided. In 1995, the Supreme Court of Justice decided that the initial structure of the community remains intact. The community becomes undivided in status but cannot be qualified as joint ownership. Later, however, the Supreme Court accepted that the community is converted into joint ownership.[2610]

COMMENT

1. Principle 4:51 follows the common core of the community systems surveyed and prescribes that the dissolution of the matrimonial regime converts the community into joint ownership.

2. The specific rules of a matrimonial regime are based on the solidarity between spouses. Therefore, the rules on administration of the community property offer the spouses more autonomy than a system of joint property. As stated in Principle 4:44(1) and in accordance with most of the legal systems surveyed either spouse is entitled to administer community property. Only

2602 See MĄCZYŃSKI, Polish Report, Q 48.
2603 See GONZÁLEZ BEILFUSS, Spanish Report, Q 48.
2604 See GONZÁLEZ BEILFUSS, Spanish Report, Q 48.
2605 See ANTOKOLSKAIA, Russian Report, Q 48.
2606 See HAŤAPKA, Slovakian Report, Q 48.
2607 § 30 para. 1 Hungarian Family Act. See WEISS/SZEIBERT, Hungarian Report, Q 48.
2608 See WEISS/SZEIBERT, Hungarian Report, Q 48.
2609 Supreme Court of Justice 1 February 1995 and 5 December 1995. See DE OLIVEIRA/MARTINS/VÍTOR, Portuguese Report, Q 48.
2610 Supreme Court of Justice 11 October 2005 and 3 April 2008. See DE OLIVEIRA/MARTINS/VÍTOR, Portuguese Report, Q 48.

important acts require joint administration. A joint owner is only entitled to acts of preservation and provisional administration. All other acts require joint administration. Since the dissolution of the matrimonial regime is a consequence of the dissolution of the marriage by death or divorce or of a decision by a competent authority ordering separation of property, marital solidarity no longer exists. Consequently in the interest of the spouses and their heirs, the rules on joint ownership apply.

LIQUIDATION
LIQUIDATION
AUSEINANDERSETZUNG

Principle 4:52 Determination and valuation of the community property
(1) Community property should be determined at the date of the dissolution of the community of acquisitions, as specified by Principle 4:50.
(2) The community assets should be valued at the date of their distribution.

Principe 4:52 Détermination et évaluation des biens communs
(1) Les biens communs sont déterminés à la date de dissolution de la communauté d'acquêts telle que précisée au Principe 4:50.
(2) Les biens communs sont évalués à la date de distribution.

Prinzip 4:52 Feststellung und Bewertung des gemeinschaftlichen Vermögens
(1) Die Feststellung des gemeinschaftlichen Vermögens erfolgt im Zeitpunkt der Beendigung der Errungenschaftsgemeinschaft wie in Prinzip 4:50 bestimmt.
(2) Die Bewertung des gemeinschaftlichen Vermögens erfolgt im Zeitpunkt der Teilung.

INTERNATIONAL INSTRUMENTS

None of particular relevance.

COMPARATIVE OVERVIEW

Most legal systems differentiate between the determination of the community and the valuation of the assets. The community is determined at the date of her dissolution between the spouses whereas the assets are valued at the date of their distribution. This applies in BELGIUM,[2611] BULGARIA,[2612] CZECH REPUBLIC,[2613]

[2611] See PINTENS/ALLAERTS/SEYNS/PIGNOLET, Belgian Report, Q 44.
[2612] See TODOROVA, Bulgarian Report, Q 44.
[2613] See MELZER, Czech Report, Q 78.

FRANCE,[2614] THE NETHERLANDS,[2615] SLOVAKIA[2616] and SPAIN.[2617] In AUSTRIA,[2618] in case of dissolution by death the key date for the determination and valuation of the community is the date of death.

COMMENT

1. Principle 4:52(1) states that the determination of the community assets takes place at the date of the dissolution of the community. This Principle is in accordance with the common core of the legal systems and reflects that the community property is fixed at the date of the dissolution. After this date the composition of the community property cannot be changed.

2. Principle 4:52(2) provides that the valuation of the assets is determined at the date of their distribution, which is in conformity with the common core of the jurisdictions surveyed. In this way the fluctuations of the market value of the assets is taken into account.

2614 Cass. 20 November 1940, Sirey 1941, I, 233, note Batiffol. See Fr. Terré and Ph. Simler, Les régimes matrimoniaux, 5th ed., Paris, 2008, p. 547 ff.

2615 Unless good faith requires otherwise, Hoge Raad 17.4.2009, NJ 1999, 550. See BOELE-WOELKI/SCHONEWILLE/SCHRAMA, Dutch Report, Q 44.

2616 See HAŤAPKA, Slovakian Report, Q 44.

2617 Art. 1397 Spanish Civil Code. See GONZÁLEZ BEILFUSS, Spanish Report, Q 44.

2618 See ROTH, Austrian Report, Q 44.

Principle 4:53 Compensation

(1) The community property should be compensated for any contribution profiting the personal property of a spouse.

(2) The personal property of a spouse should be compensated for any contribution profiting the community property.

(3) In the case of investment for the acquisition, improvement or preservation of an asset, the calculation of the compensation should take into account any resulting increase or decrease in the value of the asset.

(4) The compensation should be paid in money, unless the spouses agree otherwise.

Principe 4:53 Récompenses

(1) La communauté a droit à récompense pour toute contribution réalisée au profit des biens propres d'un époux.

(2) Une récompense est due pour toute contribution réalisée par les biens propres d'un époux au profit de la communauté.

(3) En cas d'investissement en vue de l'acquisition, de l'amélioration ou de la conservation d'un bien, il est tenu compte, lors du calcul du montant de la récompense, de la plus-value ou de la moins-value du bien au profit duquel l'investissement a été réalisé.

(4) La récompense est due sous forme monétaire, sauf accord contraire des époux.

Prinzip 4:53 Ausgleich

(1) Das gemeinschaftliche Vermögen erhält einen Ausgleich für jeden Beitrag zugunsten des persönlichen Vermögens eines Ehegatten.

(2) Das persönliche Vermögen eines Ehegatten erhält einen Ausgleich für jeden Beitrag zugunsten des gemeinschaftlichen Vermögens.

(3) Im Fall der Anlage für den Erwerb, die Verbesserung oder den Erhalt eines Vermögensgegenstands ist bei der Berechnung des Ausgleichs der gestiegene oder gesunkene Wert des Vermögensgegenstands in Betracht zu ziehen.

(4) Der Ausgleich ist in Geld zu zahlen, sofern die Ehegatten nichts anderes vereinbaren.

INTERNATIONAL INSTRUMENTS

None of particular relevance.

COMPARATIVE OVERVIEW

Compensation in proprietary rights or in value

The community and the personal property of the spouses are not always kept separate. The rules on the administration of the community allow a spouse to use assets of the community to maintain his personal property. A spouse may, for example, use community money to maintain or improve his or her own house. The creditor of a spouse can in certain cases recover a personal debt on community assets (see Principle 4:43). If at the dissolution of the matrimonial property regime no compensation has been paid, an unjust enrichment has to be rectified. The legal systems surveyed offer several solutions.

In most systems proprietary rights in the assets are not modified but compensation is due as in BELGIUM,[2619] BULGARIA,[2620] FRANCE,[2621] THE NETHERLANDS,[2622] POLAND,[2623] PORTUGAL,[2624] SLOVAKIA[2625] and SPAIN.[2626] In principle, compensation is paid in money but in exceptional circumstances a payment in kind is possible.

In other systems the court may change proprietary rights in the assets and declare personal assets improved with community funds to be community assets as in HUNGARY,[2627] LITHUANIA[2628] and RUSSIA.[2629]

Moment of compensation

In all the legal systems surveyed spouses are free to pay compensation during the marriage but they are not obliged to do so. Only after the dissolution of the community does a right to compensation become established and enforceable through the liquidation and distribution of the community.

2619 Art. 1435 Belgian Civil Code. See PINTENS/ALLAERTS/SEYNS/PIGNOLET, Belgian Report, Q 45.
2620 See TODOROVA, Bulgarian Report, Q 45.
2621 Art. 1433 and 1437 French Civil Code. See FERRAND/BRAAT, French Report, Q 45.
2622 See BOELE-WOELKI/SCHONEWILLE/SCHRAMA, Dutch Report, Q 45.
2623 See MĄCZYŃSKI, Polish Report, Q 45.
2624 See DE OLIVEIRA/MARTINS/VÍTOR, Portuguese Report, Q 45.
2625 See HAŤAPKA, Slovakian Report, Q 45.
2626 Art. 1358 Spanish Civil Code. See GONZÁLEZ BEILFUSS, Spanish Report, Q 45.
2627 See WEISS/SZEIBERT, Hungarian Report, Q 45.
2628 See MIKELENAS, Lithuanian Report, Q 45.
2629 See ANTOKOLSKAIA, Russian Report, Q 45.

Calculation of the compensation

Some legal systems calculate the compensation at the nominal value and disregard an increase or a decrease in value as in BULGARIA,[2630] POLAND,[2631] PORTUGAL[2632] and SLOVAKIA.[2633] In SPAIN,[2634] the principle of nominal compensation is applied and the real increase or decrease of the value is disregarded, but the amount is updated with the consumer price index at the date of distribution.

Other systems differentiate between compensation for investments and other compensation as in BELGIUM[2635] and FRANCE.[2636] In the former case the increase in value is taken into account, in the second category nominal compensation prevails. In the latter case the loss of the interest, for example, in case of payment of a personal debt with community assets is covered by the solidarity of the community system. In THE NETHERLANDS,[2637] the principle of nominal compensation applies, but legal doctrine advocated that this principle might in exceptional cases be set aside for reasons of good faith. Since 1 January 2012, the increase in value has to be taken into account in case of investment.[2638]

COMMENT

1. The first two paragraphs of Principle 4:53 prescribe compensation for any contribution made by one category of property to another category. This rule reflects the common core of the jurisdictions surveyed. The approach avoids unjust enrichment (see also Principle 4:38). An example: Spouse A inherits a house having a market value of 400.000 units. This house belongs to his personal property (Principle 4:36(b)). The community property immediately invests 100.000 units to improve the house. Now the house has a market value of 500.000 units. This means that the community property invested one fifth to the market value of the house. At the date of dissolution of the regime the house has a market value of 600.000 units. The community property has to pay compensation to the personal property taking into account the market value of the house at the date of the dissolution of the regime (Principle 4:52). Since the community property contributed one fifth to the market value of the house, the

2630 See TODOROVA, Bulgarian Report, Q 45.
2631 See MĄCZYŃSKI, Polish Report, Q 45.
2632 Art. 550 Portuguese Civil Code. See DE OLIVEIRA/MARTINS/VÍTOR, Portuguese Report, Q 45 and Q 46.
2633 See HAťAPKA, Slovakian Report, Q 45.
2634 See GONZÁLEZ BEILFUSS, Spanish Report, Q 45.
2635 See PINTENS/ALLAERTS/SEYNS/PIGNOLET, Belgian Report, Q 45.
2636 See FERRAND/BRAAT, French Report, Q 45.
2637 See BOELE-WOELKI/SCHONEWILLE/SCHRAMA, Dutch Report, Q 45.
2638 Art. 1:87 Dutch Civil Code.

compensation has to be fixed at one fifth of the market value at the date of dissolution of the regime being 120.000 units. If due to a decrease of the market the house only has a market value of 300.000 units at the date of the dissolution of the regime, the compensation has also to be fixed at one fifth of this market value, namely, 60.000 units.

2. Principle 4:53(3) implies that as a general rule the compensation is nominal. This applies when, for example, the community has paid a personal debt. But in the case of investment by one category of property for the acquisition, improvement or conservation of an asset belonging to another category of property the compensation should take into account the increase or decrease of the value of the asset. This rule, which reflects the common core of the legal systems surveyed, ensures that the profit made by the beneficiary category of property also benefits the category that made the investment. *Vice versa* both categories of property have to share the consequences of a decrease of the value of the asset.

3. Principle 4:53(4) follows the majority of the legal systems surveyed and provides for compensation in money, unless otherwise agreed.

Principle 4:54 Ranking of community debts
Community debts and compensation rights rank equally.

Principe 4:54 Ordre de paiement des dettes communes
Les dettes de la communauté et les droits à récompense ont le même rang.

Prinzip 4:54 Rang der gemeinschaftlichen Schulden
Gemeinschaftliche Schulden und Ausgleichsansprüche haben den gleichen Rang.

INTERNATIONAL INSTRUMENTS

None of particular relevance.

COMPARATIVE OVERVIEW

The legal systems surveyed offer two models. In the first model community debts have priority over compensation rights. This is the solution in BELGIUM,[2639] HUNGARY,[2640] ITALY,[2641] LITHUANIA[2642] and SPAIN.[2643] In BULGARIAN law,[2644] there is no statutory provision, but in practice community debts have priority.

In the second model, community debts and compensation rights have equal rank. In FRENCH law,[2645] there is no priority order. Community debts rank equally with compensation rights, with the exception that preference is given to the creditor of a community debt, for example, on the basis of a mortgage. The same rule applies in DUTCH law.[2646] There is no specific rule on priority. The majority in legal doctrine accepts that general property and contract law are applicable, which implies that a spouse who is entitled to compensation and a community creditor are concurrent creditors. POLISH[2647] and RUSSIAN[2648] law

2639 Art. 1430 para. 3 Belgian Civil Code.
2640 See WEISS/SZEIBERT, Hungarian Report, Q 47.
2641 See PATTI/CARICATO/IRTI/IANNICELLI/SERRA/DI STEFANO/PETÖ/BORTULU, Italian Report, Q 47.
2642 Art. 3.118 Lithuanian Civil Code.
2643 Art. 1399 Spanish Civil Code.
2644 See TODOROVA, Bulgarian Report, Q 47.
2645 Art. 1474 French Civil Code. See FERRAND/BRAAT, French Report, Q 47.
2646 See BOELE-WOELKI/SCHONEWILLE/SCHRAMA, Dutch Report, Q 47. Some scholars are of a different opinion.
2647 See MĄCZYŃSKI, Polish Report, Q 47.
2648 See ANTOKOLSKAIA, Russian Report, Q 47.

have no provisions on priority which means that community debts and compensation rights have equal rank.

COMMENT

1. Each model has advantages and disadvantages. Under the first model, prescribing the priority of community debts, the community creditors are placed in a better position than under the second model which prescribes an equal rank of community debts and compensation rights. This position facilitates transactions between the spouses and third persons. The position of a spouse having compensation rights is weak. When there are substantial community debts, he or she will not be able to recover his or her claim. Under the second model, the creditor is in a weaker position because he competes with the spouse entitled to compensation rights. But there is no difference between his or her position and the position of other community creditors.

2. Principle 4:54 favours the second model on the basis of a better law approach. There is no reason to put the creditor in a better position than a spouse. The Principle sets matrimonial property law in line with the general law on obligations and eliminates undefendable discrimination of the spouse.

DISTRIBUTION
DISTRIBUTION
TEILUNG

Principle 4:55 Agreement on distribution
Spouses are free to agree on the distribution of the community property.

Principe 4:55 Convention sur la répartition
Les époux peuvent conclure une convention sur la répartition des biens communs.

Prinzip 4:55 Vereinbarung über die Teilung
Die Ehegatten können eine Vereinbarung über die Teilung des gemeinschaftlichen Vermögens treffen.

INTERNATIONAL INSTRUMENTS

None of particular relevance.

COMPARATIVE OVERVIEW

Almost all of the legal systems surveyed allow the spouses to agree on the distribution of the community and to set aside or adjust the rules on division of the community property. In AUSTRIA,[2649] BELGIUM,[2650] BULGARIA,[2651] FRANCE,[2652] HUNGARY,[2653] ITALY,[2654] LITHUANIA,[2655] THE NETHERLANDS,[2656] RUSSIA,[2657] SLOVAKIA[2658] and SPAIN[2659] spouses can make an agreement without

2649 See ROTH, Austrian Report, Q 55.
2650 See PINTENS/ALLAERTS/SEYNS/PIGNOLET, Belgian Report, Q 55.
2651 See TODOROVA, Bulgarian Report, Q 55.
2652 See FERRAND/BRAAT, French Report, Q 55.
2653 See WEISS/SZEIBERT, Hungarian Report, Q 55.
2654 See PATTI/CARICATO/IRTI/IANNICELLI/SERRA/DI STEFANO/PETÖ/BORTULU, Italian Report, Q 55.
2655 See MIKELENAS, Lithuanian Report, Q 55.
2656 See BOELE-WOELKI/SCHONEWILLE/SCHRAMA, Dutch Report, Q 55.
2657 See ANTOKOLSKAIA, Russian Report, Q 55.
2658 See HAŤAPKA, Slovakian Report, Q 55.
2659 See GONZÁLEZ BEILFUSS, Spanish Report, Q 55.

any intervention of a competent authority. The agreement must not, however, violate the rights of the creditors who may find protection in specific matrimonial property law or in the law of obligations and may initiate an *actio pauliana*.[2660] In LITHUANIAN law,[2661] the agreement cannot violate the rights or interests of minor children. In MALTA,[2662] the spouses can deviate from the rules but the agreement is subject to authorisation by the competent court. In POLAND[2663] and PORTUGAL,[2664] the rules on division in equal shares are mandatory and cannot be set aside by the will of the spouses.

COMMENT

1. Principle 4:55 follows the common core of the legal systems and allows the spouses to agree on the distribution of the community property and to set aside or adjust the general rules of division. This agreement may concern all aspects of liquidation and distribution as for example the renouncement to compensation, the evaluation of the assets or the distribution in kind or in money.

2. Principle 4:55 does not provide for any intervention by a competent authority which reflects the common core. There is no need to make the agreement subject to authorisation or scrutiny by a competent authority since the spouses can find their protection in the law on obligations. Creditors too are protected in all legal systems by specific rules of matrimonial property law. In many legal systems they can also find protection in the law of obligations and initiate an *actio pauliana* when the division infringes their rights. The agreement on distribution applies as between the spouses and cannot affect the rights of third persons.

3. In cases of exceptional hardship the competent authority may set aside or adjust the agreement on distribution (see Principle 4:57).

2660 The *actio pauliana* is a remedy for the creditor against fraudulent transfers by his debtor.
2661 See MIKELENAS, Lithuanian Report, Q 55.
2662 See FARRUGIA, Maltese Report, Q 49 and 55.
2663 See MĄCZYŃSKI, Polish Report, Q 55.
2664 See DE OLIVEIRA/MARTINS/VÍTOR, Portuguese Report, Q 55.

Principle 4:56 Allocation of the family home, household goods and professional assets
In determining the distribution of community property a competent authority may, in the interest of the family and subject to payment of compensation, allocate to one of the spouses
(a) the family home and household goods;
(b) professional assets.

Principe 4:56 Attribution du logement de la famille, de meubles meublants et de biens professionnels.
Lorsqu'elle se prononce sur la répartition des biens communs, l'autorité compétente peut, dans l'intérêt de la famille et moyennant compensation financière, attribuer à l'un des époux
(a) le logement de la famille et des meubles meublants;
(b) des biens professionnels.

Prinzip 4:56 Zuweisung der Familienwohnung, der Haushaltsgegenstände und der beruflichen Vermögensgegenstände
Bei der Teilung des gemeinschaftlichen Vermögens kann die zuständige Behörde vorbehaltlich einer Ausgleichszahlung einem der Ehegatten
(a) die Familienwohnung und Haushaltsgegenstände;
(b) berufliche Vermögensgegenstände zuweisen.

INTERNATIONAL INSTRUMENTS

Recommendation R (81) 15 of the Committee of Ministers of the Council of Europe on the rights of spouses relating to the occupation of the family home and the use of the household contents deals with those rights in case of dissolution and breakdown of the marriage. In the case of divorce or judicial separation, Principle 3 states that the right to occupy the family home may be assigned, in appropriate cases and according to the conditions laid down by national law, exclusively to one of the spouses. The surviving spouse should have the same right (Principle 4). The Principle is restricted to occupancy rights and does not deal with proprietary rights. By Principle 5, Principles 1 to 4 applies to leases. According to Principle 7, the whole or part of the said household contents may, in appropriate cases and according to the conditions laid down by national law, be assigned exclusively to one of the spouses in the case of a divorce of judicial separation. Principle 8 grants the same rights to the surviving spouse.

COMPARATIVE OVERVIEW

Family home and household goods

In most jurisdictions spouses have no preferential rights to the matrimonial home and household goods belonging to the community, but the competent authority may allocate the family home and the household goods to one of the spouses on the basis of his or her interests and the interests of the children. In BELGIUM,[2665] FRANCE[2666] and LITHUANIA[2667] the allocation is possible in the case of dissolution by death as well as by divorce. In the case of death the surviving spouse has a preferential right, in the case of divorce the court decides on the merits of the case. In other jurisdictions the allocation of the property is only possible in the case of divorce whereas in the case of death the surviving spouse may use the goods for a certain period as in POLAND.[2668] In RUSSIA,[2669] the court has the power to allocate the family home and the household goods after divorce.

In SPAIN,[2670] allocation is only possible in case of death. The surviving spouse can choose between ownership and use of the family home. Unless they are of an extraordinary cultural, economic or historical value, household goods are always attributed to the surviving spouse.[2671] In MALTA,[2672] the surviving spouse only has the right to live in the family home and to use the household goods until death or remarriage.

In some jurisdictions the allocation is restricted to the use of the preferential assets. In BULGARIA,[2673] the court may order the allocation in the case of a divorce based on irretrievable breakdown of the marriage when minor children exist or when the use of the family home is indivisible and special circumstances such as the fault for the marriage breakdown or health problems can be invoked. In HUNGARY,[2674] the allocation of the use of assets is in principle restricted to the family home. Household assets can only be allocated when they are needed for minor children.

2665 Art. 1446–1447 Belgian Civil Code. See PINTENS/ALLAERTS/SEYNS/PIGNOLET, Belgian Report, Q 51.

2666 See FERRAND/BRAAT, French Report, Q 51.

2667 See MIKELENAS, Lithuanian Report, Q 51.

2668 See MĄCZYŃSKI, Polish Report, Q 51.

2669 See ANTOKOLSKAIA, Russian Report, Q 51.

2670 Art. 1407 Spanish Civil Code. See GONZÁLEZ BEILFUSS, Spanish Report, Q 51.

2671 Art. 1321 Spanish Civil Code. See GONZÁLEZ BEILFUSS, Spanish Report, Q 51.

2672 See FARRUGIA, Maltese Report, Q 51.

2673 See TODOROVA, Bulgarian Report, Q 51.

2674 See WEISS/SZEIBERT, Hungarian Report, Q 51.

Most jurisdictions restrict the allocation to those assets belonging to the community as in BELGIUM[2675] and FRANCE[2676] and exclude the reallocation of personal property. In THE NETHERLANDS,[2677] this rule also applies but the court may grant the use of the family home and the household goods belonging to the personal property of a spouse to the other one for a limited period. In BULGARIA[2678] and ITALY[2679] the family home and the household goods belonging to the personal property can be allocated but only in respect of its use and usufruct. In SPAIN,[2680] the allocation of personal property is restricted to household goods.

When the property rather than its use is allocated, compensation is due as in BELGIUM[2681] and FRANCE.[2682] In RUSSIA,[2683] the court may order compensation but is not obliged to do so. In SLOVAKIA[2684] no preferential rights exist.

Professional assets

Most jurisdictions allow allocation of professional assets as in BELGIUM,[2685] FRANCE,[2686] HUNGARY,[2687] LITHUANIA,[2688] PORTUGAL,[2689] RUSSIA,[2690] SLOVAKIA[2691] and SPAIN.[2692] In ITALY[2693] and POLAND[2694] such an allocation is not possible.

2675 See PINTENS/ALLAERTS/SEYNS/PIGNOLET, Belgian Report, Q 51.
2676 See FERRAND/BRAAT, French Report, Q 51.
2677 Art. 1:165 Dutch Civil Code. See BOELE-WOELKI/SCHONEWILLE/SCHRAMA, Dutch Report, Q 51.
2678 See TODOROVA, Bulgarian Report, Q 51.
2679 See PATTI/CARICATO/IRTI/IANNICELLI/SERRA/DI STEFANO/PETÖ/BORTULU, Italian Report, Q 51.
2680 See GONZÁLEZ BEILFUSS, Spanish Report, Q 51.
2681 Art. 1446–1447 Belgian Civil Code. See PINTENS/ALLAERTS/SEYNS/PIGNOLET, Belgian Report, Q 51.
2682 See FERRAND/BRAAT, French Report, Q 51.
2683 Art. 38 Russian Family Code. See ANTOKOLSKAIA, Russian Report, Q 51.
2684 See HAŤAPKA, Slovakian Report, Q 51.
2685 Art. 1446–1447 Belgian Civil Code. See PINTENS/ALLAERTS/SEYNS/PIGNOLET, Belgian Report, Q 52.
2686 See FERRAND/BRAAT, French Report, Q 52.
2687 See WEISS/SZEIBERT, Hungarian Report, Q 52.
2688 See MIKELENAS, Lithuanian Report, Q 52.
2689 See DE OLIVEIRA/MARTINS/VÍTOR, Portuguese Report, Q 52.
2690 See ANTOKOLSKAIA, Russian Report, Q 52.
2691 See HAŤAPKA, Slovakian Report, Q 52.
2692 See GONZÁLEZ BEILFUSS, Spanish Report, Q 52.
2693 See PATTI/CARICATO/IRTI/IANNICELLI/SERRA/DI STEFANO/PETÖ/BORTULU, Italian Report, Q 52.
2694 See MĄCZYŃSKI, Polish Report, Q 52.

In most jurisdictions the allocation takes place against payment as in BELGIUM,[2695] FRANCE,[2696] HUNGARY,[2697] LITHUANIA,[2698] THE NETHERLANDS[2699] and SLOVAKIA.[2700] In RUSSIA,[2701] however, the court can deviate from that rule if the debtor spouse is unable to pay and if the interest of that spouse so requires.

COMMENT

1. Principle 4:56(a) states that the competent authority may allocate the family home and the household goods to one of the spouses. The allocation only concerns those assets which are part of the community. Reallocation of personal assets is excluded.

2. Principle 4:56(b) allows the allocation of professional assets. Those assets are personal property when they are exclusively used for the professional activities of one spouse (Principle 4:36(e)). Therefore, Principle 4:56(b) only deals with assets that are not exclusively used for the professional activities of one spouse. This will be the case when the assets are used for the professional activities of both spouses or when those assets are also used for other purposes.

3. The main criterion for the allocation is the interest of the family, which means the interest of the spouses and the children. If, for example, the children will reside with one of the parents, their interests will prevail over those of the other spouse. The main criterion does not prevent the competent authority taking other criteria into account as, for example, the financial situation of the spouses.

4. The allocation is subject to payment of compensation. In cases of exceptional hardship the competent authority may deviate from this rule (see Principle 4:57).

2695 Art. 1446–1447 Belgian Civil Code.
2696 See FERRAND/BRAAT, French Report, Q 52.
2697 See WEISS/SZEIBERT, Hungarian Report, Q 52.
2698 See MIKELENAS, Lithuanian Report, Q 52.
2699 See ANTOKOLSKAIA, Russian Report, Q 52.
2700 See HAŤAPKA, Slovakian Report, Q 52.
2701 See ANTOKOLSKAIA, Russian Report, Q 52.

Principle 4:57 Equal sharing and adjustment

(1) The community property should be distributed equally between the spouses.

(2) In cases of exceptional hardship the competent authority can

(a) adjust the distribution;

(b) set aside or modify any spousal agreement made in accordance with Principle 4:55.

Principe 4:57 Répartition égale et adaptations

(1) Les biens communs sont répartis de façon égale entre les époux.

(2) En cas de dureté exceptionnelle, l'autorité compétente peut

(a) adapter la répartition;

(b) écarter ou modifier toute convention conclue en application du Principe 4:55.

Prinzip 4:57 Gleiche Anteile und Anpassung

(1) Das gemeinschaftliche Vermögen wird unter den Ehegatten gleich aufgeteilt.

(2) In Fälle außergewöhnlicher Härte kann die zuständige Behörde

(a) die Beteiligung anpassen;

(b) jede nach Prinzip 4:55 getroffene Vereinbarung der Ehegatten aufheben oder abändern.

INTERNATIONAL INSTRUMENTS

Resolution (78) 37 of the Committee of Ministers of the Council of Europe on equality of spouses in civil law aims to promote this equality in matters of property and financial relations of spouses. Whereas the resolution contains a recommendation concerning the default regime of separation, it does not contain a specific recommendation concerning the community of property.

Recommendation R (89) 1 of the Committee of Ministers of the Council of Europe on contributions following divorce aims to promote the idea that each spouse should be economically independent and self-supporting. The resolution recommends attaining this aim by matrimonial property regimes granting a former spouse the right to obtain a fair share in the property of the other (Principle 1).

COMPARATIVE OVERVIEW

Equal distribution of the community property after the dissolution of the regime is the common rule in the legal systems surveyed. In most of these systems a competent authority has no power to set aside or to adjust the rules on the division of the community property. This is the case in BELGIUM,[2702] PORTUGAL[2703] and SLOVAKIA.[2704] In FRENCH law,[2705] the court cannot put aside or adjust the rules on division as such, but in ordering the *prestation compensatoire,* it takes into account the property of the spouses after the liquidation of the community. The court fixes the modalities of the compensation and determines the attribution of community assets.[2706]

In some legal systems the court can deviate from an equal division in the interests of the minor children or of one of the spouses. In HUNGARY,[2707] the court can deviate in those cases and will especially do so if the application of the general rules would result in serious inequity between the spouses. POLISH law[2708] allows the courts to deviate from equal division by taking into account the contribution of each spouse. However, the courts seldom use those powers. In RUSSIA,[2709] the most common example of such a deviation is the attribution of the family home to the spouse with whom the minor children reside. Another example is when a spouse has no income without a justified reason or when he has squandered property to the detriment of the family.[2710] In BULGARIA,[2711] the court may, in the case of divorce, adjust the equal distribution, when a spouse exercises parental responsibility and this creates for him or her special difficulties or when the contribution to the marriage by a spouse significantly exceeds the contribution of the other spouse. The latter applies also in the case of termination of the regime by the competent authority. In AUSTRIA,[2712] the majority of distributions are in equal shares, although the law allows for an equitable division such that the interests of the child are to be taken into consideration.

COMMENT

1. The comparative overview shows that in a large number of the legal systems surveyed, the competent authority may not deviate from a distribution of the community property in equal shares. One of the reasons for this is that any inequality between the spouses is mitigated by the allowance of maintenance.

2702 See PINTENS/ALLAERTS/SEYNS/PIGNOLET, Belgian Report, Q 55.
2703 See DE OLIVEIRA/MARTINS/VÍTOR, Portuguese Report, Q 55.
2704 See HAŤAPKA, Slovakian Report, Q 55.
2705 Art. 271 para. 2 French Civil Code. See FERRAND/BRAAT, French Report, Q 55.
2706 Art. 274 French Civil Code.
2707 See WEISS/SZEIBERT, Hungarian Report, Q 55.
2708 Art. 43 Family and Guardianship Code.
2709 Art. 39 para. 2 Russian Family Code. See ANTOKOLSKAIA, Russian Report, Q 55.
2710 Art. 39 para. 2 Russian Family Code. See ANTOKOLSKAIA, Russian Report, Q 55.
2711 Art. 29 para. 1 and 3 Bulgarian Family Code.
2712 § 83 para. 1 Austrian Marriage Act. See ROTH, Austrian Report, Q 55.

Adopting this common core, Principle 4:57(1) states the equal distribution of the community as a general rule.

2. The legal systems having a community of property and allowing a competent authority to deviate from a division in equal shares are mostly Eastern European jurisdictions where housing problems exist and maintenance is rather low. Principle 4:57(2) takes into account that such exceptional hardship may exist and that in those cases a deviation from an equal split of the community may be justified. The competent authority may deviate from an equal distribution and even deviate from Principle 4:56 and allocate the family home and the household goods without compensation. In those cases of exceptional hardship the competent authority can also set aside or modify any spousal agreement made in accordance with Principle 4:55.

3. The hardship should be exceptional. It can arise in a case where the unequal distribution of the community is absolutely necessary to provide for the needs of a spouse who cannot rely on maintenance and social security benefits.

Principle 4:58 Recovery of community debts after distribution of the community

(1) Community debts can be recovered after the distribution of the community from the share of the community of each spouse and from the personal property of the spouse who incurred the debt.

(2) The spouse who paid a community debt after the distribution of the community has recourse against the other spouse for half of the payment.

Principe 4:58 Recouvrement des dettes de la communauté après répartition des biens communs

(1) Après répartition des biens communs, les dettes de la communauté peuvent être recouvrées sur la part de chaque époux dans les biens communs ainsi que sur les biens propres de l'époux qui a souscrit la dette.

(2) L'époux qui a payé une dette de la communauté après répartition des biens communs, dispose d'une action récursoire contre l'autre époux pour la moitié du montant acquitté.

Prinzip 4:58 Haftung für gemeinschaftliche Schulden nach Teilung der Errungenschaftsgemeinschaft

(1) Nach Teilung der Errungenschaftsgemeinschaft haften für gemeinschaftliche Schulden der Anteil jedes Ehegatten an der Gemeinschaft und das persönliche Vermögen des Ehegatten, der die Verbindlichkeit eingegangen ist.

(2) Der Ehegatte, der eine gemeinschaftliche Schuld nach Teilung der Errungenschaftsgemeinschaft beglichen hat, kann vom anderen Ehegatten die Hälfte der gezahlten Summe verlangen.

INTERNATIONAL INSTRUMENTS

None of particular relevance.

COMPARATIVE OVERVIEW

Settlement of the debts at the liquidation of the community

Until the liquidation and distribution of the community, debts are settled in accordance with the rules on the recovery of community debts (see comparative overview under Principle 4:42). In principle, community debts are settled at the liquidation of the community. Community debts are deducted from the community property. Most of the legal systems do not establish a ranking order between the community debts and apply general law as in FRANCE.[2713] This means that all community debts have the same rank, except when they are privileged or guaranteed by a mortgage. In other systems the law establishes a ranking order between the different categories of community debts. In BELGIUM,[2714] privileged debts rank first in accordance to their rank of privilege, followed by mortgages according to the day of their registration, followed by community debts that can be recovered on the community and the personal property of both spouses and finally the community debts that can be recovered from the community and the personal property of one spouse.

Settlement of the debts after liquidation and distribution

When there are insufficient assets to pay the community debts or when the debts are not yet payable at the date of liquidation and distribution of the community assets, they will have to be settled in due time after that date. The rights of a creditor do not change after the liquidation and distribution of the community.

In most of the legal systems surveyed the rules on settlement of the community debts after liquidation and distribution of the community follow in general the rules on recovery during the matrimonial property regime. In this respect, however, a distinction has to be made between the position of the creditor and the question of contribution between the spouses.

In BELGIAN law,[2715] each spouse is jointly and severally liable for community debts left after liquidation and distribution with all his assets, as well his personal assets as the assets he received as his or her share in the community.[2716] An exception is provided for the so-called incomplete community debts. Since those debts can only be recovered from the community assets and from the assets of the spouse who entered into such a debt, they can only be recovered after liquidation and distribution from all the assets of the contracting spouse. The non-contracting spouse is only liable for the community assets that were distributed to him. A spouse, who has paid a community debt, has the right to recover half of the amount from the other spouse.[2717]

2713 See FERRAND/BRAAT, French Report, Q 50.

2714 Art. 1439 Belgian Civil Code.

2715 Art. 1440 para. 2 Belgian Civil Code. See PINTENS/ALLAERTS/SEYNS/PIGNOLET, Belgian Report, Q 50.

2716 Art. 1440 para. 1 Belgian Civil Code. See PINTENS/ALLAERTS/SEYNS/PIGNOLET, Belgian Report, Q 50.

2717 Art. 1441 Belgian Civil Code.

In FRENCH law,[2718] each spouse is liable to pay with his or her personal property and his or her share of the community for the debts that entered into the community in his or her name. For community debts that entered into the community in the name of the other spouse, that spouse is liable to pay with all his or her property for half of those debts.[2719] But the spouse can invoke a *beneficium emolumentum*,[2720] when an inventory has been made. In that case he or she is only liable up to the amount of his or her share in the community.[2721] Concerning the contribution between the spouses, each spouse has to pay half of the community debts.[2722] The spouse who has paid more than his or her share, has recourse against the other spouse for the excess.[2723] BULGARIAN[2724] and DUTCH[2725] law offer similar solutions. In other legal systems each debt is attributed to one of the spouses as in MALTA,[2726] RUSSIA[2727] and SLOVAKIA.[2728]

COMMENT

1. Principle 4:58 is restricted to the settlement of community debts after the liquidation of the community and the distribution of the assets whereas the settlement of community debts during the regime and at liquidation is governed by Principle 4:42. Principle 4:58 concerns debts that were not settled at the liquidation of the community because there were no assets available to recover them or because the debts were not yet due at the liquidation.

2. Principle 4:58(1) regulates the position of the creditor and states that he may recover a debt paid after dissolution of the community from the share of the community of each spouse and from the personal property of the spouse who incurred the debt.

3. Principle 4:58(2) regulates the recourse of one spouse against the other. The spouse who paid the debt has recourse against the other for half of the payment.

2718 Art. 1482 French Civil Code. See FERRAND/BRAAT, French Report, Q 50.
2719 Art. 1483 para. 1 French Civil Code. See FERRAND/BRAAT, French Report, Q 50.
2720 A protection mesure against the insolvability of the community for the spouse who made an inventory.
2721 Art. 1483 para. 1 French Civil Code. See FERRAND/BRAAT, French Report, Q 50.
2722 Art. 1485 para. 1 French Civil Code.
2723 Art. 1487 French Civil Code.
2724 See TODOROVA, Bulgarian Report, Q 50.
2725 See BOELE-WOELKI/SCHONEWILLE/SCHRAMA, Dutch Report, Q 50.
2726 Art. 1333 Maltese Civil Code.
2727 See ANTOKOLSKAIA, Russian Report, Q 50.
2728 See HAŤAPKA, Slovakian Report, Q 55.

4. If the spouses have agreed on an unequal distribution of the community according to Principle 4:55, recourse between the spouses has to be adjusted in accordance with the shares of both spouses. The same solution applies if the competent authority has adjusted the distribution of the community according to Principle 4:58(2).

PRINCIPLES OF EUROPEAN FAMILY LAW REGARDING PROPERTY RELATIONS BETWEEN SPOUSES

PREAMBLE

Recognising that, notwithstanding the existing diversities between national family law systems, there is nevertheless a growing convergence of laws;
Recognising that the free movement of persons within Europe is hindered by the remaining differences;
Desiring to contribute to common European values regarding the equality of spouses;
Desiring to strike a balance between the spouses' private autonomy and their solidarity;
Desiring to contribute to the welfare of the family;
Desiring to secure the protection of the family home;
Desiring to guarantee each spouse a fair share in the property acquired during the marriage;
Desiring to contribute to the harmonisation of family law in Europe and to strengthen the rights of its citizens;
The Commission on European Family Law recommends the following Principles:

CHAPTER I: GENERAL RIGHTS AND DUTIES OF THE SPOUSES

Principle 4:1 General application
The Principles contained in this Chapter apply irrespective of the matrimonial property regime.

Principle 4:2 Equality of the spouses
Both spouses have equal rights and duties.

Principle 4:3 Legal capacity of the spouses

Subject to the following Principles, each spouse has full legal capacity and in particular is free to enter into legal transactions with the other spouse and with third persons.

Principle 4:4 Contribution to the needs of the family

(1) Each spouse should contribute to the needs of the family according to his or her ability.

(2) The contribution to the needs of the family encompasses contributions to the running of the household, the personal needs of the spouses and the maintenance, upbringing and education of the children.

(3) If a spouse does not fulfill his or her obligation to contribute to the needs of the family the other spouse may request the competent authority to determine the contribution.

Principle 4:5 Protection of the family home and household goods

(1) Any act of disposal of rights to the family home or household goods requires the consent of both spouses.

(2) Any act of disposal by one spouse without the consent of the other is valid if the latter ratifies it.

(3) If a spouse refuses or is unable to give consent, the other spouse may request authorisation by the competent authority.

(4) Any act of disposal in breach of the preceding paragraphs may be annulled by the competent authority upon the application of the non-consenting spouse.

Principle 4:6 Protection of the leased family home

(1) Where the family home is leased to one spouse, the lease is deemed to belong to both spouses, even if it has been concluded before the marriage.

(2) One spouse may not terminate or modify the lease without the consent of the other.

(3) The landlord should notify both spouses to terminate the lease.

Principle 4:7 Representation

(1) One spouse may authorise the other spouse to represent him or her in legal transactions.

(2) When a spouse is unable to express his or her intentions, the competent authority may authorise the other spouse

- (a) to act alone where the consent of his or her spouse would otherwise be required;
- (b) to represent his or her spouse when the latter has the power to act alone.

Principle 4:8 Duty to inform
Each spouse has the duty to inform the other about his or her assets and debts and about significant acts of administration in so far as it is necessary to enable the other to exercise his or her rights.

Principle 4:9 Freedom to enter into marital property agreements
Spouses should be free to enter into agreements determining their marital property relationship.

CHAPTER II: MARITAL PROPERTY AGREEMENTS

Principle 4:10 Concept
(1) In a marital property agreement made before the marriage the future spouses may choose their matrimonial property regime.
(2) During the marriage the spouses may modify their matrimonial property regime or change it for another regime.

Principle 4:11 Form requirements
Marital property agreements should be drawn up by a notary or other legal professional with comparable functions, be dated and should be signed by both spouses.

Principle 4:12 Disclosure
When entering into a marital property agreement the spouses should be under a mutual duty to disclose their assets and debts.

Principle 4:13 Obligations of a notary or other legal professional with comparable functions
The notary or other legal professional with comparable functions should
- (a) give impartial advice to each spouse separately,
- (b) ensure that each spouse understands the legal consequences of the marital property agreement, and
- (c) ensure that both spouses freely consent to the agreement.

Principle 4:14 Effects as against third parties
As against third parties marital property agreements are binding if at the time of making the transactions with a spouse
- (a) such information is publically documented; or
- (b) they knew of the relevant parts of the agreement.

Principle 4:15 Exceptional hardship
Having regard to the circumstances when the agreement was concluded or those subsequently arising, the competent authority may, in cases of exceptional hardship, set aside or adjust a marital property agreement.

CHAPTER III: MATRIMONIAL PROPERTY REGIMES

SECTION A: PARTICIPATION IN ACQUISITIONS

Principle 4:16 Applicability of the participation in acquisitions regime
The participation in acquisitions regime applies if the spouses have not agreed otherwise in accordance with Chapter II.

CONCEPT

Principle 4:17 Concept of participation in acquisitions
(1) Participation in acquisitions is a matrimonial property regime during which property is owned separately by the spouses.
(2) Each spouse's property comprises acquisitions and reserved property.
(3) Upon dissolution of the regime each spouse participates in the acquisitions made by the other during the regime in accordance with Principle 4:31.

ASSETS

Principle 4:18 Acquisitions
(1) The acquisitions comprise the assets acquired during the regime, other than the reserved property. In particular, the acquisitions include
- (a) each spouse's income and gains whether derived from earnings or property;
- (b) assets acquired by means of either spouse's income or gains.

(2) Assets are presumed to be acquisitions unless they are proved to be reserved property.

Principle 4:19 Reserved property
Reserved property comprises
- (a) assets acquired before the commencement of the regime;
- (b) gifts, inheritances and bequests acquired during the regime;
- (c) assets substituting reserved property;
- (d) assets that are personal in nature;
- (e) assets exclusively acquired for a spouse's profession;
- (f) increases in value of the property included in (a) to (e).

Principle 4:20 Presumption of joint ownership
Assets are presumed to be owned jointly by both spouses unless otherwise proved.

DEBTS

Principle 4:21 Personal debts
Debts incurred by one spouse are his or her personal debts.

Principle 4:22 Recovery of personal debts
Personal debts are recoverable from the debtor spouse's acquisitions and his or her reserved property.

ADMINISTRATION

Principle 4:23 Administration of property
Subject to Principles 4:6 and 4:7, each spouse is entitled to administer his or her property independently.

DISSOLUTION

Principle 4:24 Grounds for dissolution
The regime on the participation in acquisitions is dissolved by
- (a) the death of a spouse;
- (b) the annulment of the marriage, divorce or legal separation;
- (c) the change of the matrimonial property regime by agreement between the spouses; or
- (d) the decision of the competent authority based upon serious grounds.

Principle 4:25 Date of dissolution
The dissolution of the regime on the participation in acquisitions takes effect
- (a) at the date of the death of a spouse;
- (b) in the case of annulment of the marriage, divorce or legal separation, at the date of the application;
- (c) in the case of an agreement to change to another matrimonial property regime, at the date of the change; and
- (d) in the case of a decision by the competent authority, at the date of the application.

LIQUIDATION

Principle 4:26 Determination and valuation of acquisitions

(1) The acquisitions of each spouse should be determined at the date of the dissolution of the regime, as specified by Principle 4:25.
(2) The acquisitions should be valued at the date of the liquidation of the regime.

Principle 4:27 Detrimental transactions

In calculating the acquisitions of each spouse account should be taken of

(a) excessive gifts;
(b) dissipation of assets;
(c) other acts that have intentionally diminished the value of the acquisitions to the detriment of the other spouse.

Principle 4:28 Compensation

(1) The acquisitions of a spouse should be compensated for any contribution profiting his or her reserved property.
(2) The reserved property of a spouse should be compensated for any contribution profiting his or her acquisitions.
(3) Debts encumber the property in relation to which they were incurred. In cases of doubt they are presumed to encumber the acquisitions.
(4) In the case of investment for the acquisition, improvement or preservation of an asset the calculation of the compensation should take into account any resulting increase or decrease in the value of the asset.
(5) The compensation should be paid in money, unless the spouses agree otherwise.

PARTICIPATION

Principle 4:29 Agreement on participation

Spouses are free to agree on the participation in the acquisitions.

Principle 4:30 Allocation of the family home and household goods

The competent authority may, in the interest of the family and subject to payment of compensation, allocate the family home and household goods to one of the spouses.

Principle 4:31 Equal participation in the net acquisitions

(1) If one spouse's net acquisitions exceed the value of that of the other, the latter participates in the surplus to the amount of one half.
(2) Net acquisitions are the value of the acquisitions after deducting the debts.

(3) Losses made by one spouse exceeding his or her acquisitions at the date of the dissolution, should not be shared by the other spouse.
(4) The claim of participation is a monetary one, unless the spouses agree otherwise.
(5) Upon request of the debtor spouse the competent authority may, where there are serious grounds for doing so, authorise payments to be deferred or payable in instalments.

Principle 4:32 Adjustment by the competent authority
In cases of exceptional hardship the competent authority can
- (a) adjust the participation;
- (b) set aside or modify any spousal agreement made in accordance with Principle 4:29.

SECTION B: COMMUNITY OF ACQUISITIONS

Principle 4:33 Applicability of the community of acquisitions regime
The community of acquisitions regime applies if the spouses have not agreed otherwise in accordance with Chapter II.

CONCEPT

Principle 4:34 Concept of the community of acquisitions
(1) The community of acquisitions is a matrimonial property regime comprising community property and personal property.
(2) Community property is property acquired during the community of acquisitions and which is not personal property.
(3) Personal property is each spouse's own property.

ASSETS

Principle 4:35 Community property
(1) Community property comprises any property movable and immovable acquired during the regime that is not the personal property of one of the spouses.
(2) In particular, community property includes
- (a) the spouses' income and gains whether derived from earnings, community property or personal property;
- (b) assets acquired either jointly or individually by the spouses during the community of acquisitions by means of the spouses' income and gains;
- (c) gifts and bequests to both spouses or to one spouse on condition that they belong to community property.

Principle 4:36 Personal property
Personal property comprises
(a) assets acquired before entering into the community of acquisitions;
(b) gifts, inheritances and bequests acquired during the regime;
(c) assets acquired through substitution, investment or reinvestment in accordance with Principles 4:37 and 4:38;
(d) assets personal in nature, acquired during the regime;
(e) assets exclusively acquired for a spouse's profession.

Principle 4:37 Substitution
(1) Any asset substituting personal assets without extra payment should be regarded as personal property.
(2) Any asset substituting personal assets with additional payment should be regarded as personal property unless the payment provided by community property equals or exceeds the value of the substituted asset.
(3) Where additional payment is made by one category of property, compensation is payable by the other.

Principle 4:38 Investment or reinvestment
(1) Any asset acquired solely through the investment or reinvestment of personal assets should be regarded as personal property.
(2) Any asset acquired partly through the investment or reinvestment of personal assets and partly through community assets should belong to the personal property unless the payment provided by community property equals or exceeds the value of the investment or reinvestment.
(3) Where additional investment of reinvestment is made by one category of property, compensation is payable by the other.

Principle 4:39 Presumption of community property
Assets are presumed to be community property unless they are proved to be personal property in accordance with Principles 4:35 to 4:38.

DEBTS

Principle 4:40 Community debts
The community debts are
(a) debts incurred jointly by both spouses;
(b) debts incurred by one spouse in order to meet the appropriate family needs;
(c) debts related to the maintenance of children;
(d) debts incurred by one spouse for the use or administration of community assets or in the interest of the community property;
(e) debts related to a spouse's professional activities;

(f) debts related to gifts and bequests belonging to community property;
(g) debts that have not been proved to be personal debts.

Principle 4:41 Personal debts
Personal debts of a spouse are
(a) debts incurred before entering into the community of acquisitions;
(b) debts related to gifts, inheritances and bequests acquired by one spouse during the regime;
(c) debts related to personal property;
(d) debts which are personal by nature;
(e) debts incurred without the required consent of the other spouse.

Principle 4:42 Recovery of community debts
(1) Community debts can be recovered from the community property and from the personal property of the spouse who incurred the debt.
(2) If the spouses are jointly and severally liable, the debt may also be recovered from the personal property of either spouse.

Principle 4:43 Recovery of personal debts
(1) Debts which are personal to one spouse can be recovered from
(a) the debtor spouse's personal property;
(b) the debtor spouse's income and gains;
(c) the community assets to the extent of their merger with the debtor spouse's personal property.
(2) Personal debts related to tort or crime can also be recovered from half of the net value of the community property where the debtor spouse's personal property, income and gains are insufficient for recovery.

ADMINISTRATION

Principle 4:44 Administration of community property
(1) Each spouse is entitled to administer community property, but important acts require joint administration.
(2) If one spouse refuses to consent to an act requiring joint administration, the other spouse may apply to the competent authority for authorisation to act alone.

Principle 4:45 Acts requiring joint administration
Subject to Principles 4:4 to 4:8 and taking into account the economic circumstances of the spouses, acts requiring joint administration include in particular the following:
(a) acquisition, alienation and encumbrance of immovable property;
(b) entering into significant loan agreements, guarantees and sureties;
(c) making significant gifts.

Principle 4:46 Annulment of acts of administration
Acts requiring joint administration may be annulled by the competent authority upon the application of the non-consenting spouse.

Principle 4:47 Administration of personal property
Subject to Principles 4:6 and 4:7 each spouse is entitled to administer his or her personal property independently.

Principle 4:48 Divestment of the right to administer community property
(1) Upon application by one spouse the competent authority may divest the other spouse of the right to administer in whole or in part the community property on the grounds of
- (a) inability to express his or her intentions;
- (b) serious maladministration; or
- (c) serious failure to comply with the duty to inform in accordance with Principle 4:8.

(2) To the extent that one spouse has been divested of the right to administer the community property the power vests exclusively in the other spouse.
(3) Upon application of either spouse the competent authority may reinstate the divested spouse.

DISSOLUTION

Principle 4:49 Grounds for dissolution
The community of acquisitions regime is dissolved by
- (a) the death of a spouse;
- (b) the annulment of the marriage, divorce or legal separation;
- (c) the change of the matrimonial property regime by agreement between the spouses; or
- (d) the decision of the competent authority based upon serious grounds ordering separation of property.

Principle 4:50 Date of dissolution
The dissolution of the community of acquisitions regime takes effect
- (a) at the date of the death of a spouse;
- (b) in the case of annulment of the marriage, divorce or legal separation as between the spouses, either at the date of the application or, if the spouses separated earlier, at the date of their separation and as against third persons, at the date of the registration of the decision of the competent authority;
- (c) in the case of an agreement to change to another matrimonial property regime as between the spouses, at the date of the change and as against third persons, at the date of the publication of the agreement;

(d) in the case of separation of property ordered by the competent authority as between the spouses, at the date of the application and against third persons, at the date of the publication of the application.

Principle 4:51 Administration after dissolution
After the dissolution of the community of acquisitions the general rules of joint ownership apply to administration.

LIQUIDATION

Principle 4:52 Determination and valuation of the community property
(1) Community property should be determined at the date of the dissolution of the community of acquisitions, as specified by Principle 4:50.
(2) The community assets should be valued at the date of their distribution.

Principle 4:53 Compensation
(1) The community property should be compensated for any contribution profiting the personal property of a spouse.
(2) The personal property of a spouse should be compensated for any contribution profiting the community property.
(3) In the case of investment for the acquisition, improvement or preservation of an asset, the calculation of the compensation should take into account any resulting increase or decrease in the value of the asset.
(4) The compensation should be paid in money, unless the spouses agree otherwise.

Principle 4:54 Ranking of community debts
Community debts and compensation rights rank equally.

DISTRIBUTION

Principle 4:55 Agreement on distribution
Spouses are free to agree on the distribution of the community property.

Principle 4:56 Allocation of the family home, household goods and professional assets
In determining the distribution of community property a competent authority may, in the interest of the family and subject to payment of compensation, allocate to one of the spouses

(a) the family home and household goods;
(b) professional assets.

Principle 4:57 Equal sharing and adjustment

(1) The community property should be distributed equally between the spouses.

(2) In cases of exceptional hardship the competent authority can

(a) adjust the distribution;

(b) set aside or modify any spousal agreement made in accordance with Principle 4:55.

Principle 4:58 Recovery of community debts after distribution of the community

(1) Community debts can be recovered after the distribution of the community from the share of the community of each spouse and from the personal property of the spouse who incurred the debt.

(2) The spouse who paid a community debt after the distribution of the community has recourse against the other spouse for half of the payment.

PRINCIPES DE DROIT EUROPÉEN DE LA FAMILLE CONCERNANT LES RELATIONS PATRIMONIALES DES ÉPOUX

PREAMBULE

Reconnaissant que, malgré les diversités existant entre les systèmes nationaux de droit de la famille, la convergence entre les lois tend à s'accroître;
Reconnaissant que la libre circulation des personnes en Europe est entravée par les différences qui demeurent;
Souhaitant contribuer à des valeurs communes européennes concernant l'égalité des époux;
Souhaitant établir un équilibre entre l'autonomie de la volonté des époux et leur solidarité;
Souhaitant contribuer au bien être de la famille;
Souhaitant assurer la protection du logement de la famille;
Souhaitant garantir à chaque époux une part équitable dans le patrimoine acquis pendant le mariage;
Souhaitant contribuer à l'harmonisation du droit de la famille en Europe et renforcer les droits de ses citoyens;
La Commission pour le Droit Européen de la Famille recommande les Principes suivants:

CHAPITRE I: DROITS ET DEVOIRS GÉNÉRAUX DES ÉPOUX

Principe 4:1 Application générale
Les Principes contenus dans ce Chapitre sont applicables quel que soit le régime matrimonial des époux.

Principe 4:2 Egalité des époux
Chaque époux a les mêmes droits et devoirs.

Principe 4:3 Capacité juridique des époux
Sous réserve des principes suivants, chaque époux a la pleine capacité juridique, et peut en particulier conclure des actes juridiques avec l'autre époux ou avec des tiers.

Principe 4:4 Contribution aux besoins de la famille
(1) Chaque époux contribue aux besoins de la famille à proportion de ses facultés.
(2) La contribution aux besoins de la famille comprend les contributions aux charges du ménage, aux besoins personnels des époux, à l'entretien et à l'éducation des enfants.
(3) Si un époux n'exécute pas son obligation de contribuer aux besoins de la famille, l'autre époux peut demander à l'autorité compétente de fixer le montant de la contribution.

Principe 4:5 Protection du logement de la famille et des meubles meublants
(1) Tout acte de disposition des droits sur le logement de la famille ou sur les meubles meublants requiert le consentement de chaque époux.
(2) Tout acte de disposition par un époux sans le consentement de l'autre est valide si ce dernier le confirme.
(3) Si un époux refuse son consentement ou n'est pas en mesure de le donner, l'autre époux peut solliciter l'autorisation de l'autorité compétente.
(4) Tout acte de disposition passé en violation des alinéas précédents peut être annulé par l'autorité compétente à la demande de l'époux qui n'a pas consenti.

Principe 4:6 Protection du bail relatif au logement de la famille
(1) Si le contrat de bail du logement de la famille a été conclu par un seul des époux, ce bail est réputé appartenir à l'un et l'autre des époux même s'il a été conclu avant le mariage.
(2) Un époux ne peut, sans le consentement de l'autre, mettre fin au contrat de bail ou le modifier.
(3) Le bailleur notifie la résiliation du bail à chaque époux.

Principe 4:7 Représentation
(1) Un époux peut donner mandat à l'autre époux de le représenter dans les actes juridiques.
(2) Si un époux est hors d'état de manifester sa volonté, l'autorité compétente peut autoriser l'autre époux
(a) à agir seul dans le cas où le consentement de son époux serait nécessaire;
(b) à représenter son époux dans le cas où ce dernier a le pouvoir d'agir seul.

Principe 4:8 Obligation d'information
Chaque époux est tenu d'informer l'autre époux de son patrimoine ainsi que des actes importants d'administration dans la mesure nécessaire pour permettre à l'autre époux d'exercer ses droits.

Principe 4:9 Liberté de conclure des conventions patrimoniales
Les époux sont libres de conclure des conventions matrimoniales portant sur leurs relations patrimoniales.

CHAPITRE II: CONVENTIONS MATRIMONIALES PORTANT SUR LES RELATIONS PATRIMONIALES DES ÉPOUX

Principe 4:10 Notion
(1) Dans une convention conclue avant le mariage, les futurs époux peuvent choisir leur régime matrimonial.
(2) Au cours du mariage, les époux peuvent modifier leur régime ou en changer entièrement.

Principe 4:11 Conditions de forme
Les conventions matrimoniales portant sur les relations patrimoniales entre époux doivent être dressées par un notaire ou un autre professionnel du droit exerçant des fonctions comparables, être datées et doivent signées par chaque époux.

Principe 4:12 Révélation du patrimoine
Lorsque les époux concluent une convention matrimoniale, chacun d'eux est tenu de révéler à l'autre la composition de son patrimoine.

Principe 4:13 Obligations du notaire ou du professionnel du droit exerçant des fonctions comparables
Le notaire ou le professionnel du droit exerçant des fonctions comparables
- (a) conseille chaque époux séparément, en toute impartialité,
- (b) s'assure que chaque époux comprend les conséquences juridiques de la convention matrimoniale, et
- (c) s'assure que le consentement des deux époux est libre.

Principe 4:14 Effets à l'égard des tiers
Les conventions matrimoniales portant sur les relations patrimoniales entre époux sont opposables aux tiers si, au moment de la conclusion d'une convention avec un époux,
- (a) ces informations sont contenues dans un document public; ou
- (b) les tiers avaient connaissance des clauses pertinentes de la convention matrimoniale.

Principe 4:15 Dureté exceptionnelle
En cas de dureté exceptionnelle, l'autorité compétente peut, en tenant compte des circonstances dans lesquelles la convention matrimoniale a été conclue ou de circonstances postérieures, écarter ou adapter la convention matrimoniale.

CHAPITRE III: RÉGIMES MATRIMONIAUX

SECTION A: PARTICIPATION AUX ACQUÊTS

Principe 4:16 Applicabilité du régime de participation aux acquêts
Le régime de la participation aux acquêts s'applique si les époux n'ont pas conclu de convention contraire conformément au Chapitre II.

NOTION

Principe 4:17 Notion de participation aux acquêts
(1) La participation aux acquêts est un régime matrimonial pendant la durée duquel les époux sont chacun propriétaires de leur patrimoine.
(2) Le patrimoine de chaque époux se compose d'acquêts et de biens réservés.
(3) Lors de la dissolution du régime matrimonial, et conformément au Principe 4:31 chaque époux participe aux acquêts réalisés pendant la durée du régime.

L'ACTIF

Principe 4:18 Acquêts
(1) Les acquêts comprennent les biens acquis pendant le régime et qui ne sont pas des biens réservés. Les acquêts comprennent notamment
- (a) les revenus et gains de chaque époux, qu'ils proviennent de salaires ou de son patrimoine;
- (b) les biens acquis au moyen de revenus ou gains d'un époux.

(2) Les biens sont présumés acquêts sauf preuve contraire.

Principe 4:19 Propriété réservée
La propriété réservée comprend
- (a) les biens acquis avant le début du régime matrimonial;
- (b) les donations, successions et legs intervenus durant le régime;
- (c) les biens acquis en substitution de biens réservés;
- (d) les biens personnels par nature;
- (e) les biens acquis exclusivement pour la profession d'un époux;
- (f) les plus values des biens visés aux points (a) à (e).

Principe 4:20 Présomption d'indivision
Sauf preuve contraire, les biens sont présumés appartenir en indivision aux deux époux.

DETTES

Principe 4:21 Dettes personnelles
Les dettes souscrites par un époux lui sont personnelles.

Principe 4:22 Recouvrement des dettes personnelles
Les dettes personnelles peuvent être recouvrées sur les acquêts et la propriété réservée de l'époux débiteur.

ADMINISTRATION

Principe 4:23 Administration des biens
Sous réserve des principes 4:6 et 4:7, chaque époux est habilité à administrer seul ses biens.

DISSOLUTION

Principe 4:24 Motifs de dissolution
Le régime de participation aux acquêts est dissous par
(a) le décès d'un époux;
(b) l'annulation du mariage, le divorce ou la séparation de corps;
(c) le changement de régime matrimonial par accord entre les époux; ou
(d) la décision de l'autorité compétente, fondée sur des motifs graves.

Principe 4:25 Date de dissolution
La dissolution du régime de participation aux acquêts prend effet
(a) à la date du décès d'un époux;
(b) en cas d'annulation du mariage, de divorce ou de séparation de corps, à la date de la demande;
(c) en cas de convention de changement de régime matrimonial, à la date du changement; et
(d) en cas de décision de l'autorité compétente, à la date de la demande.

LIQUIDATION

Principe 4:26 Détermination et évaluation des acquêts
(1) Les acquêts de chaque époux sont déterminés à la date de dissolution du régime, telle que précisée au Principe 4:25.
(2) Les acquêts sont évalués à la date de liquidation du régime.

Principe 4:27 Opérations préjudiciables

Lors du calcul des acquêts de chaque époux, il est tenu compte

(a) des donations excessives;
(b) des biens dissipés;
(c) d'autres actes ayant intentionnellement diminué la valeur des acquêts au détriment de l'autre époux.

Principe 4:28 Compensation

(1) Une récompense est due pour toute contribution des acquêts d'un époux réalisée au profit de ses biens réservés.
(2) Une récompense est due pour toute contribution des biens réservés d'un époux réalisée au profit de ses acquêts.
(3) Les dettes grèvent le patrimoine en rapport avec lequel elles sont nées. En cas de doute, elles sont présumées grever les acquêts.
(4) En cas d'investissement en vue de l'acquisition, de l'amélioration ou de la conservation d'un bien, il est tenu compte, lors du calcul du montant de la récompense, de la plus-value ou de la moins-value du bien au profit duquel l'investissement a été réalisé.
(5) La récompense est due sous forme monétaire, sauf accord contraire des époux.

PARTICIPTATION

Principe 4:29 Convention sur la participation

Les époux peuvent conclure une convention sur la participation aux acquêts.

Principe 4:30 Attribution du logement de la famille et de meubles meublants

L'autorité compétente peut, dans l'intérêt de la famille et moyennant compensation financière, attribuer à l'un des époux le logement de la famille et des meubles meublants.

Principe 4:31 Participation égale aux acquêts nets

(1) Si les acquêts nets d'un époux dépassent en valeur ceux de l'autre époux, ce dernier participe à l'accroissement pour moitié.
(2) Les acquêts nets correspondent à la valeur des acquêts après déduction des dettes.
(3) Les pertes réalisées par un époux qui, à la date de la dissolution, sont supérieures à ses acquêts, ne sont pas partagées avec l'autre époux.
(4) La créance de participation est de nature monétaire, sauf accord contraire des époux
(5) A la requête de l'époux débiteur, l'autorité compétente peut, en présence de motifs graves, autoriser des délais de paiement ou des paiements échelonnés.

Principe 4:32 Adaptations par l'autorité compétente

En cas de dureté exceptionnelle, l'autorité compétente peut

(a) procéder à des adaptations de la participation;
(b) écarter ou modifier toute convention conclue entre les époux en vertu du Principe 4:29.

SECTION B: COMMUNAUTÉ D'ACQUÊTS

Principe 4:33 Applicabilité du régime de communauté d'acquêts
Le régime de communauté d'acquêts s'applique si les époux n'ont pas conclu de convention contraire conformément au Chapitre II.

NOTION

Principe 4:34 Notion de communauté d'acquêts
(1) La communauté d'acquêts est un régime matrimonial qui comprend le patrimoine commun et le patrimoine personnel.
(2) Le patrimoine commun est le patrimoine acquis durant la communauté d'acquêts et qui n'est pas patrimoine personnel.
(3) Le patrimoine personnel est le patrimoine propre de chaque époux.

L'ACTIF

Principe 4:35 La communauté
(1) La communauté comprend tout bien meuble et immeuble acquis durant le régime et qui n'est pas propre à un des époux.
(2) En particulier, la communauté comprend
(a) les revenus et gains provenant soit de l'activité professionnelle des époux, soit de leur patrimoine commun ou personnel;
(b) les biens acquis en commun ou séparément par les époux durant la communauté d'acquêts au moyen des revenus et gains des époux;
(c) les donations et legs faits aux deux époux, ou à un seul époux sous condition qu'ils tombent dans la communauté.

Principe 4:36 Patrimoine propre
Le patrimoine propre comprend
(a) les biens acquis avant l'existence de la communauté d'acquêts;
(b) les successions et les libéralités échues pendant le régime;
(c) les biens acquis par échange, emploi ou remploi conformément aux Principes 4:37 et 4:38;
(d) les biens personnels par nature, acquis durant le régime;
(e) les biens acquis exclusivement pour l'activité professionnelle d'un époux.

Principe 4:37 Substitution
(1) Tout bien qui se substitue à un bien propre sans paiement additionnel est lui-même propre.
(2) Tout bien qui se substitue à un bien propre avec paiement additionnel est lui-même propre, sauf si le payement additionnel fait par la communauté est égal à la valeur du bien remplacé ou l'excède.
(3) En cas de paiement additionnel fait par un des patrimoines, une récompense est due par l'autre.

Principe 4:38 Emploi ou remploi
(1) Tout bien acquis exclusivement par emploi ou remploi de biens propres est lui-même propre.
(2) Tout bien acquis en partie par emploi ou remploi de biens propres et en partie par des biens communs, appartient au patrimoine propre sauf si le paiement fait par la communauté est égal à la valeur de l'emploi ou du remploi ou bien l'excède.
(3) En cas d'emploi ou de remploi additionnel fait par un des patrimoines, une récompense est due par l'autre.

Principe 4:39 Présomption de communauté
Les biens sont présumés communs sauf si leur caractère propre est prouvé conformément aux Principes 4:35 à 4:38.

DETTES

Principe 4:40 Passif de la communauté
Le passif de la communauté se compose
- (a) des dettes contractées conjointement par les deux époux;
- (b) des dettes contractées par un époux pour les besoins appropriés de la famille;
- (c) des dettes d'aliments envers les enfants;
- (d) des dettes contractées par un époux pour l'usage ou l'administration des biens communs ou dans l'intérêt de la communauté;
- (e) des dettes relatives à l'activité professionnelle d'un époux;
- (f) des dettes relatives aux donations ou legs faisant partie de la communauté;
- (g) des dettes dont il n'est pas prouvé qu'elles sont des dettes personnelles.

Principe 4:41 Dettes propres
Les dettes propres d'un époux sont
- (a) les dettes contractées avant l'existence de la communauté d'acquêts;
- (b) les dettes grevant les successions et libéralités échues à l'époux pendant le régime;
- (c) les dettes relatives aux biens propres;

(d) les dettes personnelles par leur nature;
(e) les dettes contractées sans le consentement nécessaire de l'autre époux.

Principe 4:42 Recouvrement des dettes de la communauté
(1) Les dettes de la communauté peuvent être recouvrées sur les biens communs et sur les biens propres de l'époux qui a contracté la dette.
(2) Si les époux sont solidairement tenus, la dette peut être recouvrée également sur les biens propres de l'un ou l'autre époux.

Principe 4:43 Recouvrement des dettes propres
(1) Les dettes propres d'un époux peuvent être recouvrées sur
(a) les biens propres de cet époux;
(b) ses gains et salaires;
(c) les biens communs dans la mesure de leur confusion avec les biens propres de l'époux débiteur.
(2) Les dettes personnelles résultant d'un délit civil ou d'une infraction pénale peuvent également être recouvrées sur la moitié de la valeur nette de la communauté, si les biens personnels ainsi que les gains et salaires de l'époux débiteur ne suffisent pas pour le recouvrement.

ADMINISTRATION

Principe 4:44 Administration de la communauté
(1) Chaque époux a le droit d'administrer les biens communs. Toutefois, les actes importants requièrent une administration conjointe.
(2) Si un époux refuse de donner son consentement à un acte nécessitant une administration conjointe, l'autre époux peut solliciter de l'autorité compétente l'autorisation de passer l'acte seul.

Principe 4:45 Actes nécessitant une administration conjointe
Sous réserve des Principes 4:4 à 4:8 et en tenant compte de la situation économique des époux, les actes nécessitant une administration conjointe englobent notamment:
(a) l'acquisition, l'aliénation et la charge de biens immeubles;
(b) la conclusion de contrats de prêts, de garanties et de sûretés de valeur significative;
(c) les donations de valeur significative.

Principe 4:46 Annulation des actes d'administration
Les actes nécessitant une administration conjointe peuvent être annulés par l'autorité compétente à la requête de l'époux qui n'a pas consenti à l'acte.

Principe 4:47 Administration du patrimoine propre
Sous réserve des principes 4:6 et 4:7, chaque époux a le pouvoir d'administrer seul ses biens propres.

Principe 4:48 Retrait du droit d'administrer la communauté
(1) A la requête d'un époux, l'autorité compétente peut priver l'autre époux du droit d'administrer tout ou partie de la communauté en raison
- (a) d'une impossibilité de manifester sa volonté;
- (b) de graves fautes d'administration; ou
- (c) d'une grave violation de l'obligation d'information énoncée au Principe 4:8.

(2) L'autre époux est seul habilité à administrer la communauté dans la mesure de la privation du droit d'administration de son conjoint.
(3) A la demande de l'un ou l'autre époux, l'autorité compétente peut restituer à l'époux destitué son droit d'administration.

DISSOLUTION

Principe 4:49 Causes de dissolution
Le régime de communauté d'acquêts est dissous par
- (a) le décès d'un époux;
- (b) l'annulation du mariage, le divorce ou la séparation de corps;
- (c) le changement de régime matrimonial par convention entre les époux; ou
- (d) la séparation de biens ordonnée par l'autorité compétente pour motifs graves.

Principe 4:50 Date de la dissolution
La dissolution du régime de communauté d'acquêts prend effet
- (a) au moment du décès d'un époux;
- (b) en cas d'annulation du mariage, de divorce ou de séparation de corps, entre époux à la date de la demande ou, si les époux se sont séparés antérieurement à cette date, à la date de leur séparation, à l'égard des tiers à la date de l'enregistrement de la décision rendue par autorité compétente;
- (c) en cas de convention de changement de régime matrimonial, entre époux à la date de la convention et à l'égard des tiers à la date de la publication de la convention;
- (d) en cas de séparation de biens prononcée par l'autorité compétente, entre époux à la date de la demande et à l'égard des tiers, à la date de la publication de la demande.

Principe 4:51 Administration après dissolution
Postérieurement à la dissolution de la communauté d'acquêts, l'administration est soumise aux règles générales relatives à l'indivision.

LIQUIDATION

Principe 4:52 Détermination et évaluation des biens communs
(1) Les biens communs sont déterminés à la date de dissolution de la communauté d'acquêts telle que précisée au Principe 4:50.
(2) Les biens communs sont évalués à la date de distribution.

Principe 4:53 Récompenses
(1) La communauté a droit à récompense pour toute contribution réalisée au profit des biens propres d'un époux.
(2) Une récompense est due pour toute contribution réalisée par les biens propres d'un époux au profit de la communauté.
(3) En cas d'investissement en vue de l'acquisition, de l'amélioration ou de la conservation d'un bien, il est tenu compte, lors du calcul du montant de la récompense, de la plus-value ou de la moins-value du bien au profit duquel l'investissement a été réalisé.
(4) La récompense est due sous forme monétaire, sauf accord contraire des époux.

Principe 4:54 Ordre de paiement des dettes communes
Les dettes de la communauté et les droits à récompense ont le même rang.

DISTRIBUTION

Principe 4:55 Convention sur la répartition
Les époux peuvent conclure une convention sur la répartition des biens communs.

Principe 4:56 Attribution du logement de la famille, de meubles meublants et de biens professionnels
Lorsqu'elle se prononce sur la répartition des biens communs, l'autorité compétente peut, dans l'intérêt de la famille et moyennant compensation financière, attribuer à l'un des époux
- (a) le logement de la famille et des meubles meublants;
- (b) des biens professionnels.

Principe 4:57 Répartition égale et adaptations
(1) Les biens communs sont répartis de façon égale entre les époux.
(2) En cas de dureté exceptionnelle, l'autorité compétente peut

(a) adapter la répartition;
(b) écarter ou modifier toute convention conclue en application du Principe 4:55.

Principe 4:58 Recouvrement des dettes de la communauté après répartition des biens communs

(1) Après répartition des biens communs, les dettes de la communauté peuvent être recouvrées sur la part de chaque époux dans les biens communs ainsi que sur les biens propres de l'époux qui a souscrit la dette.

(2) L'époux qui a payé une dette de la communauté après répartition des biens communs, dispose d'une action récursoire contre l'autre époux pour la moitié du montant acquitté.

PRINZIPIEN ZUM EUROPÄISCHEN FAMILIENRECHT BETREFFEND VERMÖGENSRECHTLICHE BEZIEHUNGEN ZWISCHEN EHEGATTEN

PRÄAMBEL

In Anerkennung, dass es trotz der bestehenden Unterschiede der nationalen Familienrechte gleichwohl eine zunehmende Übereinstimmung gibt;
In Anerkennung, dass die bestehenden Unterschiede die Freizügigkeit der Personen in Europa behindern;
In dem Wunsch zu den gemeinsamen europäischen Werten in Bezug auf die Gleichheit der Ehegatten beizutragen;
In dem Wunsch einen Ausgleich zwischen der Privatautonomie der Ehegatten und ihrer Solidarität zu schaffen;
In dem Wunsch zum Wohl der Familie beizutragen;
In dem Wunsch den Schutz der Familienwohnung zu sichern;
In dem Wunsch jedem Ehegatten eine gerechte Teilhabe an dem während der Ehe erworbenen Vermögen zu garantieren;
In dem Wunsch zur Angleichung des Familienrechts in Europa beizutragen und die Rechte seiner Bürger zu stärken;
Empfiehlt die Kommission für Europäisches Familienrecht die folgenden Prinzipien:

KAPITEL I: RECHTE UND PFLICHTEN DER EHEGATTEN IM ALLGEMEINEN

Prinzip 4:1 Allgemeine Anwendbarkeit
Die Prinzipien dieses Kapitels sind unabhängig vom jeweiligen Güterstand anwendbar.

Prinzip 4:2 Gleichheit der Ehegatten
Jeder Ehegatte hat die gleichen Rechte und Pflichten.

Prinzip 4:3 Rechts-, Geschäfts- und Handlungsfähigkeit der Ehegatten
Vorbehaltlich der nachstehenden Prinzipien besitzt jeder Ehegatte vollständige Rechts-, Geschäfts- und Handlungsfähigkeit und kann insbesondere Rechtsgeschäfte mit dem anderen Ehegatten und mit Dritten vornehmen.

Prinzip 4:4 Beitrag zum Lebensbedarf der Familie
(1) Jeder Ehegatte trägt nach seinen Fähigkeiten zum Lebensbedarf der Familie bei.
(2) Der Beitrag zum Lebensbedarf der Familie umfasst Beiträge zur Führung des Haushaltes, zu den persönlichen Bedürfnissen der Ehegatten, zum Unterhalt und zur Erziehung der Kinder.
(3) Erfüllt ein Ehegatte seine Verpflichtung zu den Familienausgaben beizutragen nicht, kann der andere Ehegatte von der zuständigen Behörde verlangen, den Beitrag zu bestimmen.

Prinzip 4:5 Schutz der Familienwohnung und Haushaltsgegenstände
(1) Jedes Verpflichtungs- oder Verfügungsgeschäft bezüglich Rechten an der Familienwohnung oder bezüglich der Haushaltsgegenstände erfordert die Zustimmung beider Ehegatten.
(2) Jedes andere Verpflichtungs- oder Verfügungsgeschäft eines Ehegatten ohne Zustimmung des anderen Ehegatten ist wirksam, wenn der andere es genehmigt.
(3) Verweigert ein Ehegatte seine Zustimmung oder ist er nicht in der Lage, diese zu erteilen, kann der andere Ehegatte eine Ermächtigung bei der zuständigen Behörde beantragen.
(4) Jedes Verpflichtungs- oder Verfügungsgeschäft, das die vorangegangenen Absätze verletzt, kann auf Antrag des nicht zustimmenden Ehegatten von der zuständigen Behörde für nichtig erklärt werden.

Prinzip 4:6 Schutz der gemieteten Familienwohnung
(1) Ist die Familienwohnung an einen der Ehegatten vermietet worden, erstreckt sich das Mietverhältnis auf beide Ehegatten, selbst wenn das Mietverhältnis vor der Ehe eingegangen worden ist.
(2) Ohne Zustimmung des anderen Ehegatten kann ein Ehegatte das Mietverhältnis nicht beenden oder ändern.
(3) Der Vermieter hat beiden Ehegatten zu kündigen, um das Mietverhältnis zu beenden.

Prinzip 4:7 Vertretung
(1) Ein Ehegatte kann den anderen Ehegatten ermächtigen, ihn bei rechtlichen Geschäften zu vertreten.
(2) Ist ein Ehegatte außerstande, seinen Willen zu äußern, kann die zuständige Behörde den anderen Ehegatten ermächtigen

(a) in den Fällen, in denen die Zustimmung seines Ehegatten erforderlich wäre, alleine zu handeln;
(b) seinen Ehegatten zu vertreten, wenn letzterer berechtigt ist, alleine zu handeln.

Prinzip 4:8 Informationspflicht
Jeder Ehegatte hat die Verpflichtung, den anderen über seine Vermögensgegenstände und Schulden sowie wesentliche Verwaltungshandlungen insoweit zu informieren, wie das notwendig ist, um dem anderen die Ausübung seiner Rechte zu ermöglichen.

Prinzip 4:9 Freiheit ehegüterrechtliche Vereinbarungen zu treffen
Die Ehegatten sind frei, Vereinbarungen zur Bestimmung ihrer ehelichen Vermögensbeziehungen zu treffen.

KAPITEL II: EHEGÜTERRECHTLICHE VEREINBARUNGEN

Prinzip 4:10 Begriff
(1) In einer vor der Eheschließung getroffenen Vereinbarung können die künftigen Ehegatten ihren Ehegüterstand wählen.
(2) Während der Ehe können die Ehegatten ihren Ehegüterstand abändern oder zu einem anderen Ehegüterstand überwechseln.

Prinzip 4:11 Formerfordernisse
Ehegüterrechtliche Vereinbarungen sind von einem Notar oder einer anderen rechtskundigen Person mit vergleichbaren Funktionen auszufertigen, zu datieren und von beiden Ehegatten zu unterzeichnen.

Prinzip 4:12 Offenlegung des Vermögens
Bei Abschluss einer ehegüterrechtlichen Vereinbarung unterliegen die Ehegatten einer gegenseitigen Verpflichtung ihre Vermögensgegenstände und Schulden offenzulegen.

Prinzip 4:13 Pflichten des Notars oder einer anderen rechtskundigen Person mit vergleichbaren Funktionen
Der Notar oder eine andere rechtskundige Person mit vergleichbaren Funktionen soll
(a) jeden Ehegatten unparteiisch und getrennt beraten,
(b) sicherstellen, dass jeder Ehegatte die rechtlichen Folgen der ehegüterrechtlichen Vereinbarung versteht, und

(c) sicherstellen, dass beide Ehegatten die Vereinbarung freiwillig treffen.

Prinzip 4:14 Wirkungen gegenüber Dritten
Gegenüber Dritten wirken ehegüterrechtliche Vereinbarungen, wenn im Zeitpunkt des Abschlusses des Rechtsgeschäfts mit einem Ehegatten
(a) derartige Informationen öffentlich dokumentiert waren; oder
(b) sie die relevanten Teile der Vereinbarung kannten.

Prinzip 4:15 Außergewöhnliche Härte
Unter Berücksichtigung der Umstände bei Zustandekommen der Vereinbarung oder später entstandener Umstände kann die zuständige Behörde in Fällen außergewöhnlicher Härte die ehegüterrechtliche Vereinbarung für unwirksam erklären oder anpassen.

KAPITEL III: EHEGÜTERSTÄNDE

ABSCHNITT A: ERRUNGENSCHAFTSBETEILIGUNG

Prinzip 4:16 Anwendbarkeit des Güterstands der Errungenschaftsbeteiligung
Der Güterstand der Errungenschaftsbeteiligung gilt, sofern die Ehegatten nicht etwas anderes gemäß Kapitel II vereinbart haben.

BEGRIFF

Prinzip 4:17 Begriff der Errungenschaftsbeteiligung
(1) Die Errungenschaftsbeteiligung ist ein Güterstand, während dessen jeder Ehegatte Eigentümer seines Vermögens ist.
(2) Das Vermögen jedes Ehegatten umfasst die Errungenschaft und das Vorbehaltsvermögen.
(3) Bei Beendigung des Güterstands ist jeder Ehegatte an der während des Güterstands erworbenen Errungenschaft des anderen gemäß Prinzip 4:31 beteiligt.

AKTIVA

Prinzip 4:18 Errungenschaft
(1) Die Errungenschaft umfasst während des Güterstands erworbene Vermögensgegenstände mit Ausnahme des Vorbehaltsvermögens. Die Errungenschaft umfasst insbesondere
(a) das Einkommen und die Gewinne eines jeden Ehegatten erzielt aus dem Einkommen oder dem Vermögen;

(b) Vermögensgegenstände, die mit Mitteln aus dem Einkommen oder dem Gewinn eines Ehegatten erworben worden sind.

(2) Es wird vermutet, dass Vermögensgegenstände Errungenschaften sind, es sei denn, es wird bewiesen, dass sie Vorbehaltsvermögen sind.

Prinzip 4:19 Vorbehaltsvermögen

Vorbehaltsvermögen umfasst

(a) vor Beginn des Güterstands erworbene Vermögensgegenstände;
(b) während des Güterstands erworbene Schenkungen, Erbschaften und Vermächtnisse;
(c) Vorbehaltsvermögen ersetzende Vermögensgegenstände;
(d) Vermögensgegenstände persönlicher Natur;
(e) ausschließlich für die Berufstätigkeit eines der Ehegatten erworbene Vermögensgegenstände;
(f) Wertsteigerungen der in (a) bis (e) genannten Vermögensgegenstände.

Prinzip 4:20 Vermutung von Miteigentum

Es wird vermutet, dass Vermögensgegenstände Miteigentum beider Ehegatten sind, es sei denn, das Gegenteil wird bewiesen.

VERBINDLICHKEITEN

Prinzip 4:21 Persönliche Verbindlichkeiten

Verbindlichkeiten eines Ehegatten sind seine persönlichen Schulden.

Prinzip 4:22 Haftung für persönliche Verbindlichkeiten

Für persönliche Verbindlichkeiten haften die Errungenschaft und das Vorbehaltsvermögen des verpflichteten Ehegatten.

VERWALTUNG

Prinzip 4:23 Verwaltung des Vermögens

Vorbehaltlich der Prinzipien 4:6 und 4:7 ist jeder Ehegatte berechtigt, sein Vermögen allein zu verwalten.

BEENDIGUNG

Prinzip 4:24 Gründe für die Beendigung

Der Güterstand der Errungenschaftsbeteiligung wird beendet durch

(a) den Tod eines Ehegatten;
(b) die Nichtigerklärung der Ehe, die Ehescheidung oder die gesetzliche Trennung;

(c) die Änderung des Güterstands durch die Ehegatten; oder
(d) die Entscheidung der zuständigen Behörde aus wichtigen Gründen.

Prinzip 4:25 Zeitpunkt der Beendigung
Die Beendigung des Güterstands der Errungenschaftsbeteiligung wird wirksam im Zeitpunkt

(a) des Todes eines Ehegatten;
(b) im Fall der Nichtigerklärung der Ehe, der Ehescheidung oder der gesetzlichen Trennung der Ehegatten im Zeitpunkt der Antragstellung;
(c) im Fall einer vereinbarten Änderung des Güterstands im Zeitpunkt der Änderung; und
(d) im Fall einer Entscheidung der zuständigen Behörde im Zeitpunkt der Antragstellung.

AUSEINANDERSETZUNG

Prinzip 4:26 Feststellung und Bewertung der Errungenschaft
(1) Die Errungenschaft jedes Ehegatten wird im Zeitpunkt der Beendigung des Güterstands festgestellt, wie in Prinzip 4:25 bestimmt.
(2) Die Errungenschaft wird im Zeitpunkt der Auseinandersetzung des Güterstands bewertet.

Prinzip 4:27 Benachteiligende Handlungen
Bei der Berechnung der Errungenschaft jedes Ehegatten werden berücksichtigt

(a) übermäßige Schenkungen;
(b) Verschwendung von Vermögensgegenständen;
(c) andere Handlungen, die den Wert der Errungenschaft zum Nachteil des anderen Ehegatten absichtlich vermindert haben.

Prinzip 4:28 Ausgleich
(1) Die Errungenschaft eines Ehegatten erhält einen Ausgleich für jeden Beitrag zugunsten seines Vorbehaltsvermögens.
(2) Das Vorbehaltsvermögen eines Ehegatten erhält einen Ausgleich für jeden Beitrag zugunsten seiner Errungenschaft.
(3) Verbindlichkeiten belasten das Vermögen in Bezug auf welches sie eingegangen wurden. Im Zweifel wird vermutet, dass sie die Errungenschaft belasten.
(4) Im Fall der Anlage für den Erwerb, die Verbesserung oder den Erhalt eines Vermögensgegenstands ist bei der Berechnung des Ausgleichs der gestiegene oder gesunkene Wert des Vermögensgegenstands in Betracht zu ziehen.
(5) Der Ausgleich ist in Geld zu zahlen, sofern die Ehegatten nichts anderes vereinbaren.

BETEILIGUNG

Prinzip 4:29 Vereinbarung über die Beteiligung
Die Ehegatten können eine Vereinbarung über die Errungenschaftsbeteiligung treffen.

Prinzip 4:30 Zuteilung der Familienwohnung und Haushaltsgegenstände
Die zuständige Behörde kann, im Interesse der Familie und vorbehaltlich einer Ausgleichszahlung, die Familienwohnung und Haushaltsgegenstände einem der Ehegatten zuteilen.

Prinzip 4:31 Gleiche Beteiligung an den Netto-Errungenschaften
(1) Übersteigt der Wert der Netto-Errungenschaft eines Ehegatten den Wert der des anderen, ist letzterer zur Hälfte des übersteigenden Betrages beteiligt.
(2) Netto-Errungenschaft ist der Wert der Errungenschaft nach Abzug der Schulden.
(3) Verluste eines Ehegatten, die seine Errungenschaft im Zeitpunkt der Beendigung übersteigen, werden nicht mit dem anderen Ehegatten geteilt.
(4) Der Anspruch auf Beteiligung ist ein Anspruch in Geld, sofern die Ehegatten nichts anderes vereinbaren.
(5) Auf Antrag des verpflichteten Ehegatten kann die zuständige Behörde aus schwerwiegenden Gründen einen Zahlungsaufschub oder eine Zahlung in Raten gewähren.

Prinzip 4:32 Anpassung durch die zuständige Behörde
In Fällen außergewöhnlicher Härte kann die zuständige Behörde
- (a) die Beteiligung anpassen;
- (b) jede nach Prinzip 4:29 getroffene Vereinbarung der Ehegatten aufheben oder abändern.

ABSCHNITT B: ERRUNGENSCHAFTSGEMEINSCHAFT

Prinzip 4:33 Anwendbarkeit des Güterstands der Errungenschaftsgemeinschaft
Der Güterstand der Errungenschaftsgemeinschaft gilt, sofern die Ehegatten nicht etwas anderes gemäß Kapitel II vereinbart haben.

BEGRIFF

Prinzip 4:34 Begriff der Errungenschaftsgemeinschaft
(1) Die Errungenschaftsgemeinschaft ist ein Güterstand bestehend aus gemeinschaftlichem Vermögen und persönlichem Vermögen.

(2) Gemeinschaftliches Vermögen ist Vermögen, das während der Errungenschaftsgemeinschaft erworben wurde und nicht persönliches Vermögen ist.
(3) Persönliches Vermögen ist das eigene Vermögen jedes der Ehegatten.

AKTIVA

Prinzip 4:35 Gemeinschaftliches Vermögen
(1) Gemeinschaftliches Vermögen besteht aus beweglichem und unbeweglichem Vermögen, das während des Güterstands erworben wird und das nicht persönliches Vermögen eines der Ehegatten ist.
(2) Insbesondere umfasst das gemeinschaftliche Vermögen
- (a) Einkommen und Gewinne erzielt aus Verdienst, gemeinschaftlichem oder persönlichem Vermögen;
- (b) Vermögensgegenstände, die entweder gemeinsam oder getrennt von den Ehegatten während der Errungenschaftsgemeinschaft mit Mitteln aus Einkommen und Gewinnen erworben werden.
- (c) Schenkungen und Zuwendungen von Todes wegen an beide Ehegatten oder an einen Ehegatten unter der Bedingung, dass sie zum gemeinschaftlichen Vermögen gehören.

Prinzip 4:36 Persönliches Vermögen
Persönliches Vermögen umfasst
- (a) vor Beginn der Errungenschaftsgemeinschaft erworbene Vermögensgegenstände;
- (b) während des Güterstands durch Schenkung und von Todes wegen erworbenes Vermögen;
- (c) in Folge der Prinzipien 4:37 und 4:38 durch Ersetzung, Anlage oder Wiederanlage erworbene Vermögensgegenstände;
- (d) während des Güterstands erworbene persönliche Vermögensgegenstände;
- (e) ausschließlich für die Berufstätigkeit eines Ehegatten erworbene Vermögensgegenstände.

Prinzip 4:37 Ersetzung
(1) Jeder Vermögensgegenstand, der ohne zusätzliche Zahlung persönliche Vermögensgegenstände ersetzt, wird als persönliches Vermögen angesehen.
(2) Alle Vermögensgegenstände, die mit zusätzlicher Zahlung persönliche Vermögensgegenstände ersetzen, werden als persönliches Vermögen angesehen, es sei denn, die aus dem gemeinschaftlichen Vermögen erfolgende Zahlung hat den gleichen oder einen höheren Wert der ersetzten Vermögensgegenstände.
(3) Erfolgt eine zusätzliche Zahlung aus einem Vermögen, ist dem anderen Vermögen ein Ausgleich zu zahlen.

Prinzip 4:38 Anlage oder Wiederanlage

(1) Jeder ausschließlich durch Anlage oder Wiederanlage persönlicher Vermögensgegenstände erworbene Vermögensgegenstand ist als persönliches Vermögen anzusehen.

(2) Jeder teilweise durch Anlage oder Wiederanlage persönlicher Vermögensgegenstände und teilweise durch gemeinschaftliche Vermogensgegenstände erworbene Vermögensgegenstand gehört zum persönlichen Vermögen, es sei denn, die aus dem gemeinschaftlichen Vermögen erfolgende Zahlung hat den gleichen oder einen höheren Wert der erfolgten Anlage oder Wiederanlage.

(3) Erfolgt eine zusätzliche Anlage oder Wiederanlage aus einem Vermögen, ist dem anderen Vermögen ein Ausgleich zu zahlen.

Prinzip 4:39 Vermutung gemeinschaftlichen Vermögens

Es wird vermutet, dass Vermögensgegenstände gemeinschaftliches Vermögen sind, es sei denn, es wird bewiesen, dass sie nach den Prinzipien 4:35 bis 4:38 persönliches Vermögen sind.

VERBINDLICHKEITEN

Prinzip 4:40 Gemeinschaftliche Verbindlichkeiten

Gemeinschaftliche Verbindlichkeiten sind

(a) von beiden Ehegatten gemeinsam eingegangene Verbindlichkeiten;
(b) von einem der Ehegatten für den angemessenen Lebensbedarf der Familie eingegangene Verbindlichkeiten;
(c) Unterhaltsverpflichtungen gegenüber Kindern;
(d) von einem der Ehegatten für den Gebrauch oder die Verwaltung von gemeinschaftlichen Vermögengegenständen oder im Interesse des gemeinschaftlichen Vermögens eingegangene Verbindlichkeiten;
(e) Verbindlichkeiten in Bezug auf die berufliche Tätigkeit eines Ehegatten;
(f) im Zusammenhang mit einer Schenkung oder Zuwendung von Todes wegen an das gemeinschaftliche Vermögen entstandene Verbindlichkeiten;
(g) Verbindlichkeiten, von denen nicht bewiesen ist, dass sie persönliche Verbindlichkeiten sind.

Prinzip 4:41 Persönliche Verbindlichkeiten

Persönliche Verbindlichkeiten eines Ehegatten sind

(a) vor Eintritt in die Errungenschaftsgemeinschaft eingegangene Verbindlichkeiten;
(b) Verbindlichkeiten, die im Zusammenhang mit einer während des Güterstands erworbenen Schenkung oder einem Erbfall entstanden sind;
(c) Verbindlichkeiten, die sich auf das persönliche Vermögen beziehen;

(d) Verbindlichkeiten persönlicher Art;
(e) ohne die erforderliche Zustimmung des anderen Ehegatten eingegangene Verbindlichkeiten.

Prinzip 4:42 Haftung für gemeinschaftliche Verbindlichkeiten
(1) Für gemeinschaftliche Verbindlichkeiten haftet das gemeinschaftliche Vermögen und das persönliche Vermögen des Ehegatten, der die Verbindlichkeit eingegangen ist.
(2) Sind die Ehegatten gesamtschuldnerisch verpflichtet, haftet für die Verbindlichkeit ebenfalls das persönliche Vermögen jedes Ehegatten.

Prinzip 4:43 Haftung für persönliche Verbindlichkeiten
(1) Für persönliche Verbindlichkeiten eines Ehegatten haften
(a) das persönliche Vermögen dieses Ehegatten;
(b) seine Einkünfte und sein Gewinn;
(c) die gemeinschaftlichen Vermögensgegenstände bis zum Ausmaß ihrer Vermischung mit dem persönlichen Vermögen des verpflichteten Ehegatten.
(2) Für persönliche Verbindlichkeiten aus deliktischem oder strafbarem Handeln haftet auch die Hälfte des Nettowerts des gemeinschaftlichen Vermögens, wenn das persönliche Vermögen, das Einkommen und die Gewinne des verpflichteten Ehegatten für die Haftung nicht ausreichen.

VERWALTUNG

Prinzip 4:44 Verwaltung des gemeinschaftlichen Vermögens
(1) Jeder Ehegatte ist zur Verwaltung gemeinschaftlichen Vermögens berechtigt. Wichtige Geschäfte erfordern jedoch eine gemeinsame Verwaltung.
(2) Lehnt ein Ehegatte ab, einem Geschäft zuzustimmen, das gemeinschaftliche Verwaltung erfordert, so kann der andere Ehegatte eine Ermächtigung bei der zuständigen Behörde beantragen, das Geschäft alleine vorzunehmen.

Prinzip 4:45 Gemeinschaftliche Verwaltung erfordernde Geschäfte
Vorbehaltlich der Prinzipien 4:4 bis 4:8 und unter Berücksichtigung der wirtschaftlichen Verhältnisse der Ehegatten, gehören zu den gemeinschaftliche Verwaltung erfordernden Geschäften insbesondere die folgenden:
(a) Erwerb, Veräußerung und Belastung unbeweglichen Vermögens;
(b) Eingehung bedeutender Darlehensverträge, Bürgschaften und Garantien;
(c) Gewährung bedeutender Geschenke.

Prinzip 4:46 Nichtigerklärung von Geschäften
Geschäfte, die gemeinschaftliche Verwaltung erfordern, können auf Antrag des nicht zustimmenden Ehegatten von der zuständigen Behörde für nichtig erklärt werden.

Prinzip 4:47 Verwaltung des persönlichen Vermögens
Vorbehaltlich der Prinzipien 4:6 und 4:7 ist jeder Ehegatte berechtigt, sein persönliches Vermögen allein zu verwalten.

Prinzip 4:48 Entziehung des Rechts zur Verwaltung des gemeinschaftlichen Vermögens
(1) Auf Antrag eines Ehegatten kann die zuständige Behörde dem anderen das Recht, das gemeinschaftliche Vermögen zu verwalten, ganz oder teilweise entziehen wegen
- (a) Unfähigkeit, den eigenen Willen zu äußern;
- (b) schwerwiegender mangelhafter Verwaltung; oder
- (c) schwerwiegender Verletzung der Verpflichtung zur Information nach Prinzip 4:8.

(2) In dem Ausmaß, in dem einem der Ehegatten das Recht zur Verwaltung des gemeinschaftlichen Vermögens entzogen wird, steht die Befugnis dem anderen allein zu.
(3) Auf Antrag jedes der Ehegatten kann die zuständige Behörde dem Ehegatten das ihm entzogene Recht zur Verwaltung wieder einräumen.

BEENDIGUNG

Prinzip 4:49 Gründe für die Beendigung
Die Errungenschaftsgemeinschaft wird beendet durch
- (a) den Tod eines Ehegatten;
- (b) die Nichtigerklärung der Ehe, Ehescheidung oder gesetzliche Trennung;
- (c) die Änderung des Güterstands durch Vertrag zwischen den Ehegatten; oder
- (d) die aus wichtigen Gründen Gütertrennung anordnende Entscheidung der zuständigen Behörde.

Prinzip 4:50 Zeitpunkt der Beendigung
Die Beendigung der Errungenschaftsgemeinschaft wird wirksam im Zeitpunkt
- (a) des Todes eines Ehegatten;
- (b) im Fall der Nichtigerklärung der Ehe, Ehescheidung oder gesetzlichen Trennung der Ehegatten, zwischen den Ehegatten im Zeitpunkt der Antragstellung, oder, wenn sich die Ehegatten vorher getrennt haben, im Zeitpunkt ihrer Trennung und gegenüber Dritten im Zeitpunkt der Eintragung der Entscheidung der zuständigen Behörde;

(c) im Fall einer vereinbarten Änderung des Güterstands, zwischen den Ehegatten im Zeitpunkt der Vereinbarung und gegenüber Dritten im Zeitpunkt der Bekanntmachung der Vereinbarung;
(d) im Fall der Gütertrennung durch die zuständige Behörde, zwischen den Ehegatten im Zeitpunkt der Antragstellung und gegenüber Dritten im Zeitpunkt der Bekanntmachung des Antrags.

Prinzip 4:51 Verwaltung nach Beendigung
Nach Beendigung der Errungenschaftsgemeinschaft finden die allgemeinen Regeln über das Miteigentum auf die Verwaltung Anwendung.

AUSEINANDERSETZUNG

Prinzip 4:52 Feststellung und Bewertung des gemeinschaftlichen Vermögens
(1) Die Feststellung des gemeinschaftlichen Vermögens erfolgt im Zeitpunkt der Beendigung der Errungenschaftsgemeinschaft wie in Prinzip 4:50 bestimmt.
(2) Die Bewertung des gemeinschaftlichen Vermögens erfolgt im Zeitpunkt der Teilung.

Prinzip 4:53 Ausgleich
(1) Das gemeinschaftliche Vermögen erhält einen Ausgleich für jeden Beitrag zugunsten des persönlichen Vermögens eines Ehegatten.
(2) Das persönliche Vermögen eines Ehegatten erhält einen Ausgleich für jeden Beitrag zugunsten des gemeinschaftlichen Vermögens.
(3) Im Fall der Anlage für den Erwerb, die Verbesserung oder den Erhalt eines Vermögensgegenstands ist bei der Berechnung des Ausgleichs der gestiegene oder gesunkene Wert des Vermögensgegenstands in Betracht zu ziehen.
(4) Der Ausgleich ist in Geld zu zahlen, sofern die Ehegatten nichts anderes vereinbaren.

Prinzip 4:54 Rang der gemeinschaftlichen Schulden
Gemeinschaftliche Schulden und Ausgleichsansprüche haben den gleichen Rang.

TEILUNG

Prinzip 4:55 Vereinbarung über die Teilung
Die Ehegatten können eine Vereinbarung über die Teilung des gemeinschaftlichen Vermögens treffen.

Prinzip 4:56 Zuweisung der Familienwohnung, der Haushaltsgegenstände und der beruflichen Vermögensgegenstände

Bei der Teilung des gemeinschaftlichen Vermögens kann die zuständige Behörde vorbehaltlich einer Ausgleichszahlung einem der Ehegatten

(a) die Familienwohnung und Haushaltsgegenstände;
(b) berufliche Vermögensgegenstände zuweisen.

Prinzip 4:57 Gleiche Anteile und Anpassung

(1) Das gemeinschaftliche Vermögen wird unter den Ehegatten gleich aufgeteilt.
(2) In Fälle außergewöhnlicher Härte kann die zuständige Behörde

(a) die Beteiligung anpassen;
(b) jede nach Prinzip 4:55 getroffene Vereinbarung der Ehegatten aufheben oder abändern.

Prinzip 4:58 Haftung für gemeinschaftliche Schulden nach Teilung der Errungenschaftsgemeinschaft

(1) Nach Teilung der Errungenschaftsgemeinschaft haften für gemeinschaftliche Schulden der Anteil jedes Ehegatten an der Gemeinschaft und das persönliche Vermögen des Ehegatten, der die Verbindlichkeit eingegangen ist.
(2) Der Ehegatte, der eine gemeinschaftliche Schuld nach Teilung der Errungenschaftsgemeinschaft beglichen hat, kann vom anderen Ehegatten die Hälfte der gezahlten Summe verlangen.

BEGINSELEN VAN EUROPEES FAMILIERECHT BETREFFENDE VERMOGENSRECHTELIJKE RELATIES TUSSEN ECHTGENOTEN

PREAMBULE

Erkennende dat ondanks de bestaande verschillen in de nationale familierechten er evenwel een toenemende convergentie bestaat;
Erkennende dat de bestaande verschillen het vrij verkeer van personen in Europa beletten;
Geleid door de wens om een bijdrage te leveren aan gemeenschappelijke Europese waarden met betrekking tot de gelijkheid van de echtgenoten;
Geleid door de wens om een evenwicht te vinden tussen de partijautonomie van de echtgenoten en hun solidariteit;
Geleid door de wens om een bijdrage te leveren aan het welzijn van het gezin;
Geleid door de wens om de bescherming van de gezinswoning te verzekeren;
Geleid door de wens om elke echtgenoot een billijk aandeel in het tijdens het huwelijk verworven vermogen te verzekeren;
Geleid door de wens om een bijdrage te leveren aan de harmonisatie van het familierecht in Europa en de rechten van haar burgers te versterken;
Beveelt de Commissie voor Europees Familierecht de volgende beginselen aan:

HOOFDSTUK I: ALGEMENE RECHTEN EN PLICHTEN VAN ECHTGENOTEN

Beginsel 4:1 Algemene toepassing
De in dit hoofdstuk vervatte beginselen zijn van toepassing ongeacht het huwelijksvermogensstelsel van de echtgenoten.

Beginsel 4:2 Gelijkheid van de echtgenoten
Elke echtgenoot heeft gelijke rechten en plichten.

Beginsel 4:3 Bekwaamheid van de echtgenoten

Onder voorbehoud van de volgende beginselen geniet elke echtgenoot volledige rechts- en handelingsbekwaamheid en kan in het bijzonder rechtshandelingen aangaan met de andere echtgenoot en met derden.

Beginsel 4:4 Bijdrage in de behoeften van het gezin

(1) Elke echtgenoot draagt volgens zijn mogelijkheden bij in de behoeften van het gezin.
(2) De bijdrage in de behoeften van het gezin omvat bijdragen voor de huishouding, de persoonlijke behoeften van de echtgenoten, het levensonderhoud en de opvoeding van de kinderen.
(3) Indien een echtgenoot zijn of haar verplichting tot bijdrage in de behoeften van het gezin niet nakomt, kan de andere echtgenoot de bevoegde autoriteit verzoeken de bijdrage te bepalen.

Beginsel 4:5 Bescherming van de gezinswoning en het huisraad

(1) Elke beschikking over de rechten op de gezinswoning of het huisraad vereist de toestemming van beide echtgenoten.
(2) Elke beschikking door een echtgenoot zonder de toestemming van de andere is geldig, indien deze laatste deze bevestigt.
(3) Indien een echtgenoot zijn of haar toestemming weigert of hiertoe niet in staat is, kan de andere echtgenoot om de toestemming van de bevoegde autoriteit verzoeken.
(4) Elke beschikking verricht in overtreding van de voorgaande alinea's kan op verzoek van de echtgenoot die niet heeft toegestemd, door de bevoegde autoriteit worden vernietigd.

Beginsel 4:6 Bescherming van de gehuurde gezinswoning

(1) Werd het huurcontract over de gezinswoning door één echtgenoot afgesloten, dan wordt de huur vermoed aan beide echtgenoten toe te behoren.
(2) Een echtgenoot kan zonder toestemming van de andere echtgenoot het huurcontract niet opzeggen of wijzigen.
(3) De verhuurder moet de opzegging van het huurcontract aan beide echtgenoten betekenen.

Beginsel 4:7 Vertegenwoordiging

(1) Een echtgenoot kan de andere echtgenoot machtigen om hem of haar bij rechtshandelingen te vertegenwoordigen.
(2) Is een echtgenoot niet in staat zijn of haar wil te uiten, dan kan de bevoegde autoriteit de andere echtgenoot machtigen

- (a) om alleen te handelen in de gevallen waarin de toestemming van zijn of haar echtgenoot vereist is;
- (b) om zijn of haar echtgenoot te vertegenwoordigen in de gevallen waarin deze laatste bevoegd is om alleen te handelen.

Beginsel 4:8 Informatieplicht
Elke echtgenoot heeft de plicht de andere echtgenoot te informeren over zijn vermogen en over belangrijke bestuurshandelingen voor zover dit nodig is om deze laatste toe te laten om zijn of haar rechten uit te oefenen.

Beginsel 4:9 Vrijheid om huwelijkscontracten te sluiten
Het staat de echtgenoten vrij om huwelijkscontracten te sluiten.

HOOFDSTUK II: HUWELIJKSCONTRACTEN

Beginsel 4:10 Begrip
(1) De toekomstige echtgenoten kunnen in een vóór het huwelijk gesloten huwelijkscontract hun huwelijksvermogensstelsel kiezen.
(2) De echtgenoten kunnen tijdens het huwelijk hun huwelijksvermogensstelsel wijzigen of een ander stelsel aannemen.

Beginsel 4:11 Vormvoorschriften
Huwelijkscontracten moeten voor een notaris of een ander juridisch beroepsbeoefenaar met vergelijkbare functies worden verleden, gedateerd en door beide echtgenoten worden ondertekend.

Beginsel 4:12 Openbaring
Bij het sluiten van een huwelijkscontract hebben de echtgenoten de wederzijdse verplichting om de samenstelling van hun vermogen aan elkaar te openbaren.

Beginsel 4:13 Plichten van de notaris of van de andere juridische beoefenaar met vergelijkbare functies
De notaris of de andere juridische beoefenaar met vergelijkbare functies
- (a) geeft aan elke echtgenoot afzonderlijk onpartijdig advies;
- (b) verzekert zich ervan dat elke echtgenoot de rechtsgevolgen van het huwelijkscontract begrijpt;
- (c) verzekert zich van de vrije toestemming van beide echtgenoten.

Beginsel 4:14 Gevolgen tegenover derden
Huwelijkscontracten gelden tegenover derden, indien bij het sluiten van een overeenkomst met een echtgenoot,
- (a) deze informatie vervat is in een openbaar document; of
- (b) de derden kennis hadden van de relevante bedingen van het huwelijkscontract.

Beginsel 4:15 Buitengewoon ingrijpende omstandigheden
Rekening houdende met de omstandigheden bij de sluiting van de overeenkomst of met later ontstane omstandigheden kan de bevoegde autoriteit in geval van buitengewoon ingrijpende omstandigheden het huwelijkscontract opheffen of wijzigen.

HOOFDSTUK III: HUWELIJKSVERMOGENSSTELSELS

AFDELING A: PARTICIPATIE IN DE AANWINSTEN

Beginsel 4:16 Toepasselijkheid van het stelsel van participatie in de aanwinsten
De participatie in de aanwinsten is van toepassing voor zover de echtgenoten geen andersluidende overeenkomst hebben gesloten in overeenstemming met Hoofdstuk II.

BEGRIP

Beginsel 4:17 Begrip van participatie in de aanwinsten
(1) Participatie in de aanwinsten is een huwelijksvermogensstelsel tengevolge waarvan elke echtgenoot eigenaar van zijn vermogen is.
(2) Het vermogen van elke echtgenoot omvat de aanwinsten en het voorbehouden vermogen.
(3) Bij ontbinding van het stelsel participeert elke echtgenoot in de door de andere echtgenoot tijdens het stelsel verworven aanwinsten door toepassing van Beginsel 4:31.

BATEN

Beginsel 4:18 Aanwinsten
(1) De aanwinsten omvatten de tijdens het stelsel verworven vermogensbestanddelen met uitzondering van het voorbehouden vermogen. De aanwinsten omvatten in het bijzonder

- (a) de inkomsten en winsten van elke echtgenoot afkomstig uit inkomen of vermogen;
- (b) de goederen verworven met inkomsten en winsten van een echtgenoot.

(2) Behoudens tegenbewijs worden vermogensbestanddelen vermoed aanwinsten te zijn.

Beginsel 4:19 Voorbehouden vermogen
Het voorbehouden vermogen omvat

(a) vóór de inwerkingtreding van het huwelijksvermogensstelsel verkregen goederen;
(b) tijdens het huwelijksvermogensstelsel verkregen schenkingen, nalatenschappen en legaten;
(c) goederen verkregen ter vervanging van voorbehouden goederen;
(d) goederen van persoonlijke aard;
(e) goederen uitsluitend verworven voor het beroep van een echtgenoot;
(f) waardevermeerderingen van de onder (a) tot (e) vermelde goederen.

Beginsel 4:20 Vermoeden van mede-eigendom
Behoudens tegenbewijs worden de goederen vermoed aan beide echtgenoten in mede-eigendom toe te behoren.

SCHULDEN

Beginsel 4:21 Persoonlijke schulden
Schulden aangegaan door één echtgenoot zijn persoonlijke schulden.

Beginsel 4:22 Verhaalbaarheid van persoonlijke schulden
Persoonlijke schulden zijn verhaalbaar op de aanwinsten en het voorbehouden vermogen van de echtgenoot-schuldenaar.

BESTUUR

Beginsel 4:23 Bestuur van de vermogens
Onder voorbehoud van de Beginselen 4:6 en 4:7 is elke echtgenoot gerechtigd om zijn of haar vermogen alleen te besturen.

ONTBINDING

Beginsel 4:24 Ontbindingsgronden
Het stelsel van participatie in de aanwinsten wordt ontbonden door

(a) het overlijden van een echtgenoot;
(b) de nietigverklaring van het huwelijk, de echtscheiding of de scheiding van tafel en bed;
(c) de wijziging van het huwelijksvermogensstelsel door een overeenkomst tussen de echtgenoten, of
(d) de beslissing van de bevoegde autoriteit wegens ernstige gronden.

Beginsel 4:25 Datum van ontbinding
De ontbinding van het stelsel van participatie in de aanwinsten heeft gevolgen
(a) op het tijdstip van het overlijden van een echtgenoot;
(b) in geval van nietigverklaring van het huwelijk, echtscheiding of scheiding van tafel en bed op het tijdstip van het verzoek;
(c) in geval van een overeenkomst tot wijziging van het huwelijksvermogensstelsel op het tijdstip van de wijziging;
(d) in geval van beslissing door de bevoegde autoriteit op het tijdstip van het verzoek.

VEREFFENING

Beginsel 4:26 Vaststelling en waardering van de aanwinsten
(1) De aanwinsten van elke echtgenoot worden vastgesteld op het tijdstip van de ontbinding van het stelsel zoals bepaald in Beginsel 4:25.
(2) De aanwinsten worden op het ogenblik van de verdeling gewaardeerd.

Beginsel 4:27 Nadelige handelingen
Bij de berekening van de aanwinsten van elke echtgenoot moet worden rekening gehouden met
(a) buitensporige schenkingen;
(b) verkwiste goederen;
(c) andere handelingen die de waarde van de aanwinsten in het nadeel van de andere echtgenoot opzettelijk hebben verminderd.

Beginsel 4:28 Vergoedingen
(1) De aanwinsten van een echtgenoot verkrijgen een vergoeding voor elke bijdrage in het voordeel van zijn voorbehouden vermogen.
(2) Het voorbehouden vermogen van een echtgenoot verkrijgt een vergoeding voor elke bijdrage in het voordeel van zijn aanwinsten.
(3) Schulden belasten het vermogen met betrekking tot welke zij zijn aangegaan. Bij twijfel wordt vermoed dat zij de aanwinsten belasten.
(4) Bij investering voor de verkrijging, de verbetering of de instandhouding van een goed, wordt bij de berekening van het bedrag van de vergoeding rekening gehouden met de meerwaarde of minwaarde van dit goed.
(5) Behoudens andersluidende overeenkomst wordt de vergoeding in geld voldaan.

PARTICIPATIE

Beginsel 4:29 Overeenkomst over de participatie
De echtgenoten kunnen een overeenkomst over de participatie in de aanwinsten sluiten.

Beginsel 4:30 Toebedeling van de gezinswoning en het huisraad
De bevoegde autoriteit kan in het belang van het gezin en tegen vergoeding de gezinswoning en het huisraad aan een echtgenoot toebedelen.

Beginsel 4:31 Gelijke participatie in de netto-aanwinsten
(1) Indien de netto-aanwinsten van een echtgenoot de waarde van deze van de andere overstijgen, dan participeert deze laatste in het meerdere ter hoogte van de helft.
(2) De netto-aanwinsten zijn gelijk aan de waarde van de aanwinsten na aftrek van de schulden.
(3) De door een echtgenoot geleden verliezen die zijn aanwinsten op het ogenblik van de ontbinding van het stelsel overtreffen, worden niet met de andere echtgenoot gedeeld.
(4) Behoudens andersluidende overeenkomst tussen de echtgenoten, is de vordering tot participatie een vordering in geld.
(5) Op verzoek van de echtgenoot-schuldenaar kan de bevoegde autoriteit wegens ernstige redenen uitstel van betaling of betaling in termijnen toestaan.

Beginsel 4:32 Aanpassing door de bevoegde autoriteit
In geval van buitengewoon ingrijpende omstandigheden kan de bevoegde autoriteit

(a) de participatie aanpassen;
(b) elke bij toepassing van Beginsel 4:29 gesloten overeenkomst tussen de echtgenoten opheffen of wijzigen.

AFDELING B: GEMEENSCHAP VAN AANWINSTEN

Beginsel 4:33 Toepasselijkheid van de gemeenschap van aanwinsten
Het stelsel van de gemeenschap van aanwinsten is van toepassing voor zover de echtgenoten geen andersluidende overeenkomst hebben gesloten in overeenstemming met Hoofdstuk II.

BEGRIP

Beginsel 4:34 Begrip van de gemeenschap van aanwinsten
(1) De gemeenschap van aanwinsten is een huwelijksvermogensstelsel dat uit gemeenschappelijk en persoonlijk vermogen bestaat.
(2) Het gemeenschappelijk vermogen is het tijdens de gemeenschap van aanwinsten verworven vermogen dat geen persoonlijk vermogen is.
(3) Het persoonlijk vermogen is het eigen vermogen van elke echtgenoot.

BATEN

Beginsel 4:35 Gemeenschappelijk vermogen

(1) Het gemeenschappelijk vermogen bevat alle tijdens het stelsel verworven roerende en roerende goederen die geen persoonlijke goederen van een echtgenoot zijn.

(2) Het gemeenschappelijk vermogen bevat in het bijzonder

(a) de inkomsten en winsten afkomstig uit de professionele activiteiten van de echtgenoten en uit hun gemeenschappelijk en persoonlijk vermogen;

(b) gemeenschappelijk of door een echtgenoot afzonderlijk tijdens het stelsel verworven goederen met middelen uit inkomsten en winsten;

(c) schenkingen en legaten aan beide echtgenoten of aan een echtgenoot onder het beding dat deze tot het gemeenschappelijk vermogen zullen behoren.

Beginsel 4:36 Persoonlijk vermogen

Het persoonlijk vermogen bevat

(a) vóór de inwerkingtreding van de gemeenschap van aanwinsten verkregen goederen;

(b) tijdens het huwelijksvermogensstelsel verkregen schenkingen, nalatenschappen en legaten;

(c) goederen verkregen ter vervanging, belegging of wederbelegging zoals bepaald in de Beginselen 4:37 en 4:38;

(d) tijdens de werking van het stelsel verkregen goederen van persoonlijke aard;

(e) goederen uitsluitend verworven voor het beroep van een echtgenoot.

Beginsel 4:37 Vervanging

(1) Elk goed dat een persoonlijk goed vervangt zonder aanvullende betaling is een persoonlijk goed.

(2) Elk goed dat een persoonlijk goed vervang met aanvullende betaling is een persoonlijk goed, tenzij de aanvullende betaling met gemeenschappelijk vermogen gelijk is aan of groter dan de waarde van het vervangen goed.

(3) In geval van een aanvullende betaling door een vermogen is een vergoeding door het andere vermogen verschuldigd.

Beginsel 4:38 Belegging en wederbelegging

(1) Elk uitsluitend door belegging of wederbelegging verkregen goed is een persoonlijk goed.

(2) Elk goed gedeeltelijk verkregen door belegging of wederbelegging van persoonlijk vermogen en gedeeltelijk verkregen door gemeenschappelijk vermogen is een persoonlijk goed, tenzij de betaling door het gemeenschappelijk vermogen gelijk is aan of hoger is dan de belegging of wederbelegging.

(3) In geval van bijkomende belegging of wederbelegging door een vermogen is een vergoeding door het andere vermogen verschuldigd.

Beginsel 4:39 Vermoeden van gemeenschappelijk vermogen
Een goed wordt vermoed gemeenschappelijk te zijn, tenzij zijn persoonlijk karakter wordt bewezen door toepassing van de Beginselen 4:35 tot 4:38.

SCHULDEN

Beginsel 4:40 Gemeenschappelijke schulden
Gemeenschappelijke schulden zijn

(a) schulden aangegaan door beide echtgenoten gezamenlijk;
(b) schulden aangegaan door een echtgenoot voor de aanvaardbare behoeften van het gezin;
(c) schulden voor het levensonderhoud van de kinderen;
(d) schulden aangegaan door een echtgenoot voor het gebruik of het bestuur van het gemeenschappelijk vermogen of in het belang van het gezin;
(e) schulden met betrekking tot het beroep van een echtgenoot;
(f) schulden met betrekking tot een schenking of een legaat dat tot het gemeenschappelijk vermogen behoort;
(g) schulden waarvan het persoonlijk karakter niet bewezen is.

Beginsel 4:41 Persoonlijke schulden
Persoonlijke schulden van een echtgenoot zijn

(a) schulden aangegaan vóór de inwerkingtreding van de gemeenschap van aanwinsten;
(b) schulden met betrekking tot tijdens het stelsel verkregen schenkingen, nalatenschappen en legaten;
(c) schulden met betrekking tot de persoonlijke goederen;
(d) schulden persoonlijk door hun aard;
(e) schulden aangegaan zonder de vereiste toestemming van de andere echtgenoot.

Beginsel 4:42 Verhaalbaarheid van gemeenschappelijke schulden
(1) Gemeenschappelijke schulden zijn verhaalbaar op het gemeenschappelijk vermogen en op het persoonlijk vermogen van de echtgenoot die de schuld is aangegaan.
(2) Zijn de echtgenoten hoofdelijk aansprakelijk, dan is de schuld ook verhaalbaar op het persoonlijk vermogen van elke echtgenoot.

Beginsel 4:43 Verhaalbaarheid van persoonlijke schulden
(1) Persoonlijke schulden van een echtgenoot zijn verhaalbaar op

(a) het persoonlijk vermogen van de echtgenoot-schuldenaar;

(b) het inkomen en de winsten van de echtgenoot-schuldenaar;
(c) de gemeenschappelijke goederen in de mate van hun vermenging met persoonlijke goederen van de echtgenoot-schuldenaar.

(2) De persoonlijke schulden uit een onrechtmatige daad of een misdrijf zijn tevens verhaalbaar op de helft van de netto-baten van het gemeenschappelijk vermogen, indien de persoonlijke goederen en de inkomsten en winsten van de echtgenoot-schuldenaar voor het verhaal ontoereikend zijn.

BESTUUR

Beginsel 4:44 Bestuur van het gemeenschappelijk vermogen
(1) Elke echtgenoot heeft het recht het gemeenschappelijk vermogen te besturen, maar belangrijke handelingen vereisen gezamenlijk bestuur.
(2) Indien een echtgenoot weigert zijn of haar toestemming te verlenen tot een handeling die gezamenlijk bestuur vereist, kan de andere echtgenoot de bevoegde autoriteit om een machtiging tot alleen handelen verzoeken.

Beginsel 4:45 Handelingen die gezamenlijk bestuur vereisen
Onder voorbehoud van de Beginselen 4:4 tot 4:8 en rekening houdend met de economische situatie van de echtgenoten bevatten de handelingen die gezamenlijk bestuur vereisen, in het bijzonder:

(a) de verkrijging, vervreemding van en de instelling van een zekerheidsrecht op onroerende goederen;
(b) betekenisvolle leningen, borgstellingen en waarborgen;
(c) betekenisvolle schenkingen.

Beginsel 4:46 Vernietiging van bestuurshandelingen
Handelingen die gezamenlijk bestuur vereisen kunnen op verzoek van de echtgenoot, die niet in de handeling heeft toegestemd, door de bevoegde autoriteit worden vernietigd.

Beginsel 4:47 Bestuur van persoonlijk vermogen
Onder voorbehoud van de Beginselen 4:6 en 4:7 heeft elke echtgenoot het recht zijn persoonlijk vermogen alleen te besturen.

Beginsel 4:48 Ontneming van het recht het gemeenschappelijk vermogen te besturen
(1) Op verzoek van een echtgenoot kan de bevoegde autoriteit de andere echtgenoot het recht om het gemeenschappelijk vermogen te besturen geheel of gedeeltelijk ontnemen wegens

(a) onmogelijkheid om zijn of haar wil te uiten;
(b) ernstige fouten in het bestuur;

(c) ernstige schending van de informatieplichten zoals bepaald in Beginsel 4:8.

(2) In de mate waarin een echtgenoot het recht om het gemeenschappelijk vermogen te besturen wordt ontnomen, komt deze bevoegdheid de andere echtgenoot alleen toe.

(3) Op verzoek van elke echtgenoot kan de bevoegde autoriteit de echtgenoot in zijn ontnomen recht om te besturen herstellen.

Beginsel 4:49 Ontbindingsgronden

De gemeenschap van aanwinsten wordt ontbonden door

(a) het overlijden van een echtgenoot;
(b) de nietigverklaring van het huwelijk, de echtscheiding of de scheiding van tafel en bed;
(c) de wijziging van het huwelijksvermogensstelsel door een overeenkomst tussen de echtgenoten;
(d) de beslissing van de bevoegde autoriteit tot scheiding van goederen wegens ernstige gronden.

Beginsel 4:50 Datum van ontbinding

De ontbinding van de gemeenschap van aanwinsten heeft gevolgen

(a) op het tijdstip van het overlijden van een echtgenoot;
(b) in geval van nietigverklaring van het huwelijk, echtscheiding of scheiding van tafel en bed, tussen echtgenoten op het tijdstip van het verzoek of, indien de echtgenoten vóór dit tijdstip gescheiden leefden, op het tijdstip van hun scheiding en tegenover derden op het tijdstip van publicatie van het verzoek;
(c) in geval van een overeenkomst tot wijziging van het huwelijksvermogensstelsel, tussen echtgenoten vanaf het tijdstip van de overeenkomst en tegenover derden op het tijdstip van publicatie van de overeenkomst;
(d) in geval van een door de bevoegde autoriteit uitgesproken scheiding van goederen, tussen de echtgenoten vanaf het tijdstip van het verzoek en tegenover derden op het tijdstip van publicatie van het verzoek.

Beginsel 4:51 Bestuur na ontbinding

Na de ontbinding van de gemeenschap van aanwinsten zijn de algemene regels over mede-eigendom op het bestuur van toepassing.

VEREFFENING

Beginsel 4:52 Vaststelling en waardering van de aanwinsten

(1) Het gemeenschappelijk vermogen wordt vastgesteld op het tijdstip van de ontbinding van het stelsel zoals bepaald in Beginsel 4:50.

(2) Het gemeenschappelijk vermogen wordt op het tijdstip van de verdeling gewaardeerd.

Beginsel 4:53 Vergoedingen

(1) Het gemeenschappelijk vermogen verkrijgt een vergoeding voor elke bijdrage ten voordele van het persoonlijk vermogen van een echtgenoot.
(2) Het persoonlijk vermogen van een echtgenoot verkrijgt een vergoeding voor elke bijdrage ten voordele van het gemeenschappelijk vermogen.
(3) Bij investering voor de verkrijging, de verbetering of de instandhouding van een goed, wordt bij de berekening van het bedrag van de vergoeding rekening gehouden met de meerwaarde of minwaarde van dit goed.
(4) Behoudens andersluidende overeenkomst wordt de vergoeding in geld voldaan.

Beginsel 4:54 Rang van de gemeenschappelijke schulden

Gemeenschappelijke schulden en vergoedingen hebben dezelfde rang.

VERDELING

Beginsel 4:55 Overeenkomst over de verdeling

De echtgenoten kunnen een overeenkomst over de verdeling van het gemeenschappelijk vermogen sluiten.

Beginsel 4:56 Toebedeling van de gezinswoning, het huisraad en de beroepsgoederen

Bij de verdeling van het gemeenschappelijk vermogen kan de bevoegde autoriteit in het belang van het gezin en tegen aanvullende betaling aan een echtgenoot toebedelen

(a) de gezinswoning en het huisraad;
(b) beroepsgoederen.

Beginsel 4:57 Gelijke verdeling en aanpassing

(1) Het gemeenschappelijk vermogen wordt tussen de echtgenoten gelijk verdeeld.
(2) In geval van buitengewoon ingrijpende omstandigheden kan de bevoegde autoriteit

(a) de verdeling aanpassen;
(b) elke bij toepassing van Beginsel 4:55 gesloten overeenkomst tussen echtgenoten opheffen of wijzigen.

Beginsel 4:58 Verhaalbaarheid van gemeenschappelijke schulden na de verdeling van het gemeenschappelijk vermogen

(1) Na de verdeling van het gemeenschappelijk vermogen worden de gemeenschappelijke schulden verhaald op het aandeel van elke echtgenoot in dit vermogen en op het persoonlijk vermogen van de echtgenoot die de schuld is aangegaan.

(2) De echtgenoot die na de verdeling van het gemeenschappelijk vermogen een gemeenschappelijk schuld heeft voldaan, kan de helft van de betaalde som op de andere echtgenoot verhalen.

PRINCIPIOS DE DERECHO EUROPEO DE FAMILIA RELATIVOS A LAS RELACIONES PATRIMONIALES ENTRE LOS CÓNYUGES

PREÁMBULO

Reconociendo, que a pesar de las divergencias de los sistemas nacionales de Derecho de familia existe, no obstante, una creciente convergencia;
Reconociendo que las diferencias que subsisten obstaculizan la libre circulación de personas;
Deseando alcanzar un equilibrio entre la autonomía privada de los cónyuges y su solidaridad;
Deseando contribuir al bienestar de la familia;
Deseando asegurar la protección de la vivienda familiar;
Deseando garantizar a cada cónyuge una participación justa en el patrimonio adquirido durante el matrimonio;
Deseando contribuir a la armonización del Derecho de familia en Europa y reforzar los derechos de los ciudadanos;
La Comisión para el Derecho Europeo de Familia recomienda los siguientes Principios:

CAPÍTULO I: DERECHOS Y DEBERES GENERALES DE LOS CÓNYUGES

Principio 4:1 Aplicación general
Los Principios contenidos en este Capítulo se aplican sea cual sea el régimen económico matrimonial de los cónyuges.

Principio 4:2 Igualdad de los cónyuges
Los cónyuges tienen los mismos derechos y obligaciones.

Principio 4:3 Capacidad jurídica de los cónyuges
Sin perjuicio de lo que dispongan los siguientes Principios, cada cónyuge tiene plena capacidad jurídica y, puede, en particular, celebrar negocios jurídicos con el otro cónyuge y con terceras personas.

Principio 4:4 Contribución a las necesidades de la familia
(1) Los cónyuges han de contribuir a las necesidades de la familia de acuerdo con sus capacidades.
(2) La contribución a las necesidades de la familia comprende las contribuciones al mantenimiento del hogar, a las necesidades personales de los cónyuges y al mantenimiento y la educación de los hijos.
(3) Cuando un cónyuge incumpliere su obligación de contribuir a las necesidades de la familia, el otro cónyuge podrá solicitar a la autoridad competente que determine la cuantía de dicha contribución.

Principio 4:5 Protección de la vivienda familiar y del ajuar doméstico
(1) Todo acto de disposición de derechos relativos a la vivienda familiar y al ajuar domestico requiere el consentimiento de ambos cónyuges.
(2) Un acto de disposición realizado por uno de los cónyuges sin el consentimiento del otro será válido si es confirmado por éste.
(3) Cuando un cónyuge rehusare otorgar su consentimiento o no estuviere en condiciones de otorgarlo, el otro cónyuge podrá solicitar autorización a la autoridad competente.
(4) Todo acto de disposición que vulnere lo dispuesto en los apartados precedentes puede ser anulado por la autoridad competente a solicitud del cónyuge que no ha consentido.

Principio 4:6 Protección del arrendamiento relativo a la vivienda familiar
(1) Aunque el contrato de arrendamiento de la vivienda familiar hubiere sido concluido por únicamente uno de los cónyuges, incluso con anterioridad a la celebración del matrimonio, se entenderá que ambos cónyuges son parte del arrendamiento.
(2) Un cónyuge no puede rescindir o modificar el contrato de arrendamiento sin el consentimiento del otro.
(3) El arrendador ha de notificar la rescisión del contrato a cada uno de los cónyuges.

Principio 4:7 Representación
(1) Un cónyuge puede otorgar mandato al otro para que le represente en actos jurídicos.
(2) Si un cónyuge no estuviere en condiciones de manifestar su voluntad, la autoridad competente podrá autorizar al otro cónyuge

(a) a actuar por si solo en aquellos casos en los que el consentimiento del otro cónyuge fuere necesario;
(b) a representar a su cónyuge en aquellos casos en que éste tenga la facultad de actuar por si solo.

Principio 4:8 Obligación de informar
El cónyuge está obligado a informar al otro cónyuge acerca de su patrimonio así como sobre actos de administración importantes en la medida necesaria para permitirle ejercer sus derechos.

Principio 4:9 Libertad para concluir capitulaciones matrimoniales
Los cónyuges son libres de concluir capitulaciones matrimoniales acerca de sus relaciones patrimoniales.

CAPÍTULO II: CAPITULACIONES MATRIMONIALES ACERCA DE LAS RELACIONES PATRIMONIALES DE LOS CONYUGES

Principio 4:10 Concepto
(1) Los futuros cónyuges pueden otorgar capitulaciones estipulando su régimen económico matrimonial antes de la celebración del matrimonio.
(2) Durante el matrimonio los cónyuges pueden modificar su régimen económico matrimonial o cambiar de régimen.

Principio 4:11 Requisitos formales
Las capitulaciones matrimoniales acerca de las relaciones patrimoniales de los cónyuges deben ser concluidas ante un notario u otro profesional jurídico que ejerza funciones equivalentes, llevar fecha y ser firmadas por ambos cónyuges.

Principio 4:12 Revelación del patrimonio
Cuando los cónyuges celebren capitulaciones matrimoniales estarán recíprocamente obligados a revelar al otro cónyuge la composición de su patrimonio.

Principio 4:13 Obligaciones del notario u otro profesional jurídico que ejerza funciones equivalentes
El notario o profesional que ejerza funciones equivalentes debe
(a) asesorar imparcialmente a cada uno de los cónyuges de forma separada,
(b) asegurar que cada uno de los cónyuges entiende las consecuencias jurídicas de las capitulaciones matrimoniales, y
(c) asegurar que ambos cónyuges prestan libremente su consentimiento a las capitulaciones.

Principio 4:14 Efectos frente a terceros
Las capitulaciones matrimoniales acerca de las relaciones patrimoniales de los cónyuges son oponibles a terceros, si en el momento de la conclusión del negocio con uno de los cónyuges

(a) dicha información estuviere contenida en un documento público; o
(b) los terceros tuvieren conocimiento de las clausulas pertinentes de las capitulaciones.

Principio 4:15 Excepcional onerosidad
En caso de excepcional onerosidad, habida cuenta de las circunstancias en las que se concluyeren las capitulaciones o de las que se produjeren posteriormente, la autoridad competente podrá descartar o adaptar las capitulaciones matrimoniales.

CAPÍTULO III: REGÍMENES ECONÓMICOS MATRIMONIALES

SECCIÓN A: PARTICIPACIÓN EN LAS GANANCIAS

Principio 4:16 Aplicabilidad del régimen de participación en las ganancias
El régimen de participación en las ganancias se aplica si los cónyuges no han concluido capitulaciones matrimoniales conforme al Capítulo II.

CONCEPTO

Principio 4:17 Concepto de participación en las ganancias
(1) La participación en las ganancias es un régimen económico matrimonial durante cuya duración cada uno de los cónyuges es propietario de su patrimonio.
(2) El patrimonio de cada uno de los cónyuges comprende las ganancias y los bienes reservados.
(3) En el momento de disolución del régimen cada cónyuge participa en las ganancias obtenidas por el otro conforme al Principio 4:31.

EL ACTIVO

Principio 4:18 Ganancias
(1) Las ganancias comprenden los bienes adquiridos durante el régimen que no son bienes reservados. En particular, las ganancias incluyen

(a) los ingresos y rentas de cada cónyuge tanto derivados de salarios como de su patrimonio;
(b) los bienes adquiridos mediante dichos ingresos y rentas.

(2) Se presume que los bienes son ganancias salvo prueba en contrario.

Principio 4:19 Propiedad reservada
La propiedad reservada comprende
(a) los bienes adquiridos con anterioridad al inicio del régimen;
(b) las donaciones, herencias y legados adquiridos durante el régimen;
(c) los bienes adquiridos en sustitución de bienes reservados;
(d) los bienes que son de naturaleza personal;
(e) los bienes exclusivamente adquiridos para la profesión de un cónyuge;
(f) las plusvalías de los bienes comprendidos en (a) a (e).

Principio 4:20 Presunción de pro indiviso
Salvo prueba en contrario se presume que los bienes pertenecen en pro indiviso ordinario a ambos cónyuges.

DEUDAS

Principio 4:21 Deudas personales
Las deudas suscritas por un cónyuge son de carácter personal.

Principio 4:22 Recobro de deudas personales
De las deudas personales responden las ganancias y la propiedad reservada del cónyuge deudor.

ADMINISTRACIÓN

Principio 4:23 Administración de bienes
Sin perjuicio de los Principios 4:6 and 4:7, a cada cónyuge le corresponde la administración independiente de sus bienes.

DISOLUCIÓN

Principio 4:24 Causas de disolución
El régimen de participación en las ganancias se disuelve por
(a) el fallecimiento de uno de los cónyuges;
(b) la anulación del matrimonio, el divorcio o la separación legal;
(c) la estipulación de un régimen económico matrimonial distinto mediante capitulaciones entre los cónyuges; o
(d) la decisión de la autoridad competente fundada en causa grave.

Principio 4:25 Fecha de la disolución
La disolución de la participación en las ganancias tiene efecto
(a) en la fecha del fallecimiento de uno de los cónyuges;
(b) en caso de anulación del matrimonio, divorcio o separación legal, en la fecha de la demanda;

(c) en caso de capitulaciones estipulando un régimen económico matrimonial distinto, en la fecha del cambio; y
(d) en caso de decisión de la autoridad competente, en la fecha de la demanda.

LIQUIDACIÓN

Principio 4:26 Determinación y valoración de las ganancias
(1) Las ganancias de cada uno de los cónyuges se determinan en la fecha de disolución del régimen establecida en el Principio 4:25.
(2) Las ganancias se valoran en la fecha de liquidación del régimen.

Principio 4:27 Actos perjudiciales
Al calcular las ganancias de cada cónyuge se tendrán en cuenta
(a) las donaciones excesivas;
(b) la disipación de bienes;
(c) otros actos que hayan intencionadamente disminuido el valor de las ganancias en perjuicio del otro cónyuge.

Principio 4:28 Compensación
(1) Se hará compensación a las ganancias de un cónyuge por contribuciones a cargo de las mismas en beneficio de sus bienes reservados.
(2) Se hará compensación a los bienes reservados de un cónyuge por contribuciones a cargo de los mismos en beneficio de sus ganancias.
(3) Las obligaciones gravan el patrimonio respecto al cual han sido contraídas. En caso de duda se presume que gravan las ganancias.
(4) En los supuestos de adquisición, mejora o conservación de un bien se tendrá en cuenta en el cálculo de la compensación el incremento o disminución de valor del bien resultante de dicha inversión.
(5) La compensación se pagará en metálico, salvo acuerdo en contrario.

PARTICIPACIÓN

Principio 4:29 Convenio sobre la participación
Los cónyuges pueden concluir un convenio sobre la participación en las ganancias.

Principio 4:30 Adjudicación de la vivienda familiar y del ajuar domestico
La autoridad competente puede adjudicar, en interés de la familia y mediando el pago de una compensación, la vivienda familiar y el ajuar domestico a uno de los cónyuges.

Principio 4:31 Participación igual en las ganancias netas
(1) Si las ganancias netas de un cónyuge exceden el valor de las del otro, éste participa en el excedente por mitad.

(2) Las ganancias netas equivalen al valor de las ganancias una vez deducidas las deudas.
(3) Las pérdidas sufridas por un cónyuge, que excedan a sus ganancias en la fecha de disolución, no se comparten con el otro cónyuge.
(4) El crédito de participación es un crédito monetario, salvo acuerdo en contrario de los cónyuges.
(5) A solicitud del cónyuge deudor y mediando causa grave la autoridad competente puede autorizar el aplazamiento del pago o el pago a plazos.

Principio 4:32 Adaptaciones por la autoridad competente
En caso de excepcional onerosidad la autoridad competente puede
- (a) adaptar la participación;
- (b) descartar o modificar cualquier convenio concluido entre los cónyuges en virtud del Principio 4:29.

SECCIÓN B: COMUNIDAD DE GANANCIALES

Principio 4:33 Aplicabilidad de la comunidad de gananciales
La comunidad de gananciales se aplica si los cónyuges no han concluido capitulaciones en contrario conforme al Capítulo II.

CONCEPTO

Principio 4:34 Concepto de la comunidad de gananciales
(1) La comunidad de gananciales es un régimen económico matrimonial que comprende el patrimonio común y el patrimonio privativo.
(2) El patrimonio común es el patrimonio adquirido durante la comunidad de gananciales y que no es patrimonio privativo.
(3) El patrimonio privativo es el patrimonio propio de cada cónyuge.

EL ACTIVO

Principio 4:35 La comunidad
(1) La comunidad comprende todo bien mueble o inmueble adquirido durante el régimen que no pertenece al patrimonio privativo de uno de los cónyuges.
(2) En particular la comunidad comprende
- (a) los ingresos y rentas derivados bien de la actividad profesional de los cónyuges bien de su patrimonio común o privativo;
- (b) los bienes adquiridos conjunta o individualmente por los cónyuges durante la comunidad de gananciales mediante los ingresos y rentas de los cónyuges;
- (c) las donaciones o legados a ambos cónyuges o a uno de ellos con la condición de que pertenezca a la comunidad.

Principio 4:36 Patrimonio privativo

El patrimonio privativo comprende

(a) los bienes adquiridos antes del inicio de la comunidad;
(b) las donaciones, herencias y legados recibidos durante el régimen;
(c) los bienes adquiridos por sustitución, inversión o reinversión de acuerdo con los Principios 4:37 y 4:38;
(d) bienes de naturaleza personal, adquiridos durante el régimen;
(e) bienes exclusivamente adquiridos para la profesión de un cónyuge.

Principio 4:37 Sustitución

(1) Todo bien que sustituya a un bien privativo sin pago adicional ha de considerarse bien privativo.
(2) Todo bien que sustituya un bien privativo con pago adicional ha de considerarse bien privativo salvo que el pago adicional a cargo de la comunidad sea igual o superior al valor del bien sustituido.
(3) En caso de pago adicional a cargo de uno de los patrimonios se deberá compensación al otro.

Principio 4:38 Inversión o reinversión

(1) Todo bien adquirido únicamente mediante la inversión o reinversión de bienes privativos ha de considerarse un bien privativo.
(2) Todo bien adquirido parcialmente mediante la inversión o reinversión de bienes privativos y parcialmente mediante bienes gananciales pertenece al patrimonio privativo salvo que el pago a cargo de la comunidad iguale o supere el valor de la inversión o reinversión.
(3) En caso de inversión o reinversión adicional a cargo de uno de los patrimonios se deberá compensación al otro.

Principio 4:39 Presunción de bienes gananciales

Se presume que los bienes son gananciales salvo que se pruebe que son bienes privativos conforme a los Principios 4:35 a 4:38.

DEUDAS

Principio 4:40 Deudas gananciales

Son deudas gananciales

(a) las deudas contraídas conjuntamente por los cónyuges;
(b) las deudas contraídas por uno de los cónyuges para satisfacer necesidades apropiadas de la familia;
(c) las deudas de alimentos respecto a niños;
(d) las deudas contraídas por uno de los cónyuges para el uso o administración de bienes gananciales o en interés de la comunidad;
(e) las deudas relativas a las actividades profesionales de uno de los cónyuges;

(f) las deudas relativas a donaciones o legados pertenecientes a la comunidad;
(g) las deudas respecto a las cuales no se haya probado que sean de naturaleza privativa.

Principio 4:41 Deudas privativas
Son deudas privativas de uno de los cónyuges
(a) las deudas contraídas antes del inicio de la comunidad de gananciales;
(b) las deudas relativas a donaciones, herencias y legados recibidos por uno de los cónyuges durante el régimen;
(c) las deudas relativas al patrimonio privativo;
(d) las deudas privativas por su naturaleza;
(e) las deudas contraídas sin el necesario consentimiento del otro cónyuge.

Principio 4:42 Recobro de las deudas gananciales
(1) Respecto a las deudas gananciales responde la comunidad y el patrimonio privativo del cónyuge que contrajo la deuda.
(2) Si los cónyuges son deudores solidarios también responde de la deuda el patrimonio privativo de cada uno de los cónyuges.

Principio 4:43 Recobro de las deudas privativas
(1) De las deudas privativas de uno de los cónyuges responden
(a) el patrimonio privativo del cónyuge deudor;
(b) los ingresos y rentas del cónyuge deudor;
(c) los bienes gananciales en la medida de su confusión con los bienes privativos del cónyuge deudor.
(2) De las deudas privativas resultantes de un ilícito civil o penal responde también la mitad del valor neto de la comunidad, si el patrimonio privativo del cónyuge deudor, sus ingresos y rentas resultaren insuficientes para el pago.

ADMINISTRACIÓN

Principio 4:44 Administración de la comunidad
(1) Cada uno de los cónyuges tiene derecho a administrar los bienes gananciales por si solo, pero los actos importantes requieren una administración conjunta.
(2) Si un cónyuge rehusare prestar su consentimiento a un acto que requiere una administración conjunta, el otro cónyuge podrá solicitar a la autoridad competente autorización para realizar el acto por si solo.

Principio 4:45 Actos que requieren una administración conjunta
Conforme a los Principios 4:4 a 4:8 y teniendo en cuenta las circunstancias económicas de los cónyuges los actos que requieren una administración conjunta incluyen, en particular, los siguientes:

(a) la adquisición, alienación e hipoteca de bienes inmuebles;
(b) la conclusión de contratos de préstamo, garantía y seguros de valor significativo;
(c) las donaciones significativas.

Principio 4:46 Anulación de actos de administración
Los actos que requieren una administración conjunta pueden ser anulados por el cónyuge que no ha prestado su consentimiento al acto.

Principio 4:47 Administración del patrimonio privativo
Sin perjuicio de los Principios 4:6 y 4:7, cada uno de los cónyuges tiene la potestad de administrar por sí mismo sus bienes privativos.

Principio 4:48 Privación del derecho a administrar la comunidad
(1) A solicitud de uno de los cónyuges la autoridad competente puede privar al otro cónyuge del derecho a administrar total o parcialmente la comunidad por causa
(a) de incapacidad para manifestar su voluntad;
(b) de graves faltas de administración; o
(c) de una violación grave del deber de información conforme al Principio 4:8.
(2) En la medida en que uno de los cónyuges haya sido privado del derecho a administrar la comunidad, el otro cónyuge tendrá la potestad de administrar la comunidad por si mismo.
(3) A solicitud de cualquiera de los cónyuges la autoridad competente puede reinstaurar al cónyuge en su derecho de administración.

DISOLUCIÓN

Principio 4:49 Causas de disolución
La comunidad de gananciales se disuelve por
(a) el fallecimiento de uno cónyuges;
(b) la anulación del matrimonio, el divorcio o la separación legal;
(c) la estipulación de un régimen económico matrimonial distinto mediante capitulaciones entre los cónyuges; o
(d) la decisión de la autoridad competente ordenando la separación de bienes por causa grave.

Principio 4:50 Fecha de la disolución
La disolución de la comunidad de gananciales tiene efecto
(a) en la fecha del fallecimiento de uno de los cónyuges;
(b) en caso de anulación del matrimonio, divorcio o separación legal, respecto a los cónyuges, en la fecha de la demanda o, si los cónyuges se

separaron con anterioridad, en la fecha de su separación, y respecto a terceras personas, en la fecha de registro por la autoridad competente;

(c) en caso de capitulaciones estipulando un régimen matrimonial distinto, respecto a los cónyuges en la fecha del cambio, y respecto a terceras personas, en la fecha de publicación del convenio;

(d) en caso de separación de bienes ordenada por la autoridad competente, respecto a los cónyuges, en la fecha de la demanda, y respecto a terceras personas, en la fecha de publicación de la demanda.

Principio 4:51 Administración tras la disolución
Tras la disolución de la comunidad de gananciales la administración se rige por las reglas ordinarias sobre la comunidad pro indiviso.

LIQUIDACIÓN

Principio 4:52 Determinación y valoración de los bienes gananciales
(1) Los bienes gananciales se determinan en la fecha de disolución de la comunidad de gananciales establecida en el Principio 4:50.
(2) Los bienes gananciales se valoran en la fecha de distribución.

Principio 4:53 Compensación
(1) Se hará compensación a la comunidad por las contribuciones en beneficio del patrimonio privativo de un cónyuge.
(2) Se hará compensación al patrimonio privativo de uno de los cónyuges por las contribuciones en beneficio de la comunidad.
(3) En los supuestos de adquisición, mejora o conservación de un bien se tendrá en cuenta en el cálculo de la compensación el incremento o disminución de valor del bien resultante de dicha inversión.
(4) La compensación se pagará en metálico, salvo acuerdo en contrario.

Principio 4:54 Rango de las deudas de la comunidad
Las deudas de la comunidad y los derechos de compensación tienen el mismo rango.

DISTRIBUCIÓN

Principio 4:55 Convenio sobre la distribución
Los cónyuges pueden concluir un convenio sobre la distribución de los bienes gananciales.

Principio 4:56 Adjudicación de la vivienda familiar, el ajuar domestica y los bienes profesionales

Cuando se pronuncie sobre la distribución de los bienes gananciales la autoridad competente puede, en interés de la familia y mediando el pago de la compensación, adjudicar a uno de los cónyuges

(a) la vivienda familiar y el ajuar doméstico;
(b) los bienes profesionales.

Principio 4:57 Distribución igual y adaptaciones

(1) Los bienes gananciales han de distribuirse de forma igual entre los cónyuges.

(2) En caso de excepcional onerosidad la autoridad competente puede

(a) adaptar la distribución;
(b) descartar o modificar cualquier convenio concluido entre los cónyuges conforme al Principio 4:55.

Principio 4:58 Recobro de las deudas de la comunidad con posterioridad a la distribución de la comunidad

(1) Con posterioridad a la distribución de los bienes gananciales responde de las deudas de la comunidad la cuota de bienes gananciales de cada cónyuge y el patrimonio privativo del cónyuge que contrajo la deuda.

(2) El cónyuge que paga una deuda de la comunidad con posterioridad a la distribución de los bienes gananciales dispone de una acción de resarcimiento de la mitad del pago frente al otro cónyuge.

EUROPEISKA FAMILJERÄTTSPRINCIPER RÖRANDE MAKARS FÖRMÖGENHETSFÖRHÅLLANDEN

PREAMBEL

Med insikt om att de nationella rättsliga regleringarna rörande familj, trots rådande skillnader, ändå gradvis närmar sig varandra;
Med insikt om att kvarstående skillnader hindrar den fria rörligheten av personer inom Europa;
I avsikt att bidra till gemensamma europeiska värderingar rörande likställdhet mellan makar;
I avsikt att uppnå jämvikt mellan makars självbestämmande och deras inbördes solidaritet;
I avsikt att främja familjens välfärd;
I avsikt att säkerställa ett skydd för familjens bostad;
I avsikt att tillförsäkra varje make en rättvis andel av den egendom som förvärvats under äktenskapet;
I avsikt att bidra till harmoniseringen av familjerätten i Europa och att stärka medborgarnas rättigheter;
Rekommenderar Kommissionen för den europeiska familjerätten följande principer:

KAPITEL I: MAKARNAS ALLMÄNNA RÄTTIGHETER OCH SKYLDIGHETER

Princip 4:1 Allmän tillämplighet
Principerna i detta kapitel tillämpas oberoende av vilken äktenskaplig förmögenhetsordning som gäller.

Princip 4:2 Makarnas jämställdhet
Båda makarna har samma rättigheter och skyldigheter.

Princip 4:3 Makarnas rättsliga behörighet

Om inte annat anges i de följande principerna, har varje make full rättslig handlingsförmåga och kan följaktligen ingå rättshandlingar med såväl den andre maken som med tredje man.

Princip 4:4 Bidrag till familjens behov

(1) Varje make har att bidra till familjens behov i förhållande till sin förmåga.
(2) Bidrag till familjens behov avser bidrag till hushållsutgifter, utgifter för makarnas personliga behov samt utgifter för underhåll, uppfostran och utbildning av barnen.
(3) Om en make inte fullgör sin skyldighet att bidra till familjens behov, kan den andre maken begära att behörig myndighet beslutar om bidraget.

Princip 4:5 Skydd för familjens bostad och bohag

(1) Ett förfogande över rättigheter som hänför sig till familjens bostad eller bohag kräver samtycke av båda makarna.
(2) Ett förfogande av en make utan den andres samtycke är giltigt om den andre samtycker i efterhand.
(3) Om en make vägrar att ge samtycke eller saknar möjlighet att göra det, kan den andre maken begära tillstånd av behörig myndighet.
(4) Ett förfogande i strid med föregående punkter kan på ansökan av den som inte samtyckt förklaras ogiltigt av behörig myndighet.

Princip 4:6 Skydd för förhyrd familjebostad

(1) Om en familjebostad har förhyrts av ena maken, skall hyresrätten anses innehas av båda makarna, även om hyresavtalet har ingåtts före äktenskapet.
(2) En make får inte säga upp eller förändra hyresavtalet utan samtycke av den andre.
(3) Uppsägning från hyresvärdens sida skall tillställas båda makarna.

Princip 4:7 Ställföreträdarskap

(1) Ena maken kan uppdra åt den andre maken att företräda honom eller henne i rättsliga angelägenheter.
(2) Om en make inte har möjlighet att ge uttryck för sina avsikter, kan behörig myndighet ge den andre maken tillstånd

(a) att handla på egen hand när det annars skulle ha krävts samtycke från maken;
(b) att företräda sin make när denne har behörighet att handla på egen hand.

Princip 4:8 Informationsplikt

Varje make är skyldig att informera den andre i fråga om sina tillgångar och skulder och om väsentliga förvaltningsåtgärder i den mån det erfordras för att den andre skall kunna utöva sina rättigheter.

Princip 4:9 Rätt att ingå avtal om förmögenhetsförhållandena i äktenskapet
Makar har rätt att ingå avtal om sina äktenskapliga förmögenhetsförhållanden.

KAPITEL II: MAKARS AVTAL OM INBÖRDES FÖRMÖGENHETSFÖRHÅLLANDEN

Princip 4:10 Begrepp
(1) I ett avtal som ingås före äktenskapet kan blivande makar välja vilken förmögenhetsordning som skall tillämpas i äktenskapet.
(2) Under äktenskapet kan makarna förändra sin förmögenhetsordning eller byta den mot en annan.

Princip 4:11 Formkrav
Avtal om makars förmögenhetsförhållanden skall vara upprättade av en notarie eller en annan juridiskt utbildad person med motsvarande arbetsuppgifter, vara daterade och undertecknade av båda makarna.

Princip 4:12 Upplysningsplikt
När ett avtal om makars förmögenhetsförhållanden ingås är båda makarna skyldiga att upplysa om sina tillgångar och skulder.

Princip 4:13 Skyldigheter för en notarie eller en person med motsvarande utbildning och arbetsuppgifter
Notarien eller den person som har motsvarande utbildning och arbetsuppgifter, skall

(a) utföra opartisk rådgivning med makarna var för sig;
(b) försäkra sig om att varje make inser de rättsliga följderna av avtalet om förmögenhetsförhållandena i äktenskapet; och
(c) försäkra sig om att båda makarna frivilligt samtycker till avtalet.

Princip 4:14 Verkan mot tredje person
I förhållande till tredje person är ett avtal om makars förmögenhetsförhållanden i äktenskapet bindande, om vid tidpunkten för en rättshandling med en make

(a) information om avtalet var tillgänglig i en offentlig handling; eller
(b) tredje person hade kännedom om avtalet i relevanta delar.

Princip 4:15 Synnerlig börda
I fall där efterlevnad av ett avtal om makars förmögenhetsförhållanden, på grund av omständigheter som förelåg när avtalet ingicks eller tillkommit därefter, skulle innebära en synnerlig börda, kan behörig myndighet åsidosätta eller anpassa avtalet.

KAPITEL III: ÄKTENSKAPLIGA FÖRMÖGENHETSORDNINGAR

AVDELNING A: DELAKTIGHET I FÖRVÄRV

Princip 4:16 Tillämplighet av förmögenhetsordningen delaktighet i förvärv
Förmögenhetsordningen delaktighet i förvärv tillämpas om makarna inte har bestämt annat i enlighet med Kapitel II.

BEGREPPET

Princip 4:17 Begreppet delaktighet i förvärv
(1) Delaktighet i förvärv är en äktenskaplig förmögenhetsordning under vilken egendom ägs av makarna var för sig.
(2) En makes egendom består av förvärvad egendom och avskild egendom.
(3) Vid upplösning av förmögenhetsordningen är en make delaktig i den andre makens förvärvade egendom i enlighet med Princip 4:31.

TILLGÅNGAR

Princip 4:18 Förvärvad egendom
(1) Förvärvad egendom är tillgångar som förvärvats under förmögenhetsordningen och som inte är avskild egendom. Med förvärvad egendom avses särskilt
- (a) en makes inkomster och vinster, oberoende av om de härrör från arbete eller kapital; och
- (b) tillgångar som förvärvats med hjälp av endera makens inkomster eller vinster.

(2) Tillgångar presumeras vara förvärvad egendom såvida de inte bevisas vara avskild egendom.

Princip 4:19 Avskild egendom
Med avskild egendom avses
- (a) tillgångar som har anskaffats innan förmögenhetsordningen infördes;
- (b) tillgångar som har tillförts genom gåva, arv eller testamente under förmögenhetsordningen;
- (c) tillgångar som har ersatt avskild egendom;
- (d) tillgångar som är av personlig natur;
- (e) tillgångar som har anskaffats enbart för en makes yrkesutövning;
- (f) värdeökning av egendom som avses i (a)–(e).

Princip 4:20 Presumtion om samägande
Tillgångar presumeras tillhöra båda makarna gemensamt, om inte annat bevisas.

SKULDER

Princip 4:21 Personliga skulder
En skuld som en make ådragit sig är hans eller hennes personliga skuld.

Princip 4:22 Betalning av personliga skulder
Personliga skulder kan betalas ur den skuldsatte makens förvärvade och avskilda egendom.

FÖRVALTNING

Princip 4:23 Förvaltning av egendom
Om inte annat följer av Principerna 4:6 och 4:7 är varje make behörig att självständigt förvalta sin egendom.

UPPLÖSNING

Princip 4:24 Grunder för upplösning
Förmögenhetsordningen delaktighet i förvärv upplöses genom

(a) en makes död;
(b) annullering av äktenskapet, äktenskapsskillnad eller hemskillnad;
(c) ändring av äktenskaplig förmögenhetsordning genom avtal mellan makarna; eller
(d) beslut av behörig myndighet grundat på starka skäl.

Princip 4:25 Tidpunkt för upplösning
Upplösning av förmögenhetsordningen delaktighet i förvärv inträffar

(a) vid tidpunkten för en makes död;
(b) i fall av annullering av äktenskapet, äktenskapsskillnad eller hemskillnad, vid tidpunkten för ingivande av ansökan;
(c) i fall av avtal om en annan förmögenhetsordning, vid tidpunkten för ändringen; och
(d) i fall av beslut av behörig myndighet, vid tidpunkten för ingivande av ansökan.

AVVECKLING

Princip 4:26 Bestämning och värdering av förvärvad egendom

(1) Varje makes förvärvade egendom skall fastställas vid tidpunkten för upplösningen av förmögenhetsförordningen, såsom anges i Princip 4:25.

(2) Den förvärvade egendomen skall värderas vid tidpunkten för avvecklingen.

Princip 4:27 Skadliga handlingar

Vid beräkning av en makes förvärvade egendom skall hänsyn tas till

(a) överdrivna gåvor;

(b) förslösning av tillgångar;

(c) andra handlingar som avsiktligen har minskat den förvärvade egendomens värde till den andre makens nackdel.

Princip 4:28 Kompensation

(1) En makes förvärvade egendom kompenseras för varje bidrag till förmån för avskild egendom.

(2) En makes avskilda egendom kompenseras för varje bidrag till förmån för förvärvad egendom.

(3) Skulder belastar den egendom till vilken de hänför sig. Vid oklarhet presumeras de belasta förvärvad egendom.

(4) Vid beräkning av kompensation för utgifter för att förvärva, förbättra eller bevara en tillgång skall hänsyn tas till den ökning eller minskning av tillgångens värde som kan ha skett.

(5) Kompensation skall betalas i pengar, såvida makarna inte avtalar om annat.

DELAKTIGHET

Princip 4:29 Avtal om delaktighet

Makar har rätt att ingå avtal om delaktighet i förvärvad egendom.

Princip 4:30 Tilldelning av familjens bostad och bohag

Behörig myndighet kan, i familjens intresse och under förutsättning av betalning av kompensation, tilldela ena maken familjens bostad och bohag.

Princip 4:31 Lika delaktighet i förvärvad nettoegendom

(1) Ifall en makes förvärvade nettoegendom i värde överstiger den andre makens, är den senare delaktig i hälften av överskottet.

(2) Förvärvad nettoegendom är värdet av förvärvad egendom med avdrag för skulder.

(3) En makes förluster, som vid tidpunkten för upplösning överstiger hans eller hennes förvärvade egendom, skall inte delas av den andre maken.

(4) Anspråk på delaktighet avser pengar, såvida makarna inte avtalar om annat.
(5) På ansökan av en betalningsskyldig make kan behörig myndighet, om det finns synnerliga skäl, ge tillstånd till att betalningen uppskjuts eller sker genom avbetalning.

Princip 4:32 Jämkning av behörig myndighet
I fall av synnerlig börda kan behörig myndighet
 (a) jämka delaktigheten;
 (b) åsidosätta eller ändra ett sådant avtal mellan makar som avses i Princip 4:29.

AVDELNING B: GEMENSKAP I FÖRVÄRV

Princip 4:33 Tillämplighet av förmögenhetsordningen gemenskap i förvärv
Förmögenhetsordningen gemenskap i förvärv tillämpas om makarna inte har bestämt annat i enlighet med Kapitel II.

BEGREPPET

Princip 4:34 Begreppet gemenskap i förvärv
(1) Gemenskap i förvärv är en äktenskaplig förmögenhetsordning som omfattar gemenskapsegendom och personlig egendom.
(2) Gemenskapsegendom är egendom som förvärvats under denna förmögenhetsordning och som inte är personlig egendom.
(3) Personlig egendom är en makes enskilda egendom.

TILLGÅNGAR

Princip 4:35 Gemenskapsegendom
(1) Gemenskapsegendom omfattar all lös och fast egendom som har förvärvats under förmögenhetsordningen gemenskap i förvärv och som inte är en av makarnas personliga egendom.
(2) Med gemenskapsegendom avses särskilt
 (a) makarnas inkomster och vinster som har intjänats eller härrör från gemenskapsegendom eller personlig egendom;
 (b) tillgångar som har förvärvats gemensamt eller individuellt under förmögenhetsordningen med hjälp av makarnas inkomster eller vinster;
 (c) tillgångar som har tillförts genom gåva eller testamente, antingen till båda makarna eller till ena maken under villkor att egendomen skall vara gemenskapsegendom.

Princip 4:36 Personlig egendom
Med personlig egendom avses
- (a) tillgångar som har anskaffats innan förmögenhetsordningen infördes;
- (b) tillgångar som under förmögenhetsordningen har tillförts genom gåva, arv eller testamente;
- (c) tillgångar som har ersatt personlig egendom eller som har anskaffats genom investering eller återinvestering enligt Princip 4:37 respektive Princip 4:38;
- (d) tillgångar som är av personlig natur, anskaffade under förmögenhetsordningen;
- (e) tillgångar som har anskaffats enbart för en makes yrkesutövning.

Princip 4:37 Substitution
(1) En tillgång som ersätter personliga tillgångar utan tilläggsbetalning skall anses vara personlig egendom.
(2) En tillgång som ersätter personliga tillgångar med tilläggsbetalning skall anses vara personlig egendom, dock inte om en tilläggsbetalning med gemenskapsegendom motsvarar eller överstiger den ersatta egendomens värde.
(3) När tilläggsbetalning görs med en sorts egendom skall den andra sortens egendom kompenseras.

Princip 4:38 Investering och återinvestering
(1) En tillgång som helt har anskaffats genom investering eller återinvestering av personliga tillgångar skall anses vara personlig egendom.
(2) En tillgång som har anskaffats genom investering eller återinvestering av både personliga tillgångar och gemenskapstillgångar skall anses vara personlig egendom såvida den betalning som skett med gemenskapsegendom inte motsvarar eller överstiger värdet av det som investerats eller återinvesterats.
(3) När tilläggsbetalning i samband med investering eller återinvestering görs med en sorts egendom skall den andra sortens egendom kompenseras.

Princip 4:39 Presumtion om gemenskapsegendom
Tillgångar presumeras vara gemenskapsegendom såvida de inte bevisas vara personlig egendom i enlighet med Principerna 4:35 till 4:38.

SKULDER

Princip 4:40 Gemenskapsskulder
Med gemenskapsskulder avses
- (a) skulder som båda makarna har ådragit sig;
- (b) skulder som ena maken har ådragit sig för att tillgodose tillbörliga familjebehov;

(c) skulder som hänför sig till underhåll av barnen;
(d) skulder som ena maken har ådragit sig för användning eller förvaltning av gemenskapegendom eller i sådan egendoms intresse;
(e) skulder som hänför sig till en makes yrkesutövning;
(f) skulder som hänför sig till tillgångar som tillförts gemenskapsegendomen genom gåva eller testamente; och
(g) skulder som inte har bevisats vara personliga skulder.

Princip 4:41 Personliga skulder
Med en makes personliga skulder avses
(a) skulder som har uppkommit innan förmögenhetsordningen gemenskap i förvärv infördes;
(b) skulder som hänför sig till vad som under förmögenhetsordningen av en make erhållits genom gåva, arv eller testamente;
(c) skulder som hänför sig till personlig egendom;
(d) skulder som är av personlig natur; och
(e) skulder som en make ådragit sig utan erforderligt samtycke av den andre maken.

Princip 4:42 Återbetalning av gemenskapsskulder
(1) En gemenskapsskuld kan återbetalas ur gemenskapsegendom eller ur den personliga egendom som tillhör den make som har ådragit sig skulden.
(2) Om båda makarna solidariskt ansvarar för skulden, kan den också återbetalas ur endera makens personliga egendom.

Princip 4:43 Återbetalning av personliga skulder
(1) En makes personliga skulder kan betalas ur
(a) dennes personliga egendom;
(b) dennes inkomster och vinster;
(c) gemenskapsegendom, i den mån den skuldsatte makens personliga egendom har blandats samman med sådan egendom.
(2) Personliga skulder på grund av skadeståndsansvar eller ansvar för brott kan också betalas ur hälften av gemenskapsegendomens nettovärde, om den betalningsskyldiges personliga egendom, inkomster och vinster inte räcker för betalning.

FÖRVALTNING

Princip 4:44 Förvaltning av gemenskapsegendom
(1) Vardera maken är behörig att förvalta gemenskapsegendom, men viktiga handlingar skall företas gemensamt.

(2) Om en make vägrar att samtycka till en handling som förutsätter gemensamt beslut, kan den andre maken av behörig myndighet begära tillstånd att handla på egen hand.

Princip 4:45 Handlingar som förutsätter gemensamt beslut
Med förbehåll för vad som följer av Principerna 4:4 till 4:8 och med beaktande av makarnas ekonomiska situation, förutsätter särskilt följande handlingar gemensamt beslut:

(a) förvärv, avyttring eller belastning av fast egendom;
(b) betydande åtaganden som avser skuldsättning eller ställande av garantier eller säkerheter;
(c) betydande gåvor.

Princip 4:46 Ogiltigförklaring av förvaltningshandlingar
En handling som förutsätter gemensamt beslut kan, efter ansökan av den make som inte har samtyckt till handlingen, av behörig myndighet förklaras vara ogiltig.

Princip 4:47 Förvaltning av personlig egendom
Om inte annat följer av Principerna 4:6 och 4:7 är varje make behörig att självständigt förvalta sin personliga egendom.

Princip 4:48 Förlust av rätten att förvalta gemenskapsegendom
(1) Efter ansökan av ena maken kan behörig myndighet helt eller delvis ta ifrån den andre maken dennes rätt att förvalta gemenskapsegendom, på grund av

(a) att denne inte är förmögen att ge uttryck för sina avsikter;
(b) allvarlig misskötsel av förvaltningen;
(c) allvarlig underlåtenhet att lämna sådan information som avses i Princip 4:8.

(2) Den rätt att förvalta gemenskapsegendom som fråntagits en make tillkommer den andre maken ensam.
(3) Efter ansökan av någon av makarna kan behörig myndighet återge en make rätt att förvalta gemenskapsegendom.

UPPLÖSNING

Princip 4:49 Grunder för upplösning
Förmögenhetsordningen gemenskap i förvärv upplöses genom

(a) en makes död;
(b) annullering av äktenskapet, äktenskapsskillnad eller hemskillnad;
(c) ändring av äktenskaplig förmögenhetsordning genom avtal mellan makarna; eller
(d) beslut om egendomsskillnad av behörig myndighet, grundat på starka skäl.

Princip 4:50 Tidpunkt för upplösning
Upplösning av förmögenhetsordningen gemenskap i förvärv inträffar

(a) vid tidpunkten för en makes död;
(b) i fall av annullering av äktenskapet, äktenskapsskillnad eller hemskillnad, antingen vid tidpunkten för ingivande av ansökan eller, om makarna har separerat dessförinnan, vid tidpunkten för separationen och i förhållande till tredje person vid tidpunkten för registrering av beslut av behörig myndighet;
(c) i fall av avtal om övergång till en annan förmögenhetsordning, vid tidpunkten för ändringen, och i förhållande till tredje man vid tidpunkten för offentliggörande av avtalet; och
(d) i fall av beslut om egendomsskillnad mellan makarna av behörig myndighet, vid tidpunkten för ingivande av ansökan, och i förhållande till tredje person vid tidpunkten för offentliggörande av ansökan.

Princip 4:51 Förvaltning efter upplösning
Efter upplösning av gemenskap i förvärv bestäms förvaltningen av reglerna om samäganderätt.

AVVECKLING

Princip 4:52 Bestämning och värdering av gemenskapsegendom
(1) Gemenskapsegendomen skall fastställas vid den tidpunkt för upplösning som anges i Princip 4:50.
(2) Gemenskapstillgångarna skall värderas vid tidpunkten för fördelning av dem.

Princip 4:53 Kompensation
(1) Gemenskapsegendom kompenseras för bidrag till förmån för en makes personliga egendom.
(2) En makes personliga egendom kompenseras för bidrag till förmån för gemenskapsegendom.
(3) Vid beräkning av kompensation för en investering för att förvärva, förbättra eller bevara en tillgång skall hänsyn tas till den ökning eller minskning av tillgångens värde som kan ha skett.
(4) Kompensation skall betalas i pengar, såvida makarna inte avtalar om annat.

Princip 4:54 Rangordning av gemenskapsskulder
Gemenskapsskulder och kompensationsrättigheter är likställda.

FÖRDELNING

Princip 4:55 Avtal om fördelning
Makar har rätt att ingå avtal om fördelning av gemenskapsegendom.

Princip 4:56 Tilldelning av familjens bostad, bohag och yrkesutrustning
Behörig myndighet kan, i familjens intresse och under förutsättning av betalning av kompensation, tilldela ena maken

(a) familjens bostad och bohag;
(b) yrkesutrustning.

Princip 4:57 Lika delning och jämkning
(1) Gemenskapsegendomen skall fördelas lika mellan makarna.
(2) I fall av synnerlig börda kan behörig myndighet

(a) jämka fördelningen;
(b) åsidosätta eller ändra ett sådant avtal mellan makar som avses i Princip 4:55.

Princip 4:58 Återbetalning av gemenskapsskulder efter fördelning
(1) Efter fördelning av gemenskapsegendomen kan gemenskapsskulder återbetalas ur en makes andel av gemenskapsegendomen och ur den personliga egendom som tillhör den make som har ådragit sig skulden.
(2) Den make som efter fördelning har betalat en gemenskapsskuld har rätt till ersättning från den andre maken för halva beloppet.

European Family Law Series

1. *Legal Recognition of Same-Sex Couples in Europe*, K. Boele-Woelki and A. Fuchs (eds.)
2. *European Family Law in Action Volume I: Grounds for divorce*, K. Boele-Woelki, B. Braat and I. Sumner (eds.)
3. *European Family Law in Action Volume II : Maintenance Between Former Spouses*, K. Boele-Woelki, B. Braat and I. Sumner (eds.)
4. *Perspectives for the Unification and Harmonisation of Family Law in Europe*, K. Boele-Woelki (ed.)
5. *Family Law Legislation of the Netherlands*, I. Sumner and H. Warendorf
6. *Indépendance et interdépendance patrimoniales des époux dans le régime matrimonial légal des droits néerlandais, français et suisse*, B. Braat
7. *Principles of European Family Law Regarding Divorce and Maintenance Between Former Spouses*, K. Boele-Woelki, F. Ferrand, C. González Beilfuss, M. Jänterä-Jareborg, N. Lowe, D. Martiny and W. Pintens
8. *Inheritance Law Legislation of the Netherlands*, I. Sumner and H. Warendorf
9. *European Family Law in Action Volume III : Parental Responsibilities*, K. Boele-Woelki, B. Braat and I. Curry Sumner (eds.)
10. *Common Core and Better Law in European Family Law*, K. Boele-Woelki (ed.)
11. *All's well that ends registered?*, I. Curry-Sumner
12. *Model Family Code – From a global perspective*, I. Schwenzer and M. Dimsey
13. *Harmonisation of Family Law in Europe. A Historical Perspective*, M. Antokolskaia
14. *Brussels II bis: Its Impact and Application in the Member States*, K. Boele-Woelki and C. González Beilfuss (eds.)
15. *Tensions between Legal, Biological and Social Conceptions of Parentage*, I. Schwenzer (ed.)
16. *Principles of European Family Law Regarding Parental Responsibilities*, K. Boele-Woelki, F. Ferrand, C. González Beilfuss, M. Jänterä-Jareborg, N. Lowe, D. Martiny and W. Pintens
17. *Juxtaposing Legal Systems and the Principles of European Family Law on Divorce and Maintenance*, E. Örücü and J. Mair (eds.)
18. *Convergence and Divergence of Family Law in Europe*, M. Antokolskaia (ed.)
19. *European Challenges in Contemporary Family Law*, K. Boele-Woelki and K. Sverdrup (eds.)
20. *Children and their parents*, M. Vonk
21. *La capacité de l'enfant dans les droits français, anglais et écossais*, L. Francoz-Terminal

22. *Joint Parental Authority*, C.G. Jeppesen de Boer
23. *Debates in Family Law around the Globe at the Dawn of the 21st Century*, K. Boele-Woelki (ed.)
24. *European Family Law in Action Volume IV: Property Relations between Spouses*, K. Boele-Woelki, B. Braat and I. Curry-Sumner (eds.)
25. *Foundational Facts, Relative Truths. A Comparative Law Study on Children's Right to Know Their Genetic Origins*, R. Blauwhoff
26. *Imperative Inheritance Law in a Late-Modern Society. Five Perspectives*, Christoph Castelein, René Foqué and Alain Verbeke (eds.)
27. *Juxtaposing Legal Systems and the Principles of European Family Law on Parental Responsibilities*, Esin Örücü and Jane Mair (eds.)
28. *La justice des mineurs en Europe*, Yann Favier and Frédérique Ferrand (eds.)
29. *The Future of Family Property in Europe*, Katharina Boele-Woelki, Jo Miles and Jens M. Scherpe (eds.)
30. *The Place of Religion in Family Law: A Comparative Search*, Jane Mair and Esin Örücü (eds.)
31. *Reconstructing Marriage. The Legal Status of Relationships in a Changing Society*, Caroline Sörgjerd
32. *Legal Recognition of Same-Sex Relationships in Europe*, Katharina Boele-Woelki, Angelika Fuchs (eds.)
33. *Principles of European Family Law Regarding Property Relations Between Spouses*, Katharina Boele-Woelki, Frédérique Ferrand, Cristina González Beilfuss, Maarit Jänterä-Jareborg, Nigel Lowe, Dieter Martiny and Walter Pintens